CRIMINAL LAW

SECOND EDITION

CRIMINAL LAW

SECOND EDITION

CHARLES P. NEMETH

CRC Press
Taylor & Francis Group
Boca Raton London New York

CRC Press is an imprint of the
Taylor & Francis Group, an **informa** business

CRC Press
Taylor & Francis Group
6000 Broken Sound Parkway NW, Suite 300
Boca Raton, FL 33487-2742

First issued in paperback 2018

ISBN-13: 978-1-4398-6171-4 (hbk)
ISBN-13: 978-1-138-37451-5 (pbk)

This book contains information obtained from authentic and highly regarded sources. Reasonable efforts have been made to publish reliable data and information, but the author and publisher cannot assume responsibility for the validity of all materials or the consequences of their use. The authors and publishers have attempted to trace the copyright holders of all material reproduced in this publication and apologize to copyright holders if permission to publish in this form has not been obtained. If any copyright material has not been acknowledged please write and let us know so we may rectify in any future reprint.

Library of Congress Cataloging-in-Publication Data

Nemeth, Charles P., 1951-
    Criminal law / Charles P. Nemeth. -- 2nd ed.
    p. cm.
    Includes bibliographical references and index.
    ISBN 978-1-4398-6171-4
    1. Criminal law--United States. I. Title.

KF9219.N46 2011
345.73--dc23   2011020148

Visit the Taylor & Francis Web site at
http://www.taylorandfrancis.com

and the CRC Press Web site at
http://www.crcpress.com

Dedication

To my courageous and beautiful Anne Marie, who strives for perfection in all she does. She blossoms as a teacher in the truest sense of the vocation.

To St. Thomas Aquinas who said:

"Violence is directly opposed to the voluntary, as likewise to the natural. For the voluntary and the natural have this in common, that both are from an intrinsic principle; whereas violence is from an extrinsic principle. And, for this reason, just as things devoid of knowledge, violence affects something against nature ..."

(Summa Theologica, Volume I, Part I-II, Question 6, article 5)

Contents

Preface

Critical to any meaningful understanding of criminal law is the look back at its heritage and history. From whence does the criminal law come? So crucial is this question that most modern practitioners take for granted the enactment and application of criminal laws, as if the statutes have always been here or arose because of chance or accident. Nothing could be further from the truth. Indeed, criminal law, like every other sort of law, has a long and distinguished history. What presently exists emerges from the introspection and analysis of our predecessors who thought it worth the definition. Never undervalue the role of history in the study and analysis of legal principles.

Chapter 1 tries to tell you why the criminal codes came about and focuses its attention on the moral, religious, spiritual, and human influences that led up to our present system. Tracking all the way back to the Romans and Greeks, the chapter attempts to provide the type of historical perspective often missing in criminal law texts and affords the reader with a critical, histrionic perspective. Criminal laws, put another way, have a genealogy and are often wrapped up in religious and moral traditions, politics, and social forces, and find their way to contemporary times with this baggage—some of it good, and others bad. In sum, Chapter 1 blends the worlds of history, philosophy, ethics, and moral tradition with the modern statutory frameworks. As such, the chapter looks at great thinkers who played central roles in the shaping of criminal laws, such as Aquinas, Plato, Hobbes, Bentham, and Locke. In the final analysis, the reader will appreciate the complicated origins of criminal law and discern the diverse forces at work in the shaping of the modern American criminal law system.

Chapter 2 is primarily definitional in design and introduces the reader to myriad ways crime is described in the modern criminal justice model. Crimes are defined from varied perspectives including the issue of moral and ethical prohibition, custom and habit, mores and cultural expectation, and as judgment concerning the propriety of conduct—namely whether it be deviant or other form of aberration. Next, the reader will be introduced to the formalistic definitions commonly witnessed in criminal codes, from larceny and misdemeanors to summary offenses and minor infractions. Aside from the updated examination of Model Penal Code provisions, the text evaluates a host of state-by-state criminal codifications as well as corresponding case law that evaluates its legitimacy. Added to this is a full examination of how crime definitions are tied to potential punishments that can be inflicted for the proscribed conduct. Finally, the chapter considers how criminal participants are categorized and how their roles are designated in the form of principals and accessories, as well as new coverage on corporate and vicarious liability.

At the heart of all criminal conduct lie the elements of act and mind—the subject of Chapter 3. Actus reus, the thing done or act committed, or omitted, and mens rea, the mind and the intent of the actor, form the two seminal elements necessary for criminal culpability. Without these essential elements, criminal responsibility can never be imposed. For, in the American criminal law system, defendants taste the retribution of punishment only when demonstrably responsible for the act, both factually and mentally. In this sense, the American conception of criminal responsibility calls for a two-prong analysis: (1) what did the actor do, or fail to do under a legal duty, and (2) did the actor understand or appreciate the act chosen? Both components form the criminal proof in the prosecution. Both weigh heavily on the tactics of lawyers, the assessment of jury panels, and the scrutinies of appeals and trial judges. Aside from intentional acts, the criminal law excuses mistakes and certain forms of ignorance and fully appreciates the dynamics of coercion and duress, mental capability and infancy, and other factors that affect the voluntariness of human activity. On the mental side, the law distinguishes the severity and grades of criminal offense by the level and clarity of mental thought. The mentally focused, unburdened by disease or illness, fully plotting the resultant crime, are considered people with specific intent. Those laden with assorted psychoses, social and personal disorders, driven by passion and rage seem to have a more clouded judgment and thus less responsibility. These criminal agents have general intent, which usually represents a lower level or degree of criminal culpability. At the end of the criminal intent spectrum are those criminal actors who act carelessly or with gross negligence, those who could or should have known that injury would result from their conduct, and those whose conduct is outlawed under strict liability provisions. Add to this a look at strict liability determinations and the full panoply of mental states is covered. The mens rea analysis will be difficult and complex, but the subject matter keenly addresses what it means to be criminally culpable.

Chapter 4 commences the journey into particular criminal offenses and more specifically categorized offenses against the body that result in the death of another. Lumped under the term *homicide*, the most heinous of crimes are those offenses that involve taking the life of another either with planned intentionality, as in murder in the first degree; with rage or passion or other mitigation, as in manslaughter; or by gross negligence or in violation of a strict liability statute, such as criminally negligent homicide—a common offense in DUI murder circumstances. Principles involving provocation, mitigation, and standard defense strategy are fully covered. Special attention is given to the complicated Felony Murder Rule (FMR) that holds accountable the full range of criminal participants in a case of multiple players and often inflicts harsh and brutal results on those not intending to kill another. The ramifications for any criminal participation are quite severe under the FMR doctrine. Other homicide forms that produce controversial reactions also are assessed and critiqued, including suicide, abortion, and infanticide.

Bodily injury offenses are further scrutinized in Chapter 5, where the chief emphasis is on nonterminal, yet frightfully dangerous, criminal conduct. To be sure, all of these forms of criminal agency can evolve into potential life-and-death situations and the law delivers serious consequences for these infractions. Robbery, the property taking with violent means and physical assault, starts the treatment. Kidnapping, the multifaceted and multiintentional crime, receives extensive coverage with particular attention given to the motive, rationale, and intent of kidnapping and the underlying or corresponding felony. The various forms of assault, from aggravated to simple, continue the chapter's direction. At the chapter's end, the growing plague of those who employ terror rather than actual physical contact to achieve criminal ends is analyzed as well as the tragedy of physical injury in the family setting.

Chapter 6's distressing coverage involves all types of sexual assault and brutality. In an age when the pressure to decriminalize sexual deviance has never been stronger, when there are calls for child consent ages to be lowered, and when scandal rocks church and school, the sanctity of the human person is under severe onslaught. Rape and its modern progeny of criminal offenses take center stage in this comprehensive chapter. Aside from the common law perspective, the reader will be introduced to the dynamic reform efforts presently afoot in the criminal justice system. Topics involve gender neutrality, earnest resistance, types of penetration and sexual activity, and sexual history and character evidence. Also discussed will be the cumbersome and difficult issue of voluntary sodomy and its continuing criminalization in certain jurisdictions. Other areas of concern include the escalating plague of incest, the legitimization and argumentation about sexual activity with children, and the criminalization of HIV transmission.

Moving away from bodily offense, Chapter 7 reviews the standard property offenses in every criminal code, from larceny/theft to bribery and forgery. The chapter expends enormous time highlighting the evolution of larceny in terms of its coverage of property types and scope. Although common law larceny remains thoroughly intact, the offense has been revolutionized over the past five decades to encompass theft of once-unimagined interests including services, utilities, government benefits, and commercial and business documents. How these offenses are carried out in the world of the Internet and electronic commerce is fully evaluated. Reviewed too, are the crimes of embezzlement, forgery, and bribery, both the public and the commercial variety. In forgery, the reader is exposed to the types of instruments that can be subject to the statute and the impact technology has had on the fast evolving list of forgeable instruments.

Chapter 8 focuses on the habitation and the genre of offenses unique to its construction. If the home or domicile demands respect from the legal system, it is rooted in the traditional expectation of privacy and corresponding outrage one experiences when the home is violated. The domicile receives special treatment because of its intimate reality with the victim. This is why arson has long been held as a brutal and unacceptable offense. Arson not only destroys property, but often human life as well. In burglary, the intruder's breaking and entry undermines the tranquility that a resident has every right to expect. Whatever the felonious purpose of the burglary actor, it cannot be tolerated by a culture dedicated to the protection of its citizenry. The complexity of dual intentionalities receives focused attention in the law of burglary. The offense of trespass receives significant attention because it often lays the foundation for other criminal actions.

One of the central aims of this text has been to allow the reader a vision beyond the criminal codification. Understanding criminal law calls for much more than mere code memory and recitation. Criminal law is in the business of judgments that are legal and, just as important, moral, religious, political, and social in design. Criminal codes have over many generations regulated conduct on many fronts and with varying degrees of resistance and tolerance. Extreme restrictions on conduct, of whatever sort, do not seem to go over well in the American experience. Prohibition, for example, speaks loudly about the impossibility of eradicating a particular form of vice. Yesterday's lessons can enlighten the present. What surely will not go away will be the struggle that often occurs between those that seek a higher moral ground and those with a more tolerant perspective. Chapter 9 is all about finding a balance that involves the perennial problems of public morality. Prostitution, drug legalization, obscenity, and pornography, to name a few, are part of this legal and ethical thicket. What are the ins and outs of these conducts? Can legalization or prohibition be justified? What is obscene? How does one distinguish obscene from pornographic? And, how has the virtual world impacted determination of obscenity and pornography? What level of toleration should a culture have relative to drinking and driving? Is DUI (driving under the influence) legislation properly balanced or out of control? A host of questions regarding these matters of law and public morality will lead to reasoned inquiry.

Incomplete or "inchoate" offenses are assessed in Chapter 10. By inchoate, we mean that the offense, whatever it may be, never reaches full completion. Murder or arson, as examples, might not be completed for a variety of reasons, such as apprehension, failure, or mere bungling. The failure to complete the act should not afford a defense to a criminal actor who cannot successfully carry out his misdeed. Inchoate also implies incompleteness as to the usual criminal elements. By way of illustration, the law resists punishing those who fail in one element or the other. The act must be coupled with the intentionality, except in the case of conspiracy, which punishes the planning and preparation of criminality without concern for its completion. In this sense, conspiracy is totally inchoate, though some overt step is taken toward the completion of the criminal act. The same thesis applies to criminal attempts where the actor makes a try at the crime but cannot follow through for whatever reason. Attempts cannot go unnoticed and the law makes inchoate provision for it.

The journey into criminal law ends with a full-fledged examination of predictable defenses witnessed in criminal litigation. Chapter 11's analysis dwells upon how defenses serve to undermine a fundamental element in a crime. Defenses exonerate and set free as contrasted with mitigation, which merely affects the degree of charge that can be chosen. In defenses, the criminal hopes to obliterate either the actus reus or mens rea component. Hence, in factual impossibility claims, the defendants cannot be charged with the killing of a dead person, or the rape, depending upon jurisdiction, of a wife. It is factually not possible to do the act charged. So, too, in a case of self-defense whereby a party legitimately and proportionately defends himself or herself against harm. Here, the act is not murder, but defense of life and limb. In mens rea defenses, the strategy is to undercut the mental faculties of the defendant as much as feasible. Insanity defenses zero in on a defendant's capacity to know the nature of his or her conduct, or to at least appreciate its wrongfulness. Newer applications as to sanity are also covered including the "guilty but mentally ill" conclusion. A defendant who believes that the victim consented to conduct is equally incapable of formulating the level of mental intent for many first-degree offenses. Other defense analyses consist of entrapment, duress, and coercion; and novel defenses, such as battered spouse or repressed child memory syndrome, are weighed and debated.

As always, I look forward to corrections and insights that improve this project and pray mightily that this text touches its readers in positive ways as they prepare for a career in the justice system.

Acknowledgments

No endeavor of this scope can be constructed without the accumulation of many debts and remembrances. Aside from the sheer size of the project, I can only dream of self-reliance in the production. I have no allusions that others were not central to the project's conclusion. First and foremost, my friend and editorial assistant of nearly 23 years, Hope Haywood, has been in the forefront of these productions. As Hope blends the minutiae and the grand aspects of the project, I have developed a dependency that I hope never to lose as I continue to write. In her own right, she has embarked in an academic career that will show, in even more ways, her brilliance and zest for knowledge. Her work in the area of legal research and legal method is a valuable skill set in the orchestration of texts. Thanks again, Hope.

I have been fortunate to be tenured in both the State University of New York and the Pennsylvania State System of Higher Education and each provides an environment conducive to scholarly production. Although writing can be nothing less than agonizing on select days, the culture of SUNY rewarded those who engage in this sort of learnedness. That tradition of support and assistance surely continues at California University of Pennsylvania where Dean Len Colelli, Provost Gerri Jones, and, of course, our beloved President Angelo Armenti, Jr. could not be more supportive. In my own office, regular assistance is provided by Laurie Manderino, Rose Mahouski, Irene Chaliotis, and an excellent graduate assistant, Katie Heinnickel, whose work has been superlative.

To all the companies and providers who generously allowed usage of materials and promotional materials, I extend my gratitude. There are legions of cooperative entities that made significant contributions to this work.

Finally, the project receives much encouragement and motivation from my family—Jean Marie, whose sacrifices can no longer be counted, and the seven kids who eat and wear whatever compensation I generate from this or any other activity. They are the glory of my life and I owe much to each and every one of them. And, as they grow into adulthood, I am thankful that these former "kids" of mine have become exceptional people in every walk of life and activity they undertake. Thanks Ellie, Stephen, Anne Marie, John, Joseph, Mary Claire, and Michael Augustine.

Charles P. Nemeth

JD, Ph D, LLM

Chapter 1

The Foundation and Heritage of the Criminal Law

KEYWORDS

Codification: To reduce to a code; systematize; classify.

Common Law: The body of law developed in England primarily from judicial decisions based on custom and precedent, unwritten in statute or code, and constituting the basis of the English legal system.

Criminal Law: The public law that deals with crimes and their prosecution.

Criminology: The scientific study of crime as a social phenomenon, of criminals, and of penal treatment.

Defendant: The party against whom a criminal or civil action is brought.

Jurisprudence: The science or philosophy of law.

Marxism: The theory of materialism based on communist practice.

Offender: One that commits an offense.

Positivism: The philosophy of science that holds that we should admit as knowledge only that about which we can be absolutely certain.

Teleology: Greek term for the end, completion, purpose, or goal of any thing or activity.

Utilitarianism: The belief that morally right is whatever produces the greatest overall amount of pleasure or happiness.

INTRODUCTION: THE IDEA OF CRIMINAL LAW

The study and analysis of criminal law represents a lifetime of both experience and intellectual pursuit. For students of criminal justice, legal studies, law and police science, this conceptual journey is mandatory. At its root, the justice system depends, first and foremost, on the system known as the *criminal law,* that body of rules and legal promulgations that forbid and direct, define and limit, categorize and delineate conduct, which can be labeled criminal in design. For one who labors in the criminal justice system, it will be impossible to avoid the content of the criminal law. It will be even more impossible to achieve success in any occupation in the justice system without a true understanding of what it means to violate the content of the criminal law.

The subject of criminal law can be studied from many angles. Its codification and passage is largely the result of political and legislative processes that depend upon political science. Others view the subject matter through the prism of the psychological and psychiatric sciences searching for why and how criminal agents do what they do. In another context, the social sciences, namely criminology and sociology, look at criminal law from a social–cultural perspective employing both quantitative and qualitative means to evaluate its impacts. While all of these methods are instructive, the task herein lies mainly in the final context—that of law and jurisprudence.[1]

Within the following analysis, the reader is chiefly exposed to crimes in a legal context that searches and interprets common law, case law interpretations, and the actual text of the crimes code itself, which lays out the parameters and definitions for what constitutes a particular offense. Just as critically, the examination that follows integrates the system itself—the criminal justice system that has been erected for the sole purpose of dealing with those disobeying the law of crimes. In the final analysis, criminal law is the foundation for a justice model and its systematic underpinnings. Prisons are built for violators. Police departments exist to ferret out and corral those who aggrieve its provisions. Probation and parole officers watch over criminal offenders who now retain some level of freedom outside the prison. Courtroom employees, lawyers and judges, forensic scientists and the like, all serve the criminal law. The law of crimes lay out the general parameters for when, why, and how the justice system and its professionals should commence its work. How ludicrous it would be to have it any other way. The entire infrastructure pertinent to the justice model depends upon the law's content and definitions; the system looks to the law of crimes for guidance on what makes the actor an "offender" or "defendant."[2]

For a very easy way to understand educational module on Criminal Process, visit http://www.america.gov/st/usg-english/2008/May/20080522220810eaifas0.9525873.html

Hence, the intellectual undertaking soon to unfold is crucial to any student's understanding of how the criminal justice system operates. Like a hub on the wheel of a bicycle, the criminal law surrounds itself with an extraordinary array of functions and roles readily witnessed in the criminal justice system, whether policing, corrections, legal operations, forensic science, or the legislative process. Its subject matter provides a functional equilibrium to both role and task and reminds the many players in the justice model that criminal codes are the essential starting point for any reasoned machine. Without its definitional content, the culture would be subject to the whims and impulses of individualized moral speculation, and even more traumatically, the capricious and arbitrary tendencies so often witnessed in haphazard or ill-defined institutions. In other words, the rule of law cries out for order. Order, in both person and nation, will not occur without a sanctioned series of dos and don'ts in the moral sphere. For these reasons, the criminal law and its codification are intimately tied to how a person and nation defines itself. A nation of laws fares better than a nation ruled by anarchy. A nation with some sense of definable criminality, even though it may differ from other sovereignty, displays at least some rationality about what is or is not acceptable in terms of behavior or human activity.

To be sure, there is little that is universally agreed upon in the matter of criminal codification. Long gone are the days when uniformity of moral tradition lit up our sense of understanding. Instead, most justice models and the countries they represent are influenced by an emerging relativity in things right and wrong. To be sure, it is getting much tougher to find consensus about anything. Even once universally condemned practices, e.g., sexual intercourse with minors, manslaughter despite provocation (burning bed and spouse abuse cases), and sodomy, muster both critics and advocates for challenges to the status quo. This is all the more reason why the study of criminal law is so essential to students seeking careers in the justice system.

Aside from the historical benefits, the criminal law student will gain awareness as to why these rules exist in the first place, that their placement in codes and cases is more than mere random choice or power base representation. The study of criminal law reflects both tradition and evolution. Therefore, any reliable understanding of modern day laws cannot occur without some knowledge of its foundations. Our modern criminal law did not emerge from nothingness. Instead, the criminal law predictably mirrors the culture it serves. None of its prescriptions came about without purpose or meaning. Even the critics of a law will cite an historical misunderstanding that triggered the law in the first place. Whether the law in question represents right or wrong will be a battle long and arduously fought. What is certain is that each and every criminal codification has a history upon which it was built. In this way, the study of criminal law manifests cultural and social intentions in addition to legal and economic forces. On top of these factors, the analysis of criminal law depends on even more, from an understanding of moral and ethical tradition, religion and theology, neurology and psychology, to a keen awareness of political process and public consensus. From these varying perspectives, it is easy to see the richness of the excursion about to commence.

THE NEED FOR TRADITION AND FOUNDATION

The justice system that operates without a reasoned understanding of why its laws are right, dependable, and, most importantly, just, is devoid of justification and an anchor to keep the system steady and dependable. By anchor, we mean some fundamental awareness and appreciation for the nature of law and its application.[3]

Criminal law needs "some authority called forth in support of it, procedural devices to execute it, and methods for sustaining it."[4] It is patently insufficient to argue that laws are laws simply because of their enactment. For "the law is an instrument, a tool of moral perfection. Law facilitates individual and communal perfection; it assists the human agent in being virtuous and it aids human beings in the contemplation of proper objects and ends. In these ways, law is far more influential than its mere promulgation."[5]

For a wonderful Web location that collects legal documents that manifest our legal history in the West, visit http://aalt.law.uh.edu/

This tendency to depend solely on the enactment as a rationale is sometimes referred to as positivism. To the positivist, the law rests primarily on the promulgation itself and need not look much beyond its content. In other schools of thought, such as deconstructionism, there is a view that today's laws need to change for tomorrow and that the law of crimes needs, from time to time, to be stood on its head while it awaits another definition. For the deconstructionist, it matters not if the law has purpose; it simply exists to change this or that. For the Marxist, the law mirrors the power base and the economic order.[6]

For the utilitarian, the law has real meaning when it serves the most good for the particular situation in which it applies.[7] For others, law works its way into the community for no other reason than mere chance and accident. In the law of crimes, where so much is at stake, these postures seem insubstantial and blatantly inadequate.[8]

Police officers who arrest for infractions, judges who sentence the convicted, and prisons that incarcerate must carry out their assigned tasks with certitude and an exactitude that justifies the imposition. Somehow, we must be confident in the righteousness of the case and cause as well as the reasonableness of its punishments. Any positive enactment cannot hold the moral high ground unless and until "reverence for ancestors has been so much weakened that it is no longer thought wrong to interfere with traditional customs by positive enactment."[9] Defendants, and those that labor in the justice system, deserve this small margin of truth.

Amazingly, most justice practitioners are unaware of the ethical and moral dimension that is natural to jurisprudence. Instead of assessing the moral and ethical dimension of a particular law, the practitioner acts as if on automatic pilot. Discovering why a law is good, just, and, yes, even right is the sort of jurisprudential exercise that all justice practitioners should be exposed to. To reveal this dimension, the criminal law thinker goes back to first principles, to the foundational period of why and when criminal laws were enacted in the first place.

CRIMINAL LAW AND THE COMMON LAW

Before the age of statutes and codes, before the system awaited the rulings of appellate courts for interpretations of codified law, the legal world relied heavily on what is termed the "common law." The law of crimes and other areas of legal practice looked not to books but to an intellectual tradition, which, generation after generation, had been passed down. By common, we mean not only what is conceptually shared, e.g., ideas on culpability and defense, right to a trial and possibly a jury, but also what a commonwealth of nations, generally Western nations rooted in Anglo-Saxon legal tradition, fundamentally agrees to. America's roots are inexorably bound up in the English common law tradition although America has developed its own tradition that compliments the English model.[10]

For those in search of common law, one needs only to look back to discover how the principle evolved. In common law analysis, we discern why a crime is a crime, not because the book says so, but because our tradition has held long and fast to the criminalization. Over centuries of Anglo-Saxon, feudal, and English commonwealth traditions, the principles taken for granted today have evolved step-by-step. These prohibitions and proscriptions in criminal law have been passed down from one generation to another, to one English-speaking people after another and from one jurisdiction to another. The English Commonwealth of nations, from Britain to Australia, from New Zealand to Canada, represents a collective of communal interests not only in law but in language, economics, and moral ideology. The ideals of the West span a millennium and these rock hard principles comprise the common law. Hence, rape has always been prohibited under the common law, as has murder, robbery, and other major felonies. A book, a codification, need not be enacted to identify the wickedness of the act. The common law is therefore an unwritten law that binds the justice system not by express language, but by predominant and majoritarian thinking. It is a *lex non scripta*, an unwritten law, with ample power to bind and restrict, "enmeshed in tradition and custom. Recordation was reiteration, echoing intangible established and accepted usages and practices."[11]

Common law represents the moral consensus in mores and values and the general suppositions that a nation/state depends upon for survival. Common laws comprise customary rules of

CASE 1.1

BUCK V. BELL
274 U.S. 200 (1927)

Mr. Justice HOLMES delivered the opinion of the Court.

This is a writ of error to review a judgment of the Supreme Court of Appeals of the State of Virginia, affirming a judgment of the Circuit Court of Amherst County, by which the defendant in error, the superintendent of the State Colony for Epileptics and Feeble Minded, was ordered to perform the operation of salpingectomy upon Carrie Buck, the plaintiff in error, for the purpose of making her sterile. The case comes here upon the contention that the statute authorizing the judgment is void under the Fourteenth Amendment as denying to the plaintiff in error due process of law and the equal protection of the laws.

Carrie Buck is a feeble-minded white woman who was committed to the State Colony above mentioned in due form. She is the daughter of a feeble-minded mother in the same institution, and the mother of an illegitimate feeble-minded child. She was eighteen years old at the time of the trial of her case in the Circuit Court in the latter part of 1924. An Act of Virginia approved March 20, 1924 recites that the health of the patient and the welfare of society may be promoted in certain cases by the sterilization of mental defectives, under careful safeguard, etc.; that the sterilization may be effected in males by vasectomy and in females by salpingectomy, without serious pain or substantial danger to life; that the Commonwealth is supporting in various institutions many defective persons who if now discharged would become a menace but if incapable of procreating might be discharged with safety and become self-supporting with benefit to themselves and to society; and that experience has shown that heredity plays an important part in the transmission of insanity, imbecility, etc.

The statute then enacts that whenever the superintendent of certain institutions including the above named State Colony shall be of opinion that it is for the best interest of the patients and of society that an inmate under his care should be sexually sterilized, he may have the operation performed upon any patient afflicted with hereditary forms of insanity, imbecility, etc., on complying with the very careful provisions by which the act protects the patients from possible abuse.

The superintendent first presents a petition to the special board of directors of his hospital or colony, stating the facts and the grounds for his opinion, verified by affidavit. Notice of the petition and of the time and place of the hearing in the institution is to be served upon the inmate, and also upon his guardian, and if there is no guardian the superintendent is to apply to the Circuit Court of the County to appoint one. If the inmate is a minor notice also is to be given to his parents, if any, with a copy of the petition. The board is to see to it that the inmate may attend the hearings if desired by him or his guardian. The evidence is all to be reduced to writing, and after the board has made its order for or against the operation, the superintendent, or the inmate, or his guardian, may appeal to the Circuit Court of the County. The Circuit Court may consider the record of the board and the evidence before it and such other admissible evidence as may be offered, and may affirm, revise, or reverse the order of the board and enter such order as it deems just. Finally any party may apply to the Supreme Court of Appeals, which, if it grants the appeal, is to hear the case upon the record of the trial in the Circuit Court and may enter such order as it thinks the Circuit Court should have entered. There can be no doubt that so far as procedure is concerned the rights of the patient are most carefully considered, and as every step in this case was taken in scrupulous compliance with the statute and after months of observation, there is no doubt that in that respect the plaintiff in error has had due process at law.

The attack is not upon the procedure but upon the substantive law. It seems to be contended that in no circumstances could such an order be justified. It certainly is contended that the order cannot be justified upon the existing grounds. The judgment finds the facts that have been recited and that Carrie Buck 'is the probable potential parent of socially inadequate offspring, likewise afflicted, that she may be sexually sterilized without detriment to her general health and that her welfare and that of society will be promoted by her sterilization,' and thereupon makes the order. In view of the general declarations of the Legislature and the specific findings of the Court obviously we cannot say as matter of law that the grounds do not exist, and if they exist they justify the result. We have seen more than once that the public welfare may call upon the best citizens for their lives. It would be strange if it could not call upon those who already sap the strength of the State for these lesser sacrifices, often not felt to be such by those concerned, in order to prevent our being swamped with incompetence. It is better for all the world, if instead of waiting to execute degenerate offspring for crime, or to let them starve for their imbecility, society can prevent those who are manifestly unfit from continuing their kind. The principle that sustains compulsory vaccination is broad enough to cover cutting the Fallopian tubes. Three generations of imbeciles are enough. But, it is said, however it might be if this reasoning were applied generally, it fails when it is confined to the small number who are in the institutions named and is not applied to the multitudes outside. It is the usual last resort of constitutional arguments to point out shortcomings of this sort. But the answer is that the law does all that is needed when it does all that it can, indicates a policy, applies it to all within the lines, and seeks to bring within the lines all similarly situated so far and so fast as its means allow. Of course, so far as the operations enable those who otherwise must be kept confined to be returned to the world, and thus open the asylum to others, the equality aimed at will be more nearly reached.

Judgment affirmed.

Questions

1. What practice has been declared legal by this nation's highest court?
2. What is the definition of a feeble-minded inmate?
3. How does the Court justify the law's legitimacy?
4. Relay your thoughts on the Court's language:

"It would be strange if it could not call upon those who already sap the strength of the State for these lesser sacrifices, often not felt to be such by those concerned, in order to prevent our being swamped with incompetence. It is better for all the world, if instead of waiting to execute degenerate offspring for crime, or to let them starve for their imbecility,

> society can prevent those who are manifestly unfit from continuing their kind. The principle that sustains compulsory vaccination is broad enough to cover cutting the Fallopian tubes." (at 206)

right and moral principles that stand essentially unaltered over the course of history. The English jurist, Blackstone remarked:

> Whence it is that in our law the goodness of a custom depends upon its having been used time out of mind; or, in the solemnity of our legal phrase, time whereof the memory of man runneth not to the contrary. This it is that gives it its weight and authority; and of this nature are the maxims and customs which compose the common law, or *lex non scripta*, of this kingdom.[12]

Statutes, as contrasted with common laws, are modern inventions in the prosecution of criminal cases manifesting a shift from the power of the unwritten truth of the common law to the definition of crimes by the sovereign and their legislators. Even though nearly all modern criminal prosecutions are rooted in statutory provisions, the common law never really disappears from the legal landscape, for a statute's very existence depends upon its past. Any legitimacy attached to a criminal codification relies on its origin, and contemporary jurists are not averse to making arguments based on both statute and the common law. Within the code is our legal tradition; within the statute is the precedent, or common law, that gave birth to the criminal law. Massachusetts Chief Justice Shaw summarizes the symbiotic dependency of statute and common law:

> To a very great extent, the unwritten law constitutes the basis of our jurisprudence, and furnishes the rules by which public and private rights are established and secured, the social relations of all persons regulated, their rights, duties, and obligations determined, and all violations of duty redressed and punished. Without its aid, the written law, embracing the constitution and statute laws, would constitute but a lame, partial, and impracticable system.[13]

Tradition, the blend of history and custom, can tell us much about why laws make sense. Religious, theological, and philosophical discourse can lead to an appreciation of why the law has dependability. There is something fundamentally compelling about laws that have long and abiding histories, about laws that appear universal in application and agreed upon by the masses and where experience edifies the sensibility of the law in the first and last place. Tradition, the passing down of what precedes us, is always worth the venture, instructive and rarely unrewarding.

If this text accomplishes no other purpose, it would be one—the critical understanding of legal tradition in the formation of criminal laws. To know not only the content of the law, but also from where its content comes is crucial. By all means, be comfortable with the legislative and promulgative processes, but be more assured after discovering the root and foundation of the law. To say a particular conduct qualifies for the term *crime* has little meaning if the designation lacks a foundation.

Setting a course for a career in criminal law without charting and navigating the tradition that envelops the law of crimes is an unenlightened sojourn.[14] The same observation applies to lawyers who mimic the rulings of judges not discerning the moral and ethical impact of the finding nor caring for the correctness of the ruling in both substantive and virtuous contexts. So much of the contemporary justice model moves through its assigned tasks without any historical understanding and an amoral functionalism that justifies conduct by the enactment alone, forgetting that "law is not codification or enactment alone. ... Law encompasses man's intellectual operations and rationality; it suggests a cohesive and unified plan for social, governmental, and personal living; it lays out a schema of moral and human rights; and it insists upon an unbridled attentiveness to nature and endorses conduct consistent with our nature."[15]

To conclude that a law is nothing more than the sum of its words is to evaluate legal principles by vacuous means. Scan tradition and custom and moral predictability emerges. Become confident that the law of crimes is based on far more than fancy and whim and that its purpose and application tend to the common and the individual good. Recognize that criminal law demands much of its operatives, especially the confidence to appreciate its heritage.

A SURVEY OF LEGAL TRADITION

Those entrusted with the enactment, enforcement, decision making, and advocacy of criminal law in contemporary settings must possess an idea of what law is. Each police officer, judge, jurist, and lawyer should have a firm understanding of what the criminal law is. These foundational inquiries provide an anchor for occupational role, set a bedrock of defensible ideology to coerce and punish, and assure justice practitioners that the justice system operates from right. Where is the law rooted? From where does the criminal law derive its legitimacy and authority? What is the basis for the justness of any criminal law? How can the criminal law guarantee consistent and universal application? How is the criminal law properly interpreted? Questions regarding the criminal law's essence, its origin and enforceability, its tie to justice and injustice were commonly posed in the ancient and medieval periods of the West. Today, we seem to take it all for granted.

In short, the criminal law needs a home to spring out of into the external world. In the classical and medieval world, the aim and ambition of any legal theory was essentially one of the *telos*, the teleologies of both man and his relationship with a creator or some divine force. The roots were cosmological and ontological, driven deep and unreservedly into the nature of man, his or her constitution, reason, intellect, and rationality. By contrast, in the modern world, criminal law analysis is primarily the positivistic, the science of legislative enactment where the practitioner constructs his or her legal edifice on the indemonstrable, sociological foundation that issues no definite philosophy of man.[16] Utilitarians, in the tradition of Jeremy Bentham,[17] manufacture a criminal law's legitimacy from its inherent usefulness, a utility for the most part and for the most moments. To the Hegelian,[18] criminal law is an expression, an unfolding of man as some historical form. To the Marxian,[19] criminal law reflects the power base that wrenches both its authority and its corresponding materialism from the powerless and less influential. In any backdrop of criminal law jurisprudence, from the extremely rational to the reactionary, we yearn for a foundation.

The Ancient Idea of Law and Crime

Our ancient predecessors in Greece and Rome defined law and criminal conduct in distinctly different ways than we are accustomed. Law meant a hierarchy and a series of goods and ends[20] observed from human existence, and an overall belief in law as the rule and measure of life and the universe itself.

Hellenic thought, for example, Plato's theory of *Forms*[21] (the idea of perfection versus an imperfection) testifies to this tendency. Plato writes with regularity about law, the gods, divine and human justice, and a hierarchical perspective on morality, truth, and perfection. Plato accepts without much argument the existence of divine forces in human reality.[22] Plato portrays a reality twofold in design: one human, where the vagaries of day-to-day existence are grounded; another divine, where the divine God, or gods as the case may be, sets the example, provides or detracts from human experience. In this sense, man makes or breaks his world by his adherence to law, but, as is typical in Greek theology, may be an unwitting recipient of a divinely generated justice or injustice. At Book I in his work *Laws*, Plato urges this from the outset.

> They are correct laws, laws that make those who use them happy. Because they provide all the good things. Now, the good things are two fold: some human, some divine. The former depends on the divine goods, and, if a city receives the greater, it also will acquire the lesser. If not, it will lack both.[23]

In Plato's world, human agents depend upon and pray to the gods for justice. Man alone is inadequate to assure a just society for "if the gods are willing, the laws will succeed in making our city blessed and happy."[24] At the level of the divine, there is perfection, beauty, and justice, that simply cannot be achieved in a changeable and temporal world. As with art, music, or a craft, perfection represents the acme of accomplishment. The divine provides the blueprint for what law is and should be, since the divine is encased without error, capable of self-movement and generation and the cause of all else.[25]

Nature, too, plays a pivotal role in Plato's perspective on law. Plato perceives nature as a grounding station, a panoply of norms and universal expectations. Nature is not exclusively a hodgepodge of occurrences without rhyme or design, but, more appropriately, is a rule and measure, an operation with not only means, but proper ends, and an added entanglement with the divine. Nature is not chance, but a divinely executed action. Whether horses, eyes, organic or inorganic matter, Plato discerns a naturalism in every facet of existence. The order of things, in general, "is established by nature."[26] Plato's laws of nations and the citizenry established a perennial perspective on law as enactment or law as reflection of the universe.[27]

For a deep and insightful look at nature, and law in the world of Plato and Aristotle, see https://repository.up.ac.za/upspace/bitstream/2263/4723/1/Junker_Reading(1999).pdf

---

The Greek giant, Aristotle, dealt with the law's relationship to rationality and reason and how law, to be law at all, need not only be consistent with reason, but advance and promote the virtuous life. Reason is consistent with a good and virtuous existence, and, therefore, a lawful life, while its contrary, vice, aligns itself with irrationality and illegality. Aristotle discerns the habituating tendencies in law. Law and legislation are the means by which "all men become virtuous."[28] Aristotle poses the law's training propensity, especially for the young who "must be regulated by laws."[29]

Aristotle's language of law dwells upon goods, virtues, perfections, justice, ends and means, and a hierarchical vision that gazes far beyond promulgation. Aristotle exhorts the human agent "to become immortal as far as that is possible and do our utmost to live in accordance with what is highest in us"[30] to live life "guided by reason,"[31] for such an existence "is the best and most pleasant for man";[32] carrying out existence in accordance with the "nature proper to each thing."[33] For Aristotle, the state, the law, exists for happiness and the advancement of virtue and wisdom.[34] Individual virtue leads a collective of virtuous agents comprising the community and the communal good, Aristotle claims. Aristotle is incapable of differentiating individual conduct from its effect on the collective whole, for "it is evident that the same life is best for each individual, and for states and for mankind collectively."[35] The fact that virtue is synonymous with law is an extraordinary Aristotelian legacy.[36]

Become familiar with the many works of Aristotle now readily online at http://classics.mit.edu/Browse/browse-Aristotle.html

---

Roman jurists, in the mold of Cicero, affirmed the connection between a higher and lower form of law. Cicero's masterpiece, *De Legibus* (*On the Laws*),[37] expends considerable time laying out multiple levels in law, allowing for the necessity of positive human laws, then passionately reminding his readers not to forget the law's ultimate source—the transcendent. Cicero seems surprisingly pre-Christian in his analysis given his pagan background. Cicero's idea of communion ties together God and man.

> Inasmuch as there is no attribute superior to reason, and it is present in both God and man, it must be the essential basis for communion between man and God.[38]

When Cicero declares that God is the "supreme"[39] law, by implication and explicit meaning, he admits a continuum of laws, a series of law forms that stand atop one another, integrated, yet simultaneously existing in separate or diverse domains.

Cicero's legal dialog anticipates the role of reason in jurisprudence. Cicero recognized that human beings are capable of reason and, as a result, are qualified to create laws. Reason, especially *recta ratio*, or right reason, presumes a legal product in tune with the drafter's essential nature. Cicero describes how reason is the glue for both person and culture.

> The essential justice that binds human society together and is maintained by one law is right reason, expressed in commands and prohibitions. Whoever disregards this law, whether written or unwritten, is unjust.[40]

Nature, Cicero declares, is our other dependable guide, and, in fact, justice itself is derived from nature. Cicero relates Nature's instructive powers, which are permanent fixtures and guideposts in moral activity:

> Goodness is not just a matter of opinion; what idea is more absurd than that? Since then we distinguish good from evil by its nature, and since these qualities are fundamental in Nature, surely by a similar logic we may discriminate and judge between what is honorable and what is base according to Nature.[41]

Thus, Cicero posits the argument that behavior consistent with Nature is lawful and inconsistent is the opposite. Hence, unnatural behavior, such as incest, necrophilia, bestiality, and the like, all have identifiable natural consequences. The same naturalistic reasoning could be applied to prostitution and drug usage.

Cicero clearly had a way with words. Assess some of these excellent commentaries at http://
pirate.shu.edu/~knightna/westciv1/cicero.htm

Early Medieval Legal Thought

By the time of St. Augustine, the rudimentary, pagan conceptions of law donned a Stoic, yet
religious, Christianized attitude, a sort of supreme cosmic rationality. Augustine, a former
Roman patrician who subsequently converted to Christianity and became the Bishop of
Hippo, erects a multilevel edifice throughout his brilliant inquiries where the criminal law
resides. According to St. Augustine, the eternal law of God (the *lex aeterna*) serves as the
starting point for human operations since God is the author of the universe.[42] Creation itself
manifests the eternal law of the Supreme God who is its Author.[43] Augustine's *lex aeterna* is
not a pantheistic ideal where God is the universe itself. Instead, it is "the ineradicable and
sublime administration of all things with proceeds from the Divine Providence."[44] The *lex
aeterna* is a "divinely ordained orderliness"[45] covering every aspect of human existence. St.
Augustine states:

> To put in a few words, as best I can, the notion of eternal law that has been impressed upon our minds:
> It is that law by which it is just that everything be ordered in the highest degree [*ordinatissima*].[46]

Hovering over all levels of human existence, Augustine's *lex aeterna* perfectly represents law
as the act of legislator, law enforcement, lawyer, and the judge interpreting its content, in submission to a divine plan and a divine will.[47]

Besides this, Augustine's contribution to the hierarchical ideal in law is quite evident in his
discussion of the *lex naturalis*, the natural law. Descending down from the apex of the eternal
law, is the imprint of the Creator on beings created. This imprint, this inherency, Augustine
terms the *lex naturalis*, is participatory in the *lex aeterna*. Transcribed, implanted in the soul of
man, the *lex naturalis* is man's imperfect participation in the perfection of the eternal law. One
of Augustine's more famous quotes is: "Law is written in the hearts of men, which iniquity itself
effects not."[48]

Augustinian legal thought is essentially derivative in design since Augustine's natural law "is
to be discovered in the divinely ordained ontological order. It is the observance of this infinite
natural and moral order that forms the true substance of the Augustinian concept of law and
right, justice, and morality."[49] Human laws, particularly criminal ones, are not independent of
this order and are, in fact, partners to the natural and eternal laws. Human laws are crucial to
individual and social operations and are, according to St. Augustine, "helpful to men living in
this life."[50] Nations and states cannot exist without temporal laws, especially the criminal variety. Yet these human promulgations must be consistent with the higher order of the natural and
eternal law. When a human law is inconsistent with and contrary to the tenets of the eternal and
natural law, it loses its force and identity as law. Augustine's maxim "an unjust law is not a law
at all"[51] imparts the derivative quality of his jurisprudence. He issues this provocative argument
in *De Libero Arbitrio*. "We shall not, shall we, dare say that these laws are unjust—or rather, are
not laws at all, for I think that a law that is not just is not a law."[52] Dr. Martin Luther King, Jr., a
reader and Augustine scholar, employed Augustine's radical theory of civil disobedience during
the Civil Rights era of the 1960s. Augustine also would dramatically impact Thomas Aquinas in

the thirteenth century whose analysis of the just and unjust law would deliver exceptional benefits to even twentieth-century movements like that of Dr. King's.[53]

During the seventh century, the writings of Isidore of Seville[54] further laid down our criminal law heritage. For Isidore, human laws, including the criminal variety, were not severable from the higher laws that justify their enactment. Isidore's "natural law is a law common to all peoples (nations), and is held to be not something established by man himself, but rather a common natural instinct."[55] Quite evident in Isidore's work is the recognition of how authority, legal or otherwise, descends from God. Government and individuals both function because of the higher power not the lower. Kings, as well as subjects, were bound by the law identically. These same characters compel king and citizen to obey the law so that justice might be nurtured. Truth is the ruler's guide.[56] Isidore's prevailing imperative was to demand and search for certitude because each thing tends "one end of truth."[57]

Other questions posed by Isidore reflect a prophetic legal thinker, examples being the interplay between law and custom, the relationship and contrast between military and civilian law, and civil law with criminal law.[58] Laws, too, must be enacted without private gain, but rather a common purpose.[59]

Legal Thought in the Later Middle Ages

Between the time of Isidore and the eleventh century, there are scant contributions to legal theory, with most authors remaining true to the Augustinian model. By this time, a vigorous debate on the nature of law reemerged. Anselm of Canterbury showed little hesitation in calling for a higher form of law. Anselm's *Cur Deus Homo* advanced the proposition that God is "the supreme good, is justice himself and is the perfection all beings seek."[60] Law can only be law when compatible with justice, God being its highest and greatest good. Nothing in God is injustice or unjust.[61] At the pinnacle of justice is truth itself, and justice instructs the human person on how to live with self and others.[62] In this truth, God subsists and nothing else can.[63]

Peter Abelard's conceptual approach accepts the dominant position divine law assumes, but attempts to particularize the issues at street level. Not only is man, by committing crimes, displeasing his nature, he is displeasing his Creator. Abelard summarizes in his *Ethics*:

> If perhaps someone asks whence we can infer that the transgression of adultery displeases God more than overeating, I think divine law can teach us, which has not instituted any satisfaction of punishment to penalize the latter, but it has decreed that the former be damned not with any penalty but with the supreme affliction of death. For where the love of our neighbour, which the Apostle says is the fulfilling of the Law, is more fully damaged, more is done against it and sin is greater.[64]

The significance of Abelard's thought rests in his emphasis on particular legal and moral situations. Abelard builds a more complex series of rules that were derived from not only the Testaments, but from the natural law impressed in the psyche of the human species. Abelard's ethical theory stresses the universality and immutability of our natural law imprint. "The natural law, impressed on Christian, Jew, Muslim, and Pagan, is simultaneously revealed in Scripture and encapsulates the basic moral prohibitions of murder, stealing, and so on."[65]

Abelard also comments on the relationship of justice, the ethical life of the individual and the common good. Justice is not exclusively what is due another because any theory of reciprocity and equality is impossible without reference to the collective whole. Abelard clearly delivers this principle:

For it often happens that, when we give someone what is his due on account of his merits, what we do for one individual brings common harm. Therefore, in order to prevent the part being put before the whole, the individual before the community, to the definition [of justice] there is added "provided that the common utility is preserved." We should do all things so that we each seek not our own, but the common good, and provide for the public welfare rather than that of our families and live not for ourselves but our fatherland.[66]

Finally, Abelard's message clearly includes the formative nature of law in its most general sense, for human beings who sin or are in error are corrected by the compulsion of the law.[67]

By the twelfth century, it would be difficult to find a legal thinker who did not share the basic sentiments outlined to this point. The law, structured in tiers and escalating dimensions, anchored its legitimacy in a higher–lower continuum. The legal thought of Gratian, particularly his *Decretals*, and more specifically his *Treatise on Laws at DD 1-20*, lays solid groundwork for the modern criminal law model. Though law consists of "ordinance and usage,"[68] the term imputes justice. For Gratian, virtue is presented as essential to any definition of law, and the overall purpose of the law is to lead men to virtue so that "human temerity can be controlled, innocence can be protected in the midst of wicked people, and the capacity of the wicked to harm others can be restrained by fear of punishment."[69] These same human laws, prodding man to virtue, are legitimate only to the extent compatible with a natural law, infused by the Creator. Gratian further comments: "Now natural law similarly prevails by dignity over custom and enactments. So, whatever has been either received in usages or set down in writing is to be held null and void if it is contrary to natural law."[70]

Gratian's natural law is what is contained in the law and the Gospel. Further, Gratian's natural law, just as Abelard attempts, delivers a series of general precepts, "common to all nations"[71] and to all peoples. These primary tenets of the natural law are, by way of example:

… the union of men and women, the succession and rearing of children, the common possession of all things, the identical liberty of all, or the acquisition of things that are taken from the heavens, earth, or sea, as well as the return of a thing deposited or of money entrusted to one, and the repelling of violence by force. This, and anything similar, is never regarded as unjust, but is held to be natural and equitable.[72]

When particular determinations are examined, criminal law designs eventually unfold to protect these principles. Resistance and condemnation of human laws enacted contrarily to these contents are required. As Gratian argues, "dispensation"[73] from its content is not permitted.

Alexander of Hales dwelled upon similar subject matter in his *Summa Universae Theologiae*. A hierarchy of laws underscores Alexander's legal formula, for every law, even the positive variety, is bound to the eternal law of God.[74] This eternal law is impressed and imprinted in the souls of rational creatures.[75] Alexander's legal thinking is undeniably derivative, maintaining that every law, human or divine, derives its force from the *lege aeterna*[76] assuming that the law is just and good. The *legis aeternae* is immutable[77] and absolute.[78] An unjust law cannot be derived from the eternal law.[79]

Both human law and the natural law are derived from the eternal law as well. At the lower part of the legal continuum, human laws are integrated into his hierarchical plan.[80] The same conclusion is obvious for the natural law because every good is undeniably and universally from the eternal good just as the natural law is derived from the eternal law.[81]

Alexander is reverential about the natural law, its immutability,[82] its rationality,[83] its mandatory connection to the positive human law,[84] and, finally, its intensive leadership in helping the human agent do what is right and to forever journey to the God who implants its directives. Alexander's natural law reasoning is an intensely intimate participation with the eternal law of God.

Albert the Great (1206–1280) perceived law in both a personal and political sense: to control the masses, to maintain order, and to compel nations and states to unite. Law is a sanction, an authoritative reminder, as well as a tool for human advancement and virtue, for both individual citizen and nation.[85] Albert's definition of the natural law is universal in design and principle, it is instinctually and inherently known and understood.[86] This instinctual, inherent character, while comprehended differently by differing players, is universally experienced. While positive human law differs across the world's stage, the natural law is the same for all.[87] The natural law, strictly defined, is innate, universal, and the dictate of reason.[88] Such a law cannot be banished from memory, but its extent and quality may diminish or differ in the consideration of particular dilemmas. No dispensation from its content is possible, neither can it be altered or eliminated.[89]

Albert is equally dedicated to a perpetual dialog on justice and injustice. Justice, as well as other virtues, are intimately part of Albert's jurisprudence. Law's consistent interdependency with reason can only prompt discussion of final ends, goods, and the virtuous life. Albert's law to be law at all,[90] inevitably advances virtue.[91]

The Turning Point toward Our Modern System

When contemporary thinkers employ the term *law*, they yearn for definition, an anchor, a foundation of meaning. Exactly what a law means depends on perspective. A common conception of law is that of a rule, regulation, statute, or ordinance; a case issued by judicial authority or some other concretization of a particular legal idea or principle. Laws are as numerous and meaningful as the scope of their coverage, and are, without much argument, juridical instruments. By the thirteenth century, legal philosophy was firmly entrenched in a Christian, teleological conception, attendant to a natural law basis. No other thinker up to this time developed as sophisticated a criminal law perspective as Thomas Aquinas. In St. Thomas's view, law is a "certain rational plan and rule of operation"[92] and especially proper "to rational creatures only."[93] St. Thomas confidently asserts that "law is something pertaining to reason"[94] and a measure of human activity. If it is a measure of human action, one must presuppose there is a connection to human reason because only the human species analyzes, deliberates, and counsels about activity and movement. Law is entwined with being itself.

When dealing with the law's essence, St. Thomas imparts primary stature to reason:

> Law is a rule and measure of acts, whereby man is induced to act or is restrained from acting; for *lex* [law] is derived from *ligare* [to bind] because it binds one to act. Now the rule and measure of human acts is the reason, which is the first principle of human acts.[95]

St. Thomas Aquinas is well aware that the ordinating influence of law does not terminate with individual activity because it just as pertinently applies to the common good of a nation as it applies to the common good of its individual citizenry. In response to whether a law should be crafted for the individual or common case, St. Thomas indicates that every human law derives legitimacy from its relationship to the common interest. Laws consist of far more than individual applications, but are germane to the life of a nation. "Hence, human laws should be proportioned to the common good. Now, the common good comprises many things. Therefore, law should take account of many things, as to persons, as to matters, and as to times."[96]

With keen insight, St. Thomas discerns the futility of a law that applies in the individual scenario alone. Laws are implemented not for the single person or the one-time circumstance, but instead, law is a common precept applicable to a community of men.[97] It is for the multitude that laws exist because laws for the community are nothing more than the social sum of its members. Law, particularly the human variety, "is framed for the multitude of beings."[98]

Aquinas and the Hierarchy of Law

St. Thomas, impressed with the power of human law, though aware of its limitations, designs a multitiered construct, a hierarchical architectonic of laws in four categories: the eternal, the natural, the divine, and the human. These four types exist independently, yet dependently; distinct, yet unified and integrated. Succinctly put, the hierarchy implies unity, but is dedicated to a priority of one type of law over the others. An elementary depiction would be as shown in Figure 1.1.

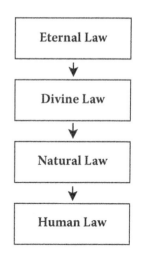

Figure 1.1   St. Thomas Aquinas's hierarchy of laws.

In the plan of God, the higher law descends to the lower law. St. Thomas sees lower forms of the law as derived from the higher form. This "derivative"[99] quality commences with the eternal law, the Divine exemplar that is the blueprint for the universe and its law. Divine revelation, centrally exposed in biblical instruction, gives clarification to the people of God. Creation, especially the rational variety, participates in the eternal law by and through the natural law. Positive laws, the promulgations of man, are a necessary component for a civil society. Unified and interdependent in design, Thomistic law is complicated yet elementary. At its peak, God's eternal law watches over the other categories. "The exemplar of divine Wisdom is the eternal law."[100] St. Thomas relates, and as a result, "all laws proceed from the eternal law."[101] At the human level, each derives its legitimacy from its superior counterpart. A judge, jurist, police officer, lawmaker, and lawyer cannot differentiate or chop up their legal inquiry, e.g., forgetting man's natural inclination in a case of incest; proclaiming a humanistic notion of individual rights at the expense of common welfare; enacting a statute, interpreting a case, applying a principle, without regard for spiritual, moral or revelatory considerations. Within the *Treatise on Law*, St. Thomas offers a series of interlocking and interdependent categories of law, each form gauged in its relationship to the others before legal action will have legitimacy.

The Eternal Law

At the pinnacle in Thomistic jurisprudence is the eternal law of God, the rational architect of the universe and its creatures. In calling God's law the "supreme exemplar,"[102] Aquinas foundationally sets the basis for all legal practice and theory in this perennial, permanent, and immutable dimension. God, the artist and the craftsman, makes only good things, and as a result, molds creatures with lawful inclinations and components. Aquinas characterizes objects or beings by the "emanation"[103] from God's being, containing or being the law itself and the "extensiveness" of God's influence on reality itself.

Even the wicked and the perverse are subject to the eternal law. Even the blessed and the damned are under the eternal law.[104] Even the ignorant cannot disavow some knowledge of the eternal law because their being still reflects the Creator by its effects. Even the lustful and the slaves of flesh cannot "dominate"[105] and destroy the good of one's nature, for "there remains in man the inclination to do the things that belong to the eternal law."[106] Nothing and no one can evade the eternal law. The eternal law, residing within, or more accurately inherently within, the God of Creation, is the measure of all activity. Thomas does not hesitate calling God's law truth itself. At Question 93, Article 1, he summarizes that "the divine intellect is true in itself, and its exemplar is truth itself."[107]

The Natural Law

Since the human species is powerless to fully learn the mind of God and His eternal law, St. Thomas recommends a look at our very natures. Nature, in a scientific, physical sense has an order, a series of operational rules. Undoubtedly, human beings, like other beings, display natural inclinations, preferences, propensities ,and dispositions that mirror the wisdom of the author. The term *natural law* references two critical Thomistic ideas: (1) the nature of a being itself and (2) law as an operation of that nature. To say someone or something has a nature is to typify its very existence. Then, apply law to that nature and that nature unfolds before us, doing what it must and should do to preserve its existence, signifies nature as well.[108]

From the Thomistic view, man is forged so tightly with the natural law that he cannot extricate himself from its influence. We can't even intend contrary to what we are, though we can will the difference—choosing evil, which "is a result apart from intention."[109] Wickedness, unlawfulness, does not reside in reason or our constitution, for "such a thing is not the necessary result of what is intended; rather, it is repugnant to what is intended."[110] St. Thomas does not compartmentalize the natural law's influence on human operations, but recognizes its determinative power. Every inclination in the human actor, particularly those touched or controlled by reason, deals with our natural law imprint.[111]

The Content of the Natural Law—Any reasoned analysis of the natural law inspects the sum and substance of its content. Thus far, descriptive terms, such as inclinations and imprints, have been employed to describe the natural law, but this is inadequate. What is it that we are inclined about? St. Thomas's theory of the natural law catalogs these inclinations as essentially self-evident, discoverable by all who engage in "slight reflection."[112] At Question 94, Article 2, a list of these first principles is announced:

> For there is in man, first of all, an inclination to good in accordance with the nature which he has in common with all substances, inasmuch, namely, as every substance seeks the preservation of its own being, according to its nature; and by reason of this inclination, whatever is a means of preserving human life, and of warding off its obstacles, belongs to the natural law. Secondly, there is in man an inclination to things that pertain to him more specially, according to that nature which he has in common with other animals; and in virtue of this inclination, those things are said to belong to the natural law which nature has taught to all animals, such as sexual intercourse, the education of offspring and so forth.[113]

These inclinations of social existence, propagation of the species, self-preservation, the inherent desire to know truth and God, are universally true in all rational beings.[114]

Other principles are labeled *secondary*, or by some, *tertiary*[115] derivations of fundamental natural law principles. The clear-cut, undeniable tenets of first principles lose their punch, or at least their ease of discovery, as one moves to more particular cases.

The Divine Law

St. Thomas's recognition of the divine exemplar, the divine intellect giving rationality to the universe, and the view that God's very being is the eternal law itself, is often considered the thesis of divine law. Divine law, while having the qualities of God's rationality and plan, is not the same as the eternal law. Divine law, in the most elementary framework, is the Old and New Testaments, which comprise the Bible. It is easy to interchangeably term the eternal law, the divine, and the divine, the eternal, for common parlance often does so. Instead, one finds St. Thomas fully cognizant of the role and purpose of Scripture in the life of the Christian, and that this same Scripture has revelatory qualities. Scripture explains the mind and particular commands of a transcendent, perfect God. Additionally, the eternal, natural, and human laws, while interdependent and unified in a teleological sense, do not, according to St. Thomas, directly address the law of salvation. He suggests divine law serves this end:

> [T]he end of the divine law is to bring man to that end which is everlasting happiness; and this end is hindered by any sin, not only of external action, but also of internal action. Consequently, that which suffices for the perfection of human law, viz., the prohibition and punishment of sin, does not suffice for the perfection of the divine law, but it is requisite that it should make man altogether fit to partake of everlasting happiness.[116]

It is obvious that St. Thomas is not just paying lip service as to the divine law's value in his jurisprudence.

Man's incompetency to do what is right and God's unbridled generosity in His revealing, through Scripture, the plan for human operations, the Divine Law anchors human kind in God's great scheme.[117] Comprehensively, St. Thomas inserts the divine promulgations of both the Old Law and the New, so that even though the "benefits of nature"[118] are not forfeited, the "benefits of grace"[119] are not lost through sin.

In short, the divine law directly enunciates the faith since human reason alone cannot fully discern the things of God.[120] In both the Old and New Testaments, St. Thomas declares the plan of salvation as proclaimed by the Creator. Whether by the Old Testament's stern deterrent mentality or the New Testament's all-encompassing charity, both scriptural domains lay out a map for salvation. The Decalogue, as an illustration, represents the divine law's capacity to guide, to instruct, to lead man to proper ends, and on the way giving one another their due.[121]

Divine law continually serves as a reminder to the Christian citizen and moral agent, transmitting its luminous beacon of moral truth to those "habituated to sin"[122] and "darkened as to what ought to be done in particular."[123]

Human Law

Those less learned about St. Thomas Aquinas often assume that human law is either incidental or deficient when compared to the eternal, natural, and divine law.[124] The things of the Earth are by no means as lofty or principled as the perfections of God. Nor are the legal musings of man as legislator, lawyer, and judge possibly on par with the divine or eternal promulgations. Despite the imperfection, human laws are essential to St. Thomas's theory of law because their content aims "at the ordering of human life … under the precepts of a life we have to lead."[125] Criminal law could be no better an example.[126]

> A Web location dedicated to Aquinas on law, nature, and justice provides links for further study at http://www.lonang.com/exlibris/aquinas/

One of the most striking features of St. Thomas's discussion of human law is its necessity—a belief that human existence would fail without legal promulgations. Human beings need commands, proscriptions, and prohibitions to carry out their individual and collective enterprise. Laws serve as a series of parameters and controls for human conduct. Although human beings are fundamentally geared to the good, and by their rational nature can identify proper ends, experience delineates the value of control. Wills, passions, and appetites tug and, at times, overwhelm the rational creature that chooses conduct contrary to their nature. Indeed, St. Thomas is bold enough to assert that a morally inclined individual has little need of human law because that person already adheres to the dictates of practical reason, the mandates of the natural law, the divine law precepts, and the blueprint of the eternal law. This type of character is rare for the theory of necessity relates to the bulk of humanity.[127] Those already disposed to virtue have less need for legal regulation while those whose "disposition is evil are not led to virtue unless they are compelled."[128]

The necessity of human law, as St. Thomas poses, "refers to the removal of evils"[129] from the world we inhabit. Law, in the human sense, is the purifier, the fortress against the onslaught of moral barbarism. From another perspective, the necessity of human law is manifest in human activity of every sort, especially in the communal setting. Positive law involves both the "law of nations and civil law."[130] Hence, human law is necessitous for both reasons of utility and man's current lack of perfection. It is, for lack of better description, a libation that the virtuous can avoid and the wicked must drink.

Any justice professional soon discovers that most law has a precedential legacy. Cases of first instance are temporary events because legal pronouncements eventually attract a following. When enough people praise the decision and enough support is generated amongst the legal community, a legal maxim and principle is born. To have any credibility, a law withstands the test of time and the clamor of the crowd. Good laws are not drafted in isolation, but rooted in tradition. Human law is derived from other sources including the theological and philosophical underpinnings espoused by St. Thomas. Even speeding, jaywalking, taxes, etc., have a derivative quality, especially in the justness behind their enactment. Kings, too, derive their authority from a higher power, although history is replete with examples of those who turn the crown into an anointing, who would "usurp that right, by framing unjust laws, and by degenerating into tyrants who preyed on their subjects."[131] Human law depends upon and looks to the eternal, natural, and divine laws. Using his integrative method, St. Thomas finds it impossible to separate human law from the natural law order so evident in rational creatures. At most, Aquinas places human law lower in his legal hierarchy because its enforceability depends upon human beings, while divine law "persuades men by means of rewards or punishments to be received from God. In this respect, it employs higher means."[132] Because law is an exercise of human reason, and reason is the rule and measure of law, St. Thomas argues that human law is derived from the natural and eternal law. The derivative relationship between the positive law and "higher" law is not one based on confrontation, but one of unity and integration.[133]

Human laws that are contrary to the tenets of the natural law are, by implication, an affront to the eternal law and not really laws in the truest sense. Radically, St. Thomas holds that every law is derived from the eternal law because of reason's role in the deliberation, and a law deviating from reason has not the nature of law in any sense.[134] A human law, inconsistent with the natural, does violence to the very notion of what law is and, ergo, cannot bind in conscience.[135] Neither, therefore, is it nor can it be law as popularly understood. Human laws inconsistent with the divine law receive no recognition from St. Thomas since any enactment "contrary to the divine law ... has not the nature of law."[136] Any human promulgation antagonistic to the eternal, divine, and natural laws will be an affront to any version of law and equity. To so hold is a radical error in jurisprudence. Thus, St. Thomas declares: "But, in so far as it deviates from reason, it is called an unjust law and has the nature, not of law, but of violence."[137]

The Enlightenment to Colonial Period

Up until the time of the Reformation, the natural law philosophy of the medieval period remained intact and is still ingrained in most prominent jurists and legal philosophers. The hierarchical construct, where the eternal, divine, and natural interlocked and intertwined with the human law, would come under scrutiny or new interpretation, but was never removed from the legal landscape. Criminal law was now more than sin or assaults on the purity of the divine. After the sixteenth century, these once ensconced ideas of law took new shape and the jurisprudential beacon pointed in different directions. Instead of the emphasis being the Divine and the universal, the attention turned to the individual and the rights attached to that personhood. For, after the Enlightenment, the idea of rights in a legal sense loses its teleological meaning and turns individualized and internal. Surely, the average legal thinker maintained the strong correlation evident in theological thinking and law, but the push now shifts to human rights in the positive realm. Laws were the product of sovereigns in power, or the image of those in the majority, or manifestations of the will of the populace. Laws were also the means to assure peace over war, tranquility over turbulence. The relationships between law, nature, and rational thinking were altered in other ways. Laws, criminal or otherwise, were tools of control and order keepers.

As proof, the revolutions in France and the United States spoke loudly of this changing of the guard; this general notion that men as free beings have rights naturally as citizens in addition to any divinely bestowed. Laws, particularly criminal ones, were then analyzed and adopted under a differing philosophical bent: Are these enactments useful? Do they serve a particular good in a collective or individual sense? Can these laws be separate from theology and some eternal oversight? Are laws permanent in any sense or merely a reflection of the struggle? Can law and morality be mixed at all? Are men and women persons of equality? Do citizens have unalienable rights and privileges? Should governmental authority go unchecked?

The text is incapable of dealing with all the major thinkers in this area, but will highlight the legal thought of three thinkers whose influence on the American experience is undeniable and whose jurisprudence influenced the shape and content of our criminal law tradition.

Thomas Hobbes

Hobbes's attention to law and human interaction is a curious mix of psychology and personal struggle. Instead of a series of interlocking and dependent goods and perfections, watched over by a providential divinity, Hobbes's world contains characters squabbling over the meager resources available to all. Replacing the natural law imprint of commands and prescriptions with a confrontational vision of human warfare, Hobbes believes that the sole purpose of law is to keep human beings from engaging in warfare, which he terms the law of nature. In the world of St. Thomas Aquinas, nature rationally orders person and the world around them. Natural law tenets are imprinted in the human constitution as the Creator intended. For Hobbes, warfare is the natural state of existence and in a world without law, chaos reigns supreme. Without the sovereign's imposition of law and order, human individualism would run without checks or balances. "Not being required to defer to anyone else's judgments, but not being able, either, to rely on others to seek the good cooperatively or benevolently, people would have rationally to expect the worst from one another and, if they thought that their safety demanded it, take preemptive action. Thus, even those who were not naturally greedy or violent might begin to see their own survival and well-being in taking as much of what they wanted as they could, or in killing anyone who might be a potential enemy, which could mean anyone."[138] Hence, a criminal codification needs enactment not necessarily because it is the moral guidepost for the nation, but because without the codification, the nation would collapse. Hobbes's compelling work, *Leviathan* (1651), paints this very bleak picture:

> To this warre of every man against every man, this also is consequent; that nothing can be Unjust. The notions of Right and Wrong, Justice and Injustice have there no place. Where there is no common Power, there is no Law: where no Law, no Injustice. Force, and Fraud, are in warre, the two Cardinall vertues. Justice, and Injustice are none of the Faculties neither of the Body, nor Mind ... It is consequent also to the same condition, that there be no Propriety, no Dominion, no Mine and Thine distinct; but onely that to be every mans, that he can get; and for so long, as he can keep it.[139]

In man's state of nature, there is war and it is the task of government and its promulgative powers in law to regulate this predictable state of affairs. Of course, this necessitous perception is a far cry from the medieval conception of the human condition, which optimistically believes that man is quite capable of human goodness and perfection and that law serves as the abiding and habituating instrument toward these ends.

Hobbes further dictates that the inherent freedom to do or not do in each human player must be given up to the commonwealth for the sake of peace. Individual preferences and attitudes must be sacrificed for the ordered society to sustain itself. And since the human person is born free, this relinquishment in an individual sense is contrary to that fundamental freedom, but a necessity for survival. As long as the sovereign government keeps its end of the bargain, namely safety and tranquility for its citizens, the individual person cannot demand unbridled freedom. If the sovereign fails to deliver the promise, then the relinquished freedoms return the citizen who seeks out another governing body. Rather than the medieval conception that the king or other monarchy or governing force was divinely ordained or under the tutelage of God, Hobbes types government in purely secular terms with obedience to it rooted in the exchange of freedom for protection. Once the protection breaks down or is corrupted, the obligation to obey ends. "The obedience springs from a transfer of right for the sake of peace. The state is thus seen as a security or peacekeeping device whose existence is in the interest of the many, rather than as a facsimile on Earth of a divine ordering of things by nobility or rank or station."[140]

The Hobbesian model of law is fluid rather than fixed and can easily justify the type of revolutionary ardor so passionately apparent in the American Revolution. In this context, we see subjects of the sovereignty, a government ordained by God under traditional terms, rise up and revolt against a whole stream of laws and regulations that oppressed the colonialists. So, too, it will be the disdain the American colonialists will have toward the severe capital offense system in place in the late eighteenth century and myriad potential offenses in a cumbersome criminal law system imposed on the colonists. For Hobbes, living under an oppressive sovereignty is not living at all. Hobbes relays the point well:

> For the use of Lawes, (which are but Rules Authorised) is not to bind the People from all Voluntary actions; but to direct and keep them in such a motion, as not to hurt themselves by their own impetuous desires, rashnesse, or indiscretion; as Hedges are set, not to stop Travellers, but to keep them in the way. And therefore a Law that is not Needfull, having not the true End of a Law, is not Good.[141]

Therefore, any criminal law system that does not maintain the promised peace and tranquility is, according to Hobbes, not worthy of our allegiance and in need of overturn.

John Locke

Locke's many discourses on law and government are innovative and lively and few would argue that the Lockean influence was both deep and abiding in the Constitution's framers. In John Locke's world, there was a contagious optimism about the human condition rather than the miserable lot of warfare and greed posited by Hobbes. For Locke believed, as did Aristotle and Aquinas, that God implanted man and woman with a rational character to live correctly, and that, as a rule, human beings are "pretty decent fellow[s]"[142] whom if they think long and incisively enough will discern, this rational ideology of law. Locke remarks in his *Second Treatise on Government*:

> The state of Nature has a law of Nature to govern it, which obliges every one, and reason, which is that law, teaches all mankind who will but consult it, that being all equal and independent, no one ought to harm another in his life, health, liberty or possessions; for mean being all the workmanship of one omnipotent and infinitely wise Maker; all the servants of one sovereign Master, sent into the world by His order and about His business.[143]

In the Lockean perspective, the citizen precedes the governmental entity, the rights and ambitions of the inhabitant exist despite the rise or fall of governments since these rights are rooted in the law of nature as ordained by God. "And, so the chief lesson John Locke learned from the law of nature was that even before government existed men were free, independent, and equal in the enjoyment of inalienable rights, chief among them being life, liberty and property."[144] Locke conceives the human player as independent of government in a truly noble and serious sense and, when constitutionalists use the term "unalienable rights," Locke's vision could not be better expressed.[145]

For this reason, Locke wrote extensively of property rights, the value of labor, due process imperatives, and the fundamental right of redress against errant governments. This is an ideology built on nature, but a nature built on individual liberties. When compared to Aquinas's ideal of nature, one witnesses a divine plan rooted from the bottom up in the world of Locke. Put another way, Locke sees the human agent as free willing and moving, in accordance with the divine plan, and endowed with a series of rights and privileges that attach to personhood because of personhood. For Augustine and Aquinas, the rights we so continuously hear about emanate from the divine being who makes all things plausible and possible. Rights descend downward never upward. While the contrast may be academic, the fundamental difference has clearly impacted the American experience in the criminal justice system.

It should not be surprising, therefore, that the United States zealously guards individual rights in a constitutional and statutory sense more than most of its European and even Canadian counterparts. This is a nation built on individual protections like no other. And, in Locke, we see the fervor for individual integrity and protection, as he indicates:

I easily grant that civil government is the proper remedy for the inconveniences of the state of nature, which must certainly be great where men may be judges in their own case; since it is easy to be imagined that he who was so unjust as to do his brother an injury will scarce be so just as to condemn himself for it; but I shall desire those who make this objection to remember that absolute monarchs are but men, and if government is to be the remedy of those evils, which necessarily follow from men's being judges in their own cases, and the state of nature is therefore not to be endured, I desire to know what kind of government that is, and how much better it is than the state of nature.[146]

After all, there is a natural and unending suspicion of government in this revolutionary setting known as America. Whether or not criminal laws are involved, the citizenry exerts great pain to check and balance the power of the sovereign. This democratization of human personhood spills into property ownership, resistance to tyranny, and Locke's belief that government must have inherent checks and balances, runs deep in the American character. The fact that our system of governance has three major powers, all of which are separate, is not an accident. In Locke's mind, limitations on government were not signs of weakness, but strength in national character. This is a dramatic shift away from the monarchy form so prevalent in his time.

The Lockean jurisprudence is one that will not tolerate abuse of its citizenry. In his *Second Treatise*, Locke is unequivocal about the sovereign obligations to the public and in the event it fails to deliver, revolution and dissolution remains the chief course of action. Rising up, confronting legal authority, revolting are not timid exhortations, but the fire and brimstone of the civil libertarian that will influence the American legal system from the outset. Locke's language displays reasoned passion:

And hence it is that he who attempts to get another man into his absolute power does thereby put himself into a state of war with him, it being to be understood as a declaration of a design upon his life; for I have reason to conclude that he who would get me into his power without my consent would use me as he pleased when he got me there, and destroy me, too, when he had a fancy to it; for nobody can desire to have me in his absolute power unless it be to compel me by force to that which is against the right of my freedom, i.e., to make me a slave.[147]

Visit an Oregon State University site dedicated to John Locke at http://oregonstate.edu/instruct/phl302/philosophers/locke.html

---

Jeremy Bentham

Whether a law is useful for most individuals is the guiding premise in the jurisprudence of Bentham. Useful, or of utility, are the buzzwords of the school of utilitarianism of which Bentham and John Stuart Mill were fervent advocates. Bentham's approach has been characterized as cynical and self-serving because his ideology affords little in the forms of moral dependability or theological foundations. To be sure, Bentham had little regard for religious thought in the matter of law because its absolute and doctrinaire qualities were always at odds with his utility. For Bentham, the law should permit what the majority wants. For Bentham, a law is good if the bulk of masses like it, or if most of the citizenry benefits or if the positive results from enforcement outweigh the negative effects. A utilitarian operates in an amoral world with little or no dependency on the divine imprint, nature, natural law, or inalienable rights. Utilitarians measure cause and effect and then reach conclusions about the efficacy and sensibility of a law.

Utility to Bentham is "that property in any object, whereby it tends to produce benefit, advantage, pleasure, good, or happiness (all this in the present case comes to the same thing) or (what comes again to the same thing) to prevent the happening of mischief, plain, evil, or unhappiness."[148]

Utility, according to Bentham, is an evaluation of attendant pains and pleasures. Hence, corrective discipline would be assessed in light of whether the pain satisfactorily alters conduct. Pleasure would be scrutinized to determine whether the populace reaps major benefits from an activity either proposed as legal or proscribed.

Bentham was unreserved in his criticism of his predecessors whom he labeled "religionists and moralists."[149] The quest for legal certitude does not reside in religious melancholy and sentimentalism for its strength, and breadth can only be discerned in the measure of its worth. Worth or value, benefit or gain, loss or detriment are just some of the yardsticks employed by Bentham as he promulgates a jurisprudence of utility. Right and wrong cannot be discovered in the context of legal enforcement or legislative drafting, especially if it is based on what Bentham calls the "sympathy and antipathy" inherent in the classical and medieval model.[150] Bentham is out to turn the world on its head, to ground his legal system in a relative world where he opines that law varies by whim and fancy. Bentham blasts the universality principle evident in the medieval models discussed thus far.

> Now of the infinite variety of nations there are upon the Earth, there are no two which agree exactly in their laws, certainly not in the whole, perhaps not even in any single article, and let them agree to-day, they would disagree tomorrow.[151]

These books are meaningless exercises since today's law will be tomorrow's freedom from intrusion. Bentham's disdain for permanency, indisputability, and the teleological vision could not be plainer in his *Introduction to the Principles of Morals and Legislation.*

> It follows that, if there are any books which can, properly speaking, be styled books of universal jurisprudence, they must be looked for within very narrow limits. Among such as are expository, there can be none that are authoritative ... To be susceptible of an universal application, all that a book of the expository kind can have to treat of, is the import of words: to be, strictly speaking, universal, it must confine itself to terminology.[152]

Bentham's correctional model adopts similar principles by calling upon the penal system to react to criminality with sufficient pain to deter the activity. As if in a Pavlovian experiment, Bentham assuredly argues that criminal laws and their corresponding punishments must inflict sufficient pain to prevent the wrongdoing. Pain will on occasion be good, as well as pleasure. It is the measure of each that gives law credibility. On balance, the law should produce pleasurable results for the greatest number of citizens. Mathematically, Bentham calculates the pleasure–pain continuum as so:

> Sum up all the values of all the pleasures on the one side, and those of all the pains on the other. The balance, if it be on the side of pleasure, will give the good tendency of the act upon the whole, with respect to the interest of that individual person; if on the side of pain, the bad tendency of it upon the whole.[153]

The Bentham measure provides no allegiance to a moral framework and explicitly rejects theological bases for its justification. The system Bentham proposes peers into the future to see whether the benefit or loss is worth the law's enactment. "Right action is justified by future states of affairs rather than by past events."[154] Departing dramatically from his predecessors, Bentham's propositions open the door for an American experience that embraces legal decision making stripped of moral or ethical frameworks. If the majority of the populace wants an express benefit and, for the moment that gain spurs on individual freedom, then the law should be honored that affects this end. If the law causes undue harm to too many natives, and the resulting pain outstrips any reasonable benefit, it will not deter any future conduct by the deprivation caused, Bentham would be adverse. For all of its talk of majoritarianism, Bentham's premise appears close to the libertarian school of individuality where laws should not be enacted for education or moral reasons, or should the enactment be grounded in some sense of right. Instead, Bentham's rule meanders aimlessly while latching onto nothing. His pain/pleasure measure cannot be calculated under any quantifiable or qualitative scheme and the most he can hope for is the computation of individual preferences counted en masse. How is pain and pleasure measured? Is not pain sometimes good and pleasure often licentiousness? What formula is employed to calculate? What percentage? Bentham's legacy will eventually invade the American ideal in ways more subtle. "Don't tell me what I can and cannot do, especially if most of us want to do it!" "If it is pleasurable, it must feel right and, therefore, must be good." Like hippies and Epicureans, the Benthamites can only tell you it feels good, but know not whether the underlying conduct is worthy of our respect or allegiance. A criminal law system built on the fragile moral framework of Jeremy Bentham leads only to oblivion.

John Stuart Mill

John Stuart Mill, another utilitarian idealist, scathingly critiqued Bentham's vision as chaotic and ill-defined. Mill urged the utilitarian school to do better than Bentham when he argued:

> If, then, it is asserted that there is a comprehensive formula, including all things which are in themselves good, and that whatever else is good is not as an end but as a means, the formula may be accepted or rejected, but is not a subject of what is commonly understood by proof. We are not, however, to infer that its acceptance or rejection must depend on blind impulse or arbitrary choice. There is a larger meaning of the word "proof," in which this question is as amenable to it as any other of the disputed questions of philosophy. The subject is within the cognizance of the rational faculty; and neither does that faculty deal with it solely in the way of intuiton.[155]

Mill attempted to center "goodness and happiness" as the key variable in the utility equation; not the fleshy happiness of the lustful and physically addicted, the salvation religion provides, or the certitude in knowing that certain types of conduct are good and others bad, but that which advances and contents the human species. Goodness partially reverts back to the Aristotelian conception, that what is truly beneficial to man is consistent with reason and in tune with the virtuous disposition, but not knowing why. Mill rightfully points out the flaw in the pleasure principle advanced by Bentham.

> If this supposition were true, the charge could not be gainsaid, but would then be no longer an imputation; for, if the sources of pleasure were precisely the same to human beings and to swine, the rule of life, which is good enough for the one would be good enough for the other. The comparison of the Epicurean life to that of beasts is felt as degrading, precisely because a beast's pleasures do not satisfy a human being's conceptions of happiness. Human beings have faculties more elevated than the animal appetites and, when once made conscious of them, do not regard anything as happiness, which does not include their gratification.[156]

What is of use to the human person consists of those activities that uplift the human spirit and the human condition. What is of utility relates to the elevation and prolongation of the happy life. However, Mill stands not in the classical or medieval field, but with the undaunting optimism that utility, the usefulness for the greater good, without religious or moral fervor, can accomplish the same effect as any other system of moral coercion. In this fashion, Mill and Bentham propose a manifesto for humanism and secularism. For them crimes are crimes because of their glaring opposition to the pleasure and happiness of others, not because the offenses are morally suspect. Mill argues that happiness and rationality go hand in hand, but then opens the floodgates by literally allowing any approach to achieve happiness or define its essence. In the final analysis, critics charge that Mill fails to logically wrap up his jurisprudence in any sensible way particularly since the word *utility* is incapable of singular and universal definition.

An excellent Web location is maintained by the New School in New York City at http://homepage.newschool.edu/het//profiles/mill.htm

What remains on the American legal landscape of utilitarianism is quite apparent in moral dilemmas like abortion, homosexuality, lifestyle experimentation, eugenics, cloning, and suicide. Most advocacy groups for these and other ethical dilemmas engage in the utilitarian dialog, not the moral absolutes so central to our general tradition. Things are right or wrong not because of the quality of the act or its effects, but whether it advances the collective happiness in the greatest numbers. The legality debate of *Roe v. Wade*[157] is certainly constitutional yet utilitarian. In the absence of express constitutional language, the courts employ language of personal privacy, health of the mother, care and love of children, personal freedom, and changing sexual mores to justify the switch to legalization. For this court and many others like it, the benefits outweighed the costs for continued maintenance of illegality. How one reconciles tradition, common law heritage, and the novel approaches of our current legal ideology will be a cumbersome dilemma for legal thinkers in the generation to come.

CHAPTER DISCUSSION QUESTIONS

1. How can criminal laws be known and understood without a specific writing or codification?
2. What are some of the historical bases for how crimes were defined?
3. Is there still a relationship between how the ancient and medieval legal thinkers define criminal laws and how the modern criminal justice system does?
4. How could a legal thinker and lawyer like Cicero believe that criminal law, as well as all law, is essentially discovered in nature?
5. Argue on behalf of a criminal law system that incorporates religious principles and ideals.
6. Why is "positivism" contrary to the medieval idea of criminal legislation?
7. Does natural law reasoning still reside in certain judicial decisions?
8. How does nature differ from natural law?

9. What are the advantages and differences of a criminal law system based on natural law thinking?

10. What other options are there for creating a foundation for the criminal law system?

SUGGESTED READINGS

Adler, F., F. Cullen, C. Jonson, and A. Myer. 2010. *The origins of American criminology: Advances in criminological theory.* Vol. 16. Piscataway, NJ: Transaction Publishers.

Berch, J. J., M. A. Berch, R. W. Berch, and R. S. Spritzer. 2010. *Introduction to legal method and process: Cases and materials.* 5th ed. Eagan, MN: West Law School Publishers.

Berman, H. J,. and S. N. Saliba. 2009. *The nature and functions of law.* 7th ed.. Eagan, MN: West Law School Publishers.

Bloom, A. D. 1990. *Confronting the Constitution.* Washington, D.C.: AEI Press.

Brownstein, A. E., and L. Jacobs.. 2008. *Global issues in freedom of speech and religion: Cases and materials.* Eagan, MN: West Law School Publishers.

Duff, R. A., and S. Green. 2011. *Philosophical foundations of criminal law.* New York: Oxford University Press.

Ewin, R. E. 1991. *Virtues and rights: The moral philosophy of Thomas Hobbes.* San Francisco: Westview Press.

Finnis, J. 1980. *Natural law and natural rights.* New York: Oxford University Press.

Gierke, O. F. von. 1934. *Natural law and the theory of society.* Cambridge, U.K.: The University Press.

Griffin, L. C. 2010. *Law and religion: Cases and Materials.* 2nd ed. Eagan, MN: West Law School Publishers.

Jones, M. 2011. *History of criminal justice.* 5th ed. Scotch Plains, NJ: Anderson Publishers.

Lowey, A. 2011. *Criminal law in a nutshell.* 5th ed. Eagan, MI: Gilbert Law Publishing.

Maine, H. S. 1963. *Ancient law.* Boston: Beacon Press.

Noonan Jr., Hon. J. T., and E. McGlynn Gaffney. 2011. *Religious freedom: History, cases and other materials on the interaction of religion and government.* 3rd ed. Eagan, MN: West Law School Publishers.

Presser, S. B., and J. S. Zainaldin. 2009. *Cases and materials on law and jurisprudence in American history.* 7th ed. Eagan, MN: West Law School Publishers.

Roth, M. P. 2010. *Crime and punishment: A history of the criminal justice system.* 2nd ed. Florence, KY: Wadsworth Publishing.

Stinchcomb, J. B. 2011. *Corrections: Foundations for the future (criminology and justice studies).* 2nd ed. Florence, KY: Routledge Publishers.

Strauss, L. 1953. *Natural right and history.* Chicago: University of Chicago Press.

Weinreb, L. L. 1987. *Natural law and justice.* Cambridge, MA: Harvard University Press.

ENDNOTES

1. *See* Matthew Ross, Contemporary Criminal Law: Concepts, Cases, and Controversies, (2009); Douglas Husak, The Philosophy of Criminal Law: Selected Essays (2010).

2. Rolando V. Del Carmen, Criminal Procedure: Law and Practice (2006).

3. Harold J. Berman, Law and Revolution: The Formation of the Western Legal Tradition (1983); H. Patrick Glenn, *A Western Legal Tradition?* 49 Sup. Ct. L. Rev. 601 (2010).

4. William L. Clark & William L. Marshall, A Treatise on the Law of Crimes §102, at 11 (6th ed. 1958).

5. Charles P. Nemeth, Aquinas in the Courtroom 110–11 (2001).

6. T. B. Bottomore, A Dictionary of Marxist Thought (1991); Eric Engle, *A Primer on Left Legal Theory: Realism, Marxism, CLS & PoMo,* 3 Crit 64–78 (2010), at http://www.thecritui.com/articles/engle2.pdf

7. *See generally* THOMAS E. DAVITT, THE NATURE OF LAW (1953); GERALD J. POSTEMA BENTHAM AND THE COMMON LAW TRADITION (1989); GEORG WILHELM FRIEDRICH HEGEL, HEGEL'S SCIENCE OF LOGIC (A. V. Miller trans., 1969).
8. *See* POSTEMA, *supra* note 7.
9. WILLIAM GRAHAM SUMNER, FOLKWAYS 55 (1940).
10. OLIVER WENDELL HOLMES, JR., THE COMMON LAW (2010) (1881).
11. CLARK AND MARSHALL, *supra* note 4, §1.03, at 18.
12. 1 SIR WILLIAM BLACKSTONE, COMMENTARIES 67 (1941).
13. *Comm. v. Chapman*, 13 Metc (Mass) 68.
14. See HEINRICH A. ROMMEN, THE NATURAL LAW (1948).
15. NEMETH, COURTROOM, *supra* note 5, at 50.
16. The classic treatise by THOMAS E. DAVITT, THE NATURE OF LAW (1951) assesses the comparative foundations of positivism and Thomism.
17. *See* POSTEMA, *supra* note 7.
18. *See* HEGEL, *supra* note 7.
19. *See* ROMMEN, *supra* note 14, at 91, 125.
20. RAYMOND KLIBANSKY, THE CONTINUITY OF THE PLATONIC TRADITION DURING THE MIDDLE AGES 29–31 (1939). Klibansky deduces that the mere might of Platonic thought through the ages would alone cause Thomas to be aware of its basic underpinnings. The Middle Ages, as even today, saw Platonism "as a force continuously stimulating scientific thought, aesthetic feeling, and religious consciousness," at 37.
21. Plato's theory of *Forms* is apparent in a multiplicity of his works including SYMPOSIUM, PHAEDO, REPUBLIC and PHAEDRUS.
22. An example being: "First, there's the earth, the sun, the stars, and all things, and this beautiful orderliness of the seasons, divided into years and months. Then there's the fact that all Greeks and barbarians believe the gods exist." PLATO, THE LAWS OF PLATO b X 886a (Thomas L. Pangle, ed., 1980).
23. *Id.* at b I 631b-c.
24. *Id.* at b IV 718b.
25. RICHARD O. BROOKS, PLATO AND MODERN LAW (2007).
26. LEO STRAUSS, THE ARGUMENT AND THE ACTION OF PLATO'S LAWS 8 (1975). *See also* Jerome Hall, *Plato's Legal Philosophy*, 31 IND. L. J. 204 (1955–1956).
27. *See* Plato's REPUBLIC.
28. ARISTOTLE, NICOMACHEAN ETHICS X, 9, 1180a (Martin Ostwald trans., 1962).
29. *Id.* at X, 9, 1180a.
30. *Id.* at X, 8, 1178a.
31. *Id.* at X, 8, 1178a.
32. *Id.* at X, 8, 1178a.
33. *Id.* at X, 8, 1178a.
34. Aristotle, *Politics, in* THE BASIC WORKS OF ARISTOTLE VII, 3, 11325b (Richard McKeon ed., 1941).
35. *Id.* at VII, 3, 11325b.
36. FRED D. MILLER JR., NATURE, JUSTICE, AND RIGHTS IN ARISTOTLE'S POLITICS (1997).
37. MARCUS TULLIUS CICERO, DE RE PUBLICA (ON THE REPUBLIC) , DE LEGIBUS (ON THE LAWS) (Clinton W. Keyes trans., 1928).
38. Marcus Tullius Cicero, *On the Laws, in* SELECTED WORKS OF CICERO Book One at 228 (1948).
39. *Id.* at Book One at 228-229.
40. *Id.* at Book One at 237.
41. *Id.* at Book One at 239. *See also* CICERO, DE REPUBLICA.
42. ST. AUGUSTINE, ON FREE CHOICE OF THE WILL Book 2, 10, 115 (Anna S. Benjamin & L.H. Hackstaff trans., 1964).
43. "And this physical and moral order, which in its sublime rationality and perfection is eternal and immutable, possesses all the characteristics of a law or norm, which is also declaratory of an absolute and perfect universality, necessity, and rationality." Anton-Hermann Chroust, *The Philosophy of Law of St. Thomas Aquinas: His Fundamental Ideas and Some of His Historical Precursors*, 19 AM. J. JURIS. 3 (1975).

44. AUGUSTINE, *supra* note 42, at Book I, 6.

45. Chroust, *supra* note 43, at 2.

46. AUGUSTINE, *supra* note 42, at Book I, 6, 51.

47. Anton-Herman Chroust's precise inquiry into legal thought preceding St. Thomas captures the Augustinian way. "The *lex aeterna*, according to St. Augustine, defines and determines man's relations to God, to the universe, and to his fellow men. In brief, it constitutes the surest road to God. At the same time, the *lex aeterna* is the most concise as well as the most sublime manifestation of God's infinite wisdom, perfect intellect, and boundless love. In this, it is a deliberate act of God and, as such, the ultimate and absolute justification and, at the same time, encompasses everything created." Chroust, *supra* note 43, at 3.

48. 1 ST. THOMAS AQUINAS, SUMMA THEOLOGICA bk. I, pt. II, Q. 94, a. 6, sed contra (English Dominican Friars trans., 1947).

49. Anton-Hermann Chroust, *The Philosophy of Law from St. Augustine to St. Thomas Aquinas*, 20 N. SCHOLASTICISM 27 (1946).

50. AUGUSTINE, *supra* note 42, at Book I, 6.

51. *Id.* at Book I, 5, 33.

52. *Id.* at Book I, 5, 33.

53. *See* CHARLES P. NEMETH, AQUINAS ON CRIME (2008).

54. St. Thomas references Isidore 25 times in I–II, Q 90–97 and 7 times in I–II, Q 98–108. *See* Jean Tonneau, *The Teaching of the Thomist Tract on Law*, 34 THOMIST 31 (1970).

55. ST. ISIDORE OF SEVILLE, ISIDORI HISPALENSIS EPISCOPI ETYMOLOGIARUM SIVE ORIGINUM LIBRI XXX, bk V, 4–6 (W. Lindsay ed., 1962).

56. MARIE R. MADDEN, POLITICAL THEORY AND LAW IN MEDIEVAL SPAIN 26 (1930).

57. ST. ISIDORE OF SEVILLE, THE LETTERS OF ST. ISIDORE OF SEVILLE Letter VI, at 32, 33 (Gordon B. Ford, Jr. trans., 2d ed. 1970).

58. *See* ISIDORE, *supra* note 55, at bk. V.

59. *Id.* at bk. V, pt. XXI, at 5.

60. 2 St. Anselm, *Cur Deus Homo, in* OPERA OMNIA Capit. I, p. 98, at 3–5 (Franciscus Salesius Schmitt trans., 1940).

61. 2 St. Anselm, *De Conceptu Virginali et de Originali Peccato, in* OPERA OMNIA Capit. IV, p. 145, at 30–31 (Franciscus Salesius Schmitt trans., 1940).

62. 1 St. Anselm, *De Veritate, in* OPERA OMNIA Capit. XII, p. 191, at 27–29 (Franciscus Salesius Schmitt trans., 1984).

63. *Id.* at Capit, XIII, p. 199, at 27–28.

64. PETER ABELARD, ETHICS 75 (D. E. Luscombe trans., 1971).

65. JOHN MARENBON, THE PHILOSOPHY OF PETER ABELARD 270 (1997).

66. PETER ABELARD, COLLATIONES, pt. 118: 2068–pt. 119: 2075.

67. ABELARD, *supra* note 64, at 41.

68. GRATIAN, THE TREATISE ON LAWS (DECRETUM DD. 1-20) D. 1, C. 2 (James Gordley trans., 1993).

69. *Id.* at D. 4, C. 1.

70. *Id.* at D. 8, Part 2.

71. *Id.* at D. 1, C. 6 ' 2.

72. *Id.* at D. 1, C.7 ' 3.

73. *Id.* at D. 13, Part 1.

74. ALEXANDER OF HALES, SUMMA UNIVERSAE THEOLOGICA, bk. IV, pars II, Inq 1, Q Unica, Caput VII Art. IV, solutio (1948).

75. *Id.* at bk. IV, pars II, Inq 1, Q. I, Caput I, ad obiecta 3.

76. *Id.* at bk. IV, pars II, Inq. I, Q. I, Caput VII.

77. *Id.* at bk. IV, pars II, Inq. I, Q. I, Caput V, Ad oppositum, a.

78. *Id.* at bk. IV, pars II, Inq. I, Q. I, Caput VI.

79. *Id.* at bk. IV, pars II, Inq. I, Q. I, Caput VII, articulus I.

80. *Id.* at bk. IV, pars II, Inq. I, Q. I, Caput VII, art. III Solutio.

81. *Id.* at bk. IV, pars II, Inq. I, Q. I, Caput VII, Art IV, Ad oppositum.
82. *Id.* at bk. IV, pars II, Inq. II, Q. III, Caput II.
83. *Id.* at bk. IV, pars II, Inq. II, Q. I, Caput I.
84. *Id.* at bk. IV, pars II, Inq. II, Q. IV, Membrum II, Caput II.
85. ALBERTI MAGNI, DE BONO t 5, Q. II, Art. 1, Solutio (1951).
86. *Id.* at t 5, Q. I, Art. I, Solutio.
87. *Id.* at t 5, Q. I, Art. I, (23).
88. *Id.* at t 5, Q. I, Art. I, Solutio (16).
89. *Id.* at t 5, Q. I, Art. 4, (3).
90. Alberti Magni, *Super Ethica, in* OPERA OMNIA XIV, Pars II, Liber X, Lectio XVIII (1987).
91. *Id.* at XIV, Pars II, Liber X, Lectio XVIII, Quinto videtur.
92. 3 ST. THOMAS AQUINAS, SUMMA CONTRA GENTILES bk. III, pt. II, at 114 (Vernon J. Bourke trans., 1975).
93. *Id.* at bk. III, pt. II, at 114.
94. 2 St. Thomas Aquinas, *Summa Theologica, in* BASIC WRITINGS OF SAINT THOMAS AQUINAS bk. I, pt. II, Q. 90, a. 1, sed contra (Anton C. Pegis ed., 1945).
95. Aristotle, *Metaphysics, in* THE BASIC WORKS OF ARISTOTLE bk. II, pt. 9, at 200a 22 (Richard McKeon ed., 1941); AQUINAS, BASIC WRITINGS, *supra* note 94, at bk. I, pt. II, Q. 90, a. 1, c.
96. *Id.* at bk. I, pt. II, Q. 96, a. 2, c.
97. *Id.* at bk. I, pt. II, Q. 96, a. 1, ad 2.
98. *Id.* at bk. I, pt. II, Q. 96, a. 2.
99. ST. THOMAS AQUINAS, THE TREATISE ON LAW 149 (R.J. Henle ed., 1993).
100. AQUINAS, BASIC WRITINGS, *supra* note 94, at bk. I, pt. II, Q. 93, a. 3, sed contra.
101. *Id.* at bk. I, pt. II, Q. 93, a. 3, sed contra.
102. *Id.* at bk. I, pt. II, Q. 93, a. 1.
103. *Id.* at bk. I, Q. 45, a.3.
104. *Id.* at bk. I, pt. II, Q. 93, a. 6, ad. 3.
105. *Id.* at bk. I, pt. II, Q. 93, a. 6, ad. 2.
106. *Id.* at bk. I, pt. II, Q. 93, a. 6, ad. 2.
107. *Id.* at bk. I, pt. II, Q. 93, a. 1, ad 3.
108. Alasdair MacIntyre's often cited work, *Whose Justice? Which Rationality?* warns the critic and ally alike that the natural law is not merely a registry of pre- and proscriptions. "Obeying the precepts of the natural law is more than simply refraining from doing what those precepts prohibit and doing what they enjoin. The precepts become effectively operative only as and when we find ourselves with motivating reasons for performing actions inconsistent with those precepts; what the precepts can then provide us with is a reason which can outweigh the motivating reasons for disobeying them, that is, they point us to a more perfect good than do the latter." ALASDAIR MACINTYRE, WHOSE JUSTICE? WHICH RATIONALITY? 194 (1988).
109. AQUINAS, GENTILES, *supra* note 92, at bk. III, pt. I, ch. 4, at 2.
110. *Id.* at bk. III, pt. I, ch. 6, at 5.
111. AQUINAS, BASIC WRITINGS, *supra* note 94, at bk. I, pt. II, Q. 94, a. 2, ad 2.
112. *Id.* at bk. I, pt. II, Q. 100, a. 3.
113. *Id.* at bk. I, pt. II, Q. 94, a. 2, c.
114. Ralph McInerny cautions interpreters not to confuse natural law reasoning with the physical laws or imperatives. "Natural law is not simply the rational recognition of physical imperatives, nor is it a judgment of how we should act, which ignores the given teleology of the physical. Natural law relates to inclinations other than reason, which have their own ends, by prescribing how we should humanly pursue them. For St. Thomas, natural law is a dictate of reason, not a physical law." RALPH MCINERNY, ETHICA THOMISTICA: THE MORAL PHILOSOPHY OF THOMAS AQUINAS 46 (1982).
115. *See* AQUINAS, LAW, *supra* note 99.
116. AQUINAS, BASIC WRITINGS, *supra* note 94, at bk. I, pt. II, Q. 98, a. 1, c.
117. 3 Rev. Patrick M. J. Clancy, *St. Thomas on Law, in* ST. THOMAS AQUINAS, THE SUMMA THEOLOGICA, 3275 (Fathers of the English Dominican Province trans., 1947).

118. AQUINAS, BASIC WRITINGS, *supra* note 94, at bk. I, pt. II, Q. 98, a. 5.

119. *Id.* at bk. I, pt. II, Q. 98, a. 5; Clancy, *supra* note 117, at 3275.

120. *Id.* at bk. I, pt. II, Q. 100, a. 1.

121. *Id.* at bk. I, pt. II, Q. 100, a. 8, c.

122. *Id.* at bk. I, pt. II, Q. 99, a. 2, ad. 2.

123. *Id.* at bk. I, pt. II, Q. 99, a. 2, ad. 2.

124. For a full commentary on the essential nature of a criminal law system, *see* NEMETH, CRIME, *supra* note 53.

125. AQUINAS, BASIC WRITINGS, *supra* note 94, at bk. I, pt. II, Q. 99, a. 4, ad. 1.

126. *See* NEMETH, CRIME, *supra* note 53.

127. Charles Skok portrays Thomas's vision as realistic rather than pessimistic. "St. Thomas often made reference to men in their present condition. Not many men are truly virtuous or highly virtuous. Laws have to be made for the general run of the people in the state in which they are found. This is not pessimism but realism." CHARLES D. SKOK, PRUDENT CIVIL LEGISLATION ACCORDING TO ST. THOMAS AND SOME CONTROVERSIAL AMERICAN LAW 119 (1967).

128. AQUINAS, BASIC WRITINGS, *supra* note 94, at bk. I, pt. II, Q. 95, a. 1, ad. 1.

129. *Id.* at bk. I, pt. II, Q. 95, a. 3.

130. *Id.* at bk. I, pt. II, Q. 95, a. 4, c.

131. *Id.* at bk. I, pt. II, Q. 105, a. 1, ad 5.

132. *Id.* at bk. I, pt. II, Q. 99, a. 6, ad. 2.

133. *See* CHARLES P. NEMETH, AQUINAS AND KING (2010); *see also* Mark R. Macguigan, *Civil Disobedience and Natural Law*, 52 KY. L.J. 347-362 (1964); Howard Zinn, *Law, Justice and Disobedience*, NOTRE DAME J. L. ETHICS & PUB. POL'Y 899-919 (1991); Noel Dermot O'Donoghue, *The Law Beyond The Law*, 18 AM. J. JURIS. 164 (1973); Robert M. Palumbos, *Within Each Lawyer's Conscience a Touchstone: Law, Morality, and Attorney Civil Disobedience*, 153 U. PA. L. REV. 1058 (2005); Paul Butler, *By Any Means Necessary: Using Violence and Subversion to Change Unjust Law*, 50 UCLA L. REV. 752 (2003).

134. AQUINAS, BASIC WRITINGS, *supra* note 94, at bk. I, pt. II, Q. 93, a. 3, ad. 2.

135. *Id.* at bk. I, pt. II, Q. 93, a 3.

136. *Id.* at bk. I, pt. II, Q. 93, a. 3, ad 1.

137. *Id.* at bk. I, pt. II, Q. 93, a. 3, ad 2.

138. Tom Sorell, *Hobbes, in* THE BLACKWELL COMPANION TO PHILOSOPHY 532 (Nicholas Bunnin and E. P. Tsui-James eds., 1996).

139. THOMAS HOBBES, LEVIATHAN ch. XIII (A. R. Waller, ed., 1904).

140. Sorell, *supra* note 138, at 534.

141. HOBBES, *supra* note 139, at ch. XXX.

142. JOHN LOCKE, SECOND TREATISE ON GOVERNMENT xii (Thomas P. Peardon ed., 1980) (1952).

143. JOHN LOCKE, TWO TREASTISES OF CIVIL GOVERNMENT, bk. II, ch. II, at 6.

144. JOHN LOCKE, SECOND TREATISE ON GOVERNMENT xiii (1997).

145. C. FRED ALFORD, NARRATIVE, NATURE, AND THE NATURAL LAW: FROM AQUINAS TO INTERNATIONAL HUMAN RIGHTS (2010); JOHN LOCKE, ESSAYS ON THE LAW OF NATURE AND ASSOCIATED WRITINGS (W. von Leyden ed., 2002); J. BUDZISZEWSKI, WRITTEN ON THE HEART: THE CASE FOR NATURAL LAW (1997).

146. LOCKE, SECOND, *supra* note 144, at ch. 2, at 13.

147. *Id.* at ch. 3, at 17.

148. Jeremy Bentham, *An Introduction to the Principles of Morals and Legislation, in* COLLECTED WORKS ch. 1 (J. H. Burns ed., 1968).

149. JEREMY BENTHAM, AN INTRODUCTION TO THE PRINCIPLES OF MORALS AND LEGISLATION ch. 2, at 5 (Wilfred Harrison ed., 1948).

150. *See Id.*

151. *Id.* at ch. 17, at 2.

152. *Id.*

153. *Id.* at ch. 4, at 5.

154. Ross Harrison, *Bentham, Mill and Sidgwick, in* THE BLACKWELL COMPANION TO PHILOSOPHY 628 (Nicholas Bunnin & E. P. Tsui-James eds., 1996).

155. JOHN STUART MILL, UTILITARIANISM 7 (Oskar Piest ed., 1985).

156. *Id.* at 11.

157. 410 U.S. 113 (1973).

Chapter 2

Definitions of Crime

KEYWORDS

Actus reus: The substance of a crime that must be proven and that consists of an injury or loss and the criminal act that resulted in it.

Civil law: The law that applies to private rights.

Corpus delicti: The substance of a crime that consists of an injury or loss and the criminal act that resulted in it.

Crime: Conduct that is prohibited and has a specific punishment prescribed by public law.

Felony: A crime that has a greater punishment imposed by statute than that imposed on a misdemeanor.

Infraction: A violation.

Mens rea: A culpable mental state; one involving intent or knowledge and forming an element of a criminal offense.

Mala in se: An offense that is evil or wrong from its own nature irrespective of statute.

Mala prohibita: An offense prohibited by statute, but not inherently evil or wrong.

Misdemeanor: A crime that carries a less severe punishment than a felony.

Modus operandi: A distinct pattern or method of operation especially that indicates or suggests the work of a single criminal in more than one crime.

Principal: One who commits a crime or instigates, encourages, or assists another to commit it especially when constructively or actually present.

Principal in the first degree: A principal under common law who intentionally commits and is actually or constructively present at the commission of a crime.

Principal in the second degree: A principal under common law who aids, encourages, or commands another to commit a crime and is actually or constructively present when it is committed.

Punishment: A penalty inflicted on an offender through the judicial and criminal process.

Tort: A wrongful act other than a breach of contract that injures another and for which the law imposes civil liability.

Treason: The offense of attempting to overthrow the government of one's country or of assisting its enemies in war.

Vicarious liability: Liability that is imposed for another's acts because of imputed or constructive fault.

DEFINING CRIME

Most people recognize crime without a definition. Crime affronts persons and property and subjects the communal good to harm and evil. The law of crimes is very different than most other areas of law and litigation because it tends to the personal; it breeds fear and trepidation and elicits a host of reactions from retribution to vengeance. Crime is relational by design and encompasses a cause and effect: a crime and then a victim.[1]

On the one hand, the perpetrator identifies a specific target for the infliction of a particular harm, whether person or property, while on the other hand, the harm is judged as a collective or communal harm that the state should not tolerate. In both individual and communitarian terms, crime is defined in radically different ways than in the civil system. In the law of torts, negligence and strict liability, where injuries ensue from mistaken and errant conduct, the remedy and the philosophy of making whole is dramatically individualized. Television commercials with lawyers promising damage awards and protection from insurance companies do not represent the law of crimes, but that of individualized harm and injury. The law of torts and civil remedies is intertwined with the law of crimes, but, for the most part, stands far apart. The compatibility and contrast between the law of crimes and torts is charted at Figure 2.1.

Crime undermines the public tranquility and unnerves the populace. Left unchecked, criminals and the conduct performed will overwhelm the collective stability taken for granted in orderly societies.

Exactly how crime is defined varies greatly in most jurisdictions, yet the basic elements that make up each crime appear fairly consistent.

> For an excellent power point presentation on criminal definitions, visit http://crab.rutgers.edu/~jasiegel/Ch2_%20Defining_Crime.pdf

Crime, that conduct declared unacceptable and, therefore, restricted by the populace, achieves this status because of some outrage or unease caused by the behavior. If we weren't bothered in the first place, the conduct's prohibition would make little sense. Clark and Marshall's *Treatise on Crimes* delivers a very workable definition:

	Civil Wrongs (Torts)	Criminal Wrongs
Harm	Personal harm	Harm against society
Intentional Behavior	Not required	Required
Proof	Preponderance of the evidence	Beyond a reasonable doubt
Other Prosecutions	May also prosecute criminally	May also prosecute civilly
Results	Damage awards generally compensatory and sometimes punitive in nature	Fines, imprisonment, community service, probation or orders of restitution

Figure 2.1   Characteristics of civil and criminal wrongs.

A crime is any act or omission prohibited by public law for the protection of the public, and made punishable by the state in a judicial proceeding in its own name. It is a public wrong, as distinguished from a mere private wrong or civil injury to an individual.[2]

The crime also can be analyzed holistically and then by the sum of its parts. The body of the crime, the *corpus delicti*, its elemental qualities, so to speak, the content of the offense, comprises the act known as crime. So, a murder is an act that consists of various elements that constitute the body of a crime, namely the actor acting, the victim killed, and the actor's wish and desire to simultaneously affect this end. Dean Wigmore's classic treatise on evidence sums up this definition precisely:

It is clear that an analysis of every crime, with reference to this element of it, reveals three component parts, first, the occurrence of the specific kind of injury or loss (as, in homicide, a person deceased***); ... secondly, somebody's criminality (in contrast, e.g., to accident) as the source of the loss, these two together involving the commission of a crime by somebody; and, thirdly, the accused's identity as the doer of this crime.[3]

Within the pages that follow, the reader will analytically dissect the body, the components and elements that make up specific offenses. By learning the parts, one gains the fullest understanding of what crimes are, and what content of proof is necessary to convict or defend. From the conception of the whole, we arrive at particular determinations of crimes. In each crime exists these rudimentary elements:

- The Act: Actus Reus
- The Mind: Mens Rea
- The Causation: The Act Triggered by Mind

With rare exception, these criteria and elemental authorities are needed in the proof and defense of any criminal case. "At the core of criminal law rests the basic principle that people should be responsible for any harm that results from their unlawful actions."[4] Prosecutors weave facts that tell a story of a free-willing agent who knows and desires the criminal purpose. Defense attorneys and public defenders undercut and cripple these same arguments by showing a contrary mind or a mistaken action. In the combat of criminal litigation, each side needs to erect or destroy the elements of criminal responsibility.

This methodology of dissection and parsing the elements is what nurtures the keen criminal thinker, who cuts through facts with legal standards or recasts facts in a light most favorable to client or cause. Learn the elements of each and every offense. If a police officer, one should be religiously attentive to facts pertinent to the offense, for facts lead not only to evidentiary certainty, but also legal proof. Forcing facts to fit charges is a sure way to undermine a case before ever entering the courthouse door. Investigate with the elements in mind. Prove not only that dead men are dead, but that the suspected perpetrator was the agent and willful perpetrator of death. Never lose sight of the structural elements that shore up criminal prosecutions and defenses. Never be afraid to choose wisely those offenses that fit nicely into the picture that emerges during the investigation. In the study of criminal law, the world must square with the criminal law chosen.[5]

Crime as a Moral and Religious Judgment

Every government or political–social structure has declared some types of conduct as unacceptable. From the time of ancient society, a system of criminal law and aligned corrective powers has existed. The Latin word, *crimen*, meaning "sin," says much about our criminal heritage. While the political and social system declares behavior illegal for practical and communal reasons, criminal behavior has also been characterized as sinful, wrong, an affront to God or the gods and an act inconsistent with theological order. In this sense, crime defines itself by political, social, and cultural realities, but also by judgments that involve correctness and good. Crime, in each situation, represents the judgment of others, the finding that certain types of conduct are wrong and reprehensible, and penalties are properly inflicted on those who engage in this activity. In criminal law, we discern a "soft or hard coercion and a series of guiding influences to keep the citizen morally erect. Punishment is 'especially necessary against those who are prone to evil.'[6] Rewards as well as punishments ... are devised 'so that men may be drawn away from evil things and toward good things.'[7] Laws not backed by correction would be hollow admonitions."[8]

The business of criminal law is tied tightly to moral judgment—a conclusion that some behaviors are fundamentally suspect. Hence, murder, incest, theft, and maiming others garner legitimacy from few quarters. These offenses are prohibited because their content is essentially or inherently evil. This type of conduct, amongst others, is labeled and defined *mala in se*—corrupt in and of themselves and devoid of any rational defense. For the classical and medieval mind, crime was more the sin than the infraction. Crime was an affront to nature, to communal goods, and the moral ordering inherent in the human person. Cicero, the esteemed Roman jurist, saw crime as a confrontation with nature itself and bound to lead its perpetrators to a life of misery and corruption.

> Goodness is not just a matter of opinion: What idea is more absurd than that? Since then we distinguish good from evil by its nature, and since these qualities are fundamental in Nature, surely by a similar logic we may discriminate and judge between what is honorable and what is base according to Nature.[9]

Crime corrupts the human player, rots being and psyche, and fosters vice instead of virtue. In this way, crime corrodes the soul and destroys the sanctity of human good. From a religious perspective, crime's definition can be discerned in theological sources. Certainly the entire legal infrastructure of Judaism and Islam defines conduct in criminal terms. Indeed, in Christian tradition, the Son of God was executed for blasphemy—the insult to the true God based upon Jewish law. When Jesus Christ indicated he was, in fact, the Messiah, his legal fate was sealed in the Sanhedrin, the pharisaical court, which lodged no objection. Roman law deferred to the finding and history tells us the rest.

The Talmud and its judicial system are clear predecessors to our vision of how crime interrelates with moral, spiritual, and theological judgments. The 613 Mitzvot[10] (commandments), along with the biblical passages they are based on, are reproduced in the Appendix. An examination of the Mitzvot demonstrates the extraordinary influence these religious traditions have upon the definition of crime.

The Koran, the holy book of Islam, addresses criminal conduct in similar ways:

> Yet whoso doeth evil or wrongeth his own soul, then seeketh pardon of Allah, will find Allah Forgiving, Merciful. Whoso committeth sin committeth it only against himself. Allah is ever knower, Wise. And whoso committeth a delinquency or crime, then throweth (the blame) thereof upon the innocent, hath burdened himself with falsehood and a flagrant crime.[11]

In the medieval world, the view that crime was sin and personal error continued with the likes of St. Augustine and St. Thomas Aquinas. Augustine's influential work on free will, *De Libero Arbitrio*, sets a tone for generations of thinkers when he relates:

> Or how does a man gain a happy life through his will, when although all want to be happy, there are so many unhappy men ... The eternal law, to which it is time now to turn our attention, established with immutable firmness the point that merit lies in the will, while happiness and unhappiness are a matter of reward and punishment.[12]

Crime and personal responsibility became the hallmark of Western jurisprudence, that the actor is ultimately responsible for the criminality. Crime then represents personal failure and human frailty, and, most importantly, a corrosion and corruption of the soul. For Aquinas, crime was a manifestation of human failure and even more. Crime, the very word, has religious connotations because it is derived from the root Latin word *crimen*, which means "sin."[13]

> Moreover, as good things are owed to those who act rightly, so bad things are due to those who act perversely. But, those who act rightly, at the end intended by them, receive perfection and joy. So, on the contrary, this punishment is due to sinners, that from those things in which they set their end they receive affliction and injury.[14]

Aquinas developed a very elaborate discourse in his *Summa Theologica* on not only the nature of crime,[15] but the specific elements and qualifications for major felonies. His treatment of murder and self-defense is keenly attuned to the many nuances and definitions of crime that are applicable even today.[16] Even in the thirteenth century, Aquinas fully comprehends the dynamic of provocation and the impact of passion on the actor. His treatment of the death penalty edifies how completely responsible human beings are for their actions. As free beings, choosing crime evidences a deevolution; to the beast level where the actor forfeits his right to live. "[T]he insubordinate and the degenerate are allotted physical punishments like beatings and other chastisements, censure, and loss of their possessions. However, the absolutely incurable are exterminated—the bandit, for instance, is hanged."[17] Justifying the death of sinners to the betterment of the common good, Thomas Aquinas proclaims "[w]hen, however, the good incur no danger, but rather are protected and saved by the slaying of the wicked, then the latter may be lawfully put to death."[18]

The tradition of mixing religious principles into criminal definitions continued unabated into the colonial American experience as well. The early colonies penalized crime by employing terms like *unnatural*, an *affront to God, gravest acts contrary to the law of God and man*, taking lessons from early English Law. Terms, such as *contra gravissima natura,* were common in early codifications. Compare the construction of these early laws with South Carolina's current definition of "buggery."

> **The Buggery Act of 1533**—Forasmuch as there is not yet sufficient and condign punishment appointed and limited by the due course of the Laws of this Realm, for the detestable and abominable Vice of Buggery committed with mankind or beast.[19]

Indian Penal Code of 1860—Unnatural offences. Whoever voluntarily has carnal intercourse against the order of nature with any man, woman, or animal, shall be punished with imprisonment for life, or with imprisonment of either description for a term which may extend to ten years and shall also be [fined].[20]

South Carolina Code (2009)—Whoever shall commit the abominable crime of buggery, whether with mankind or with beast, shall, on conviction, be guilty of felony and shall be imprisoned in the penitentiary for five years or shall pay a fine of not less than five hundred dollars, or both, at the discretion of the court.[21]

This fervent alchemy of religion and law was viewed as compatible and normal. Card playing and dancing were illegal because of temptation and wantonness that might evolve, restrictions on economic and social activities on Sundays existed to honor the Sabbath, and rules relative to homosexuality, adultery, fornication, marriage, and drinking were promulgated based on religious and legal foundations. The distinct and radical separation of religion from legal and moral judgment is primarily a phenomenon of the past 40 years. For most of Western tradition, the moral and spiritual standards rested comfortably in criminal definition.

Visit Emory University's Center for the Study of Religion and Law at http://cslr.law.emory.edu/

Crime as Deviance and Aberration

Another approach regarding defining crime involves the nature of deviancy and what constitutes normalcy in human behavior.[22] What is normal and what is deviant was once firmly entrenched in general custom and moral standards. Certain types of behavior were criminal because of their inherency and universal condemnation. Even today, despite an increasingly liberal toleration of once suspect human behavior, we have our standards and thresholds of acceptability. Some conducts are still designated deviant or errant in design. While exceptional dissents exist, these types of conduct are, for the most part, universally condemned. Who could argue that these conducts are generally condemned?

Bestiality: Sexual relations with animals.
Incest: Sexual relations with one's own offspring or other immediate relative.
Pedophilia: Sexual relations with small children.
Murder: The unlawful killing of another.
Property theft: The unlawful taking of another's tangible interest.

For most of us, these seem hardly debatable, but there are those that wish to sweep away every sort of restriction urging a new day of understanding and toleration. In sexual offenses, lobby groups advocate liberalization of laws with children and offspring.

The move to decriminalize once universally agreed upon prohibitions extends to all sectors of communal life including economic systems. Those seeking the overthrow of governments and

STORY 2.1

ORGANIZATION OF PEDOPHILIAS

Even more shocking, there are a few groups that advocate sexual activity between adults and children. Many of these organizations prepare various pamphlets and newsletters advocating, if not encouraging, sex with children. They want to legalize sexual relations between adults and children so that the social discrimination that pedophiles face is removed. They maintain that pedophilia (or intergenerational sex) is a sexual orientation or preference just like homosexuality or heterosexuality; that age should not be a factor. Of recent outrage, has been the blatant publication of the manual, *The Pedophile's Guide to Love and Pleasure*, that exhorts the benefits and techniques of pedophilia, published by Philip Ray Greaves (Figure 2.3). Just recently sold on Amazon. com, the book has now been removed from that site.

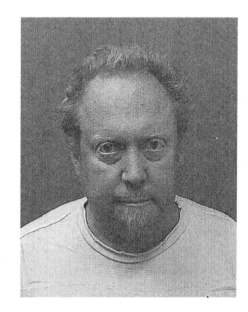

Figure 2.3   Philip Ray Greaves.

Read about Philip Ray Greaves and his recent arrest at http://www.washingtontimes.com/news/2010/dec/20/author-pedophilia-guide-arrested-obscenity-charged/

Child pornography laws, which address photos and videos, as well as include written material that advocates or encourages sex with children, hope to eradicate and combat these disturbing conclusions.[1]

Even pornographic materials involving children are not the perfectly safe haven they used to be. In the virtual world, there has been an explosion of materials available for general consumption. The virtual world has opened up new vistas and interpretive mentalities that once would have never been envisioned. In *Ashcroft v. The Free Speech Coalition*,[2] the U.S. Supreme Court considered the question of whether children, depicted in virtual, pornographic contexts, should be free from law enforcement scrutiny in the same way as actual children would be. The decision shocked many, in a 6–3 vote, the Court agreed with the virtual pornographers and distinguished virtual acts from real ones. The dissent, by Justice Scalia, Thomas, and Rehnquist, responded in amazement.

Other than computer-generated images that are virtually indistinguishable from real children engaged in sexually explicitly conduct, the Child Pornography Prevention Act of 1996 (CPPA) can be limited so as not to reach any material that was not already unprotected before the CPPA. The CPPA's definition of "sexually explicit conduct" is quite explicit in this regard. It makes clear that the statute only reaches "visual depictions" of:

> [A]ctual or simulated ... sexual intercourse, including genital–genital, oral–genital, anal–genital, or oral–anal, whether between persons of the same or opposite sex; ... bestiality; ... masturbation; ... sadistic or masochistic abuse; ... or lascivious exhibition of the genitals or pubic area of any person. 18 U. S. C. §2256(2).3

This is but one case law determination dealing with child pornography on the Internet. In response to this decision, Congress made numerous legislative efforts to ban the practices, in addition to the CPPA.[4]

Obscene Visual Representations of the Sexual Abuse of Children—**18 U.S.C. § 1466a (2008)**

Certain Activities Relating to Material Constituting or Containing Child Pornography—**18 U.S.C. § 2252a (2008)**

Sexual Exploitation of Children—**18 U.S.C. § 2251 (2008)**

Certain Activities Relating to Material Constituting or Containing Child Pornography—**18 U.S.C. § 2252a (2008)**

See, also, a more recent ruling from the Supreme Court at *United States v. Williams*, 553 U.S. 285 (2008).

The Internet has made it easier for pedophiles to communicate with each other, to acquire material and ply victims more readily. In a report by the *Seattle Times* in October 1999, they stated that by 1998, over 1,500 suspected pedophiles in just 32 states had been identified through various popular chat rooms. In 2007, an investigation by U.S. and British authorities of an online global pedophile ring netted 700 suspects from at least four different countries.[5] The Internet provides unlimited and unrestricted access to vulnerable children and less risk in the virtual world of interaction than personal contact.[6]

Some of the more notorious groups advancing various sorts of perversion involving children include:

North American Man-Boy Love Association (NAMBLA)
Formed: 1978 in Boston
Conferences: Yearly in New York
Activities: Help defend men accused of child sexual abuse, lobby against laws that prohibit child sexual abuse, hold marches and conferences.

NAMBLA has produced a professional Web location that justifies its criminality. Visit, with both caution and reservation, at http://www.nambla.org/

The Rene Guyon Society
Formed: 1962
Motto: "Sex by age eight, or it's too late."

Activities: Abolishment of laws prohibiting pedophilia (want adults to be able to perform anal sex on children as young as four, say that children performing oral sex on adults will end thumb-sucking.), newsletters.[7]

Childhood Sensuality Circle (CSC)

Formed: 1971

Activities: Pamphlets, such as "Porno for Children," and "Letters from Sucky Lucy, Age 11," "A Child's Sexual Bill of Rights." A police raid in 1987 put the CSC out of business.[8]

Pedophile Information Exchange (PIE)

Formed: 1974

Joined with the Pedophile Action for Liberation (PAL) in 1977 when PAL disbanded.

Activities: Building a sense of community for pedophiles, provide a public forum for debate. *Magpie* is a magazine with a contact page for pedophiles, to campaign for the legal and social acceptance of pedophilia love, abolishment of the age of consent.

Lewis Carroll Collectors Guild

Disbanded in 1988

Activities: Published a newsletter called *Wonderland*, which contained some nude photos of preteens, contact pages for pedophiles.

Howard Nichols Society

Formed: 1981 by David Sonenschein, a former consultant to the 1970 Presidential Committee on Obscenity and Pornography and a pedophile, wrote the pamphlet, "How to Have Sex with Kids."

The Internet can be employed aggressively against these perpetrators by investigators and prosecutorial staff who need be forever vigilant. Some of the more successful Web locations dedicated to ferreting out the child molester and other similar ilk are:

- www.childlures.com: Program that informs children, parents, and educators of safety issues regarding children and adults, and also offers an Internet safety pact that your child can read and sign.
- www.cyberangels.org: Promotes child safety and abuse prevention methods.
- www.enough.org: Web site that warns adults and children of the threat of pornography on the web.
- www.pedowatch.org: One of the oldest Web sites in existence that works in conjunction with law enforcement to combat pornography and child seducing on the Internet.
- www.prevent-abuse-now.com: Home for Inside Pandora's Box, a wealth of information regarding children and Internet access.
- www.troopers.state.ny.us: The home for the Internet Crimes against Children Task Force in the State of New York.
- www.officer.com: Provides hundreds of links to a wide array of police agencies in every state in America. No matter where you live, you will find a police agency close to home.

NOTES

1. Dannielle Cisneros, *"Virtual Child" Pornography on the Internet: A "Virtual" Victim?*, 2002 DUKE L. & TECH. REV. 0019 (2002), at http://www.law.duke.edu/journals/dltr/articles/2002dltr0019.html (accessed August 16, 2011).
2. 535 U.S. 234 (2002).
3. *Id*. at 268.
4. Child Pornography Prevention Act of 1996, 18 U.S.C. §§ 2252, 2252A (2000).
5. 700 Pedophile Suspects Identified as Global Ring Is Broken Up, N.Y. TIMES ONLINE, June 19, 2007, at http://www.nytimes.com/2007/06/19/world/europe/19pedophile.html (accessed August 16, 2011).
6. For an overview of the problem, *see* Ryan C. W. Hall & Richard C. W. Hall, *A Profile of Pedophilia: Definition, Characteristics of Offenders, Recidivism, Treatment Outcomes, and Forensic Issues*, 82 MAYO CLINIC PROCEEDINGS 457–471 (2007).
7. Read more about this group in STEPHEN T. HOLMES & RONALD M. HOLMES, SEX CRIMES: PATTERNS AND BEHAVIOR 124 (2008).
8. ERICH GOODE & D. ANGUS VAIL, EXTREME DEVIANCE 145 (2008).

economic systems, in the mold of Trotsky, Mao, and Marx, radically deconstruct once-accepted condemnations. Property offenses are justified under redistributionist theories and the elixir of social justice. Even radical theologians, spouting off liberation rationales, find room for justification in property offenses. Even offenses against humanity that were once universally condemned have seen serious dismantling in the past 100 years. The Third Reich's Final Solution against the Jews during World War II speaks loudly about how deviance can be rationalized. Here, the murder of innocent people, based on arbitrary classifications, eugenics, and an even falser logic justified mass extermination, all of it under the guise and protection of German law. Murder of mental defectives, homosexuals, and political dissidents was legitimized under theories of moral efficiencies and eugenic cost-benefit analysis (Figure 2.4)

Others now argue that deviance is really nothing more than a human convention and an ephemeral invention that cannot be rooted in permanent or perennial precepts. Time, by its simple passage, will alter our view, its proponents argue. This unfolding, so to speak, represents the natural evolution of moral understanding and makes deviance a temporary state of affairs. Of course, our mores and cultural toleration of all sorts of behavior over the past 50 years convince many of deviance's relativity.

The decriminalization of sodomy is often touted as a self-evident proof of relativity in deviance stereotypes. So, too, the proliferation of illegal sexual activity outside or within marriage, from fornication to adultery, conducts that were once frowned upon in the American experience. The same types of arguments are regularly heard in the debate relative to drug legalization and prostitution; topics fully covered and analyzed in Chapter 9. Here, the pressure has been, and continues to be, liberalization of once widely accepted proscriptions. Here, the clamor is for a removal of stigma and judgmental stereotype. Prostitutes, by perverse logic, are now characterized as free beings utilizing all necessary resources for economic empowerment. "If prostitution were sufficiently transformed to make it completely nonoppressive to women, though commercial transactions involving sex might still exist, prostitution as we now know it would not."[23] Contemporary perceptions of once deviant behavior shake the foundations of these concepts and cause uneasiness in judgment and reaction. Efforts to legalize historical definitions are afoot in every locale and every quarter.

Just a few decades ago, the psychiatric definition of homosexual behavior, as an illustration, could only be construed as deviant within the American Psychological Association's (APA)

Figure 2.4   American military personnel view corpses in the Buchenwald concentration camp. This photo was taken after the liberation of the camp, Germany, April 18, 1945. (Photo courtesy of the United States Holocaust Memorial Museum.)

Diagnostic and Statistical Manual. In 1973, the Board of Directors of the APA removed homosexuality from *the Diagnostic and Statistical Manual of Mental Disorders* (*DSM*). A new diagnosis, ego-dystonic homosexuality, was created for the *DSM*'s third edition in 1980 and was indicated by: "(1) a persistent lack of heterosexual arousal, which the patient experienced as interfering with initiation or maintenance of wanted heterosexual relationships, and (2) persistent distress from a sustained pattern of unwanted homosexual arousal. In 1986, the diagnosis was removed entirely from the *DSM*.[24]" At the same time, there is an undeniable tension especially unique to the American way of life, which hopes to allow its people the pursuit of happiness and individual freedom to live honorably and charitably with others. On the other hand, it is difficult to fathom a nation-state, in the genre of the American experience, to root out individuals because of their sexual proclivities with consenting adults. What is so troubling is how readily these judgments are bandied about, how change so easily comes about, and how history is purged without much reservation. While it can be agreed that previous judgments on human conduct may not always be correct given social, moral, and cultural understanding, change should at least be deliberative. Instead of pathology or deviance, lifestyle changes cannot fully eradicate what was once morally challenged. Something more substantive is essential. At the same time, criminal law thinkers must avoid personal attacks and uncharitable animus to others engaged in conduct not universally agreed upon, while not casting away the heritage that is ingrained in the American experience.

Crime as Severity and Grade

Another definitional approach in the meaning of crime will relate to its classification by severity and grade. Crimes vary according to subject matter and harmful effects. Hence, the common law

and codified definitions of specific crimes reflect the act's severity. Crimes are further differentiated on other bases.

First, the blueprint for crime was generally broken down into a few categories relating to the
act's subject matter. Thus, the law recognized crimes by the aim the actor took in its commission—property offenses for tangible goods; public offenses, such as disorderly conduct and incit-
ing a riot; administration of justice offenses, such as bribery and perjury; and personal offenses
like murder, rape, and assault. Most titles to crime codes do exactly the same thing by defining
crimes according to the ultimate end the criminal agent desires.

In addition to this approach, criminal codes further divide up the offense categories according
to degree. Murder in the first degree, second degree, and third degree; rape in the first and second
degree all offer glimpses into a statutory design that distinguishes criminal acts from both factual
and penalty perspectives. Generally, the codifier uses a higher–lower continuum to subsume each
imaginable category of the named offense, for murderers commit murder under varied facts and
motivations. The premeditating murderer is a radically different animal than the passionate one
whose intent is clouded by emotion and provocation. Definitionally, the degree system recognizes
that every crime's facts go beyond a universal template, where all perpetrators are adjudged identically. The degree continuum understands the level and sophistication of the criminal agent and
metes out punishment and elemental requirements in accordance with these differences.

§ 775.081. Classifications of Felonies and Misdemeanors

1. Felonies are classified, for the purpose of sentence and for any other purpose specifically
   provided by statute, into the following categories:
   (a) Capital felony
   (b) Life felony
   (c) Felony of the first degree
   (d) Felony of the second degree
   (e) Felony of the third degree

   A capital felony and a life felony must be so designated by statute. Other felonies are of
   the particular degree designated by statute. Any crime declared by statute to be a felony
   without specification of degree is of the third degree, except that this provision shall not
   affect felonies punishable by life imprisonment for the first offense.

2. Misdemeanors are classified, for the purpose of sentence and for any other purpose specifically provided by statute, into the following categories:
   (a) Misdemeanor of the first degree
   (b) Misdemeanor of the second degree

   A misdemeanor is of the particular degree designated by statute. Any crime declared by
   statute to be a misdemeanor without specification of degree is of the second degree.[25]

Other gradation methods may employ separate classifications for offenses, such as Class A, B,
C, E, and so on. The "lower" the letter the worse the offense. The same may be true with a number-
ing system that seeks to define criminal offenses into Class 1, 2, and 3, respectively.

§ 55.05. Classifications of Felonies and Misdemeanors

1. Felonies are classified, for the purpose of sentence, into five categories as follows:

    (a) Class A felonies
    (b) Class B felonies
    (c) Class C felonies
    (d) Class D felonies
    (e) Class E felonies

Class A felonies are subclassified, for the purpose of sentence, into two categories as follows: subclass I and subclass II, to be known as class A-I and class A-II felonies, respectively.

2. Misdemeanors are classified, for the purpose of sentence, into three categories as follows:
    (a) Class A misdemeanors
    (b) Class B misdemeanors
    (c) Unclassified misdemeanors[26]

There is no magic in this, only a concerted effort to grade offenses according to level of criminal culpability and the depth and breadth of criminal participation. Any system that lumps offenders en masse cannot do justice in criminal adjudication.

Severity and seriousness also can be measured by how an offense is designated. One classic example is the *mala in se/mala prohibita* classification. In the former instance, the offense is inherently wrong, without defense and reasonable explanation. *Mala in se* crimes are wrong in their moral gravity and egregiousness. To kill without justification, rape, and theft all qualify for this designation. The Latin *mala*, meaning wrong or bad, is coupled with *in se*, which is defined as in itself, needing no other basis or justification for the conclusion.[27]

Contrasted with *in se* offenses will be those classified as *mala prohibita*. For example, tax offenders shoulder less moral responsibility because the infraction was an invention of the legislature. So, too, for the most part, are traffic offenses. Traveling at 45 mph in a 35 mph zone connotes almost nothing about the moral character of the driver nor does the additional 10 miles per hour over the speed limit manifest a faulty moral conscience. The act's wrongfulness depends on the prohibition, not the inherent gravity of the movement. Failure to shovel a sidewalk in a snowstorm or to register or inspect a vehicle or violation of a zoning law, illustrate infractions without much moral dimension and, as a result, are designated *mala prohibita* rather than *mala in se*. In the overall scheme, most prohibited criminal offenses provoke less outrage from the community. It will be rare for public clamor to reach a crescendo over a tax cheat or consumer fraud case although the very opposite is true with those offenses declared *mala in se*.

CLASSIFICATION OF OFFENSES

At common law, criminal offenses were defined in a threefold way: treason, felony, and misdemeanor. The distinctions were largely a reflection of the offense's subject matter and its inherent gravity.

Treason

Treason was and is a very specialized offense dealing with the betrayal of country. Acts of treason have certainly been highlighted by the case of FBI Agent Robert Hansen (Figure 2.5) whose clan-

STORY 2.2

ROBERT PHILIP HANSSEN

From: FBI National Press Office, Washington D.C., February 20, 2001.

Attorney General John Ashcroft, FBI Director Louis J. Freeh, and U.S. Attorney Helen Fahey announced today that a veteran FBI counter-intelligence Agent was arrested Sunday by the FBI and charged with committing espionage by providing highly classified national security information to Russia and the former Soviet Union.

At the time of the arrest at a park in Vienna, Virginia, Robert Philip Hansen, age 56, was clandestinely placing a package containing highly classified information at a prearranged, or "dead drop," site for pick-up by his Russian handlers. Hansen had previously received substantial sums of money from the Russians for the information he disclosed to them.

FBI Director Louis J. Freeh expressed both outrage and sadness. He said the charges, if proven, represent "the most serious violations of law—and threat to national security.

"A betrayal of trust by an FBI Agent, who is not only sworn to enforce the law but specifically to help protect our nation's security,

Figure 2.5   Robert Philip Hanssen. (Photo courtesy of the FBI.)

is particularly abhorrent. This kind of criminal conduct represents the most traitorous action imaginable against a country governed by the Rule of Law. It also strikes at the heart of everything the FBI represents—the commitment of over 28,000 honest and dedicated men and women in the FBI who work diligently to earn the trust and confidence of the American people every day.

"These kinds of cases are the most difficult, sensitive and sophisticated imaginable. I am immensely proud of the men and women of the FBI who conducted this investigation. Their actions represent counterintelligence at its very best, reflecting dedication to both principle and mission. It is not an easy assignment to investigate a colleague, but they did so unhesitatingly, quietly and securely."

Hansen was charged in a criminal complaint filed in Federal court in Alexandria, Virginia, with espionage and conspiracy to commit espionage, violations that carry a possible punishment of life in prison, and under certain circumstances, the death penalty. Following the arrest, FBI Agents began searching Hansen's residence, automobiles, and workspace for additional evidence.

A detailed affidavit, filed in support of the criminal complaint and search warrants, provides a troubling account of how Hansen first volunteered to furnish highly sensitive documents to KGB intelligence officers assigned to the Soviet embassy in Washington, D.C. The affidavit chronicles the systematic transfer of highly classified national security and counterintelligence information by Hansen in exchange for diamonds and cash worth more than $600,000. Hansen's activities also have links to other, earlier espionage and national security investigations, including the Aldrich Ames and Felix Bloch cases, according to the affidavit.

The affidavit alleges that on over 20 separate occasions, Hansen clandestinely left packages for the KGB, and its successor agency, the SVR, at dead drop sites in the Washington area. He also provided over two dozen computer diskettes containing additional disclosures of information. Overall, Hansen gave the KGB/SVR more than 6,000 pages of valuable documentary material, according to the affidavit.

The affidavit alleges that Hansen compromised numerous human sources of the U.S. Intelligence Community, dozens of classified U.S. Government documents, including "Top Secret" and "codeword" documents, and technical operations of extraordinary importance and value. It also alleges that Hansen compromised FBI counterintelligence investigative techniques, sources, methods, and operations, and disclosed to the KGB the FBI's secret investigation of Felix Bloch, a foreign service officer, for espionage.

Freeh said that although no formal damage assessment could be conducted before the arrest without jeopardizing the investigation, it is believed that the damage will be exceptionally grave.

During the time of his alleged illegal activities, Hansen was assigned to New York and Washington, D.C., where he held key counterintelligence positions. As a result of his assignments, Hansen had direct and legitimate access to voluminous information about sensitive programs and operations. As the complaint alleges, Hansen effectively used his training, expertise, and experience as a counterintelligence Agent to avoid detection, to include keeping his identity and place of employment from his Russian handlers and avoiding all the customary "tradecraft" and travel usually associated with espionage. The turning point in this investigation came when the FBI was able to secure original Russian documentation of an American spy who appeared to the FBI to be Hansen, which subsequent investigation confirmed.

Freeh said the investigation that led to the charges is a direct result of the combined and continuing FBI/CIA effort ongoing for many years to identify additional foreign penetrations of the U.S. intelligence community. The investigation of Hansen was conducted by the FBI with direct assistance from the CIA, Department of State, and the Justice Department, and represents an aggressive and creative effort, which led to this counterintelligence success. Freeh said, "We appreciate the unhesitating leadership and support of Attorney General John Ashcroft from the moment he took office."

Freeh also expressed his gratitude to Helen Fahey, U.S. Attorney for the Eastern District of Virginia, Assistant U.S. Attorney Randy Bellows, and senior Justice Department officials Robert Mueller, Frances Fragos Townsend, John Dion, and Laura Ingersoll for their contributions to the case.

United States Attorney Fahey said, "In the past decade, it has been our unfortunate duty to prosecute a number of espionage cases—Ames, Pitts, Nicholson, Squillacote, Kim, Boone, and others. With each case, we hope it will be the last. Today, however with the arrest of Robert Hansen, we begin again the process of bringing to justice a U.S. Government official charged with the most egregious violations of the public trust. The full resources of the Department of Justice will be devoted to ensuring that those persons who would betray their country and the people of the United States are prosecuted and severely punished.

"I want to express my appreciation for the outstanding work done by the National Security Division and the Washington Field Office of the FBI in this investigation. Their superlative work in this extraordinarily sensitive and important investigation is testament to their professionalism and dedication. We also express our deep appreciation for the outstanding assistance provided by the Internal Security Section of the Criminal Division of the Department of Justice."

Freeh and CIA Director George Tenet kept the Intelligence Committees of Congress, because of the clear national security and foreign policy implications, informed about the case.

As a result of Hansen's actions, Freeh has ordered a comprehensive review of information and personnel security programs in the FBI. Former FBI Director and Director of Central Intelligence William H. Webster will lead the review. Webster, currently in private law practice, brings a "unique experience and background in government management and counterintelligence," Freeh said. "Moreover, the respect he enjoys throughout the intelligence community and elsewhere in government is second to none. Judge Webster will have complete access and whatever resources that are necessary to complete the task and will report directly to Attorney General Ashcroft and me. I will share his report with the National Security Council and then Congress as well," Freeh said.

destine and secret activities in union with Russian spies is one of this nation's most notorious cases.

Selling secrets to the enemy, exchanging information for money to the detriment of one's own homeland represents a daring untrustworthiness that must be dealt with harshly. In Hansen's case, the offenses committed over a three-decade period led to death and leaks in national security. So serious are these types of infractions that the Founding Fathers of this nation spelled out the crime in explicit detail within the Constitution.

Treason against the United States shall consist only in levying war against them, or in adhering to their enemies, giving them aid and comfort. No person shall be convicted of treason unless on the testimony of two witnesses to the same overt act, or on confession in open court. The Congress shall have power to declare the punishment of treason; but no attainder of treason shall work corruption of blood or forfeiture except during the life of the person attainted.[28]

Since medieval times, the offense has further been defined as either high or petit (lower), though this distinction has largely been lost in contemporary settings. Federal criminal codifications still employ the language of treason though it is no longer separate from the felony/misdemeanor classification.

Sec. 2381. Treason—Whoever, owing allegiance to the United States, levies war against them or adheres to their enemies, giving them aid and comfort within the United States or elsewhere, is guilty of treason and shall suffer death, or shall be imprisoned not less than five years and fined under this title but not less than $10,000; and shall be incapable of holding any office under the United States.[29]

Treason has also been typed an "infamous crime" since the emergence of the common law tradition. The term *infamous* described a corrupt disqualification from giving testimony in any legal forum, a deceit and fraudulent character, and a general untrustworthiness that the law could not tolerate. To be infamous is to be famous for all the wrong reasons just as FBI agent Robert Hanson has now become.

Figure 2.6   John Walker Lindh.

Another case of notoriety involves John Walker Lindh (Figure 2.6), an American citizen, who joined Taliban field forces and battled against the United States in its theatre of war in the Middle East. Lindh eventually plea bargained to avoid the treason punishment, which could have been death. He is presently serving a 20-year term.

Read the original federal complaint for John Walker Lindh's arrest at http://www.justice. gov/ag/criminalcomplaint1.htm

---

Betrayal of country also may fall under other statutory constructs, such as sedition and espionage.[30]

Felonies

The more serious of the major crime classifications, felonies constitute the bulk of first- and second-degree crimes, or the common law capital or forfeiture offenses. A capital offense at common law could result in the imposition of death and it was nearly impossible for the death penalty to be inflicted in misdemeanor cases. A forfeiture offense signified a loss of property rights or interest in personalty or realty. Common law felonies were cataloged as follows:

Murder
Manslaughter
Rape
Sodomy
Robbery
Larceny
Arson
Burglary
Mayhem

Felonies are the gravest offenses in the criminal law model with corresponding punishments equally severe. The common list of felony categories has been liberally expanded over the past century since criminal activity has become more sinister and sophisticated than our forbearers ever envisioned. Hence, drugs, obscenity and sexual pandering, fraud, tax and other official misrepresentation, sexual crimes beyond rape and sodomy, and firearms offenses, to name a few, have been added to an ever-growing list of felonious conduct. The gravity of the offense in question provides one barometer of when a felony is appropriately designated.

Felonies are labeled such because of statutory constructions as well. At both the state and federal level, the designation "felony" is attached when the legislative process so dictates. As a result, certain former misdemeanors at common law or codified, may be upgraded to the felony status if the legislature deems prudential. The seriousness of an offense may be less related to its inherent corruption and wickedness than to its pressing political stress. For example, drug possession offenses, habitual offender statutes, and other enhancement provisions involving hate crimes and ethnic intimidation, may not be, on close inspection, as morally grave as other conduct that still retains a misdemeanor title. Even so, these politically influenced offenses have achieved felony status. New York's nonparole drug offense has been attacked for more than 20 years for its extraordinary harshness by launching smaller crimes into a larger, graver sphere.[31]

Driving under the Influence (DUI) and other intoxication offenses, once the province of the petty misdemeanor category, have been recast in felonious mode due to the harm inflicted and the public outcry. In other words, things once minor can become major if the pressure is substantial enough. Criminal offenses, whether discerned or not, are subject to the push and pull of political factions and public demand. For this reason alone, one should not become too comfortable holding that all felonies are fundamentally more serious than misdemeanor counterparts.[32]

A further distinction in the felony/misdemeanor contrast can be gleaned from the level of punishment inflicted. Aside from the gravity of the offense, the felony definition rests upon how long an accused can be incarcerated or whether the death penalty is possible. As a general rule of thumb, felonies allow a minimum of 365 days of incarceration or death while misdemeanor penalties are less than 365 days and afford no chance of death penalty imposition. It is a crude but very telling qualification since the felony actor incurs harsher penalty results than the misdemeanant.

Blackstone, an influential legal thinker in Western tradition, laid this out in his Commentaries more than three centuries ago:

> A crime, or misdemeanor, is an act committed, or omitted, in violation of a public law, either forbidding or commanding it. This general definition comprehends both crimes and misdemeanors; which properly speaking are mere synonymous terms: though, in common usage, the word, "crimes," is made to denote such offences as are of a deeper and more atrocious dye; while smaller faults, and omissions of less consequence, are comprised under the gentler name of "misdemeanors" only.[33]

In this way, one looks to the penalty possibilities outlined in the statute governing the offense.[34]

In either determinant or indeterminate sentencing schemes, an express time period, say 10 years, or between two to five years of potential incarceration, will be listed. The more onerous the punishment, anything beyond 365 days, will mean the offense is a felony. Less, and the opposite conclusion is drawn. "Under such a statute, it is the potential punishment that may be imposed which determines whether an offense is a felony, and not the punishment that is actually imposed in a particular case."[35]

Misdemeanors

In addition to the term of incarceration, the misdemeanor qualification rests on grounds of gravity, seriousness, and diversion to alternative disposition. For the most part, misdemeanors are lower grade or degree offenses in criminal codifications and of lesser gravity and seriousness. Just as in the evolution of felonies, misdemeanors go through varying degrees of growth and ebb, whereby the transgression offends our sensibilities depending on the state of our knowledge and moral outrage. Obviously, certain sodomy offenses were once designated capital, felony offenses punishable by death during the bulk of this nation's history, even the consensual variety. Today, many of these statutes have been decriminalized based on constitutional grounds.[36] The story of drug law tells a similar story. As the push to decriminalize continues, we regularly see once bedrock criminality turned into less severe offenses, or as public pressure increases to the level of contagion, once tolerable behavior is recast in satanic terms. In general, however, misdemeanors do not undercut the greater good as intensely as the felony counterpart.

Misdemeanor punishments are more commonly diverted to alternative disposition. Instead of filling our prison facilities with less despicable offenders than the felony audience, the penalty infrastructure recognizes the worthiness of other penalty approaches, such as community service, probation, work release, or simply far less time spent in correctional facilities.

Visit the ABA Web location on ADR to see how it is employed in criminal cases at http://new.abanet.org/sections/criminaljustice/CR100000/Pages/default.aspx; you can also watch their video at http://www.myspace.com/video/vid/62259035

DUI/DWI litigation has shown a systematic willingness to divert a large population of offenders to alternative disposition and allow the justice model to penalize the infractions with diverse approaches not usually witnessed in the world of felonies. A sample statute that represents the misdemeanor format is below.

§ 3803. Grading

(a) BASIC OFFENSES—Notwithstanding the provisions of subsection (b):

(1) An individual who violates section 3802(a) (relating to driving under influence of alcohol or controlled substance) and has no more than one prior offense commits a misdemeanor for which the individual may be sentenced to a term of imprisonment of not more than six months and to pay a fine under section 3804 (relating to penalties).

(2) An individual who violates section 3802(a) and has more than one prior offense commits a misdemeanor of the second degree.

(b) OTHER OFFENSES—

(1) An individual who violates section 3802(a)(1) where there was an accident resulting in bodily injury, serious bodily injury or death of any person or in damage to a vehicle or other property, or who violates section 3802(b), (e) or (f) and who has no more than one prior offense commits a misdemeanor for which the individual may be sentenced to a term of imprisonment of not more than six months and to pay a fine under section 3804.

(2) An individual who violates section 3802(a)(1) where the individual refused testing of blood or breath, or who violates section 3802(c) or (d) and who has no prior offenses commits a misdemeanor for which the individual may be sentenced to a term of imprisonment of not more than six months and to pay a fine under section 3804.

(3) An individual who violates section 3802(a)(1) where there was an accident resulting in bodily injury, serious bodily injury or death of any person or in damage to a vehicle or other property, or who violates section 3802(b), (e) or (f) and who has more than one prior offense commits a misdemeanor of the first degree.

(4) An individual who violates section 3802(a)(1) where the individual refused testing of blood or breath, or who violates section 3802(c) or (d) and who has one or more prior offenses commits a misdemeanor of the first degree.[37]

Defendants are keenly aware of the procedural differences granted the misdemeanant when compared to the felony case. Legal tradition has long provided less protection, regarding both constitutional and process rights, to these lower crimes rather than the higher ones. The Constitution itself distinguishes rights based on the "capital" nature of offenses. Hence, if a defendant is entitled to a felony form of due process and receives the rights due a misdemeanant, it may serve as a basis for an appeal.[38]

Summary/Petty Offenses

Farther down the hierarchical schema of crime classifications are the designations of *summary* or *petty* offenses. The word summary indicates the fluid, almost automatically dispositional nature of the offense, meaning the system deals with the offense summarily. Petty, from the French adjective *petit*, means small or insignificant. As a rule, summary offenses are minor in nature and are defined as such to allow the justice system to dispense with them readily. Disorderly conduct or vagrancy, as illustrations, are witnessed with regularity in the justice system. It would be insensible to dedicate the full machinery of the justice system to offenses of this nature and far more rational to dispose of them expeditiously. Public intoxication, loitering, first time shoplifting, and other similar offenses neatly fit this category and allow the justice model to process these recurring cases quickly and efficiently. Common law tradition provides no precedential authority for enactment of these types of offenses. Legislative tinkering with basic felony and misdemeanor categories erects this lower infrastructure of criminality.

§ **168-13. Specific acts and penalties**—The following shall be considered violations and penalties for improper parking and, as such, are prohibited acts:

B. Specific acts and penalty.
   (1) The following are prohibited acts:
      (a) Parking in a no-parking zone
      (b) Parking in an intersection or in a marked bus stop
      (c) Parking so as to impede traffic
      (d) Parking double
      (e) Parking in a no-standing area
   (2) The penalty for any violation of this subsection is $17.[39]

Finally, the term *infraction* is sometimes employed in the criminal realm and by most accounts refers to traffic or other municipal offense, such as failure to shovel a sidewalk or obtain licensure for a pet. Infractions are so innocuous that imprisonment remains impossible, with fines and other collections being the sole means of enforceability and correction.

PARTIES TO CRIMES

Aside from the actor who carries out the offense itself, there are often other parties involved in the criminality. The law of complicity, dealing with parties to the criminal act, covers these classifications and can sometimes be complicated. At first glance, the interpreter of fact and law searches out the actual doer, the perpetrator/offender, in order to attach liability. This is simple enough and requires the utilization of the system's many investigative arms to ferret out the criminal. Evidence is amassed that points directly and inferentially to the primary criminal agent under the suspected felony or misdemeanor. The "doer" of the deed represents only one facet of the law of complicity since other second and third parties may participate directly and indirectly. There are those who will aid and abet, encourage and solicit, incite and cheer, and those who will provide help and assistance to carry out the criminal deed. These parties bear responsibility in equal or varied ways.

Depending on jurisdiction and statutory construction, these parties may be held accountable identically or under less severe terms. Some statues lump the parties together with little distinction, the end result being shared responsibility. The U. S. Code, at Title 18 section 2 defines a principal as:

Sec. 2. Principals

(a) Whoever commits an offense against the United States or aids, abets, counsels, commands, induces or procures its commission, is punishable as a principal.
(b) Whoever willfully causes an act to be done which if directly performed by him or another would be an offense against the United States, is punishable as a principal.[40]

The Model Penal Code (MPC) declares that the primary agent and any accomplices in the criminal deed are all responsible regardless of the level of participation and involvement and generally dispenses with the common law designations of principal and accessory. Instead, the MPC labels parties broadly as those who encourage, solicit, aid, abet, facilitate, and cause the crime to occur. For the MPC, complicity sweeps in those who participate willingly and even those who stood by and did nothing to prevent the offense when legal duty commanded a preventive reaction. A portion of the MPC includes this language:

(1) A person is guilty of an offense if it is committed by his own conduct or by the conduct of another person for which he is legally accountable, or both.
(2) A person is legally accountable for the conduct of another person when:
   (a) Acting with the kind of culpability that is sufficient for the commission of the offense, he caused an innocent or irresponsible person to engage in such conduct; or
   (b) He is made accountable for the conduct of such other person by the Code or by the law defining the offense; or
   (c) He is an accomplice of such other person in the commission of the offense.[41]

The law of complicity seeks to assign culpability based on the intimacy of the act and the relationship of offender to the victim. Complicity measures the degree of participation by the criminal collective and holds them accountable.

The participants in the criminal act fall into these major categories (Figure 2.7):

Principal		Accessory	
First Degree	**Second Degree**	**Before the Fact**	**After the Fact**
The person who, with the required state of mind, performed the criminal act or directly caused the criminal result, either by his own hand, with an instrument, non-human, or innocent human agent.	A person who was actually or constructively present at the scene of the crime and with the required state of mind, who aided, counseled, commanded, or encouraged the principal in the first degree	A person, neither actively or constructively present at the crime scene who, with the required state of mind, who ordered, counseled, encouraged, or otherwise aided and abetted, the principal in the first degree.	A person who, knowing of the commission of an offense by an offender, concealed the offender or gave the offender other assistance to prevent their detection, arrest, trial or punishment.

Figure 2.7   Parties to felonies.

Principals

The primary criminal agent is known as the principal, the party predominantly responsible for the offense committed and the party who can be shown to possess the requisite mental state to commit the act. Principals author the criminal enterprise and carry it to fruition. Principals bear the most severe level of culpability because of their direction and control of events and circumstances.

Principals in the second degree are equally guilty because their level of participation is so closely aligned to the act of the principal in the first degree. For example, this type of party may not pull the trigger, but you can bet they delivered the gun for purposes of killing. Principals in the second degree may not artificially hide behind the acts of another when they are, in fact, a driving force in the commission of the offense.[42]

Principals in the second degree watch and witness the crime unfold, encourage and insist on its completion, and aid and abet the primary offender. Clark and Marshall lay out three requirements for this finding.

> To constitute one as a principal in the second degree, (1) there must be a guilty principal; in the first degree, (2) the principal in the second degree must be present when the offense is committed, but his presence may be constructive, and (3) he must aid or abet the commission of the offense, for some participation is necessary, though it need not necessarily be active.[43]

The key issues that continually emerge in this area are whether the defendant was present at the time of the commission of the offense and whether the defendant was an actual participant to some degree. Presence could either be actual or constructive. In the latter case, the defendant may orchestrate the entire event from afar, such as setting up the bank robbery, remaining outside while his colleagues carry out the planned deed, or acting as mastermind for the entire crime yet remaining physically away during its commission. Principals in the second degree are not getaway car drivers or peripheral parties to the act, but central and crucial players in its commission. As long as the offender might "render assistance in some manner, not necessarily physical, in the commission of the offense,"[44] he or she may be principals in the second degree.

Participation is the other crucial factor in principal analysis. What role the criminal offender plays in the overall modus operandi speaks loudly of the level of participation. Extraneous, tangential activities are less likely to prove the level of participation necessary for this type of party status, but those who plan, prepare, engage in substantial activity, and supervise in some way the implementation of the offense are strong candidates for principals in the second degree. These determinations are always factual and depend heavily on the evidentiary and investigative record. A reasonable arbiter can perceive the difference between the small contributor and the brains behind the enterprise. Deductive reasoning can identify those who don the role of major player and those who merely contribute to a portion of the criminal operation. Principals in the second degree are heavy hitters in the crime's unraveling and are held to severe consequence.

Accessories

Less involved in the criminal deed, though still bearing a level of culpability, are those designated as accessories. An accessory assists in the commission of the offense either before or after. Hence, criminal accessories may provide preparatory assistance that allows the criminality to occur, such as funding or weaponry, or aid the principals after the deed is done, by assisting in escape or hiding the felon. Nonreporting of the felony, hiding what a party knows to be a felony undetected, was the crime of misprision at common law. Citizens were expected to affirmatively report the commission of a felony to lawful authorities.

Accessories are more actively engaged in the crime because their tasks or roles are essential to success. Escape car drivers make possible the completion of the offense so that the fruits of illegality might be shared or spent. Parties who solicit, command, or procure the commission of a particular offense are those who originate the criminal design and influence the primary doers. Accessories before the fact develop the criminal enterprise and issue some sign of consent and willingness that the deed be done. Mere bystanders and onlookers will not suffice nor will parties who may be aligned to a criminal conspiracy but do not entice or incite others to engage in particular criminal conduct. An accessory before the fact procures, counsel, and commands the act. Once beyond this preparatory stage, such as presence at the crime scene, either constructively or actually, then the accessory ceases to be an accessory and evolves into a principal in the second degree.

Accessories after the fact provide relief, assistance, and comfort to those known to be criminal offenders.[45] When compared to the accessory before the fact, the role of this type of accessory is less intellectual and more reactionary. By this we mean the participant works after the crime has been committed and in more limited ways. Instead of planning and procuring the means to commit the crime, the accessory after the fact attempts to hide the act, affords a means of escape and nondetection, and helps avoid detection for purposes of trial or punishment and otherwise provides aid and comfort to the felonious party.

Title 18 of the United States Code at section three includes these and other descriptors of after the fact activity.

Sec. 3. Accessory After the Fact—Whoever, knowing that an offense against the United States has been committed, receives, relieves, comforts or assists the offender in order to hinder or prevent his apprehension, trial or punishment, is an accessory after the fact.

Except as otherwise expressly provided by any Act of Congress, an accessory after the fact shall be imprisoned not more than one-half the maximum term of imprisonment or (notwithstanding section 3571) fined not more than one-half the maximum fine prescribed for the punishment of the principal, or both; or if the principal is punishable by life imprisonment or death, the accessory shall be imprisoned not more than 15 years.[46]

CASE 2.1

PEOPLE V. BATTERSON
2 N.Y.S. 376, 50 Hun 44 (NY Sup. 1888).

The appellant was indicted jointly with Stephen Adwin, John McKibben, and Dennis Reardon, with having on the 18th day of July, 1886, at the city of Rochester, in and upon one Sophia Kaisar, violently and feloniously made an assault, and her, the said Sophia Kaisar, then and there, against her will, and without her consent, and by forcibly overcoming her resistance, feloniously and forcibly did ravish, carnally know, and have sexual intercourse. It is contended in the first place that the verdict is against the weight of evidence. It appears from the evidence that Sophia Kaisar was at the time unmarried, and was a servant girl in the employ of one Westfall, on Harvard street, in the city of Rochester. That she was keeping company with one George Bahls, whom she subsequently married. That on Sunday evening, the 18th of July, 1886, she went for a walk with Mr. Bahls, through Nicholas Park, in that city. That while in the park they met the four persons indicted, who came to them, one saying to Bahls that he wanted him to come with him, and the defendant, Batterson, took hold of the shawl of Miss Kaisar; but that they got away from them at that time, and went on walking in another part of the park. That about a half an hour afterwards the same four persons again came up with them, and McKibben, Reardon, and Batterson took hold of Bahls, one by the throat, the defendant, Batterson, having a club, and pushing from behind, and took him away from the girl, while Adwin took hold of her, and threw her upon the ground. That she cried and hollered, and succeeded in getting up. Adwin then went off with her a little way, and threw her down again. She called for George, the police, and tried to get up, but he held her down. That McKibben and Reardon returned to them, and they held their hands over her mouth, holding her to the ground, while each of the three in turn violated her person. Bahls, after getting away from the persons who took him away from the girl, went for assistance, and found a policeman; and Reardon was arrested the same evening. The defendant, Batterson, gave himself up to the police on Tuesday morning, after having remained away from home over Monday night. The only substantial conflict is in the evidence of the defendant, Batterson, who denied that he took part in pushing Bahls away from the girl, but he admits that when they came up with Bahls and the girl that Adwin addressed him by saying, "Officer, do your duty." That he then put his hand upon the shoulder of Bahls, and said, "Here, my good fellow, you know this is not a fit place for you to do this. Why don't you take your girl and go home?" That he did nothing further, and then went off home. He further admitted that he supposed he knew the intention of the other men in following the girl, and supposed that they were going to have intercourse with her. It is not pretended that the appellant personally had intercourse with the girl, but it is claimed that he was present aiding and assisting the others in accomplishing that crime by forcibly taking from her Mr. Bahls, who was her escort and protector. We regard the evidence as ample to sustain the verdict upon this theory.

It is contended, in the second place, that there is a variance between the evidence and the indictment; that the indictment should have charged specifically the acts of the defendant, Batterson, which they sought to prove upon the trial as constituting the crime; and the case of *People v. Dumar* ... is relied upon to sustain this claim. It will be observed that the four persons are indicted together as principals. Section 29 of the Penal Code defines the principal as "a person concerned in the commission of a crime, whether he directly commits the acts constituting the offense, or aids and abets in its commission, and whether present or absent; and a person who directly or indirectly counsels, commands, induces, or procures another to commit a crime," etc. No question is made but that this provision is broad enough to cover the acts of the defendant, and make him a principal. But, it is claimed that his acts should be set forth showing that he was a principal within the provisions of this section. While the provisions of the section defining a principal are broader and more comprehensive than the prior statutes, and embrace what was before known as an accessory before the fact, we do not understand it to have changed the form of pleading in the cases where a person was principal at common law or under the statute. Such we regard the defendant, Batterson. The crime was commenced when these persons took hold of Bahls and the girl to separate them. Batterson was then present, and, by taking part in pushing Bahls away from the girl, was aiding and assisting in their separation, so that the other three could have connection with her, and not be prevented by her friend and escort, Bahls. This would make Batterson a principal at common law as much as though he was present, aiding and assisting burglars in the breaking open of a house, although he did not personally enter.

A more serious question is raised in reference to the admission of evidence. Upon the trial Mrs. Westfall was sworn as a witness on behalf of the people, and gave evidence, as to the condition that Miss Kaisar was in on her return to the house on the evening in question, to the effect that she was very much agitated and excited, and appeared much frightened; that her hair was disordered, her face red, eyes swollen; that she was crying, and continued crying for some time afterwards; she appeared very different from usual, and as though she had something on her mind which was greatly troubling her; that she cried a great many nights nearly all night long; and then, under objection, testified to her having threatened to take her own life; that before that she was a girl of a very happy disposition and of pleasant manners. The decisions in the different states of the Union are not in exact harmony upon the question here presented. The subject was under consideration in this court in the case of *People v. Clemens* ... in which case many of the authorities are cited and considered. The rule in this state doubtless is that on the trial of an indictment for rape proof of the fact that the prosecutrix make complaint recently after the commission of the offense is competent; while details given by her as to how the offense was committed, and by whom, is not competent as evidence in chief; that it is also competent to show the condition of the prosecutrix, mentally and otherwise, immediately after the offense, in order that the jury may judge more accurately as to the credit that should be given to her testimony. The evidence as to her disheveled hair, her frightened appearance, red face, and swollen eyes, and of her crying, was doubtless competent. The testimony to the effect that she also threatened suicide some days afterwards is going a step beyond the well-authenticated rule. While I am not prepared to say that it was such an error as would make a new trial necessary, my associates are of that opinion. They think it was incompetent, and tended to prejudice the jury against the defendant. ... No other questions are raised which it is necessary to here consider. The judgment and conviction reversed, and new trial ordered, and the proceedings remitted to the court of sessions of Monroe County to proceed thereon. So ordered.

Questions

1. What criminal offense was charged?
2. How many criminal agents were involved?
3. Which party appealed the finding of Principal in the second degree and to what effect?

Whoever, knowing that an offense against the United States has been committed, receives, relieves, comforts, or assists the offender in order to hinder or prevent his apprehension, trial or punishment, is an accessory after the fact.

The impact of the accessory finding is quite draconian since many after the fact accessories have little or nothing to do with the actual commission of the offense, but more to do with assisting the perpetrator in postcrime activities, and yet the penalty inflicted on the doer and the accessory may be identical. Defense counsel has a long and sterling history of innovative challenges to the accessory claim. One argument deals with the quality, content, and proof of mens rea. Here, the defendant argues that, as an accessory, his or her mens rea may or may not match that of the actual principal, and that to be a just resolution, the parties should have intended the same result. From another vantage point, what if the accessory had no idea that a principal was about to engage in criminal conduct as when a gun seller sells a gun to a person soon to use it as a criminal tool. What if the accessory is being honest and forthright about this lack of knowledge? To this question, the courts are utterly split.[47]

Some courts hold that the accessory may be subject to a distinct analysis as to knowledge while others conclude that the principal's mens rea will be imputed to the accessory. What is certain is that this form of mens rea analysis is in a "state of chaos."[48]

DEFENSE STRATEGIES

If the Principal is acquitted, the accessory charge is legally impossible.

If a felony was committed, the charged accessory was unaware of it.

If a felony was committed, the charged accessory's aid and assistance must coincide with the timing of underlying felony charged.

If the felony is plea bargained to a misdemeanor, the accessory charge must be dropped.

If the charged accessory did not know that the person assisted was the felon, there can be claim of accessory after the fact.

The alleged accessory renounced the plan of assistance before fully carrying it out and gave notice to lawful authorities.

The alleged accessory affirmatively withdrew from any participation in the assistance of the offender.

The MPC and other statutory authority allow any accused the defense of renunciation of and withdrawal from the criminal enterprise, but these actions cannot be inferred. To avail oneself of these defenses, affirmative and clear-cut steps of both disavowal and notification are mandated.

Check closely the jurisdictional rules regarding these various parties before issuing judgments, because statutory authority has greatly reformed these basic tenets of party law and responsibility. Each day, our court and legislative houses witness new and innovative efforts to hold accountable more than the actual committer of the offense and to spread the widest possible net to catch perpetrators from diverse angles of participation. A controversial tactic is known as vicarious liability.

VICARIOUS LIABILITY

Long a part of the civil system of torts and related causes of action, the notion of vicarious liability is new to criminal law. As in civil litigation, holding someone other than the actual wrongdoer liable is a means to remedy harm and hold accountable those entrusted with certain undeniable responsibilities. To be vicariously liable is to be culpable by implication, by transfusion, by status and role, similar to a parent being ultimately responsible for the conduct of children, a guardian for a ward, or a public safety officer or emergency personnel for the safety and well-being of the public. The theory of vicarious liability finds a nonoffender guilty of the offense even though the party committed no act and never intended the act be done. This is a radical departure from a criminal law jurisprudence that insists that each offense be proved by the elements that constitute the offense: the act (actus reus) and the mental state and intentionality (mens rea). In its place, innovative criminal law framers implant the offender's elements into a third party. So dramatically changed is the status quo that the imposition can only be in select and narrow cases. For example, offenses involving weapons and the abuse of children will sometimes witness the imposition of vicarious liability. Hence, if a child dies by a handgun or kills another by an unlocked weapon owned legally by a parent, the parent may be vicariously liable for the death caused.[49]

Case and statutory law support the finding of culpability on a parent whose child destroys property, sets fire to school facilities, and wreaks property havoc. Rhode Island, for example, places the onus of responsibility on the parents of the troubled child, and does so unapologetically. "The Rhode Island law penalizes a parent who permits or suffers such child to habitually associate with vicious, immoral, or criminal persons, or to grow up in ignorance, idleness, or crime, or to wander about the street of any city in the nighttime without being in any lawful business or occupation, or to enter any house of ill fame, policy shop, or place where any gambling is carried on or gaming device is operated, or to enter any place where intoxicating liquors are sold."[50]

The thrust behind vicarious liability is to ensure that parents and other responsible parties do not avoid liability for the errors of their children.[51] "The laws uniformly take some wrongdoing of the child's as evidence of improper parenting rather than focusing on specific acts of parenting engaged in by the adult. The exception is the almost omnipresent defense of showing that the parent took reasonable steps to control the behavior of the juvenile."[52] So pronounced are these types of problems in modern society that these extreme measures encounter little resistance or criticism.[53] Labeled "parental responsibility laws," the tolerance threshold has now been achieved when it comes to legislative patience and the activities of minors.[54]

For these reasons, vicarious liability has been characterized as strict liability criminality since neither proof of act nor proof of intentionality is required for a conviction. The sole element in proof is "being a parent and having a child who has committed an act of delinquency, truancy, or curfew breaking."[55]

CASE 2.2

U.S. V. MERCADO

610 F.3d 841 (2010)

Domingo Mercado ("Mercado") appeals the District Court's order denying his motion for judgment of acquittal. Because we find the evidence was sufficient to support the verdict, we will affirm the District Court's order.

I.

On September 10, 2008, a grand jury indicted Mercado and his two co-defendants, Dionel Rodriguez-Nunez ("Rodriguez-Nunez") and Hiram Coira-Soto, otherwise known as Morrisette ("Morrisette"), on one count of possession with intent to distribute 100 grams or more of heroin, and aiding and abetting the possession with intent to distribute, in violation of 21 U.S.C. § 841(a)(1) and (b)(1)(B). The grand jury also indicted them on one count of possession with intent to distribute, and aiding and abetting the possession with intent to distribute, within 1,000 feet of a school, in violation of 21 U.S.C. § 860(a). Rodriguez-Nunez pled guilty to both counts pursuant to a cooperation plea agreement. Morrisette was scheduled to plead guilty on February 5, 2009, but instead absconded. Mercado proceeded alone to trial on February 17, 2009.

At trial, the Government presented evidence that the Drug Enforcement Agency (DEA) had been working with a confidential informant, whom Rodriguez-Nunez knew as Poppy. On two occasions prior to the charges in question, Poppy completed controlled substance purchases from Rodriguez-Nunez. On August 13, 2008, at 11:00 a.m., DEA agents instructed Poppy to contact Rodriguez-Nunez and request 250 grams of heroin. Rodriguez-Nunez told Poppy he did not have that much heroin but would travel to New York City to pick some up and call Poppy when he returned.

Rodriguez-Nunez, however, did not go to New York City. Instead, he contacted Morrisette about getting heroin to sell to Poppy. Rodriguez-Nunez testified that he had never done business with Morrisette before, but believed that Morrisette could provide for his customer's needs.

On August 14, 2008, starting at 7:00 a.m., DEA agents set up surveillance at the 200 block of East Allegheny Avenue across the street from Rodriguez-Nunez's residence. Rodriguez-Nunez left his house at approximately 11:00 a.m. He made one stop and then arrived at a barber shop located at the intersection of Front and Lippincott in Philadelphia at 11:40 a.m., less than three blocks from his house. Rodriguez-Nunez stayed in the area around the barber shop for most of the afternoon, talking to numerous people.

Although DEA agents did not observe Rodriguez-Nunez talking with Morrisette or Mercado in front of the barber shop, Rodriguez-Nunez testified that he talked to them twice throughout the day. He said Morrisette pulled up in a black Ford Taurus sometime before noon. Mercado sat in the passenger seat. Rodriguez-Nunez stood outside the passenger-side window of the car and spoke with Morrisette about purchasing heroin. Then, Morrisette and Mercado drove away. A short time later, Morrisette dropped by the barber shop again with Mercado in the passenger seat. This time, Morrisette was driving a maroon

GMC Envoy registered in his name. Standing on the street and speaking to Morrisette through the passenger-side window, Rodriguez-Nunez and Morrisette further discussed which drugs Morrisette had available to sell to Rodriguez-Nunez.

Rodriguez-Nunez testified that he and Morrisette exchanged several calls over cellular phones throughout the day. Originally, Rodriguez-Nunez agreed to pay $62 for each gram of heroin, but in a later call he asked Morrisette if he could decrease the price to $60 per gram. Morrisette responded by saying he would "patch [Rodriguez-Nunez] on with the owner of [the] stuff." (J.A. 115.) Immediately thereafter, a new voice spoke into the phone and confirmed that the price was $62 a gram. Neither Morrisette nor the "owner" ever identified the new voice by name.

Another confidential informant called Rodriguez-Nunez between 4:30 p.m. and 5:00 p.m. to ask if Rodriguez-Nunez had succeeded in acquiring some heroin. Rodriguez-Nunez responded that he was returning from picking up the heroin and was going to meet with Poppy at the Cousin's Supermarket parking lot across the street from his house. Based on this information, law enforcement set up surveillance in the supermarket's parking lot.

Poppy and Rodriguez-Nunez met at 5:15 p.m. Rodriguez-Nunez told Poppy he did not have the heroin yet, but that Poppy should come back in ten minutes. Then Rodriguez-Nunez left the parking lot, briefly stopped by the barber shop, and returned to his residence on Allegheny Avenue. Rodriguez-Nunez waited on his stoop for Morrisette to arrive with the heroin.

Sometime later, Morrisette pulled up in front of Rodriguez-Nunez's house in the black Ford Taurus. Again, Mercado was in the passenger seat. Rodriguez-Nunez walked over to the passenger-side window and reached into the car. Someone handed him a wrapped package of heroin, which he put directly in his pocket. Rodriguez-Nunez testified that he is unsure whether Mercado or Morrisette passed him the package. Surveillance officers were also unable to see which one transferred the package to Rodriguez-Nunez.

Morrisette drove away. Rodriguez-Nunez crossed the street to deliver the package to Poppy, but DEA agents arrested Rodriguez-Nunez before he could [deliver the package]. DEA agents took Rodriguez-Nunez inside his residence, executed a search of his house, and recovered the heroin package from his right, rear pocket. Rodriguez-Nunez, through a Spanish interpreter, immediately began cooperating. He told the DEA agents he received the heroin from a man named Morrisette, which he had yet to pay for, and that he was supposed to call when he had the money.

At the DEA agents' direction, Rodriguez-Nunez called Morrisette at 6:20 p.m. and told him to come pick up the money. A short while later, Morrisette and Mercado drove up, this time in the maroon GMC Envoy. The DEA agents arrested both Morrisette and Mercado.

Rodriguez-Nunez testified that although he saw Mercado with Morrisette every time he saw Morrisette that day, he never conversed with Mercado. When asked if Mercado had anything to do with the drugs, Rodriguez-Nunez stated, "I wasn't dealing with that man. Whatever they did among themselves, you know, Morrisette's the one that knows. It's their business." (J.A. 139.)

Agent Poules testified that after DEA agents arrested Rodriguez-Nunez, Morrisette, and Mercado, he confiscated their cellular phones. The phone he took from Rodriguez-Nunez was registered to the same number Poppy used to call Rodriguez-Nunez. The number for

Morrisette's phone was consistent with the number Rodriguez-Nunez dialed to request that Morrisette pick up the money. Agent Poules also retrieved Mercado's phone and subpoenaed the toll records relating to the three phones.

The toll records revealed that the phones registered to the parties exchanged several phone calls on August 14, 2008, before 11:00 a.m. Of course, the toll records do not show that the parties themselves made these calls. Relevant to this case, however, is the fact Rodriguez-Nunez's phone called Morrisette's phone two times that morning, both resulting in short voice messages. Of particular note is the fact that, before Morrisette responded to Rodriguez-Nunez, three short calls were placed between Morrisette's phone and Mercado's phone. Only after those calls were made did Morrisette respond to Rodriguez-Nunez's call. There were no phone calls between Mercado and Rodriguez-Nunez, only between Mercado and Morrisette and Morrisette and Rodriguez-Nunez.

The Government's case also included three stipulations: the package recovered contained heroin, the distance between the parking lot and the school is less than 1,000 feet, and law enforcement maintained the proper chain of custody for documents recovered until the point the documents were introduced into evidence.

Mercado moved for a Rule 29 judgment of acquittal after the Government presented all of its evidence, save one witness. The District Court listened to brief arguments on the motion, but deferred the ruling until after the jury verdict. The jury convicted Mercado on both counts.

After the jury verdict, the District Court asked counsel to reargue the motion, focusing their Rule 29 arguments on Mercado's potential liability as an aider or abettor or via constructive possession. It stated:

> It's no secret that I disagree with the jury verdict in this case. I'm not saying that the defendant is not guilty. I think looking hard at the meaning of "reasonable doubt," if I had been sitting as a juror, I would have voted for a verdict of not guilty. But, that's not the test. My disagreement with the jury verdict doesn't carry the day for the Defense, and yet I'm driven to this conclusion. By the Government's argument, I think the fact that the defendant was present four times takes this case out of the rule that mere presence, where the drugs are being delivered, and mere presence in the car in which they're being delivered, is not enough. Mere presence once, yes. Mere presence four times, I say no. That prevents me from saying that no rational trier of the fact could find the defendant guilty beyond a reasonable doubt.

(J.A. 268-69.) Thus, the District Court denied the motion for judgment of acquittal.

II.

The District Court had subject matter jurisdiction over this case pursuant to 18 U.S.C. § 3231, and we have appellate jurisdiction pursuant to 28 U.S.C. § 1291.

We apply a particularly deferential standard when determining if a jury verdict rests on sufficient evidence because a reviewing court "must be ever vigilant, not to usurp the role of the jury by weighing credibility and assigning weight to the evidence." *United States v. Boria*, 592 F.3d 476, 480 (3d Cir. 2010) (quoting *United States v. Brodie*, 403 F.3d 123, 133 (3d Cir. 2005)). Therefore, we view the evidence in the light most favorable to the prosecution and sustain the verdict unless it is clear that no rational trier of fact could have found the essential elements of the crime beyond a reasonable doubt. *United States v. Cunningham*, 517 F.3d 175, 177 (3d Cir. 2008). Thus, an insufficiency of the evidence claim places a heavy burden on the appellant because we will only find the evidence insufficient when the prosecution's failure is clear. *United States v. Soto*, 539 F .3d 191, 194 (3d Cir. 2008); Brodie, 403 F.3d at 133. The prosecution may satisfy its burden entirely through circumstantial evidence. *United States v. Bobb*, 471 F.3d 491, 494 (3d Cir. 2006) .

III.

Mercado does not dispute that he had full knowledge that Morrisette was engaging in the substantive crime of possession and distribution of a controlled substance. He claims, however, that the Government offered insufficient evidence from which a reasonable juror could infer that he in some way aided or facilitated in the crime. Instead, he contends the evidence establishes he was merely a passive spectator.

The relevant inquiry on appeal is whether any reasonable juror could find that Mercado facilitated the drug transaction between Morrisette and Rodriguez-Nunez. One who aids and abets the possession, manufacture, or distribution of a controlled substance in violation of 21 U.S.C. § 841(a)(1) is punishable as a principal. 18 U.S.C. § 2(a). One is guilty of aiding and abetting if the government proves: (1) that another committed a substantive offense, and (2) the one charged with aiding and abetting knew of the commission of the substantive offense and acted to facilitate it. *United States v. Cartwright*, 359 F.3d 281, 287 (3d Cir. 2004). Additionally, we require proof that the defendant had the specific intent to facilitate the crime. *United States v. Garth*, 188 F.3d 99, 113 (3d Cir. 1999). One can aid or abet another through use of words or actions to promote the success of the illegal venture. *United States v. Xavier*, 2 F.3d 1281, 1288 (3d Cir. 1993).

We have emphasized that "facilitation" for aiding and abetting purposes is "more than associat[ion] with individuals involved in the criminal venture." Soto, 539 F.3d at 194 (quoting *United States v. Dixon*, 658 F.2d 181, 189 (3d Cir. 1981)). Rather, the defendant must "participate in" the criminal enterprise. Id. Thus, to convict for aiding and abetting, the Government must prove the defendant associated himself with the venture and sought by his actions to make it succeed. *United States v. Powell*, 113 F.3d 464, 467 (3d Cir. 1997). The Government need only show some affirmative participation which, at least, encourages the principal offender to commit the offense. *United States v. Frorup*, 963 F.2d 41, 43 (3d Cir. 1992). An aiding and abetting conviction can be supported solely with circumstantial evidence as long as there is a "logical and convincing connection between the facts established and the conclusion inferred." Soto, 539 F.3d at 194 (quoting Cartwright, 359 F.3d at 287).

The evidence produced at trial revealed that Mercado accompanied Morrisette as a passenger in his two cars on four occasions during an ongoing drug transaction where Morrisette discussed, delivered, and attempted to receive payment for more than 100 grams of heroin. Additionally, phones registered to Morrisette, Rodriguez-Nunez, and Mercado exchanged calls prior to 11:00 a.m. on August 14, 2008, and Morrisette put Rodriguez-Nunez on the phone with the "owner" of the heroin, who was in Morrisette's immediate proximity.

There is no direct evidence that Mercado aided or encouraged Morrisette during the ongoing drug transaction. The Government, however, maintains that a reasonable juror could infer from the circumstantial evidence of Mercado's repeated presence in Morrisette's car, and the pattern of the phone calls, that Mercado aided and abetted Morrisette. Id. Specifically, the Government argues that, by switching cars with Morrisette on three occasions, a reasonable juror could infer Mercado affirmatively acted to help Morrisette frustrate surveillance of the drug transaction. Additionally, because Rodriguez-Nunez testified he received the heroin after reaching into the passenger-side window, a reasonable juror could infer that Mercado handed him the heroin. Finally, the Government asserts that a reasonable juror could infer from the pattern of the calls between Rodriguez-Nunez, Morrisette, and Mercado that Rodriguez-Nunez called Morrisette to "announce that he was available to do the deal; [Morrisette] immediately called Mercado to pass this information along and arrange to acquire the drugs; Mercado made arrangements and then informed [Morrisette]; and, finally, [Morrisette] called Rodriguez-Nunez to tell him the deal was on." (Gov't Br. 29.) At argument, the Government alternatively proposed a reasonable juror could infer Mercado served as Morrisette's "muscle," and accompanied him to ensure the drug sale went smoothly.

Mercado claims there is insufficient evidence to support his conviction by arguing that a reasonable juror is prohibited from inferring anything from the telephone calls under *United States v. Thomas*, 114 F.3d 403 (3d Cir. 1997), and that evidence of Mercado sitting in Morrisette's car merely establishes his presence at the scene of the crime, not his participation in the crime. Soto, 539 F.3d at 194. We address each argument in turn.

In Thomas, we reversed a jury verdict and judgment convicting Thomas of conspiring to possess cocaine with an intent to distribute. Thomas, 114 F.3d at 404. We determined the prosecution failed to prove that Thomas, who in exchange for $500 went into a hotel room to confirm a suitcase was inside, knew the suitcase contained controlled substances. Id. at 404–05. The Government offered evidence of calls between a co-conspirator's phone and Thomas's home phone, pager, and cellular phone, to establish that Thomas knew the suitcase contained drugs. Id. at 405–06. There was no evidence of the calls' contents. We noted the Government's case depended on the jury inferring that the caller informed Thomas that there was cocaine in the suitcase. Id. at 406. We determined it was "speculative to conclude that Thomas knew that drugs were involved," and that we could not uphold a jury verdict based on speculation alone. Id.

Contrary to Mercado's assertions, Thomas does not broadly proscribe jurors from making inferences about phone calls when there is no evidence of their contents. See id. It more narrowly prohibits jurors from inferring that a defendant gained knowledge of the subject of an illegal conspiracy based the existence of a call alone. Id. Because Rodriguez-Nunez's testimony provides ample evidence Mercado had knowledge of the ongoing heroin transaction, Thomas is distinguishable.

Mercado's claim that evidence of his repeated presence only establishes that he was "merely present" as a passive spectator is unpersuasive. This argument implicates two cases where we reached contrary results. In *United States v. Jenkins*, we determined evidence that (1) a defendant was sitting on a couch in his friend's apartment, (2) in boxer shorts, (3) near to a table supporting three bags of cocaine, established that the defendant was "merely present" at the scene of the crime and was insufficient to support a conviction for aiding and abetting. 90 F.3d 814, 816, 821 (3d Cir. 1996). We found evidence of "[h]is close proximity to the drugs and firearms, state of dress, and acquaintance with Stallings, who committed the principal offense," was insufficient because it did not suggest the defendant associated himself with, or participated in, the drug distribution scheme. Id. at 821.

In contrast, in *United States v. Leon*, we affirmed an aiding and abetting conviction where the evidence established: (1) law enforcement spotted the defendant at a rest stop in the vicinity of two co-defendants (who had U-Haul trucks and a tractor trailer under their control) the day before a large quantity of drugs were unloaded, and (2) the following day the defendant was found lying face down on a tugboat after police ordered individuals to freeze a short distance from where a large quantity of drugs had been seen in a "secluded area" on a trailer, the same trailer that was seen at the rest stop the night before. 739 F.2d 885, 892 (3d Cir. 1984). We acknowledged that the defendant's proximity to the location where a large quantity of drugs was unloaded merely established his presence near the drugs, and might be insufficient evidence from which to infer his participation in the drug distribution scheme. Id. at 892–93. We concluded, however, that a reasonable juror could infer from the defendant's proximity to where the drugs were unloaded, and his presence near the co-defendants the previous night, "that [the defendant] was not present for some innocuous reason, but was involved in the conspiracy." Id. at 893.

Unlike in Jenkins, Mercado was not present during the drug transaction on one occasion, but repeatedly. Evidence of repeated presence suggests Mercado was not present by accident, but rather participated in and facilitated the drug possession. See Leon, 739 F.2d at 893 (concluding a reasonable juror could find a defendant's presence was not innocuous based on evidence that he was present on two occasions); see also *United States v. Paone*, 758 F.2d 774, 776 (1st Cir. 1985) (concluding a jury could reasonably infer a defendant aided and abetted based on his "repeated presence at important junctures of th[e] drug deal"). This is particularly true because Morrisette and Mercado switched cars on three occasions during the day; thus, Mercado got out of one of Morrisette's cars and chose to get into another car on three separate instances to continue accompanying Morrisette at important junctures during a prolonged drug transaction. Evidence of Mercado's presence considered in conjunction with the phone call patterns, which establish Mercado's association with Morrisette, is more evidence than we had before us when we affirmed the jury's conviction in Leon. See Leon, 739 F.2d at 892.

This is admittedly a close case. We are constrained by a deferential burden that requires us to sustain the jury's verdict unless the prosecution's failure is clear. Brodie, 403 F.3d at 133. Although we realize other inferences are possible from the evidence offered, we believe that if the evidence is viewed in the light most favorable to the Government, a reasonable juror could infer that Mercado, at a minimum, encouraged Morrisette to possess and distribute heroin based on his repeated presence in Morrisette's cars and their phone communications. Frorup, 963 F.2d at 43; see *United States v. Cooper*, 567 F.2d 252, 254 (3d Cir. 1977) ("The evidence does not need to be inconsistent with every conclusion save that of guilt if it does establish a case from which the jury can find the defendant guilty beyond a reasonable doubt.") (*internal quotation marks and citation omitted*). Therefore, we will affirm the judgment. Soto, 539 F.3d at 194.

Mercado predicts that affirming his conviction will be tantamount to imposing criminal liability on people who associate with criminals. We disagree. A person cannot be considered an aider and abettor if he or she is present, even under extremely suspicious circumstances, near drugs on one occasion. Id.; Jenkins, 90 F.3d at 821. Rather, we will only affirm a jury's conviction for aiding and abetting liability if evidence of a defendant's presence, taken in consideration with the totality of the evidence, supports an inference that the defendant acted in a way to progress the crime. Soto, 539 F.3d at 194. If such an inference could not be drawn, drug suppliers could regularly monitor their drug distributors and avoid prosecution simply by not handling the product or talking to the buyers.

We hold that a defendant's presence on multiple occasions during critical moments of drug transactions may, when considered in light of the totality of the circumstances, support an inference of the defendant's participation in the criminal activity. Such an inference is appropriate in this case. See also *United States v. Lema*, 909 F.2d 561, 570 (1st Cir. 1990) (affirming a jury conviction for aiding and abetting based on, *inter alia*, evidence that a defendant was present at two separate drug transactions); Paone, 758 F.2d at 776.

VI.

We, therefore, hold there was sufficient evidence for a jury to find Mercado guilty of aiding and abetting the possession with intent to distribute heroin beyond a reasonable doubt.

Questions

1. Why is the issue of mere presence critical to the defense argument? Is there another type of presence?
2. Do the facts show that Mercado actually possessed controlled substances for the purposes of sale and distribution?
3. How would you describe the judge's view when it regards the validity and sanctity of a jury verdict?
4. What does the Court mean when it references the "totality of circumstances"?
5. What does the Court say a reasonable juror could do in this case?

IMPUTING CRIMINALITY TO CORPORATE ACTION

Under historical interpretation, it is legally impossible to apply the criminal elements of act and mind to a nonbeing in the form of a corporate entity or nonprofit association. These entities will do nothing, though the employees who labor under their roof could act in criminal ways. Finding corporations guilty of criminal offenses is technically a pipedream. How can a corporation act as a human agent would? How can it think and rationalize the plan of action? What type of mens rea does a business entity possess?

Both corporations and individuals may be convicted of actual criminal code violations, though in the former instance, this is an exceedingly rare event. This liability can attach either in an individual or vicarious sense. By vicarious we mean that the employer is responsible for the conduct of their employees. Most jurisdictions, however, do impose a higher burden of proof in a case of vicarious liability because "the prosecution must prove that the employer knowingly and intentionally aided, advised, or encouraged the employee's criminal conduct."[56]

CASE 2.3

STATE V. PITTS
714 P.2d 582, 584 (N.M. 1986)

The case before us today was initiated as a delinquency proceeding in children's court.

Defendant William Wayne Pitts was seventeen years and eight months old at the time of the sexual offenses in question, and the victim was a twelve-year-old boy. The proceeding was transferred to district court for criminal prosecution, pursuant to NMSA 1978, Section 32-1-30 (Repl.Pamp. 1981). Defendant there was convicted of two counts of criminal sexual penetration of a minor, five counts of contributing to the delinquency of a minor, and three counts of criminal sexual contact of a minor.

Defendant appealed his convictions on several grounds. The Court of Appeals reversed and remanded to children's court, holding that defendant had been denied the effective assistance of counsel both in the children's court and the district court proceedings. That decision is not challenged in this Court. The Court of Appeals also held that the district court should have dismissed the charges of contributing to the delinquency of a minor because, as a matter of law under NMSA 1978, Section 30-6-3 (Repl.Pamp. 1984), no minor can be convicted of that offense. We granted certiorari to review this holding, and we reverse.

Section 30-6-3 states: "Contributing to delinquency of minor consists of any person committing any act, or omitting the performance of any duty, which act or omission causes, or tends to cause or encourage the delinquency of any person under the age of eighteen years.

Whoever commits contributing to delinquency of minor is guilty of a fourth degree felony."

The Court of Appeals, citing cases from other jurisdictions and a law review article, decided that this statutory language required construction. It held that the legislative intent in enacting Section 30-6-3 was to protect children from harmful adult conduct. It, therefore, construed "any person" and "whoever" to mean any adult human being.

The intent of the Legislature is to be sought first in the meaning of the words used, and when they are free from ambiguity no other means of interpretation should be resorted to. ... We believe the Court of Appeals here exceeded its authority, for "it is not the business of the courts to look beyond the plain meaning of the words of a clearly drafted statute in an attempt to divine the intent of the Legislature." ...

The Criminal Code, NMSA 1978, Sections 30-1-1 to 30-28-3 (Repl. Pamp. 1984), defines "person" as any human being or legal entity. NMSA 1978, § 30-1-12(E) (Repl. Pamp. 1984). The Legislature clearly limited that definition to human beings when it employed the phrase "any person under the age of eighteen." See NMSA 1978, § 30-6-3 (Repl. Pamp. 1984); see also NMSA 1978, § 12-2-2 (rules of construction). On the other hand, the Legislature did not choose to modify or limit that definition when it used the phrases "any person committing any act" and "whoever commits." See NMSA 1978, § 30-6-3 (Repl. Pamp. 1984).

We do not believe that the unambiguous language of this statute requires judicial construction. We cannot agree with the Court of Appeals interpretation, which requires us to read the words "adult" and "human being" into phrases the Legislature used without limitation. We hold that a minor can be prosecuted under Section 30-6-3, and can be convicted of contributing to the delinquency of a minor.

Our conclusion would be no different if we assumed, for the sake of argument, that the statute is ambiguous and that statutory interpretation is appropriate. We disagree with the Court of Appeals reading of the statute, the precedents, and the Legislature's intent. First, the fact that the offense in question was placed in Article 6 of the Criminal Code among "Crimes Against Children and Dependents" is utterly irrelevant to our consideration of who properly may be prosecuted under the statute.

Secondly, neither in *State v. Favela* ... nor in *State v. Cuevas* ... did this Court hold that the contributing to delinquency statute authorizes only the prosecution of adults. Because the defendant in each case was an adult, the question before us now did not arise. In mere dicta, each opinion did state, however, that the legislative purpose of the statute is to protect children from harmful adult conduct. ... To the extent Favela and Cuevas suggest that the statute is addressed only to adult conduct, they are overruled.

Finally, this Court has long recognized that the intent of the Legislature in enacting Section 30-6-3 and its predecessors was to extend the broadest possible protection to children, who may be led astray in innumerable ways. In order to realize this legislative purpose, we have consistently rejected narrow constructions of the statute that would limit its usefulness in protecting children. ... This Court has held the statute constitutional despite the vagueness of its description of the proscribed acts and omissions. ... Our Court of Appeals similarly has rejected a vagueness challenge arguing that an inattentive parent might be convicted as "any person" contributing to the delinquency of a minor. ... Furthermore, we have tacitly approved the Court of Appeals holding that the statute is constitutional, although it imposes criminal sanctions for acts committed without criminal intent. ...

In short, even if we considered statutory interpretation necessary in this case, we would disagree with the Court of Appeals conclusion that the statute authorizes the prosecution of adults only. In light of the statute's protective purpose, we believe it defies reason to infer that the Legislature intended to exclude acts of minors against minors when it chose to punish "any person" who contributed to the delinquency of a minor.

For the reasons stated, we hold that a minor, properly transferred from children's court to district court, may be tried and convicted of contributing to the delinquency of a minor under Section 30-6-3. We, therefore, reverse that portion of the Court of Appeals decision holding that the trial court erred in denying defendant's motion to dismiss the charges of contributing to the delinquency of a minor. This case is remanded to the Court of Appeals for orders consistent with this opinion.

Questions

1. Cite the exact statute at issue.
2. Does the statute hold the parents strictly liable for the conduct of their children?
3. For what type of offense was this imposed liability upheld?
4. Do you agree or disagree with the Court?

> Visit the Yale Law Journal's recent treatment of corporate criminal liability at http://www.yalelawjournal.org/images/pdfs/729.pdf

Other legal issues make difficult a prosecution against corporations for criminal behavior. A broad critique of corporate criminal intent can be summarized as follows:

How can a corporation formulate specific or general intent, the mens rea necessary for a criminal conviction?

More particularly, in violent acts of criminality, such as rape, murder, or robbery, to whom or on whose authority within the corporate structure would the responsibility lie?

Both queries pose difficult legal dilemmas. While it is common to hear a sort of class warfare critique of the corporate heads of state, this type of "them versus us" will simply not do. To be culpable requires knowledge of the crime and its purpose. In the evolving analysis of corporate crime, a trend toward corporate responsibility has emerged.[57] Does a corporate officer and director who has actual knowledge of criminal behavior on the part of subordinates within the corporation bear some level of responsibility? Is a corporation responsible, as principal, for the acts of its agents both civilly and criminally? While "officers may be held criminally responsible on the presumption that it authorized the illegal acts"[58] that judgment will depend on the facts and circumstances of each case.

There are other rationales for imposing criminal culpability on the corporate officers and directors. Criminal charges are regularly brought forth and eventual liability sometimes imposed for failure to uphold the rules and regulatory standards promulgated by government agencies, such as:

Occupational Health and Safety Act (OSHA)
The Food and Drug Administration (FDA)
National Labor Relations Board (NLRB)
Environmental Protection Act (EPA)
Homeland Security Administration (HSA)
National Transportation Safety Board (NTSB)

Government agencies are empowered to charge and assess criminal penalties and fines. OSHA is the classic federal agency with these sweeping powers.

> Review the penalty power and authority under criminal prosecution for OSHA at http://www.ktvu.com/news/23874131/detail.html

Other common corporate areas of criminality in business crime include securities fraud, antitrust activity, bank fraud, tax evasion, violations against the Racketeer Influenced and Corrupt Organizations Act (RICO), and acts involving bribery, international travel, and business practices.[59] Finding corporations criminally responsible for particular actions is not the insurmountable task it once was.

Unless special rules of liability are crafted, none of these questions can be sensibly answered. No corporation, whether General Motors or Ford, Enron, AIG, CNN or Microsoft, can actualize and intellectualize as the street criminal does or as the definitions of crime require. This is a factual and a legal impossibility except under special legislation. "Criminal violations normally entail two elements, mens rea and actus reus. Since corporations are purely incorporeal legal entities, they cannot actually do or intend anything."[60] Corporations and other businesses are no more than "fictional beings."[61] This is not to say that government cannot impose criminal liability for infractions and violations, from environmental pollution to OSHA hazards in the workplace. Congress has delegated not only rulemaking power to various agencies of government, but simultaneously granted it enforcement powers that are broad and include criminal correction.[62] In the federal system particularly, legislation enables governmental authority to punish business and other entities by various measures including:

1. Mechanisms to remedy harm caused by an organization, including restitution, remedial measures, and community service.
2. Probation, ranging from the requirement that no further crimes be committed during the prohibition term to the issuance of surprise audits and periodic reports.
3. The imposition of monetary fines, largely determined by calculating the base level, base fine, and culpability factor.

Section B also discusses the structure and implications of compliance programs designated to enable organizations to reduce potential liability by self-policing.[63]

The Environmental Protection Agency is blessed with these sweeping powers to sanction the business entity. "Criminal prosecutions and fines have increased markedly in recent years. The EPA pursues criminal sanctions when there is significant environmental harm and culpable conduct. EPA enforcement policy emphasizes both cross-media environmental problems, and cooperation with other administrative agencies. The EPA identifies three national industry sectors for priority attention at any given time."[64] An example of one of its many legislative directives is the Federal Insecticide, Fungicide, and Rodenticide Act (FIFRA)that is reproduced below.

TITLE 7 UNITED STATES CODE (2010)

Section 136. Definitions

For purposes of this subchapter:

  (e) Certified applicator, etc.

    (1) Certified applicator

        The term "certified applicator" means any individual who is certified under section 136i of this title as authorized to use or supervise the use of any pesticide, which is classified for restricted use. Any applicator who holds or applies registered pesticides, or uses dilutions of registered pesticides consistent with subsection (ee) of this section, only to provide a service of controlling pests without delivering any unapplied pesticide to any person so served is not deemed to be a seller or distributor of pesticides under this subchapter.

    (2) Private applicator

        The term "private applicator" means a certified applicator who uses or supervises the use of any pesticide which is classified for restricted use for purposes of producing any agricultural commodity on property owned or rented by the applicator or the applicator's employer or (if applied without compensation other than trading of personal services between producers of agricultural commodities) on the property of another person.

(3) Commercial applicator
The term "commercial applicator" means an applicator (whether or not the applicator is a private applicator with respect to some uses) who uses or supervises the use of any pesticide which is classified for restricted use for any purpose or on any property other than as provided by paragraph (2).

Section 136j. Unlawful Acts

(a) In general
(1) Except as provided by subsection (b) of this section, it shall be unlawful for any person in any State to distribute or sell to any person:
(A) any pesticide that is not registered under section 136a of this title or whose registration has been canceled or suspended, except to the extent that distribution or sale otherwise has been authorized by the Administrator under this subchapter;
(B) any registered pesticide if any claims made for it as a part of its distribution or sale substantially differ from any claims made for it as a part of the statement required in connection with its registration under section 136a of this title;
(C) any registered pesticide the composition of which differs at the time of its distribution or sale from its composition as described in the statement required in connection with its registration under section 136a of this title;
(D) any pesticide which has not been colored or discolored pursuant to the provisions of section 136w(c)(5) of this title;
(E) any pesticide which is adulterated or misbranded; or
(F) any device which is misbranded.
(2) It shall be unlawful for any person:
(A) to detach, alter, deface, or destroy, in whole or in part, any labeling required under this subchapter;
(B) to refuse to:
(i) prepare, maintain, or submit any records required by or under section 136c, 136e, 136f, 136i, or 136q of this title;
(ii) submit any reports required by or under section 136c, 136d, 136e, 136f, 136i, or 136q of this title; or
(iii) allow any entry, inspection, copying of records, or sampling authorized by this subchapter;
(C) to give a guaranty or undertaking provided for in subsection (b) of this section which is false in any particular, except that a person who receives and relies upon a guaranty authorized under subsection (b) of this section may give a guaranty to the same effect, which guaranty shall contain, in addition to the person's own name and address, the name and address of the person residing in the United States from whom the person received the guaranty or undertaking;

(D)   to use for the person's own advantage or to reveal, other than to the Administrator, or officials or employees of the Environmental Protection Agency or other Federal executive agencies, or to the courts, or to physicians, pharmacists, and other qualified persons, needing such information for the performance of their duties, in accordance with such directions as the Administrator may prescribe, any information acquired by authority of this subchapter which is confidential under this subchapter;

(E)   who is a registrant, wholesaler, dealer, retailer, or other distributor to advertise a product registered under this subchapter for restricted use without giving the classification of the product assigned to it under section 136a of this title;

(F)   to distribute or sell, or to make available for use, or to use, any registered pesticide classified for restricted use for some or all purposes other than in accordance with section 136a(d) of this title and any regulations thereunder, except that it shall not be unlawful to sell, under regulations issued by the Administrator, a restricted use pesticide to a person who is not a certified applicator for application by a certified applicator;

(G)   to use any registered pesticide in a manner inconsistent with its labeling;

(H)   to use any pesticide which is under an experimental use permit contrary to the provisions of such permit;

(I)   to violate any order issued under section 136k of this title;

(J)   to violate any suspension order issued under section 136a(c)(2)(B), 136a-1, or 136d of this title;

(K)   to violate any cancellation order issued under this subchapter or to fail to submit a notice in accordance with section 136d(g) of this title;

(L)   who is a producer to violate any of the provisions of section 136e of this title;

(M)   to knowingly falsify all or part of any application for registration, application for experimental use permit, any information submitted to the Administrator pursuant to section 136e of this title, any records required to be maintained pursuant to this subchapter, any report filed under this subchapter, or any information marked as confidential and submitted to the Administrator under any provision of this subchapter;

(N)   who is a registrant, wholesaler, dealer, retailer, or other distributor to fail to file reports required by this subchapter;

(O)   to add any substance to, or take any substance from, any pesticide in a manner that may defeat the purpose of this subchapter;

(P)   to use any pesticide in tests on human beings unless such human beings (i) are fully informed of the nature and purposes of the test and of any physical and mental health consequences which are reasonably foreseeable therefrom, and (ii) freely volunteer to participate in the test;

(Q)   to falsify all or part of any information relating to the testing of any pesticide (or any ingredient, metabolite, or degradation product thereof), including the nature of any protocol, procedure, substance, organism, or equipment used, observation made, or conclusion or opinion formed, submitted to the Administrator, or that the person knows will be furnished to the Administrator or will become a part of any records required to be maintained by this subchapter;

(R)   to submit to the Administrator data known to be false in support of a registration; or

(S)   to violate any regulation issued under section 136a(a) or 136q of this title.

(b) Exemptions

The penalties provided for a violation of paragraph (1) of subsection (a) of this section shall not apply to:

(1)   any person who establishes a guaranty signed by, and containing the name and address of, the registrant or person residing in the United States from whom the person purchased or received in good faith the pesticide in the same unbroken package, to the effect that the pesticide was lawfully registered at the time of sale and delivery to the person, and that it complies with the other requirements of this subchapter, and in such case the guarantor shall be subject to the penalties which would otherwise attach to the person holding the guaranty under the provisions of this subchapter;

(2)   any carrier while lawfully shipping, transporting, or delivering for shipment any pesticide or device, if such carrier upon request of any officer or employee duly designated by the Administrator shall permit such officer or employee to copy all of its records concerning such pesticide or device;

(3)   any public official while engaged in the performance of the official duties of the public official;

(4)   any person using or possessing any pesticide as provided by an experimental use permit in effect with respect to such pesticide and such use or possession; or

(5)   any person who ships a substance or mixture of substances being put through tests in which the purpose is only to determine its value for pesticide purposes or to determine its toxicity or other properties and from which the user does not expect to receive any benefit in pest control from its use.

Section 136l. Penalties

(a) Civil penalties

(1)   In general

Any registrant, commercial applicator, wholesaler, dealer, retailer, or other distributor who violates any provision of this subchapter may be assessed a civil penalty by the Administrator of not more than $5,000 for each offense.

(2)   Private applicator

Any private applicator or other person not included in paragraph (1) who violates any provision of this subchapter subsequent to receiving a written warning from the Administrator or following a citation for a prior violation, may be assessed a civil penalty by the Administrator of not more than $1,000 for each offense, except that any applicator not included under paragraph (1) of this subsection who holds or applies registered pesticides, or uses dilutions of registered pesticides, only to provide a service of controlling pests without delivering any unapplied pesticide to any person so served, and who violates any provision of this subchapter may be assessed a civil penalty by the Administrator of not more than $500 for the first offense nor more than $1,000 for each subsequent offense.

(b) Criminal penalties
    (1) In general
        (A) Any registrant, applicant for a registration, or producer who knowingly violates any provision of this subchapter shall be fined not more than $50,000 or imprisoned for not more than 1 year, or both.
        (B) Any commercial applicator of a restricted use pesticide, or any other person not described in subparagraph (A) who distributes or sells pesticides or devices, who knowingly violates any provision of this subchapter shall be fined not more than $25,000 or imprisoned for not more than 1 year, or both.
    (2) Private applicator
    Any private applicator or other person not included in paragraph (1) who knowingly violates any provision of this subchapter shall be guilty of a misdemeanor and shall on conviction be fined not more than $1,000, or imprisoned for not more than 30 days, or both.
    (3) Disclosure of information
    Any person, who, with intent to defraud, uses or reveals information relative to formulas of products acquired under the authority of section 136a of this title, shall be fined not more than $10,000, or imprisoned for not more than three years, or both.
    (4) Acts of officers, agents, etc.
    When construing and enforcing the provisions of this subchapter, the act, omission, or failure of any officer, agent, or other person acting for or employed by any person shall in every case be also deemed to be the act, omission, or failure of such person as well as that of the person employed.

Section 136p. Exemption of Federal and State Agencies

The Administrator may, at the Administrator's discretion, exempt any Federal or State agency from any provision of this subchapter if the Administrator determines that emergency conditions exist which require such exemption. The Administrator, in determining whether or not such emergency conditions exist, shall consult with the Secretary of Agriculture and the Governor of any State concerned if they request such determination.

Questions

1. FIFRA applies to what entities?
2. FIFRA can only criminalize private and not commercial applicators. True or False?
3. FIFRA provides criminal sanctions for a variety of specific offenses. Name three.
4. What level of imprisonment does FIFRA provide?

CASE 2.4

U.S. V. HAYES INT'L CORP.
786 F.2d 1499 (11ᵗʰ Cir)

The degree of knowledge necessary for a conviction under 42 U.S.C. § 6928(d)(1), unlawful transportation of hazardous waste, is the principal issue in this appeal. The district court granted judgments of acquittal notwithstanding the jury verdicts. The court held that the government had not presented sufficient evidence of knowledge to support convictions of Hayes International Corp. and L. H. Beasley. A decision of the district court setting aside a jury verdict of guilty is entitled to no deference, *United States v. Burns*, 597 F.2d 939, 941 (5th Cir. 1979), and we have conducted our own review of the evidence and find it sufficient. Accordingly, we reverse.

Hayes International Corp. (Hayes) operates an airplane refurbishing plant in Birmingham, Alabama. In the course of its business, Hayes generates certain waste products, two of which are relevant to this case. First, Hayes must drain fuel tanks of the planes on which it works. Second, Hayes paints the aircraft with spray guns and uses solvents to clean the paint guns and lines, thereby generating a mix of paint and solvents.

L. H. Beasley was the employee of Hayes responsible for disposal of hazardous wastes. In early 1981, Beasley orally agreed with Jack Hurt, an employee of Performance Advantage, Inc., to dispose of certain wastes. Under the agreement, Performance Advantage would obtain from Hayes the valuable jet fuel drained from the planes; Performance Advantage would pay twenty cents per gallon for the jet fuel, and, at no charge, would remove other wastes from the Hayes plant including the mixture of paint and solvents. Performance Advantage was a recycler, and used the jet fuel to make marketable fuel. Wastes were transported from Hayes to Performance Advantage on eight occasions between January 1981 and March 1982.

Beginning in August 1982, government officials discovered drums of waste generated by Hayes and illegally disposed of by Performance Advantage. Approximately six hundred drums of waste were found, deposited among seven illegal disposal sites in Georgia and Alabama. The waste was the paint and solvent which Performance Advantage had removed from Hayes. Some of the drums were simply dumped in yards, while others were buried. The prosecutions in this case were brought under the Resource Conservation and Recovery Act.

42 U.S.C. §§ 6901-6987. The Act creates a cradle to grave regulatory scheme to ensure that hazardous wastes are properly disposed of. Generators of waste are required to identify hazardous wastes, 42 U.S.C. § 6922(1), and use a manifest system to ensure that wastes are disposed of only in facilities possessing a permit. 42 U.S.C. § 6922(5).

The regulatory scheme sets forth two different methods of identifying a hazardous waste. 40 C.F.R. § 261.3. A waste is hazardous if it appears on a list of wastes adopted by the Environmental Protection Agency. The list appears at 40 C.F.R., Subpart D. A waste is also hazardous if it possesses certain characteristics. These characteristics are set forth in 40 C.F.R., Subpart C. The mixture of paint waste and solvent involved in this case was a characteristic waste based on its ignitability. n1 40 C.F.R. § 261.21.

Beasley and Hayes each were convicted of eight counts of violating 42 U.S.C. § 6928(d) (1), which provides criminal sanctions for "Any person who (1) knowingly transports any hazardous waste identified or listed under this subchapter to a facility which does not have a permit under section 6925 of this title."

Hayes' liability is based on the actions of Beasley. It is undisputed that Performance Advantage did not have a permit. In their motion for judgment notwithstanding the verdict and on appeal, the appellees raise three basic theories of defense, and argue that the government's evidence was insufficient to refute any of them. First they contend that they did not commit any "knowing" violation because they misunderstood the regulations. Second, they contend that they did not "know" that Performance Advantage did not have a permit. Third, they contend that they did not commit a knowing violation because they believed that Performance Advantage was recycling the waste. Under the regulations in force at the time, characteristic hazardous waste was not regulated if it was "beneficially used or re-used [sic] or legitimately recycled or reclaimed." 40 C.F.R. § 261.6(a)(1), superseded effective July 5, 1985, 50 Fed.Reg. 665.

On appeal, the government argues that the first two defenses are legally insufficient, and that the jury could have rejected the third on the basis of the evidence. We cannot precisely discern from the district court's order whether it accepted all three of these defenses. Moreover, in the course of considering the sufficiency of the evidence, the district court held that several of the inferences advanced by the government were impermissible. Accordingly, to properly evaluate the appellees' contentions we must first consider the nature of the criminal offense involved.

Whether Knowledge of the Regulations Is Required

In certain cases, the Court has held that an offense requires no mental element, but simply requisite actions. In *United States v. Freed* ... the defendant was charged with violating a statute making it unlawful "to receive or possess a firearm which is not registered to him."... The Court held that no element of scienter was necessary for conviction; a person need not even have known that the grenades were unregistered. The Court reasoned that the statute itself set forth no mental element, and that the statute was "a regulatory measure in the interest of the public safety, which may well be premised on the theory that one would hardly be surprised to learn that possession of hand grenades is not an innocent act." ...

The Court has had greater difficulty with statutes in which Congress has created an offense of "knowingly violating a regulation." In *United States v. International Minerals & Chemical Corp.* ... the defendant was charged with "knowingly" violating an I.C.C. regulation. The regulation prohibited shipping hazardous materials without showing them on the shipping papers. The Court held that knowledge of the regulation was not an element of the offense; the use of "knowingly" in the statute referred only to the defendant's knowledge that the materials being shipped were dangerous. The Court noted the general maxim that ignorance of the law is no excuse, but also reasoned that where "obnoxious waste materials are involved, the probability of regulation is so great that anyone who is aware that he is in possession of them or dealing with them must be presumed to be aware of the regulation." ... The Court interpreted a similar statute in *Boyce Motor Lines v. United States* ... : the statute also punished "knowing" violations of

I.C.C. regulations. The regulation at issue required shippers of dangerous materials to select the least crowded route. The Court stated that a conviction would require that the shipper knew of a safer route or willfully neglected to consider a safer route. ...

The Court reached a different result in a recent case involving food stamps, *Liparota v. United States* ... The statute in Liparota provided punishment for anyone who "knowingly uses, transfers, acquires, alters, or possesses coupons or authorization cards in any manner not authorized by [the statute] or the regulations." ... The government argued that "knowingly" simply referred to knowledge of acquiring or possessing food stamps, and that the defendant need not have known the acquisition was in violation of the regulations. The Court disagreed, holding that knowledge of illegality was necessary. The Court reasoned that to hold "otherwise would be to criminalize a broad range of apparently innocent conduct." ... The Court also noted that the statute was distinguishable from those in Freed and International Minerals, because it did not involve "a type of conduct that a reasonable person should know is subject to stringent public regulation and may seriously threaten the community's health and safety." ...

The appellees contend that our interpretation of section 6928(d)(1) should be controlled by Liparota. They argue that a violation of section 6928(d)(1) therefore requires knowledge of transportation, knowledge that the waste is a waste within the meaning of the statute, knowledge that disposal sites must have a permit, and knowledge that the site in question does not have a permit. In short, they contend that the defendants must have known that their actions violated the statute. The appellees find some support for their position in the recent decision of *United States v. Johnson & Towers.* ...

We conclude that Liparota does not control this case. First, section 6928(d)(1) is not drafted in a manner which makes knowledge of illegality an element of the offense. The statute in Liparota, paraphrased, prohibited "knowing violation of a regulation," and reading a legal element into the offense therefore made linguistic sense. In addition, section 6928(d)(1) is undeniably a public welfare statute, involving a heavily regulated area with great ramifications for the public health and safety. As the Supreme Court has explained, it is completely fair and reasonable to charge those who choose to operate in such areas with knowledge of the regulatory provisions.

Indeed, the reasonableness is borne out in this case, for the evidence at trial belied the appellees' profession of ignorance. Accordingly, in a prosecution under 42 U.S.C. § 6928(d)(1), it would be no defense to claim no knowledge that the paint waste was a hazardous waste within the meaning of the regulations; nor would it be a defense to argue ignorance of the permit requirement.

Questions

1. What is the exact language of the statute when it refers to the hazardous quality of waste?
2. From the facts available in the case, can it be inferred that the defendant knew or should have known?
3. Will ignorance of the law work as a defense in this case?
4. How do you reconcile the Court's decision with the explicit language of the statute relative to mens rea?

Figure 2.8   Defective tire that caused a fatal accident.

Over the course of the twentieth century, various states and the federal government have felt comfortable imputing criminal liability when the agent/employee of the corporation commits an infraction. As parent with child, the law vicariously imputes responsibility to the employer, as justifiable under common law theories of *respondeat superior*, and strictly holds liable the corporation for the acts of these agents, as long as the employee is acting within the scope of the employment.[65]

Unfortunately for the business world, courts with reformist outlooks are not averse to stretching the mens rea element of "knowingly" beyond its usual meaning. Knowingly should mean that the corporation was aware or, under reasonable circumstances, could or should have been aware of a particular regulation.

Other jurisdictions qualify the liability by looking to the managerial status of the employee, usually higher up officers and directors of the company because it is they that wield the power of the corporation, not the full array of employees from secretarial to the vice presidency.[66]

The Model Penal Code at §2.07 expresses its preference for this narrow approach by noting that the suspected act must be:

> The commission of the offense was authorized, requested, commanded, performed, or recklessly tolerated by the board of directors or by a high managerial agent acting in behalf of the corporation within the scope of his office or employment.[67]

If there is any trend to identify, it seems reasonable to conclude that corporate criminal liability will increase in twenty-first century especially since corporations lumber over the common employee and the residential community with power and might. While some may argue that this trend tells us much about the class warfare mentality and the lack of unity between labor and management, others say the confrontation with America's corporate form is politically motivated. Whether the criminal law is capable of exerting any serious pressure on the corporate mentality remains to be seen. In the end, to survive, a corporation must deliver products and services worthy of their price, and befriend employee and community alike (Figure 2.8).

DISCUSSION QUESTIONS

1. How does the length of incarceration relate to a crime's definition?
2. What is the policy behind "vicarious" liability?
3. Why or how does decriminalization influence the severity of crimes?
4. Explain how principals may be other than the actual actor.
5. Explain how grading criminal offenses reflects various needs of the system and particular defendants.
6. Discuss how criminal law images the moral traditions of a nation.
7. Can deviance always be translated into a crime?
8. How does treason differ from the other categories of criminal offenses?
9. How can criminal liability be imputed?
10. What are the more common summary offenses?

SUGGESTED READING

Anderson, J. F. 2008. *Criminal justice and criminology: Terms, concepts, and cases.* Lanham, MD: University Press of America.

Boyce, R. N., D. A. Dripps, and R. M. Perkins. 2010. *Criminal law and procedure,* 11th ed. Eagan, MN: West Law School Publishers.

Carrasco, C. E., and M. K. Dupee. 1999. Corporate criminal liability. *American Criminal Law Review* 36 (Summer): 445.

Dictionary of criminal justice terms. 1990. Longwood, FL: Gould Publications.

Dix, G. E. 2011. *Gilbert law summaries on criminal law,* 18th ed. Eagan, MN: West Law School Publishers.

Douglas, J. E. 1997. *Crime classification manual.* San Francisco: Jossey-Bass Publishers.

Downes, D. and P. Rock. 2011. *Understanding deviance: A guide to the sociology of crime and rule-breaking.* New York: Oxford University Press.

Duff, R. A., and S. Green, Stuart. 2011. *Philosophical foundations of criminal law.* New York: Oxford University Press.

Padfield, N. 2010. *Criminal law: Core text.* New York: Oxford University Press.

Rush, G. E. 2005. *Criminal justice terms and definitions.* San Clemente, CA: LawTech Publishing.

ENDNOTES

1. George F. Cole & Christopher E. Smith, Criminal Justice in America 37 (2007).
2. William L. Clark & William L. Marshall, A Treatise on the Law of Crimes §2.01 at 92 (6th ed. 1958).
3. *Id.* at §2.04 at 127.
4. Eric Henkel, *Two Crimes for the Price of One: Reshaping Felony Homicide in State v. Russell,* 71 Mont. L. Rev. 205 (2010).
5. *See* Marcus Felson & Rachel Boba, Crime and Everyday Life (2009).
6. 2 Thomas Aquinas, *Summa Theologica, in* Basic Writings of Saint Thomas Aquinas, bk. I, pt. II, Q. 100, a. 7, ad. 4 (Anton C. Pegis ed., 1945).
7. 4 Thomas Aquinas, Summa Contra Gentiles bk. III, pt. II, ch.142, 3 (Vernon J. Bourke trans., 1975).
8. Charles P. Nemeth, Aquinas in the Courtroom 165-166 (2001).
9. Cicero, *On the Laws, in* Selected Works of Cicero Book One at 239 (1948).
10. Judaism 101, *A List of the 613 Mitzvot* (2007) available at http://www.jewfaq.org/613.htm (accessed August 3, 2011).
11. Holy Koran, surah AN NISAA', at 4:110–112.

12. St. Augustine, On Free Choice of the Will, bk. I, 14, 100-101 (Anna S. Benjamin & L. H. Hackstaff trans., 1964).

13. John Dombrink & Daniel Hillyard, Sin No More: From Abortion to Stem Cells, Understanding Crime, Law, and Morality in America (2007).

14. 2 St. Thomas Aquinas, The Summa Theologica bk. II, pt. II, Q. 108, a. 3 (Fathers of the English Dominican Province trans., 1947).

15. *See* Charles P. Nemeth, Aquinas on Crime (2008).

16. *See* Nemeth, Courtroom, *supra* note 8.

17. St. Thomas Aquinas, Commentary On The Nicomachean Ethics X. L.XIV:C 2151 (C. I. Litzinger trans., 1964).

18. Aquinas, Theologica, *supra* note 14, at II-II, Q. 64, a. 2, ad 1.

19. The Buggery Act, 1533, 25 Hen. 8, c. 6.

20. Indian Penal Code §377 (1860).

21. S.C. Code Ann. § 16-15-120 (2009).

22. Handbook on Crime and Deviance (Marvin D. Krohn, Alan J. Lizotte & Gina Penly Hall eds., 2009); *see also* Olena Antonaccio et al., *The Correlates of Crime and Deviance: Additional Evidence*, 47 J. Res. Crime & Delinq. 297-328 (2010).

23. Laurie Shrage, *Should Feminists Oppose Prostitution?* 99 Ethics 347, 359 (1989).

24. Gregory M. Herek, *Facts About Homosexuality and Mental Health*, University of California at Davis, available at http://psychology.ucdavis.edu/rainbow/html/facts_mental_health.html (accessed August 3, 2011) (2009); *see also* American Psychiatric Association, Diagnostic and Statistical Manual of Mental Disorders (4th ed., 1994).

25. Fla. Stat. § 775.081 (2010).

26. N.Y. Penal § 55.05 (McKinney 2010).

27. Anthony Walsh & Craig Hemmens, Introduction to Criminology: A Text/Reader 17 (2008).

28. U.S. Const. amend. III, § 3.

29. 18 U.S.C. § 2381 (2010).

30. 18 U.S.C. §§ 792 (2010).

31. *See* N. Y. Penal Law §70.00, 220.00 (McKinney 2010).

32. *See*, for example, the disparity between the punishment set out in the Iowa Criminal Code for class D felons and a person convicted of an aggravated misdemeanor. "A class "D" felon, not an habitual offender, shall be confined for no more than five years, and in addition shall be sentenced to a fine of at least seven hundred fifty dollars, but not more than seven thousand five hundred dollars. A class "D" felon, such felony being for a violation of section 321J.2, may be sentenced to imprisonment for up to one year in the county jail." (Iowa Code § 902.9(5) (2010)) "When a person is convicted of an aggravated misdemeanor, and a specific penalty is not provided for, the maximum penalty shall be imprisonment not to exceed two years. There shall be a fine of at least five hundred dollars but not to exceed five thousand dollars. When a judgment of conviction of an aggravated misdemeanor is entered against any person and the court imposes a sentence of confinement for a period of more than one year the term shall be an indeterminate term."(Iowa Code § 903.1(2) (2010)).

33. 4 Sir William Blackstone, Commentaries 5 (1941).

34. Sometimes the blending of offenses leads to higher penalties, especially under recidivists statutes. For an interesting dilemma of where state offense can be coupled with federal offenses for the purpose of misdemeanor elevation to felony, *see* Joy Sander, *Legal Trends: U. S. Supreme Court Rules Noncitizen with Two of More Misdemeanor or Possession Convictions are Not Automatic Aggravated Felons*, Hous. Law., July/Aug. 2010, at 47; *see also Carachuri-Rosendo v. Holder*, Case No. 09-60, 560 U. S. ___ (June 14, 2010).

35. Clark & Marshall, *supra* note 2, at § 2.02 at 113.

36. *Lawrence v. Texas*, 539 U.S. 558 (2003).

37. 75 Pa. Cons. Stat. § 3803 (2010).

38. Melissa B. Schlactus, *Annual New York Constitutional Issue: Due Process: Court of Appeals of New York*, 26 Touro L. Rev. 955 (2010); *see also People v. Davis*, 912 N.E.2d 1044 (N.Y. 2009).

39. Code Of The Town Of West Hartford, Connecticut § 168-13(B) (2001).

40. 18 U.S.C. § 2 (2010).

41. MODEL PENAL CODE § 2.06 (Proposed Official Draft 1962).

42. *See* IDAHO CODE ANN. §18-204 (2005).

43. CLARK & MARSHALL, *supra* note 2, at § 8.02 at 507.

44. *Id.* at §8.02 at 511.

45. LA. REV. STAT. §14:25 (2006).

46. 18 U.S.C. § 3 (2001).

47. James O'Connor, *"But I Didn't Know Who He Was!": What is the Required Mens Rea for an Aider and Abettor of a Felon in Possession of a Firearm*, 32 W. NEW ENG. L. REV. 245 (2010).

48. *Id.* at 252; *see also* Stephen R. Klein, Note, *A Shot at Mens Rea in Aiding and Abetting Illegal Firearms Possession Under 18 U.S.C. § 922(g)*, 7 AVE MARIA L. REV. 639 (2009).

49. Delaware statute holds the parent accountable in no uncertain terms: "... intentionally or recklessly stores or leaves a loaded firearm within the reach or easy access of a minor and where the minor obtains the firearm and uses it to inflict serious physical injury or death upon the minor or any other person." DEL. CODE tit. 11, § 1456(a) (2010), as does Kentucky: "... permits the juvenile to possess a handgun knowing that there is a substantial risk that the juvenile will use a handgun to commit a felony offense." KY. REV. STAT. § 527.110 (West 2010).

50. Paul W. Schmidt, *Dangerous Children and the Regulated Family: The Shifting Focus of Parental Responsibility Laws*, 73 N.Y.U. L. REV. 667, 678 n. 75 (May 1998). *See* R.I. GEN. LAWS 11-9-4 (1994).

51. I. Freckelton, Vicarious Liability and Criminal Prosecutions for Regulatory Offences, 14 J. LAW MED. 24-26 (2006).

52. Schmidt, *supra* note 50, at 682.

53. A 67.3 percent increase in juvenile violent crime between 1986 and 1995 and a 31.4 percent increase in adult violent crime during the same period, and 15 and .5 percent increase in juvenile and adult violent crime, respectively, were reported between 1991 and 1995. FEDERAL BUREAU OF INVESTIGATION, U.S. DEPT. OF JUSTICE, UNIFORM CRIME REPORTS FOR THE UNITED STATES 1995, 212, 214 (1996). *See* Ralph A. Rossum, *Reforming Juvenile Justice and Improving Juvenile Character: The Case for the Justice Model*, 23 PEPP. L. REV. 823, 824 (1996).

54. Schmidt, *supra* note 50.

55. *Id.* at 683. *See* OR. REV. STAT. § 163.577(1) (1995). *See also* a stirring report on how criminals may eventually defer personal responsibility to parents whose gene pool they inherited, Celia Wells, *'I Blame the Parents': Fitting New Genes in Old Criminal Laws*, 61 MODERN L. REV. 724 (Sept. 1998).

56. Schnabalk, *The Legal Basis of Liability, Part II*, 27 SEC. MGMT. 29 (1983). *See also* Lawrence Friedman, *In Defense of Corporate Criminal Liability*, 23 HARV. J. L. & PUB. POL'Y 833 (2000); WILLIAM A. SIMPSON, CORPORATE CRIMINAL INTENT (August 5, 2009), available at http://ssrn.com/abstract=1444543 (accessed August 3, 2011); *County of Santa Clara v. Southern Pacific Railroad Company* 118 U.S. 394 (1886); *Arthur Andersen LLP v. United States* 544 U.S. 696 (2005); *New York Cent. & H.R.R. Co. v. U.S.*, 212 U.S. 481 (1909); *U.S. v. Bank of New England, N.A.*, 821 F.2d 844 (1st Cir. 1987).

57. *See W.T. Grant Co. v. Superior*, 23 Cap. App. 3d 284 (1972); *N.Y. Central & Hudson Railroad v. U.S.*, 212 U.S. 481 (1908); *People v. Canadian Fur Trappers Corp.*, 161 N.E. 455 (N.Y. 1928); *see generally* Shirley Baccus-Lobel, *Criminal Law*, 52 S.M.U. L. REV. 881, 910-11 (1999); Rolando V. del Carmen, *An Overview of Civil and Criminal Liabilities of Police Officers and Departments*, 9 AM. J. CRIM. L. 33 (1981); Rolando V. del Carmen, *Civil and Criminal Liabilities of Police Officers*, in POLICE DEVIANCE (T. Barker & D. L. Carter eds., 1994); Rolando V. del Carmen & Victor E. Kappeler, *Municipal and Police Agencies as Defendants: Liability for Official Policy and Custom*, 10 AM J. POLICE 1-17 (1991).

58. ARTHUR J. BILEK, JOHN C. KLOTTER, & R. KEEGAN FEDERAL, LEGAL ASPECTS OF PRIVATE SECURITY 144 (1980).

59. Schnabalk, *supra* note 56.

60. Cynthia E. Carrasco & Michael K. Dupee, *Corporate Criminal Liability*, 36 AM. CRIM. L. REV. 445, 448 (1999).

61. *Id.* at 446. *See* V. S. Khanna, *Corporate Criminal Liability*, 109 HAR. L. REV. 1477, 1479-80 (1996).

62. *See* 18 U.S.C. §3551-3742 (2010); 28 U.S.C. § 991-998 (2010); U.S. SENTENCING GUIDELINES MANUAL (1998).

63. Carrasco & Dupee, *supra* note 60, at 447–48.
64. Reid Page et al., *Environmental Crimes*, 36 AM. CRIM. L. REV. 515, 516 (1999). *See* 42 U.S.C. §§ 6901-6992(k) (1994); 15 U.S.C. §§ 2601-2692 (1994); 7 U.S.C. § 136 (1994), 42 U.S.C. §§ 7451-7671 (1994), 5 U.S.C. App. (1994).
65. *U.S. v. A & P Trucking*, 358 U.S. 121 (1958); *Mylan Lab., Inc. v. Akzo, N.V.*, 2 F.3d 56, 63 (4th Cir. 1993); *U.S. v. Hilton Hotels Corp.*, 467 F.2d 1000, 1007 (9th Cir. 1972); *W. T. Grant Co. v. Superior*, 23 Cap. App. 3d 284 (1972); *N.Y. Central & Hudson Railroad v. U.S.*, 212 U.S. 481 (1908); *People v. Canadian Fur Trappers Corp.*, 161 N.E. 455 (N.Y. 1928); *County of Santa Clara v. Southern Pacific Railroad Company* 118 U.S. 394 (1886); *Arthur Andersen LLP v. United States* 544 U.S. 696 (2005); *New York Cent. & H.R.R. Co. v. U.S.*, 212 U.S. 481 (1909); *U.S. v. Bank of New England, N.A.*, 821 F.2d 844 (1st Cir. 1987).
66. ARIZ. REV. STAT. § 13-305 (West 2010); DEL. CODE tit. 11, § 281 (2010); OHIO REV. CODE § 2901.23 (2011). *See State v. Smokey's Steakhouse, Inc.*, 478 N.W.2d 361, 362 (N.D. 1991); *State v. Christy Pontiac-GMC, Inc.*, 354 N.W.2d 17, 20 (Minn. 1984); *State v. Adjustment Credit Bureau, Inc.*, 483 P.2d 687, 691 (Idaho 1971).
67. MODEL PENAL CODE § 2.07(1)(c) (1985).

Chapter 3

Actus Reus and Mens Rea

KEYWORDS

Corpus delicti: The body of evidence that constitutes the offense; the objective proof that a crime has been committed.

General intent: The intent that must exist in all crimes.

Intent: A state of mind wherein the person knows and desires the consequences of his act which, for purposes of criminal liability, must exist at the time the offense is committed.

Judgment: A declaration by a court of the conviction of a criminal defendant and the punishment to be imposed.

Knowledge: Awareness that a fact or circumstance probably exists.

Negligence: Failure to exercise the degree of care expected of a person of ordinary prudence in like circumstances in protecting others from a foreseeable and unreasonable risk of harm in a particular situation.

Omission: The act, fact, or state of leaving something out or failing to do something that is required by duty, procedure, or law.

Reckless: Characterized by the creation of a substantial and unjustifiable risk to the lives, safety, or rights of others, and by a conscious and sometimes wanton and willful disregard for or indifference to that risk that is a gross deviation from the standard of care a reasonable person would exercise in like circumstances.

Specific intent: Intent that is essential to certain crimes and, which, as an essential element of the crime, must be proved beyond a reasonable doubt.

Strict liability: Liability in a crime where no specific or general mens rea is required. The conduct itself, even if innocently engaged in, results in criminal liability.

Willful blindness: Deliberate failure to make a reasonable inquiry of wrongdoing despite suspicion or an awareness of the high probability of its existence.

IDEA AND MENTAL STATE IN CRIMINAL CULPABILITY

Crimes, for the most part, require two major components: an act, known as actus reus, and a mind, known as mens rea. And these two components need an integration of sorts. In other words, simply acting without thinking or intending a particular result or end may not be enough for criminal culpability. Conversely, thinking without acting is rarely, if ever, a crime. Mental thoughts, the content and substance of what is going on in the intellect, will not suffice for a criminal prosecution. So, in a sense, these two components are bound together in order for criminal responsibility to attach. The actor must think of the act and intend its outcome. This central conclusion constitutes the chapter's coverage—discerning how culpability depends on both doing and willing a particular result. Acts alone do not suffice. The sum and substance of criminal culpability assumes not only the act, but also the corresponding mindset, which manifests intentionality. In Western jurisprudence, more than movement is required. An acts plus the required mental state triggers culpability:

$$\text{ACTUS REUS} + \text{MENS REA} = \text{CULPABILITY}$$

Side by side with the act ride the mental faculties of those accused of wrongdoing. One's act, coupled with a particular mindset, inevitably leads to criminal responsibility. Acts are prompted and nourished by intention. Acts, without thought, cannot prompt the type of punitive consequences envisioned in criminal codification. Even so, just as thought alone provides an insufficient basis, a criminal charge will not be sustained without activity of some sort. Proving each element is never an easy undertaking for the justice professional. The greater challenge lies in the world of mind, that mental state that demonstrates the intentionality. Criminal code provisions that speak of *knowing* expressly require actual knowledge. When a statute includes the term *intentionally*, we are pretty sure the proof of what is on the mind must be specific. Though not all statutes are precisely drafted in these terms, one such code requirement is that the defendant has a "reasonable cause to believe" that the act will end with a certain result.[1] While it is nearly impossible to precisely define, the mind has both objective and subjective definition. If we are lucky, the offender will discharge his mind in a letter, a tape, or online message. If lucky, the jury will directly hear of the plan and criminal design—unadulterated and clear in delivery. In these ways, the mind is as objective as we can decipher. Few would argue that objective proof of the mental is heavily preferred. Some commentators see a need for objective proof in major felonies, though this is not a set legal standard.[2]

Most of what we discover is inferential. As the *corpus delicti* is examined, we impute a way of thinking to the defendant, and, in this sense, we engage the subjective reality of mind. Both are instructive and both are necessary to any criminal prosecution.[3]

The Nature of a Criminal Act

Criminal conduct generally assumes some specific, executed activity. In a free society, it would be inconsistent with the ideas of individual autonomy and personal liberty to punish thoughts or ideas. As strange as it may sound, thoughts can be dastardly or disturbing, hideous and heinous, and incomprehensively evil, yet still not be sufficient to fashion any criminal liability. The "thought police" have gained no foothold in this democracy, though some critics of political correctness and hate speech have warned of the possibility. In a free society, the contemplation is as free as the individual that thinks the thought and until some "overt" action is brought about by the thought, there is no crime.

The term *actus reus* means the thing done or carried out, and, in the case of a criminal charge, it is elemental that the prosecutor be able to point to an act that constitutes the very essence of the offense. Indeed, the Model Penal Code (MPC) declares the impossibility of being labeled or adjudged criminal unless he or she commits or omits when bound under a legal obligation. Section 2.01 of the MPC states in part:

(1) A person is not guilty of an offense unless his liability is based on conduct which includes a voluntary act or the omission to perform an act which he is physically capable.[4]

Stated simply, to be a criminal, one must do rather than merely think of doing.[5]

In contrast, certain theological perspectives do not divide up acts and thoughts. In other words, one can sin by doing as well as thinking about doing. One can sin by thought, word, and deed. As Jesus of Nazareth tells his followers of this multiple possibility:

> You have heard that it was said, "YOU SHALL NOT COMMIT ADULTERY"; but I say to you that everyone who looks at a woman with lust for her has already committed adultery with her in his heart. If your right eye makes you stumble, tear it out, and throw it from you; for it is better for you to lose one of the parts of your body, than for your whole body to be thrown into hell.[6]

Former President Jimmy Carter caused quite a stir during an interview when he indicated that he had committed adultery, not by the actual conduct of sexual intercourse with another person while married, but the "lusting after and desiring others" in thought alone. This mental offense, at least in Christian tradition, theologically equalizes offenders in thought and deed. A secular justice system could hardly function under this type of conclusion. A rapist could rape by either thinking the idea or doing the deed, or a thief would pay a price without having stolen a thing, or even making an attempt to do same, if it be thought desirous. Hence, temporal judicial systems look for real action coupled with demonstrable intent.

Hate crime legislation illustrates the tricky and oftentimes dangerous intrusion into the thought patterns of a criminal actor. Looked at squarely, the murderer who murders with racial or gender motivation or who assaults a party with a differing sexual orientation, performs the assault irrespective of the victim's attributes. Fundamentally, to look much beyond the act itself—the killing, the maiming, or the assault—seems a psychic exercise with no clear measure. That the offender should be more severely punished for "acts" committed with hate in one's heart, based on these criteria, seems to expand the notion of actus reus into uncharted territory.

Actus Reus: Voluntariness and Free Choice

Coupling acts with the requisite state of mind encompasses criminal agency. Without the two elements conjoined, the prosecution of the stated charge is a legal impossibility. Acts, for criminal purposes, are volitional rather than the product of compulsion, accident, reflex, or somnambulism. To be criminal, the act is prompted by free choice and free will in the human person. We can only hold accountable those whose wills and desires conform to the chosen activity. Hence, our system resists punishing actors who are careless, mistaken, or ignorant of events and circumstances. The act must be the product of volition. Accountability inures to those who have chosen the path of wrong over right.

The MPC delivers amazingly clear instructions on the nature of voluntariness.

(2) The following are not voluntary acts within the meaning of this section:
- (a) A reflex or convulsion;
- (b) A bodily movement during unconsciousness or sleep;
- (c) Conduct during hypnosis or resulting from hypnotic suggestion;
- (d) A bodily movement that otherwise is not a product to the effort or determination of the actor, either conscious or habitual.[7]

CASE 3.1

U.S. V. WILLIAMS
332 F. Supp. 1 (Md. 1971)

Herbert F. Murray, District Judge. In this case the defendant was charged in a two-count indictment under Title 18, U.S.C.A. Sections 2113(a) and (b) with robbery of a branch of the Maryland National Bank in Cambridge, Maryland, on December 4, 1970. The case was tried nonjury on September 13 and 14, 1971.

The basic facts are not in dispute. In a stipulation signed by government counsel, the defendant and his counsel, it was agreed that on the date set out in the indictment, the defendant went into the bank in Cambridge, Maryland, and requested a loan from a branch officer of the bank. The officer declined to grant the defendant a loan. Thereafter, the defendant walked up to Mrs. Martina Bennett, a teller, and handed to her a note stating "This is a stickup." Mrs. Bennett gave him all her cash, and defendant then left the bank with the money. It was also stipulated that Mrs. Bennett was intimidated by defendant giving her the note and for that reason turned over to defendant the funds in her drawer. An audit made immediately after the robbery showed the defendant had taken $4,727 of the bank's money.

While defendant thus does not contest the fact that a robbery occurred and he committed it, his counsel urges upon the Court that an essential element of the crime is lacking. It is contended that the two sections of the bank robbery statute on which the counts in the indictment are based both require a specific intent to steal, and that at the time of the robbery defendant was so intoxicated from alcohol and drugs that he was incapable of forming such specific intent.

The threshold legal questions thus are whether voluntary intoxication can [have] negative specific intent as an element of crime and, if so, whether the offenses charged in either or both counts of the indictment require proof of specific intent. If specific intent is an element of the offense in either count of the indictment, the factual question then arises as to whether on all the evidence the degree of defendant's intoxication was such as to create a reasonable doubt that defendant had a specific intent to steal when the robbery took place.

It is clear from the cases that while voluntary intoxication is ordinarily no defense to crime, it may have that effect if specific intent is an element of the crime. ...

Did Congress in the several subsections of the bank robbery statute create "general intent" crimes or "specific intent" crimes? Some cases uncritically lump all subsections of the statute under the "specific intent" label. Other cases ascribe more careful draftsmanship to the Congress, and find a specific intent an element of the crime only in those subsections of the statute where the language "with intent" is used.

Thus, in *United States v. DeLeo* ... the indictment was under 18 U.S.C.A. Sections 2113(a) and (d). On appeal, the defendant contended that the crime was of the common law larceny genus requiring allegation and proof of specific intent. The Court rejected this argument, stating at pages 490–491:

"Six specific crimes are set out in Section 2113. Felonious intent is specifically incorporated in the definition of two of them: entering a federally insured institution with intent to commit a felony (a—second paragraph), and taking property with intent to steal or purloin (b). However, it is not made part of the crimes of taking by force and violence or by intimidation (a—first paragraph); knowingly receiving stolen property (c); assaulting or putting in jeopardy the life of a person by a dangerous weapon (d); or killing a person, or forcing a person to accompany him, while in the course of committing one of the other offenses or avoiding apprehension or confinement for any of them (e).

"This differentiation shows careful draftsmanship. Entering and taking can be innocent acts, and, therefore, require felonious intent to constitute crime; receiving stolen property can be innocent, unless done knowingly. However, the other offenses describe acts which, when performed, are so unambiguously dangerous to others that the requisite mental element is necessarily implicit in the description. ..."

The Court in the present case concludes as a matter of law ... that the act of the defendant, which he admits of taking by intimidation from the presence of another money belonging to the bank, constitutes a violation of subsection (a) of the statute as charged in Count I of the indictment. The Court rejects as a defense to the crime charged in Count I of the indictment any voluntary intoxication of the defendant.

As to Count II of the indictment, the Court feels that historically and legally the contention of the defendant is correct, and that a specific intent to steal is an element of the crime. The Court on a review of all the evidence in the case is satisfied beyond a reasonable doubt that defendant when he took and carried away money belonging to the bank exceeding $100 in value did so with the intent to steal or purloin.

The Court in finding as a fact that defendant had the intent to steal is not unmindful of the fact that there was substantial evidence to show that defendant had imbibed significant quantities of alcohol and drugs, but the Court from all the evidence finds beyond a reasonable doubt that he both had the capacity to and did intend to steal when he took the bank's money. The basis for the Court's finding in this regard requires some reference to the evidence of defendant's taking of alcohol and drugs and his condition at the time of the robbery.

In testifying on his own behalf, defendant claimed that as a result of an argument with his wife he started drinking with a companion around 9:00 a.m. on December 3, 1970, the day before the robbery and over the next fourteen hours the two consumed three fifths of whiskey, of which defendant had about half. During this period defendant also took 6 or 7 "yellow jackets" or barbiturate pills. Between midnight on December 3 and the occurrence of the robbery around 1:00 p.m. on December 4, defendant claims that he and a companion drank an additional one or one and a half fifths of whiskey, of which defendant had all but half a pint. In addition, sometime in this latter period defendant took some LSD pills, with the result that he had only "spotty" recollection of events the morning of the robbery. Defendant does recall going into the bank and talking with the branch officer, and leaving the bank stuffing money under his jacket, but disclaims any recollection of confronting the teller, presenting her with a "stickup" note and actually receiving from her over $4,000 in cash.

The witnesses who actually observed the defendant on the day of the robbery indicate he had been drinking, but not that he was drunk. A cab driver named Hopkins who drove the defendant at 6:00 a.m. to redeem his watch and then to a drive-in said his eyes were red and he had been drinking. His speech was "heavy" and he did not seem to walk normally.

Mrs. Florence Brannock, a teller in the bank, spoke briefly with defendant when he asked for the loan department and directed him to the branch officer. She felt he smelled strongly of cheap wine or alcohol and that his speech, while understandable, was not normal—it was a little "slurred" or "thick."

Branch Officer John Bramble testified that the defendant came into his office seeking a $400 loan for Christmas. In their conversation, defendant gave his place of employment, said he owned a 1969 Chevrolet, and had an account in the Farmer's and Merchant's bank across the street. The witness said he could smell a strong odor of alcohol on the defendant's breath and felt he was under the influence of liquor and that he also appeared somewhat nervous. After declining to grant the defendant a loan, the witness watched the defendant walk toward the lobby of the bank and could not remember anything unusual about the defendant's walk.

Mrs. Martina Bennett, a cash teller, recalled that a little after 1:00 p.m. a man approached from the side aisle of the bank. She recalled having seen him previously at Mrs. Brannock's desk. He put a note on her counter and said nothing. At first she thought he might be deaf and read the note. It was printed in pencil on a torn piece of paper and read "This is a stickup." She noticed that he had his right hand in his jacket pocket which was thrust forward pointing at her as though he had a gun. She was terrified and afraid he was going to shoot her. She put all her money on the counter, but she did not see what he did with it, although she believes he dropped some and then picked it up. She noticed nothing unusual about the defendant's appearance and did not smell any alcohol. When he was standing before her he did not appear to waver, but his eyes did appear sleepy. She watched him walk away from her counter and down a flight of four steps leading to the lobby entrance.

A cab driver witness named Wilson Wright testified the defendant and two other men approached him around 5:00 p.m. on December 4, 1970, in Salisbury, Maryland. He took the men to two different destinations in Salisbury and then the defendant and one of the men hired him to take them to Hartsville, South Carolina, where the other man, "Charles," lived. The witness noticed the defendant had a large sum of money in a bag, which the defendant said was earned in five years of work in Vietnam. The witness said the defendant looked and acted normal while they were in Salisbury, but en route to Virginia the defendant and his companions were drinking from two fifths of whiskey and the defendant fell into a deep sleep about 8:30 p.m. About 4:00 a.m. the witness left the two men off at a house in Hartsville, South Carolina, and that was the last he saw of the defendant.

The testimony as to acts of the defendant closest in time to the robbery was given by the owner of a small store in Cambridge, George Heist. His store is located about two blocks from the bank. He recalled that the defendant came into his store about noon and asked for a piece of paper to figure a bill. The defendant reached for a sales pad but the witness did not want the defendant to use the pad and gave him a piece of paper instead. The defendant turned around with his back to the witness and put the piece of paper on top of some stocking boxes and started to write. Apparently dissatisfied, he balled up the piece of paper and threw it on the floor. Defendant reached again for the witness' sales paid, which the witness again refused to give him, tearing off a piece of old calendar paper instead. Defendant again turned around and wrote some more, and then left the store.

The witness said that the defendant while in his store seemed coherent, didn't stagger, and acted normally except for trying to take his sales pad twice. However, because the defendant "seemed a little high on something" he decided, after the defendant left the store, to read what was on the balled up piece of paper. It read "This is a stick." Although defendant on leaving the store walked away from and not towards the bank, the witness appropriately concluded a robbery might be in prospect and got a policeman to whom he gave a description of the defendant. Later he heard the fire whistle blow about 1:00 p.m., which was a signal that the bank had been robbed.

Dr. Leonard Rothstein, a private psychiatrist called by the defendant, had an interview examination with defendant on May 24, 1971, and also talked to the defendant's wife. The defendant gave the doctor a history of abusing alcohol since age 19, and told the doctor he was drinking beer all day before the robbery and took some "yellow jackets" in the evening, and some LSD in the morning before the robbery. Dr. Rothstein found no significant evasiveness in the defendant and no discrepancies between defendant's account and his wife's.

On the basis of defendant's account to him and his examination, the doctor expressed the opinion that at the time of the offense the defendant had no psychosis or structural alteration in the brain. However, the doctor concluded from what the defendant told him of his ingestion of alcohol and drugs that the higher centers governing the making of judgments, control of behavior and retention of experience in memory had been affected. While the defendant knew what he was doing, his judgment about the appropriateness of his actions and his ability to control them were severely impaired. From the history the doctor concluded the defendant had taken the alcohol and drugs voluntarily and with knowledge from previous experience of their probable effect. In response to a hypothetical question asked on cross examination by counsel for the government, the doctor admitted that if the defendant had not taken alcohol and drugs before the offense, he would at the time have had no psychiatric illness and would have had the capacity to conform his conduct to the requirements of the law.

Dr. William Fitzpatrick, who had examined the defendant on July 15, 1971, at the request of the government, was called as an expert psychiatric witness by the defense. He related a personal history and account of the offense given him by the defendant very similar to that related by defendant's own expert, Dr. Rothstein. He found the defendant of normal intelligence with no evidence of psychosis or structural brain disorder. From the history, he judged the defendant to be a passive dependent personality of the type more likely to abuse alcohol than the average person. Although from defendant's own account, he was an episodic heavy user of alcohol and drugs, he did not find evidence that he was an alcoholic or a drug addict. He felt that because defendant was a passive dependent type he had a condition something short of total mental health. However, had the defendant not taken alcohol and drugs at time of the offense, he would not consider that defendant lacked criminal responsibility or capacity to conform his conduct to the requirements of the law. Although the doctor did not know the quantity of alcohol or drugs defendant consumed before the offense, he assumed the defendant was intoxicated at the time and that his intoxication was self-induced with knowledge on the part of the defendant that he would get drunk if he drank. He admitted that if he assumed a lesser degree of intoxication he would have to alter his opinion, but his opinion that defendant at the time of the offense could not conform his conduct to the requirements of the law was based on assumed intake of large quantities of alcohol. However, the doctor honestly disclaimed any opinion on whether defendant could specifically intend to rob a bank.

In expressing their conclusions, both psychiatrists obviously had in mind the ALI formulation contained in Model Penal Code, Section 4.01, approved in this circuit in *United States v. Chandler*. However, defense counsel disclaimed any contention that this standard was applicable in determining the issue of the criminal responsibility of this defendant. In this connection, it is noted that Section 2.08(3) of the Model Penal Code provides "Intoxication does not, in itself, constitute mental disease within the meaning of Section 4.01."

As then Circuit Judge Burger stated in *Heideman v. United States* ...: "Drunkenness, while efficient to reduce or remove inhibitions, * does not readily negate intent. *" (* Footnotes omitted)

The Court believes that the defendant had taken alcohol and drugs to the point of being "under the influence," but that he was not so intoxicated as not to understand what he was doing or to not have the intention to steal from the bank. There is a marked difference between the accounts of the persons who observed the defendant and the defendant's own account as to his condition. It appears from a witness called by the defense that he was able to write a "stickup" note shortly before the robbery, go into the bank, hold a coherent conversation about a loan, present the note, obtain over $4,000 in cash, none of which has been returned, and make good his escape. The Court concludes beyond a reasonable doubt that the defendant had the intent to steal from the bank as required for conviction under Count II, and that he is in any event guilty under Count I of the indictment. If an intent to steal is an element of the offense charged in Count I, the Court finds that intent proved as to Count I also. The Court therefore finds the defendant guilty as charged in both counts of the indictment.

Questions

1. What events led up to the defendant's voluntary intoxication? Do you believe this has any bearing on the case?
2. Is specific intent an essential element in the crime of robbery?
3. Did the court find that voluntary intoxication can negate the element of either the act or the intent? Why or why not?

Accountability and responsibility can only be directed to those aware of surrounding circumstances. The sleepwalker and the hypnotically induced do not decide freely. Just as pertinent, the undesired reflex displays acts without rationality and thus must be nonvolitional; in the same way the party suffering from an epileptic seizure or comatose party is incapable of free choice. At the heart of voluntariness is not the complete intellectual understanding that resides in mens rea, but, rather, the capacity to choose an action freely. This appraisal is not always easy to discern since extreme confusion, mental instability, and other neurological impairment can cloud the judgment of choice. Subconscious influences, the pressures of socialization, and behavioral explanations touted by modern thinkers further muddy the waters of choice.

On the other hand, a strong potential for misapplication and abuse of discretion exists in this interpretive domain. In the current age, often sarcastically labeled "The Age of Victimization," an onslaught of defense theories and mitigation arguments has diluted the concept of personal responsibility. When one hears that music causes murder, cupcakes create killers, and premenstrual syndrome explains away a murder charge, it has surely become more convenient for defendants to live in the land of the involuntary act. In essence, defendants have posited every imaginable argument to vanquish any sense of will or choice in criminal activity. For some, the movement of the body results from unconscious forces. Quite telling is the MPC's fourth category of an involuntary act, which consists of "bodily movement not the product of the effort of the determination or effort of the actor, either conscious or habitual."[8] To paraphrase, "actions are not my responsibility since I am neither conscious of them nor aware of my learned habits." The heroin addict can tell that story better than any other character. So can the pedophile or other sexual predator that knits an endless yarn.

States continuously grapple with the fine line between a human act that results from self-determination and others caused and affected by other forces. It is too simplistic to characterize defendants as spineless buoys, buffeted about on the oceans of self-control. Yet, this is exactly how the system sometimes classifies them. This picture caricatures the human species. A better portrayal would be to show, on occasion, that certain human acts are solely the result of impulse and reflex, or to recognize that certain cases of duress and coercion are substantial enough to overwhelm the will of even the strongest player. Beyond this, it is a safe bet that the words "involuntary" and "voluntary" have lost ordinary meaning if one accepts the current mitigation environment.

Actus Reus: Commission versus Omission

To act implies a motion of sorts, the doing, the carrying out, the physical reality of bodily motion relating to a particular deed. "Commission" properly and most uniformly describes actus reus. Commission signifies that the criminal agent has carried through on a chosen course of conduct. Commission puts in actual motion what the will and free choice wants and desires. For criminal purposes, the agent must voluntarily act rather than be a mover unaware of circumstance or condition. To hold otherwise would be contrary to our most fundamental notions of criminal responsibility whereby a conviction would be improper unless the actor "committed some act in furtherance of the intent."[9] So, in a burglary, one needs to break and enter into a domicile or other facility in order to do the requisite act required for the burglary crime, or the arsonist must act by burning, singeing, imploding or exploding, charring, or blistering a structure. To rape, the doer penetrates a requisite orifice of the body lacking permission, right, or consent. These things done, these *acti rei*, are the deed themselves.

While commission represents the primary meaning of actus reus, a failure to act (the omission) is the other path. Instead of commission, the criminal act finds its substance in inactivity or failure to do what is required. A parent who fails to watch vigilantly over a child while swimming may not intend the drowning, but by the failure to exercise due care, the parent's omission constitutes the actus reus.

The MPC clearly lays out the distinction:

(3) Liability for the commission of an offense may not be based on an omission unaccompanied by action unless;
   (a) the omission is expressly made sufficient by the law defining the offense; or
   (b) a duty to perform the omitted act is otherwise imposed by law.[10]

The concept of omission is particularly complicated because it blends the subtleties of moral and legal obligation. In other words, there are many things we should do in the moral sphere,

CASE 3.2

PEOPLE V. HEITZMAN
886 P.2d 1229 (Cal. App. 1994)

Penal Code section 368, subdivision (a), is one component of a multifaceted legislative response to the problem of elder abuse. The statute imposes felony criminal liability on "[a]ny person who, under circumstances or conditions likely to produce great bodily harm or death, willfully causes or permits any elder or dependent adult, with knowledge that he or she is an elder or dependent adult, to suffer, or inflicts thereon unjustifiable physical pain or mental suffering, or having the care or custody of any elder or dependent adult, willfully causes or permits the person or health of the elder or dependent adult to be injured, or willfully causes or permits the elder or dependent adult to be placed in a situation such that his or her person or health is endangered. ..."

In this case, we must decide whether the statute meets constitutional standards of certainty. As we shall explain, we conclude initially that, on its face, the broad statutory language at issue here fails to provide fair notice to those who may be subjected to criminal liability for "willfully ... permit[ting]" an elder or dependent adult to suffer pain, and similarly fails to set forth a uniform standard under which police and prosecutors can consistently enforce the proscription against "willfully ... permit[ting]" such suffering. Under these circumstances, section 368(a) would be unconstitutionally vague absent some judicial construction clarifying its uncertainties.

We conclude that the statute may properly be upheld by interpreting its imposition of criminal liability upon "[a]ny person who ... permits ... any elder or dependent adult ... to suffer ... unjustifiable pain or mental suffering" to apply only to a person who, under existing tort principles, has a duty to control the conduct of the individual who is directly causing or inflicting abuse on the elder or dependent adult. Because the evidence in this case does not indicate that defendant had the kind of "special relationship" with the individuals alleged to have directly abused the elder victim that would give rise to a duty on her part to control their conduct, she was improperly charged with a violation of section 368(a). We, therefore, reverse the judgment of the Court of Appeal.

I. Facts

The egregious facts of this case paint a profoundly disturbing family portrait in which continued neglect of and apparent indifference to the basic needs of the family's most vulnerable member, an elderly dependent parent, led to a result of tragic proportion. Sixty-seven-year-old Robert Heitzman resided in the Huntington Beach home of his grown son, Richard Heitzman, Sr., along with another grown son, Jerry Heitzman, and Richard's three sons. On December 3, 1990, police were summoned to the house, where they discovered Robert dead in his bedroom. His body lay on a mattress that was rotted through from constant wetness, exposing the metal springs. The stench of urine and feces filled not only decedent's bedroom, but the entire house as well. His bathroom was filthy, and the bathtub contained fetid, green-colored water that appeared to have been there for some time.

Police learned that Jerry Heitzman was primarily responsible for his father's care, rendering caretaking services in exchange for room and board. Jerry admitted that he had withheld all food and liquids from his father for the three days preceding his death on December 3. Jerry explained that he was expecting company for dinner on Sunday, December 2, and did not want his father, who no longer had control over his bowels and bladder, to defecate or urinate because it would further cause the house to smell.

At the time of his death, decedent had large, decubitus ulcers, more commonly referred to as bed sores, covering one-sixth of his body. An autopsy revealed the existence of a yeast infection in his mouth, and showed that he suffered from congestive heart failure, bronchial pneumonia, and hepatitis. The forensic pathologist who performed the autopsy attributed decedent's death to septic shock due to the sores which, he opined, were caused by malnutrition, dehydration, and neglect.

Twenty years earlier, decedent had suffered a series of strokes that paralyzed the left side of his body. Defendant, 31-year-old Susan Valerie Heitzman, another of decedent's children, had previously lived in the home and had been her father's primary caregiver at that time. In return, defendant's brother Richard paid for her room and board. Richard supported the household by working two full-time jobs, and supplemented this income with decedent's monthly Social Security and pension checks.

One year prior to her father's death, defendant decided to move away from the home. After she moved out, however, she continued to spend time at the house visiting her boyfriend/nephew Richard, Jr. Since leaving to live on her own, she noticed that the entire house had become filthy. She was aware that a social worker had discussed with Jerry the need to take their father to a doctor. When she spoke to Jerry about it, he told her he had lost the doctor's telephone number the social worker had given him. She suggested to Jerry that he recontact the social worker. She also discussed with Richard, Jr., the need for taking her father to the doctor, but she never made the necessary arrangements.

In the last six weekends before her father died, defendant had routinely visited the household. She was last in her father's bedroom five weeks prior to his death, at which time she noticed the hole in the mattress and feces-soiled clothing lying on the floor. Another of decedent's daughters, Lisa, also visited the house that same day.

Two weeks prior to her father's death, defendant spent the entire weekend at the house. On Sunday afternoon, she saw her father sitting in the living room, and noticed that he looked weak and appeared disoriented. A week later, during Thanksgiving weekend, and several days prior to decedent's death, defendant again stayed at the house. Decedent's bedroom door remained closed throughout the weekend, and defendant did not see her father. On the day decedent died, defendant awoke midmorning and left the house to return to her own apartment. Around one o'clock in the afternoon, Jerry discovered decedent dead in his bedroom.

...

II. Discussion

A. Criminal Liability for a Failure to Act

[1] Section 368(a) purportedly reaches two categories of offenders: (1) any person who willfully causes or permits an elder to suffer, or who directly inflicts unjustifiable pain

or mental suffering on any elder, and (2) the elder's caretaker or custodian who willfully causes or permits injury to his or her charge, or who willfully causes or permits the elder to be placed in a dangerous situation. The statute may be applied to a wide range of abusive situations, including within its scope active, assaultive conduct, as well as passive forms of abuse, such as extreme neglect.

[2a] Defendant here was charged under section 368(a) with willfully permitting her elder father to suffer the infliction of unjustifiable pain and mental suffering. It was thus her failure to act, i.e., her failure to prevent the infliction of abuse on her father, that created the potential for her criminal liability under the statute. [3] Unlike the imposition of criminal penalties for certain positive acts, which is based on the statutory proscription of such conduct, when an individual's criminal liability is based on the failure to act, it is well established that he or she must first be under an existing legal duty to take positive action.

A legal duty to act is often imposed by the express provisions of a criminal statute itself. Welfare and Institutions Code section 15630 provides an example. That statute specifically requires care custodians, health practitioners, adult protective services employees, and local law enforcement agencies to report physical abuse of elders and dependent adults. Those subject to the statutory duty to report who fail to do so face criminal liability. Notably, the statutory scheme encourages any person who knows or suspects that an elder or dependent adult has been the victim of abuse to report the abuse, but does not appear to impose the legal duty to do so.

When a criminal statute does not set forth a legal duty to act by its express terms, liability for a failure to act must be premised on the existence of a duty found elsewhere. A criminal statute may thus incorporate a duty imposed by another criminal or civil statute. In *Williams v. Garcetti* (1993) 5 Cal.4th 561, for example, we concluded that the language of section 272, making parents criminally liable if they fail to exercise reasonable care, supervision, protection, and control over their children, incorporated the definitions and limits of parental duties that have long been a part of California's dependency and tort law.

A criminal statute may also embody a common law duty based on the legal relationship between the defendant and the victim, such as that imposed on parents to care for and protect their minor children. Similarly, other special relationships may give rise to a duty to act. Thus, in *People v. Oliver* (1989) 210 Cal. App.3d 138, the court relied on the existence of a special relationship recognized in California civil cases and the Restatement Second of Torts to affirm the defendant's conviction of involuntary manslaughter for her failure to seek medical aid for the victim, a man she had met at a bar and brought to her home who later died of a heroin overdose.

[2b] Accordingly, in order for criminal liability to attach under section 368(a) for willfully permitting the infliction of physical pain or mental suffering on an elder, a defendant must first be under a legal duty to act. Whether the statute adequately denotes the class of persons who owe such a duty is the focus of the constitutional question presented here.

B. Vagueness

[4] The Fourteenth Amendment to the United States Constitution and article I, section 7 of the California Constitution, each guarantee that no person shall be deprived of life, liberty,

or property without due process of law. This constitutional command requires "a reasonable degree of certainty in legislation, especially in the criminal law ..." (In re Newbern (1960) 53 Cal.2d 786, 792) "[A] penal statute [must] define the criminal offense with sufficient definiteness that ordinary people can understand what conduct is prohibited and in a manner that does not encourage arbitrary and discriminatory enforcement." (*Kolender v. Lawson* (1983) 461 U.S. 352, 357.)

It is established that in order for a criminal statute to satisfy the dictates of due process, two requirements must be met. First, the provision must be definite enough to provide a standard of conduct for those whose activities are proscribed. Because we assume that individuals are free to choose between lawful and unlawful conduct, "we insist that laws give the person of ordinary intelligence a reasonable opportunity to know what is prohibited, so that he [or she] may act accordingly. Vague laws trap the innocent by not providing fair warning." (*Grayned v. City of Rockford* (1972) 408 U.S. 104, 108)

Second, the statute must provide definite guidelines for the police in order to prevent arbitrary and discriminatory enforcement. When the Legislature fails to provide such guidelines, the mere existence of a criminal statute may permit "a standardless sweep" that allows police officers, prosecutors and juries "to pursue their personal predilections."

[2c] As to the first prong of our inquiry, in determining whether the relevant language of section 368(a) is sufficiently certain to meet the constitutional requirement of fair notice, "we look first to the language of the statute, then to its legislative history, and finally to the California decisions construing the statutory language." This analytical framework is consistent with the notion that we "require citizens to apprise themselves not only of statutory language, but also of legislative history, subsequent judicial construction, and underlying legislative purposes."

In relevant part, section 368(a) makes it a felony for any person to willfully permit the infliction of pain or suffering on an elder. Defendant claims that the statute is unconstitutionally vague because it purports to impose a legal duty to prevent the infliction of physical or mental abuse on an elder on those, such as herself, who might not reasonably know they have such a duty. The People argue that the statute has no constitutional infirmity because, in clear and unambiguous terms, section 368(a) itself imposes the duty giving rise to criminal liability. According to the People, the statute provides fair notice to every individual that he or she is charged with the responsibility to prevent the infliction of abuse on any elder.

For several reasons, we reject the People's contention that the statute itself imposes a blanket duty on everyone to prevent the abuse of any elder. The wide net cast by a statutory interpretation imposing such a duty on every person is apparent when we consider that it would extend the potential for criminal liability to, for example, a delivery person who, having entered a private home, notices an elder in a disheveled or disoriented state and purposefully fails to intervene.

[5] Under general principles of tort law, civil liability is not imposed for the failure to assist or protect another, absent some legal or special relationship between the parties giving rise to a duty to act.

[2d] In the absence of any indication, express or implied, that the Legislature meant to depart so dramatically from this principle, well established at the time section 368(a) was enacted, it would be unreasonable to interpret the statute as imposing a more serious form

of liability, indeed, felony criminal liability, on every person who fails to prevent an elder from suffering abuse, absent some legal or special relationship between the parties.

Moreover, such a reading of the statutory language would create the anomaly of imposing on every individual the duty to prevent abuse, while a different statutory scheme, adopted after the enactment of section 368(a), expressly excludes everyone but a small number of healthcare, social services, and public safety individuals from the duty to report abuse. Thus, because section 368(a) may not be read as imposing a duty on every person, the facial language of the statute does not convey adequate notice to those who may be under a duty to prevent the infliction of abuse on an elder. We, therefore, look to section 368(a)'s legislative history as a guide to its interpretation.

...

[6] The legislative history thus indicates that, like the purpose underlying the felony child abuse statute from which it derives, section 368(a) was enacted in order to protect the members of a vulnerable class from abusive situations in which serious injury or death is likely to occur. The Legislature was presumably aware that, under the proposed legislation, some individuals would be subject to criminal liability for conduct not previously unlawful. How far the Legislature intended the potential reach of the new law to extend is not, however, entirely clear.

...

Our review of the case law indicates that although the constitutionality of section 368(a) has been considered by several courts, no decision has construed the statute for the purpose of clarifying who owes a duty to protect elders from the infliction of abuse. In *People v. McKelvey* (1991) 230 Cal.App.3d 399, 404 [281 Cal.Rptr. 359], the court opined that the portion of the statute at issue here was uncertain because it "does not describe those persons liable for permitting or causing a dependent adult to suffer." The court went no further in its analysis, however, because it rejected the defendant's vagueness challenge on the basis that his conduct was clearly encompassed by a different portion of section 368(a), in that he had assumed the care and custody of the elderly victim. (*People v. McKelvey*, supra, 230 Cal.App.3d at p. 404.)

...

Three of the decedent's adult children, Richard, Sr., Jerry, and defendant were jointly charged with a violation of section 368(a). At the preliminary hearing, the prosecutor argued that both Richard, Sr., and Jerry had the care and custody of decedent and could therefore be held to answer under that portion of the statute pertaining to caretakers or custodians. The prosecutor argued further that, although defendant was not responsible for the care or custody of her father, she was properly charged under the first clause of section 368(a) as "any person" who willfully permitted any elder to suffer abuse.

Richard, Sr., and Jerry were not the only family members residing with decedent. Richard, Sr.'s three sons also lived in the home. One of these individuals, Richard, Jr., was defendant's boyfriend. For the last six weekends before her father's death, defendant had routinely been in the house visiting with Richard, Jr. Approximately one month before her father died, defendant discussed with Richard, Jr., the possibility of his helping her take decedent to the doctor. The record therefore would appear to support an inference that whatever defendant knew about her father's deteriorating condition, Richard, Jr., knew as well. Under the prosecutor's reading of the statutory language, the first part of section 368(a) would also appear to be applicable to decedent's grandson, Richard, Jr. He was, however, neither arrested nor charged.

Lisa, a fourth Heitzman sibling who, like defendant, did not reside in the same house as her father and brothers, had visited the home five weeks before decedent's death. She was present in the home when defendant entered their father's room for the last time and discovered the hole where the mattress had rotted through. The record also indicates that at one point Lisa contacted the Orange County Department of Social Services concerning her father's condition, but that the agency did not follow up on her call. It would thus appear that Lisa, like defendant, was well aware of decedent's situation. Unlike defendant, however, Lisa was neither arrested for nor charged with a violation of section 368(a).

We recognize there may be many reasons for choosing to prosecute one person but not to prosecute others who may appear to be similarly situated, not the least of which is the prudent expenditure of limited prosecutorial resources. Thus, an uneven application of the law is not necessarily a consequence of the statute's failure to provide any clear standard as to who is under a duty to prevent the infliction of pain or suffering on an elder. What is apparent, however, is that, under the statute as broadly construed, officers and prosecutors might well be free to take their guidance not from any legislative mandate embodied in the statute, but rather, from their own notions of the proper legal obligation owed by a grown child to his or her aging parent. This lack of statutory guidance is at least potentially troublesome where, as here, regardless of any perceived moral obligation on defendant's part to protect her father from abuse, she cannot be held criminally liable for her failure to come to his aid in the absence of a corresponding legal duty. As one treatise has noted, although "[g]eneral principles of morals and ethics form a [large] part of the raw materials out of which law is made, ... the boundaries are not identical." (Perkins & Boyce, Criminal Law, supra, Imputability, p. 660.)

In sum, contrary to constitutional requirements, neither the language nor subsequent judicial construction of section 368(a) provides adequate notice to those who may be under a duty to prevent the infliction of abuse on an elder. Moreover, the statute fails to provide a clear standard for those charged with enforcing the law. Although the selective prosecution of defendant does not conclusively demonstrate the presence of arbitrary or discriminatory enforcement, it arguably lends support to the view that the potential exists for such impermissible enforcement.

Questions

1. Cite the precise language of the provision that indicates the duty and responsibility of some parties to the elderly.
2. Does the Court find this provision unconstitutional?
3. Do the facts demonstrate negligence involving the care of the elderly?
4. How does the Court distinguish responsibility based on these siblings?
5. What is your view on how the Court should have decided?

but are not legally obligated to perform. Omission looks for a certain linkage between parties who have specified obligations. For example, a parent has various obligations and responsibilities that involve the care and maintenance of offspring, e.g., education, food, shelter, and supervision. These well-known responsibilities are rooted in the social and human domain while simultaneously being normative, legal requirements. It would be absurd to not hold parents accountable for the neglect of their children. This same expectation, however, would not be assigned to strangers and detached citizens, even though there is some moral and spiritual sense of communal obligation to others. Even though troubling, nonobliged parties, who see and hear of abuse heaped on others, may have little or no obligation to intervene. To omit aiding an injured motorist would be criminal for the emergency medical technician (EMT) and police personnel though hardly criminal for the rubber-necker who drives by. It may be bothersome in a moral sense, but hardly illegal. In the case of an EMT, there is an occupational duty to act. So, too, with parents, lifeguards, case workers, teachers, and others entrusted with the care of others. In omission, we find not only a failure to act, but also a legal requirement to do otherwise.

Aside from occupational duties and responsibilities, the criminal law often contains codifications that designate omission as criminal act. Thus, a failure to supervise, a failure to provide oversight over children or assets, or other function may entail the type of criminal agency suitable for prosecution. In the final analysis, to hold a party liable for a failure to act, the proponent will have to advocate that the law imposes a duty or obligation upon the party to act. Inactivity without legal responsibility cannot evolve into criminal agency.

DEFINING MENS REA

At the heart of every criminal prosecution rests the mental state of the offender. In historic terms, the term *mens rea* signified what and how the perpetrator thought as he or she carried out the offense.[11] From its Latin translation, "things thought" or "mind things," this essential component of every criminal offense delves into a region unseen. How can a mind and its content be measured? How are thoughts cataloged and computed? So private, so intimate are human thought patterns that this province may be the last truly safe haven from intrusive social and behavioral scientists. Try as we might, it will always be difficult to know what another thinks. It may be even more difficult finding out what criminals dwell upon.

Mens rea is the intellectualization of criminality; it is the mental formulation of malevolent design and plan, and the overall thought process by which offenders offend. It means, at a minimum, that a "person intends the natural and probable consequences of his act."[12] Mens rea can be proved by direct action, or by reasonable interpretation and evaluation of particular facts that speak in and of themselves. In the latter instance, the precision arises from deductive reasoning rather than straightforward evidence of a mind's intent.[13]

Much more than motive, mens rea depicts the criminal's mindset during the commission of the felonious conduct. Criminal statutes usually include language demonstrating mens rea using terms such as intentional, willful, with malicious purpose, with depraved indifference to human life, recklessly, premeditatedly, carelessly, with knowledge and foresight, knowingly, with depraved heart. These words connote the mental faculty of the perpetrator and represent what the law demands as proof of mental choice.

The Model Penal Code sets out four main categories of mental state that leads to criminal responsibility when coupled with actus reus:

CASE 3.3

TOBACCO MURDER: A LEGAL BRIEF FOR PROSECUTING
TOBACCO PUSHERS: MERCHANTS OF DEATH

Fundamental Principles of Law

"No one has a right to have his property burn, if thereby the property of others is endangered. The right to extinguish fires ... is a part of the police power. ... It may be exercised not only without the consent of the owner of the property on fire, but against his will." ... The fire aspect intended by the manufacturer is, of course, of the essence in smoking. (Cigarettes without fire are not what the problem is about!)

What is at issue is an "ultrahazardous activity" as that term is defined in professional material. See an analysis of the concept by the U.S. Supreme Court in the case of *Laird v Nelms*. ... There, sonic booms and dynamite blasting are discussed in context of "ultrahazardous activity." Each produces a spreading effect. Cigarettes do that via fires and via their toxic chemicals, superheated, moving at high speed. In contrast to sonic booms and dynamite blasting, cigarettes kill 37,000,000 in the U.S. alone, and constitute a "holocaust." This is the most ultrahazardous activity on earth. The point, in law, is that in dealing with "ultrahazardous activity," there is "strict liability" for all consequent damages, even if negligence is not proven.

The U.S. Supreme Court states that it is not "unfair to require that one who deliberately goes perilously close to an area of proscribed conduct shall take the risk that he may cross the line."

In a cigarette death case (two firemen killed due a smokers' smoking), the Pennsylvania Supreme Court ruled that a toxic substance "is the prototype of forces" or substances "which the ordinary man knows must be used with special caution because of the potential for wide devastation ['universal malice']."

It is well established that a single act can violate more than one legal principle or restriction. The initial violation may be no more than a minor one, as in Hughes, a work rule violation (the no smoking rule). The violation of that seemingly minor rule caused a fire which, in turn, produced "the death of two firemen," leading to "two counts of involuntary manslaughter." Both counts were upheld by the Pennsylvania Supreme Court. Tobacco involves two, not just one, prototypic hazards, i.e., toxic chemicals and fire. ...

The Safety Duty

The Supreme Court states that by law, Congress places "the 'benefit' of worker health above all other considerations." Disregard of safety and "violation of the regulations [here, the principles herein] is evidence of negligence to be considered with the other facts and circumstances."

"In Michigan, violation of a statute is negligence per se." The "unqualified and absolute" safety adjective requires foresight and vigilance for compliance: What foresight and vigilance consist of and require of executives and tobacco sellers are described by the Supreme Court as follows:

"The requirements of foresight and vigilance imposed on responsible corporate agents are beyond question demanding, and perhaps onerous, but they are no more stringent than the public has a right to expect of those who voluntarily assume positions of authority in ... enterprises whose services and products affect ... health and well-being. ..."

This was in answer to a convicted business official (Park) who argued all the way to the Supreme Court that the legal duty set is too high! Re tobacco, there is no question but that it does adversely "affect ... health and well-being ..." up to and including causing death.

"The accused [executive or tobacco seller], if he does not will the violation, usually is in a position to prevent it. ... "

That is certainly the case here with tobacco, as each "defendant had, by reason of his position ... responsibility and authority either to prevent in the first instance, or promptly to correct, the violation complained of, and ... failed to do so."

In that case, the company president personally was arrested and convicted. He argued that he had delegated to his subordinates. In rebuttal, the Supreme Court said that he (the convicted executive) in law "could not rely on his system of delegation to subordinates to prevent or correct" the violation. The business executive has personal responsibility to act when there is a safety hazard. Safety involves a stringent duty of this nature, said the Supreme Court, as safety does "touch phases of the lives and health of the people, which, in the circumstances of modern industrialism, are largely beyond self-protection. A conscious, intentional, deliberate, voluntary decision [to ignore others' safety] properly is described as willful."

This principle covers "conscious, intentional, deliberate, voluntary decisions" to engage in tobacco production and selling and resultant adverse consequences including the above-holocaust level of deaths.

"[T]he distinction between 'misfeasance' and 'nonfeasance' (the distinction between active misconduct and passive inaction) is deeply rooted in the law of negligence. ..."

Violation of Duties of Prevention and Aid

Poison/toxic chemicals and fire involve a potential for wide devastation. The known susceptibility of smokers, nonsmokers including babies and fetuses subjected to toxic chemicals, and cocaine addicts to sudden death requires law tobacco executives and retailers, to not just NOT do as here is being done (mass death above the holocaust level), but also requires them to obey the pertinent laws and aid the victims of their past and current violations, while ceasing and desisting to commit more. The duty of prevention and of aid is ancient, e.g., as shown in a 1913 conviction based on failure to meet the duty:

"The defendant was charged with the duty to see to it that ... life was not endangered; and it is apparent he could have performed that duty ..." [And] "To constitute murder, there must be means to relieve and willfulness in withholding relief."

All company, corporate, and retail officials have this duty. Tobacco deaths can easily be prevented by the simple act of not producing it! Self-control is not onerous! Producers must produce safe products, i.e., must "see to it that ... life [is] not endangered." That is duty one, which is obviously being violated.

Duty two relates to aid. Tobacco producers and executives have made no provision to aid the victims that already exist. Indeed, they are in process of creating new and additional victims. This is rampant "willfulness in withholding relief," a holocaust of "universal malice" run rampant.

This is especially evident in view of the Michigan law, the cigarette control law, MCL § 750.27, MSA § 28.216, to prevent people from manufacturing or selling cigarettes. It is illegal to sell them cigarette one. Tobacco manufacturers and sellers could easily have obeyed the law. They never did, 1909 to present. This is a clear-cut case of mass murder, above the holocaust level. Even after the numerous lawsuits alleging harm, they continued the en masse violations. They had the means to relive the harm. They did not.

Even in no-murder, nonlife-threatening situations, i.e., simply as a routine duty, "A tortfeasor has a duty to assist his victim. The initial injury creates a duty of aid and the breach of the duty is an independent tort.

Tobacco pushers' centuries of universal malice (throughout the slavery era 1620–1865, and its many evils, including mass casualties) leads nonsmoker children, nonaddicts, into the starter drug, then down the road, to subsequent addictions, by hooking them on tobacco, a known mind-altering drug. In effect, such drug is a mind poison, causing abulia.

Since before 1858, the criminal prosecution for doing that to a person—providing a person a mind-altering drug—this has been illegal. As a result of ingesting such a drug, the person may come to harm, even if NOT from the drug, so providing it is a crime. This is true even though injury and death may be delayed, e.g., hooking a child on tobacco at age 12, but death does not occur until some decades later. The initial act is the crime, just as the initial shooting is, even though death be delayed.

Similarity of Murder Offenses in Law

In law, certain classifications of acts are equated, e.g., the California Supreme Court states thus:

"All murder which shall be perpetrated by means of poison, or lying in wait, torture, or by another kind of willful, deliberate and premeditated killing ... shall be deemed murder of the first degree." Tobacco meets all these criteria; meeting any one is enough for a murder verdict, as a matter of law.

Questions

1. Do the facts support cigarette manufacturers being held strictly liable for deaths due to cigarettes?
2. Do the facts support cigarette company executives being found guilty of negligence?
3. Do the facts set forth above lead you to the conclusion that cigarette companies and executives are guilty of "mass murder, above the holocaust level?"
4. Discuss your thoughts on the following statement as it may relate to cigarette manufacturers. Is the prosecution of manufacturers under this theory realistic or not?

   "All murder which shall be perpetrated by means of poison, or lying in wait, torture, or by another kind of willful, deliberate and premeditated killing ... shall be deemed murder of the first degree."

Except as provided in Section 2.05, a person is not guilty of an offense unless he acted purposely, knowingly, recklessly or negligently, as the law may require, with respect to each material element of the offense.[14]

Without its proof, the charging authority has no chance of success.
Described in other ways, mens rea stands for:

- Mental choice resulting from deliberation
- Will and motive to engage in criminal conduct
- Purposeful intention to commit criminal conduct
- Offender thought patterns that trigger overt action
- Offender rationalizations and justifications for criminal conduct

Each state designates this basic element in felony and misdemeanor conduct and lays out the required level of mental acuity and purpose necessary for conviction.

Visit the Lexis/Nexis Capsule Summary for Criminal States of Mind at http://www.lexis-nexis.com/lawschool/study/outlines/html/crim/crim05.htm

---

Examples from Delaware and Missouri are selectively reproduced to highlight the mental element central to criminal codification.
Delaware Code annotated:

§ 231. Definitions relating to state of mind

(a) "Criminal negligence." A person acts with criminal negligence with respect to an element of an offense when the person fails to perceive a risk that the element exists or will result from the conduct. The risk must be of such a nature and degree that failure to perceive it constitutes a gross deviation from the standard of conduct that a reasonable person would observe in the situation.

(b) "Intentionally." A person acts intentionally with respect to an element of an offense when:
  (1) If the element involves the nature of the person's conduct or a result thereof, it is the person's conscious object to engage in conduct of that nature or to cause that result; and
  (2) If the element involves the attendant circumstances, the person is aware of the existence of such circumstances or believes or hopes that they exist.

(c) "Knowingly." A person acts knowingly with respect to an element of an offense when:
  (1) If the element involves the nature of the person's conduct or the attendant circumstances, the person is aware that the conduct is of that nature or that such circumstances exist; and
  (2) If the element involves a result of the person's conduct, the person is aware that it is practically certain that the conduct will cause that result.

(d) "Negligence." A person acts with negligence with respect to an element of an offense when the person fails to exercise the standard of care which a reasonable person would observe in the situation.

(e) "Recklessly." A person acts recklessly with respect to an element of an offense when the person is aware of and consciously disregards a substantial and unjustifiable risk that the element exists or will result from the conduct. The risk must be of such a nature and degree that disregard thereof constitutes a gross deviation from the standard of conduct that a reasonable person would observe in the situation. A person who creates such a risk but is unaware thereof solely by reason of voluntary intoxication also acts recklessly with respect thereto.[15]

Missouri Revised Statutes:

§ 562.016. Culpable mental state

1. Except as provided in section 562.026, a person is not guilty of an offense unless he acts with a culpable mental state, that is, unless he acts purposely or knowingly or recklessly or with criminal negligence, as the statute defining the offense may require with respect to the conduct, the result thereof or the attendant circumstances which constitute the material elements of the crime.
2. A person "acts purposely," or with purpose, with respect to his conduct or to a result thereof when it is his conscious object to engage in that conduct or to cause that result.
3. A person "acts knowingly," or with knowledge:
    (1) With respect to his conduct or to attendant circumstances when he is aware of the nature of his conduct or that those circumstances exist; or
    (2) With respect to a result of his conduct when he is aware that his conduct is practically certain to cause that result.

4. A person "acts recklessly" or is reckless when he consciously disregards a substantial and unjustifiable risk that circumstances exist or that a result will follow, and such disregard constitutes a gross deviation from the standard of care which a reasonable person would exercise in the situation.
5. A person "acts with criminal negligence" or is criminally negligent when he fails to be aware of a substantial and unjustifiable risk that circumstances exist or a result will follow, and such failure constitutes a gross deviation from the standard of care which a reasonable person would exercise in the situation.[16]

The concept of mens rea encompasses the most critical question the justice model poses: *What does the criminal think?*[17] The answer can only be derived from an incisive and deep examination of the offender's psychological, mental, and emotional state coupled with a conjecture as to the intellectual processes operating in the offender's mind at the time of the crime. Stated another way, how does the justice system get inside the brain of the offender? How do we really know what another person thinks as action follows deliberation? Do we ever really know what another person thinks and conceptualizes? Can we ever really appreciate the motivations of other individuals? Try as we might, this jumping into the mind of another is a sheer impossibility. Is it possible to really understand the mind of John Wayne Gacy, who sodomized and ritualistically executed almost three dozen teenagers? What of Jeffrey Dahmer whose victims' body parts were stored in chemical containers and freezer bags for perverted usage?

STORY 3.1

THE MINDS OF MASS MURDERERS

John Wayne Gacy

John Wayne Gacy, Jr. was admired and liked by most who had known him. He was thought of as a generous, friendly, and hard-working man, devoted to his family and community. Gacy was involved in organizations like Chi Rho Club, Catholic Inter-Club Council, the Federal Civil Defense for Illinois, the Chicago Civil Defense, Holy Name Society, and the Jaycees. Gacy was the second of three children, raised Catholic and attended Catholic schools on the north side of Chicago. John Wayne Gacy, Sr. was an alcoholic who physically abused his wife and verbally abused his children.

In the spring of 1968, Gacy was indicted by a grand jury in Black Hawk County for allegedly committing the act of sodomy with a teenage boy named Mark Miller. Four months later, Gacy was charged with hiring an eighteen-year-old boy to beat up Miller. A judge ordered Gacy to undergo psychiatric evaluation to find if he was mentally competent to stand trial. Gacy was found to be mentally competent, but was considered to be an antisocial personality who would probably not benefit from any known medical treatment. Soon after health authorities submitted the report, Gacy pleaded guilty to the charge of sodomy. Gacy received ten years at the Iowa State Reformatory for men. Shortly after Gacy entered prison, his first wife divorced him.

Ten years later, on Friday, December 22, 1978, Gacy confessed to police that he killed at least thirty people and buried most of the remains of the victims beneath the crawl space of his house, some still had their underwear lodged in their throats. By the 28th of December, police had removed a total of twenty-seven bodies from Gacy's house. (Another body found weeks earlier and several others were recovered from the Des Plaines River.) All but nine of his victims were finally identified.

Gacy was found guilty in the deaths of thirty-three young men and he had the "singular notoriety of having been convicted of more murders than anyone else in American history" (Terry Sullivan and Peter T. Maiken (Mass Market Paperback, 1997)). Gacy received the death penalty and was sent to Menard Correctional Center where, after years of appeals, he eventually was killed by lethal injection.

Jeffrey Dahmer

Jeffrey Dahmer had fantasies about killing men and having sex with their corpses as early as age fourteen. He finally acted on his fantasy in June of 1978. His first victim was a hitchhiker named Steven Hicks. They had sex and drank beer, but when Hicks wanted to leave, Dahmer struck him in the head with a barbell and killed him. His second victim was Steven Toumi. They had been drinking heavily in one of the popular gay bars. When Dahmer woke, Toumi was dead and blood was on his mouth. He stuffed the body inside a large suitcase he bought and took Toumi's corpse to his grandmother's basement, had sex with it, masturbated on it, dismembered it, and threw it in the garbage. His third victim was a fourteen-year-old Native American boy named Jamie Doxtator.

On September 25, 1988, he offered a thirteen-year-old boy $50 to pose for some pictures. He drugged the boy and fondled him. The boy's parents realized there was something wrong with their child and took him to the hospital. Dahmer was arrested for sexual exploitation of a child and second-degree sexual assault. On January 30, 1989, he pled guilty, although he claimed that he thought that the boy was much older than he was.

On May 14, 1990, Dahmer moved to a 924 North 25th Street apartment. During the next fifteen months, Dahmer would take the lives of twelve more men. All but three of his victims were black; one was white, one was Laotian, and one was Hispanic. Most were homosexual or bisexual. The youngest was fourteen and the oldest was thirty-one.

Dahmer would select his prey at gay bars or bathhouses, lure his victims by offering them money to pose for photographs or ask them to drink some beer and watch some videos. He would drug them with his prescribed sedatives and serve them in a drink, strangle them, masturbate on the body, or have sex with the corpse. Dahmer would take pictures with his Polaroid to preserve the entire experience so that he could remember each and every murder. He would keep the skull or other body parts as souvenirs and masturbate in front of them for gratification.

He disposed of most of the bodies by dismemberment. But, he also experimented with various chemicals and acids to turn the flesh and bone to a black, foul-smelling muck, which he would pour down a drain or toilet. Sometime he would keep the heads and genitals as trophies. He preserved the genitals in formaldehyde. The heads were boiled until the flesh came off and then painted gray to look like plastic.

In his attorney's summation at trial he drew a chart for the jury in the shape of a wheel. The hub of the wheel was Dahmer and all of the spokes coming out from the wheel were the elements of his deviance. He read them off quickly:

"Skulls in locker, cannibalism, sexual urges, drilling, making zombies, necrophilia, drinking alcohol all the time, trying to create a shrine, lobotomies, defleshing, calling taxidermists, going to grave yards, masturbating ... This is Jeffrey Dahmer, a runaway train on a track of madness ..."

Prosecution rebutted with, "He wasn't a runaway train, he was the engineer!" Dahmer was found guilty and sane on fifteen counts of murder and sentenced to fifteen consecutive life terms or a total of 957 years in prison.

Dahmer adjusted well to life at the Columbia Correctional Institute in Portage, Wisconsin. Initially not part of the general population of the prison, he eventually convinced the prison authorities to allow him more contact with other inmates. He was eventually able to eat and work with other teams of inmates. On November 28, 1994, he was paired up with Jesse Anderson, a white man who had murdered his wife and blamed it on a black man, and Christopher Scarver, a black delusional schizophrenic who thought he was the son of God, who was in for first-degree murder. The guard left the three men alone to do their work. When the guards came back twenty minutes later, Dahmer's head was crushed and Anderson was fatally injured. Jeffrey Dahmer was pronounced dead at 9:11 a.m.

Leaping into the mental space of another, while neurologically impossible, is inferentially plausible. One can infer and deduce another's mindset by merely examining courses of action and[18] reducing the end result of criminal activity to a certain motive or evil design. Mens rea analysis can never be so quantitatively sophisticated as to be scientifically reducible to formula or equation. Its discovery is highly complicated, a "concept of many colors."[19]

Just like criminal activity, mens rea inquiry is a dark and confusing business. At times, the emphasis tends to rationality, whether the actor knows and understands the criminality of the action chosen.[20] At other times, the emphasis is on the objective reality of the offense, its elements and provisos whereby the prosecution must show that the defendant understood the precise nature of each component of the crime. Sometimes, the statute is utterly clear as what the expectations for mens rea should be, but appellate courts have "ignored the concept and have frequently failed to expressly seek a definition of the concept."[21]

Visit the FBI's Web location on Serial Killers at: http://www.fbi.gov/news/stories/2008/july/serialmurder_070708

Exactly what the criminal desires and pines for can never be precisely proved. Then again, criminals themselves may confess, or memorialize their mind in a letter or signed confession. Their mental state could be recorded on tape, in letters, or memoranda, in ransom notes or perverse sexual materials, or by wiretap, electronic eavesdropping, or a perusal of e-mail. In short, the business of proving mind-set is not as daunting as it first appears. True, we are incapable of invading in any real sense the mental domain of another, though we are most capable of reaching conclusions about what a person thinks through other means. This is the primordial task of the prosecution team—to show mental states coupled with completed or attempted action. To prove the overwhelming bulk of criminal charges, proof will be proffered that manifests the intentionality of the accused. Mental motivations, mental plans and designs, desires, choices, and wills are fundamental to any successful prosecution. From the defense perspective, disproof of these very same requirements frees the accused. The defense approach focuses on how an accused may mistakenly have acted, or did so without the requisite malice or reckless disregard, or operated without grave indifference to human life. From either vantage point, mens rea acts as a lynchpin as the criminal case unfolds. The most efficacious prosecution or defense depends upon its proof or disproof. In the final analysis, mens rea drives juror or judicial thinking as the ultimate issue of guilt or innocence is evaluated. Jurors can readily discern whether acts have been done, e.g., murder, arson, or rape, because, as witnesses to reality, we decipher motion and activity during our day-to-day existence. As for how a defendant thinks, the task is much more cumbersome and despite this obvious difference in evidentiary proof, demonstration of the defendant's mental faculty is no less mandatory. Proof of the mind, the mens rea, remains the hallmark of the American justice model even while knowing full well our lack of any meaningful understanding of how others think things through. Proof of intention, of will, of choice and desire, take criminal prosecution far beyond the simplistic screening of act and motion since human acts lack culpability unless coupled with a mind-set that prompts and agrees with the acts. That dual proof is the crux of the matter and the thing that so markedly distinguishes the American model of burdens and sufficiency from so many of its counterparts. Responsibility lies with those responsible. Automatons and robots lack the mental activity to want or wish for anything. It is the human player alone that dons the role of criminal, for the human agent alone is capable of willing and yearning for the end result the criminal action brings. For these and other reasons, our system exonerates those suffering from such significant mental diseases and defects that they lack the capacity to formulate the required mens rea. The insane, the gravely ill, the comatose, cannot author the mind for crime, nor can criminal culpability attach to those who act solely from reflex or bona fide sleepwalking, unintentionality, gracelessness, or even negligence. Mistakes and accidents do not constitute the mens rea necessary for criminal responsibility.

In this sense, the American experience favors the defendant because it affirmatively requires the government to prove what the perpetrator thinks. Defendants, protected by a score of constitutional barriers to self-incrimination, cannot be forced to divulge what they thought, what they did or wished to do. Defendants can sit back and watch the state or federal authority scramble to show motive and intentionality. The defense need not say a thing. The prosecution has little choice but to pose evidence that tells of the defendant's mental state during the commission of the offense in question. A failure to do so will only result in an acquittal. At first glance, this evidentiary advantage may appear unfair to the victim, although, on closer inspection, the wisdom of this defense benefit becomes apparent. In any state proclaiming justice at its foundation, criminal responsibility should only be imputed to those who intend the ultimate end of the conduct chosen. To allow the prosecution of acts alone, without a corresponding proof of intention, would rain down havoc on the common good. Imagine a legal system that had no other requirement than tying an accused to an act; agency being the singular requirement for conviction. Then compare a system that demands the agency be adjoined to a felonious mind that intends and knows the endgame of the criminal action. In the former system, the prosecution would lazily offer a case centered on the criminal act without much reference to motive, will, intention, and overall desire of the accused. In the latter case, the prosecution must offer agency blended with human motivation and intentionality, all of which explains holistically the act and the actor. If acts alone were the source of culpability, then acts would take on a life detached from actors. Responsibility would lie less with the perpetrator and more with the act. But, when an act is joined with an actor, then meaningful responsibility can be assigned and final judgment will be just. Judgment ultimately depends upon choice and will of the actor not the act itself. Judgment can be confident when the gravity of the criminal charge links itself to the gravity of the offender's mind.

TYPES OF MENS REA

As varied as the descriptors are for the nature of mens rea, it is equally obvious that various types of mens rea have evolved in the history of Western jurisprudence. Some of the distinctions are essentially artificial and in need of elimination, though the law convincingly recognizes that people are held accountable in different ways depending upon their actions and the level of mental firmness and clarity. Premeditating criminals suffer greater consequence than those who act with general indifference or criminal negligence. On the other hand, those acting recklessly or with disregard for safety of others will not be as culpable as those who unreservedly intend and coldheartedly plot and plan the activity. Degrees of mental involvement and mental sophistication are translated each day on charge sheets. First degree murder naturally calls for a higher level of mental proof than the vehicular homicide case arising from intoxication. Mental states will be defined and gauged in accordance with the clarity of the rational faculty. Accordingly, criminal codifications rooted in common law tradition will generally divide mens rea into three main categories: specific, general, and strict liability.

Specific Intent

As the word specific implies, this type of intentionality incorporates the clear thinking actor whose agency is unreserved and unqualified, and who not only generally intends some illegal result, but also targets more precisely a specific course of conduct. The label is often attached to offenses that delineate a specific type of knowledge in the statutory design that need be part of the prosecutorial burden. While most criminal charges fall into a generic type of mens rea, a term known as general, some are more exacting in their demands. First degree, higher to highest level felonies regularly call for not only the intent to engage in general criminality, but also the specific intentionality regarding a type of conduct. For example, one cannot be convicted of first-degree burglary if one believes they are entering their own home. Accordingly, one could not be charged specifically with first-degree rape if the accused believed consent was present. At issue is not whether these matters are arguable or even credible, but instead whether the code provision sets out a type of intent that particularizes its elements in such a way that the defendant must be shown to have specifically intended to violate them.

Criminal offenses calling for specific intent zero in on identifiable conduct that the offender objectively and subjectively possessed. It is not enough to argue that the defendant wanted to abuse and sexually assault a victim in a first-degree rape charge, but it will suffice when the prosecution shows that the accused selectively targeted a victim and was in full awareness that consent was not given. To specifically intend is to operate with express desire for a specific end. The Mafia hit man, paid by illicit contract to rub out an enemy of the enterprise, classically fits the category. Here, the agent moves dispassionately and kills for clear purpose and financial reward. Here, the actor carries out the design without mitigation, excuse, or the usual recipe of conditions, syndromes, and other attendant circumstances that provide for explanation. Here, the actor calculates, plots, plans, and authors a criminality without equivocation. The spouse who deliberately and over long periods of time, poisons a mate resides in this category as does the party who purchases weaponry for the express purpose of killing another. Absent in these types of cases are passion and intense emotion that muddle up the thinking being and provide some level, however unconvincing, of mitigation or excuse. This is why prosecutors rarely would charge murder in the first degree in a case of domestic violence and prefer lower degreed murder or even manslaughter charges. In this scenario, the accused operates with less mental precision than the cold-blooded killer, though the conduct is by no means excusable.

To specifically intend a criminal consequence requires the accused party to intellectualize the result with such clarity and unambiguity that the chain of mental state and criminal act is perfectly connected. Specific intent matches actors with objects sought and correlates the mental vision with the victimization soon to happen. This is why specific intent offenses are the most brutal offenses against individual and common goods because explanations are hard to come by. The criminality rests not in antagonism or heated emotionalism, nor in mental aberration and defect or provocation, but instead in cold-blooded will and choice. One kills because of blank and unadorned desire. One rapes and sodomizes, not because of an unfortunate childhood, but for the perverse satisfaction derived from sexual assault and the ability to dominate and control the victim.

Listen to a podcast or radio stream from the FBI's Behavioral Unit at http://www.fbi.gov/news/podcasts/inside/behavioral-science-unit-2013-part-ii/view

---

Those who specifically intend don't look back or second guess the consequences. Within this panorama, defense counsel attacks vigorously, offering up explanations for conduct sure to derail the specific intent claim. Impoverished childhood, drugs and alcohol, food addictions,

CASE 3.4

PEOPLE V. ERICKSON

No. 25854 (Ca. Super. Ct. 1997)

Appellant had been sexually and physically abused by her parents as a teenager. She experienced several unsuccessful relationships as an adult, including at least one previous relationship that involved serious physical abuse of appellant by her husband.

Appellant began living with the victim, Ron Pruitt, in early 1993. Soon after appellant started living with Pruitt, he became highly critical of her, was bossy and controlling, and drank a great deal of alcohol. Appellant moved out in June of 1993; she returned in September after Pruitt agreed to go to Alcoholics Anonymous. Pruitt failed to live up to this promise, however, and his previous negative behavior increased in intensity.

Around Thanksgiving of 1993, appellant came home from work to discover Pruitt in bed with another woman. As a result, appellant and Pruitt decided appellant would continue to live in the house, but in a separate bedroom; they no longer would have a romantic relationship. Nevertheless, Pruitt made it clear he still wanted to have sex with appellant. She complied with his requests for sex as a result of physical force, threats of eviction and threats to report appellant to the police for perceived criminal behavior.

Pruitt taunted appellant with claims that he knew she liked forcible sex because that was the way her father had done it. Pruitt had several guns in his home, and he threatened to kill appellant "a good two dozen times" during this period.

By July of 1994, appellant considered Pruitt's behavior intolerable. She made plans to move in with Pruitt's adult son and the son's girlfriend and to take a job where the son worked. Pruitt found out about this plan and told appellant she could neither move nor take the job; Pruitt pushed appellant around during this argument. Appellant left and spent the night at the son's house.

The next day, Pruitt went to the son's house and sent appellant home. He went to the potential employer (which was another division of the agricultural employer for whom Pruitt also worked) and arranged to cancel appellant's job offer. When Pruitt came home that evening, he was intoxicated. He argued with appellant about her plans and told her she could not move out. Pruitt became more and more intoxicated. He told appellant he would kill her if she tried to move out. Eventually, Pruitt grabbed appellant by the hair and forced her to orally copulate him. Afterwards, Pruitt pushed appellant into her bedroom. He told her that he would find and kill her if she tried leaving that night.

After Pruitt fell asleep, appellant went to a pay telephone and called her son, Keith. He told her to come to his house. Once there, appellant described to Keith the night's events. They decided to kill Pruitt; Keith would cut Pruitt's throat. Together with Keith's girlfriend, they returned to Pruitt's house.

Appellant went inside first, to make sure Pruitt was still asleep. She then summoned Keith. Keith got a knife from the kitchen. While appellant went to her own room, Keith decided he could not kill Pruitt with the knife and went outside to vomit. When he returned, Keith asked appellant to procure the handgun Pruitt kept by his bed. She got the gun. Keith took it and fired two shots into Pruitt's neck and head. Appellant and Keith decided to make it appear Pruitt had been killed during a robbery. They removed personal property and all the guns from the house. They threw most of these items into a lake. Appellant returned home about 6 a.m. and called 9-1-1.

She and Keith initially denied any knowledge of the crime; both eventually confessed.

On October 31, 1994, appellant was charged by information with murder (Pen. Code, § 187) with a firearm enhancement (Pen. Code, § 12022, subd. (a)(1)). Jury trial began on August 28, 1995. On September 20, 1995, the jury found appellant guilty of first degree murder and found true the enhancement allegation. After denying appellant's motion for new trial, the court sentenced appellant on October 18, 1995, to a prison term of 25 years to life, plus 1 year for the enhancement. Appellant filed a notice of appeal.

By motion *in limine* at the beginning of the defense case, the prosecutor sought restrictions on "expert speculations/opinions regarding the defendant's actual state of mind at the time that this killing of Mr. Ronald Pruitt was perpetrated." After argument, the court ruled that defense experts would be able to testify with regard to battered women's syndrome, "including its physical, emotional, and/or mental effects upon [appellant's] beliefs, perceptions, or behavior. But your expert will not be able to testify as to what [appellant's] belief was or wasn't, perception was or wasn't, behavior was or wasn't." After further discussion, the court reiterated its ruling, as follows: "[Y]ou can't ask your expert did Mrs. Erickson believe this or that. You can ask your expert how did battered women's syndrome affect Mrs. Erickson's belief about this subject, perception about this subject, behavior about this subject."

The first defense expert to testify was Dr. Randall Epperson, a neuropsychologist. He interviewed and administered tests to appellant. He concluded appellant was a battered woman with a lifelong history of being battered. He determined she had organic brain damage in the left hemisphere, probably from birth. Appellant's verbal IQ was 74, on the borderline of being considered retarded. She suffered from learning disabilities. As a result of her various problems, she suffered from long-term depression and viewed herself as a victim in a hostile world. Epperson concluded appellant would have a very difficult time perceiving the nature of the problems that confronted her and would have a very limited capacity of reasoning out a solution to the problems. She would, in Epperson's opinion, be likely to suffer through problems, allowing her frustrations to build up. When a problem became intolerable, her response would be confused and she would not have a reasoned approach to solving the problem.

Dr. Robin Schaeffer also testified for the defense; he is a clinical psychologist with an extensive history of working with battered women. He described in detail the battered women's syndrome and the behavior associated with it. He described the characteristics commonly associated with "the battered woman." Schaeffer examined appellant. He concluded she "does fit the psychological profile of being a battered woman." When asked whether he concluded she had "any kind of disorder," he answered that she had a cognitive disorder as described by Dr. Epperson. "[H]er cognitive disabilities resulted in increased passive dependency and lack of self-reliance and ... this made it hard for her to think through alternative solutions to her dilemma. It also made it hard for her to regulate the emotions that were generated in her by the relationship."

Defense counsel asked Schaeffer how "the fact of being a battered woman" affected appellant's perceptions of danger at the beginning of her relationship with Pruitt. He answered: "In my opinion, at the beginning ... her experiences did not cause her to perceive herself in significant danger." Defense counsel then asked: "How about at the end of the relationship?" Schaeffer answered that appellant's "experiences caused her to perceive that her life was in danger" at the end of the relationship. The prosecutor objected and the court sustained the objection, admonishing the jury to disregard the answer.

Next, defense counsel asked Schaeffer: "Doctor, listen to me carefully. How did the battered wife syndrome affect [appellant's] perception of the imminence of danger? What was the affect [*sic*] of being a battered woman?" Schaeffer began to answer, "it caused her to perceive that –" The prosecutor again objected and the court instructed the witness as follows:

"Doctor, regardless of whatever her perception might be, which I ruled you cannot state, you can state how the battered wife syndrome, her experiences, would affect or lead her to come to any perception. Again, the court's ruling you can't state what she actually perceived.

"[Schaeffer]: Okay. In my opinion, at the end of — at the time frame of the end of the relationship, the battered wife syndrome caused Deborah — affected Deborah Erickson that it did have affect on her perception that there was a danger. ... Also, at that time the battered wife syndrome did affect her perceptions as to what measures were necessary to take [to protect herself]."

Schaeffer's testimony on direct ended with his conclusion that appellant's reduced verbal IQ meant that she had less ability than the average person to think of options to protect herself. Dr. Valerie Broin took the witness stand as the defense's final expert. She was an associate professor of philosophy at California State University, Stanislaus, and taught women's studies courses. She described battered women's syndrome generally and discussed distinguishing features of battered women who kill their batterers. She expounded on particular issues present in ordinary battering relationships and in those relationships that end in the killing of the batterer.

The prosecution's expert witness, Dr. Philip Trompetter, testified in rebuttal. He testified that he examined appellant for a total of about 11 hours. He described her psychological and intellectual makeup as he saw it. He described battered women's syndrome, and concluded that appellant displayed many aspects of the syndrome, while she did not display other important aspects of it. He listed 13 common features of battered women who kill their batterers and concluded that appellant did not display those characteristics. At the close of Trompetter's testimony for the day, the prosecutor asked him: "Do you have an opinion, given your conclusion ... that the defendant suffers from the battered women's syndrome, regarding whether that syndrome affected the defendant's perception of — of danger?" He said he did, and the prosecutor asked for the opinion. Trompetter replied: "It's my opinion that she did not view herself in imminent danger of being killed by Mr. Pruitt or even significantly harmed." On defense counsel's objection, the court instructed the jury to disregard that answer.

The next day, the prosecutor began his examination of Trompetter by asking about a hypothetical woman who lacked a substantial number of the features of a battered woman who kills, but who still suffered from battered women's syndrome and killed her batterer. He asked if such a person's perception of personal danger was affected by battered women's syndrome. Trompetter answered: "Given the inconsistencies [with the profile of battered women who kill], there would be nothing to cause a battered woman to believe that they were in imminent danger of loss of life had they stayed in that battering relationship."

Questions

1. How would you characterize the relationship between Pruitt and the accused?
2. What facts about the appellant, other than the battered women's syndrome, could you see as contributing to a lack of mens rea?
3. Do you feel that battered women's syndrome is a factor that should be considered in this instance? Why or why not?

television and media enslavement, victimization by abuse, provocation, and an endless panoply of syndromes all undermine the specific intent mens rea. Think of the OJ Simpson case. Do the acts offered up at trial, on their own, tell us something about the perpetrator? Was the prosecution effective in typing Simpson as the premeditated killer that the acts seem to impute? Slashing a neck from side to side, counting the dozens of stab wounds, the viciousness of the attack, the stalk and wait, and the overall ferocity of the engagement, paint a picture of an actor operating with specific purpose. These facts do not tell a story of strict passion and spontaneity. However, there is little debate about the emotional qualities surrounding the relationship of the accused and the victim. Nor is there much confusion about Simpson's propensity to engage in violent activity within the domestic setting. The question before the tribunal involves a great deal more than the act itself. The tougher question is whether or not the agent specifically intended the end result of the attack and murder. The call is harder than most think. For, in the Simpson case, many of the traditional qualities associated with first-degree murder, a specific intent crime, are evident, but so too are these same qualities apparent in the second degree or manslaughter case.

In Simpson, we see love and hate, passion and irrationality, provocation and rage, jealousy and envy, race and gender issues, adultery and estrangement in proximity with plot, plan and time for criminal reflection.[22]

On the other hand, the accused followed and stalked the victim and could not plausibly argue spontaneity. In these facts, both the clarity and confusion of specific intent emerge and the crossover characteristics of specific and general intent come to the forefront. Put another way, an accused may be possibly charged under both schema since they may intend some things with specificity while others are more the product of blind rage and blur. Hence, multiple charges of murder and manslaughter are not incongruous inconsistencies, but sensible reflections of complexity of human minds. Amazingly, the human agent can operate with mechanical dispassion while being concurrently enraged and provoked.

Specific intent seeks to target those offenders whose offenses cannot be justified or mitigated on any grounds. Hence, first-degree felonies are reserved for this type of intent as are egregiously indefensible conducts that display gross indifference to protection of self and property.

STORY 3.2

EDMUND KEMPER

Edmund Kemper, born December 18, 1948, had a history of brutality. He mutilated two of the family cats and was caught playing games with his sister portraying death rituals. He was shipped off to his grandparent's farm. He was bored and agitated and made to stay in the house with his grandmother. He killed her with a .22 caliber shotgun, then stabbed her repeatedly with a knife. When his grandfather returned from the field he shot him as well.

The senseless murder of his grandparents earned Kemper the diagnosis of "personality trait disturbance, passive aggressive type" and a commitment to the Atascadero State Hospital for the Criminally Insane. He was released in 1969 against objections of psychiatrists and placed into his mother's custody. Kemper was 21 years of age, 6' 9" and weighed around 300 lbs.

On May 7, 1972, Kemper picked up Mary Ann Pesce and Anita Luchessa. He took them to a secluded area where he stabbed them to death and then took the bodies home to his mother's, where he dissected them, playing with various organs and took Polaroids™. He packed up their remains in plastic bags and buried them in the Santa Cruz mountains, tossing the heads into a deep ravine beside the road. On September 14, he picked up Aiko Koo, suffocated her, and then raped her corpse. He took her home and dissected her. The next morning, he had a monitoring visit by a state psychiatrist. At the end of the visit, he was ruled "no longer a threat to himself or others." It was recommended that his juvenile record be sealed. The entire time Koo's head lay in the trunk of his car. On January 9, 1973, he picked up Cindy Schall. He forced her into his trunk and shot her, had sex with her corpse, dissected her, bagged the remains and tossed them off a cliff into the ocean. By this time, he had been titled "the Coed Killer." His next victims were Rosalind Thorpe and Alice Liu. That Easter, as his mother lay asleep in her bed, he attacked her, repeatedly beating her with a claw hammer. He decapitated her and raped the headless corpse. He removed her larynx and tried to feed it through the garbage disposal because "[i]t seemed appropriate, as much as she had bitched and screamed at me over the years." Next he invited a friend of his mother's over for a surprise dinner. She was clubbed, strangled, and decapitated, then left in his bed. Easter morning he left in his car. When he reached Pueblo, Colorado, and wasn't a national celebrity, he called the Santa Cruz Police Department and confessed to the murders and being the Coed Killer. He waited for the police to pick him up. Edmund Kemper was convicted on eight counts of first-degree murder. When he was asked what he considered to be appropriate punishment for his crimes, he stated "death by torture."

Stripped away from all excuse and explanation, the specifically intending criminal wants the end result, yearns for the harm, and thirsts for victimization.[23]

General Intent

That criminals intend the natural and probable consequences of their acts summarizes the concept of general intent. The law rightfully presumes that conduct is voluntary, that criminal perpetrators are sane, and that free choice prompts human activity. This workhorse-type of intent serves as a bulwark in the criminal justice model and covers just about all criminal conduct in one way or the other. Certain lower-graded felony offenses and most misdemeanors fall under its umbrella. In select jurisdictions, this type of intent rests comfortably even in higher level felonies. The broad designation "general intent" covers conduct that the actors know or should know inflicts unwarranted harm on another. Look at the third-degree rape statute from New York, below.

A person is guilty of rape in the third degree when:

1. He or she engages in sexual intercourse with another person who is incapable of consent by reason of some factor other than being less than seventeen years old;
2. Being twenty-one years old or more, he or she engages in sexual intercourse with another person less than seventeen years old; or
3. He or she engages in sexual intercourse with another person without such person's consent where such lack of consent is by reason of some factor other than incapacity to consent.

Rape in the third degree is a class E felony.[24]

Any system to the contrary would generate an endless series of challenges to personal responsibility. While a defendant may claim he did not specifically intend to kill another, he or she will have few believers if a gun was used in a robbery and death occurred during the commission. One who carries a lethal weapon may not exactingly intend to employ it, but, under general intent principles, can be presumed to have known its potential for actual usage.

From another angle, general intent represents the accused's factual, though not necessarily legal, desires. The bulk of criminals sitting in jail deny culpability under a wide array of theories. Some claim they never intended to do this or that in a legal sense, but admit they did something. Confused? Let's address this critical point. Any criminal can allege he did not intend to embezzle in the first degree, but yet admits some other offense or not admits anything except that he took money, but intended something else. Ponder some typical embezzler justifications. "I was only borrowing the funds." "I am underpaid and deserve more." "My family needed the money and I really did not mean it." "I didn't realize it was embezzlement. I thought it was petty theft." Within this sphere, we see criminals parsing with a skill that makes politicians look infantile. Instead of assault, label the conduct a fight; instead of rape, label the conduct kinky consensual sex; instead of murder, label it a threat gone awry; instead of robbery, label it reclamation. Alternative explanations go on ad infinitum. Justice practitioners soon learn that no criminal ever really admits to anything in either a factual or legal sense because admission breaks down the gamesmanship essential to legal challenges. A defendant can always claim a different intent or desire than that posed by the prosecution, especially since the prosecution has no credible way of proving the actual mens rea of any given defendant. Inside the intellectual province known as mind, defendants can play games like school kids on recess—parsing words, admitting to some but never all of the facts, skipping around hard facts with slippery explanations, and generally mincing responses so that proof of intent can never really be pinned down. Within the rules of criminal culpability, the accused plays to win. Within the concept known as "general intent," the chances of winning are less because the law looks to a free moving agent whose acts bespeak intentionality of some sort. To hold otherwise would be an invitation to universal nonresponsibility.

Strict Liability

To be held strictly liable under a criminal statute is to be adjudged without proving the requisite intent ordinarily witnessed in criminal cases. In fact, strict liability statutes void the intentionality requirement when compared to specific and general intent offenses. Strict liability means that the accused's mental state is irrelevant to guilt or innocence and that the chief evidentiary proof rests in acts and acts alone.[25]

How and why would the legislative process dispense with the usual intellectual requirements discussed thus far? What rationale supports the dispensation? The answer is rather complex. First, certain types of criminality are deemed so urgently in need of restriction that traditional requirements are waived. Possession of weapons and drugs, felony murder deaths, theft of government property, DUI/DWI, domestic/child abuse cases, public welfare/assistance fraud, and tax cases seem to be the popular offenses where mens rea dons a limited or even nonexistent role. These offenses are characterized as so pressing and damaging that acts alone suffice. Consider the tax liability case. Here the taxpayer may not really understand or even appreciate in any sense the fraudulent reporting of income or deductions on a tax return. This ignorance will not negate culpability even though the defendant can claim: "I did not realize or I did not know that was against the law!" What about the teenage youth riding in a car with drugs that he or she personally proclaims a lack of ownership over? Will this claim exonerate? Will a claim of nonpossession of weapons make innocent some or all of the parties in weapons possession cases?

In each of these circumstances, we witness compelling public policy reasons for holding all parties accountable regardless of what the content of mens rea is or was. Granted, it is conceivable that, in a case of possession of drugs or weapons or stolen property, a party's mental state may be as pure as the driven snow. Strict liability holds the party responsible despite reasonable protestations. A few courts have labeled this "implied mens rea."[26] Other case law decisions are unapologetic about the elimination of the mens rea requirement because it serves a larger and more noble good. Welfare fraud is a frequent target of this type of public policy exception to this fundamental element.[27] This mens rea qualification should not be confused with legal concepts like "willful blindness" or "constructive knowledge," which imputes knowledge of criminality to the offender because the defendant knows or should know of the illegality. One cannot be too ignorant and then rely on the protections inherent in mens rea proof, or possess "actual knowledge disguised by pretended ignorance."[28]

Strict liability cares not a lick about what the defendant knows or doesn't and by comparison centers its attention exclusively on the actus reus. Strict liability crimes generally are lumped together under public welfare, necessity, or greater good categories.[29]

Welfare fraud, by way of illustration, continues to be an urgent drain on the taxpayer coffers, so remedial steps to halt this economic bloodletting are justified under the greater common good theory. Other offenses primarily relate to administrative agencies in government since Congress or the states understand the lack of resources to fully protect institutional interests or to fully prosecute those impinging upon agency subject matters. Explained another way, strict liability offenses are necessitated by their sheer magnitude and repetition. If the IRS had to prove intentional fraud in each and every tax case, its collection possibilities and penalty imposition would be a pipedream.

Social problems also drive the strict liability train. DUI/DWI (driving under the influence/driving while intoxicated) prosecutions rarely delve into the mens rea of the accused, choosing instead to emphasize the act of intoxication, that computation in excess of the legal limit. Who can truly prove whether or not the intoxicated offender wanted to be at this level of inebriation upon testing? Who really can discern the mental faculties of the DUI driver above and beyond the will and wish to drink in the first place. Since DUI is a current reform target, and the legislative process has listened intently to the special interest groups that lobby on behalf of DUI victims, the mens rea component loses it punch in this type of litigation. Strict liability squarely gazes on the breathalyzer's readings in excess of .08 and looks askance at the accused's intentionality. Here, the social dynamics of drinking and driving outweigh the jurisprudence of mens rea. One can disagree in good faith with the radical dispensation.[30]

Another approach justifying the growth of the strict liability trend has been the unique quality of the offenses, especially when considering penalties and punishments. For generations, strict liability offenses were considered too small and petty to exact a level of harm on the accused that should cause us to be wary of potential injustice. In *Morrisette v. U.S.*, the Supreme Court recognized this tendency yet expressed reservations:

> This has confronted the courts with a multitude of prosecutions, based on statutes or administrative regulations, for what have been aptly called "public welfare offenses." These cases do not fit neatly into any of such accepted classifications of common law offenses, such as those against the state, the person, property, or public morals. Many of these offenses are not in the nature of positive aggressions or invasions, with which the common law so often dealt, but are in the nature of neglect where the law requires care, or inaction where it imposes duty.[31]

Those uneasy with the practice have every right to challenge the evolving character of these offenses. As if Pandora's Box opened, the past 20 years has scanned the legal horizon for a revolution in this type of offense and got a mini revolt. Who would ever have envisioned a conviction for murder arising from the sale and distribution of street drugs? While the felony murder rule has many nuances that can only be described as strict liability in design, the list of felonies that qualify has not historically included drug sales, only the prime and most egregious of felonies. More is forthcoming on the Felony Murder Rule in the Chapter 4 (Crimes against the Person: Homicide). New Jersey has imposed the strict liability design on deaths resulting from drug sales. Its statute reads in part:

2C:35-9 Strict liability for drug-induced deaths

a. Any person who manufactures, distributes or dispenses methamphetamine, lysergic acid diethylamide, phencyclidine or any other controlled dangerous substance classified in Schedules I or II, or any controlled substance analog thereof, in violation of subsection a. of N.J.S. 2C:35-5, is strictly liable for a death which results from the injection, inhalation or ingestion of that substance, and is guilty of a crime of the first degree.[32]

New Jersey's enactment rests on predictable strict liability grounds citing the scourge of drugs, the compelling public policy bases, and the greater good achieved from such draconian measures. But, are existing laws, already laden with mens rea requisites, insufficient to achieve these goals? Some commentators have called the law "a harsh legislative overreach" and a statute riddled with "causation and mens rea problems, in addition to basic fairness problems."[33] Supporters claim that skimping at due process, while undesirable, pales in comparison to the havoc drugs generate and denies the original agency of the dealer/distributor in the first instance. What folly it is to forget who originated the exchange that caused the demise of the user. How can one be exonerated from a sequence of events that can eventually be traced back to the drug seller? The Supreme Court of Connecticut displayed minimal sympathy for a drug seller whining about how remote his responsibility was in the death of his customer.[34] As harsh as the results may be, it is difficult to deny the chain of events that inexorably wind their way back to the original defendant.

Similar arguments are posed about the brutality and unfairness of loitering and vagrancy laws. When does a person know or identify the state of personal loitering?[35] When does an individual evolve or de-evolve from ordinary citizen to vagrant? Aside from the continuous constitutional attacks based on void for vagueness, over breadth and free speech infringement challenges, these types of laws resist in the mens rea component. For the most part, states have waived or keenly minimized any mental element from these types of prosecutions. Public policy, greater good, and collective security are often touted as the justifiers as is the *de minimis* quality and consequence of these offenses. Let it be said that mens rea requirements are hard to discern in statutes dedicated to the elimination of vagrancy and loitering, one example from Louisiana being:

The following persons are and shall be guilty of vagrancy:

(1) Habitual drunkards; or
(2) Persons who live in houses of ill fame or who habitually associate with prostitutes; or
(3) Able-bodied persons who beg or solicit alms, provided that this article shall not apply to persons soliciting alms for bona fide religious, charitable or eleemosynary organizations with the authorization thereof; or
(4) Habitual gamblers or persons who for the most part maintain themselves by gambling; or
(5) Able-bodied persons without lawful means of support who do not seek employment and take employment when it is available to them; or
(6) Able-bodied persons of the age of majority who obtain their support gratis from persons receiving old age pensions or from persons receiving welfare assistance from the state; or
(7) Persons who loaf the streets habitually or who frequent the streets habitually at late or unusual hours of the night, or who loiter around any public place of assembly, without lawful business or reason to be present; or
(8) Persons found in or near any structure, movable, vessel, or private grounds, without being able to account for their lawful presence therein; or
(9) Prostitutes.

Whoever commits the crime of vagrancy shall be fined not more than two hundred dollars, or imprisoned for not more than six months, or both.[36]

What does it mean to wander? How does one formulate the intent to wander or be somewhere without apparent reason? Aimless meandering would appear to require very little mental sophistication by its inherent nature. It is doubtful that those who look like they are "without lawful means of support who do not seek employment and take employment when it is available to them" really forge mental states that incorporate these broad and imprecise descriptors. In this sense, mens rea is thrown to the wolves. On the other hand, the public intrusion, the annoyance that some individuals cause others by their seeming purposelessness and unwelcome visitations is a bona fide concern to those living in certain areas. Public peace and tranquility cannot be assured in an environment where wanderlust goes perpetually unchecked.

In these and other types of select offenses, the gray and murky world of strict liability finds its home.

MENS REA AND THE DEGREES OF KNOWLEDGE

The imprecision of the mental typologies discussed above has long been a subject of debate in the legal community. Exactly where the lines are drawn between specific and general intent is fuzzy and inarticulate and certainly the legislative attempts to give clarity to these nebulous legal concepts has only been partially successful. What the law seeks is the gradation of offenses according to varying degrees of intentionality—from graver to the more inconsequential—its chief aim is to provide meaningful distinctions in the level of premeditation. Justice demands that those driven by malice and planned malevolence ought to be punished more than the criminally negligent.

In its place, the Model Penal Code (MPC) Committee defines mental culpability in four major categories hoping to achieve the same end. They include:

- Purpose
- Knowledge
- Recklessness
- Negligence

The MPC recognizes, as do the majority of American jurisdictions, that mental clarity can be derived at diverse states of intellectual operations. In "purpose," we discern an agent who intends the end and who has crafted his or her criminal design with a plan in mind to affect it. In "knowledge," we encounter a criminal mover who cognitively understands the nature and dynamic of the conduct chosen and who can intellectually rationalize its operation. In "reckless," we meet those whose minds ravage the countryside before them, knowing that certain types of conduct are bound to injure others, whether it be lack of care for children, firearms in a crowd, drunken rampages, or Russian roulette. In "negligent," we engage those whose errors and mistakes are more substantive than usual, yet still the product of human stupidity and arrogance—the DUI, excessive speeding and dare, neglect supervision for the ill and the infirm, auto infractions leading to injury, and other violations. Herein lies another avenue to differentiating the level of mens rea and the charges that correspondingly fit the fact pattern. Lacking scientific precision, it is at least another valiant attempt to separate the egregious from the regrettable.

Mens Rea with Purpose

At the top of the hierarchy, purposeful and willful conduct symbolizes the truest form of intentionality. Devoid of mitigation, or with scant evidence of it, the purposeful malefactor not only knows, but prepares for the deed. Purpose implies a great deal more than knowledge and includes the premeditative, the calculating, and the plotting character about to engage in criminal conduct. While this contrast may appear petty, the consequence for the person who simply knows and the person who purposely plots and plans are remarkably distinct. In murder cases, who will be the likelier candidate for execution?

Purpose implies full use of the will in conjunction with the mental faculties of the agent. Criminals, each and every day, know and appreciate the wrongfulness of their conduct, but engage in it spontaneously, without much reflection. The purposeful perpetrator knows full well what is about to unfold and wills in advance the prohibited deed. The MPC curiously divides up purposefulness as dealing with two facets of the crime: first, the intent to commit the crime element by element, and second, the intent to cause a specific end result to the crime's victim. The MPC remarks:

A person acts purposely with respect to a material element of an offense when:

(i) if the element involves the nature of his conduct or a result thereof, it is his conscious object to engage in conduct of that nature or to cause such a result; and

(ii) if the element involves the attendant circumstances, he is aware of the existence of such circumstances or he believes or hopes that they exist.[37]

Therefore, the willful or purposeful criminal has all his or her ducks lined up for the ultimate kill. "'Willfully,' the most stringent standard, implies either a full understanding of both the law and the facts or an understanding of egregious facts that indicate the defendant knew she was doing something wrong."[38]

For the most part, prosecution teams reserve this degree of intentionality for the premeditated class of crimes. The "knowing" category subsumes most of the remaining felonies.

Mens Rea with Knowledge

Central to American jurisprudence is the insistence that responsibility lies with those who know and understand the scope and extent of behavior. Criminal defenses based on insanity, incompetence and incapacity, duress, coercion, and physical infirmity negate or mitigate the assertion that the defendant knew and appreciated the wrongfulness of the chosen conduct. Knowledge denotes awareness and understanding—an essential prerequisite to free choice and will. Only a freely moving being can live in a world of comprehension because choice implies understanding.

To know is to understand the nature of the conduct that leads to criminal liability. To know is to possess a full and complete understanding that a course of action chosen will violate some law. To know is to comprehend the chosen conduct even if unsure about subsequent findings of illegality. From these perspectives, knowledge provides the catalyst for conduct engaged in. Intentional conduct depends upon a deposit of knowledge. What that deposit exactly is has been the subject of fierce debate.[39] Select jurisdictions rest the knowledge requirement in the understanding of the conduct chosen irrespective of statutory awareness.[40] Others have determined that the proof of the accused's knowledge, awareness, and understanding of the statute violated should be proved. In certain jurisdictions, the prosecution's burden resides in both categories.[41]

The MPC offers up a valiant effort to accommodate these aligned positions:

A person acts knowingly with respect to a material element of an offense when:

(i) if the element involves the nature of his conduct or the attendant circumstances, he is aware that his conduct is of that nature or that such circumstances exist; and

(ii) if the element involves a result of his conduct, he is aware that it is practically certain that his conduct will cause such a result.[42]

Courts stumble often in this thicket of word and phrase, especially when trying to decipher at what phase of the criminal action a person knows anything. Appellate courts frequently grapple with 1st Amendment cases involving pornography to determine whether the material is legal as it relates to obscenity statutes, but also whether the owner, disseminator, producer, or supplier knows about its content in any meaningful sense.[43] Review the case below and analyze the questions that follow.

CASE 3.5

U.S. V. X-CITEMENT VIDEO
513 U.S. 64; 115 S. Ct. 464; 130 L. Ed. 2d 372 (1994)

The Protection of Children Against Sexual Exploitation Act of 1977, as amended, prohibits the interstate transportation, shipping, receipt, distribution, or reproduction of visual depictions of minors engaged in sexually explicit conduct. 18 U.S.C. § 2252. The Court of Appeals for the Ninth Circuit reversed the conviction of respondents for violation of this Act. It held that the Act did not require that the defendant know that one of the performers was a minor, and that it was, therefore, facially unconstitutional. We conclude that the Act is properly read to include such a requirement.

Rubin Gottesman owned and operated X-Citement Video, Inc. Undercover police posed as pornography retailers and targeted X-Citement Video for investigation. During the course of the sting operation, the media exposed Traci Lords for her roles in pornographic films while under the age of 18. Police Officer Steven Takeshita expressed an interest in obtaining Traci Lords tapes. Gottesman complied, selling Takeshita 49 videotapes featuring Lords before her 18th birthday. Two months later, Gottesman shipped eight tapes of the underage Traci Lords to Takeshita in Hawaii.

These two transactions formed the basis for a federal indictment under the child pornography statute. The indictment charged respondents with one count each of violating 18 U.S.C. §§ 2252 (a)(1) and (a)(2), along with one count of conspiracy to do the same under 18 U.S.C. § 371.

Evidence at trial suggested that Gottesman had full awareness of Lords' underage performances. ... The District Court convicted respondents of all three counts. The court first held that 18 U.S.C. § 2256 met constitutional standards in setting the age of minority at age 18, substituting lascivious for lewd, and prohibiting actual or simulated bestiality and sadistic or masochistic abuse. It then discussed § 2252, noting it was bound by its conclusion in Thomas to construe the Act as lacking a scienter requirement for the age of minority. The Court concluded that case law from this Court required that the defendant must have knowledge at least of the nature and character of the materials. The Court extended these cases to hold that the First Amendment requires that the defendant possess knowledge of the particular fact that one performer had not reached the age of majority at the time the visual depiction was produced. Because the court found the statute did not require such a showing, it reversed respondents' convictions. We granted certiorari, and now reverse.

Title 18 U.S.C. § 2252 (1988 ed. and Supp. V) provides, in relevant part:

(a) Any person who —
    (1) knowingly transports or ships in interstate or foreign commerce by any means including by computer or mails, any visual depiction, if —
        (A) the producing of such visual depiction involves the use of a minor engaging in sexually explicit conduct; and
        (B) such visual depiction is of such conduct;

(2)   knowingly receives, or distributes, any visual depiction that has been mailed, or has been shipped or transported in interstate or foreign commerce, or which contains materials which have been mailed or so shipped or transported, by any means including by computer, or knowingly reproduces any visual depiction for distribution in interstate or foreign commerce or through the mails, if —

(A)   the producing of such visual depiction involves the use of a minor engaging in sexually explicit conduct; and

(B)   such visual depiction is of such conduct; ...

shall be punished as provided in subsection (b) of this section.

The critical determination that we must make is whether the term "knowingly" in subsections (1) and (2) modifies the phrase "the use of a minor" in subsections (1)(A) and (2)(A).The most natural grammatical reading, adopted by the Ninth Circuit, suggests that the term "knowingly" modifies only the surrounding verbs: transports, ships, receives, distributes, or reproduces. Under this construction, the word "knowingly" would not modify the elements of the minority of the performers or the sexually explicit nature of the material because they are set forth in independent clauses separated by interruptive punctuation. But, we do not think this is the end of the matter, both because of anomalies that result from this construction, and because of the respective presumptions that some form of scienter is to be implied in a criminal statute even if not expressed, and that a statute is to be construed where fairly possible so as to avoid substantial constitutional questions.

If the term "knowingly" applies only to the relevant verbs in § 2252— transporting, shipping, receiving, distributing, and reproducing—we would have to conclude that Congress wished to distinguish between someone who knowingly transported a particular package of film whose contents were unknown to him, and someone who unknowingly transported that package. It would seem odd, to say the least, that Congress distinguished between someone who inadvertently dropped an item into the mail without realizing it, and someone who consciously placed the same item in the mail, but was nonetheless unconcerned about whether the person had any knowledge of the prohibited contents of the package.

Some applications of respondents' position would produce results that were not merely odd, but positively absurd. If we were to conclude that "knowingly" only modifies the relevant verbs in § 2252, we would sweep within the ambit of the statute actors who had no idea that they were even dealing with sexually explicit material. For instance, a retail druggist who returns an uninspected roll of developed film to a customer "knowingly distributes" a visual depiction and would be criminally liable if it were later discovered that the visual depiction contained images of children engaged in sexually explicit conduct. Or, a new resident of an apartment might receive mail for the prior resident and store the mail unopened. If the prior tenant had requested delivery of materials covered by § 2252, his residential successor could be prosecuted for "knowing receipt" of such materials. Similarly, a Federal Express courier who delivers a box in which the shipper has declared the contents to be "film" "knowingly transports" such film. We do not assume that Congress, in passing laws, intended such results.

Our reluctance to simply follow the most grammatical reading of the statute is heightened by our cases interpreting criminal statutes to include broadly applicable scienter requirements, even where the statute by its terms does not contain them.

Questions

1. What term exactly describes the actus reus in this case?
2. What does the criminal agent have to know?
3. Does the decision require actual knowledge of pornographic content?
4. Would a literal, textual reading of the statute call for awareness of content?
5. How does Justice Antonin Scalia resolve the issue in the dissent?

Drug paraphernalia cases often are defended on knowledge grounds because many of the items classified as paraphernalia have alternative uses. Storeowners selling cigarette papers or shops selling what appears to be a normal pipe can be caught, rightly or wrongly, in the web of implied knowledge derived from the possession alone. What type of knowledge would be required under this act?

21 USC § 863. Drug paraphernalia

(a) In general

It is unlawful for any person—

(1) to sell or offer for sale drug paraphernalia;

(2) to use the mails or any other facility of interstate commerce to transport drug paraphernalia; or

(3) to import or export drug paraphernalia.

(b) Penalties

Anyone convicted of an offense under subsection (a) of this section shall be imprisoned for not more than three years and fined under title 18.

...

(d) "Drug paraphernalia" defined

... It includes items primarily intended or designed for use in ingesting, inhaling, or otherwise introducing marijuana, cocaine, hashish, hashish oil, PCP, methamphetamine, or amphetamines into the human body, such as—

(1) metal, wooden, acrylic, glass, stone, plastic, or ceramic pipes with or without screens, permanent screens, hashish heads, or punctured metal bowls;

(2) water pipes;

(3) carburetion tubes and devices;

(4) smoking and carburetion masks;

(5) roach clips: meaning objects used to hold burning material, such as a marihuana cigarette, that has become too small or too short to be held in the hand;

(6) miniature spoons with level capacities of one-tenth cubic centimeter or less;

(7) chamber pipes;

(8) carburetor pipes;

  (9)   electric pipes;

(10) air-driven pipes;

(11) chillums;

(12) bongs;

(13) ice pipes or chillers;

(14) wired cigarette papers; or

(15) cocaine freebase kits.

(e) Matters considered in determination of what constitutes drug paraphernalia

In determining whether an item constitutes drug paraphernalia, in addition to all other logically relevant factors, the following may be considered:

(1) instructions, oral or written, provided with the item concerning its use;

(2) descriptive materials accompanying the item which explain or depict its use;

(3) national and local advertising concerning its use;

(4) the manner in which the item is displayed for sale;

(5) whether the owner, or anyone in control of the item, is a legitimate supplier of like or related items to the community, such as a licensed distributor or dealer of tobacco products;

(6) direct or circumstantial evidence of the ratio of sales of the item(s) to the total sales of the business enterprise;

(7) the existence and scope of legitimate uses of the item in the community; and

(8) expert testimony concerning its use.[44]

Does the language of this federal prohibition require the seller know the drug-related purposes behind the sale? Can a storeowner claim ignorance when products put into commerce are generally known to be used for these express purposes? In *Posters n Things, Ltd v. U.S.*,[45] the Supreme Court concluded that:

> [T]he Government must establish that the defendant knew that the items at issue are likely to be used with illegal drugs, it need not prove specific knowledge that the items are "drug paraphernalia" within the meaning of the statute.[46]

Does the Court really lay out a sufficient standard to deal with the knowledge issue? The danger in mandating too much knowledge will lead any polished defense counsel to assuredly employ the defense of ignorance and mistake of fact. If ignorance of all or any portion of a law became a vital defense in a criminal action, guess what would happen to the collective IQ of the prison population. If the accused only need show a lack of knowledge of some facet or aspect of the case at hand, prosecutions would invariably fail. As the U.S. Supreme Court noted in its well-reasoned Staples decision:

> The mens rea presumption requires knowledge only of the facts that make the defendant's conduct illegal, lest it conflict with the related presumption, "deeply rooted in the American legal system," that, ordinarily, "ignorance of the law or mistake of law is no defense to criminal prosecution."[47]

In the final analysis, all the justice system can hope to produce is what a reasonable person is likely to know. Courts are not hesitant to impute knowledge that is common, or to realize that most people are aware of the world around them and the conducts chosen to be engaged in. To know imputes understanding of action. To be aware makes one responsible. Though exactly what one must know and how much of it need be comprehended will be the subject of erudite law reviews for generations to come.

Mens Rea with Recklessness

Slightly lower in intellectual hierarchy is the mens rea based on recklessness. Reckless conduct differs markedly from purposeful and premeditated planning and is usually a reflection of crazed, erratic, and highly irresponsible behavior. It is not the stuff of mistake and accident, but more gross indifference to consequence along with a high level of carelessness that can cause extraordinary harm to others. At the reckless stage, the accused thinks less cogently about conduct chosen and the effects sought. In fact, the reckless person displays minimal cognitive process yet wreaks extraordinary injury to both community and commonwealth. Even so, the accused understands the escalating possibility of harm to others, or as Evangelista labels it, the "contingency" of harm that emanates from recklessness.[48]

Recklessness is conscious and intentional risk creation and it usually involves a gross deviation from the usual course of conduct expected of the human player. Examples might be shooting a weapon into a crowd, starting fires, dangerous pranks, or sale of questionable drugs.

Farther down the intentionality continuum, recklessness manifests a general indifference to others and an acute absence of care for the safety and welfare of neighbors.[49]

The MPC defines reckless intentionality as:

> A person acts recklessly with respect to a material element of an offense when he consciously disregards a substantial and unjustifiable risk that the material element exists or will result from his conduct. The risk must be of such a nature and degree that, considering the nature and purpose of the actor's conduct and the circumstances known to him, its disregard involves a gross deviation from the standard of conduct that a law-abiding person would observe in the actor's situation.[50]

The MPC dissects recklessness into various parts, none more persuasive than its requirement for a "high degree" of potential injury or harm. In this sense, recklessness does not involve juvenile pranks and trivial accidents, but an intense, more chaotic actor who lives on the edge of danger to others. This cutting distinction should be remembered as we move to the last category of mens rea: negligence.

For an excellent overview of recklessness and negligence in the formation of criminal intent, visit CALI at http://www.cali.org/lesson/467

Mens Rea and Negligence

Negligence for the most part belongs in the civil realm where its definition of breach of due care owed others is longstanding. To be negligent, one owes another a duty, and that same duty must be breached, which causes damages to an injured party. Doctors, for example, owe patients due care during the relationship as would an attorney to client. Civil remedies often sit closely by the world of crimes and have slowly but surely seen integration into the criminal law model.[51] Columbia University of Law Professor John Coffee, Jr. argues that the tort/crime distinction continues its onward march toward merger. He states:

CASE 3.6

KENTUCKY V. MITCHELL

98-CA-1546-MR (Ken. /Sup. 2001)

On the evening of November 30, 1995, Corey Mitchell, his wife, and three children began a drive to a friend's house in the family automobile. The oldest child sat unrestrained in the front seat between her parents. The twins, Mackenzie and Demi, rode in the back seat in baby seats, which were not buckled and were not fastened to the automobile seat. A collision occurred when the father, Corey Mitchell, failed to yield the right of way to an oncoming pickup truck. The father and one of his infant daughters, Mackenzie, were thrown from the automobile as a result of the impact. Both were injured and Mackenzie eventually died from her injuries. More than nine months after the tragic incident, the Commonwealth obtained an indictment for second-degree manslaughter from the grand jury. The father was convicted of reckless homicide by a trial jury and was sentenced to one year imprisonment, which was probated by the trial judge for three years.

The Court of Appeals reversed the conviction in a 2 to 1 decision. The majority held that the failure to secure a child to a child seat and to secure the child seat to the automobile seat was a violation of KRS 189.125, but that because the violation of the statute could not create tort negligence, it therefore could not possibly constitute recklessness under a criminal statute. The Court of Appeals opinion also found that the failure to secure Mackenzie to the child restraints could in no way be the immediate or direct cause of her death. This Court accepted discretionary review. The crucial issue is whether there was sufficient evidence to support a finding of guilt on the charge of reckless homicide. A person is guilty of reckless homicide when, with recklessness, he causes the death of another person. KRS 507.050. KRS 501.020(4) states in pertinent part:

> A person acts recklessly with respect to a result or to a circumstance described by a statute defining an offense when he fails to perceive a substantial and unjustifiable risk that the result will occur or that the circumstance exists. The risk must be of such a nature and degree that failure to perceive it constitutes a gross deviation from the standard of care that a reasonable person would observe in the situation.

A divided Court of Appeals panel reversed the conviction on the basis that the trial judge should have granted a directed verdict of acquittal because a violation of KRS 189.125, the Kentucky Seatbelt Statute does not provide the mental state necessary for a reckless homicide conviction. We agree. KRS 189.125 provides as follows:

(3) Any driver of a motor vehicle, when transporting a child of 40 inches in height or less in a motor vehicle operated on the roadways, streets, and highways of this state, shall have the child properly secured in a child restraint system of a type meeting the federal motor vehicle safety standards ...

(5) Failure to wear a child passenger restraint shall not be considered as contributory negligence, nor shall such failure to wear said passenger restraint system be admissible in the trial of any civil action. Failure of any person to wear a seat belt shall not constitute negligence per se.

KRS 189.990(24) provides a penalty of a $50 fine for the failure to comply with the seatbelt statute. The legislature did not intend to elevate a violation of this statute to the Class D felony status of reckless homicide. *Baker v. Commonwealth* holds that statutes which create criminal offenses should do so in express terms, and criminal liability should not rest upon implication or inference as to what the General Assembly intended but did not expressly state. There is no indication that the legislature intended any additional penalty in this regard. In *Lofthouse v. Commonwealth,* a majority of this Court determined that evidence that a defendant should have been aware of a substantial risk that the victim would die from ingesting cocaine and heroin was insufficient to support a conviction of reckless homicide for providing those drugs. Here, the Commonwealth presented no evidence to support its position that the conduct of the father was reckless other than the failure to secure the infant in a proper child restraint system. This conduct, standing alone, without any other evidence of recklessness is not sufficient to constitute the standard of recklessness required by KRS 507.050, which is a gross deviation from the standard of care that a reasonable person would observe in the situation.

The Court of Appeals reasoned that if the legislature recognized that failure to restrain did not constitute civil negligence per se, then the violation could not satisfy the gross deviation requirement of recklessness. This is a reasonable rationale in this case and should not be interpreted as a bar to criminal prosecution in general. Here, the evidence was insufficient to support a conviction for reckless homicide. The decision of the court of appeals is affirmed.

Questions

1. Do the facts of the case prove Cory Mitchell to be in violation of KRS 501.020(4)? Why or why not?
2. Do you feel that the two statutes in question, KRS 501.020(4) and KRS 189.125, are at odds with one another? Why do you think the legislature enacted KRS 189.125?
3. Do you think a reasonable person believes there is a "substantial risk" in not properly securing an infant in a car seat?

The upshot of these trends is that the criminal law seems much closer to being used interchangeably with civil remedies. Sometimes, identically phrased statutes are applicable to the same conduct— one authorizing civil penalties, the other authorizing criminal sanctions. More often, the criminal law is extended to reach behavior previously thought only civilly actionable. Either way, this practice of defining the criminal law to reach all civil law violations in a particular field of law in order to gain additional deterrence may distort the underlying legal standard.[52]

Because crimes and tortious causes of action like negligence serve differing yet similar purposes, we must be mindful to maintain the integrity of both remedies and avoid the dilution of a crime's severity while resisting the criminalization of once purely private harms. In this litigation crazy age, with aggrieved parties trekking toward courthouses for remediation of every harm, the temptation may be a bit too strong.[53] In the criminal sphere, negligence fence sits. On the one hand, the issues of duty and respective duty still are bandied about, while on the other, the term negligence is measured on a broader spectrum. Negligence in criminal court represents the grossest variety. Not only are mistakes made, the faulty conduct is exceptionally grave and causes harsh results. Drunken drivers may never intend to kill others, but they do. Under purposeful, knowing, and reckless constructions, the mental state of the typical drunk driver will not count. No one who speeds excessively sets out to kill people during the journey. Heroin addicts whose children are born with heroin addiction do not specifically intend to transmit this condition to their offspring.[54] Ironically, attempts to criminalize the abuse of a fetus run smack against the abortion rights mantra that the fetus is not a human being.[55] In each of these scenarios, the mental intent can only be proved inferentially, and even then, it is not a very convincing story. These case examples fit neatly into the negligence domain whereby criminal liability attaches to those who fail in some way, who breach in their responsibility or leadership role who engage in conduct that could only be termed dumb and inexcusable. Overall, the chief rationale for applying negligence principles to criminal action, has yet to be fully analyzed or assessed for efficacy since its primary aim is deterrence.[56] In sum, the negligent criminals are the ones with the least convincing case of mens rea and those teetering on the edge of civil harm.

The MPC understands that human error can translate into more than mistake and tort and will climb the next step into the domain of crime when the actor should have known, could have known, should have realized and contemplated that certain risks were associated with behavior. The MPC cogently defines the essence of the criminally negligent mental state at § 2.02 as:

> The risk must be of such a nature and degree that the actor's failure to perceive it, considering the nature and purpose of his conduct and the circumstances known to him, involves a gross deviation from the standard of care that a reasonable person would observe in the actor's situation.[57]

It is failure to predict the ensuing harm that contrasts negligence from recklessness. The reckless offender confidently aggrieves others knowing only a portion of the harm soon to be caused or appreciating only some aspect of the story to unfold, while the negligent offender cannot even envision, in a mental sense, what will soon occur. Unlike the other three forms of mens rea discussed, negligence is aptly described as a state of unawareness when the actor should be bright-eyed and bushytailed. The punishment for this lack of awareness hopes to foster a vigilant citizenry that will know better before engaging in the type of carelessness that the law seeks to avoid.[58] In hindsight, drunken drivers always know the foolishness of their chosen path, but when people die as a result, the actor's failure to perceive the risk and the associated harm can result in criminal judgment.

Find out about Drug Driving and weigh whether these traditional negligence standards should apply at http://www.drugabuse.gov/PDF/Infofacts/driving09.pdf

---

DISCUSSION QUESTIONS

1. Explain how a DUI/DWI case could be characterized "strict liability."
2. What impact does mitigation have upon charge selection in the prosecutor's office?
3. Compare and contrast the idea of mitigation with criminal defense?

4. Explain how the definition of a crime is a combination of act and mind?
5. Is it possible to be guilty of any criminal offense by merely thinking rather than doing?
6. Which of the "intent" levels is the most difficult to prove?
7. Which of the "intent" levels is the most difficult to defend?
8. Describe how omission constitutes actus reus?
9. What types of offenses constitute the intent of recklessness?
10. Compare and contrast the mental intent of "purposeful" and "knowing."

SUGGESTED READING

Douglas, J. and M. Olshaker. 1999. *The anatomy of motive.* New York: Scribner.

Katz, L. 1987. *Bad acts and guilty minds: Conundrums of the criminal law.* Chicago: University of Chicago Press.

Duff, R. A., L. L. Farmer, S. E. Marshall, M. M. Renzo, and V. V. Tadros. 2011. *The boundaries of the criminal law.* (Criminalization Series). New York: Oxford University Press.

Lagier, D. G. 2010. *The paradoxes of action: (Human action, law and philosophy).* (Law and Philosophy Library). New York: Springer Publishing Company.

Moore, M. S. 2010. *Placing blame: A theory of the criminal law.* New York: Oxford University Press.

Rhodes, R. 1999. *Why they kill: The discoveries of a maverick criminologist.* New York: Alfred A. Knopf.

Robinson, P. H. 2008. *Criminal law: Case studies and controversies,* 2nd ed. New York: Aspen Publishers, Inc.

Samenow, S. E. 1984. *Inside the criminal mind.* New York: Times Books.

Taylor, L. 1984. *Born to crime: The genetic causes of criminal behavior.* Westport, CT: Greenwood Press.

Yaffe, G. 2011. *Attempts: Trying and attempted crimes.* New York: Oxford University Press.

Zilboorg, G. 1968. *The psychology of the criminal act and punishment.* New York: Greenwood Press.

ENDNOTES

1. Jonathan L. Hood, Comment: What is Reasonable Cause to Believe? The Mens Rea Required for Conviction Under 21 U.S.C. Section 841, 30 PACE L. REV. 1360, 1364, 1365 (2010).
2. *Id.*
3. For an interesting discussion of how our EU friends weigh and interpret mens rea, see Johan D. Van Der Vyver, *Prosecutor v. Jean-Pierre Bemba Gombo*: International Criminal Court Pre-Trial Decision on Burdens of Proof in Prosecution Under the I.C.C. Statute, 106 *A. J. I. L.* 241 (2010).
4. MODEL PENAL CODE § 2.01 (Proposed Official Draft 1963).
5. A person's state of character, coupled with a mens rea seems to be influential in eventual sentencing. *See* Kenneth W. Simons, Does Punishment for Culpable Indifference Simply Punish for Bad Character—Examining the Requisite Connection between Mens Rea and Actus Reus, 6 BUFF. CRIM. L. REV. 219 (2002–2003).
6. 5 Matthew 27–29.
7. MODEL PENAL CODE § 2.01 at 2 (Proposed Official Draft 1963).
8. *Id.*
9. *See* SUMM. PA. JUR. §1:6 at 7.
10. MODEL PENAL CODE § 2.01(3) (Proposed Official Draft 1955).
11. Steven Powles, Joint Criminal Enterprise: Criminal Liability By Prosecutorial Ingenuity and Judicial Creativity?, 2 J. INT. CRIM. JUST. 606-619 (2004).
12. SUMM. PA. JUR. § 5:9 at 84.
13. When judging the mind of a genocidal defendant, the Court must interpret more than the objective in proving mens rea. *See* Johan D. Van Der Vyver, *International Criminal Law: Genocide—Mens Reas—Standards of Proof—Superior Responsibility,* 104 A. J. I. L. 461 (2010).
14. MODEL PENAL CODE § 2.02 (1) (Proposed Official Draft 1955).

15. DEL. CODE ANN. tit. 11, § 231 (2010).

16. MO. REV. STAT. § 562.016 (2010).

17. KÄREN M. HESS, CHRISTINE HESS ORTHMANN, INTRODUCTION TO LAW ENFORCEMENT AND CRIMINAL JUSTICE 54 (2008).

18. FBI BEHAVIORAL ANALYSIS UNIT, SERIAL MURDER: MULTI-DISCIPLINARY PERSPECTIVES FOR INVESTIGATORS (2008) at http://www.fbi.gov/news/stories/2008/july/serialmurder_070708 (accessed August 3, 2011); *see also* James L. Knoll & Robert R. Hazelwood, *Becoming the Victim: Beyond Sadism in Serial Sexual Murderers*, AGGRESSION AND VIOLENT BEHAVIOR: A REVIEW JOURNAL, March/April 2009, at 106–114.

19. Dannye Holley, *Mens Rea Evaluations by the United States Supreme Court: It Does Not Have the Tools and Only Occasionally Displays the Talent: A Sixty Year Report: 1950-2009*, 35 OKLA. CITY U. L. REV. 401 (2010).

20. *Id.* at 406.

21. *Id.* at 420; *see also Cunningham v. California*, 127 S.Ct. 856 (2007).

22. Andrew G. Hodges, *Suicidal Threats: Reading between the Lines of O.J. Simpson's Suicide Note*, in SUICIDE AND LAW ENFORCEMENT, 315-325 (Donald C. Sheehan & Janet I. Warren eds., 2001).

23. Jeremy Wright & Christopher Hensley, *From Animal Cruelty to Serial Murder: Applying the Graduation Hypothesis*, INT'L J. OFFENDER THERAPY & COMP. CRIMINOLOGY, Feb. 2003, at 71–88.

24. N.Y. PENAL LAW § 130.25 (McKinney 2010).

25. The oft quoted *Morrisette v. U.S.* decision, 342 U.S. 246 (1952), represents the U.S. Supreme Court's most significant contribution to the area of strict liability. Here the accused picked up used shell casings on government lands not realizing the illegality of the taking. Unconvinced was the Court about how pressing these takings were on the national psyche that it wrote: "The Government asks us by a feat of construction radically to change the weights and balances in the scales of justice. The purpose and obvious effect of doing away with the requirement of a guilty intent is to ease the prosecution's path to conviction, to strip the defendant of such benefit as he derived at common law from innocence of evil purpose, and to circumscribe the freedom heretofore allowed juries. Such a manifest impairment of the immunities of the individual should not be extended to common-law crimes on judicial initiative." (*Morrissette*, 342 U.S. at 263).

26. *See Staples v. U.S.*, 511 U.S. 600 (1994).

27. In Dotterweich the Court held: "A public welfare offense dispenses with the conventional requirement for criminal conduct—awareness of some wrongdoing. In the interest of the larger good, it puts the burden of acting at hazard upon a person otherwise innocent, but standing in responsible relation to a public danger." *U.S. v. Dotterweich*, 320 U.S. 277, 281 (1943). *See also U.S. v. Freed*, 401 U.S. 601 (1971); *U.S. v. Balint*, 258 U.S. 250 (1922).

28. Jonathan L. Marcus, *Model Penal Code section 2.02(7) and Willful Blindness*, 102 YALE L.J. 2231, 2232 (1993).

29. Paul R. Bonney, *Manufacturers' Strict Liability for Handgun Injuries: An Economic Analysis*, 73 GEO. L.J. 1437 (1984-1985).

30. Strict Liability has also been used to tie higher levels of criminality when firearms are employed. *See* VIOLENCE POLICY CENTER, ENDGAME: ANY SETTLEMENT OF FIREARMS LITIGATION MUST ADDRESS THREE SPECIFIC AREAS OF GUN INDUSTRY CONDUCT AND INCLUDE A STRICT ENFORCEMENT MECHANISM, NCJ 183196 (1999), available at http://www.vpc.org/studies/endcont.htm (accessed August 3, 2011).

31. *Morrissette v. U.S.*, 342 U.S. 246 (1952).

32. N.J. STAT. ANN. § 2C:35-9 (West 1995); *see also* FLA. STAT. §782.04 (2010); MINN. STAT. § 609.195 (1987).

33. Blair Talty, *New Jersey's Strict Liability for Drug-Induced Death: The Leap from Drug Dealer to Murder*, 30 RUTGERS L.J. 513, 537 (1999).

34. The Court held a dealer strictly liable since the Court "found the statute valid under the due process clauses of both the federal and state constitutions with regard to the effect of a drug dealers' lack of mens rea in this type of situation. The New Jersey Supreme Court also concluded that application of the statute in question did not constitute cruel and unusual punishment. Finally, the court found that the language of the statute was not vague or ambiguous." *Id.* at 518–19. *See State v. Maldonado*, 645 A.2d 1165 (N.J. 1994); N.J. STAT. ANN. § 2C:35-9 (West 2010).

35. *See* Harry Simon, *The Criminalization of Homelessness in Santa Ana, California: A Case Study*, 29 Clearinghouse Rev. 725 (1995).
36. La. Rev. Stat. Ann. *§14:107 (2010)*.
37. Model Penal Code, § 2.02 at 2 (Proposed Official Draft 1955).
38. Katherine R. Tromble, *Humpty Dumpty on Mens Rea Standards: A Proposed Methodology for Interpretation*, 52 Vand. L. Rev. 521, 522 (1999).
39. *See Posters n Things, Ltd. v. U.S.*, 511 U.S. 513, 524 (1994) (holding that a defendant must know that the items sold are likely to be used with illegal drugs, but not that the items are "drug paraphernalia" within the meaning of the statute); *Babbitt v. Sweet Home Chapter of Communities for a Greater Oregon*, 515 U.S. 687, 696 n. 9 (1995) (discussing the significance of Congress's changing the mens rea requirement from "willfully" to "knowingly" in 1978 in order to make a violation of the Endangered Species Act a general intent crime); *Moskal v. U.S.*, 498 U.S. 103, 108 (1990) (requiring only that the defendant knows he altered a car title to be convicted).
40. *See Note: Mens Rea in Federal Criminal Law*, 111 Harv. L. Rev. 2402 (1998).
41. For a thorough review of these conflicting views, *see* Tromble, *supra* note 38.
42. Model Penal Code, § 2.02 (Proposed Official Draft 1955).
43. *Staples v. U.S.*, 511 U.S. 600 (1994).
44. 21 U.S.C. § 863 (2010).
45. *Posters n Things, Ltd v. U.S.*, 511 U.S. 513 (1994).
46. *Id.* at 524.
47. *Staples*, at 622 n.3. For an interesting discourse on how courts ferret out the feigned or connived ignorance from the real, *see* Marcus, *supra* note 28.
48. *See* 2 Robert Evangelista, Pennsylvania Trial Guide Supp. §22.22 (1994).
49. *See Id.*
50. Model Penal Code § 2.02 (2)(c) (Proposed Official Draft 1955).
51. *See* John C. Coffee, Jr., *Does "Unlawful" mean "Criminal"?: Reflections on the Disappearing Tort/Crime Distinction in American Law*, 71 B.U. L. Rev. 193 (1991).
52. *Id.* at 198.
53. For a compelling analysis on how a civil malpractice case, coupled with a surgeon's desire to kill a patient, should be eligible for both remedies, *see* G.R. Sullivan, *Bad Thoughts and Bad Acts*, 1990 Crim. L. Rev. 559 (1990).
54. The dramatic rise of cocaine babies has prompted state legislatures to enact laws that criminalize once civil sanctions for neglect of children. *See* Shona B. Glink, *The Prosecution of Maternal Fetal Abuse: Is this the Answer?* 1991 U. Ill. L. Rev. 533 (1991); Fla. Stat. § 39.823 (2010); 705 Ill. Comp. Stat. 405/2-3 (2010); Minn. Stat. §§ 145.88, 145.882 (2010).
55. *See People v. Stewart* (San Diego County Ct. Feb. 23, 1987); *Reyes v. Superior Court*, 75 Cal. App. 3d 214, 141 Cal. Rptr. 912 (1977).
56. Paul H. Robinson & John M. Darley, *The Role of Deterrence in the Formulation of Criminal Law Rules: At Its Worst When Doing Its Best*, 91 Geo. L.J. 949 (2003).
57. Model Penal Code § 2.02(2) (d) (Proposed Official Draft 1955).
58. *See* Summ. Pa. Jur. 2d §5:7.

Chapter 4

Crimes against the Person: Homicide

KEYWORDS

Abortion: The termination of a pregnancy after, accompanied by, or closely followed by the death of the embryo or fetus; the medical procedure of inducing expulsion of a human fetus to terminate a pregnancy.

Aggravating circumstance: A circumstance relating to the commission of an act that increases the degree of liability or culpability.

Criminal homicide: Homicide committed by a person with a criminal state of mind.

Felony murder: A murder that occurs in the commission of a serious felony, such as burglary or sexual battery.

Flagrante delicto: In the very act of committing a misdeed; in the midst of sexual activity.

Malice: The intention or desire to cause harm to another through an unlawful or wrongful act without justification or excuse.

Malice aforethought: Actual or implied malice existing in or attributed to the intention of one that injures or kills without justification or excuse and usually requiring some degree of deliberation or premeditation or wanton disregard for life.

Manslaughter: The unlawful killing of a human being without malice.

Mitigating circumstance: A circumstance in the commission of an act that lessens the degree of criminal culpability.

Murder: To kill a human being unlawfully and under circumstances constituting murder.

Negligent homicide: Homicide caused by a person's criminally negligent act.

Premeditation: Consideration or planning of an act beforehand.

Proximate cause: A cause that sets in motion a sequence of events uninterrupted by any superseding causes and that results in a foreseeable effect that would not otherwise have occurred.

Suicide: The voluntary and intentional killing of one's self; suicide was a felony at common law, but modern statutory law is not unanimous in classifying it as a crime.

Vehicular homicide: Homicide committed by the use of a vehicle.

INTRODUCTION: THE NATURE OF HOMICIDE

The commission of murder represents the gravest act in the world of criminal law. Murder is the terminal criminal act because of its irreversibility, its depraved effect on individuals, families, and communities, and its immoral control over another's destiny. The justice system is driven to action because of the repulsive deed, its universal condemnation, and the need to secure communities.[1] Our punishment system lays out the harshest retaliation and leaves open the possibility of the imposition of the death penalty in select jurisdictions.

Under the broad rubric of "homicide," the legislative design lays out acceptable and unacceptable conduct and distinguishes the act of murder by various categories of seriousness and gravity and defines the parameters of self-defense and the reasonableness of force itself. Homicide need not be a criminal act and, in some cases, is lawful and appropriate.

JUSTIFIABLE HOMICIDE

- When a police officer returns fire on a fleeing criminal with death resulting, the homicide is justifiable.
- When a soldier kills an oncoming enemy, according to the rules of engagement, homicide occurs, but the act is noncriminal.
- When a fire, triggered by faulty equipment, takes the life of a resident, the killing can still be labeled a homicide, although characterized as accidental.
- When Timothy McVeigh, the murderer of nearly 170 people in Oklahoma City, felt the terminal effects of the lethal injection, his homicide was lawful and privileged.
- When a private citizen is accosted with a weapon during the commission of a robbery, the citizen's use of a lethal weapon to protect life is lawful based on a theory of self-defense.
- When legislative changes authorize once proscribed conduct, such as euthanasia and abortion, homicide is no longer unlawful but lawful.

These examples elucidate the dualistic qualities inherent in homicide analysis. Do not assume, in every case, that the taking of life constitutes a criminal deed. Never forget that the act alone, the killing itself, suffices in the evidentiary arena for murder; manslaughter and the like depend on intentionality. The act alone falls short. Explanations, mitigating factors, excuse and defense, license and authority effect eventual culpability and it is the complex task of the legal interpreter to apply facts to the codes in question.

In the illegal framework, homicide falls into three main categories:

- Murder, first, second
- Manslaughter, first, second
- Involuntary and/or Negligent Homicide (vehicular and DUI cases)

Where the legal assessment fits depends on many factors. Each requires proof of death—a *corpus delicti*. In fact, common law prosecutions were nigh impossible without production of the victim's body. Today, given the sophistication of body disposal and the increasing means to hide the deed, a judgment of murder or manslaughter is still possible. Thomas Capano, Delaware's former assistant attorney general and high roller in local politics, was found guilty of the first-degree murder of Ann Marie Fahey, the former secretary of the Delaware governor, without presentation of the body.

STORY 4.1

THOMAS CAPANO

Thomas J. Capano (Figure 4.1) was a prominent and politically connected lawyer from a wealthy and influential family with a successful home construction business. He served as legal counsel to former Delaware Governor Michael N. Castle and as an aide to Governor Thomas Carper.

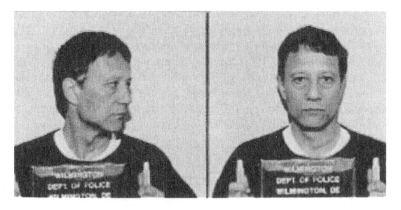

Figure 4.1   Thomas Capano. (Photo courtesy of the Wilmington, Delaware Police Department.)

Anne Marie Fahey was scheduling secretary to Governor Carper. It was sometime in 1993 when Fahey met Thomas Capano. The two began a three-year affair that was known only to a small group of friends and staffers at the governor's office. Capano was obsessive, overbearing, and extremely jealous. Fahey grew weary of his ways and longed to be free of him. Because she was afraid of him, when she began dating another man, she did not tell Capano. Capano and Fahey were last seen together dining out on the evening of June 27, 1996. On June 29th, after hearing nothing from her for two days, Fahey's family reported her missing to the Wilmington Police Department (WPD). The WPD contacted the FBI for assistance, so the Wilmington Resident Agency (RA) of the FBI's Baltimore office teamed with the WPD to chart their course of action in the investigation.

Because of Fahey's relationship with Capano, investigators quickly zeroed in on Capano as a suspect. He stated he had invited Anne Marie to dinner and he saw her home. According to Capano, they parted on good terms. The WPD/FBI investigative team used a number of creative investigative techniques to determine what actually happened that night, including toll record analysis, seizure of e-mails from Capano's law firm and Fahey's office, surveillance, analysis of gun purchase records, four search warrants including a four-day search of two landfills, psychological profiling, and analysis of financial records.

A search of Fahey's apartment uncovered letters written to Fahey from Capano. Fahey's diary spoke of their past, showing that months before her disappearance Fahey had tried to break off the relationship. Authorities also searched Capano's home and car for blood and hair samples, ultimately finding bloodstains on a radiator cover and some woodwork. A Red

Cross blood bank search helped recover a container of blood that Fahey had donated weeks earlier, and forensic exams linked Fahey's blood to the blood found in Capano's house.

Further investigation revealed that Capano's brothers, Gerard and Louis, were involved in a conspiracy to cover up evidence of Fahey's murder, but they were reluctant to cooperate with authorities. Then, after Gerard's arrest in November of 1997 on various drug and weapons charges, he had a change of heart and agreed to help. Once Gerard agreed to cooperate, Louis followed suit. Both pled guilty in federal court on charges related to the cover-up of the crime. Gerard and Louis became witnesses for the prosecution.

In their account, after Thomas murdered Fahey, he forced her 5-foot 11-inch body into a 192-quart, large fishing cooler he had purchased about two months earlier. The pair then drove a boat some 70 miles off the New Jersey coast and dumped the cooler into the Atlantic Ocean. Gerard Capano testified that the cooler wouldn't sink, so he shot it full of holes with a 12-gauge shotgun he kept onboard for shark fishing. The cooler still wouldn't sink, so Thomas lifted the body of Anne Marie Fahey out of the cooler, wrapped a chain and anchor around it, and threw it overboard, watching it sink. He then threw the cooler back into the water. About a week after Anne Marie Fahey's death, the cooler was discovered by a fisherman, who pulled it from the sea. He plugged the holes in it and began using it to keep his catch of the day. It was not until a year later, with Capano's arrest and the story about the cooler, that the fisherman got in touch with authorities and reported his find (Figure 4.2).

Thomas Capano was arrested by FBI Agents in November of 1997. The U.S. Attorney and Delaware Attorney General decided the best course of action was to dismiss the federal charge against Capano and institute a state first-degree murder charge. In January of 1999, they voted to convict him for the murder of Anne Marie Fahey. On March 16, 1999, he was sentenced to death. He died in his cell on September 19, 2011.

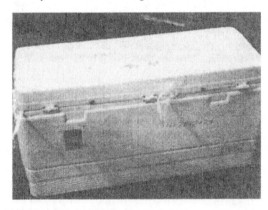

Figure 4.2   Cooler in which Anne Marie Fahey's body was placed. (Photo courtesy of the Wilmington, Delaware Police Department.)

Capano's blind rage and jealousy triggered the brutal death of Ms. Fahey. The body's subsequent disposal far out in the Atlantic Ocean further edifies this grim deed and the malevolent and premeditated intention of Capano. Capano's defense heavily depended on the prosecution's failure to produce the body, but to no avail. The *corpus delicti* was proved by other means, such as:

- Presence of blood and fibers
- Proof of motive
- Testimony of the brother implicating and describing the body's disposal in the high seas
- Motive and rage through phone and correspondence

- Purchase of cooler to place body
- Opportunity and means

With the rise of forensic science and the aggressive use of other sources of corroboration, homicides are now proven circumstantially. Defense counsel will surely dwell on the absence of the body as proof positive of other explanations, such as the alleged victim is missing, hiding, or has wandered away. While circumstantial evidence may be persuasive, it never really eliminates the fundamental question in every homicide case: Where is the body?[2] Challenges by defense counsel keenly address the reliability of the remains, the custodial identification of the *corpus delicti,* and the sufficiency of these types of identification under standard forensic practices.[3] The tougher issues center on the question of intentionality.

In the murder category, the prosecution needs to show a high level of intentionality. Most murder in the first and second degree statutes call for specific intent on the part of the actor. Hence, the act is premeditated, willful and purposeful, and without serious mitigation or attendant circumstances. Manslaughter generally comprises fact patterns that demonstrate a recklessness or gross disregard for the safety of others or the commission of homicide in emotional and passionate settings. Manslaughter is murder with passion and provocation joined with the type of general intent that imputes understanding and desire.

The last category, involuntary manslaughter, possesses the most imprecise form of intentionality, if intent exists at all. Some have described this form of homicide as strict liability in design since the actor does not intend the consequences directly. Drunk drivers may not will the death of another, but the actor should or could have known that death might occur if they drove while intoxicated. In each of these three cases, the terminality of the result is only too obvious. Any system that proclaims justice as its centerpiece will respond accordingly.

MURDER IN THE FIRST DEGREE

ELEMENTS:

- The killing of another without privilege or right
- With premeditation, deliberateness, and intentional knowledge
- With specific intent

Intentionality reaches its full blossom in the crime of murder. At no place in the killing of another do we find the clarity of knowledge and will of movement where the actor desires the termination of another with little, if any, reservation. Murder means purposeful annihilation of another and begets the final end of a breathing, functioning human being. Most murder statutes define the seriousness of the offense with clear-cut terms, such as premeditation, willfulness, knowing, and intentional.

> Visit the Bureau of Justice Statistics Web location and review its many resources on homicide at http://bjs.ojp.usdoj.gov/content/homicide/homtrnd.cfm

Tennessee's template for first-degree murder reflects standard practice in the United States.

(a) First-degree murder is:

    (1) A premeditated and intentional killing of another;

    (2) A killing of another committed in the perpetration of or attempt to perpetrate any first-degree murder, act of terrorism, arson, rape, robbery, burglary, theft, kidnapping, aggravated child abuse, aggravated child neglect, rape of a child, aggravated rape of a child or aircraft piracy; or

    (3) A killing of another committed as the result of the unlawful throwing, placing or discharging of a destructive device or bomb.[4]

Within this design rests the archetypal elements of the murder charge, namely premeditation, intentional killings, plots and plans that utilize bombs and other destructive devices, and deaths caused during the commission of a major felony. Classic conspiracy plans have been repeatedly held as sufficient evidence for conviction under murder 1 rules. Telling others of the intent to kill, making public threats to kill, and drawing up plans to carry out the kill, signify the type of mental preparation necessary for the most heinous crime.[5]

As Timothy McVeigh so coldly and calculatingly wove his justification and basis for the Oklahoma City bombing, one would be hard pressed not to recognize the distinct markings of the murder 1 persona. In his particular case, the pounds of explosives, the rental truck, the communications and articulations of purpose and method, and, most importantly, the eventual rationalization of how 168 human beings were killed for a cause. McVeigh (Figure 4.3) is the measure of the murderer without remorse or regret, with a perverse assuredness that did not wane until his lethal injection.

At common law, murder convictions depended on a finding of premeditation—the thought process that occurs before the event, followed by an exercise of will to carry out the task. To premeditate was to plan in advance, to contemplate the sequence to unfold. This intellectual

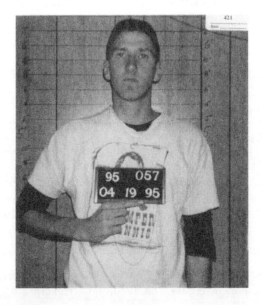

Figure 4.3   Timothy McVeigh. (Photo courtesy of the FBI.)

process also has been labeled "deliberation" and "malice aforethought." Murder was a more unified crime with fewer degrees and grades as the learned scholar Wharton noted:

> Although at common law there were no degrees of murder, most jurisdictions have subdivided murder into two or more degrees.[6]

In contemporary settings, the distinction has dissolved somewhat being redeployed in the sentencing phase more than the charge component. By this, the legal system spends less of its energy trying to prove the purity of the defendant's mental processes and more of its time arguing on behalf of harsher punishments for those who premeditate. Undoubtedly, the death penalty appears reserved for those who revel and choose with wild abandon and less for those who act in spontaneity and passion. "Murder in the first degree" culprits knew exactly what they were going to do and when they were going to do it. Today, the murder construct erects many more degrees and gradations in the definition of murder by adding provisions that account for passion, provocation, gross negligence, and depraved indifference to others.

While the evolution of murder and its progeny may be rapid, the apex of criminals still belongs to the murder convict, for these are the players who murder without hesitation. Actions do not arise from provocative behavior induced by rage or other emotion, nor would a murderer be aptly described if acting in response to grave emotional harm, physical duress, or other coercion. This will be no easy task since the bulk of homicides occur under less than sterile circumstances. The Bureau of Justice Statistics charts the rationales longitudinally in Figure 4.4.[7]

Neither would a premeditated thinker exist if time did not warrant or allow for any sort of meaningful reflection. Harvard Law Professor Michael J. Pauley poses the dilemma just as it should be:

> If premeditated means thought about beforehand, it strains credulity to say that a murder can be premeditated in a fraction of a second. It strains it even more to say that such a murder is deliberate in the sense that the killer carefully weighed the alternatives with calmness and depth of thought. All in a fraction of a second? Surely, this is enough time to form an intent to kill. But to weigh alternatives? To consider calmly and deeply? That seems a different matter.[8]

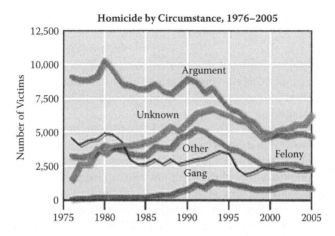

Figure 4.4   Homicide by Circumstance, 1976–2005.

Hence, the task of prosecutor and defense counsel in the resolution of charges is whether or not the facts warrant a finding sufficient to achieve this level of intellectual clarity. Combustible events will usually not qualify, nor will circumstances laden with emotional abuse and social pathology. An examination of the crime's attendant circumstances will tell us much about whether murder 1 or murder 2 sticks. The lines of inquiry might be:

- How much activity previous to the murder?
- How much time?
- How much corroboration of plan and purpose?
- What tools, weaponry, or other artifices were employed?
- What is the manner of killing?
- How many killings?
- What is the defendant's motive?
- What does the evidence manifest about intentionality?
- What level of corroboration exists?
- What is the emotional state of the defendant?

Just precisely what first-degree murder is cannot always be predicted. It is clear that facts and circumstances, defense personalities and profiles play a major role in deciphering when the act can be called "premeditated" and when it can be called "depraved and grossly indifferent." The lines are murky because the mental faculty of the deranged and the rational person can inevitably lead to the same result. The mentally limited, the retarded, and the intellectually challenged are not good candidates for capital murder, according to the U.S. Supreme Court's ruling in *Penry V. Lynaugh*,[9] since intentionality is negatively influenced by errant cognitive operations.[10]

Edmund Kemper, the hideous yet highly intelligent murderer and necrophile of his own mother, provides a contrast in the art of Murder 1 formulation. On its face, his acts are so dastardly that one could only imagine the deep-seated psychological trauma with which he was burdened. Even so, his convictions on the highest degree of murder, reflect the level of premeditation.

Find out about select criminals under the umbrella of Murder 1 at the FBI's Web location at http://www.fbi.gov/wanted/murders/wanted-group-view?b_start:int=30&-C=

Those who torture and maim the victim slowly to cause a lingering and brutal death, kill with a vicious clarity. Those who stalk, lay hidden and snatch up the victims, and whose perversion and obsession prompt horrific deaths are Murder 1 candidates, even when laden with mental mitigation. Having the time, reasoning things through, weighing and evaluating all consequences illustrate intentionality.[11]

The lines of distinction between Murder 1 and Murder 2 can be tough to decipher. Even the most learned of legal professionals tend to confuse the two, or take the gamble that the tougher charge just might work in the jury's mind. On this prediction, they are frequently right. In response, defendants endlessly appeal the suitability of the charges and subsequent conviction, urging the appellate court to overturn what it sees as a misapplication of law. They, too, are often right. Thus, an upset and emotionally enraged father's original conviction of murder, for flinging his three-month-old child to the pavement out of frustration, was struck down to manslaughter because his act was grossly reckless though not intentional.[12] While arguments are legitimate on both sides of the offense, particularly when one considers the tragic death of this innocent

CASE 4.1

PENRY V. LYNAUGH
492 US 302, 109 S. Ct. 2934 (1989).

In this case, we must decide whether petitioner, Johnny Paul Penry, was sentenced to death in violation of the Eighth Amendment because the jury was not instructed that it could consider and give effect to his mitigating evidence in imposing its sentence. We must also decide whether the Eighth Amendment categorically prohibits Penry's execution because he is mentally retarded.

On the morning of October 25, 1979, Pamela Carpenter was brutally raped, beaten, and stabbed with a pair of scissors in her home in Livingston, Texas. She died a few hours later in the course of emergency treatment. Before she died, she described her assailant. Her description led two local sheriff's deputies to suspect Penry, who had recently been released on parole after conviction on another rape charge. Penry subsequently gave two statements confessing to the crime and was charged with capital murder. At a competency hearing held before trial, a clinical psychologist, Dr. Jerome Brown, testified that Penry was mentally retarded. As a child, Penry was diagnosed as having organic brain damage, which was probably caused by trauma to the brain at birth. Penry was tested over the years as having an IQ between 50 and 63, which indicates mild to moderate retardation. Dr. Brown's own testing before the trial indicated that Penry had an IQ of 54. Dr. Brown's evaluation also revealed that Penry, who was 22 years old at the time of the crime, had the mental age of a 6½-year-old, which means that "he has the ability to learn and the learning or the knowledge of the average 6½-year-old kid." Penry's social maturity, or ability to function in the world, was that of a 9- or 10-year-old. Dr. Brown testified that "there's a point at which anyone with [Penry's] IQ is always incompetent, but, you know, this man is more in the borderline range." The jury found Penry competent to stand trial. The guilt–innocence phase of the trial began on March 24, 1980. The trial court determined that Penry's confessions were voluntary, and they were introduced into evidence. At trial, Penry raised an insanity defense and presented the testimony of a psychiatrist, Dr. Jose Garcia. Dr. Garcia testified that Penry suffered from organic brain damage and moderate retardation, which resulted in poor impulse control and an inability to learn from experience. Dr. Garcia indicated that Penry's brain damage was probably caused at birth, but may have been caused by beatings and multiple injuries to the brain at an early age. In Dr. Garcia's judgment, Penry was suffering from an organic brain disorder at the time of the offense, which made it impossible for him to appreciate the wrongfulness of his conduct or to conform his conduct to the law.

Penry's mother testified at trial that Penry was unable to learn in school and never finished the first grade. Penry's sister testified that their mother had frequently beaten him over the head with a belt when he was a child. Penry was also routinely locked in his room without access to a toilet for long periods of time. As a youngster, Penry was in and out of a number of state schools and hospitals until his father removed him from state schools altogether when he was 12. Penry's aunt subsequently struggled for over a year to teach Penry how to print his name. The State introduced the testimony of two psychiatrists to rebut the testimony of Dr. Garcia. Dr. Kenneth Vogtsberger testified that, although Penry was a person of limited mental ability, he was not suffering from any mental illness or defect at the time of the crime, and that he knew the difference between right and wrong and had the potential to honor the law. In his view, Penry had characteristics consistent with an antisocial personality, including an inability to learn from experience and a tendency to be impulsive and to violate society's norms. He testified further that Penry's low IQ scores underestimated his alertness and understanding of what went on around him. Dr. Felix Peebles also testified for the State that Penry was legally sane at the time of the offense and had a "full-blown antisocial personality." In addition, Dr. Peebles testified that he personally diagnosed Penry as being mentally retarded in 1973 and again in 1977, and that Penry "had a very bad life generally, bringing up." In Dr. Peebles' view, Penry "had been socially and emotionally deprived and he had not learned to read and write adequately." Although they disagreed with the defense psychiatrist over the extent and cause of Penry's mental limitations, both psychiatrists for the State acknowledged that Penry was a person of extremely limited mental ability, and that he seemed unable to learn from his mistakes.

The jury rejected Penry's insanity defense and found him guilty of capital murder. Tex. Penal Code Ann. 19.03 (1974 and Supp. 1989). The following day, at the close of the penalty hearing, the jury decided the sentence to be imposed on Penry by answering three "special issues":

(1) whether the conduct of the defendant that caused the death of the deceased was committed deliberately and with the reasonable expectation that the death of the deceased or another would result;
(2) whether there is a probability that the defendant would commit criminal acts of violence that would constitute a continuing threat to society; and
(3) if raised by the evidence, whether the conduct of the defendant in killing the deceased was unreasonable in response to the provocation, if any, by the deceased. Tex. Code Crim. Proc. Ann., Art. 37.071(b) (Vernon 1981 and Supp. 1989).

If the jury unanimously answers "yes" to each issue submitted, the trial court must sentence the defendant to death. Arts.37.071(c)-(e). Otherwise, the defendant is sentenced to life imprisonment. Ibid.

Defense counsel raised a number of objections to the proposed charge to the jury. With respect to the first special issue, he objected that the charge failed to define the term "deliberately." With respect to the second special issue, he objected that the charge failed to define the terms "probability," "criminal acts of violence," and "continuing threat to society." Defense counsel also objected to the charge because it failed to "authorize a discretionary grant of mercy based upon the existence of mitigating circumstances" and because it "fail[ed] to require as a condition to the assessment of the death penalty that the State show beyond a reasonable doubt that any aggravating circumstances found to exist outweigh any mitigating circumstances." In addition, the charge failed to instruct the jury that it may take into consideration all of the evidence whether aggravating or mitigating in nature which was submitted in the full trial of the case. Defense counsel also objected that, in light of Penry's mental retardation, permitting the jury to assess the death penalty in this case amounted to cruel and unusual punishment prohibited by the Eighth Amendment.

These objections were overruled by the trial court. The jury was then instructed that the State bore the burden of proof on the special issues, and that before any issue could be answered "yes," all 12 jurors must be convinced by the evidence beyond a reasonable doubt that the answer to that issue should be "yes." The jurors were further instructed that in answering the three special issues, they could consider all the evidence submitted in both the guilt–innocence phase and the penalty phase of the trial. The jury charge then listed the three questions, with the names of the defendant and the deceased inserted.

The jury answered "yes" to all three special issues, and Penry was sentenced to death. The Texas Court of Criminal Appeals affirmed his conviction and sentence on direct appeal. That court held that terms, such as "deliberately," "probability," and "continuing threat to society" used in the special issues need, not be defined in the jury charge because the jury would know their common meaning. The court concluded that Penry was allowed to present all relevant mitigating evidence at the punishment hearing, and that there was no constitutional infirmity in failing to require the jury to find that aggravating circumstances outweighed mitigating ones or in failing to authorize a discretionary grant of mercy based upon the existence of mitigating circumstances. The court also held that imposition of the death penalty was not prohibited by virtue of Penry's mental retardation. This Court denied certiorari on direct review.

...

JUSTICE BRENNAN, with whom JUSTICE MARSHALL joins, concurring in part and dissenting in part.

...

I agree that the jury instructions given at sentencing in this case deprived petitioner of his constitutional right to have a jury consider all mitigating evidence that he presented before sentencing him to die. I would also hold, however, that the Eighth Amendment prohibits the execution of offenders who are mentally retarded and who thus lack the full degree of responsibility for their crimes that is a predicate for the constitutional imposition of the death penalty.

...

JUSTICE STEVENS, with whom JUSTICE BLACKMUN joins, concurring in part and dissenting in part.

...

In Part IV-A, the Court decides that a rule that the Eighth Amendment prohibits the execution of a mentally retarded person ought to apply retroactively. Assuming retroactivity is pertinent, I agree that the first exception to Justice Harlan's nonretroactivity doctrine "should be understood to cover not only rules forbidding criminal punishment of certain primary conduct, but also rules prohibiting a certain category of punishment for a class of defendants because of their status or offense," ante, at 330, and that this claim lies within that exception. *

The remaining sections of Part IV adequately and fairly state the competing arguments respecting capital punishment of mentally retarded persons. In my judgment, however, that explication, particularly the summary of the arguments advanced in the Brief for American Association on Mental Retardation et al. as Amici Curiae, compels the conclusion that such executions are unconstitutional. I would therefore reverse the judgment of the Court of Appeals in its entirety.

...

JUSTICE SCALIA, with whom THE CHIEF JUSTICE, JUSTICE WHITE, and JUSTICE KENNEDY join, concurring in part and dissenting in part.

...

I disagree with the holding in Part II-B of the Court's opinion that petitioner's contention, that his sentencing was unconstitutional because the Texas jury was not permitted fully to consider and give effect to the mitigating evidence of his mental retardation and background of abuse, does not seek the application of a "new rule" and is therefore not barred by Teague. I also disagree with the disposition of the merits of this contention, in Part III of the Court's opinion. ...

I turn briefly to the place of today's holding within the broad scheme of our constitutional jurisprudence regarding capital sentencing, as opposed to the immediately applicable precedents. It is out of order there as well. As noted at the outset of this discussion, our law regarding capital sentencing has sought to strike a balance between complete discretion, which produces "wholly arbitrary and capricious action," and no discretion at all, which prevents the individuating characteristics of the defendant and of the crime to be taken into account. That is why, in Jurek, we did not regard the Texas Special Issues as inherently bad, but to the contrary thought them a desirable means of "focus[ing] the jury's objective consideration of the particularized circumstances," or, as the plurality put it in Franklin, "channel[ing] jury discretion ... to achieve a more rational and equitable administration of the death penalty." In providing for juries to consider all mitigating circumstances insofar as they bear upon (1) deliberateness, (2) future dangerousness, and (3) provocation, it seems to me Texas had adopted a rational scheme that meets the two concerns of our Eighth Amendment jurisprudence. The Court today demands that it be replaced, however, with a scheme that simply dumps before the jury all sympathetic factors bearing upon the defendant's background and character, and the circumstances of the offense, so that the jury may decide without further guidance whether he "lacked the moral culpability to be sentenced to death," "did not deserve to be sentenced to death," or "was not sufficiently culpable to deserve the death penalty." The Court seeks to dignify this by calling it a process that calls for a "reasoned moral response," but reason has nothing to do with it, the Court having eliminated the structure that required reason. It is an unguided, emotional "moral response" that the Court demands be allowed—an outpouring of personal reaction to all the circumstances of a defendant's life and personality, an unfocused sympathy. Not only have we never before said the Constitution requires this, but the line of cases following Gregg sought to eliminate precisely the unpredictability it produces.

The decision whether to impose the death penalty is a unitary one; unguided discretion not to impose is unguided discretion to impose as well. In holding that the jury had to be free to deem Penry's mental retardation and sad childhood relevant for whatever purpose it wished, the Court has come full circle, not only permitting but requiring what Furman once condemned. "Freakishly" and "wantonly," have been re-baptized "reasoned moral response." I do not think the Constitution forbids what the Court imposes here, but I am certain it does not require it.

Questions

1. On what legal theory was the imposition of death penalty challenged?
2. How did the Texas lower courts justify the imposition of the death penalty?
3. What did the dissenting opinion argue?

child, the law on homicide directs us to fit facts to charges, not punishments to emotional satisfactions. For murder to be sustained, that father would have had to premeditated and intended the death of the three month old. Rather, the defendant's rage spurred on a passionate attack against a set of circumstances that the father could no longer control intellectually and emotionally. By no means does the father's conduct become excusable; it is more a question of what form of guilt and responsibility he must bear until his last days. The lines cross and bend, twist and traverse through all sorts of alternatives and as facts unfold, laws are interpreted. At times, fact patterns so eerily merge that most prosecutors feel comfortable choosing both charges as part of the indictment's content. Clearly defendants prefer, at least in some cases, the all or nothing approach. Murder in the first degree's burden is hefty and affords defendants a host of ways to get out of personal responsibility. The mental troubles of any charged murderer are bound to influence the clarity of mind, and by implication the capacity to formulate in premeditated ways. But, isn't this inconsistent? How can the actor be both? In Illinois, a few appellate courts allow for the state itself to amend and issue jury instructions that might include both because of these semantic complexities.[13]

The United States Supreme Court weighed one example of how this problem presents itself in day-to-day litigation in *Jackson v. Virginia*.[14] Under Virginia law, murder in the first degree's premeditation could not be countered by evidence of voluntary intoxication. In Jackson, the defendant's appeal rested on many grounds including how intoxication might either defend or mitigate the charge of murder in the first degree. The Court upheld a long line of cases that restricts voluntary intoxication as a defense, but opened the door to its usage as a mitigator relative to intentionality. It is a complicated call since defendants could always allege drunkenness and would ready themselves in advance of the premeditation, getting sauced just enough to mitigate the criminality. This would be an unfortunate result. But, Jackson goes down that road only so far. It would be impossible to assert a pure defense, although a state of intoxication materially reflects the defendant's state of mind at the time the offense was committed. This recognition does not excuse or make innocent, but causes jury and judges alike to think and assess a little harder. In Jackson, the sufficiency of the evidence depends on proof of each material element. Mens rea in the world of murder in the first rejects an actor having no real awareness of reality and rightfully insists that the court and the jury consider how a material element of a particular offense might be affected. The Court held that intoxication should not be excluded from the overall evaluation.

This familiar standard gives full play to the responsibility of the trier of fact fairly to resolve conflicts in the testimony, to weigh the evidence, and to draw reasonable inferences from basic facts to ultimate facts. Once a defendant has been found guilty of the crime charged, the fact finder's role as weigher of the evidence is preserved through a legal conclusion that upon judicial review all of the evidence is to be considered in the light most favorable to the prosecution. The criterion thus impinges upon "jury" discretion only to the extent necessary to guarantee the fundamental protection of due process law.[15]

In the final analysis, Murder 1 zeroes in on the defendant who wants the death of another and under the ordinary interpretation knows that someone will die. One cannot point a weapon at someone, pull the trigger, then say, "I did not mean to kill." This is factually and morally unacceptable.[16]

Hence, when three students aimed and fired at police and killed their high school principal, they could not hide behind the specious defense that their intentions were not formulated. Engaging in a deadly gun battle with lawful authorities can be properly designated Murder 1 intentionality.[17] When mitigation emerges, the murder in the first charge loses a part of its punch. When this occurs, a lower grade of murder may be in order.

MURDER IN THE SECOND DEGREE

ELEMENTS

- The killing of another without privilege or right
- With general intent

When the facts lack the necessary clarity to meet the murder in the first degree threshold, a lower grade of murder may be in order. Legislatures fully recognize that a murder may not be preplanned and thought out in advance, yet still be a calculated act. Murder in the second degree focuses on the knowledge factor more than the plot. To know and accept the death to be inflicted is to have rationalized and thought about it. To know is to understand the full implications, yet still proceed with the criminal agency.

§ 14-17. Murder in the first and second degree defined; punishment

A murder that shall be perpetrated by means of a nuclear, biological, or chemical weapon of mass destruction as defined in G.S. 14-288.21, poison, lying in wait, imprisonment, starving, torture, or by any other kind of willful, deliberate, and premeditated killing, or which shall be committed in the perpetration or attempted perpetration of any arson, rape or a sex offense, robbery, kidnapping, burglary, or other felony committed or attempted with the use of a deadly weapon shall be deemed to be murder in the first degree ... All other kinds of murder, including that which shall be proximately caused by the unlawful distribution of opium or any synthetic or natural salt, compound, derivative, or preparation of opium, or cocaine or other substance described in G.S. 90-90(1) d., or methamphetamine, when the ingestion of such substance causes the death of the user, shall be deemed murder in the second degree.[18]

Some jurisdictions have designated certain actions as so depraved and indifferent that the inference of knowledge is permissible. In other words, how else can conduct be rationally explained except that the actor desired the particular end. While no advance planning took place, the acts committed can only be termed murderously depraved. Put another way, premeditation takes a back seat to general intentionality. Nebraska' statute could not be plainer about this:

> Murder in the second degree; penalty. (1) A person commits murder in the second degree if he causes the death of a person intentionally, but without premeditation.[19]

At common law, the trier searched for a level of "malice" that subjectively explained objective actions. Why else would the defendant kill except for maliciousness and evil heart. Malice imputes wrongfulness in the actor and partially explains the criminality. However, murderers come in many shapes and sizes and may or may not operate with depravity, malice, or evil at the base of the conduct. The contract "hit man" kills even people he may know or like and rationalizes the conduct as "business" and an occupational risk. Malice may explain some forms of intentionality, but not all of them. Hence, the contemporary perspective is to weigh the conduct as either expressly or impliedly instructive of the actor's intentions. It is fair to impute and infer from conduct the corresponding depravity and bad motive. It is acceptable to adjudge another's intentions from the results of their decision making. "American law followed the general pattern of the English common law. To the present, American casebooks and treatises consistently define malice as:[20]

> (1) An intent to kill someone, not necessarily the victim ... (2) An intent to commit "serious" or "grievous" bodily injury upon someone. (3) A wanton and reckless disregard of a very great risk of causing death or serious bodily injury ... The older statutes use language such as "depraved heart" or an "abandoned and malignant heart" to refer to this type of culpability. (4) Malice is also implied when the defendant or his accomplice commits a killing in the perpetration of certain felonies."[21]

Indeed, any finding of intentionality relies on deductive reasoning from the reality that surrounds the players in criminal conduct. Murder 2 mindsets know but do not open up about knowledge. A rational jury also could infer that the defendant acted "knowingly" in regard to the attempted second-degree murder charges. Whether an accused "knowingly" attempted to kill his or her victim is a question of fact for the jury.[22] "Intent, which can seldom be proven by direct evidence, may be deduced or inferred from the character of the assault, the nature of the act, and from all the circumstances of the case in evidence."[23]

While hardly scientific, the fact finder has little choice in the assessment of the case before the bar. A defendant without a plan and short on premeditation is assuredly one who will proclaim spontaneity and provocation in the defense. Murder in the second degree represents those whose intellectual processes are confused yet understood. Murder 2 pulls in those whose actions can only be explained as knowing, depraved, and wanton in design. Murder 2 candidates cannot argue lack of awareness or cognitive failure, but external influences that touch the clarity of thought. One common place where this offense is more appropriate than Murder 1 is in domestic circumstances, though others argue that the passion of intense domestic turmoil belongs mostly in the manslaughter category.[24]

The *Commonwealth v. Malone* decision educates the legal thinker on another aspect of the Murder 2 phenomena, namely the "depraved heart" component. Sounding emotional, the "depraved" standard tells us a great deal about the M2 player. Here, the actor wantonly engages in conduct even the feebleminded can appreciate. Here, the actor shoots into a crowd, derails a

---

CASE 4.2

COMMONWEALTH V. MALONE

42 A.2d 445 (1946)

Visit your local county law library or a law library at a local college or university or use Lexis/Nexis or WestLaw and obtain the above case, then answer the following questions.

Questions

1. What type of actions did the defendants engage in?
2. What level of mens rea did the defendants possess? Premeditated? Planned or depraved?
3. Did the defendants specifically intend to kill another?
4. Would these facts qualify for M1? Why or why not?

---

train, sets fire to the building as a "joke," and then defends whatever sliver of honor possessed with the argument of no intentionality. Hiding in the thicket of chaotic movement, the defendant expects the court to believe that these chosen deeds are detached from mental deliberations and the result of movement for its own sake. Any system willing to separate human activity from the very persona causing it is on the low road to confusion.

MANSLAUGHTER

ELEMENTS:

- The killing of another without privilege or right
- Mitigating factors, or provocation exist
- May be accidental or negligent

Descending downward on the scale of homicidal responsibility, one next encounters the crime of manslaughter. Manslaughter is murder with passion, provocation, and mitigation—circumstances that take the perpetrator out of the realm of the cold and calculating. It comes in two varieties: voluntary and involuntary. In the involuntary form, it is an act of extreme or gross negligence. The voluntary form closely resembles murder except for the presence of compelling mitigation and provocation. The manslaughter offender kills because of mitigation, which is roughly defined as any explanation prompting the criminal agent to act. The homicide occurs because or on account of:

- The defendant's emotional rage and jealousy
- The defendant's mental, familial, and economic pathology
- The defendant's addictions and history of substance abuse
- The defendant's psychological profile

- The defendant's syndromes, from battered spouse to junk food deprivation
- The defendant's reaction to provocation
- The defendant's gross indifference to others but lack of direct intention
- The defendant's psychiatric profile

A lack of time to deliberate and think things through rationally provides the backdrop for manslaughter when compared to the intellectual choice so evident in murder. Hence, in a rare reversal, a New York appellate court overturned the finding of the trial court when a security guard, reacting to death of his partner, shot an assailant. Here, three youths pummeled a colleague with a steel pipe. Enraged, the security guard fired upon the youths killing one of them. Reversing the conviction of murder, the opinion relates:

> The entire incident, including the shooting, unfolded within a matter of seconds leaving defendant with no opportunity for deliberation other than to react emotionally to the extreme circumstances confronting him.[25]

In this case, we identify a man under charged circumstances whose emotions are intense and reactionary. This emotional aura correctly mitigates the claim of the deliberation and premeditation. So, too, is the result witnessed in passionate and emotionally laden settings, such as:

- Battered spouses[26]
- Sexual abuse
- Terroristic threats and harassment
- Love, sex, and betrayal
- Envy, jealousy, and rage

Like it or not, homicide occurs in less than deliberate venues. The complexity of human relationships, the unreliability of emotional reaction and overreaction, and the existence of human frailty guarantees some homicidal activity that falls short of the planned and premeditated.[27]

Review the manslaughter finding in the major construction accident in New York City at http://www.foxnews.com/us/2010/07/22/verdict-expected-manslaughter-case-nyc-crane-collapse-killed-injured/

To be sure, every person has threatened another with the undignified affront: "I could kill you!" Parents, children, and estranged lovers have heard it, so, too, teachers and police.[28] When the threat becomes more than idle chatter, criminality occurs. Manslaughter takes in these complicated confrontations and dares not afford exoneration for the acts, but only another classification for the finding of culpability. Simply, manslaughter allows the defendant to explain why the homicide occurred in the first place, not necessarily in the sense of excuse or acquittal, but as to influence and determinism. The criminal actor moves with forces above and beyond the usual freedom of the human agent. The human agent saddled with mitigation makes intentionality less apparent. Mitigation and mitigating factors are what the defense uses to explain, to elucidate the conduct in question. It is mitigation that catapults the thinking, intentional mind into another dimension filled with obtuse and ill-defined terms like: passion, provocation, mental illness, abuse as a child and spouse, syndromes, addictions and obsessions, jealousy and paramours,

STORY 4.2

MOTHERS WHO KILL

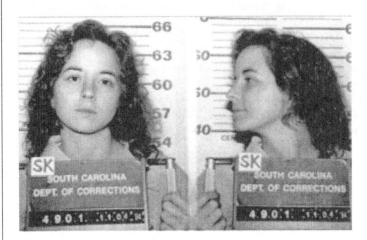

Figure 4.5   Susan Smith.

Susan Smith

On October 25, 1994, Susan Smith, 23, (Figure 4.5) told Union County deputies a black man jumped into her car and forced her to drive at gunpoint. He then made her get out and then drove away with her two children still in the car. After weeks of investigation, Smith finally confessed to the murder. Smith was depressed about her relationship with boyfriend Tom Findlay, and was planning on committing suicide and killing the boys so they wouldn't have to go on without her. She prepared to let her Mazda drift down a boat ramp into John D. Long Lake. For some reason, Smith exited the car before it immersed.

It took an hour and a half for 11 jurors to decide that Susan Smith should receive a life sentence after she was found guilty of murdering her two sons, Michael, 3, and Alexander, 14 months. Smith will be eligible for parole on November 4, 2024, after serving a minimum of 30 years.

Figure 4.6   Darlie Routier.

Darlie Routier

The evening of June 5, 1996, Darin Routier, 27, and baby Drake went upstairs to bed. Darlie, 26, (Figure 4.6) and the couple's other two sons, Devon, 6, and Damon, 5, slept in front of the TV on the couches in the main floor living room. Hours later, Darlie called 911 to report an attack on the two boys by unknown intruders. Darlie alleges that she observed one or more intruders flee the house through the kitchen and utility room into the garage, having dropped a knife onto the utility room floor. She allegedly chased the man, picked up the knife, then went back to the kids. She says she screamed, waking her husband. Darin immediately came down the stairs wearing his jeans and glasses. She then called 911 while Darin performed CPR and first aid to the dying boys. Devon was dead on the scene as a result of multiple stab wounds to his chest.

Damon was transported to the hospital but died enroute of similar wounds. Darlie was treated and transported to the hospital where she underwent emergency surgery to clean, observe, and close the 9-inch slice to her neck and lesser stab wounds to her arm and shoulder.

Dallas District Attorney eventually charged Darlie Routier with the murder of her own children, accusing her of inflicting the near-fatal injuries on herself. Darlie Routier was convicted of murder and sentenced to death by lethal injection. She is at present on Death Row in Gatesville, Texas, awaiting execution at an as-yet undetermined future date.

Darlie's case has been the subject of much speculation. There have been allegations of inconsistencies in the court transcripts, mishandling and improper processing of evidence, as well as allegations that Routier was tried by the media and not in court.

Most recently, in 2008, Ms. Routier has filed a First Motion for Discovery in a Federal Habeas proceeding that was granted in part.

Andrea Yates

Most recently, Andrea Yates, 36, was charged in the death of her five children on June 20, 2001. She admitted to a police investigator methodically drowning her five children one-by-one in a bathtub in a "zombie-like fashion." It is reported that when 7-year-old Noah came upon the body of his 6-month-old sister floating in the bathtub, he asked his mother, "What's wrong with Mary?" Then he fled. Yates allegedly chased the boy and dragged him back to the bathtub.

The bodies of Luke, 2; Paul, 3; John, 5; and 6-month-old Mary were found with a sheet over them on a bed in one room. The body of Noah was still in the bathtub. Under Texas law she could face the death penalty if convicted.

According to Yates' husband, she has been battling postpartum depression. But, someone close to the investigation has reported that Yates told investigators she had been thinking of killing her children for months, that she believes she was a bad mother and felt that her children were disabled and that they were not developing normally.

In March 2002, a jury found Yates guilty, rejecting her insanity defense. Although the prosecution had sought the death penalty, the jury refused that option. The trial court sentenced Yates to life imprisonment in the Texas Department of Criminal Justice with eligibility for parole in 40 years.

On January 6, 2005, a Texas Court of Appeals reversed the convictions, because California psychiatrist and prosecution witness Dr. Park Dietz admitted he had given materially false testimony during the trial. On January 9, 2006, Yates again entered pleas of not guilty by reason of insanity. On February 1, 2006, she was granted release on bail on the condition that she be admitted to a mental health treatment facility.

On July 26, 2006, after three days of deliberations, Yates was found not guilty by reason of insanity, as defined by the state of Texas. She was thereafter committed to the North Texas State Hospital, Vernon Campus. In January 2007, Yates was moved to a low security state mental hospital in Kerrville, Texas.

intoxication and remembrance, neglect, Satanism and the occult, television and music, junk food and chemical imbalance, breastfeeding and bottles, astrological signs and witchcraft, XYY chromosomes and genetic imbalance, religion and messages from God, dogs and other animal instructions, mental disease and defect, ethnic rage, love, estrangement, and betrayal.

Mitigation extends as far as human imagination journeys and just as distant as the creative energies of defense counsel can muster. It seems impossible to conceive of other, even more avant garde theories coming to the legal forefront, but like "talk show" content, the surprises will continue.[29]

The point, however, remains consistent: That murder charges encompass a deliberate, thinking actor who has planned and chosen the result while the party engaged in manslaughter carries on with a mind driven by nonintellectual forces, whether passion or hate, psychiatric disturbance or novel syndrome. Mothers who kill their own flesh and blood, small children and babies, act either with clear-cut intentionality or a mushy cogency determined by other dynamics, some of which are more believable than others. Postpartum blues, a rather nondescript syndrome experience by some mothers who have recently delivered children, is touted as explanatory of why a mother would drop her child off a 34th-floor apartment porch.

If not accidental, what other explanation would suffice in a case so egregious. Do mothers intentionally desire the death of their offspring? Is first-degree murder a suitable charge in these tragic cases? Or does the actor operate under some burden that makes intentionality a mix of thought, desire, and mitigation? One cannot discount the possibility of first-degree activity in this type of case, because mothers, like any other homicidal perpetrator, are capable of acting with express purpose and premeditation. However, it is far more plausible that the mother suffers in some sense for whatever reasons, from continuous abuse, from poverty or individual decline, from addiction or instability.[30]

Read the *Newsweek* article on When Mothers Kill Their Own Children at http://www.newsweek.com/2008/01/10/annals-of-filicide.html

Whether the defense has any credibility is not the issue. Whether the actor finds forces driving her ambitions, no matter how perverse, is the issue. Much to our dismay, we hear too many stories of babies left in trash cans and dumpsters, buried in backyards, and left in hotel rooms, by the very mothers who bore them. From all possible perspectives, the manslaughter statute fits better because of the inexplicability of it all. Naturally, at least in most cases, mothers protect and nourish their offspring. Mothers who kill their own are an irregularity, yet a growing and very disturbing trend in a culture said to value children. With a mix of liberalism, feminism, and tolerance, certain commentators are questioning our tendency to value children while posing excuses for the women who kill their offspring. The concealment of a pregnancy should be construed as the fundamental opposite any other form of murder or manslaughter, but seems to be in its own league. DePaul University Professor Michelle Oberman incisively describes the dilemma:

> First, an extraordinarily high number of infants are killed within twenty-four hours of birth. In medical circles, these cases are known as "neonaticides," and they constitute almost half of the cases in my sample. The circumstances that surround neonaticides are remarkably consistent and, on the whole, entirely distinguishable from the fact patterns associated with the homicide deaths of older infants and children. As a result, my analysis is divided into two groups—neonaticide and infanticide—depending upon the age of the victim. Second, in spite of the factual differences between neonaticide and infanticide, society's response to both of these crimes reflects a profound sense of confusion, ambivalence, and general unwillingness to equate these homicides with murder.[31]

In these sorts of facts, in the postpartum world, manslaughter, the offense of the mitigated, works nicely. Review the statute below:

§ 2503. Voluntary manslaughter

(A) GENERAL RULE —A person who kills an individual without lawful justification commits voluntary manslaughter if at the time of the killing he is acting under a sudden and intense passion resulting from serious provocation by:
   (1) the individual killed; or
   (2) another whom the actor endeavors to kill, but he negligently or accidentally causes the death of the individual killed.[32]

As in murder, the act of killing another is mandated. The distinction between these offenses can be identified in the language of provocation. To suffer from provocation is to experience some intense emotion or pressure, not the coercive variety, but the type that prompts the average person to react and to do so in ways that an individual normally would not. Thus, discovering a lover sleeping with another person, in *flagrante delicto*, qualifies, as does subsequent injuries in a heated domestic quarrel that cause death. These scenarios present a vastly different picture of homicidal behavior: one reflective, the other spontaneous and less reasoned.[33]

Provocation as Mitigator

Provocation stimulates courses of conduct that the agent typically would not engage in, spurring on fits of rage and uncontrollable anger, and generating retaliatory responses that cross the line between civility and criminality.[34] Every person experiences anger, but the manslaughterer goes forward uncontrollably.[35]

This type of provocation does not excuse or fully defend, only mitigates to the lower charge. Our analysis does not presently address the justification defense nor use provocation as the basis for self-defense analysis. Instead, the examination seeks only to show how the purposeful and deliberative mind de-evolves into the enraged and provoked mind that thinks with less precision and clarity. In this neurological region, manslaughter reigns.

Provocation results from unreasonable circumstances and, therefore, affects reasonable people in unreasonable ways. Provocation is not the stuff of trifles and trivialities, but the sum and substance of those conditions and events that push us over the edge—to a place one would not ordinarily trek. "Common experience teaches that, at some point, anger becomes so intense that people find it extremely difficult to control themselves and respond constructively, rather

---

CASE 4.3

SCHICK V. STATE
570 N.E.2d 918 (Ind. Ct. App. 1991).

In *Schick v. State*, the seventeen-year-old defendant hitched a ride with the victim after his car broke down. The two allegedly drove around looking for women to have sex with. The defendant stated he asked the victim where he could get "a blow job?" and the victim answered, "I can handle that." After cruising for a period of time, they stopped for cigarettes and then drove to a baseball field. The two walked into the shadows where the victim pulled down his pants and underwear, grabbed the defendant around the waist and tried to take hold of the defendant's penis. Schick kneed the victim in the stomach, punched him in the face, then continued to brutally stomp on the victim, who later died from the injuries. Before fleeing the scene, the defendant took money from the victim's wallet.

Questions

1. What type of conduct qualifies for reasonable provocation?
2. Does the Court allow this type of provocation to serve as a pure defense?
3. Does the Court allow the provocation to lower the type of homicide charge?
4. Locate the case decision and review the court's decision. What is your opinion of the eventual finding?
5. Do you feel it is reasonable to conclude the advance was a form of provocation?

---

than violently, to the anger-producing stimulus. Therefore, when A kills P because his reason is "disturbed or obscured by passion to an extent which might render ordinary men, of fair average disposition, liable to act rashly or without due deliberation or reflection, and from passion, rather than judgment,"[36] he is less to blame than if he killed P while he was calm. This is because it is harder for A to control his actions when he is angry than when he is calm."[37]

Granted, this human frailty does not allow a carte blanche acceptance in every case. Other factors must be considered, such as:

- The timing and contiguousness of the provocation with the homicide
- The element of surprise, shock, and previous level of defendant's knowledge
- The lack of time off to cool off from the influence of provocation
- Alternative ways of handling the dilemma
- Past history of the defendant and the target[38]
- Credibility of the claim
- The adequacy of the provocation in the first place

The call here is sometimes very fuzzy. Naturally, a charged defendant will seek out the least onerous offenses and hope to cast off the most severe. Manslaughter carries far less severe penalties than M1 and M2. What about the OJ Simpson case? Some commentators have called into question the wisdom of an M1 charge under the very turbulent facts of this infamous case. Fifty-seven stab wounds, a sliced head, almost detached, lying in wait, the brutality of the force exerted and the injuries, and the death of another party with little interest one way or the other relegates the offense to the murder category, does it not? Or are the mitigating factors so compelling in the case to prompt the lower manslaughter charge? Mitigation assumed many forms in this unfortunate case, including:

- Passion and rage
- Jealousy
- Sexual infidelities
- Controlling and manipulative personality
- Race and gender
- A History of domestic abuse
- Previous police interaction
- Victim forgiveness
- Children and custody[39]

The point in the Simpson case, and a host of others, rests in the mitigation environment. Does manslaughter fits these facts more squarely than murder?

Professor George Anastaplo's cutting review of the OJ Simpson case raises some profound issues when he notes:

> I have considered what the jurors, and to some extent the judge, in the Simpson case were thinking. I have also considered what the lawyers in the case were thinking. What about Mr. Simpson himself? If he did do the two killings, it could not have been altogether on impulse. That is, there are indications that the killer made preparations, if only with respect to the knife, clothing, and schedule relied upon. If Mr. Simpson did the killings, what did he believe would happen? Did he wonder whether he, a "likely" suspect, would have an adequate alibi? How could Mr. Simpson, if he set out to kill, be sure that no one would see him in the neighborhood? The thoughtlessness evident here may be seen as well in the spousal-abuse episodes connected to him, episodes that would immediately make him a suspect when his ex-wife was slaughtered. Those episodes testify to passions that may be hard to predict or to control altogether. Certainly there were intense passions exhibited in the killings themselves, especially in the extension of the violence against what seems to have been an innocent bystander, the companion of the apparently targeted woman.[40]

In the Simpson case, the glaring closeness of the premeditated and emotional rage is self-evident. Choosing a charge can alter the outcome of a case and, when chosen improperly, the consequences for the common good can be most negative. With the findings in Simpson, we have witnessed nothing short of racial polarization and a full realization that facts do not matter, and that the usual accoutrements witnessed in the legal system can be tossed to the wayside if emotions run free.

Manslaughter typically confuses criminal intent, a hazy, sort of fogged up intellectualism that destroys the purity of intention. Its world of passion and provocation may appear to readily reduce personal responsibility although that is not the essence of the offense. Manslaughter does not exculpate the offender, it only accepts the glaring reality that some minds are clearer than others. Some killers kill with crystalline intent, others with minds severely touched by mitigation.[41] In the latter case, manslaughter makes good sense. Manslaughter targets the perpetrators who kill with depravity and enhanced emotion, those who care little for the ultimate consequences for the ultimate act of crime.

Find out how one legally defines provocation in the Wisconsin statute at http://www.lawserver.com/law/state/wisconsin/wi-laws/wisconsin_laws_939-44

FELONY MURDER RULE

ELEMENTS:

- Death of another: Any victim, any perpetrator
- That results from, during, and because of a specific felony
- Specific intent to commit an underlying felony
- No intent to kill another is necessary

One of the stranger legal principles students of criminal law encounter early on involves the theory of felony murder. Much of what has been offered so far becomes foreign to the analysis, for in felony murder emerges a type of strict liability for the murderous act. In felony murder, defendants find little solace in the mitigation, lack of intentionality, and other traditional defense mechanisms. The theory of felony murder holds the convicted accountable with little or no proof of mens rea and searches for cooperation between various parties to the underlying felon. The Felony Murder Rule (FMR) holds not only the trigger puller responsible, but the accessories before and after the fact that planned and participated, as if they, too, pulled the trigger. FMR makes all involved accountable for murder when part of a scheme and event results in the death of another. The FMR has two fundamental aims: "(1) to impose liability on a felon for an unintended homicide committed by the felon or someone working in concert with the felon during a felony, and (2) to deter a person from committing a felony because of the liability that is attached if a homicide occurs during the felony."[42]

A felony murderer not only kills, but does so while committing a distinct and underlying felony delineated in the statutory design. Within the world of felony murder, defendants fight hard to save themselves from harsh convictions of Murder 1 and Murder 2 even when not intending to kill a soul.

Felony murderers kill during the commission of a specified felony (i.e., robbery, arson, rape, or battery). A quick review of representative state jurisdictions show unique designs with a similar purpose, although the FMRs are "conceived as legislatures saw fit."[43] Felony murderers comprise a unique and distinctive class of accused because guilt may be imposed without achieving the requisite elements of criminal law culpability. Actus reus is what rides the horse not mens rea. It is the commission of some type of specifically designated felony that the legislature deems so unsavory that stern measures are justified. The mental state of the defendant is imputed by the defendant's choice of conduct and may or may not be devoid of intentionality. In this way, the penalties of felony murder are extraordinarily harsh in select cases and proportionate in others. Look at the dilemma from this perspective. Assume you have a defendant who burns a structure with the clear-cut intention of killing a targeted victim who sleeps within. Under classical criminal jurisprudence, the agent intends two separate felonies: arson and Murder 1. However, these same two events may be intended in different ways by other criminal actors. One defendant might lack the desire to kill another and instead is driven by economic or other motivation. If a death does occur, despite the absence of intent, felony murder imputes the felonious intent to the arson actor. Murder 1 is the end result in either case. The domain of felony murder is properly described as a form of strict liability.

Qualifying Felonies

Central to any real understanding of the felony murder doctrine is the requirement that the death of another occur during the commission of particular category of felony. Not all felonies qualify. Legislatures list *ad seriatim* those felonies that trigger the rule; an example being:

> All murder which shall be committed in the perpetration of, or attempt to perpetrate, any rape in any degree, sexual offense in the first or second degree, sodomy, mayhem, robbery, carjacking or armed carjacking, burglary in the first, second, or third degree, a violation ... of this article concerning destructive devices, kidnapping as defined ... this article, or in the escape or attempt to escape from ... any institution or facility under the jurisdiction of the Division of Correction of the Division of Pretrial Detention and Services, or from any jail or penal institution in any of the counties of this State, shall be murder in the first degree.[44]

The Illinois Code provides useful language as well:

> Treason, first degree murder, second degree murder, predatory criminal sexual assault of a child, aggravated criminal sexual assault, criminal sexual assault, robbery, burglary, residential burglary, aggravated arson, arson, aggravated kidnapping, kidnapping, aggravated battery resulting in great bodily harm or permanent disability or disfigurement and any other felony which involves the use or threat of physical force or violence against any individual.[45]

While there is no unassailable prescription, it is fair to say that serious felonies usually suffice, though there has been a tendency to expand the list. For example, some argue that if the driver of an automobile that is in an accident leaves the scene, and the victim dies, the FMR should apply. So "accident" tethers itself to the FMR.[46]

Major felonies, such as robbery and rape, are properly characterized as so severe that the penalty of death be properly assigned under an FMR philosophy. When armed robbers take money by force, the law has every right to impose liability on perpetrators who just so happen to kill others in the process. One cannot rob and then disingenuously argue he or she never intended harm. So, too, with arson defendants who proclaim that their intentionality could never have mulled the potential death of another as the incendiary activity occurs. These dangerous activities bear all types of fruit, even the terminal, deadly variety. These defendants are not lambs to the slaughter, but criminal agents perfectly capable of anticipating and projecting the serious harm that arises in felonious activity.

To keep track of the diverse felonies that qualify for FMR coverage, the anagram at Figure 4.7 should assist the reader.

Any Victim

Another oddity of the felony murder doctrine relates to victimhood. The severity of the rule can be gleaned from the rule's liberal net of potential victims as the underlying felony plays out. In short, any party who dies prompts the rule's application and includes intended and unintended parties.[47]

L	ARCENY
A	RSON
B	URGLARY
R	APE/ROBBERY
E	XTORION
A	SSAULT
E	SCAPE FROM PRISON
M	URDER

Figure 4.7   LABREAEM Anagram.

Critics of the felony murder rule are many and varied. See how one group assesses FMR at http://www.prisonsfoundation.org/letters/what's_wrong_with_the_felony_murder_rule. html

Thus, the concept of victimhood spreads wide under the FMR principle and includes:

- The intended victim
- Any inadvertent victim
- A by-passer
- An onlooker
- A public safety officer responding to the scene
- EMS/fire personnel
- A rescuer or good Samaritan
- Other defendants and perpetrators
- An accomplice, conspirator, or other participant

Felony murder spoons out these tough and unapologetic results by allowing the broadest perspective of victim classes, even those remote under ordinary circumstances and those beyond the ken of the perpetrator. For example, robbery partners usually do not set out early in the criminal enterprise hoping to kill one another. Why would the gun-toting bank robber wish to eliminate his or her means of escape from the crime scene? How could a bank robber envision that a private citizen would engage in a feeble rescue attempt that caused the death to self or others? These cases amplify how unintentional felony murder really is, yet how severe the law reacts to the unintended results of felonious activity. A price must be paid for the gamble of criminal enterprise. For felons, stained by the muck of felonious assault and battery, rape, and arson, escape and extortion, the FMR will stick to them in any of their surroundings.

Any Perpetrator—Any Victim is the basic parameter of the FMR. Draconian as it might appear, courts have shown little willingness to overturn the FMR. The resistance is grounded in the chain of events that lead to another's death. Undeniably, victims would not exist if defendants had not engaged in criminal conduct in the first instance. For this reason, defendants are often labeled the "proximate cause" of the killing and correctly so. In *People v. Lowery*, an appeals court relays the theory of proximate cause with eloquence:

> It is equally consistent with reason and sound public policy to hold that when a felon's attempt to commit a forcible felony sets in motion a chain of events which were or should have been within his contemplation when the motion was initiated, he should be held responsible for any death which by direct and almost inevitable sequence results from the initial criminal act.[48]

The "any victim" standard has been challenged by numerous commentators. The rub amongst defense counsel sits not at some level of culpability, but the severe nature of penalty and culpability assigned to these acts. To critics, Murder 1 and 2 are misplaced codifications in the world of felony murder. Some other form of homicide may be more fitting, especially one less onerous. Others have suggested that in the objectifiable case where the defendant lacks any provable intentionality, felony murder can apply, but with far less stringent aftereffects. Why should an unintending agent be punished at the same level as the intending, premeditating, and plotting

CASE 4.4

PEOPLE V. DEKENS
182 Ill. 2d 247, 695 N.E.2d 474 (Ill 1998).

This appeal presents the question whether a defendant may be charged with first degree murder, on a felony murder theory, when the decedent is a co-felon who is killed by an intended victim of the defendant and co-felon.

The defendant was charged in the circuit court of Kankakee County with murder, criminal drug conspiracy, and attempted armed robbery. Prior to trial, the defendant moved to dismiss the murder charge, which was based on a felony murder theory. The defendant contended that he could not be charged with that offense because the decedent in this case was a co-felon, who was shot and killed by the victim of the robbery attempt. For purposes of resolving the defendant's motion, the prosecution and the defense stipulated to the facts underlying the case. According to the parties' stipulation, an undercover police officer arranged to buy drugs from the defendant at a residence in Kankakee on January 5, 1996. Prior to the meeting, the defendant and the decedent, Peter Pecchenino, formulated a plan to rob the officer. During the drug transaction, the defendant pointed a shotgun at the officer and threatened him. In response, the officer fired several shots at the defendant. As the officer was leaving the residence, he was grabbed by Pecchenino. The officer shot Pecchenino, who later died as a result of those wounds. The defendant was subsequently charged with Pecchenino's murder, under a felony murder theory.

In *People v. Lowery*, this court recently reviewed the nature of the felony murder doctrine and the opposing theories on which liability may be based. As Lowery explains, Illinois follows the "proximate cause" theory of liability for felony murder. Under that theory, liability attaches "for any death proximately resulting from the unlawful activity, notwithstanding the fact that the killing was by one resisting the crime." The other principal theory of liability under the felony murder doctrine is the agency theory, which is followed by a majority of jurisdictions. Under the agency theory, "the doctrine of felony murder does not extend to a killing, although growing out of the commission of the felony, if directly attributable to the act of one other than the defendant or those associated with him in the unlawful enterprise." There is no liability under the agency theory when the homicide is committed by a person resisting the felony. Morris, relied on by the trial judge in this case, is an expression of the agency theory of liability.

We believe that a charge of felony murder is appropriate in these circumstances. Here, the intended victim shot and killed the defendant's co-felon. We do not believe that the defendant should be relieved from liability for the homicide simply because of the decedent's role in the offense. Nor do we believe that application of the doctrine depends on whether or not the decedent was an innocent party. To hold otherwise would import the agency theory of felony murder into our law. As we have noted, Illinois has long followed the proximate cause theory. Consistent with that view, then, we conclude that a defendant may be charged with murder under a felony murder theory when an intended victim of the felony shoots and kills a co-felon of the defendant.

> **Questions**
>
> 1. Who actually killed in the case?
> 2. Who was the victim?
> 3. Who was found guilty of felony murder?
> 4. Did the convicted party kill the victim?

murderer? Why not reserve the most severe penalties for those engaging in the most heinous and calculating of human activities? As Clark and Marshall cogently remark:

> At common law, malice was implied as a matter of law in cases of homicide arising while the defendant was engaged in the commission of some other felony; such a killing was murder whether death was intended or not. The fact that the party was engaged in the commission of a felony was regarded as sufficient to apply the element of malice ... On this principle, it was murder at common law unintentionally to kill another while committing, or attempting to commit, burglary, arson, rape, robbery, or larceny. The doctrine has repeatedly been recognized and applied in this country, and is to be regarded as still in force.[49]

DEFENSE STRATEGIES

Defense counsel has significant challenges in FMR cases. Strategies that have shown promise include:

- To demonstrate a lack of causation between the felony and the killing
- To challenge a felony murder statute on due process grounds
- To challenge the severity of punishments and the assignment of culpability under constitutional theories involving the Eighth Amendment and its cruel and unusual punishment clause
- To pose Eighth Amendment challenges under the "excessive fines and penalties" clause of the Eighth
- To challenge a lack of equal protection as designated under the 14th Amendment since unintentional criminal agents suffer stringent penalties despite their role in the offense
- To discern and argue some intervening cause, which prompted the death of the victim
- To hold the trigger man or woman, the actual doer of the deed, to a higher standard than the mere accomplice or accessory.

Any Perpetrator

Another facet of the felony murder rule that intrigues legal commentators and jurists relates to how the principal's act will bind all the principal's cohorts, whether accessories, conspirators, accomplices or possibly solicitors, aiders, and abettors. In other words, the FMR grabs each defendant involved in the deed and declares each equally accountable. As harsh as it seems, no one can sever ties to the other; no one can relinquish responsibility for all of the outcomes and no

CASE 4.5

STATE V. OIMEN
184 Wis. 2d 423, 516 N.W.2d 399 (Wis. 1994).

This is a review of an unpublished decision of the court of appeals affirming a judgment of the Dane County circuit court, Judge George A. W. Northrup, convicting James Oimen, pursuant to a jury verdict, of felony murder, sec. 940.03, Stats., as a party to a crime and convicting Oimen of attempted armed robbery, secs. 943.32(1)(b) and (2), Stats., and 939.32(1), Stats., also as a party to a crime. We accepted review limited to the following two issues: whether the felony murder statute, sec. 940.03, Stats., [Section 940.03, Stats. 1991-1992, states:

Whoever causes the death of another human being while committing or attempting to commit a crime specified in s. 940.225(1) or (2)(a) [first degree sexual assault and second degree sexual assault with use or threat of force or violence], 943.02 [arson], 943.10(2) [armed burglary] or 943.32(2) [armed robbery] may be imprisoned for not more than 20 years in excess of the maximum period of imprisonment provided by law for that crime or attempt.] applies to a defendant whose co-felon is killed by the intended felony victim; and whether the circuit court erred in instructing the jury on the elements of felony murder.

We conclude that under sec. 940.03, a defendant can be charged with felony murder for the death of a co-felon when the killing was committed by the victim of the underlying felony. Sec. 940.03 limits liability to those deaths caused by a defendant committing or attempting to commit a limited number of inherently dangerous felonies, but it contains no other limitations on liability. The state need only prove that the defendant caused the death, and that the defendant caused the death while committing or attempting to commit one of the five listed felonies. The defendant's acts need not be the sole cause of death. Thus, Oimen was appropriately charged with felony murder for the death of a co-felon, Shawn Murphy McGinnis, who was killed by Tom Stoker, the victim of the underlying felony. ...

We affirm the decision of the court of appeals.

The evidence at trial indicated that in late December of 1988, James Oimen, Shawn Murphy McGinnis, and David Hall made plans to rob Tom Stoker, a "bookie" who occasionally had large sums of money at his house. Over the course of several meetings, Oimen, who had placed bets with Stoker on numerous occasions, told Hall and McGinnis that Stoker was a quiet person who was "meek and mild" and did not carry a gun. Oimen stated that Stoker could have up to $200,000 in the house, but would not report a theft because the money was gained illegally. Oimen drew a diagram of the layout of Stoker's house and told the other two men where the money was likely to be. Oimen added that Stoker would turn over his money if the two men merely threatened to destroy the computer Stoker used to keep track of point spreads. Oimen also explained that he did not want to go into the house himself because Stoker knew him.

On January 2nd, 1989, McGinnis borrowed a gun described as either a pellet gun or a BB gun. Hall testified that the gun looked real and he was only able to discern that it was a BB gun because it had a small hole at the end. That evening, the three men drove to Stoker's house and parked down the street. Hall and McGinnis went up to the house and Oimen remained in Hall's pickup. McGinnis carried the BB gun. Hall carried a pool cue butt, a small billy club and a pocket knife. Before attempting the break-in, McGinnis cut Stoker's phone lines.

At approximately 11:30 p.m., Stoker was attempting to call his daughter when the phone line went dead. Suspicious that something had happened, Stoker laid his Winchester 308 automatic hunting rifle out in the bedroom. Stoker then walked through the house to look out the windows. In the kitchen, he turned on the porch light and pulled aside curtains on a window in the kitchen door. He did not open the door. McGinnis and Hall were standing right outside this door, with masks covering their heads. McGinnis, who was pointing the BB gun about four inches from Stoker's head, yelled something such as, "We want your money, you bookie." Stoker testified that the gun looked like a large hand gun.

The next sequence of events occurred in less than forty-five seconds. Stoker ran back to his bedroom, grabbed the rifle and loaded it. Meanwhile, McGinnis broke down the kitchen door and the two men ran into the house. While Stoker was loading his gun, he saw McGinnis standing down the hall in the bathroom doorway, pointing a gun straight at Stoker. Stoker could not see Hall, but he saw what looked like another gun pointed out from the stairway.

Stoker pointed his gun at McGinnis. After McGinnis said, "He's got a gun," Hall and McGinnis turned and began to run back in the direction from which they had come. Stoker walked down the hall after the men. When Stoker reached the kitchen, it appeared to him that McGinnis, who was on the porch, was coming back into the house. Stoker testified that McGinnis pointed his gun at Stoker, who responded by firing his rifle. The shot hit McGinnis, who fell backwards into the snow outside.

Hall heard the rifle shot and then McGinnis screaming that he had been hit. While Hall helped McGinnis toward the road, he heard his pickup start up. He left McGinnis and went up the street to where Oimen had agreed to wait if there was any trouble. Oimen was not there—Hall could hear the pickup driving away in the distance. Hall went back to where McGinnis lay near the road, but ran away once he heard police sirens. Meanwhile, McGinnis died. On January 5, Hall turned himself into the police. In return for an agreement with the district attorney's office that he would only be charged with one count of armed burglary, Hall described what had happened that night and the preceding days.

Oimen was arrested and charged with attempted armed robbery, felony murder, and armed burglary, as a party to the crime on each count. Attempted armed robbery was the underlying felony in the felony murder charge. Oimen moved to dismiss the felony murder charge, arguing that sec. 940.03, Stats., the felony murder statute, did not apply to a co-felon when the victim of the underlying felony killed one of the other felons. The Dane County circuit court denied the motion and the case proceeded to trial.

At the end of Oimen's trial, Dane County Circuit Court Judge George Northrup instructed the jury. The jury was instructed on all three theories of party to a crime liability—direct actor, conspirator, and aider and abettor. In relevant part, Judge Northrup gave the following instruction on felony murder:

Felony murder, as defined in § 940.03 of the Criminal Code of Wisconsin, is committed by one who causes the death of another human being while committing or attempting to commit the crime of armed robbery. Before the defendant may be found guilty of felony murder, the State must prove by evidence which satisfies you beyond a reasonable doubt that the following two elements of this offense were present.

First, that the defendant caused the death of Shawn Murphy McGinnis.

Second, that the defendant caused the death of Shawn Murphy McGinnis while attempting to commit the crime of armed robbery.

The first element requires that the relation of cause and effect exists between the death of Shawn Murphy McGinnis and the act of the defendant. Before the relation of cause and effect can be found to exist, it must appear that the defendant's act was a substantial factor in producing the death.

The second element requires that the defendant caused the death of Shawn Murphy McGinnis while committing the crime of armed robbery.

In determining whether the defendant was in the act of committing an attempted armed robbery, you should be guided by the law and instructions as have already been given to you by this Court.

Questions

1. What type of cause does the court utilize to find the defendant guilty under felony murder?
2. Who was the victim in this case?
3. Who actually killed the victim?
4. Can you envision a sound defense in these facts under the existing law?

one can selectively choose which part of the criminal enterprise to be tuned into while escaping the remainder. Under the "any perpetrator" rule, it is one for all and all for one. Courts rightfully resist the claim of separation and selective culpability when hearing appellate cases over the FMR. Hence, the escape driver may not pull the trigger while passing time for the getaway, though he or she might as well have.[50] The "Any Perpetrator" theory subsumes each and every colleague into the web of culpability. Naïve, dumbfounded, and surprised defendants cannot withstand the tug of the FMR.[51]

The Dilemma of Dual Intents

One final curiosity of the FMR relates to its competing intentionalities. While mens rea becomes somewhat irrelevant under the unusual FMR fact pattern, since the legislative pattern imposes strict liability, this exemption on proof becomes available only in cases where a demonstration of the underlying felony's mens rea has been proven. In other words, proof of the rape, the robbery, or other qualifying felony mandates satisfactory evidence of the defendant's mental state. Strict liability in FMR must extend to the felony, which affords the Rule's very existence. A prosecutor unable to convict based on the root felony stands in legal quicksand on felony murder grounds. Hence, to avail oneself of the FMR, proof of the qualifying felony is mandatory. Otherwise, the defendant will be prosecuted as any other murderer is—under the fundamental elements of both act and mind. In the last instance, the prosecutor works much harder than the smooth sailing strict liability affords. From this perspective, FMR really contains two forms of intentionality:

QUALIFYING FELONY + HOMICIDE = FELONY MURDER RULE

CASE 4.6

STATE V. RUSSELL
198 P.3d 271 (2008)

Following a jury trial in the Thirteenth Judicial District, Rusty Lee-Ray Russell ("Russell") was found guilty of deliberate homicide (under a felony homicide theory), aggravated assault, robbery by accountability, and aggravated assault by accountability. He was sentenced to eighty years (with ten suspended) for the deliberate homicide. He also received ten years for each of the remaining counts, including the aggravated assault which was the predicate felony for the felony homicide charge. Russell appeals, arguing his conviction for aggravated assault violates the double jeopardy clause of the Montana Constitution. Russell also challenges the jury instructions given in the case, and claims he was denied effective assistance of counsel. We affirm in part, and reverse in part.

We restate the issues as follows:

I. Did the District Court err by denying Russell's motion to dismiss his conviction for aggravated assault, where his felony homicide conviction was predicated on the same assault?

...

Background

On Monday night, April 25, 2005, Russell and his friend Brandon Spotted Wolf ("Spotted Wolf") spent the evening drinking their way across Billings. Though they were underage, they convinced two people to buy them a couple bottles of whiskey, which they drank in various back alleys and in a private residence over the course of the evening. Early the next morning, they found themselves outside the Saint Vincent De Paul Thrift Store, where they ran into Henry Rideshorse ("Rideshorse"). Rideshorse had a bottle of vodka; the boys had about half a bottle of whiskey left. They decided to share the two bottles amongst the three of them, and moved into the back alley behind the thrift store where they could drink without being seen by police.

Near the loading docks behind the store, several transients were sleeping. Spotted Wolf approached one of the sleeping men, Dale Wallin. Spotted Wolf demanded money or alcohol from Wallin, but Wallin did not respond. Russell drew a knife and gave it to Spotted Wolf. Spotted Wolf slashed Wallin's face, gave the knife back to Russell and said, "Show me what you're made of, man, show me what you can do." Russell took the knife and stabbed Wallin several times in the back.

Russell turned and walked further back into the alley, still holding the knife. There he saw another transient, John Gewanski, sleeping next to a dumpster. Both Rideshorse and Spotted Wolf testified that they saw Russell approach Gewanski, and heard Gewanski make several grunting noises, as if he were being punched or stabbed. The record contains conflicting evidence as to whether or not Spotted Wolf joined Russell in assaulting Gewanski. Blood from both victims was found on both Russell's and Spotted Wolf's clothing. Gewanski sustained numerous stab wounds and died in the makeshift shelter where he had been sleeping when he was attacked.

Russell and Spotted Wolf turned their attention back to Wallin, and began attacking him again. Rideshorse intervened and tried to protect Wallin. Russell punched Rideshorse, and said to Spotted Wolf, "Let's do this guy, man." Spotted Wolf testified that he convinced Russell not to kill Rideshorse, and the two fled the scene. Rideshorse helped Wallin to his feet, ran to the street, and flagged down a police car for help. In the meantime, Wallin stumbled several blocks to the Rescue Mission, where he was taken to the hospital. Wallin survived his multiple stab wounds.

Spotted Wolf was found the next morning, passed out with a blood alcohol level exceeding 0.3, blood on his clothing, and a bloody knife in his pants. He was taken to the hospital and treated for alcohol poisoning, and later arrested. Russell was apprehended by the police the following day.

Spotted Wolf pled guilty to one count of deliberate homicide by accountability, one count of aggravated assault, and one count of robbery. In exchange for his plea and testimony, Spotted Wolf received a reduced sentence.

Russell was charged with four offenses: the deliberate homicide of Gewanski, the aggravated assault of Wallin, robbery by accountability, and aggravated assault of Gewanski by accountability. The deliberate homicide charge was brought under § 45-5-102(1)(b), MCA, the felony homicide statute. The information identified the *304 aggravated assault of Wallin as the underlying felony for the felony homicide charge.

Spotted Wolf testified against Russell at his trial. When asked why he and Russell attacked Wallin, Spotted Wolf replied, "I don't know, because we were drunk."

At the close of trial, Russell requested that the court specifically instruct the jury that, if they convicted Russell of deliberate homicide under a felony homicide theory, they must all agree on the particular act or acts he committed. The District Court refused the instruction, but issued a general unanimity instruction instead. The jury found Russell guilty on all four counts.

Prior to sentencing, Russell moved to dismiss his conviction for aggravated assault. Russell argued that his conviction resulted in multiple punishments in violation of Article II, Section 25 of the Montana Constitution. The District Court denied Russell's motion to dismiss, and sentenced Russell to eighty years, with ten suspended, for the felony homicide. Russell also received ten years for each of the remaining counts, to run consecutively with the eighty-year sentence, but concurrently with each other.

Discussion

I. Did the District Court err by denying Russell's motion to dismiss his conviction for aggravated assault, where his felony homicide conviction was predicated on the same assault?

We review a district court's denial of a motion to dismiss in a criminal case *de novo*. *State v. Burkhart*, 2004 MT 372, ¶ 39, 325 Mont. 27, ¶ 39, 103 P.3d 1037.

Russell argues that the District Court erred in refusing to grant his motion to dismiss his conviction for aggravated assault. The felony homicide charge in Count I was predicated on the charge for aggravated assault in Count II. Thus, Russell asserts, the underlying felony in Count II should have been merged with the felony homicide charge in Count

I. Russell claims that the District Court's refusal to dismiss his conviction for aggravated assault placed him in double jeopardy for the same aggravated assault charge, a result prohibited by Article II, Section 25 of the Montana Constitution.

Although Russell frames the issue as a double jeopardy issue under Article II, Section 25 of the Montana Constitution, "we have repeatedly recognized that courts should avoid constitutional issues whenever possible." In re S.H., 2003 MT 366, ¶ 18, 319 Mont. 90, ¶ 18, 86 P.3d 1027, ¶ 18. Here, determining whether the District Court erred in failing to dismiss Count II can be resolved through application of our code of criminal procedure §§ 46-11-410(2)(a) and 46-1-202(9), MCA.

Section 46-11-410, MCA, states, in pertinent part, as follows:

(1) When the same transaction may establish the commission of more than one offense, a person charged with the conduct may be prosecuted for each offense.
(2) A defendant may not, however, be convicted of more than one offense if:
    (a) one offense is included in the other. ...

Section 46-1-202(9), MCA, defines "included offense" as follows:

"Included offense" means an offense that:

    (a) is established by proof of the same or less than all the facts required to establish the commission of the offense charged. ...

As used in § 46-1-202(9)(a), MCA, the term "facts" refers to the statutory elements of the offense, not the individual facts of the case. State v. Beavers, 1999 MT 260, ¶ 30, 296 Mont. 340, ¶ 30, 987 P.2d 371, ¶ 30.

Here, Russell was charged with felony homicide under § 45-5-102(1)(b), MCA. Felony homicide can be accomplished by multiple means under the statute.

A person commits the offense of deliberate homicide if ... the person attempts to commit, commits, or is legally accountable for the attempt or commission of robbery, sexual intercourse without consent, arson, burglary, kidnapping, aggravated kidnapping, felonious escape, assault with a weapon, aggravated assault, or any other forcible felony and in the course of the forcible felony or flight thereafter, the person or any person legally accountable for the crime causes the death of another human being.

Section 45-5-102(1)(b), MCA. The statute lists a myriad of possible predicate felonies: robbery, sexual intercourse without consent, arson, burglary, kidnapping, and so on. The State charged Russell by information with deliberate homicide under § 45-5-102(1)(b), MCA, and identified aggravated assault as the predicate felony. The court defined the felony homicide charge to include aggravated assault in its instructions to the jury. Thus, the charge, as applied to Russell, included aggravated assault as an element of felony homicide.

At oral argument, the State conceded that the same evidence was used to prove the stand-alone aggravated assault charge in Count II, and the predicate felony relied upon in the felony homicide charge in Count I. An offense is an included offense if it "is established by proof of the same or less than all the facts required to establish the commission of the offense charged. ..." Section 46-1-202(9)(a), MCA. In the unique context of felony homicide, the predicate offense is, of necessity, an included offense, as well as an element of the felony homicide itself. As applied in this case, aggravated assault is both an included offense and an element of felony homicide.

Under § 46-11-410(1)-(2)(a), MCA, "A defendant may not ... be convicted of more than one offense" arising out of "the same transaction" if "one offense is included in the other. ..." Assuming that the assault on Wallin and the killing of Gewanski were part of the same transaction, then under § 46-11-410(2)(a), MCA, Russell's conviction of felony homicide precludes a conviction on the aggravated assault charge in Count II.

In his dissent, Justice Rice relies heavily on our 1981 decision in *State v. Close*, 191 Mont. 229, 623 P.2d 940 (1981). The Close decision is of very limited value in the present case. The basic premise of the Close rationale is false. The Close Court engaged in a Blockburger analysis and held that "it is clear that proof of felony homicide will not [a] necessarily require proof of either robbery or aggravated kidnapping." *Close*, 191 Mont. at 246, 623 P.2d at 950. "One can commit felony homicide without committing robbery, or commit aggravated kidnapping without committing felony homicide. Therefore, Blockburger does not require the conclusion that felony homicide and the underlying felony merge." *Close*, 191 Mont. at 247, 623 P.2d at 950. Although the Court was correct that, in the abstract, one can commit felony murder without necessarily committing aggravated kidnapping or can commit aggravated kidnapping without committing felony homicide, a defendant cannot commit the offense of felony homicide without committing a predicate felony offense. Thus, when the State uses an offense (such as kidnapping or robbery or, as here, assault) as a predicate offense in its charge of felony homicide, the accused cannot be found guilty of felony homicide without having committed the predicate offense of kidnapping, robbery, or assault. When the State chooses to charge the offenses in that fashion, the offenses merge. The predicate offense becomes a lesser included offense of the felony homicide charge. Sections 46-11-410, 46-1-202(9), MCA.

The dissent argues that where there are two victims, the State should be able to hold the defendant separately accountable for each crime. The dissent's criticism is valid but misdirected. The discretion to charge whom with what lies with the State, not this Court. Here, the State could have charged Russell with felony homicide of Gewanski using robbery as the predicate felony, and then charged Russell separately with felony assault of Wallin, in which case there would have been no merger of the assault and the homicide convictions. Alternatively, the State could have avoided merger altogether by charging Russell with all three crimes separately: first, the deliberate homicide of Gewanski under § 45-5-102(a), MCA; second, robbery by accountability under §§ 45-4-401(1)(a) and 45-2-302(3), MCA; and finally, the aggravated assault of Wallin under § 45-5-202, MCA. Contrary to the dissent's characterization, the merger of the homicide and assault convictions in this felony homicide case arises not from a "stupefying leap" by this Court, but from the State's choice in framing the charges.

Our decision does not, as the dissent suggests, give Russell a "free pass" for Wallin's assault. As we painstakingly outline above, the State had to prove each element of aggravated assault in order to convict Russell for felony homicide in this case. Russell was punished for both the predicate offense, Wallin's assault, and Gewanski's homicide, when he was charged and convicted under § 45-5-102, MCA.

Finally, under § 45-5-102, MCA, felony homicide is punishable by death, by life imprisonment, or by imprisonment for a term of not less than 10 years or more than 100 years. The dissent's hyperbolic "free pass" argument ignores the fact that where the felon is sentenced to death or life in prison for felony homicide, any additional punishment for the underlying felony would have no practical effect.

Accordingly, we hold that the District Court erred in refusing to dismiss Russell's conviction for aggravated assault under Count II.

...

Conclusion

We reverse the District Court's order denying Russell's motion to dismiss his conviction for aggravated assault. Aggravated assault was an included element of felony homicide under § 45-5-102(1)(b), MCA, as charged and applied in this case. Article II, Section 25 of the Montana Constitution prohibits the State from convicting and punishing Russell again for the same aggravated assault. Accordingly, we vacate Russell's conviction for aggravated assault under Count II of the information. We conclude that the District Court did not abuse its discretion in denying Russell's proposed specific unanimity jury instruction. Finally, Russell's ineffective assistance of counsel claim is not record-based, thus we dismiss it without prejudice.

Defendants have creatively attacked this formula for generations arguing various lines.

Any failure in the equation negates the FMR case. Because, if a killing does not occur, the issue of murder in any degree, outside of the attempted category, will not meet the threshold. If an underlying felony is not satisfactorily proved, FMR remains illusory also, and only the murder case survives. The problems of dual intent multiply across the legal system for many believe that FMR is by nature an unfair penalty. In *State v. Russell*,[52] the defendant argues that if he is guilty of specific intent felonious homicide, he cannot be guilty of FMR—the strict liability version.[53] In addition, he claims that the underlying felony need be causally connected to the actual murder. See *State v. Russell* at Case 4.6.

DEFENSE STRATEGIES FOR FMR

- If Defendant (D) did not succeed in carrying out the underlying felony, FMR fails.
- If D admits to manslaughter or lower form of criminal homicide, FMR could not be a proper charge.
- If D moves to dismiss FMR and not an M1 or M2 charge, does D gamble with better evidentiary cards? Because the burden on unadorned M1 or 2 demands proof of specific or general intent, D may be right.
- If D desired only to perform the underlying felony, how could D intend any other outcome?
- D's conviction as mere participant violates the Fifth, Eighth, and Fourteenth Amendments of the Constitution.
- If D renounced participation in anything beyond the underlying felony, can D be exonerated from FMR?

- If D's commission of the underlying felony is detached by time and space from the eventual death of another, how can FMR apply?
- What if the State is unable to distinguish the dual intentionalities as the crimes play out? For example, if the initial aggravated assault evolves into a criminal homicide, can't D argue that these intentionalities merge? In this way is there no distinct felony from the homicide itself?

Defense counsel may move energetically against FMR for a host of reasons, none more compelling than the extreme difficulty in launching a meaningful defense in an offense that bypasses mens rea. One can always expect the defense to urge unity rather than severability in the root offense and the killing. A kidnapper who terrorizes another with threats to kill may intend only to kill in the end and could care less about the elements of kidnapping. Sexual degenerates who prey on children, drifters, and the like, expend limited energy severing their actions and are primarily aiming for the purpose of the kidnapping in the first instance. FMR should be declared inapplicable when the prosecution cannot highlight the distinct nature of the two felonies in question. As learned Justice Samuel Cardozo cautioned, failure to do so is nothing more than a "futile attempt to split into unrelated parts an indivisible transaction."[54] Defense counsel posits that if it's murder, just say so and we will defend. However, wily prosecutors and DAs are enticed by the unassailability of the FMR as much as defense counsel cringe at its power. In the end, prosecutorial teams must be perpetually cognizant of how unique and intricate the FMR dynamic can be and to avoid being caught in the web of dueling intentionalities. Another aspect of these competing mental states relates to whether offenses eventually merge together or, put another way, whether the original offense dissipates upon the commission of the second and final offense. For example, does not an assault merge into murder or manslaughter when the originally assaulted victim dies? In *People v. Chun*,[55] that is exactly what occurred when the court labeled the "assaultive aspect"[56] blends into the actual homicide.[57]

CASE 4.7

PEOPLE V. MORAN
246 NY 100 (1927).

Visit your local county law library or a law library at a local college or university or online at Lexis/Nexis or WestLaw and obtain the above case and answer the following questions.

Questions

1. Which two felonies were questioned as not being sufficiently distinct to enable the FMR?
2. How does the Court rule on the issue?
3. Do you agree with the Court's decision? Explain.

NEGLIGENT HOMICIDE (INVOLUNTARY MANSLAUGHTER)

ELEMENTS:

- Killing of another
- By criminal negligence, gross, or reckless conduct
- Without proof of criminal intent

As the excursion into the law of homicide travels degree by degree, at the lower ebb of the criminal continuum rests the law of negligent homicide. The term "involuntary" means just what it says—unwilling. One can kill unwillingly yet still be held to some level of culpability. The term "negligence" connotes a failure of obligation and person. To be negligent is to err, to make mistakes not out of malevolence and depraved indifference, but from a gross carelessness that cannot be brooked. Not to be confused with mere accident, where the law excuses the human agent, negligence garners a level of personal responsibility that our legal system cannot ignore. Criminal negligence includes any act in which "a person acts negligently with respect to a material element of an offense when he should be aware of a substantial and unjustifiable risk that the material element exists or will result from his conduct."[58] In the criminal realm, negligence means a great deal more than the law of torts where we look to due care and diligence, duty owed and breached, and personal damages amassed. Criminal negligence encompasses personal harm and injury to be sure, but appreciates the individual injury in a greater, communal context by criminalizing the conduct. The Model Penal Code (MPC) offers a circuitous definition of negligent homicide by indicating that "criminal homicide constitutes negligent homicide when it is committed negligently."[59]

Find out about how faith-healing parents, who refused treatment for their own children, were subsequently charged with involuntary manslaughter at http://www.msnbc.msn.com/id/35207710/ns/us_news-crime_and_courts/

It will be rare to find those who kill negligently that really intend to do so. These are the individuals who could or should have known better. The driver who had one too many to drinks, the substance abuser who forgets about her child, or the guardian that lets his watchful eye lapse can kill not by accident but by the type of omission that the common good cannot tolerate. The law assumes and presumes an incomplete and unformed notion of will and volition in the matter. As such, the offense is correctly designated "involuntary." See Figure 4.8[60] for a graphic representation on the statistics regarding DUI Fatalities, a classic form of involuntary manslaughter.

The variety of criminal laws addressing these principles is impressive, though not uniform in approach. "There is considerable diversity concerning the unlawful acts that do or should suffice to make a killing involuntary manslaughter. There also is considerable uncertainty regarding the meaning of the 'criminal negligence' that will make a killing involuntary manslaughter under the alternative route contained in traditional definitions of the offense."[61] Some jurisdictions see very little difference between the involuntary manslaughter and the case of negligent homicide. Others take the view that various categories of lower

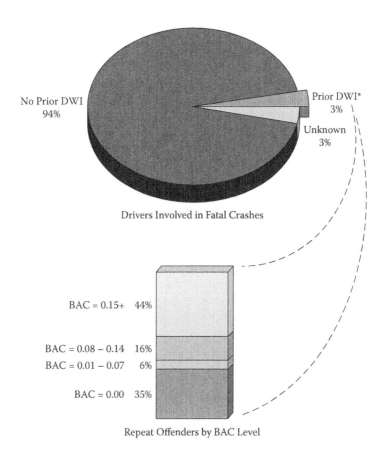

Figure 4.8   Repeat offenders by BAC Level.

level homicide are needed by separating the offenses according to types of conduct, e.g., use of a vehicle, killing as a result of substance abuse, death as a result of some failed duty, and so forth and so on. The distinctions represent a maze that spins the intellect of even experienced practitioners.

Again, we see the law strictly adjudging those who may not wish the death of another, but could have predicted the eventual outcomes. By employing common sense, it is proper to impute culpability when one could or should have known the outcome. As in the federal murder rule, mens rea takes a back seat to the action itself. Review the statute below to discern the emphasis.

§ 2504. Involuntary manslaughter

(A)   GENERAL RULE.—A person is guilty of involuntary manslaughter when as a direct result of the doing of an unlawful act in a reckless or grossly negligent manner, or the doing of a lawful act in a reckless or grossly negligent manner, he causes the death of another person.[62]

So common has been vehicular homicide that novel code provisions have been enacted to react to this unfortunate increase. Vehicular homicides occur because of traffic infractions like excessive speeding and running signals or in driving under the influence cases. In some jurisdictions, the involuntary manslaughter requirements may yet call for proof of some sort of general intent whereby the defendant could be shown to have had some level of cognition about what would take place. California refers to this intellectual plane as "due caution and circumspection."[63] Put another way, should not the reasonable person know that some injury may evolve from the circumstances? The actor in this setting lacks the malignant heart and the depravity that constitutes gross recklessness, but still displays a careless disregard that should not go unnoticed. Thus, when heroin users share illegal drugs that cause death, as took place in *Commonwealth v. Bowden*,[64] a murder conviction could not be sustained due to a paucity of intentionality. The zeal to eradicate drugs has caused certain jurisdictions to impose even greater penalties than have been historically appropriate in drug death cases. New Jersey, for example, has chosen to impose a strict liability murder finding in these cases instead of the negligent or involuntary homicide. Its statute, presented in part, tramples old notions:

a. Any person who manufactures, distributes or dispenses methamphetamine, lysergic acid diethylamide, phencyclidine or any other controlled dangerous substance classified in Schedules I or II, or any controlled substance analog thereof, in violation of subsection a. of N.J.S. 2C:35-5, is strictly liable for a death which results from the injection, inhalation or ingestion of that substance, and is guilty of a crime of the first degree.
b. The provisions of N.J.S. 2C:2-3 (governing the causal relationship between conduct and result) shall not apply in a prosecution under this section. For purposes of this offense, the defendant's act of manufacturing, distributing or dispensing a substance is the cause of a death when:
   (1)   The injection, inhalation or ingestion of the substance is an antecedent but for which the death would not have occurred; and
   (2)   The death was not:
      (a)   too remote in its occurrence as to have a just bearing on the defendant's liability; or
      (b)   too dependent upon conduct of another person which was unrelated to the injection, inhalation or ingestion of the substance or its effect as to have a just bearing on the defendant's liability.

c. It shall not be a defense to a prosecution under this section that the decedent contributed to his own death by his purposeful, knowing, reckless or negligent injection, inhalation or ingestion of the substance, or by his consenting to the administration of the substance by another.[65]

The policy has strong opposition in many quarters. Antagonists see these designs as nothing more than a "harsh legislative overreach"[66] that disregards "causation and mens rea problems, in addition to basic fairness problems."[67] For many, drug-induced deaths represent a careless, negligent homicide rather than murder or pure manslaughter, though these matters are arguable.

From another slant, involuntary manslaughter charges were usually a tinge tougher than the errant vehicle operator whose carelessness causes the death of another. All of these distinctions are reduced to very fine lines when you think about it. Vehicular homicide (or auto manslaughter as it is sometimes referred) focuses on the relationship of vehicle, victim, and operator. A few jurisdictions employ language like "death as a result of any violation of law while operating a motor vehicle," or "death is the direct result of operating a motor vehicle while under the influence," to zero in on specific conduct and even more particular types of defendants.[68] When alcohol or other controlled substances are involved, the conduct is always construed as graver than the traffic infraction fatality. To supporters, public policy and the level of harm caused by drunk drivers justify the differentiation.

At its heart, the proponent of negligent homicide has a far greater burden than the demonstration of carelessness on the part of the human player. Instead, the careless conduct goes beyond ordinary mistake and leaps into the realm of predictability and responsibility. To engage in careless conduct is one thing, to test the limits of safety and communal tranquility is quite another. Drunk drivers know only too well the eventual possibilities. So do speeders and drag racers, drug users, and substance abusers. In this world, the mistake is transformed into inexcusable error that is grossly hostile to others. Running a red light, without the influence of mind-altering substances, may or may not be a simple mistake. The facts will have to be evaluated closely. As a lawyer, one is sure to encounter a case that treads both sides of the ocean: one in the sea of culpable recklessness and the other in the waters of unfortunate accident. This author recalls such a scenario in his own practice. How would you have handled these facts:

The driver, a 41-year-old mother of three, is proceeding in a westerly direction on a very curvy road. She obeys all traffic signs as to speed and operates her vehicle without any external illegal influences. Suddenly, a small boy darts in front of her, running from a wooded area. The vehicle rams into the 12-year-old child and flings him onto the windshield where the mother and her children see the tragic events unfold.

- As to criminal negligence, the County District Attorney was asked to rule on the possibility of criminal charges. How should the DA so find?
- As to civil negligence, the privately retained attorney was asked by the family to determine a potential avenue for the redress of damages? How should the attorney weigh this possibility?
- On what basis should the DA base the decision to prosecute or not? How would you rule?
- Can you think of a solid legal argument that would justify the charge of negligent homicide?
- As for the private attorney, has the driver of the vehicle breached any duty to the deceased?
- If you were a lawyer, would you litigate the case?[69]

SUICIDE

ELEMENTS:

- Taking of one's own life (common law) or the assistance or solicitation of same
- With intent
- By machine or mechanical instrument or device (in some cases)

The taking of one's own life was a criminal offense according to common law. The proscription had minimal deterrent or practical utility because those aggrieved enough to end existence cannot feel the lash of the justice system. It seems insensible to have any law on the books for individual victims except for its message. More convincingly, the law does punish those who aid and abet others to commit suicide. Physicians and medical personnel, friend and foe, relative and intimate partner should not wield such influence. Consider the contrary proposition. What if suicide was promoted as a thing of value and merit? What if the society took no umbrage with those who enticed and solicited others to end their lives? What value would the nation be offering up to its citizens? From another slant, would the promotion or toleration of suicidal practices contribute to the advancement of the common good? Would enough people be convinced of its legitimacy to enter into the suicide pact that would not be otherwise? Delicate as these questions are, they are on the front burner in the twenty-first century, and argued from a myriad of vantage points.

First, the spectrum that comprises individual freedom and rights, includes the demand, on the part of a select constituency, that what an individual does to self is not the province of others. "My body, my rights," the mantra is. Personal privacy and freedom from governmental intrusion are championed in the advocacy of assisted suicide legalization.[70] A decade or so ago, freedom arguments relative to assisted suicide may have had a friendlier ear in the federal courts in particular. Courts are increasingly resisting the expansionist view of individual liberties unless it can be shown that the intrusion is in "the 'realm of personal liberty which the government may not enter.'"[71] They essentially argue that the Fourteenth Amendment protects fundamental 'liberty' interests from undue government restriction if they involve 'the most intimate and personal choices a person may make in a lifetime, choices central to personal dignity and autonomy.'"[72,73] Today, the question of suicide practice has been construed so contrary to our moral heritage that legalization remains only a remote possibility.[74]

Second, for a growing minority, suicide should receive some type of constitutional protection, as if some express or evolving legal right portended by the Founding Fathers. Suicide, it would seem, is guaranteed by the First Amendment, or under a property clause of the Fourteenth Amendment. Edward Rubin argues that such laws are a "coercive imposition of the Christian-based morality of higher purposes on citizens, and are thus unconstitutional under the First Amendment."[75]

This exact claim was deliberated on extensively by our own Supreme Court in *Washington v. Glucksberg.*[76] In addressing the right to physician-assisted suicide, the court unanimously refused to extend the constitutionalism to this quarter. Chief Justice Rehnquist argued passionately against the legalization of the practice:

> We begin ... by examining our Nation's history, legal traditions, and practices. In almost every State—indeed, in almost every western democracy—it is a crime to assist a suicide. Rather, they are longstanding expressions of the States' commitment to the protection and preservation of all human life. Indeed, opposition to and condemnation of suicide—and, therefore, of assisting suicide—are consistent and enduring themes of our philosophical, legal, and cultural heritages.[77]

History, tradition, moral order, and our own instincts argue against the legalization the Court so held. In this rare, unanimous opinion, the door was closed for legitimated suicide.

The matter of suicide, physician-assisted or otherwise, has significant popular support in the American theatre. Nearly all states ban all aspects of suicide, though there are three states, Oregon, Washington, and California, that have "Death with Dignity Acts" of provisions.[78] These Acts tend to distinguish assisted suicide that is aggressive, euthanasia which is systematically

CASE 4.8

WASHINGTON V. GLUCKSBERG
117 S. Ct. 2258, 521 US 702 (1997).

The question presented in this case is whether Washington's prohibition against "causing" or "aiding" a suicide offends the Fourteenth Amendment to the United States Constitution. ...

It has always been a crime to assist a suicide in the State of Washington. In 1854, Washington's first Territorial Legislature outlawed "assisting another in the commission of self-murder." Today, Washington law provides: "A person is guilty of promoting a suicide attempt when he knowingly causes or aids another person to attempt suicide." Wash. Rev. Code 9A.36.060(1) (1994). "Promoting a suicide attempt" is a felony, punishable by up to five years' imprisonment and up to a $10,000 fine. §§ 9A.36.060(2) and 9A.20.021(1)(c). At the same time, Washington's Natural Death Act, enacted in 1979, states that the "withholding or withdrawal of life-sustaining treatment" at a patient's direction "shall not, for any purpose, constitute a suicide." Wash. Rev. Code § 70.122.070(1).

Petitioners in this case are the State of Washington and its Attorney General. Respondents Harold Glucksberg, M.D., Abigail Halperin, M.D., Thomas A. Preston, M.D., and Peter Shalit, M.D. are physicians who practice in Washington. These doctors occasionally treat terminally ill, suffering patients, and declare that they would assist these patients in ending their lives if not for Washington's assisted-suicide ban. In January 1994, respondents, along with three gravely ill, pseudonymous plaintiffs who have since died and Compassion in Dying, a nonprofit organization that counsels people considering physician-assisted suicide, sued in the United States District Court, seeking a declaration that Wash Rev. Code 9A.36.060(1) (1994) is, on its face, unconstitutional.

The plaintiffs asserted "the existence of a liberty interest protected by the Fourteenth Amendment which extends to a personal choice by a mentally competent, terminally ill adult to commit physician-assisted suicide." Id., at 1459. Relying primarily on *Planned Parenthood v. Casey*, and *Cruzan v. Director, Missouri Dept. of Health*, the District Court agreed, and concluded that Washington's assisted-suicide ban is unconstitutional because it "places an undue burden on the exercise of [that] constitutionally protected liberty interest." The District Court also decided that the Washington statute violated the Equal Protection Clause's requirement that "'all persons similarly situated ... be treated alike.'"

A panel of the Court of Appeals for the Ninth Circuit reversed, emphasizing that "in the two hundred and five years of our existence no constitutional right to aid in killing oneself has ever been asserted and upheld by a court of final jurisdiction." *Compassion in Dying v. Washington*. The Ninth Circuit reheard the case *en banc*, reversed the panel's decision, and affirmed the District Court. *Compassion in Dying v. Washington*. Like the District Court, the *en banc* Court of Appeals emphasized our Casey and Cruzan decisions. The court also discussed what it described as "historical" and "current societal attitudes" toward suicide and assisted suicide, and concluded that "the Constitution encompasses a due process liberty interest in controlling the time and manner of one's death—that there is, in short, a constitutionally recognized 'right to die.'" After "weighing and then balancing" this interest against Washington's various interests, the court held that the State's assisted-suicide ban was unconstitutional "as applied to terminally ill, competent adults who wish to hasten their deaths with medication prescribed by their physicians." The court did not reach the District Court's equal-protection holding. We granted certiorari, and now reverse.

We begin, as we do in all due-process cases, by examining our Nation's history, legal traditions, and practices. In almost every State—indeed, in almost every western democracy—it is a crime to assist a suicide. The States' assisted-suicide bans are not innovations. Rather, they are longstanding expressions of the States' commitment to the protection and preservation of all human life. Indeed, opposition to and condemnation of suicide—and, therefore, of assisting suicide—are consistent and enduring themes of our philosophical, legal, and cultural heritages.

More specifically, for over 700 years, the Anglo-American common-law tradition has punished or otherwise disapproved of both suicide and assisting suicide. In the 13th century, Henry de Bracton, one of the first legal-treatise writers, observed that "just as a man may commit felony by slaying another so may he do so by slaying himself." The real and personal property of one who killed himself to avoid conviction and punishment for a crime were forfeit to the king; however, thought Bracton, "if a man slays himself in weariness of life or because he is unwilling to endure further bodily pain ... [only] his movable goods [were] confiscated." Thus, "the principle that suicide of a sane person, for whatever reason, was a punishable felony was ... introduced into English common law." Centuries later, Sir William Blackstone, whose Commentaries on the Laws of England not only provided a definitive summary of the common law, but was also a primary legal authority for 18th and 19th century American lawyers, referred to suicide as "self-murder" and "the pretended heroism, but real cowardice, of the Stoic philosophers, who destroyed themselves to avoid those ills which they had not the fortitude to endure. ..." Blackstone emphasized that "the law has ... ranked [suicide] among the highest crimes," ibid, although, anticipating later developments, he conceded that the harsh and shameful punishments imposed for suicide "border a little upon severity."

For the most part, the early American colonies adopted the common-law approach. For example, the legislators of the Providence Plantations, which would later become Rhode Island, declared in 1647, that "self-murder is by all agreed to be the most unnatural, and it is by this present Assembly declared, to be that, wherein he that doth it, kills himself out of a premeditated hatred against his own life or other humor: ... his goods and chattels are the king's custom, but not his debts nor lands; but in case he be an infant, a lunatic, mad or distracted man, he forfeits nothing." Virginia also required ignominious burial for suicides, and their estates were forfeit to the crown.

Over time, however, the American colonies abolished these harsh common-law penalties.

William Penn abandoned the criminal-forfeiture sanction in Pennsylvania in 1701, and the other colonies (and later, the other States) eventually followed this example. Zephaniah Swift, who would later become Chief Justice of Connecticut, wrote in 1796 that "there can be no act more contemptible, than to attempt to punish an offender for a crime, by exercising a mean act of revenge upon lifeless clay, that is insensible of the punishment. There can be no greater cruelty, than the inflicting [of] a punishment, as the forfeiture of goods, which must fall solely on the innocent offspring of the offender. ... [Suicide] is so abhorrent to the feelings of mankind, and that strong love of life which is implanted in the human heart, that it cannot be so frequently committed, as to become dangerous to society. There can of course be no necessity of any punishment."

This statement makes it clear, however, that the movement away from the common law's harsh sanctions did not represent an acceptance of suicide; rather, as Chief Justice Swift observed, this change reflected the growing consensus that it was unfair to punish the suicide's family for his wrongdoing. Nonetheless, although States moved away from Blackstone's treatment of suicide, courts continued to condemn it as a grave public wrong.

That suicide remained a grievous, though nonfelonious, wrong is confirmed by the fact that colonial and early state legislatures and courts did not retreat from prohibiting assisting suicide.

Swift, in his early 19th-century treatise on the laws of Connecticut, stated that "if one counsels another to commit suicide, and the other by reason of the advice kills himself, the advisor is guilty of murder as principal." This was the well-established common-law view, as was the similar principle that the consent of a homicide victim is "wholly immaterial to the guilt of the person who caused [his death]." And the prohibitions against assisting suicide never contained exceptions for those who were near death. Rather, "the life of those to whom life had become a burden—of those who [were] hopelessly diseased or fatally wounded—nay, even the lives of criminals condemned to death, [were] under the protection of law, equally as the lives of those who [were] in the full tide of life's enjoyment, and anxious to continue to live."

The earliest American statute explicitly to outlaw assisting suicide was enacted in New York in 1828, Act of Dec. 10, 1828, ch. 20, § 4, 1828 N. Y. Laws 19 (codified at 2 N. Y. Rev. Stat. pt. 4, ch. 1, tit. 2, art. 1, § 7, p. 661 (1829)), and many of the new States and Territories followed New York's example. Between 1857 and 1865, a New York commission led by Dudley Field drafted a criminal code that prohibited "aiding" a suicide and, specifically, "furnishing another person with any deadly weapon or poisonous drug, knowing that such person intends to use such weapon or drug in taking his own life." By the time the Fourteenth Amendment was ratified, it was a crime in most States to assist a suicide. The Field Penal Code was adopted in the Dakota Territory in 1877, in New York in 1881, and its language served as a model for several other western States' statutes in the late 19th and early 20th centuries. California, for example, codified its assisted-suicide prohibition in 1874, using language similar to the Field Codes. In this century, the Model Penal Code also prohibited "aiding" suicide, prompting many States to enact or revise their assisted-suicide bans. The Code's drafters observed that "the interests in the sanctity of life that are represented by the criminal homicide laws are threatened by one who expresses a willingness to participate in taking the life of another, even though the act may be accomplished with the consent, or at the request, of the suicide victim."

Though deeply rooted, the States' assisted-suicide bans have in recent years been reexamined and, generally, reaffirmed. Because of advances in medicine and technology, Americans today are increasingly likely to die in institutions, from chronic illnesses. Public concern and democratic action are therefore sharply focused on how best to protect dignity and independence at the end of life, with the result that there have been many significant changes in state laws and in the attitudes these laws reflect. Many States, for example, now permit "living wills," surrogate health-care decision making, and the withdrawal or refusal of life-sustaining medical treatment.

At the same time, however, voters and legislators continue for the most part to reaffirm their States' prohibitions on assisting suicide. The Washington statute at issue in this case, Wash. Rev. Code § 9A.36.060 (1994), was enacted in 1975 as part of a revision of that State's criminal code. Four years later, Washington passed its Natural Death Act, which specifically stated that the "withholding or withdrawal of life-sustaining treatment ... shall not, for any purpose, constitute a suicide" and that "nothing in this chapter shall be construed to condone, authorize, or approve mercy killing . ..." In 1991, Washington voters rejected a ballot initiative which, had it passed, would have permitted a form of physician-assisted suicide. Washington then added a provision to the Natural Death Act expressly excluding physician-assisted suicide.

California voters rejected an assisted-suicide initiative similar to Washington's in 1993. On the other hand, in 1994, voters in Oregon enacted, also through ballot initiative, that State's "Death With Dignity Act," which legalized physician-assisted suicide for competent, terminally ill adults. Since the Oregon vote, many proposals to legalize assisted-suicide have been and continue to be introduced in the States' legislatures, but none has been enacted. And just last year, Iowa and Rhode Island joined the overwhelming majority of States explicitly prohibiting assisted suicide. Also, on April 30, 1997, President Clinton signed the Federal Assisted Suicide Funding Restriction Act of 1997, which prohibits the use of federal funds in support of physician-assisted suicide.

Thus, the States are currently engaged in serious, thoughtful examinations of physician-assisted suicide and other similar issues. For example, New York State's Task Force on Life and the Law—an ongoing, blue-ribbon commission composed of doctors, ethicists, lawyers, religious leaders, and interested laymen—was convened in 1984 and commissioned with "a broad mandate to recommend public policy on issues raised by medical advances." Over the past decade, the Task Force has recommended laws relating to end-of-life decisions, surrogate pregnancy, and organ donation. After studying physician-assisted suicide, however, the Task Force unanimously concluded that "legalizing assisted suicide and euthanasia would pose profound risks to many individuals who are ill and vulnerable. ... The potential dangers of this dramatic change in public policy would outweigh any benefit that might be achieved."

Attitudes toward suicide itself have changed since Bracton, but our laws have consistently condemned, and continue to prohibit, assisting suicide. Despite changes in medical technology and notwithstanding an increased emphasis on the importance of end-of-life decision making, we have not retreated from this prohibition. Against this backdrop of history, tradition, and practice, we now turn to respondents' constitutional claim.

Questions

Locate the remainder of the opinion online to answer the following:

1. Exactly what law was under the Court's scrutiny?
2. How does Justice Scalia resolve the arguments?
3. How does Justice Ginsburg arrive at her conclusion?
4. Would you have decided differently?

imposed by governmental authorities, and the rights of patients to passive choice in withdrawing or refusing treatment.[79]

Most public opinion polls signify a majority of citizens wish the freedom to end lives in cases of terminal illness under conditions unlikely to improve. A remarkable portion of the citizenry also believes that governmental intrusion in this area is an affront to personal liberty.[80] The case of Dr. Jack Kevorkian, the suicide doctor, portrays this national ambivalence.

Throughout the later stages of his career, Kevorkian became the poster child of the libertarians who shun governmental involvement. To those opposed to the practice of physician-assisted suicide, he became the pariah. To the state of Michigan, he was a major thorn to a legal system attempting to thwart his increasing boldness in the suicide market. Under a series of laws, enacted and reenacted, Kevorkian became the target. In most prosecutions, the doctor walked free. In his last trial, his luck ran out as he was prosecuted under the following statute:

752.1027 Prohibited acts; violation; penalties; applicability of subsection (1); exceptions Sec. 7:

(1) A person who has knowledge that another person intends to commit or attempt to commit suicide and who intentionally does either of the following is guilty of criminal assistance to suicide, a felony punishable by imprisonment for not more than 4 years or by a fine of not more than $2,000.00, or both:
   (a)   Provides the physical means by which the other person attempts or commits suicide.
   (b)   Participates in a physical act by which the other person attempts or commits suicide.

(2) Subsection (1) shall not apply to withholding or withdrawing medical treatment.
(3) Subsection (1) does not apply to prescribing, dispensing, or administering medications or procedures if the intent is to relieve pain or discomfort and not to cause death, even if the medication or procedure may hasten or increase the risk of death.[81]

Michigan, like its sister states, walks a fine and delicate line of tolerance in the passage of life. To those who have witnessed terminal patients deteriorate and decay, the practice seems fair and even merciful. Human misery is never a pleasant sight and its elimination should be an honorable task. But, human existence cannot avoid its inevitable tragedy either since death, injury, and illness begets all of us. Watching patients die with courage and dignity affords the rest of the populace a lesson in what makes the human spirit flourish. There is beauty even in this sadness and instruction to the rest of us to count our blessings. At times, greatness arises from human misery since the maintenance of life in the most tenuous of circumstances, screams loudly of human endurance and the will to survive. To the end, the human person craves self-preservation.

Read the Hastings Center Report on Dying with Dignity at http://www.thehastingscenter. org/Publications/HCR/Detail.aspx?id=4538

The unbridled intrusion of the scientific and the medical communities has muddled our sensibilities. Longevity in life has become both friend and enemy. Suicide becomes legitimated by a philosophy of medical intervention that knows no boundaries and which superimposes itself on human decision making. Hospital wards see residents who "live" by machine and pill, yet whose quality of life could never be envisioned by our forefathers. The confusion of technological intervention at all costs fosters the dilemma. Death with dignity is not too much to ask. Death to avoid all pain and suffering may be too generous an accommodation. In an age when pain has largely been eliminated by the use of drug therapies, pain cannot rationalize the premature end to human life. Questions of quality and dignity are not to be forgotten either. "Living" as a vegetable or being mechanically propped up, is devoid of what it truly means to be human. Moralists who condemn each and every case sometimes fail to visualize the grayness in the panorama. Libertarians are just as blind since their self-serving approach to personal freedom provides no assurances of whether this conduct achieves some level of moral defensibility. In between all this, the law trudges along trying to choose wisely. The ambiguity sprinkles right into our legal system which parades the value of life and at the same time understands public sentiment, which resists the extraordinary and sometimes uncalled maintenance of human life by means utterly unnatural. This natural progression is what the human species seeks—to operate in accordance with natural laws and operations. As the Michigan Supreme Court held in the matter of Dr. Jack Kevorkian:

> Whereas suicide involves an affirmative act to end a life, the refusal or cessation of life-sustaining medical treatment simply permits life to run its course, unencumbered by contrived intervention.[82]

Neither the medical community, Dr. Kevorkian, or popular interest groups that tout rights like cheap shillings for the taking seems to understand this dynamic. Suicide, whether by hand or machine, is not what it used to be.

Finally, there have been a few jurisdictions that have had to deal with parental refusal to seek or accept lifesaving medical care for their offspring. Grounded in religious objections, the parents, by making a decision for an underage child, essentially guarantee their demise. Aside from this having the connotations of a homicide charge, the refusal of life-saving treatment finely borders the suicide question. An Ohio decision, *in re Clark*[83] rejected the parents' demand when it held that while the parents may cling to any religious formula for their own sakes, but "the right of theirs ends where somebody else's right begins."[84] Other states have tried to balance constitutional express involving religious practice and the right of a child to a continued life.[85]

ABORTION

Since *Roe v. Wade*,[86] a popular consensus has developed regarding the lack of criminality in the practice of abortion.[87] While *Roe* opened the door for legalized abortion, in direct contravention to the overwhelming majority of American jurisdictions, it never set out to eliminate every aspect of criminality from the practice. On close inspection of the *Roe* opinion, one quickly discerns the limited liberalization of the practice in the first and second trimesters, and the reinforced condemnation of third trimester activity.

(a) For the stage prior to approximately the end of the first trimester, the abortion decision and its effectuation must be left to the medical judgment of the pregnant woman's attending physician.

(b) For the stage subsequent to approximately the end of the first trimester, the State, in promoting its interest in the health of the mother, may, if it chooses, regulate the abortion procedure in ways that are reasonably related to maternal health.

CASE 4.9

PEOPLE V. KEVORKIAN
527 NW 2d 714, 728 (Mich. 1994)

These cases raise three issues with regard to the state's imposition of criminal responsibility on persons who assist others in committing suicide. Two questions are presented by the appeals in Docket Nos. 99591, 99752, 99758, and 99759: (1) Whether the Michigan assisted suicide statute, MCL 752.1027; MSA 28.547(127), was enacted in violation of Const 1963, art 4, § 24.

(2) Whether the criminal provisions of MCL 752.1027; MSA 28.547(127) violate the United States Constitution. In Docket No. 99674, a case predating the assisted suicide statute, the question presented is: (3) Whether the circuit court erred in quashing the information charging the defendant with murder.

We conclude: (1) the assisted suicide provisions of the statute were validly enacted and do not violate the Title-Object Clause of the Michigan Constitution; (2) the United States Constitution does not prohibit a state from imposing criminal penalties on one who assists another in committing suicide; (3) in the murder case, the motion to quash must be reconsidered by the circuit court to determine if the evidence produced at the preliminary examination was sufficient to bind the defendant over for trial.

People v. Kevorkian **(Docket No. 99591)**

The "Wayne County Assisted Suicide Case"

Also after the enactment of the assisted suicide statute, defendant Kevorkian is alleged to have assisted in the death of Donald O'Keefe. The defendant was charged under the statute and bound over after preliminary examination. He moved to dismiss, and the circuit court granted the motion. The court rejected the art 4, § 24 challenges to the statute, but found a due process interest in the decision to end one's life, and that the law impermissibly burdened that interest.

The court held an evidentiary hearing to determine if the facts satisfied the four-part test that it had set forth in its opinion. Following the hearing, the court issued an order concluding that the facts of the case met the standard and dismissed the charge. The prosecutor appealed to the Court of Appeals.

The "Oakland County Assisted Suicide Case"

Defendant Kevorkian was charged in two separate files with assisting in the suicides of Merion Frederick and Ali Khalili. The defendant was bound over after a preliminary examination in one case and waived examination in the other. The circuit court granted the defendant's motion to dismiss. The court discussed the potential privacy and liberty interests in ending one's life, concluding that a person does have the right to commit suicide. However, it further concluded that defendant Kevorkian lacked standing to challenge the statute. The court also found that the statute was unconstitutional because it had more than one object and because its purpose was changed during its passage through the Legislature. The prosecuting attorney appealed.

People v Kevorkian **(Docket No. 99674)**
The "Oakland County Murder Case"

Before the statute was enacted, defendant Kevorkian allegedly assisted in the deaths of Sherry Miller and Marjorie Wantz on October 23, 1991. He was indicted by a citizens' grand jury on two counts of murder. After a preliminary examination, the defendant was bound over for trial. In the circuit court, the defendant moved to dismiss, and the circuit judge granted the motion, concluding that assisting in suicide does not fall within the crime of murder. The prosecutor appealed.

II

The Court of Appeals issued its decisions in two sets of opinions on May 10, 1994. One decision dealt with the cases involving the assisted suicide statute. The majority concluded that the assisted suicide statute was unconstitutional because the act had more than one object, in violation of art 4, § 24. Though recognizing that it arguably was not necessary to deal with the remaining issue, the majority went on to consider whether the statute violated the United States Constitution. The majority concluded that there was no violation, and that the state was free to make it a criminal offense to assist another in committing suicide.

The appeal regarding the murder case was decided separately. The majority concluded that the circuit court erred in quashing the information.

III

The prosecuting authorities in each of the assisted suicide cases appealed the conclusion that the assisted suicide statute was enacted in violation of Const 1963, art 4, § 24. Defendant Kevorkian filed a cross appeal with regard to the United States constitutional issue in the Wayne County assisted suicide case, and the plaintiffs in the declaratory judgment action filed their own application for leave to appeal on that issue. In the murder case, defendant Kevorkian filed an application for leave to appeal. On June 6, 1994, we granted the applications and the cases were argued on October 4, 1994.

Questions

1. Identify the statute under which Dr. Kevorkian was prosecuted.
2. What was the basis of his appeal?
3. How did the majority opinion deal with the merits of the appeal?
4. What is your own view on the matter of physician-assisted suicide? How would you reconcile the Court's arguments?

(c) For the stage subsequent to viability, the State in promoting its interest in the potentiality of human life may, if it chooses, regulate, and even proscribe, abortion except where it is necessary, in appropriate medical judgment, for the preservation of the life or health of the mother.[88]

It is not an easy area of law to conquer. It never has been since the time of the Greeks and the Romans. Even great medievalists in the person of St. Thomas Aquinas, the angelic doctor of the

Roman Catholic Church, while condemning the practice of abortion, was unwilling to criminalize the practice in every period of gestation. While the practice was always a mortal sin, with the aligned consequence of eternal damnation, it was not murder in every instance. It is sin due to its meddling with nature and the natural ends of an ordered and rational universe.[89] The strength of the natural law tradition since the time of the Middle Ages served as a backdrop for resistance to abortion, but fumbled with, just as we do, when a human is a human, when quickening or movement occurs, when viability emerges, and when the life is self-sufficient.[90] Current theological postures don't make the criminal law's position much clearer. If we concede that life begins at conception and that human life in its potentiality is identical to developed and actual life, then the justice model would have a multitude of prosecutions on its hands. If we conclude that conception and the early stages of fetal development are a mushy, disorganized cell mass lacking any organic logic, we shall rarely be concerned about things like fetal health and maternal responsibility. If we simply dwell on this issue from a constitutional perspective, we shall find no solace or tranquility in the mire of political and moral disagreement. If anything is true since *Roe v. Wade*, it is our state of abject polarization and general antagonism to opposing viewpoints.

Any law or case decision that promotes this level of turmoil has failed its central goal of justice and rationality. Indeed, the scientific community's current understanding of fetal life and human development is light years ahead of *Roe*.[91] Reading the infantile science of *Roe* should at least cause the community to revisit the issue. Politics aside, abortion remains a criminal matter whether we like it or not. Some examples include:

- Unqualified abortion operators
- False abortion providers
- Illegal abortion at late term without medical necessity
- Procurement of illegal abortions
- Sale of fetal byproducts
- Sale of illegal abortifacients
- Underage and nonconsensual abortions
- RU 486 (The "day after" pill)

Since *Roe*, lawmakers on both sides of the aisle have tried mightily to expand or diminish the right. For pro-choice advocates, any restriction on the practice is met with an almost blind resistance. One commentator opined, under efforts to place any restrictions on abortion, that the *Roe* legacy corrodes a little at a time, and regulations that once were considered a burden on that right "do not necessarily constitute an undue burden."[92]

At common law, abortion law did not come into play until the fetus moved or quickened. "Prior to quickening, the common law deemed abortion to be no crime at all for any party concerned,[93] and American courts that adjudicated prosecutions for abortion at common law consistently adhered to this view. Courts in several states dissented, but acknowledged their contravention of the common law. Furthermore, although abortionists were prosecuted for performing postquickening abortions, no American case reports a common-law prosecution of a woman for procuring an abortion, either pre- or postquickening; dicta, however, runs both for and against the woman's liability."[94]

For an overview of abortion through history, visit: http://www.lcms.org/graphics/assets/media/WRHC/187_A%20Historical%20Summary%20of%20Abortion.PDF

For a wide array of rationales, abortion law eventually becomes a codified and universally condemned practice except in cases involving the life of the mother. Health, communicable diseases, puritanical sexual mores, chivalric compassion for women, and the inherent dangers seemed to top the lists of legislative motivations.[95]

Throughout the history of abortion in America, the legal system has targeted the provider rather than the patient. Very few prosecutions have ever occurred that punish the mother of the aborted child. Instead, pre-*Roe* activity[96] concentrated its power on providers in statutes, a tendency that continues today, such as Pennsylvania's:

§ 3217. Civil penalties

Any physician who knowingly violates any of the provisions of section 3204 (relating to medical consultation and judgment) or 3205 (relating to informed consent) shall, in addition to any other penalty prescribed in this chapter, be civilly liable to his patient for any damages caused thereby and, in addition, shall be liable to his patient for punitive damages in the amount of $5,000, and the court shall award a prevailing plaintiff a reasonable attorney fee as part of costs.

§ 3218. Criminal penalties

(a) APPLICATION OF CHAPTER.— Notwithstanding any other provision of this chapter, no criminal penalty shall apply to a woman who violates any provision of this chapter solely in order to perform or induce or attempt to perform or induce an abortion upon herself. Nor shall any woman who undergoes an abortion be found guilty of having committed an offense, liability for which is defined under section 306 (relating to liability for conduct of another; complicity) or Chapter 9 (relating to inchoate crimes), by reason of having undergone such abortion.[97]

Other criminal infractions deal not with the woman seeking the abortion, but with how the processes of the abortion were carried out, such as consent of minors, licensure, and term of the abortion.[98]

As the story of pro-life and pro-choice unfolds, the paralysis evident in the exchange will not be settled any time soon, unless and until our Courts do a better job of sorting the question out in a jurisprudential way.[99]

Visit the First Amendment Center, which lays out the proper protocol for protest as to abortion at: http://www.firstamendmentcenter.org/assembly/topic.aspx?topic=buffer_zones

---

The politics of abortion are strange and miserable bedfellows to laws on abortion. If law is an exercise of reason and rational activity, what law makes sense in this quagmire? Is it simply a matter of personal right without regard for the fetus? Or is it a matter that relates to the body alone? Professor Jennifer Hendricks seems to posit an abortion jurisprudence that heavily relies on the personal integrity of the woman's body as a sufficient rationale and that the reason why abortion restrictions of any sort come about is male sexism. She remarks:

This division between the body and the social suggests that women's liberty can be protected only by breaking it into pieces that have analogs with men's experiences. When men are the norm, women's rights become derivative.[100]

While the argument is creative, how does the critic account for the bulk of female objection to every form of abortion? Professor Hendricks acts as if women are strictly homogenous, a monolithic group that think in only one way—without restriction or dissent. The arguments, that either support or object to abortion, tend to be more eclectic than the body argument alone. Arguments on either side of the wall consider perennial questions of justice. Is abortion a practice that advances the collective good? Does the elimination of abortion advance any particular end relating to justice or is the proliferation of abortion a guarantor of human freedom? Or is it just the opposite?

As a young college student, this author recalls the debate of *Roe* and its quest to decriminalize the act of abortion. The proponents passionately argued that "each child would be special, that no unwanted children would come into the world, that the quality of our lives would increase accordingly." The antagonists to the Court screamed the slaughter of the innocents and the violation of God's law. Today, children have never been in worse shape—neglected, abused, and forgotten in numbers never dreamt of in pre-*Roe* times. As for God's law, God is the arbiter of that supreme dominion, the jurisdiction not available in the temporal sphere. There is uneasiness about this debate that gnaws at both conservative and liberal alike. Something, somewhere will have to be done about this extremely complicated issue that tugs at conscience and autonomy. For some jurists, in the shape of Antonin Scalia, the scourge of abortion is both personal and communal, and largely the result of those who crafted the *Roe* opinion by paying only nominal lip service to what the law is obliged to do.

> That is, quite simply, the issue in this case: Not whether the power of a woman to abort her unborn child is a "liberty" in the absolute sense, or even whether it is a liberty of great importance to many women. Of course, it is both. The issue is whether it is a liberty protected by the Constitution of the United States. I am sure it is not. I reach that conclusion not because of anything so exalted as my views concerning the "concept of existence, of meaning, of the universe, and of the mystery of human life." Rather, I reach it for the same reason I reach the conclusion that bigamy is not constitutionally protected because of two simple facts: (1) the Constitution says absolutely nothing about it, and (2) the longstanding traditions of American society have permitted it to be legally proscribed.

> The authors of the joint opinion, of course, do not squarely contend that *Roe v. Wade* was a correct application of "reasoned judgment," merely that it must be followed, because of *stare decisis*. But, in their exhaustive discussion of all the factors that go into the determination of when *stare decisis* should be observed and when disregarded, they never mention "how wrong was the decision on its face?" Surely, if "[t]he Court's power lies ... in its legitimacy, a product of substance and perception," the "substance" part of the equation demands that plain error be acknowledged and eliminated. Roe was plainly wrong, even on the Court's methodology of "reasoned judgment," and even more so (of course) if the proper criteria of text and tradition are applied.[101]

For Scalia's polar counterpart, Justice Judith Ginsburg, the unease is just as pointed as she seeks a way out of the morass.

> After considering the fundamental constitutional questions resolved by Roe, principles of institutional integrity, and the rule of *stare decisis*, we are led to conclude this: The essential holding of *Roe v. Wade* should be retained and once again reaffirmed.
>
> It must be stated at the outset and with clarity that Roe's essential holding, the holding we reaffirm, has three parts. First is a recognition of the right of the woman to choose to have an abortion before viability and to obtain it without undue interference from the State. Before viability, the

CASE 4.10

STENBERG V. CARHART
192 F. 3d 1142 (8th Cir. 2000).

We again consider the right to an abortion. We understand the controversial nature of the problem. Millions of Americans believe that life begins at conception and consequently that an abortion is akin to causing the death of an innocent child; they recoil at the thought of a law that would permit it. Other millions fear that a law that forbids abortion would condemn many American women to lives that lack dignity, depriving them of equal liberty and leading those with least resources to undergo illegal abortions with the attendant risks of death and suffering. Taking account of these virtually irreconcilable points of view, aware that constitutional law must govern a society whose different members sincerely hold directly opposing views, and considering the matter in light of the Constitution's guarantees of fundamental individual liberty, this Court, in the course of a generation, has determined and then redetermined that the Constitution offers basic protection to the woman's right to choose. We shall not revisit those legal principles. Rather, we apply them to the circumstances of this case.

Three established principles determine the issue before us. We shall set them forth in the language of the joint opinion in Casey. First, before "viability ... the woman has a right to choose to terminate her pregnancy."

Second, "a law designed to further the State's interest in fetal life, which imposes an undue burden on the woman's decision before fetal viability," is unconstitutional. An "undue burden is ... shorthand for the conclusion that a state regulation has the purpose or effect of placing a substantial obstacle in the path of a woman seeking an abortion of a nonviable fetus."

Third, "subsequent to viability, the State in promoting its interest in the potentiality of human life may, if it chooses, regulate, and even proscribe, abortion except where it is necessary, in appropriate medical judgment, for the preservation of the life or health of the mother."

We apply these principles to a Nebraska law banning "partial birth abortion." The statute reads as follows:

"No partial birth abortion shall be performed in this state, unless such procedure is necessary to save the life of the mother whose life is endangered by a physical disorder, physical illness, or physical injury, including a life-endangering physical condition caused by or arising from the pregnancy itself."

The statute defines "partial birth abortion" as:

"an abortion procedure in which the person performing the abortion partially delivers vaginally a living unborn child before killing the unborn child and completing the delivery." '28 326(9).

It further defines "partially delivers vaginally a living unborn child before killing the unborn child" to mean "deliberately and intentionally delivering into the vagina a living unborn child, or a substantial portion thereof, for the purpose of performing a procedure that the person performing such procedure knows will kill the unborn child and does kill the unborn child."

The law classifies violation of the statute as a "Class III felony" carrying a prison term of up to 20 years, and a fine of up to $25,000. "28 328(2), 28 105. It also provides for the automatic revocation of a doctor's license to practice medicine in Nebraska. '28 328(4).

We hold that this statute violates the Constitution.

I.

A. Dr. Leroy Carhart is a Nebraska physician who performs abortions in a clinical setting. He brought this lawsuit in Federal District Court seeking a declaration that the Nebraska statute violates the Federal Constitution, and asking for an injunction forbidding its enforcement. After a trial on the merits, during which both sides presented several expert witnesses, the District Court held the statute unconstitutional. We granted certiorari to consider the matter.

B. Because Nebraska law seeks to ban one method of aborting a pregnancy, we must describe and then discuss several different abortion procedures. Considering the fact that those procedures seek to terminate a potential human life, our discussion may seem clinically cold or callous to some, perhaps horrifying to others. There is no alternative way, however, to acquaint the reader with the technical distinctions among different abortion methods and related factual matters, upon which the outcome of this case depends. For that reason, drawing upon the findings of the trial court, underlying testimony, and related medical texts, we shall describe the relevant methods of performing abortions in technical detail. ...

II.

The question before us is whether Nebraska's statute, making criminal the performance of a "partial birth abortion," violates the Federal Constitution, as interpreted in Planned Parenthood of *Southeastern Pa. v. Casey*, and *Roe v. Wade*. We conclude that it does for at least two independent reasons. First, the law lacks any exception "for the preservation of the ... health of the mother." Second, it "imposes an undue burden on a woman's ability" to choose a D&E abortion, thereby unduly burdening the right to choose abortion itself. We shall discuss each of these reasons in turn.

A. The Casey joint opinion reiterated what the Court held in Roe, that "subsequent to viability, the State in promoting its interest in the potentiality of human life may, if it chooses, regulate, and even proscribe, abortion except where it is necessary, in appropriate medical judgment, for the preservation of the life or health of the mother."

The fact that Nebraska's law applies both pre- and postviability aggravates the constitutional problem presented. The State's interest in regulating abortion previability is considerably weaker than postviability. Since the law requires a health exception in order to validate even a postviability abortion regulation, it at a minimum requires the same in respect to previability regulation.

The quoted standard also depends on the state regulations "promoting [the State's] interest in the potentiality of human life." The Nebraska law, of course, does not directly further an interest "in the potentiality of human life" by saving the fetus in question from destruction, as it regulates only a method of performing abortion. Nebraska describes its interests differently. It says the law "show[s] concern for the life of the unborn," "prevent[s] cruelty to partially born children," and "preserve[s] the integrity of the medical profession." But, we cannot see how the interest related differences could make any difference to the question at hand, namely, the application of the "health" requirement.

Consequently, the governing standard requires an exception "where it is necessary, in appropriate medical judgment for the preservation of the life or health of the mother," for this Court has made clear that a State may promote but not endanger a woman's health when it regulates the methods of abortion.

Justice Thomas says that the cases just cited limit this principle to situations where the pregnancy itself creates a threat to health. He is wrong. The cited cases, reaffirmed in Casey, recognize that a State cannot subject women's health to significant risks both in that context, and also where state regulations force women to use riskier methods of abortion. Our cases have repeatedly invalidated statutes that in the process of regulating the methods of abortion, imposed significant health risks. They make clear that a risk to a women's health is the same whether it happens to arise from regulating a particular method of abortion, or from barring abortion entirely. Our holding does not go beyond those cases, as ratified in Casey. ...

B. The Eighth Circuit found the Nebraska statute unconstitutional because, in Casey's words, it has the "effect of placing a substantial obstacle in the path of a woman seeking an abortion of a nonviable fetus." It thereby places an "undue burden" upon a woman's right to terminate her pregnancy before viability. Nebraska does not deny that the statute imposes an "undue burden" if it applies to the more commonly used D&E procedure as well as to D&X. And we agree with the Eighth Circuit that it does so apply.

Questions

1. What issues does the court examine in this case?
2. What is the definition given of a "partial birth abortion?"
3. What are the courts findings as to the constitutionality of the practice?
4. In your opinion, and using a murder statute, do you believe that partial birth abortion is murder?

State's interests are not strong enough to support a prohibition of abortion or the imposition of a substantial obstacle to the woman's effective right to elect the procedure. Second is a confirmation of the State's power to restrict abortions after fetal viability if the law contains exceptions for pregnancies which endanger the woman's life or health. And third is the principle that the State has legitimate interests from the outset of the pregnancy in protecting the health of the woman and the life of the fetus that may become a child. These principles do not contradict one another; and we adhere to each.[102]

DISCUSSION QUESTIONS

1. What type of intentionality is required in a case of Murder 1?
2. Which homicide offense considers the effects and influences of mitigation?
3. What standard measures the issue of provocation?
4. Why is the Felony Murder Rule a form of strict liability?
5. Describe how abortion can result in a criminal charge?
6. Reconcile the right to privacy with physician-assisted suicide?
7. What types of perpetrators are likely premeditated killers?
8. What types of perpetrators are more likely charged with manslaughter over murder?
9. What is the Felony Murder Rule's list of qualifying felonies?
10. When is homicide justifiable?

SUGGESTED READINGS

Gorsuch, N. M. 2009. *The future of assisted suicide and euthanasia*. Princeton, NJ: Princeton University Press.
Holmes, R. M. and S. T. Holmes. 1994. *Murder in America*. Thousand Oaks, CA: Sage Publications.
Kachur, S. P. 1995. *Suicide in the United States, 1980–1992*. Atlanta: National Center for Injury Prevention and Control.
Kocsis, R. N. 2010. *Serial murder and the psychology of violent crimes*. New York: Humana Press.
Lattimore, P. K. and C. A. Nahabedian. 1997. *The mature of homicide: Trends and changes*. Washington, D.C.: National Institute of Justice.
Liebert, J. 2011. *Suicidal mass murderers: A criminological study of why they kill*. Boca Raton, FL: CRC Press.
Marseken, S. F., L. M. Surhone, and M. T. Timpledon. 2010. *Voluntary manslaughter*. Saarbrücken, Germany: Betascript Publishing.
Nolan, K. G. 2010. *Abortion: Legislative and legal issues (laws and legislation)*. Hauppauge, NY: Nova Science Publishers Inc.
Petersen, K. 2011. *Abortion law and policy: An equal opportunity perspective* (Biomedical Law & Ethics Library). Boca Raton, FL: Routledge-Cavendish Publishers.
Wiest, J. B. 2011. *Creating cultural monsters: Serial murder in America*. Boca Raton, FL: CRC Press.
Wolfgang, M. E. 1975. *Patterns in criminal homicide*. Montclair, NJ: Patterson Smith.

ENDNOTES

1. *See* RANDOLPH ROTH, AMERICAN HOMICIDE (2009).
2. A former defense lawyer, Thomas Liotti put it well when he asked "Without a corpus delicti, how do you prove the fact of death or the cause of death? ... You need a great deal of circumstantial evidence on those subjects." Michael A. Riccardi, *Prosecution Tells Tale of Murder Without Body*, N.Y. L.J., Feb. 15, 2000, at 1.
3. *See State of Tennessee v. Robbie Davidson*, No. M1997-00130-CCA-R3-CD (Tenn. Crim. App. 2000).
4. TENN. CODE ANN. § 39-13-202(a) (2010).
5. *See Tennessee v. Larry S. Brumit*, No. M1999-00154-CCS-R3-CD (Tenn. Crim. App. 2000). Drug dealers and other unsavory characters frequently engage in this type of conversation of one rubbing the other out. Mindsets are gleaned from the conversation and past bad blood.
6. 2 FRANCIS WHARTON, WHARTON'S CRIMINAL LAW 247-248 (Charles E. Torcia ed., 15th ed., 1993).
7. Bureau of Justice Statistics, *Homicide Trends in the U.S. – Homicide by Circumstance*, 1976-2005, available at http://bjs.ojp.usdoj.gov/content/homicide/circumst.cfm (accessed August 3, 2011).
8. Matthew A. Pauley, *Murder by Premeditation*, 36 AM. CRIM. L. REV. 145, 155 (1999).

9. *Penry v. Lynaugh*, 492 U.S. 302 (1999).

10. *See* Shirley Baccus-Lobel, *Criminal Law*, 52 SMU L. REV. 881, 910-11 (1999).

11. *See Midgett v. State*, 729 S.W.2d 410 (Ark. 1987), where the defendant, a six-foot tall, 300-pound man was found guilty of first-degree murder for killing his 8-year-old son, who weighed only 40 pounds. It was obvious from evidence presented at trial that the defendant had brutally beaten the child many times over his short life, that the child was malnourished, and that rib fractures and severe bruises were present on his body at the time of death. On appeal, the Arkansas Supreme Court reversed his conviction, stating that the defendant intended only to beat his son, not kill him, and if he did kill him, he did so in a fit of drunken rage and was not capable of premeditating at that time.

12. *R. v. Woollin*, 1 Cr. App. R. 97 (Court of Appeal, Criminal Division, House of Lords, 1997).

13. Patrick A. Tuite & Ronald D. Menaker, *Ruling Broadens Reach of Murder Statute*, 145 CHI. DAILY L. BULL. Nov. 3, 1999, at 5.

14. *Jackson v. Virginia*, 61 L.Ed.2d 560 (1979).

15. *Id.* at 573–574.

16. *See* the recent case involving Nathaniel Brazill, a 14-year-old who killed his teacher in Florida. "A Florida jury convicted Nathaniel Brazill of second-degree murder with a firearm for shooting Barry Grunow, deciding that the boy did not plan to kill his seventh-grade English teacher ... [T]he jury, instructed by Judge Wennet that premeditation meant thinking 'long enough to allow reflection,' decided that the boy was not guilty of the higher charge. They also convicted Brazill of aggravated assault with a firearm." Sam Handlin, *Brazill Convicted of Second-Degree Murder, Sentencing Looms* (May 16, 2001) COURT TV, at http://www.courttv.com/trials/brazill/verdict_ctv.html (accessed July 27, 2001).

17. *People v. Russell*, 693 N.E.2d 193 (N.Y. 1998).

18. N.C. GEN. STAT. § 14-17 (2010).

19. NEB. REV. STAT. § 28-304 (2010).

20. John Rockwell Snowden, *Second Degree Murder, Malice, and Manslaughter in Nebraska: New Juice for an Old Cup*, 76 NEB. L. REV. 399, 410 (1997).

21. PHILLIP E. JOHNSON, CRIMINAL LAW 160 (5th ed. 1995). *See* RICHARD J. BONNIE et al., CRIMINAL LAW 658 (1997); GEORGE E. DIX & M. MICHAEL SHARLOT, CRIMINAL LAW 400 (4th ed. 1996); Jonathan Matthew Purver, *The Language of Murder*, 14 UCLA L. REV. 1306, 1308-11 (1967).

22. *State v. Elder*, 982 S.W.2d 871, 876 (Tenn. Crim. App. 1998).

23. *State v. Mitchell*, No. W1999-06610-CCA-R3-CD, 4 (Tenn. Crim. App. 1998), *citing State v. Elder*, 982 S.W.2d 871, 876 (Tenn. Crim. App. 1998).

24. *See* Carolyn B. Ramsey, *Provoking Change: Comparative Insights on Feminists Homicide Law Reform*, 100 J. CRIM. L. & CRIMINOLOGY 33 (2010): *See also* Jeffrey S. Adler, *"I Loved Joe But I Had to Kill Him": Homicide by Women in Turn-of-the-Century Chicago*, 92 J. CRIM. L. & CRIMINOLOGY 867 (2002).

25. *People v. Roldan*, 666 N.E.2d 553 (1996).

26. *See* Bernadette McSherry, *Men Behaving Badly: Current Issues in Provocation, Automatism, Mental Impairment and Criminal Responsibility*, 12 PSYCHIATRY, PSYCHOL. & L. 15 (2005); *see also* PHIL CLEARY, GETTING AWAY WITH MURDER: THE TRUE STORY OF JULIE RAMAGE'S DEATH 28-30 (2005).

27. *See* Ramsey, *supra* note 24.

28. An incorrect application of manslaughter charges is quite evident in the prosecution of a Brooklyn High School student who raised his hand against a teacher. The teacher died the following day of a heart attack. *See* Ann Snider, *Pupil Cleared in Death of School Aide: Judge Finds Manslaughter Charge to be Unsupported*, 218 N.Y.L.J., May 22, 1998, at 1.

29. Bernie Auchter, *Men Who Murder Their Families: What the Research Tells Us*, NIJ J., June 2010, at 10.

30. *See* Michelle Oberman, *Mothers Who Kill: Coming to Terms With Modern American Infanticide*, 34 AMER. CRIM. L. REV. 1 (1996); Ania Wilczynski & Allison Morris, *Parents Who Kill Their Children*, 1993 CRIM. L. REV. 31, 32; Ania Wilczynski, *Images of Women Who Kill Their Infants: The Mad and the Bad*, 2 WOMEN & CRIM. JUST. 71, 73 (1991).

31. Oberman, *supra* note 30, at 22; *See* James J. Dvorak, *Neonaticide: Less than Murder?*, 19 N. ILL. U. L. REV. 173 (1998). So common is this unfortunate event that certain states have decided to craft unique provisions that deal with the infanticide and neonaticide, examples being CAL. PENAL CODE § 187 (West 2010) and CONN. GEN. STAT. § 53a-54a (2010).

32. 18 Pa. Cons. Stat. § 2503 (2010).

33. *See* Robert L. Evangelista, Pennsylvania Trial Guide – Criminal 318 (3rd ed. 1995).

34. Jeremy Horder, Provocation And Responsibility (1992); Joshua Dressler, *Provocation: Partial Justification or Partial Excuse?*, 51 Mod. L. Rev. 467 (1988); Joshua Dressler, *Rethinking Heat of Passion: A Defense in Search of a Rationale*, 73 J. Crim. L. & Criminology 421 (1982); Finbarr McAuley, *Anticipating the Past: The Defense of Provocation in Irish Law*, 50 Mod. L. Rev. 133 (1987); Andrew Von Hirsch & Nils Jareborg, Provocation And Culpability In Responsibility, Character, And The Emotions 241 (Ferdinand Schoeman ed., 1987).

35. *See* Evangelista, *supra* note 33, at 319–320.

36. 570 N.E.2d 918 (Ind. Ct. App. 1991).

37. *Maher v. People*, 10 Mich. 212, 220 (1862) (defining "adequate provocation").

38. Joshua Dressler, *When "Heterosexual" Men Kill "Homosexual" Men: Reflections on Provocation Law, Sexual Advances, and the "Reasonable Man" Standard*, 85 J. Crim. L. & Criminology 726, 747-748 (1995).

39. When children are killed in the family circle, in a hostile environment, charges may vary due to the mitigation inherent in family situations. *See* Ashley Brittain et al., *Investigating the Justice System Response in Missouri in Child Homicides to Hostile Environments*, 66 J. Mo. B. 263 (2010).

40. George Anastaplo, *The O.J. Simpson Case Revisited*, 28 Loy. U. Chi. L.J. 461, 472–473 (1997).

41. As to the involuntary version of manslaughter, the courts impute very little intentionality or violence in the event. As such, involuntary manslaughter will not be used for recidivist enhancement since it is not a violent crime in most jurisdictions. *See Recent Case Law: Criminal Law-Sentencing Guidelines-Seventh Circuit Holds that Involuntary Manslaughter is Not a Crime of Violence for Sentencing Guidelines' Recidivism Enhancement*, 123 Harv. L. Rev. 760 (2010); *see also United States v. Woods*, 576 F.3d 400 (7th Cir. 2009).

42. Kara M. Houck, *People v. Dekens: The Expansion of the Felony-Murder Doctrine in Illinois*, 30 Loy. U. Chi. L.J. 557, 584 (1999).

43. Kevin D. Brown, *Murder Liability and Leaving the Scene of an Accident: An Argument for an Extension of the Felony Murder Rule in Missouri*, 79 UKMC L. 195, 198 (2010).

44. Houck, *supra* note 42, at 584. *See* Md. Code Ann., Crim. Law § 2-201 (West 2010). *See also* S.D. Codified Laws § 22-16-4 (2010); Ark. Code Ann. § 5-10-104(a)(4) (2010); Tex. Penal Code Ann. § 19.02(b)(3) (West 2010).

45. 720 Ill. Comp. Stat. 5/2-8 (2010).

46. Brown, *supra* note 43, at 195.

47. *See* Case Note, *Criminal Law—Application of Felony Murder Rule Sustained Where Robbery Victim Killed Defendant's Accomplice*, 5 DePaul L. Rev. 298, 302 (1956) (noting that jurisdictions deviate when the situation is more complex than what is generally provided for in the felony-murder statutes).

48. *People v. Lowery*, 687 N.E.2d 973, 976 (Ill. 1997).

49. William L. Clark & William L. Marshall, A Treatise On The Law Of Crimes §10.07 at 656-57 (15th ed. 1958).

50. *See People v. Payne*, 194 N.E. 539, 543 (Ill. 1935).

51. Widespread differences in how the killing of a co-felon will impact the felony murder rule exist. Some case law refused to extend the FMR to co-felon deaths. *See Weick v. State*, 420 A.2d 159, 163-64 (Del.1980) (concluding that the felons were not responsible for the death of a co-felon because the felons did not commit the homicide); *State v. Murrell*, 585 P.2d 1017, 1019 (Kan. 1978) (noting that the jury acquitted a felon charged with felony-murder rule because during the armed robbery either the policy or the robbery victim killed the co-felon). A few legal locales simply transfer the intent of the felony to not only the subsequent killing but to all the actors involved. The doctrine of transferred intent differs from strict liability in that in the latter case no finding of mens rea is required while in the former a mental state is imputed. Criminals choosing the path of felonious activity have much to answer for under these stringent principles.

52. 198 P.3d 271 (Mont. 2008).

53. See a serious analysis of Russell in Eric Henkel, *Two Crimes for the Price of One: Reshaping Felony Homicide in State v. Russell*, 71 L. Rev. 295 (2010).

54. *People v. Moran*, 158 N.E. 35, 36 (N.Y. 1927).

55. 45 Cal. 4th 1172 (2009).

56. *Id.* at 1200.

57. *See also* David Mishook, *People v. Chun—In its Latest Battle with Merger Doctrine, Has the California Supreme Court Effectively Merged Second-Degree Felony Murder Out of Existence*, 15 BERKELEY J. CRIM. L. 127 (2010).

58. Model Penal Code § 2.02 (2) (d) (Proposed Official Draft 1962).

59. *Id.* at § 210.63.

60. CENTURY COUNCIL, STATE OF DRUNK DRIVING FATALITIES IN AMERICA (2009), available at http://www.centurycouncil.org/files/material/files/SODDFIA.pdf (accessed August 3, 2011).

61. GEORGE E. DIX & M. MICHAEL SHARLOT, BASIC CRIMINAL LAW 502 (2nd ed. 1980).

62. 18 PA. CONS. STAT. § 2504 (2010).

63. CAL. PENAL CODE § 192 (West 2010).

64. 309 A.2d 714 (Pa.1973).

65. N.J. STAT. ANN. § 2C:35-9 (West 2011).

66. Blair Talty, *Note: New Jersey's Strict Liability for Drug-Induced Deaths: The Leap from Drug Dealer to Murderer*, 30 RUTGERS L.J. 513, 537 (1999).

67. *Id.* at 537; *See also* Leste Grinspoon & James B. Bakalar, *The War on Drugs—A Peace Proposal*, 330 NEW ENG. J. MED. 357 (1994).

68. 75 PA. CONS. STAT. §§ 3732, 3735 (2010).

69. The author's legal colleagues exhorted him to try any plausible legal argument to test the waters so to speak since the jury award could be in the millions. The author refused and told the insurance company he could not in good conscience pursue a case without merit since he could find no plausible argument supporting the negligence theory. The DA's ruling indicated a complete absence of criminal negligence on the part of the driver. What impact did this finding have on a subsequent civil case?

70. Questions of privacy and personal freedom have long consumed the operations of the U.S. Supreme Court in cases involving contraception (*Griswold v. Connecticut*, 381 U.S. 470 (1965)), abortion (*Roe v. Wade*, 410 U.S. 113 (1973)), and more recently, parental consent requirement, spousal notification, waiting periods and recordkeeping requirements for abortions (*Planned Parenthood v. Casey*, 505 U.S. 833, 112 S.Ct. 2791 (1992)).

71. *Casey*, 112 S.Ct. at 2804.

72. *Id.* at 2807.

73. David W. Meyers & J. K. Mason, *Physician Assisted Suicide: A Second View from Mid-Atlantic*, 28 ANGLO-AMERICAN L. REV. 265, 271 (1999); *See Washington v. Glucksberg*, 521 U.S. 702 (1997); *Cruzan v. Director, Missouri Department of Health*, 497 U.S. 261 (1990).

74. Another interesting slant on suicide takes place on college campuses and whether college officials are responsible for student suicides. *See* Richard Fossey & Heather E. Moore, *Counterpoint Introduction: Tort Liability for Student Suicide: The Sky is Not Falling*, 39 J. L. & EDUC. 235 (2010).

75. Edward Rubin, *Assisted Suicide, Morality, and Law: Why Prohibiting Assisted Suicide Violates the Establishment Clause*, 63 VAND. L. REV. 763, 767 (2010); See also RONALD DWORKIN, FREEDOM'S LAW: THE MORAL READING OF THE AMERICAN CONSTITUTION 130-43 (1996); Louis Seidman, *Confusion at the Border: Cruzan, "The Right to Die," and the Public/Private Distinction*, 1991 SUP. CT. REV. 47, 49-55.

76. 521 U.S. 702 (1997).

77. *Id.* at 710-11.

78. *See* OR. REV. STAT. § 127.805 (1) (2010); *See also* Cyndi Bollman, *A Dignified Death? Don't Forget about the Physically Disabled and Those Not Terminally Ill: An Analysis of Physician-Assisted Suicide Laws*, 34 S. ILL. U. L. REV. 395 (2010); Glen R. McMurray, *An Unconstitutional Death: The Oregon Death with Dignity Act's Prohibition against Self-Administered Lethal Injection*, 32 U. DAYTON L. REV. 441 (2007).

79. Bollman, *supra* not 78, at 399.

80. *See Compassion in Dying v. State of Washington*, 79 F.3d 790, 810 (9th Cir., 1996), cert. granted and reversed, 117 S.Ct. 2258 (1997); *Poll Shows Strong Support for Assisted Suicide*, SAN FRANCISCO CHRONICLE, July 31, 1998, at A5.

81. MICH. COMP. LAWS § 752.1027(7) (2001).

82. *People v. Kevorkian*, 527 N.W.2d 714, 728 (Mich. 1994).

83. 185 N.E.2d 128 (Ohio Com. Pl., 1962).

84. Id. at 185.

85. Emily Catalano, *Healing or Homicide?: When Parents Refuse Medical Treatment for Their Children on Religious Grounds*, 18 BUFF. WOMEN'S L. J. 157, 176 (2010).

86. 410 U.S. 113 (1973).

87. For an excellent summary and update on the Roe progeny until the present, see: Erin Helling & Jenny Nam, Ed., *Eleventh Annual Review of Gender and Sexuality Law: Health Care Chapter: Abortion*, 11. GEO. J. GENDER & L. 341 (2010).

88. *Roe*, 410 U.S. at 164-65.

89. *See* CHARLES P. NEMETH, AQUINAS IN THE COURTROOM (2001).

90. Samuel W. Buell, *Note: Criminal Abortion Revisited*, 66 N.Y.U. L. REV. 1774 (1991).

91. Some keenly understand the disconnect and discord between Court rulings and public sentiment. See Linda Greenhouse, *Democracy and the Courts: The Case of Abortion*, 61 HASTINGS L.J. 1333 (2010).

92. *See Evans v. People*, 49 N.Y. 86, 90 (1872).

93. Buell, *supra* note 90, at 1785.

94. *See* Means, *The Phoenix of Abortional Freedom: Is a Penumbral or Ninth Amendment Right about to Arise from the Nineteenth Century Legislative Ashes of a Fourteenth Century Common Law Liberty?*, 17 N.Y.L.F. 335, 336-62 (1971).

95. *See* J. MOHR, ABORTION IN AMERICA 3-226 (1978) (describing hegemony of criminal-abortion laws by the end of the nineteenth century). *See also* Note, *Criminal law—Abortion*, 23 S. CA. L. REV. 523, 523 (1950).

96. Case law on abortion generally deals with constitutional claims that directly affect governmental efforts to regulate the practice. Most restrictions have been struck down, such as: *Thornburg v. American College of Obstetrics and Gynecologists*, 476 U.S. 747, 759-71 (1986) (invalidating PA Law requiring physicians to inform women of the risks of abortion, availability of prenatal care, agencies willing to assist in pregnancy; report information about women seeking abortion; and attempt to preserve the life of the fetus); *Akron v. Akron Center for Reproductive Health*, 462 U.S. 416, 433-51 (1983) (invalidating OH law requiring that all abortions after the first trimester be performed in a hospital; parental consent or court order for abortions for women under 15; that physician inform woman of viability of fetus, risks of abortion, and availability of state assistance; and 24-hour waiting period between woman's consent and abortion).

97. 18 PA. CONS. STAT. §§ 3217, 3218 (2010).

98. Not even the procedural aspects of protest on the question have been neatly sorted out. Bubble zones, prophylactic domes, and other criteria have tried to balance protest and the right of abortion. See Article, *Constitutional Law— Freedom of Speech — Third Circuit Strikes Down Prophylactic Regulations Governing Speech Surrounding Health Care Facilities Providing Abortions*, 123 HARV. L. REV. F. 1779 (2010); *see also Brown v. City of Pittsburgh*, 586 F.3d 263 (3d Cir. 2009).

99. Kristen L. Burge, *When It Rains, It Pours: A Comprehensive Analysis of the Freedom of Choice Act and its Potential Fallout on Abortion Jurisprudence and Legislation*, 40 CUMB. L. REV. 181, 202 (2009-2010); *See also* Congressional efforts to eliminate any restrictions on abortion in its Freedom of Choice Act, H.R. 3700, 101st Congress (1989); S. 1912, 101st Cong. (1989); Janessa L. Bernstein, Note, *The Underground Railroad to Reproductive Freedom: Restrictive Abortion Laws and the Resulting Backlash*, 73 BROOK. L. REV. 1463 (2008); Mark H. Woltz, Note: *A Bold Reaffirmation? Planned Parenthood v. Casey Opens the Door for States to Enact New Laws to Discourage Abortion*, 71 N.C. L. REV. 1787 (1993); Natalie Wright, Note, *State Abortion Law after Casey: Finding "Adequate and Independent" Grounds for Choice in Ohio*, 54 OHIO ST. L.J. 891 (1993).

100. Jennifer S. Hendricks, *Body and Soul: Equality, Pregnancy, and the Unitary Right to Abortion*, 45 HARV. R.R.- C. L. L. 329. 330 (2010).

101. *Planned Parenthood v. Casey*, 505 U.S. 833, 980, 982-983 (1992).

102. *Id.* at 845-46.

Chapter 5

Crimes against the Person: Assault and Other Offenses

KEYWORDS

Abduct: To carry or lead a person away by threat or use of force or often by fraud.

Aggravated assault: A criminal assault that is committed with an intent to cause or that causes serious bodily injury, especially through the use of a dangerous weapon; a criminal assault accompanied by the intent to commit or the commission of a felony.

Asportation: The carrying away of someone else's property that is an element of larceny.

Assault: The crime or tort of threatening or attempting to inflict immediate offensive physical contact or bodily harm that one has the present ability to inflict and that puts the victim in fear of such harm or contact.

Battery: The crime or tort of intentionally or recklessly causing offensive physical contact or bodily harm that is not consented to by the victim.

Domestic violence: Violence committed by one family or household member against another.

False imprisonment: The tort of intentionally restraining another by physical force or the threat of physical force without privilege or authority.

Force: Violence, compulsion, or constraint exerted upon or against a person or thing.

Harassment: Connotes purposeful actions and conduct motivated by a malicious or discriminatory purpose.

Hate crime: A crime that violates the victim's civil rights and that is motivated by hostility to the victim's race, religion, creed, national origin, sexual orientation, or gender.

Kidnapping: An act or instance or the crime of seizing, confining, abducting, or carrying away a person by force or fraud often with a demand for ransom or in furtherance of another crime.

Mayhem: Willful and permanent crippling, mutilation, or disfigurement of any part of another's body.

Probable cause: A reasonable ground in fact and circumstance for a belief in the existence of certain circumstances.

Reasonable suspicion: An objectively justifiable suspicion that is based on specific facts or circumstances and that justifies stopping and sometimes searching a person thought to be involved in criminal activity at the time.

Robbery: The unlawful taking away of personal property from a person by violence or by threat of violence that causes fear.

Simple assault: A criminal assault that is not accompanied by any aggravating factors.

Stalking: The act or crime of willfully and repeatedly following or harassing another person in circumstances that would cause a reasonable person to fear injury or death especially because of express or implied threats.

Threat: An expression of an intention to injure another.

INTRODUCTION: PERSONAL OFFENSES THAT INFLICT HARM

Aside from murder and rape, as the preeminent personal offenses, attacks against the person can fall under other categories. This chapter weighs and evaluates other personal harm offenses. Assault and the traditional battery depict the personal offenses that, while not necessarily life threatening, can and do cause significant personal harm. One who assaults either attempts or actually inflicts injury upon another without right or justification. The injuries are not mere scuffles or petty insults, but serious, severe, and even potentially grave injuries. In aggravated assault, the perpetrator usually employs a weapon or other artifice. The degrees of assault descend by level of severity from aggravated assault to simple assault. Robbery, while primarily a property offense, is also a theft with force and has serious connotations for both the criminal agent and the victim. Robbery requires proof of force and it is generally directed toward the victim in a physical manner. Other personal offenses include nonbodily confrontation in the form of terroristic threats, harassment, and stalking. Even though the words themselves cannot inflict actual harm or injury, the future quality of those threats caused meaningful and measurable emotional harm.

ROBBERY

ELEMENTS

- Theft by taking
- Either attempted or actual
- By force

When compared to the other property offenses, robbery distinguishes itself by its violent nature. While larceny and theft deal primarily with the nature of personal property and its taking, robbery goes a step farther. The offense includes all the traditional elements witnessed in most theft statutes, but evolves further by making that same taking a forcible and confrontational act. The federal criminal code dwells more intently on the nature of robbery as it relates to federally insured and regulated banking institutions.

(a) Whoever, by force and violence, or by intimidation, takes, or attempts to take, from the person or presence of another, or obtains or attempts to obtain by extortion any property or money or any other thing of value belonging to, or in the care, custody, control, management, or possession of, any bank, credit union, or any savings and loan association; or

    Whoever enters or attempts to enter any bank, credit union, or any savings and loan association, or any building used in whole or in part as a bank, credit union, or as a savings and loan association, with intent to commit in such bank, credit union, or in such savings and loan association, or building, or part thereof, so used, any felony affecting such bank, credit union, or such savings and loan association and in violation of any statute of the United States, or any larceny—

Shall be fined under this title or imprisoned not more than twenty years, or both.

(b) Whoever takes and carries away, with intent to steal or purloin, any property or money or any other thing of value exceeding $1,000 belonging to, or in the care, custody, control, management, or possession of any bank, credit union, or any savings and loan association, shall be fined under this title or imprisoned not more than ten years, or both; or

Whoever takes and carries away, with intent to steal or purloin, any property or money or any other thing of value not exceeding $1,000 belonging to, or in the care, custody, control, management, or possession of any bank, credit union, or any savings and loan association, shall be fined not more than $1,000 or imprisoned not more than one year, or both.

(c) Whoever receives, possesses, conceals, stores, barters, sells, or disposes of, any property or money or other thing of value which has been taken or stolen from a bank, credit union, or savings and loan association in violation of subsection (b), knowing the same to be property which has been stolen shall be subject to the punishment provided in subsection (b) for the taker.[1]

Violence is what causes some to argue that the crime is less a property offense and more aptly labeled an attack against the person.[2] Sentencing guidelines and historical patterns of imposing penalties reflect this hybrid reality. Any reasonable comparison between theft and robbery and the gravity and seriousness of robbery far outweighs the drama of theft.

Keep in mind that this distinction should not generate a forgetfulness of the principles learned thus far. In fact, hold fast to the basic elements germane to the theft charge since these are discovered in robbery as well. To fathom robbery, one need only evaluate an additional element of force.

Hence, robbery statutes display uniform and consistent qualities like:

Robbery is the felonious taking of personal property in the possession of another, from his person or immediate presence, and against his will, accomplished by means of force or fear.[3]

Police departments, at least the larger ones, dedicate some portion of their personnel to robbery alone. Visit the Miami-Dade PD for a solid example at http://www.miamidade.gov/mdpd/BureausDivisions/bureau_Robbery.asp

The Taking

No attempt is made to rehash the taking requirement in the ordinary case of larceny. Taking another's property, without a legitimate claim or right, is felonious conduct in its own right. If the offender meets the requirements of carrying away (asportation) the stolen property, and the fact finder determines the property subject to the thievery has value, and then prosecutorial staff can rest easy on meeting the evidentiary demands of a larceny case. The same would be true of robbery except that the issue of force will have to be proved.

CASE 5.1

COMMONWEALTH V. CRUZADO

No. 07-P-1398 (2009)

This is the defendant's direct appeal from his convictions of unarmed robbery and assault and battery by means of a dangerous weapon and from his sentence to life in prison on the charge of unarmed robbery, imposed as a habitual criminal under G.L. c. 279, § 25. He argues that the Commonwealth failed to prove all essential elements of the unarmed robbery and the assault and battery by means of a dangerous weapon charges and that the convictions thus violated his right to due process. He also claims that the life sentence imposed under the habitual criminal statute relative to his unarmed robbery conviction constitutes cruel and unusual punishment. We affirm.

Facts

We summarize the facts the jury could have found. Christopher Adams, an employee of Jack's Gas, a gas station in Cambridge, was not on duty at the time of the events in question, but was at the station working on his own vehicle. Tommy Tompkins, also an employee, had parked his white Honda Civic automobile in front of the station on Massachusetts Avenue. A sign indicating that Jack's Gas performed State vehicle inspections was leaning against the rear of Tompkins's Honda. Adams was eating lunch inside the station with other employees when he heard a loud slapping noise that turned out to be the sign falling over. As Adams and others ran out of the station, they saw that Tompkins's Honda had been taken and that it was two blocks away. Adams and another employee jumped in a truck and gave chase.

The driver of the Honda, the defendant, stopped at a traffic light, and Adams jumped out of the truck, ran up to the Honda, and "ripped" the door open. The defendant stepped on the gas pedal and drove through the red light. After proceeding through the intersection, the Honda was traveling thirty to forty miles per hour. Adams's foot was stuck next to the seat, and he held onto the Honda by putting one hand on the inside of the roof of the Honda and holding onto the door with the other.

While driving, the defendant kept trying to grab Adams's hands to push him off the Honda. As the defendant proceeded through the intersection, another vehicle pulled in front of the Honda, and the defendant swerved out into oncoming traffic, crossing the solid double yellow line in the road. When the Honda swerved, the door swung completely open and then swung back. Adams's foot became dislodged, and he could only hold onto the door. The defendant traveled three to four blocks with Adams continuing to hold onto the Honda. Seeing a gap between vehicles in the oncoming traffic lane, Adams jumped from the Honda to the side of the road, slid across the pavement, hit the front left tire of a parked vehicle, and spun around. Police were called and gave chase. The defendant was apprehended after he drove in the wrong direction around a rotary, struck an automobile, and crashed into a guardrail.

Discussion 1: Unarmed Robbery

The unarmed robbery statute draws substantially from the common law of robbery and requires a showing of a larceny from a person by force and violence or by assault and putting in fear. Robbery is distinguished from larceny by its requirement of actual or constructive force.

The defendant claims that the Honda was not taken from Adams's person or from an area within his control, and thus no robbery was established. In essence, he alleges that he was not in the "presence" of Adams until "well after the theft was complete" when Adams "ripped" open the door to the Honda after pursuit.

"While the statute ... speaks of a taking from the victim's 'person,' the offense is understood 'to include the common law conception of taking in a victim's presence' ... and ... cover[s] cases where the victim could have prevented the taking had he not been intimidated." *Commonwealth v. Lashway*, 36 Mass.App.Ct. 677, 679-680 (1994), quoting from *Commonwealth v. Rajotte*, 23 Mass.App.Ct. 93, 95-96 (1986). A larceny may be converted to a robbery where the assault is committed on a victim who has a protective concern for the goods and where the victim interferes with the completion of the theft. Here, a rational jury could have found that the Honda was taken from Adams's person as the robbery was not complete when the defendant was still fleeing the scene while being pursued by Adams. The defendant accelerated the car and pushed at Adams's hands to attempt to remove the car from Adams's grasp and to complete the theft.

We also reject the defendant's argument that the element of force was not proved beyond a reasonable doubt. "Robbery includes all of the elements of larceny and in addition requires that force and violence be used against the victim or that the victim be put in fear." *Commonwealth v. Goldstein*, 54 Mass.App.Ct. 863, 867 (2002). In Goldstein, the defendant argued that because a knife was brandished after control of the shopping cart holding the stolen merchandise had been relinquished, only larceny could be established. As we said there, "[a] larceny may be converted into a robbery where ... a person who has protective concern for the goods taken interferes with the completion of the robbery." Ibid. See *Commonwealth v. Rajotte*, supra at 94. "[T]he nexus between the force or fear and the taking may be relatively loose and yet encompass a robbery." Goldstein, supra at 868, quoting from *Commonwealth v. Lashway*, supra at 680. See Model Penal Code § 222.1 & comment 2 (1980) (robbery includes force or threat of force occurring "in the course of committing a theft," as well as a period of flight after commission).

The jury here could have found that Adams's chasing the defendant and his attempt to recover the Honda by jumping onto it occurred in the course of the theft. Accordingly, the defendant's use of force—by accelerating the Honda with Adams still holding on and by attempting to dislodge Adams's hands from the Honda—was employed to perpetrate that theft.

We also reject the defendant's argument that the Commonwealth failed to show that Adams had a "protective interest" in the Honda. "The essence of robbery is the exertion of force, actual or constructive, against another in order to take personal property of any value whatsoever, with the intention of stealing it, from the protection which the person of that other affords. ... It is not affected by the state of the legal title to the goods taken."

Commonwealth v. Levia, 385 Mass. 345, 348 (1982), quoting from *Commonwealth v. Weiner*, 255 Mass. 506, 509 (1926). Adams had an adequate protective concern for Tompkins's car, which was stolen from outside their place of employment. See *Commonwealth v. Grassa*, 42 Mass.App.Ct. 204, 207–208 (1997), and cases cited.

Discussion 2: Assault and Battery by Means of a Dangerous Weapon (As provided by G.L. c. 265, § 15A(b), as appearing in St. 2002, c. 35, § 2:)

"Whoever commits assault and battery upon another by means of a dangerous weapon shall be punished by imprisonment in the state prison for not more than ten years or in a house of correction for not more than 2½ years, or by a fine of not more than $5,000, or both such fine and imprisonment."

A weapon can be dangerous per se—"an instrumentality designed and constructed to produce death or great bodily harm"—or dangerous as used, where the object is capable of inflicting serious bodily injury or causing death. *Commonwealth v. Appleby*, 380 Mass. 296, 303-304 (1980). See *People v. Buford*, 69 Mich.App. 27, 30 (1976) (automobile may be a dangerous weapon as used). It is a question for the fact finder whether an instrument is used as a dangerous weapon. Appleby, supra at 304.

The defendant argues that his conviction of assault and battery by means of a dangerous weapon, the Honda, must be reversed as the Commonwealth did not prove all elements of the offense beyond a reasonable doubt. "[T]he offense of assault and battery by means of a dangerous weapon under G.L. c. 265, § 15A, requires that the elements of assault be present, that there be a touching, however slight, that that touching be by means of the weapon, and that the battery be accomplished by use of an inherently dangerous weapon, or by use of some other object as a weapon, with the intent to use that object in a dangerous or potentially dangerous fashion." Id. at 308 (citations omitted). The second theory of assault and battery is that it is "the intentional commission of a wanton or reckless act (something more than gross negligence) causing physical or bodily injury to another." *Commonwealth v. Burno*, 396 Mass. 622, 625 (1986). The jury was instructed on both theories.

The defendant contends the battery was not accomplished because it was Adams who brought himself into contact with the Honda. The evidence was sufficient to sustain the conviction of assault and battery by means of a dangerous weapon under either theory.

Supporting conviction under the intentional theory of battery, the jury could have found that the defendant intended to use both the Honda and his hands in a dangerous or potentially dangerous fashion. While driving, he intentionally accelerated the Honda as Adams was holding onto it, drove the Honda through a red light, swerved in traffic, and traveled several blocks at a speed of thirty to forty miles per hour. At the same time, the defendant used his hands to attempt to dislodge Adams from the Honda.

Alternatively, the defendant's conviction can be upheld under a wanton and reckless theory of battery. The jury could have found that the defendant's decision to accelerate with a person holding onto the door and frame of the Honda was heedless of the potential danger to Adams. Not only was the defendant driving the Honda in a dangerous fashion, but he was also attempting to push Adams from the Honda with his hands. The reckless conduct resulted in Adams jumping from the moving Honda and suffering injuries.

Discussion 3: Sentencing as a Habitual Criminal

A jury found the defendant guilty under the habitual criminal statute, which requires that he be "punished by imprisonment in the state prison for the maximum term provided by law as a penalty for the felony for which he is then to be sentenced." G.L. c. 279, § 25. For unarmed robbery the maximum term is life in prison. G.L. c. 265, § 19(b). The defendant's arguments that this sentence constitutes cruel and unusual punishment under the Eighth Amendment to the United States Constitution and art. 26 of the Massachusetts Declaration of Rights were rejected in *Commonwealth v. Tuitt*, 393 Mass. 801, 813 (1985).

Judgments affirmed.

Questions

1. In these facts, what other offenses can be simultaneously charged that align with robbery?
2. What "force" did the Court conclude was sufficient for an unarmed robbery?
3. Is it reasonable to conclude that the victim believed that these actions constituted a taking by force?
4. The defendant argues about an insufficient presence. Exactly what does this mean?

Defendants are well versed in these distinctions especially when one considers the harsh penalties associated with robbery as compared to larceny. Accused parties challenge robbery charges by affirmatively asserting and even admitting the taking. Their resistance to robbery coalesces on the force and violence front due to the tough sanctions associated with the crime. In essence, choosing larceny over robbery is an easy choice for any defendant. In *Zanders v. U.S.*,[4] the defendant successfully appealed a robbery conviction under a robbery statute, which read as:

> Whoever by force or violence, whether against resistance or by sudden or stealthy seizure or snatching, or by putting in fear, shall take from the person or immediate actual possession of another anything of value, is guilty of robbery, and any person convicted thereof shall suffer imprisonment for not less than two years nor more than 15 years.[5]

The majority opinion dismissed both robbery counts against the defendant on facts that amounted to nothing more than a subway pickpocketing. The victim was completely unaware until a later time that he had lost his wallet. With this lack of apprehension, it is conclusive that the accused carried out their design without the infliction or threat of imminent harm. The *Zanders* court found neither direct nor indirect evidence of any taking committed by the appellants.[6]

Another way of looking at these distinctions is to view robbery as a combination of other offenses, namely assault and theft. This characterization affords defense teams another alternative in the search for a way out of robbery's rigor. The charge of two separate offenses may result in less punishment than a singular charge of robbery.[7]

Force

Determining the nature of force in robbery cases subjects both the investigative and prosecutorial team to intense investigative fact finding. A mistake in the review can result in a dismissal of the robbery charge when other charges might have made more sense. Embarking on a robbery prosecution is unwise unless evidence of force exists. To achieve this standard, the evidence will have to demonstrate some, but not necessarily all, of the following criteria:

- Infliction of physical injury
- Real and serious threats to inflict physical injury or harm
- Threats to perform another felony on the person subject to the robbery
- Cause the crime victim to be in fear of real and immediate bodily injury
- Take the property by means of force

Central to any proof of force is evidence that the taking took place under the stress of physical force. Courts at the appellate level grapple each day with subtle nuances of exactly what level of force satisfies. Victims understand the difference and distinction although criminal appellants generally assert that force was insufficient to meet the legal threshold. The use of firearms and blunt instruments offers no real confusion. Even fake guns made from wood qualify because the measure of fear of immediate and imminent harm is not in the mind of the offender, but those subject to the threat.

The troubling case law involves threats, words, and aggressive motions. These will qualify if the threat has immediacy, meaning it can and will likely occur. How these activities are measured suffers from some individualized perceptions. However, the law demands that the reaction be that of the reasonable person rather than the easily frightened or over-reactive. Hurling assault words and insults will not do, nor will threats from those incapacitated or incapable of affecting such force. To be persuasive, the party alleging force reacts as the normal, ordinary person reacts. When a gangbanging street thug states: "I am going to break your legs unless you give me the television," it is reasonable to believe the threat. The same threat coming from a 5 year old simply will not wash. As a result of this relativity, each case must be evaluated in light of the reasonable person standard. Each case differs dramatically.

Using the rape analogy regarding penetration, some jurisdictions have employed the measure, "however slight" to weigh the sufficiency of force employed. While the comparison has some validity, the robber lives in a very different world than the rapist. Penetration in a rape case should have an exceptionally lenient standard to protect the crime victim. To do otherwise would generate another form of assault and affront to the victim. But, for the robber, the act of violence seems somewhat at odds with the "slight" duplication. How can violence be slight? How does one assault another slightly and yet meet the demand for force and violence? Slight or minimally violent intrusions may fit other felonies or misdemeanors, such as theft, petty theft, purse snatching, or harassment. If a victim is aware that his/her wallet is being taken, and the wallet is ripped out of the pocket of the victim, has the force standard been met? The answer here is probably yes, but the reality of choosing this offense to prosecute over others, seems remote. Defense attorneys will harp endlessly about the real lack of force in this very common fact pattern. Prosecutors may be technically on safe ice, but given the lack of severity relating to violence, one can predict the plea bargain for the pickpocket. One also may find that the imposition of force is out of sync in a temporal sense with the actual taking. Courts view the totality of the victim's circumstances when deciding whether the force or threat thereof is sufficiently linked to the taking.[8]

A victim unaware of the taking, even if by force, due to coma or unconsciousness, cannot be robbed. Robbery requires a victim's awareness and apprehension. A corpse raided of its possessions cannot be robbed in the legal sense, either. In the final analysis, the robbery codification opens a wide array of possible approaches in prosecution and defense. The offender can be convicted by actual infliction of injury as swiftly as the same conviction will be upheld when only threat to do the same is offered.

DEFENSE STRATEGIES

Was force insufficient for robbery?
Was force independent of the taking?
Was the victim aware of the taking and force?
Was the victim's reaction reasonable?
Was the perpetrator capable of carrying out a threat?

States are now cataloging crime date as well. Search the Michigan crime data base on robbery at http://www.michigan.gov/msp/0,1607,7-123-1645_3501_4621-25744--,00.html

KIDNAPPING AND RELATED OFFENSES

ELEMENTS:

- Unlawful confinement and restraint by force
- Movement (asportation)
- For unlawful purpose—ransom, sexual, commission of a felony
- With specific intent

At common law, the crime of kidnapping was grave and serious. A person's freedom of movement and expectation that he or she be free of personal intrusion was sacrosanct in Western tradition. Additionally, kidnapping's surreptitious quality puts the victim in an exceptionally unpredictable and dangerous situation.[9] The kidnapper is usually driven by clear motives. Motive instructs why the criminal agent sought to carry out the deed. Motive explains the offender's mind.[10] While proof of motive is not a fundamental element of kidnapping, an absence of a rationale for the criminal conduct may trigger needless doubt in the jury. The motivations primarily fall into these categories:

- Economic: For money and other pecuniary gain
- Sexual: Transportation for the purpose of sexual activity without consent
- Political: Radical movement unlawfully restrains others for purposes of statement of change
- Random violence: Thrill seeking, irrational dominance of others

CASE 5.2

DILLINGHAM V. KENTUCKY

98-SC-429-MR (Ken.Sup. 1999)

Appellants, Kenneth Ray Dillingham and Robert Jurell Hicks, were convicted respectively of first-degree robbery and complicity to first-degree robbery. Dillingham and Hicks were sentenced to twenty years imprisonment. ...

The Edmonton State Bank in Center, Kentucky, was robbed at 11:30 a.m. on December 1, 1997. A neatly dressed man walked into the bank and handed a note to a clerk, Clifton Thompson. The note read, "This is a robbery. Don't push any buttons or call the police." The man stated that he had a gun. However, according to the testimony at trial, no witness actually saw a weapon.

A bank employee, Bernice Wisdom, emptied the teller drawers and handed the contents to the robber pursuant to his demands. The man placed the money in a briefcase with his left hand while keeping his right hand in his pocket. The man exited the bank, got into the passenger side of a waiting light blue Lincoln Town Car, and fled the scene. ...

Bank employees Clifton Thompson and Bernice Wisdom positively identified Dillingham as the man who robbed the Edmonton State Bank. Further, a customer testified that he saw Dillingham in the bank just prior to the robbery. Next, while no witness testified that he or she saw a weapon, there was sufficient evidence adduced at trial to convict Dillingham of first-degree robbery. ...

Almost $13,000 was stolen from the bank, which included a number of twenty dollar bills in "bait money," which are bills that the bank keeps a record of the serial numbers. The bait money only is to be removed from the drawer during the course of a robbery in order to facilitate capture of the robber. Wisdom testified that on the day of the robbery each of the three teller drawers at the bank contained $200 in bait money. She further testified that she emptied all three teller drawers and handed the contents to the robber.

A search of Hick's residence uncovered a coffee can filled with over $4,000 in currency of different denominations. Included with this currency were thirteen twenty dollar bills, the serial numbers of which matched the serial numbers of some of the bait money stolen from the bank. Additionally, Hick's wallet contained over $1,000 in cash, including a twenty dollar bill the serial number of which matched one of the serial numbers on the bait money list. Finally, a search of Hick's vehicle produced a set of clothes that were identified in court by two witnesses as being the same or similar to the clothes worn by the bank robber.

Questions

1. Is the force satisfactory in these facts? Explain.
2. If you were the defense attorney, what would your best argument be as it relates to the reasonable person standard?
3. If you were an investigator for the District Attorney, who would you interview in order to show force and why?
4. Is this a case of actual or potential force?
5. Does its location have anything to do with upholding the conviction?

Equally conclusive regarding the offense of kidnapping is its negative and harsh impacts on victims and families. "In short, whereas kidnapping inherently involves violation of the autonomy of the person and inhuman treatment ... it is difficult not to argue in favor of recognition as a human rights violation. The global kidnapping epidemic is not primarily based on political ideology, but more based on economic incentive."[11] Kidnapping is an "atrocious" and "devastating" act.[12]

Kidnappers are unpredictable and often self-righteous. The political ones are crusaders and change agents; radicals that see any means as satisfactory to the end. The irrational actors are impossible to decipher because they live on the edge, for it is the violence that drives; the charge and thrill of the dominance that stimulates. Sexual predators kidnap because they are spurred on by lust, by overwhelming passion that blots out reason, and by an unquenchable thirst to hide and control events they know only too acutely are corrupt and fiendish. Sexual predators use the movement of kidnapping to control the circumstances of the felonious conduct, especially the disposal of evidence and the bodies defiled. Economic offenders use the crime for economic gain.

> For an excellent overview of kidnapping from a corporate perspective, see http://www.claytonconsultants.com/pdf/CCKRB-EN-0409.pdf

Most criminal codifications describe in particular terms the reason for the abduction, whether it be ransom, facilitation of another offense, or abject violence. The Model Penal Code's (MPC) provision is regularly emulated.

A person is guilty of kidnapping if he unlawfully removes another from his place of residence or business, or a substantial distance from the vicinity where he is found, or if he unlawfully confines another for a substantial period in a place of isolation, with any of the following purposes:

(a) to hold for ransom or reward, or as a shield or hostage; or
(b) to facilitate commission of any felony or flight thereafter; or
(c) to inflict bodily injury on or to terrorize the victim or another; or
(d) to interfere with the performance of any governmental or political function.[13]

While motive is instructive, it does explain the full complement of issues that arise in a kidnapping prosecution. Much like the Felony Murder Rule (FMR), kidnapping has competing intents and legal cross currents. Some commentators identify one aspect as the "piggyback" quality. By piggyback, we mean the offense rests on other offenses, such as the original rapist, who specifically intends to rape another, but to effectuate the offense, restrains and moves the victim to another location. The simple geographic shift makes the rape into something more—a kidnapping. In this sense, the offense is evolutionary, as changing and as transient as the offender's itinerary. As the offender moves through time and space, while forcibly dragging along the target of the original intent, kidnapping charges evolve out of other offenses. For this reason, kidnapping facilitates the commission of underlying offenses, e.g., burglary changes to rape, rape metamorphoses to murder. As long as the movement accompanies the evolving offenses, kidnapping applies.

Defense attorneys, as one can imagine, seek to thwart this tendency toward transference and evolution. Statutory constructions tend to dwell on the factors witnessed in the North Carolina law below:

§ 14-39. Kidnapping

(a) Any person who shall unlawfully confine, restrain, or remove from one place to another, any other person 16 years of age or over without the consent of such person, or any other person under the age of 16 years without the consent of a parent or legal custodian of such person, shall be guilty of kidnapping if such confinement, restraint or removal is for the purpose of:

   (1) Holding such other person for a ransom or as a hostage or using such other person as a shield; or

   (2) Facilitating the commission of any felony or facilitating flight of any person following the commission of a felony; or

   (3) Doing serious bodily harm to or terrorizing the person so confined, restrained or removed or any other person; or

   (4) Holding such other person in involuntary servitude in violation of G.S. 14-43.12.[14]

The Nature of Movement

Movement, geographic displacement, is a central element in the proof of kidnapping. To kidnap, one must move the victim from one point to another, from one place to another setting. North Carolina emphasizes the geographic movement in express language, "from one place to another." This spatial and linear displacement is mandatory in most jurisdictions and without proof of movement the charge fails on the merits. As in some property offenses like larceny/theft, the law cannot meet its burden unless the property has been asported to some variable location. "Carrying away" describes the asportation component of kidnapping in a very similar way that property offenses do. How much movement is required is not clearly enunciated in the codes. Each case will present differing factual issues that will impact the measure of any movement. Cases in which the defendant drives 30 miles after an abduction is surely satisfactory. So, too, will a dragged victim who is subsequently assaulted and killed. What the law requires is a separation of space from initial location to another space being the subsequent location. The crux of kidnapping resides in altered states and shifting geography. New Mexico employs the verbs "taking, restraining, transporting, or confining" to delineate the requirement.[15]

A cautionary note regarding geography is worth mentioning. Do not confuse the coincidental or identical movement of the underlying felony with the transitory state of kidnapping. While kidnapping can be charged when the movement's primary aim is the successful commission of a felony, prosecutorial teams can always predict the defense argument that attacks the theory altogether. For these professionals, the issue is not movement alone, but a separateness of purpose in the movement.[16] Movement, in order to qualify under kidnapping schemes, must be sufficiently independent of the underlying felony; a fact sometimes lost on those who stress the facilitation end of kidnapping law. That movement should mutate, so to speak, from the initial offense into another, independently standing offense. Illustrations might be that the assault changes to rape as the movement unfolds, the burglary degenerates into a sadistic sodomy when the victim moves from one spatial point to another. It is not always easy to differentiate the dual criminal enterprises and the reality of merger. The inclusion of lesser offenses into the main criminal conduct will be a continually appraised issue in kidnapping cases.[17]

Think of a fleeing defendant under a hail of bullets from law enforcement. Is his escape an independent movement or part of the original felony's history? What if the same defendant breaks into a house to elude the police? Does this break-in now constitute the new crime of kidnapping if someone just happens to be in the house?

It may sound too convenient that one crime turns into another, but many commentators insist that each crime has little life of its own and that the movement during the commission of one felony has no inherent ability to be reborn into a second offense. Thus, prosecution teams collect and catalog evidence that shows not only geographic movement, but also facts that confirm and corroborate the purpose of said movement.

The Nature of Force

Kidnapping belongs in the category of violent offense and the typical statutory designs mention and mandate the requirement of force or other coercion. Force presents itself in many ways, from outright violence to fraud and deception. New Mexico portrays the force component as: "by force, intimidation or deception, with intent."[18]

If the element of force is missing, then lower level offenses such as false imprisonment or unlawful confinement may be better choices. Simply stated, kidnapping involves more than inconvenience and dispute between parties and instead harkens for an intensely violent setting, based on seriously injurious circumstances. Despite this general characterization, the twists and turns of the kidnapper's mind accomplish his goal with trickery and deception, which is violence to the will of the victim.

What at first appears a lowly misdemeanor or a nonviolent offense may eventually become a higher grade of criminality. In *Haynie v. Furlong*,[19] the unlawful taking commenced as a custody dispute between divorced parents. As will be seen shortly, this type of custodial dispute has special legislative construction that precludes the use of kidnapping to affect the return of the child to the custodial parent. When that custodial dispute evolves into other tragedy, the kidnapping remedy can be resurrected. In Haynie, the father sexually abused his children—an unfortunate fact that supports a finding of force.

Be careful not to confuse lesser offenses, which lack separate elements, and are thereby merged into the primary offense. Some courts have little choice but to dismiss some in a series of multiple charges when the facts and circumstances support one offense. In *New Mexico v. Laguna*,[20] the enticement of a child offense was held severable and a different offense than a kidnapping by deception charge. The Court held that double jeopardy forbids the prosecution of two charges over one transaction or instance.[21] However, the Court was satisfied that kidnapping, which constituted the movement of a child for the purposes of molestation, was sufficient for a kidnapping charge. The argument that the victim willingly got in the car with the perpetrator did not impress the Court, which described the plan as deceptive and intimidating.

> While there does not appear to be any evidence of intimidation in getting Robert into the car, the evidence of what occurred during the ride could reasonably lead the fact finder to conclude that Defendant intimidated Robert during transportation. ... To intimidate is to "make timid, to inhibit or discourage by or as if by threats"[22]... may result from words or conduct ... creates an apprehension of danger ... reducing victim's ability to resist. Robert was in a moving car, strapped in his seatbelt, when Defendant made demonstrative sexual advances. Defendant changed the intended destination. Robert was afraid ... did not think defendant could let him out of the car. Defendant was an adult ... jury could reasonably infer that Robert was transported or confined by intimidation.[23]

CASE 5.3

NEW MEXICO V. LAGUNA
992 P.2d 896 (N.M. App. 1999)

The victim, Robert H., two months away from fifteen years old, decided to walk to his girl-friend's house on a hot, Las Cruces, July afternoon. Getting there would take about an hour. A car passed by. The driver, Defendant, waved, and Robert waved back. Defendant pulled off the street and motioned for Robert to come over. Robert went to the vehicle and Defendant asked Robert if he had a sister. Robert replied that he did. Defendant asked her name, which Robert supplied. Defendant indicated that he knew her. During cross-examination, Robert testified that he did not know if it was true that Defendant knew his sister and that his sis-ter knew a lot of people. After the small talk about Robert's sister, Defendant asked Robert if he needed a ride.

Robert accepted, got in the car and gave Defendant directions. Robert testified that he got in the vehicle because he wanted a ride, not because Defendant knew his sister. However, on redirect, Robert testified that he felt more comfortable getting in the vehicle because Defendant said he knew his sister. Nevertheless, because it was hot, he would have taken a ride from anyone that day.

As Defendant was driving in the direction indicated by Robert, he placed his closed hand on Robert's leg and began to rub and move his hand up Robert's leg. Robert pushed Defendant's hand away. Again, Defendant placed his hand on Robert's leg and worked it up the leg toward his crotch. Robert testified that this touching happened more than twice. Robert continued to push Defendant's hand away. On at least one of those touchings, Defendant grabbed Robert's leg. Defendant turned on a street that was not in the direction of Robert's destination. Defendant pulled over to a house, and asked, "Can we stop at my friend's house real quick?"

Robert told Defendant that if he did, he, Robert, was "just going to leave." Defendant drove on, continuing in the direction that Robert had given him. By this time, Robert was trying to think of a way to get away from Defendant and he told Defendant that he needed to stop at a Shell station they were passing. Robert then quickly changed his mind about the Shell station and directed Defendant to his sister's boyfriend's house, which was nearby. Robert was thinking, "Well, because like if I had to struggle or anything, I could tell [her boyfriend]." Defendant drove to the house and stopped in front of it.

At some point or points during the ride, Robert thought that Defendant might rape him and that Defendant would not let him out of the car. At the sister's boyfriend's house, while the engine remained running and before Robert could unfasten his seatbelt and exit the vehicle, Defendant grabbed for Robert's crotch. According to Robert, Defendant "tried to grab my penis, but he grabbed the pants" instead. Robert instantly and reactively punched Defendant, who then let go of the pants. Robert unfastened his seatbelt, got out of the car, went into the house and told the mother of his sister's boyfriend what happened. He then began to walk to his girlfriend's house. Defendant pulled up and called to Robert from the car. Robert told Defendant, "No. I'm going to kill you. ..." Defendant left, and Robert went into a nearby house and called the police.

Defendant contends that this evidence is insufficient to support the conviction of first degree kidnapping. Substantial evidence is relevant evidence that a reasonable mind would accept as adequate to support a conclusion. See *State v. Carrasco*, 1997 NMSC 47, P11, 124 N.M. 64, 946 P.2d 1075. We review the evidence in the light most favorable to the verdict, resolving all conflicts and indulging in all permissible inferences to uphold the conviction and disregarding all evidence and inferences to the contrary. See *State v. Rojo*, 1999 NMSC 1, P19, 126 N.M. 438, 971 P.2d 829. We must decide whether the evidence could justify a finding by a rational trier of fact that each essential element of the crime charged has been established beyond a reasonable doubt. See *State v. Huff*, 1998 NMCA 75, P10, 125 N.M. 254, 960 P.2d 342.

Kidnapping is the "unlawful taking, restraining, transporting or confining of a person, by force, intimidation or deception, with intent ... to inflict death, physical injury, or a sexual offense on the victim." Section 30-4-1(A). Kidnapping is a first degree felony that can be reduced to a second degree felony when the defendant "voluntarily frees the victim in a safe place and does not inflict great bodily harm upon the victim." Section 30-4-1(B).

Defendant concedes that there was evidence that he took or transported Robert with the intent to commit a sexual offense. Defendant does not argue that the evidence was insufficient to prove unlawfulness. He contends, however, that there was no evidence of force, intimidation, or deception at any stage. He argues that the State relied only on deception, but did not meet its burden of proving deception. The record shows that the State argued both intimidation and deception in the taking and transporting of Robert. The use of force is not an issue. While there does not appear to be any evidence of intimidation in getting Robert into the car, the evidence of what occurred during the ride could reasonably lead the fact finder to conclude that Defendant intimidated Robert during transportation. Defendant argues that there was no testimony of any threats or use of intimidating words or gestures. We disagree. To intimidate is to "make timid[; t]o inhibit or discourage by or as if by threats." *Webster's II New College Dictionary* 581 (1995). Intimidation includes "putting in fear." *Black's Law Dictionary*, 737 (6th ed. 1990); see also *State v. Sanchez*, 78 N.M. 284, 285, 430 P.2d 781, 782 (Ct. App 1967). Intimidation may result from words or conduct. Intimidation creates an apprehension of danger of bodily harm while also reducing the victim's ability to resist the advances toward that harm. See Sanchez, 78 N.M. at 285, 430 P.2d at 782.

Robert was in a moving car, strapped in his seatbelt, when Defendant made demonstrative sexual advances. Defendant changed the intended destination. Robert was afraid that Defendant was going to rape him. He did not think Defendant would let him out of the car. Defendant was an adult, in control of the vehicle, making demonstrative sexual advances toward a young teenager. We believe these are circumstances from which the jury could reasonably infer that Robert was transported or confined by intimidation. ...Defendant has two double jeopardy concerns. He prevails on both.

His first is based on the prohibition against multiple punishments for the same conduct. In analyzing this contention, we must first determine if Defendant's conduct was unitary so that the same acts were used to prove a violation of both statutes. See *State v. Livernois*, 1997 NMSC 19, P19, 123 N.M. 128, 934 P.2d 1057. If the conduct is not unitary, there is no double jeopardy violation. See id. P 22. If the conduct is unitary, we must determine "'whether the legislature intended to create separately punishable offenses.'" Id. P 19 (quoting *Swafford v. State*, 112 N.M. 3, 13, 810 P.2d 1223, 1233 (1991)).

The State concedes that the enticement-of-a-child charge was based on the same conduct that supported the kidnapping-by-deception charge. We find no clear indication that the Legislature intended to create separately punishable offenses under these circumstances. Indeed, we have held that enticement of a child is a lesser included offense of kidnapping by deception. See Garcia, 100 N.M. at 125, 666 P.2d at 1272. The conviction of the lesser charge cannot stand.

Defendant's second double jeopardy contention concerns the two attempted CSCMs.

The State charged Defendant in two separate counts with attempted CSCM, reciting the elements of the statute. One instruction covered both counts. Defendant argues that there were not two separate and distinct offenses of attempted CSCM. See *State v. Herron*, 111 N.M. 357, 361-62, 805 P.2d 624, 628-29 (1991) (setting forth a number of factors to be considered in determining the appropriate unit of prosecution). It is unclear from the record and the jury instructions what conduct constituted the two instances of attempted CSCM.

The State argues that there was evidence of two separate and distinct acts of attempted CSCM even apart from the final crotch grab. According to the State, this evidence includes Robert's testimony that Defendant rubbed his leg, moving up toward his crotch several times in a continual manner. Each time Robert pushed his hand away. Under the factors set forth in Herron, however, we believe that this was simply one continuous attempt to reach Robert's private parts. The touchings occurred over a very short time period, and there was no intervening event aside from Robert pushing Defendant's hand away. We conclude that this repeated touching was a single ongoing attempt to reach Robert's private parts.

Questions

1. In what way does the court discern force between the perpetrator and his child victim?
2. Why did the court find merger?
3. What types of conduct signified an atmosphere of intimidation?

Finally, don't fall prey to the spurious defense that questions the sufficiency of evidence as to the defendant's mental state at the time of the abduction. Abduction alone signifies a dishonorable purpose. It is not the prosecution's responsibility to explain the motivation of the mover because this state of mind can be inferred from the facts and the acts of the defendant. Thus, a defendant who abducted a victim he repeatedly raped could not avail himself of the claim that there was no proof that he intended to perform these acts when unlawfully restrained.[24] The appeals court held that "any rational trier of fact could have found the essential elements of the crime beyond a reasonable doubt."[25]

FALSE IMPRISONMENT

ELEMENTS

- Knowing intent to confine
- Without claim, privilege, or right
- Confinement and restraint as to liberty

The primary distinguishing characteristic in the crime of false imprisonment as compared to kidnapping is the level of inflicted violence.[26] States that mention serious bodily injury do so without expecting the actual infliction. Other jurisdictions have removed references to violent activity altogether. While both offenses unlawfully restrain and confine the freely moving being, and do so without claim of privilege or right, the perpetrator of false imprisonment does not generate the level of force and violence to achieve this purpose. Defense tactics often include this glaring inconsistency when the charges are made together. The defense will ask how can someone be an offender of kidnapping and false imprisonment at the same time? This answer will depend on how the facts unravel. False imprisonment can escalate into more violent actions, but the contrary would be very unlikely. Then again, restraint has subjective qualities about it since some victims feel any confinement and movement as a violent intrusion, while others can appreciate the difference. Courts look to the reasonable person to contrast the violence of one offense and the infringement of liberty in the other. This does not mean that the lines are not sometimes fuzzy and awfully close to one another, and, in fact, some statutory constructions are so similar one wonders about the distinction in the first place.[27] Nebraska offers up befuddling language that sounds like, walks like, and acts like the duck known as kidnapping.

> (1) A person commits false imprisonment in the first degree if he or she knowingly restrains or abducts another person (a) under terrorizing circumstances or under circumstances which expose the person to the risk of serious bodily injury; or (b) with intent to hold him or her in a condition of involuntary servitude.[28]

The Model Penal Code moves in a completely different direction by emphasizing the restraint of liberty over the violent means to achieve the nefarious end. The MPC is strikingly softer:

> A person commits a misdemeanor if he knowingly restrains another unlawfully so as to interfere substantially with his liberty.[29]

Pennsylvania law mimics the design by qualifying the act to include any restraint that unlawfully "interfere substantially with his liberty".[30] Other states employ terms like "substantially" so as not to confuse the civil action and corresponding remedies for the tort known as "false imprisonment".[31] The legislative intent behind this offense does not include the actions of individuals operating under mistake or ignorance, but includes the offender who knows and intends to imprison without claim, privilege, or right. Improperly identified shoplifters cannot avail themselves of this type of criminal prosecution, nor can parties whose arrest was factually unjustified make this allegation against a peace officer carrying out duties in good faith. Immunity and privilege protects these law enforcement officers from mistakes made, as long as there are no civil rights violations that would prompt other remedial action. The defense of sovereign immunity generally protects police officers as long as the basis for the arrest was grounded in probable cause.[32]

CUSTODIAL INTERFERENCE

ELEMENTS:

- Knowingly and recklessly taking a child
- In violation of a court order
- Without claim, privilege, or right

One of the inevitable downsides of staggering rates of divorce in the American scene is the criminalization of custody questions.[33] Emotions run high during the battles over children and placement. If a party "takes" a child in violation of an existing court order or decree, without the privilege or right to do so, movement of the child may facilitate felonious conduct. Within this fact pattern, one also may witness the movement of a child without the child willingly participating. Even within these sorts of facts, it is possible that the higher level kidnapping charge might stick, though that is surely not the intent of these particular provisions. A typical law might be fashioned as so:

§ 2904. Interference with custody of children

(a) OFFENSE DEFINED—A person commits an offense if he knowingly or recklessly takes or entices any child under the age of 18 years from the custody of its parent, guardian, or other lawful custodian, when he has no privilege to do so.

(b) DEFENSES —It is a defense that:
   (1) the actor believed that his action was necessary to preserve the child from danger to its welfare; or
   (2) the child, being at the time not less than 14 years old, was taken away at its own instigation without enticement and without purpose to commit a criminal offense with or against the child; or
   (3) the actor is the child's parent or guardian or other lawful custodian and is not acting contrary to an order entered by a court of competent jurisdiction.[34]

The complexities of these estrangements offer little solace to an already beleaguered system. The law of crimes must concern itself with major criminal actions and not get bogged down by dates of visitation. Our civil system is already under water with the bickering and acrimony of support and custody litigation. This type of case demands significantly more than the angry and displaced parent; it requires a willful and knowing violator of custody grants, a person who appreciates the ramifications of custodial interference and decides not to adhere to the judicial controls currently in place. This is not an offense of heated emotion, but a purposeful and contrived plan to displace not only the Court's order, but also the child who is subject to it.

Lawmakers know the state of the world requires a unique legislative response to the common dispute of custody battles. Parents do take children over the objection of the custodial parent. Children are often employed as pawns during and after divorce proceedings. Some parents suffer from so many mental and addictive disorders that placement with the dysfunctional parent can, and sometimes does, cause measurable harm and even physical injury. A few cases witnessed thus far have even demonstrated how thin the line is between custody problems and actual kidnapping. The offender who custodially interferes, then sexually abuses his child, cannot hide behind the special protection these laws provide. That case, as already noted, transforms into kidnapping. In the average case, argument and disagreements over placement, visitation, child support and sharing of time and responsibility, are not the stuff of violent criminality. Often, the acts are driven by desperation and parental frustration and even in some settings, by incredibly poor custodial decision making from the Court entrusted with jurisdiction. The fact remains that disputes of this sort need unique and specialized laws.

See how the State of Idaho, County of Bannock, educates its citizenry on the complexities of custodial interference at http://www.co.bannock.id.us/prosecutor/child_custody_interference.html

An interesting defense approach in custodial cases is related to the enforceability of the underlying decree. Is it legally possible to violate a child custody decree yet to be judicially determined and finalized? Another fascinating dilemma in custody law, and how it interrelates with this offense, is the existence of any presumptions granted a parent, such as the mother, under the Tender Years Doctrine. Under this presumption, the mother is assumed better suited to care for and love the child. If the defendant knows the mother is incapable or less loving than he, does the presumption make the taking of the child more or less likely a violation under custodial interference laws? See Figure 5.1 for a list of state parental kidnapping statutes in the United States.

Some states incorporate a series of defenses that relate to the urgency of child upbringing. If a father knows that his child, placed under the presumption of Tender Years with the mother, in fact, is in some type of jeopardy or possible physical harm, the taking is defensible. The taker can carefully defend if he believed the action was necessary to protect "the child from danger to its welfare."[35] Finally, a legitimate defense exists to the claims of custodial interference when the child, of sufficient age, affirmatively chooses to be with the noncustodial parent.

CRIMES INVOLVING BODILY INJURY

In cases where death does not occur, though physical injury is inflicted, the law reserves a wide range of crimes that are relevant to these bodily harms. Injuries from altercations, fights and other disputes are an unfortunate, common occurrence in modern society. Commentators continuously groan over the violent and rough shod way people so often interact and that coarseness often seems to replace gentility. Certainly, stereotypical images of the American way of dealing with problems, according to many continental Europeans, usually consists of gun-toting, baseball bat-flinging fighters who cannot resolve differences. Our wild, western heritage reinforces this view that violence is an acceptable avenue for resolving problems. Our television and media spew a wide range of violent conducts into the cultural mainstream and the bloodlust forever-increasing violent forms of entertainment partially confirms this view. Few could argue that the ravages of violent behavior are not evident in each sector of the community, from schools to

State	Citation
AL	Ala. Code § 13a-6-45 (2004)
AK	Alaska Stat. §§ 11.41.320, 11.41.330 (Michie 2004)
AZ	Az. Rev. Stat. §§ 13-1302, 13-1302c, 13-1305 (2004.
AR	Ark. Code Ann. §§ 5-26-501, 5-26-502 (Michie 2003)
CA	Cal. Penal Code §§ 278, 278.5, 278.7 (Deering 2004)
CO	Colo. Rev. Stat. § 18-3-304 (2003)
CT	Conn. Gen. Stat. §§ 53a-97, 53a-98 (2003)
DE	Del. Code Ann. § 785 (2004)
DC	D.C. Code Ann. §§ 16-1022, 16-1023 (2004)
FL	Fla. Stat. §§ 787.03, 787.04 (2003)
GA	Ga. Code Ann. § 16-5-45 (2004)
HI	Haw. Rev. Stat. §§ 707-726, 707-727 (2003)
ID	Idaho Code § 18-4506 (Michie 2004)
IL	720 Ill. Comp. Stat. §§ 5/10-5, 5/10-5.5 (2004)
IN	Ind. Code Ann. § 35-42-3-4 (Michie 2004)
IA	Iowa Code § 710.6 (2003)
KS	Kan. Crim. Code Ann. §§ 21-3422, 21-3422a (West 2003)
KY	Ky. Rev. Stat. § 509.070 (Michie 2004)
LA	La. Rev. Stat. §§ 14:45, 14:45.1 (2004)
ME	Me. Rev. Stat. Ann. 17-A § 303 (West 2003)
MD	Md. Fam. Law Code Ann. §§ 9-304, 9-305, 9-306 (2003)
MA	Mass. Ann. Laws § 26a (Law. Co-Op 2004)
MI	Mich. Comp. Laws §§ 722.27a(6)(H), 750.350a (2004)
MN	Minn. Stat. § 609.26 (2004)
MS	Miss. Code Ann. § 97-3-51 (2003)
MO	Mo. Rev. Stat. §§ 565.150, 565.153, 565.156, 565.160(3) (2003)
MT	Mont. Code Ann. §§ 45-5-304, 45-5-631, 45-5-632, 45-5-633, 45-5-634 (2003)
NE	Neb. Rev. Stat. § 28-316 (2004)
NV	Nev. Rev. Stat. Ann. § 200.359 (Michie 2004)
NH	N.H. Rev. Stat. Ann. § 633:4 (2003.
NJ	N.J. Rev. Stat. §§ 2c:13-1, 2c:13-4 (2004)
NM	N.M. Stat. Ann. § 30-4-4 (Michie 2004)
NY	N.Y. PENAL LAW §§ 135.45, 135.50 (Mckinney 2003)
NC	N.C. Gen. Stat. §§ 14-320.1, 14-41 (2004)
ND	N.D. Cent. Code § 12.1-18-05 (2003)
OH	Ohio Rev. Code Ann. § 2919.23 (Anderson 2004)

Figure 5.1   State Parental Kidnapping Statues in the U.S.   (*continued*)

State	Citation
OK	Okla. Stat. §§ 567a, 891 (2004)
OR	Or. Rev. Stat. §§ 163.245, 163.257 (2003)
PA	18 Pa. Cons. Stat. §§ 2904, 2909 (2004)
RI	R.I. Gen. Laws §§ 11-26-1.1, 11-26-1.2 (2004).
SC	S.C. Code Ann. § 16-17-495 (Law Co-Op. 2003)
SD	S.D. Codified Laws §§ 22-19-9, 22-19-11 (Michie 2003)
TN	Tenn. Code Ann. § 39-13-306 (2004)
TX	Tex Penal Code Ann. §§ 25.03, 25.04 (Vernon 2004)
UT	Utah Code Ann. §§ 76-5-303, 76-5-305 (2004)
VT	13 Vt. Stat. Ann. § 2451 (2003)
VA	Va. Code Ann. §§ 18.2-47, 18.2-49.1 (2003)
WA	Wash. Rev. Code §§ 9a.40.060, 9a.40.070, 9a.40.080 (2003)
WV	W. Va. Code § 61-2-14d (2003)
WI	Wis. Stat. § 948.31 (2003)
WY	Wyo. Stat. Ann. § 6-2-204 (Michie 2003)

Figure 5.1   (*continued*) State Parental Kidnapping Statues in the U.S.

neighborhoods, from athletic fields to entertainment centers.[36] It is a culture that tolerates far more violence than its predecessors would, and it would be inane to claim a lack of impact. Enter most American schools in troubled neighborhoods, and the pathology will be obvious. Consider the behavior of parents at athletic events who protest and critique a coach's performance with violent means. Remember how gangbangers carry out their enforcement techniques, and how the neighborhood streets are filled with signs of retaliation.

The dearth of manners and polite behavior further manifest this seemingly unalterable march toward coarseness and brutality. Teachers assaulted, police officers abused, citizens insulted by public officials, authority figures generally suspect, represent this upward tick in violence and declining civility in human relations. In this framework, justice professionals sit and marvel at how people act and react, at how cheaply and cavalierly people employ force to achieve their ends. It is a world where five-year-olds carry guns and parents train their children to attack others, where lovers and their respective quarrels are resolved by battle and onslaught, and where insult meets with reactions once exclusively reserved for the most hardened criminals. (See Table 5.1[37] for the latest statistics on school violence.)

As long as humans have roamed the Earth, dispute and disagreement have followed them in daily life. However, this inevitability, kept in the proper perspective, is not what unravels in the twenty-first century. Without institutional order and with a general collapse in the meaning and nature of authority, the chaotic responses so apparent in all bodily injury offenses can only multiply. When a spouse is abused, the resolutions are now utterly unpredictable, from death to castration. When a child is physically disciplined by parents, and for good cause, so sensitive and simultaneously jaded we have become that we label the parent as a child abuser and the gangbanger a cultural icon. When a teacher asserts proper authority, the system takes offense and attacks the professionalism of the authority figure and allows the vagabond child to run free. When schoolyard fights break out, intervention by police officials is labeled an overreaction and

Table 5.1 Number of incidents of crime that occurred at school reported to police by incident type and selected school characteristics: School year 2007-2008.

School Characteristic	Violent Incidents Reported to Police				Serious Violent Incidents Reported to Police				Theft Reported to Police[3]				Other Incidents Reported to Police[4]			
	Number of schools	Percent of schools	Number of incidents	Rate per 1,000 students	Number of schools	Percent of schools	Number of incidents	Rate per 1,000 students	Number of schools	Percent of schools	Number of incidents	Rate per 1,000 students	Number of schools	Percent of schools	Number of incidents	Rate per 1,000 students
All public schools	31,410	38	302,600	6	10,420	13	29,400	1	25,690	31	133,800	3	40,430	49	267,800	6
Level[5]																
Primary	9,840	20	49,700	2	3,500	7	5,400	#	8,080	16	18,200	1	16,570	34	45,800	2
Middle	9,850	64	107,300	11	2,740	18	10,900	1	7,160	47	32,000	3	10,490	69	70,500	7
High school	8,890	75	131,400	11	3,140	26	11,500	1	7,800	65	74,500	6	10,170	85	139,000	11
Combined	2,840	43	14,100	5	1,040	16	1,600!	1	2,650	40	9,200	3	3,190	48	12,500	5
Enrollment size																
Less than 300	4,450	23	18,000	5	1,390	7	2,200	1	3,870	20	7,400	2	5,630	29	17,500	4
300–499	6,660	27	34,100	3	1,960	8	3,300	#	4,660	19	11,600	1	9,680	40	28,900	3
500–999	13,000	43	110,100	5	4,180	14	10,200	1	10,830	36	46,900	2	16,950	56	86,500	4
1,000 or more	7,290	78	140,300	10	2,890	31	13,700	1	6,340	68	67,900	5	8,160	88	134,900	10
Urbanicity																
City	9,600	45	123,800	9	3,440	16	13,300	1	8,080	38	42,600	3	12,760	60	96,800	7
Suburb	8,230	34	82,800	5	2,920	12	7,500	#	6,330	26	44,200	3	11,760	49	84,600	5
Town	4,800	41	38,800	6	1,370	12	3,700	1	3,610	31	17,500	3	5,440	46	29,900	5
Rural	8,780	34	57,200	5	2,690	10	4,900	#	7,680	29	29,500	3	10,460	40	56,500	5
Crime level where students live[6]																
High	2,860	46	35,300	10	1,020	16	5,000!	1!	3,400	55	13,100	4	3,720	60	35,800	10
Moderate	8,010	47	96,500	9	2,980	17	8,500	1	5,410	32	33,800	3	10,500	61	78,900	8
Low	16,030	33	106,700	4	4,830	10	10,000	#	13,430	27	64,900	2	20,560	42	112,500	4

Mixed	4,510	43	64,100	9	1,590	15	5,900	1	3,450	33	21,900	3	5,640	54	40,700	5
Regular use of law enforcement[9]															
Regular use	20,750	54	255,900	9	7,530	20	25,100	1	17,150	45	112,800	4	24,180	63	220,100	8
No regular use	10,660	24	46,700	2	2,890	6	4,300	#	8,540	19	21,000	1	16,240	36	47,700	3
Number of serious discipline problems[10]															
No problems	16,620	29	129,100	4	4,580	8	9,800	#	14,890	26	67,300	2	23,890	42	126,700	4
1 problem	8,130	50	68,300	7	3,180	20	8,200	1	6,130	38	30,600	3	9,500	59	61,400	6
2 problems	3,240	62	41,400	12	1,240	24	3,300	1	2,140	41	13,800	4	3,310	64	29,600	8
3 or more problems	3,410	71	63,700	16	1,420	30	8,200	2	2,530	53	22,200	6	3,730	77	50,100	13

[1] Violent incidents include rape or attempted rape, sexual battery other than rape, physical attack or fight with or without a weapon, threat of physical attack with or without a weapon, and robbery with or without a weapon.

[2] Serious violent incidents include rape or attempted rape, sexual battery other than rape, physical attack or fight with a weapon, threat of physical attack with a weapon, and robbery with or without a weapon.

[3] Theft or larceny (taking things worth over $10 without personal confrontation) was defined for respondents as "the unlawful taking of another person's property without personal confrontation, threat, violence, or bodily harm. This includes pocket picking, stealing a purse or backpack (if left unattended or no force was used to take it from owner), theft from a building, theft from a motor vehicle or of motor vehicle parts or accessories, theft of a bicycle, theft from a vending machine, and all other types of thefts."

[4] Other incidents include possession of a firearm or explosive device; possession of a knife or sharp object; distribution, possession, or use of illegal drugs or alcohol; and vandalism.

[5] Primary schools are defined as schools in which the lowest grade is not lower than grade 3 and the highest grade is not higher than grade 8. Middle schools are defined as schools in which the lowest grade is not lower than grade 4 and the highest grade is not higher than grade 9. High schools are defined as schools in which the lowest grade is not lower than grade 9 and the highest grade is not higher than grade 12. Combined schools include all other combinations of grades, including K-12 schools.

[6] Respondents were asked, "How would you describe the crime level in the area(s) in which your students live?" Response options included "high level of crime," "moderate level of crime," "low level of crime," and "students come from areas with very different levels of crime."

[9] Respondents were asked, "During the 2007–2008 school year, did you have any security guards, security personnel, or sworn law enforcement officers present at your school at least once a week?"

[10] Serious discipline problems include student racial/ethnic tensions, student bullying, student sexual harassment of other students, student verbal abuse of teachers, widespread disorder in classrooms, student acts of disrespect for teachers other than verbal abuse, gang activities, and cult or extremist group activities. If a respondent reported that any of these problems occurred daily or weekly in their school, each was counted once in the total number of serious discipline problems.

Note: # = rounded to zero. Interpret data with caution; ! = The standard error for this estimate is from 30 to 50 percent of the estimate's value. "At school" was defined for respondents to include activities happening in school buildings, on school grounds, on school buses, and at places that hold school-sponsored events or activities. Detail may not sum to totals because of rounding. Responses were provided by the principal or the person most knowledgeable about crime and safety issues at the school.

Source: U.S. Department of Education, Institute of Education Sciences, National Center for Education Statistics (NCES), 2007–2008 School Survey on Crime and Safety (SSOCS), 2008.

brutal. When police officers defend their physical integrity by forcibly restraining an assaulter, professional competence is questioned. Sadly, our sensibilities about what violence is and how it plays out in a very violent world, are keenly distorted. In a time with such rampant violence, how does the justice model react to quell the plague witnessed everywhere? Which laws are capable of deterring? In short, what can the system accomplish concerning violence and brutality?[38]

Assault

ELEMENTS:

- Threat or actual commission of serious bodily injury by offensive touching
- With general or specific intent depending on grade
- If threat, the harm is imminent
- If aggravated assault, employment of weapon or other instrument

---

The threat or the actual commission of serious bodily injury to another has long been criminalized in Western jurisprudence. Assault forbids another from inflicting any type of injury on the person of another and grades its level of severity by the means and method of the assault. Fist fights and barroom altercations are usually reserved for the lower grade assault while assault using weaponry or other instruments is reserved for the higher grades. At common law, assault was distinguished from battery since the latter occurred when the touching or contact actually took place while the assault, the injury by threat, was one of expectancy. Naturally, battery was deemed a more serious offense because the criminal agent carried out the threat to its physical fruition while the assaulter merely threatened to do so. Nearly every state has merged the two offenses under the assault umbrella leaving open the possibility of either imminent threat or actual physical touching. Hence, the distinction is primarily academic.

Assault cases all contain core elements, from simple to aggravated. First, the harm threatened or done must be of a serious nature, not the petty trifles and insults that civil damages cover. By serious, we mean substantive. One cannot assault another with a feather or spaghetti noodle, nor can a two-day-old baby inflict injury on another. The type of injury warranted in assault has pathological and medical substance: the smash to the face, the broken bone, the tear or laceration, the bruise or contusion. The substantiality of the injury directly correlates to its severity and the law of assault requires something measurable.[39]

Second, the reaction of the injured party must be one of reasonableness. Threats of imminent harm and injury should be kept in some rational perspective, according to how the average and most reasonable person might react. Thus, if a Mafia enforcer tells you that he is going to break your face if your payment is not to him by tomorrow, the average Mary and Joe Blow appreciate the sincerity of the threat. On the other hand, if a seven-year-old screams at an adult that "I am going to break every bone in your body," the threat is illusory and without reasonable potential. To be a threat in any sense, the harm offered must have a bona fide possibility of being inflicted, and the party communicating the threat needs to have the capacity to carry it out. Reasonable persons know what these words mean and just as intelligently can differentiate the idle or silly insult from the purposeful words of an impending assaulter. In short, the criminal actor need have the present and actual ability to carry out the threatened bodily injury.

Third, the person accused must possess the requisite intent set out in the statute. In the graver versions of assault, the actor wills and intends specifically, while, in the lower varieties, the actor knows or should know that injury is an inevitable outcome of the confrontation. Accidental touching does not qualify for criminal responsibility, though mistaken contact can be remedied by damages in the civil courts.[40]

Fourth, if a high grade of assault, such as aggravated, the prosecution team may have to produce a weapon or other instrument capable of inflicting harm. Weapons in the form of firearms and knives will always qualify, but so do blunt instruments like tire irons and tools, wooden planks and baseball bats, chains and steel bars. Aggravated cases also may involve the commission of a concurrent felony like rape or kidnapping that generates a greater degree of culpability because of the forcible actions.

In general, the law of assault should not pose many problems for the justice professional as long as the facts fit nicely into the statutory definition.

Simple Assault

Lowest in criminal gravity, simple assault covers a lot of territory in human interaction. While every form of assault can be deemed harmful, the simple version wreaks the least amount of personal havoc. Simple assault is applicable in the most usual of cases law enforcement deals with on a day-to-day basis, such as:

- Barroom brawls
- Intense rivalries
- Domestic disputes
- Street fights and disorderly riots
- Jealous rages and quarrels
- Racial disputes
- Gang wars
- Fights and scuffles

In the bulk of American jurisdictions, the offense is a misdemeanor and usually results in some type of diversion or alternative disposition due to its commonality. A typical statute might be as follows:

(a) A person commits the offense of simple assault when he or she either:
   (1) Attempts to commit a violent injury to the person of another; or
   (2) Commits an act which places another in reasonable apprehension of immediately receiving a violent injury.[41]

The coverage of these types of laws become fairly comprehensive by labeling the unacceptable conduct as negligent, reckless, careless, and even intentionally. The statute has been often labeled a "catch all" because it affords so much prosecutorial discretion. Within any series of facts where an altercation occurs, the statute predictably has some applicability. To the consternation of defense teams, assault at its most basic level, is almost impossible to defend against if other qualifying elements for higher grades of assault are available. Thus, one who brandishes a weapon while assaulting another surely falls under the generic coverage of assault. The question of aggravation will not be guaranteed.

The Model Penal Code delivers the word "attempt" into its mix of what assault can be and is. Not only the touching, not only the threat, but even the attempt to do any harm will meet its threshold. In addition, the MPC references weaponry within its coverage, holding open these multiple possibilities for prosecutorial charge.

A person is guilty of assault if he:

(a) attempts to cause or purposely, knowingly or recklessly causes bodily injury to another; or
(b) negligently causes bodily injury to another with a deadly weapon; or
(c) attempts by physical menace to put another in fear of imminent serious bodily injury.[42]

Precisely what serious bodily injury is has been the subject of endless legal and academic debate. Lower forms of assault display a liberal leaning to apparently small injury. The contact need not produce a medical diagnosis or resulting damages. Evaluate whether "spitting" can cause bodily injury in Case 5.4.

Aggravated Assault

ELEMENTS:

- Actual or offensive touching
- Serious bodily injury
- With weapon or deadly instrument

At the upper echelons of assault resides the aggravated form. "Aggravated" means that the infliction is more than the garden variety of push and shove and results in significant injury. To find aggravation, one must evaluate both the mind of the actor, who specifically intends the outcome, and the means or instrumentality utilized to reach the desired end. A major felony with extraordinary penalties attached, aggravated assault inhabits territory closely aligned to felonious homicide because the means to kill accompany the assaulter. The means do not necessarily translate into the specific intent to kill, but can impute a lower form of homicidal intent if death occurs. This is why the offense is viewed as seriously as it is.

A cursory look at any statute will contain these types of qualifications:

- That the actor acts with extreme indifference to human life
- That the actor offends knowingly, intentionally, and recklessly
- That the actor offends using a weapon or other instrumentality
- That the actor targets special victims, such as teachers, EMS, and police

The Model Penal Code delivers a crystal clear picture of how this offense differs from assault.

A person is guilty of aggravated assault if he:

(a) attempts to cause serious bodily injury to another, or causes such injury purposely, knowingly or recklessly under circumstances manifesting extreme indifference to the value of human life; or
(b) attempts to cause or purposely or knowingly causes bodily injury to another with a deadly weapon.[43]

The crux of the offense is its pure and unadulterated intentionality. There is no mistaking the mindset of the accused for he or she cannot offer up alternative explanations for why they

---

CASE 5.4

STATE V. HUMPHRIES

21 Wash. App. 405, 586 P.2d 130 (1978).

On the evening of January 17, 1977, Seattle police officers responded to a radio call seeking to locate defendant Humphries concerning some traffic and robbery warrants. The officers went to an address they had been given, and upon arriving knocked on the door, and entered when a woman opened it. Officer Burtis testified that the woman opened the door quite wide and he walked in. The woman controverted the officer's statement and testified that the officers pushed the door open and elbowed their way in.

A birthday party was in progress and numerous people were present. When the officers asked for Humphries, an argument broke out concerning their presence and the apparent lack of a warrant. Humphries appeared and joined the argument. The officers testified that during the argument Humphries spat twice in Officer Burtis' face. Burtis then informed Humphries that he was under arrest for obstructing. A fight ensued as Humphries pushed the officer out the open front door into the yard while Burtis simultaneously was attempting to consummate the arrest. As the fight ensued, Humphries was able to break free and ran back into the house. A few moments later, Burtis also went back into the house. Humphries retreated onto the front staircase, with two women standing at the bottom of the stairway shielding him.

Burtis felt that Humphries was not going to escape, so he did not attempt to immediately arrest him but waited for backup units for help. During this lull Humphries reached between the two women and struck Burtis on the jaw with his fist. Burtis, with the aid of other officers, then placed Humphries under arrest.

Humphries' version of the altercation was that as he stood on the staircase an officer reached to grab him and he knocked the officer's hand away. He stated that Officer Burtis then subdued him by choking him into submission. ...

Humphries was convicted of simple assault, a lesser included offense of third-degree assault. An instruction regarding a lesser included offense may be given when evidence is introduced which would warrant the jury in believing the accused guilty only of a lesser degree of the offense with which he is charged. RCW 9A.36.030 provides:

"Assault in the third degree. (1) Every person who, under circumstances not amounting to assault in either the first or second degree, shall assault another with intent to prevent or resist the execution of any lawful process or mandate of any court officer, or the lawful apprehension or detention of himself or another person shall be guilty of assault in the third degree."

RCW 9A.36.040 provides:

"Simple assault. (1) Every person who shall commit an assault or an assault and battery not amounting to assault in either the first, second, or third degree shall be guilty of simple assault."

Defendant argues that the court erroneously allowed the prosecutor to characterize spitting as an assault. ...

At trial and over objection, the prosecutor in her final argument characterized spitting as an assault.

An assault is an attempt to commit a battery, which is an unlawful touching; a touching may be unlawful because it was neither legally consented to nor otherwise privileged, and was either harmful or offensive. See R. Perkins, Criminal Law, ch. 2, § 2.A.1, at 107-08 (2d ed. 1969); 6 Am. Jur. 2d Assault and Battery § 5, 10 (1963). ...

Under the facts and circumstances of this case, we find no error in the prosecutor characterizing "spitting" as an assault.

Questions

1. Does "spitting" qualify for offensive touching?
2. Do you agree with the Court's finding?
3. Does it make any difference where the "spit" was aimed?
4. Can spitting cause bodily injury?

precariously placed the victim in harm's way. When a criminal actor directs the path of a vehicle toward an intended victim, when the perpetrator fires weapons into a crowd, or when the actor concentrates on one member of the body hoping to impair its usage, aggravated assault exists.

When aggravated assault charges are coupled with other aligned offenses, the inference that the offender desires to inflict serious bodily injury knowingly and recklessly is reasonable. Using a knife to threaten a rape victim meets the aggravated standard, as does the robber and other attacker. Defense strategy often dwells on the "merger" of an aggravated assault into the other offense. Therefore, the rape charge solely exists rather than accompanied by the aggravated assault. In other words, defense wants the aggravated assault merged into the rape. For defendants, one charge is preferable to two.

DEFENSE STRATEGIES

- Consent by victim
- Mutual agreement
- Self defense at an altercation not provoked by defendant
- Defense of property, especially the domicile
- Insufficient force
- Incapacity as to injury
- Merger with other offenses
- An attempted murder, not an aggravated assault
- Lack of intent as to level of injury
- Insufficient evidence as to weapon or instrumentality

Whether a weapon or other instrumentality possesses the power to inflict serious bodily injury is another defense question. Many devices capable of inflicting injury have a dual purpose. Thus, while a stapler or staple gun can be used for nonviolent means, its operation can be felonious. A plank of wood or a crescent wrench has lawful, benign purposes when used appropriately. These same items can evolve into the type of weaponry and instrumentality quite capable of serious injury. Mixing use with the facts at hand allows defendants to raise reasonable doubts about the applicability of instrumentality in the case at bar.

Mayhem

ELEMENTS:

- As in aggravated assault, plus:
- Removal, excision, or destruction of a bodily appendage
- With malice

The common law offense of mayhem has largely been incorporated in the provisions of aggravated assault. For those states that maintain the distinction, it is largely an artificial one. The essence of aggravated assault, as mayhem, is the infliction of serious bodily injury that potentially can kill or maim the individual. As noted already, this type of offense is far more than the rough and tumble argument with clenched fists. Mayhem represents a special category of aggravated assault since the act focuses primarily on the "members" of the human physique. Arms, legs, ears, nose, eyes, and genitalia are the appendages that the mayhem artist cuts away. At common law, the motivation had to be malicious in design, though one would be hard pressed to explain the hacking away under some other guise. In our time, Lorena Bobbit's hacking away at her husband's penis while he was asleep is a fabulously famous example. Urging the jury to understand the cutting as a form of self-defense, Lorena Bobbitt failed to successfully persuade a jury that her act was justified. She lacked oft-heard exculpatory explanations in other cases of severe domestic violence: she was not impoverished, she had no children, and she had alternative places to go to avoid the reprehensible husband with which she was burdened.

STORY 5.1

LORENA BOBBITT

Lorena and John Wayne Bobbitt were not an ideal couple. They fought continuously and called the police on several occasions. On June 21, 1992, Lorena Bobbitt requested a restraining order against her husband, but decided not to appear before a judge. Two days later, while John was fast asleep on his back, Lorena went into the kitchen, got a knife, and cut off John's penis.

Following that act of mayhem, Lorena got into her car and took the severed penis with her. She tossed it out the car window and onto the highway.

In defense of the mutilation of her husband, Lorena claims that he had raped her twice. She does not explain why she did not call the police immediately after either of the alleged rapes.

After four hours of deliberating, a jury of nine women and three men acquitted John Bobbitt of rape charges. Lorena Bobbitt was charged with malicious wounding for dismembering her husband, John. She claimed she attacked him after he raped her and was not responsible for her actions due to temporary insanity. On January 21, 1994, Bobbitt was found not guilty by reason of insanity and committed to a mental health facility for 45 days for observation.

HARASSMENT

ELEMENTS:

- Intentional and knowing harassment
- Repetitive acts that alarm the target of the harassment
- That causes reasonable fear of physical injury

Assault charges dwell upon the actual or imminent potential harm that is deemed serious. What about those situations in which no actual touching takes place? A great deal of human activity can be classified as abusive, yet there is a complete lack of physical aggression. People can be harassed in grotesque and frightening ways without any offensive contact. Are these behaviors capable of criminal definitions? The crime of harassment attempts to fill the void and is also instructive about motive and past association with those suffering an even greater criminality. In *State v. Anne Marie Stout*,[44] the state's highest court found evidence of harassment based on divorce and infidelity, which subsequently led to a murder, admissible and probative. Former lovers, obsessed stalkers and followers, abusive former friends, sadistic persons, and disgruntled employees are prime harassers. New York's first-degree harassment fits like a glove corralling these criminals.

> A person is guilty of harassment in the first degree when he or she intentionally and repeatedly harasses another person by following such person in or about a public place or places or by engaging in a course of conduct or by repeatedly committing acts that places such person in reasonable fear of physical injury.[45]

The key term "repeatedly" says much about the statute's direction. Repetitive conduct means numerous rather than few events.[46] Delaware's statute reads in part:

> (a) A person is guilty of harassment when, with intent to harass, annoy, or alarm another person:
> (1) That person insults, taunts, or challenges another person or engages in any other course of alarming or distressing conduct which serves no legitimate purpose and is in a manner which the person knows is likely to provoke a violent or disorderly response or cause a reasonable person to suffer fear, alarm, or distress; ...[47]

Harassment calls for more than bickering and disagreement, but proof of a systematic pattern of behavior that truly offends the ordinary sensibilities of the average person. In the first degree case, the accused parameters may involve some type of physical injury. In lower degrees of harassment, the intent is annoyance and actual or real threats of less severity. Harassment in the second degree might look like this:

> A person is guilty of harassment in the second degree when, with intent to harass, annoy or alarm another person:
>
> 1. He or she strikes, shoves, kicks or otherwise subjects such other person to physical contact, or attempts or threatens to do the same; or
> 2. He or she follows a person in or about a public place or places; or
> 3. He or she engages in a course of conduct or repeatedly commits acts which alarm or seriously annoy such other person and which serve no legitimate purpose.[48]

CASE 5.5

STECKEL V. DELAWARE
711 A.2d 5 (De Sup. Ct. 1998).

This is an automatic and direct appeal after a capital murder trial and a penalty hearing by the appellant/defendant, Brian D. Steckel ("Steckel"). On October 2, 1996, a jury convicted Steckel on three counts of murder first degree, two counts of burglary second degree, one count of unlawful sexual penetration first degree, one count of unlawful sexual intercourse first degree, one count of arson first degree, and one count of aggravated harassment, related to the rape and murder of Sandra Lee Long and to the harassment of Susan Gell.

Pursuant to 11 Del. C. § 4209(b)(1), a separate penalty hearing was conducted, at the conclusion of which the same jury recommended the death penalty by a vote of eleven to one. After consideration of the factors enumerated in 11 Del. C. § 4209(d), the Superior Court concurred with the jury's recommendation and imposed a sentence of death for each of the three convictions of first degree murder.

On appeal, Steckel challenges both the convictions and death sentences. We find no error with respect to either the guilt phase or the penalty phase of Steckel's trial and, therefore, affirm both the convictions and the death sentences.

The evidence presented at trial reflected the following events. Around noon on September 2, 1994, Steckel gained entrance to Long's apartment under the pretense of needing to use her telephone. Once inside, he ripped the telephone cord out of the wall. He then savagely attacked Long, strangling her to the point of unconsciousness with both nylon stockings and a tube sock that had been brought for that purpose. Before losing consciousness, Long fought back, biting Steckel's finger hard enough to cause it to bleed profusely. Steckel next proceeded to rape Long anally, at one point achieving penetration with a flat-head screwdriver that he had also brought for that purpose. Long regained consciousness during this part of the attack. When finished with the attack on Long, Steckel sought to conceal his crime by setting fire to the apartment in two places with the final item he brought to the crime scene, a cigarette lighter. On his way out, he locked the door behind him to minimize the possibility of escape or rescue. Despite heroic efforts of passersby, the fire consumed the apartment and killed Long even as she sought to escape the searing flames through her bedroom window.

That afternoon, *The News Journal* received a phone call from an anonymous male who claimed responsibility for Long's murder and named Susan Gell as his next victim. The *News Journal* immediately alerted Wilmington police, who contacted Gell and placed her in protective custody. Gell informed police that, over the course of the previous month, she had received threatening phone calls, which eventually had been traced to Steckel. According to Gell, these calls were lurid and sexual and included references to anal rape. Police soon concluded that Steckel was a likely suspect in the attack on Long, and they succeeded in apprehending him early the next morning.

Over the course of several interviews on September 3—during which police repeatedly advised him of his Miranda rights—Steckel confessed to the rape and murder of Long. His account of the incident was accurate down to the most disturbing details, including his use of the screwdriver and the manner in which he set fire to the apartment. He told police where to find the items used in the attack, which were recovered. Steckel's identity as the assailant was later confirmed through DNA testing and analysis of the bite marks inflicted by Long during the struggle.

Steckel stood trial on various charges arising from the incident. After an eleven-day trial, a Superior Court jury found Steckel guilty of all counts. The trial proceeded to the penalty phase, where the jury was instructed that, by its guilty verdicts on the felony murder counts, the existence of a statutory aggravating circumstance had been proven beyond a reasonable doubt. See 11 Del. C. § 4209(e)(1)j.

At the penalty hearing, the State presented evidence that the following nonstatutory aggravating circumstances existed: (i) the vicious circumstances surrounding the commission of the murder; (ii) premeditation and substantial planning; (iii) victim impact; (iv) Steckel's prior criminal record; (v) Steckel's other criminal activities, including obscene phone calls, assault, terroristic threats, and disorderly conduct; (vi) Steckel's plan and intent to escape from prison and commit murder as evidenced by his letters n3; (vii) Steckel's total cruelty and lack of remorse in writing seven letters to the victim's mother; (viii) Steckel's prison record regarding disciplinary actions and lack of respect toward authority; (ix) the victim was defenseless; and (x) the murder was committed without provocation.

The defense presented evidence that the following mitigating factors existed: (i) cooperation with police in confessing to the crime; (ii) history of alcohol and substance abuse; (iii) childhood neglect and emotional abuse; (iv) childhood sexual abuse; (v) limited education; (vi) diagnoses of Attention Deficit Disorder and Antisocial Personality Disorder, as testified to by psychiatrists; (vii) Steckel's value and contribution to his family; and (viii) remorse. Steckel testified during the presentation of this evidence and exercised his right of allocution pursuant to 11 Del. C. § 4209(c)(2).

Questions

1. Does Steckel's behavior toward Gell constitute harassment?
2. Should Steckel's harassment of Gell be considered in Long's murder trial?
3. Could Steckel's letter writing to Long's mother be considered harassment?

When telephones or other communication devices are utilized as the instrument of harassment, legislatures have crafted menacing or aggravated harassment statutes that mete out some severe penalties.[49] Without a pattern of communication, one that is continual and repetitive, the aggravated charge of menacing or harassment will not hold up.[50] If the conversations are infrequent and erratic, the charge is insufficient.[51]

Obscene phone calls have been the setting for a harassment charge when the content of the communications are demonstrably offensive to the average person.[52] Those who have been on the receiving end of obscene telephone calls understand the unsettling nature of the behavior. Defendants counter with free speech claims, though First Amendment protections are unsuitable for the protection of "lewd, lascivious, threatening or obscene words, language, drawings, or caricatures,"[53] which is used expressly to harass.[54]

In the area of sexual harassment on the job, the proponent typically takes advantage of civil remedies rather than criminal prosecutions. State and federal remedies for sexual harassment, particularly in employment settings, are extensive and are based on gender discrimination or the maintenance of a hostile work environment. EEOC (Equal Employment Opportunity Commission) remedies are not usually a criminal law matter, although cases can degenerate into subsequent liability.[55]

OTHER BODILY OFFENSES

Over the past few decades, there has been a staggering increase in the amount of bodily offenses that add to the traditional assault schema. The problems of domestic and spousal abuse are so astronomical that legislators continue to be hopeful that new laws will stem the tide.[56] (See Table 5.2 for statistics regarding violence against intimates.[57])

Visit the American Bar Association's Commission on Domestic Abuse and Violence at http://new.abanet.org/domesticviolence/Pages/Statistics.aspx

Acts of racial hatred, ethnic intimidation, and other hate crimes also have come to the fore-front as innovative solutions to a distressing wave of violence that targets special groups and classes of individuals. (See Table 5.3[58] for Hate Crime Statistics from the FBI's 2009 Uniform Crime Report.)

Visit the FBI's Hate Crimes Web Portal at http://www2.fbi.gov/ucr/hc2009/incidents.html

Table 5.2   Violence by intimate partners by type of crime and gender of victims, 2008.

	Total Number	Total Rate	Female Number	Female Rate	Male Number	Male Rate
Overall violent crime	652,660	2.6	551,590	4.3	101,050	0.8
Rape/sexual assault	44,000	0.2	35,690	0.3^	8,310	0.1^
Robbery	38,820	0.2^	38,820	0.3^	--	--
Aggravated assault	111,530	0.4	70,550	0.5	40,970	0.3^
Simple assault	458,310	1.8	406,530	3.1	51,770	0.4

Note: Victimization rates are per 1,000 persons age 12 or older. The difference in male and female intimate partner victimization rates is significant at the 95-percent confidence level for overall violent crime, robbery, and simple assault. There is no significant difference in the rate of male and female intimate partner victimization for aggravated assault.^Based on 10 or fewer sample cases; -- No cases were present for this category.

Source: Bureau of Justice Statistics, National Crime Victimization Survey, 2008.

Table 5.3   Incidents, offenses, victims, and known offenders by bias motivation, 2009.

Bias motivation	Incidents	Offenses	Victims[1]	Known offenders[2]
Total	**6,604**	**7,789**	**8,336**	**6,225**
Single-Bias Incidents	**6,598**	**7,775**	**8,322**	**6,219**
Race:	**3,199**	**3,816**	**4,057**	**3,241**
Anti-white	545	652	668	753
Anti-black	2,284	2,724	2,902	2,160
Anti-American; Indian/Alaskan Native	65	84	87	88
Anti-Asian/Pacific Islander	126	147	149	108
Anti-multirace group	179	209	251	132
Religion:	**1,303**	**1,376**	**1,575**	**586**
Anti-Jewish	931	964	1,132	353
Anti-Catholic	51	55	59	25
Anti-Protestant	38	40	42	17
Anti-Islamic	107	128	132	95
Anti-other religions	109	119	131	51
Anti-multireligious group	57	60	68	38
Anti-atheism/agnosticism/etc.	10	10	11	7
Sexual Orientation:	**1,223**	**1,436**	**1,482**	**1,394**
Anti-male homosexual	682	798	817	817
Anti-female homosexual	185	216	227	197
Anti-homosexual	312	376	391	349
Anti-heterosexual	21	21	21	14
Anti-bisexual	23	25	26	17
Ethnicity/National Origin:	**777**	**1,050**	**1,109**	**934**
Anti-Hispanic	483	654	692	649
Anti-other ethnicity/national origin	294	396	417	285
Disability:	**96**	**97**	**99**	**64**
Anti-physical disability	25	25	25	25
Anti-mental disability	71	72	74	39
Multiple-Bias Incidents[3]	**6**	**14**	**14**	**6**

[1]The term *victim* may refer to a person, business, institution, or society as a whole.

[2]The term *known offender* does not imply that the identity of the suspect is known, but only that an attribute of the suspect has been identified, which distinguishes him/her from an unknown offender.

[3]In a *multiple-bias incident*, two conditions must be met: (a) more than one offense type must occur in the incident and (b) at least two offense types must be motivated by different biases.

Why the existing laws cannot deter has yet to be adequately debated or answered. Politicians are perpetually hopeful that social problems and violent behavior can be legislated away. If laws effectively minimized spousal abuse, why does the plague continue unabated? If legislative enactments could mediate racial disharmony, why does our nation witness increasing levels of hostility for racial minorities, gays and lesbians, and certain religious groups? However well-intentioned these laws may be, enforceability is at best selective and efficacy is minimal. With good faith in the promulgation, the justice system attempts to isolate and end bodily harm crimes based on family, spouse, and race. Below are some of the more typical legislative efforts.

Protection from Abuse/Domestic Abuse

The inadequacy of current assault legislation can be proved, according to some, with numbers alone. Skyrocketing rates of spousal abuse paint a forlorn picture of domestic tranquility. The findings are quite sobering with annual compilations of "more than one million women suffer[ing] nonfatal violence at the hand of someone close to them."[59] Domestic violence encompasses "one person's use of emotional, physical, or sexual violence, or threat of violence to obtain control of another family member or intimate. Domestic violence may occur in the context of marriage, common-law relationships, or dating relationships and does not discriminate; it affects people from all walks of life, regardless of age, race, religious beliefs, educational background, income, or sexual preference."[60]

The fundamental dilemma for prosecution, under the historical offenses of assault, is the difficulty of proving a level of intentionality sufficient above and beyond the misdemeanor assault. Spousal abuse is far more complicated than a barroom brawl. On top of this, there is a general unwillingness on the part of the judicial system to invade the domestic province too aggressively. Courts do many things well, but guarding the internal affairs of the family is not its forte. Arguments and sometimes very heated exchanges between partners are natural over the life of any relationship. The fine and intricate lines between abuse and normal bickering are sometimes murky. Add to this the usual reticence witnessed in spouses that fight vigorously, yet still hope to achieve a successful relationship; the emotional crosscurrents can buffet the parties to positions that may not work in the world of common law assault. Any experienced law enforcement officer will tell amazing and befuddling stories of how complicated these affairs can be, of how today's diatribe and flood of words and flying hand becomes forgiven before the first witness takes the stand. The complications of love and hate spoil the elemental logic of bodily injury, the intent to inflict, and lack of privilege to do so. By no means are these arguments excuses for abusing spouses and the cowardly character of those inflicting these wounds. An illustrative statute might be:

> The Legislature hereby finds that spousal abusers present a clear and present danger to the mental and physical well-being of the citizens of the State of California. The Legislature further finds that the concept of vertical prosecution, in which a specially trained deputy district attorney, deputy city attorney, or prosecution unit is assigned to a case after arraignment and continuing to its completion, is a proven way of demonstrably increasing the likelihood of convicting spousal abusers and ensuring appropriate sentences for those offenders. In enacting this chapter, the Legislature intends to support increased efforts by district attorneys' and city attorneys' offices to prosecute spousal abusers through organizational and operational techniques that have already proven their effectiveness in selected cities and counties in this and other states.[61]

In our zeal to eradicate the obvious harm and as a reflection of the impotence of former laws to squash this recurring nightmare, new laws of abuse are enacted daily.[62] Somewhere and somehow an antidote will be discovered, or one can hope. For states like Georgia, simple assault and battery were unsatisfactory in this war. As a result, a new and enhanced version of domestic abuse has been enacted that issues a far harsher penalty than misdemeanor assault. The Crimes against Family Members Act of 1999[63] adds a subsection that mandates elevated "high and aggravated" misdemeanor treatment for simple assault committed between parties having certain "domestic relationships."[64] The specifics of the Act include:

(d) If the offense of simple assault is committed between past or present spouses, persons who are parents of the same child, parents and children, stepparents and stepchildren, foster parents and foster children, or other persons excluding siblings living or formerly living in the same household, the defendant shall be punished for a misdemeanor of a high and aggravated nature. In no event shall this subsection be applicable to corporal punishment administered by a parent or guardian to a child or administered by a person acting in *loco parentis*.[65]

Elevating the misdemeanor to a "high and aggravated" status, penalties for infraction are substantially longer prison terms. In fact, the minimum incarceration period for aggravated assault/battery is one year, while the same act in a domestic situation carries a three-year term. Aside from the obvious equal protection problems, does this punishment seem proportionate? Should a special class of perpetrator be singled out for harsher treatment?

Another novel approach is for the legislative design to water down some due process protections normally expected in criminal prosecutions, but now unavailable in an offense such as domestic abuse. In Pennsylvania,[66] the probable cause standard has been waived for justifying an arrest when an assault occurs in the home. Based on the world of the complainant, the accused cannot expect the same constitutional protections as other defendants will receive. With an emergency mentality, the legislature has waived these protections for a greater end. North Carolina enhances the penalties and the level of felony in cases where a pregnant woman has been injured in the commission of a crime.[67] "The added section provides that a person is guilty of a felony that is one class higher than the felony committed if that person, during the commission of a felony, causes injury to a pregnant woman that results in miscarriage or stillbirth and that person knows the woman to be pregnant."[68]

These enhancements seek to remedy a problem no one disputes, though the method chosen has its share of detractors. Too much fervor never compliments detached and dispassionate legal thinking.

Visit the federal government's special Office of Victim Assistance and find out about resources dedicated to those suffering from domestic abuse at http://ovc.ncjrs.gov/Topic.aspx?topicid=27

Hate Crimes

Recent cases involving death or assaults based on racial, gender, or sexual motivation have certainly caught the public eye. Dragged from the rear of a pickup truck in Texas, or lynched unmercifully from a tree, these types of offenses strike a most disconcerting chord in the American conscience.[69] Witnessed as national tragedy, they triggered a host of legislative responses at both the state and federal level (Figure 5.2).[70]

Yet, why are these offenses so specialized and differentiated from traditional assault offenses? Is not the beaten man the same as the beaten black youth? How does a person of one sexual orientation suffer any differently than the heterosexual whose face was smashed in or arms broken in a vicious attack? Objectively, the results are identical. Subjectively, does the assaulter who fights and attacks with rage, anger, jealousy, and envy, appear slightly less malevolent than the predator waiting for a person of the Jewish faith or a gay man leaving work? Certainly, the motivators vary, but the physical injury remains similar. If this be so, why craft "hate" crimes? The popular legislative consensus has been to enact competing versions of hate crime legislation.[71] Commencing with "ethnic intimidation" statutes, our political process sought to identify criminal acts that were reserved and motivated on account of ethnic or racial hatred. The act addresses criminal agents that possess more than the usual level of animus in the commission of the felony or misdemeanor since the object of the offense is grounded in racial, ethnic, or other motivation and by a "malicious intention."[72] See the statute from California below.

(a) No person, whether or not acting under color of law, shall by force or threat of force, willfully injure, intimidate, interfere with, oppress, or threaten any other person in the free exercise or enjoyment of any right or privilege secured to him or her by the Constitution or laws of this state or by the Constitution or laws of the United States in whole or in part because of one or more of the actual or perceived characteristics of the victim listed in subdivision (a) of Section 422.55.[73]

The federal system has adopted a sophisticated civil rights labyrinth for victims to avail when suffering from this offense. Either by money damages or criminal sanction, the United States Code addresses the issue of hate-motivated criminality in various quarters.[74] The FBI, especially as a result of fringe groups and historical terrorists like the KKK, has long been adept at strategies for ferreting out those inclined to such activities. In the FBI's Training Guide, the following recommendations are posed for law enforcement:

The types of factors to be considered by the Reporting Officer in making a determination of whether the incident is a Suspected Bias Incident are:
- Is the motivation of the alleged offender known?
- Was the incident known to have been motivated by racial, religious, disability, ethnic, or sexual-orientation bias?
- Does the victim perceive the action of the offender to have been motivated by bias?
- Is there no other clear motivation for the incident?
- Were any racial, religious, disability, ethnic, or sexual-orientation bias remarks made by the offender?
- Were there any offensive symbols, words, or acts that are known to represent a hate group or other evidence of bias against the victim's group?
- Did the incident occur on a holiday or other day of significance to the victim's or offender's group?
- What do the demographics of the area tell you about the incident?[75]

Federal law now requires hate crime statistics to be included in the Uniform Crime Report (UCR).[76] (See the FBI Hate Crime Incident Report form at Figure 5.2a.)

1-699 (Rev. 1-20-06)

OMB No. 1110-0015
Expires 10-31-10

HATE CRIME INCIDENT REPORT

Initial ☐ Adjustment ☐ ORI ☐☐☐☐☐☐☐☐☐ Date of Incident ___/___/___ (Month Day Year)

Incident No. ☐☐☐☐☐☐☐☐☐☐☐☐ **Page** ☐ **of** ☐ **of Same Incident**

Offense *(Enter an offense code and number of victims for each bias-motivated offense.)*

#1 Offense ☐☐ - # of victims ☐☐☐ #3 Offense ☐☐ - # of victims ☐☐☐

#2 Offense ☐☐ - # of victims ☐☐☐ #4 Offense ☐☐ - # of victims ☐☐☐

01 Murder
02 Forcible Rape
03 Robbery
04 Aggravated Assault
05 Burglary
06 Larceny-Theft
07 Motor Vehicle Theft
08 Arson
09 Simple Assault
10 Intimidation
11 Destruction/Damage/Vandalism

Location *(Check one for Offense #1.)*

01 ☐ Air/Bus/Train Terminal
02 ☐ Bank/Savings and Loan
03 ☐ Bar/Night Club
04 ☐ Church/Synagogue/Temple
05 ☐ Commercial/Office Building
06 ☐ Construction Site
07 ☐ Convenience Store
08 ☐ Department/Discount Store
09 ☐ Drug Store/Dr.'s Office/Hospital
10 ☐ Field/Woods
11 ☐ Government/Public Building
12 ☐ Grocery/Supermarket
13 ☐ Highway/Road/Alley/Street
14 ☐ Hotel/Motel/etc.
15 ☐ Jail/Prison
16 ☐ Lake/Waterway
17 ☐ Liquor Store
18 ☐ Parking Lot/Garage
19 ☐ Rental Storage Facility
20 ☐ Residence/Home
21 ☐ Restaurant
22 ☐ School/College
23 ☐ Service/Gas Station
24 ☐ Specialty Store (TV, Fur, etc.)
25 ☐ Other/Unknown

Enter a Location for each offense having a different location than Offense #1:

#2 ☐☐
#3 ☐☐
#4 ☐☐

Bias Motivation *(Check one for Offense #1.)*

Race
11 ☐ Anti-White
12 ☐ Anti-Black
13 ☐ Anti-American Indian/Alaskan Native
14 ☐ Anti-Asian/Pacific Islander
15 ☐ Anti-Multiple Races, Group

Ethnicity/National Origin
32 ☐ Anti-Hispanic
33 ☐ Anti-Other Ethnicity/National Origin

Religion
21 ☐ Anti-Jewish
22 ☐ Anti-Catholic
23 ☐ Anti-Protestant
24 ☐ Anti-Islamic (Muslim)
25 ☐ Anti-Other Religion
26 ☐ Anti-Multiple Religions, Group
27 ☐ Anti-Atheism/Agnosticism

Sexual Orientation
41 ☐ Anti-Male Homosexual (Gay)
42 ☐ Anti-Female Homosexual (Lesbian)
43 ☐ Anti-Homosexual (Gay & Lesbian)
44 ☐ Anti-Heterosexual
45 ☐ Anti-Bisexual

Disability
51 ☐ Anti-Physical Disability
52 ☐ Anti-Mental Disability

Enter a Bias Motivation for each offense having a different bias motivation than Offense #1:

#2 ☐☐
#3 ☐☐
#4 ☐☐

Victim Type *(Check all applicable victim types for each offense listed above.)*

	Offense #1	Offense #2	Offense #3	Offense #4
1 Individual*	☐	☐	☐	☐
2 Business	☐	☐	☐	☐
3 Financial Institution	☐	☐	☐	☐
4 Government	☐	☐	☐	☐
5 Religious Organization	☐	☐	☐	☐
6 Society/Public	■	■	■	■
7 Other	☐	☐	☐	☐
8 Unknown	☐	☐	☐	☐

*Indicate the total number of individuals (persons) who were victims in the incident. Total # of Victims ☐☐☐

Number of Offenders ☐☐ *(Use "00" for Unknown Offender.)*

Race of Offender(s) as an individual or group *(Check one.)*

1 ☐ White
2 ☐ Black
3 ☐ American Indian/Alaskan Native
4 ☐ Asian/Pacific Islander
5 ☐ Multiple Races (group only)
6 ☐ Unknown

Figure 5.2a Hate Crime Incident Report.

INSTRUCTIONS FOR PREPARING *QUARTERLY HATE CRIME REPORT* **AND** *HATE CRIME INCIDENT REPORT*

This report is authorized by Title 28, Section 534, U.S. Code, and the Hate Crime Statistics Act of 1990. Even though you are not required to respond, your cooperation in using this form to report hate crimes known to law enforcement during the quarter will assist the FBI in compiling timely, comprehensive, and accurate data regarding the incidence and prevalence of hate crime throughout the Nation. Please submit this report quarterly, by the 15th day after the close of the quarter, and any questions to the FBI, Criminal Justice Information Services Division, Attention: Uniform Crime Reports/Module E-3, 1000 Custer Hollow Road, Clarksburg, West Virginia 26306; telephone 304-625-4830, facsimile 304-625-3566. Under the Paperwork Reduction Act, you are not required to complete this form unless it contains a valid OMB control number. The form takes approximately 7 minutes to complete. Instructions for preparing the form appear below.

GENERAL

This report is separate from and in addition to the routine Summary UCR submission. In hate crime reporting, there is no Hierarchy Rule. Offense data (not just arrest data) for Intimidation and Destruction/Damage/Vandalism of Property should be reported. On this form, all reportable bias-motivated offenses should be included regardless of whether arrests have taken place. Please refer to the publication *Hate Crime Data Collection Guidelines* for additional information.

QUARTERLY HATE CRIME REPORT

At the end of each calendar quarter, each reporting agency should submit a single *Quarterly Hate Crime Report*, together with an individual *Incident Report* for each bias-motivated incident identified during the quarter (if any). If no hate crimes occurred during the quarter, the agency should submit only the *Quarterly Hate Crime Report*.

The *Quarterly Hate Crime Report* should be used to identify your agency, to state the number of bias-motivated incidents being reported for the calendar quarter, and to delete any incidents previously reported that have been determined during the reporting period not to have been motivated by bias.

HATE CRIME INCIDENT REPORT

The *Incident Report* should be used to report a bias-motivated incident or to adjust information in a previously reported incident. Include additional information on separate paper if you feel it will add clarity to the report.

Indicate the type of report as Initial or Adjustment. Provide the Originating Agency Identifier (ORI) and Date of Incident.

INCIDENT NUMBER: Provide an identifying incident number, preferably your case or file number.

UCR OFFENSE: Provide codes for all offenses within the incident determined to be bias motivated and the number of victims for each offense. In multiple offense incidents, report only those offenses determined to be bias motivated. Should more than four bias-motivated offenses be involved in one incident, use additional *Incident Reports* and make an appropriate entry in the Page ☐ of ☐ portion of each form.

LOCATION: Provide the most appropriate location of each bias-motivated offense.

BIAS MOTIVATION: Provide the nature of the bias motivation for each bias-motivated offense.

VICTIM TYPE: Provide the type of victim(s) identified within the incident. Where the type of victim is Individual, indicate the total number of individuals (persons) who were victims in the incident. Society/Public is applicable only in the National Incident-Based Reporting System (NIBRS).

NUMBER OF OFFENDERS: Provide the number of offenders. Incidents involving multiple offenders must not be coded as Unknown Offender. Indicate an Unknown Offender when nothing is known about the offender including the offender's race. When the Race of Offender(s) has been identified, indicate at least one offender.

RACE OF OFFENDER(S): Provide the race of the offender(s), if known. If there was more than one offender, provide the race of the group as a whole. If the number of offenders is entered as Unknown Offender, then the offender's race must also be indicated as Unknown.

Figure 5.2b   Hate Crime Incident Report.

Figure 5.3   Shortly after the German annexation of Austria, Nazi Storm Troopers stand guard outside a Jewish owned business. Graffiti painted on the window states: "You Jewish pig may your hands rot off!" Vienna, Austria, March 1938. (Photo courtesy of the United States Holocaust Memorial Museum.)

These types of codifications do not have unfailing support and they rankle many. Why should the justice model single out certain types of offenders for a harsher reality because of what they believe? Granted, the belief system may be warped, but how does this errancy cause a more oner-ous justice response? One can fully appreciate that repeat, habitual offenders and three time recidivists are targeted for stiffer penalties than the first time offender. This is as it should be. What cannot be left unexplained is how two offenders, one with bad thoughts and the other indifferent to race, color, etc., yet possessing similar criminal histories, should be punished with ferocity on the one hand and judicial tepidness on the other. Let's face it, prisons are filled with all sorts of characters from free-love, soft drug users to baby killers and mass murderers. To no one's amazement, some of these inhabitants have racist views—a fact evident in all sectors of the American experience. Should we reserve a harsher place for them, build them a meaner prison, and feed them lumpier gruel?

Finally, critics of these acts are quick to type these laws as having a chilling impact on free speech rights that might even be applied to "religious leaders" if their "sermons were traced to a violent act."[77] The longstanding condemnation of homosexual conduct in select religious circles could be unfairly targeted with a narrowing perception of what hate speech is or isn't. Other applications of hate crime legislation may prompt even more cumbersome speech dilemmas, especially in regard to political or moral viewpoints. Advocates of the homeless claim that any crime inflicted on the homeless population, which it labels a "vulnerable" population, should qualify as hate crimes.[78] Does the tragedy of homelessness figure prominently in hate crime anal-ysis when other offenses relate to race or ethnicity, heritage, or religion? A few commentators see little difference between a homeless or homosexual person, while others urge the maintenance of long held distinctions.[79]

CASE 5.6

COMMONWEALTH V. WHITE
335 A 2d 436 (1975)

At trial, the complainant, Walesca Rodriquez, an eight-year-old girl, testified that in July of 1973, she was playing outside her home located in Philadelphia, when a man, who she later identified as the appellant, came over to her and placed his hand over her mouth and shined a flashlight on her face. The child further testified that the appellant carried her to the back of an abandoned house located on the same block as her own home. Once inside, the appellant told the girl he was going to grab her. The child then testified that the appellant held her against a wall by her shoulders and proceeded to pull her skirt up approximately six inches when she suddenly saw a neighbor, Edwin Negron, passing a window. The child called out to Mr. Negron that the appellant wanted to kill her. At this point, the appellant left the child alone and fled the house with Mr. Negron unsuccessfully giving chase.

The appellant testified that on the night of the incident, he was using his flashlight in search of his dog in the vicinity of the abandoned house. Appellant further testified that, as he was leaving the old house, Mr. Negron confronted him and asked him what he was doing. When Mr. Negron advanced towards him, the appellant fled. The appellant also testified that he never touched the complainant, nor was she with him when he entered the old house. The appellant called four witnesses to testify in his behalf. In essence, these witnesses testified to the effect that the defendant told them he was going to look for his dog on the night in question.

With respect to his conviction for attempted indecent assault, appellant contends that in the first instance, the evidence was insufficient to constitute the crime and, in any event, since he was specifically indicted for indecent assault he could not be convicted of attempted indecent assault. We do not agree with either contention.

The recently enacted Pennsylvania Crimes Code, Act of December 6, 1972, P.L. 1482, No. 334, § 1, eff. June 6, 1973, 18 Pa. C.S. § 101 et seq., controls the disposition of this appeal since the alleged offenses occurred subsequent to June 6, 1973. The crime of indecent assault is defined in § 3126 of Title 18 as follows: "A person who has indecent contact with another not his spouse, or causes such other person to have indecent contact with him is guilty of indecent assault, a misdemeanor of the second degree, if: (1) he knows that the contact is offensive to the other person; ..." "Indecent contact" is defined as: "Any touching of the sexual or other intimate parts of the person for the purpose of arousing or gratifying sexual desire, in either person." 18 Pa. C.S. § 3101 (1973). An accused is guilty of attempt when, "with intent to commit a specific crime, he does any act which constitutes a substantial step toward the commission of that crime." 18 Pa. C.S. § 901 (1973). Application of the above statutes to the facts at bar, i.e., the appellant's act of carrying the complainant to the back of an abandoned house; holding her shoulders, threatening to grab her, and lifting her skirt up approximately six inches, all of which occurred against the complainant's will, demonstrates that the appellant had the requisite intent to commit, at the minimum, an indecent assault and, furthermore, had taken substantial steps towards the completion of the reprehensible act.

Appellant concedes that under the Act of June 24, 1939, P.L. 872, § 1107, 18 P.S. § 5107, a conviction for an attempt upon an indictment charging a substantive crime would have been proper. Appellant argues, however, that since 18 P.S. § 5107 has been repealed by the new Crimes Code, his conviction for attempted indecent assault cannot stand. We reject this argument for several reasons. Initially, appellant's argument fails because 18 Pa. C.S. § 905 specifically provides, inter alia, that the punishment for attempt shall be of the same grade and degree as the most serious offense which is attempted. In addition, neither the Crimes Code nor the Pennsylvania Rules of Criminal Procedure contain any provision requiring a conviction of the substantive offense, as distinguished from the attempt, when the indictment charges the actual offense. Furthermore, when appellant was convicted of attempted indecent assault, he was necessarily convicted of a crime which is an integral part of the substantive crime of indecent assault, since the consummated act of indecent assault cannot exist without first the attempt to commit an indecent assault. Therefore, appellant could not seriously claim that he was caught by surprise, insomuch as his defense against the charge of indecent assault also constituted a defense against the attempt to commit such an act. For all of the foregoing reasons we hold that the appellant was properly convicted of attempted indecent assault.

Questions

1. From the conduct of the defendant, what was the threat?
2. What was the felony where the threat was defined?
3. What would be the best defense for the accused in this case?
4. Do you agree with the Court's finding?

Terroristic Threats

ELEMENTS

- Threat to commit an act of violence or other public harm
- With general intent

Special legislative designs have been implemented to address situations in which touching or injury does not occur. As experience tells us, much can be coerced or extorted from people by threat, by the subtle manipulation of words and the play on emotion. The Russian KGB's victims often remarked that being killed was less troubling than anticipation of where and when a confrontation would occur. It is the threat that manipulates the psyche. It is the threat that leaves open the question of potential or actual injury. In this world of indecision and fear, the party who threatens knows the true story of the threat—the victim can only surmise and remain on edge.

If the threatening party denies the sincerity of the threat, the charge will still stick since it is the victim's reasonable perspective that drives the analysis. We cannot know what the defendant intends internally, but we can discern what the words of the threat represent. In the *United States v. Myers*,[80] the First Circuit of the Court of Appeals evaluated the meaning of threat in the mind of both the speaker and the recipient. For it to be a threat, it must have the capacity to "create apprehension that its originator will act according to its tenor."[81] To constitute threat, the trier assesses how the recipient of the message could be expected to react under the "factual context in which the statement was made."[82]

Threats that force the evacuation of public buildings and places of assembly are prime locales for this criminal act. Schools receiving bomb threats may rely on the language of the terroristic threat statute.

Threatening actions that involve felonious conduct certainly fit the requirements of this important statute. Analyze the case below.

Finally, do not confuse the nature of a criminal threat with pranks and the act of hazing. To those on the receiving end of hazing—oft-times university pledges and sorority/fraternity members or military trainees in elite units—the practices of hazing can prompt dire and deadly circumstances. Binge drinking, pranks that risk health and limb, and retaliatory action out of control can no longer be tolerated. University liability for failure to supervise has already caused extraordinary damage claims in the civil courts.

States recognize the injury that can result from these activities that remain unchecked and unregulated. Colorado has passed a hazing law which states:

(2) As used in this section, unless the context otherwise requires:

   (a) "Hazing" means any activity by which a person recklessly endangers the health or safety of or causes a risk of bodily injury to an individual for purposes of initiation or admission into or affiliation with any student organization; except that "hazing" does not include customary athletic events or other similar contests or competitions, or authorized training activities conducted by members of the armed forces of the state of Colorado or the United States.[83]

DISCUSSION QUESTIONS

1. Distinguish robbery from larceny/theft?
2. How does the question of "movement" appear in various criminal offenses?
3. Why does motive take on added importance in the kidnapping case?
4. Compare and contrast kidnapping from false imprisonment?
5. What type of bodily injury is required for an aggravated assault charge?
6. Why are hate crimes sometimes labeled "thought crimes"?
7. Which offense severely punishes those who remove appendages?
8. Why is assault often termed a "merged" offense?
9. What type of force is required in a robbery case?
10. Does harassment usually involve physical injury?

SUGGESTED READINGS

Alpert, S. N. 2008. *The birthday party: A memoir of survival.* New York: Berkley Trade.

Das, D. K., and O. N. I. Ebbe. 2009. *Criminal abuse of women and children: An international perspective.* Boca Raton, FL: CRC Press.

Fass, P. S. 1997. *Kidnapped: Child abduction in America*. New York: Oxford University Press.

Harries, K. D. 1990. *Serious violence: Patterns of homicide and assault in America*. Springfield, Ill.: Thomas Publishing Company.

Marquez, G. G. 2008. *News of a kidnapping*. London: Vintage Publishers.

Moore, R. 2010. *Cybercrime*, 2nd ed.; *Investigating high-technology computer crime*, 2nd ed. Scotch Plains, NJ: Anderson Publishers.

National Institute of Justice. 1996. *Domestic violence, stalking, and anti-stalking legislation*. Washington, D.C.: National Institute of Justice.

Russell, K. K. 1998. *The color of crime*. New York: New York University Press.

Snow, R. L. 2008. *Child abduction: Prevention, investigation, and recovery*. Santa Barbara, CA: Praeger Publishers.

Wright, R., and S. H. Decker. 1997. *Armed robbers in action: Stickups and street culture*. Boston: Northeastern University Press.

ENDNOTES

1. 18 U.S.C. § 2113 (2011).
2. *See* MARTHA J. SMITH, ROBBERY OF TAXI DRIVERS, NCJ 209729.
3. CA. PENAL CODE § 211-215 (West 2010).
4. 678 A.2d 556 (D.C. App. 1996).
5. D.C. CODE § 22-2901 (1989 Repl.).
6. *Zanders*, 678 A.2d at 564.
7. Defendants will claim double jeopardy violation if the facts of the robbery are inside the fact of an aligned offense. It usually does not work well. *See Taylor v. Kentucky*, No. 97-SC-578-MR (Ken. Sup. 1999), which addressed the potential mix of assault and robbery. In resolving, the Court dismissively and correctly held that the argument fails when the offenses differ even as to one element. It notes in part: "Thus, conviction of either the assault or the robbery of McCreary required proof of an element not required to prove the other. The conviction of robbery required proof of a theft, which was not required to convict of assault. The conviction of assault required proof of a physical injury to McCreary, whereas the conviction of robbery required proof only that Appellant used or threatened the use of physical force upon McCreary while armed with a .22 rifle." *Id*. at 6.
8. M. SCHEB & JOHN M. SCHEB II, CRIMINAL LAW AND PROCEDURE 165 (1994).
9. FOX VALLEY TECHNICAL COLLEGE, FAMILY RESOURCE GUIDE ON INTERNATIONAL PARENTAL KIDNAPPING (NCJ 215476) (2007), available at https://www.ncjrs.gov/pdffiles1/ojjdp/215476.pdf (accessed August 3, 2011); Colin V. Ram, *Regulating Intrastate Crime: How The Federal Kidnapping Act Blurs The Distinction Between What Is Truly National And What Is Truly Local*, 65 WASH. & LEE L. REV. 767 (2008).
10. David A. Alexander & Susan Klein, *Hostage-Taking: Motives, Resolution, Coping and Effects*, 16 ADVANCES PSYCHIATRIC TREATMENT 176–183 (2010).
11. Cecilia M Baillet, *Toward Holistic Transnational Protection, An Overview of International Public Law Approaches to Kidnapping*, 38 DENV. INT'L L. & POL'Y 581 (2010).
12. *Id*. at 592.
13. MODEL PENAL CODE § 212 (Proposed Official Draft 1962).
14. N.C. GEN. STAT. §14-39 (2010).
15. N.M. STAT. ANN. §30-4-1 (West 2010).
16. *See People v. Adams*, 192 N.W.2d 19 (Mich. App.1971).
17. The U.S. Supreme Court weighed in on a scheme of drugs and guns that covered five states in *U.S. v. Moreno*, 526 U.S. 275 (1999). In a rare disagreement between Justice Thomas and Scalia, we see the importance of geography. Justice Thomas: "A kidnapping, once begun, does not end until the victim is free. It does not make sense, then, to speak of it in discrete geographic fragments." *Id*. at 280. Scalia replies that the statute in question textually demands that the use of a weapon, which constituted the force, and the place where the weapon was used was unrelated to the kidnapping. Scalia is hard to disagree with when he comments: "The short of the matter is that this defendant, who has a constitutional

right to be tried in the State and district where his alleged crime was 'committed,' (U.S. Cons., art. III, §2, cl. 3; amend. VI.) has been prosecuted for using a gun during a kidnapping in a State and district where all agree he did not use a gun during a kidnapping. If to state this case is not to decide it, the law has departed further from the meaning of language than is appropriate for a government that is supposed to rule (and to be restrained) through the written word." *Moreno*, 526 U.S. at 285.

18. N.M. STAT. ANN. § 30-4-1 (West 2010).
19. No. 98-1177, 1999 U.S. App. 2390 (10th Cir. 1999).
20. 992 P.2d 896 (N.M. App. 1999).
21. *Id.* at 903.
22. WEBSTER'S NEW COLLEGE DICTIONARY 581 (1995).
23. *Laguna*, 992 P.2d at 899.
24. *See Howard v. Nelson*, No. 97-3297 (10th Cir. 1998).
25. *Id.* at 5 quoting *Jackson v. Virginia*, 443 U.S. 307, 319 (1979).
26. THOMAS J. GARDNER & TERRY M. ANDERSON, CRIMINAL LAW 288 (2008); MATTHEW ROSS LIPPMAN, CONTEMPORARY CRIMINAL LAW: CONCEPTS, CASES, AND CONTROVERSIES 365 (2008).
27. The law of crimes on false imprisonment is often eerily close to the elemental standards necessary for the tort of false imprisonment. See Shari-Ann Harris, *Lay a Hand On Me Brother: Why Definitional Balancing and Consent Doctrine Should Apply to the Religious False Imprisonment and Assault Claims in Pleasant Glade Assembly of God v. Schubert*, 11 RUTGERS J. L. & RELIG. 406 (2010).
28. NEB. REV. STAT. § 28-314 (2010).
29. Model Penal Code § 212.3 (Proposed Official Draft 1962).
30. *See* 18 PA. CONS. STAT. § 2903 (2010). Note that Pennsylvania has adopted an intermediate crime, which resides between the offense of kidnapping and false imprisonment and which requires a "threat" of serious bodily injury rather than its actual infliction. *See Id.* at § 2903.
31. *See* Colorado's benign language at COLO. REV. STAT. §18-3-303 (2010). *See Rose v. City of Denver*, 990 P.2d 1120 (Co. App. 1999).
32. Being subsequently acquitted of an offense charged and arrested affords no basis for the claim of false imprisonment since probable cause for arrest prevents liability for false imprisonment. *See Beyer v. Young*, 513 P.2d 1086 (Colo. App. 1973).
33. Nancy S. Erickson, *The Parental Kidnapping Prevention Act: How Can Non-Marital Children Be Protected?*, 18 GOLDEN GATE U. L. REV. 529 (1988); Annette M. Gonzalez & Linda M. Rio Reichmann, *Representing Children in Civil Cases Involving Domestic Violence*, 39 FAM. L.Q. 197 (2005); Lynn D. Wardle, *Form and Substance in Parentage Law*, 15 WM. & MARY BILL RTS. J. 203 (2006).
34. 18 PA. CONS. STAT. § 2904(1) (2010).
35. See how close violence comes to amounting to one crime or the other in the violent child custody dispute witnessed in *Poll v. Poll*, 588 N.W.2d 583 (Neb. 1999).
36. See the case of the convicted Massachusetts man, Thomas Junta. Junta was found guilty of involuntary manslaughter and sentenced to six to ten years in prison for the death of Michael Costin. Costin was beaten to death by Junta during a fight after their son's hockey game. *Com. v. Junta*, 815 N.E.2d 254 (Mass. App. Ct. 2004).
37. U.S. DEPARTMENT OF EDUCATION, INSTITUTE OF EDUCATION SCIENCES, NATIONAL CENTER FOR EDUCATION STATISTICS (NCES), 2007–08 SCHOOL SURVEY ON CRIME AND SAFETY (SSOCS) Table 2 (2008), available at http://nces.ed.gov/surveys/ssocs/tables/all_2008_tab_02.asp (accessed August 3, 2011).
38. The prevalence of violence appears to leave no place unscathed. Even government itself contends with the reality. *See* GOVERNMENT ACCOUNTABILITY OFFICE, BRIEFING TO CONGRESSIONAL COMMITTEES, PREVALENCE OF DOMESTIC VIOLENCE, SEXUAL ASSAULT, DATING VIOLENCE, AND STALKING, GAO-07-148R (2006), available at http://www.gao.gov/new.items/d07148r.pdf (accessed August 3, 2011).
39. MICHAEL S. SCOTT & KELLY DEDEL, ASSAULTS IN AND AROUND BARS, NCJ 215877 (2nd ed. 2006).
40. To the dismay of many, assaultive behavior frequently targets pregnant women. *See* HAROLD B. WEISS ET AL., PREGNANCY-ASSOCIATED ASSAULT HOSPITALIZATIONS: PREVALENCE AND RISK OF HOSPITALIZED ASSAULTS AGAINST WOMEN DURING PREGNANCY, NCJ 199706 (2004); VIOLENCE AGAINST WOMEN AND FAMILY VIOLENCE: DEVELOPMENTS IN RESEARCH, PRACTICE, AND POLICY, NCJ-199701 (Bonnie Fisher ed., 2004).

41. GA. CODE ANN. § 16-5-20 (2010); *See also* 18 PA. CONS. STAT. § 2701 (2010).

42. Model Penal Code § 211.1 (Proposed Official Draft 1962).

43. *Id.* at § 211.1(2).

44. 237 P.3d 37, 43 (2010).

45. N.Y. PENAL LAW § 240.25 (McKinney 2010).

46. In the area of sexual harassment, based on workplace behavior and in violation of employment and Civil Rights laws are increasingly considering nonworkplace harassment behavior as pattern evidence. Alisha M. Patterson, *None of Your Business: Barring Evidence of Non-Workplace Harassment For Title VII Hostile Environment Claims*, 10 U. C. DAVIS BUS. L.J. 237 (2010).

47. DEL. CODE ANN. tit. 11, § 1312(a)(1) (2011).

48. N.Y. PENAL LAW § 240.26 (McKinney 2010).

49. *Id.* at § 240.30.

50. *See People v. Rusciano*, 171 Misc. 2d 908, 656 N.Y.S. 2d 822 (Town of Eastchester Justice Ct., Westchester Co. 1997), where court emphasized the telephone as central to the aggravated case. "The gravamen of the crime of aggravated harassment is the use of the telephone, but for which the accompanying offending conduct would constitute, other elements being present, simple harassment." *Id.* at 913.

51. *See N.Y. v. Price*, 178 Misc. 2d 778, 683 N.Y.S.2d 417 (City of New York Criminal Court, New York County, 1998).

52. Harassment also has a civil remedy grounded in traditional torts in Civil Rights acts depending upon the basis for the harassment. *See Employment Law—Title VII-Third Circuit Issues Split Decision in Case Involving Gay Man's Harassment*, 123 HARV. L. REV. 1027 (2010); *See also Prowel v. Wise Business Forms*, 579 F.3d 285 (3d Cir. 2009).

53. 18 PA. CONS. STAT. § 1312(1) (2010).

54. *See Delaware v. Horowitz*, 1998 Del. Super. 227 (1998).

55. For close calls that might allow the victim to avail of either civil or criminal remedies, *see Fowler v. Kootenai County*, 918 P.2d 1185 (Id. Sup. Ct., 1996) and *Norris v. Hathaway*, 1999 Neb. App. 4 (No. A-97-916) (1999).

56. *See* ERICA L. SMITH & DONALD J. FAROLE, JR., PROFILE OF INTIMATE PARTNER VIOLENCE CASES IN LARGE URBAN COUNTIES, NCJ 228193 (2009), available at http://bjs.ojp.usdoj.gov/content/pub/pdf/pipvcluc.pdf (accessed August 3, 2011); *See also* SHANNAN CATALANO ET AL., FEMALE VICTIMS OF VIOLENCE, NCJ 228356 (2009), available at http://bjs.ojp.usdoj.gov/content/pub/pdf/fvv.pdf (accessed August 3, 2011).

57. CATALANO ET AL., *supra* note 57, at 1.

58. U.S. DEPARTMENT OF JUSTICE, FEDERAL BUREAU OF INVESTIGATION, HATE CRIME STATISTICS, 2009 Table 1 (2010), available at http://www2.fbi.gov/ucr/hc2009/data/table_01.html (accessed August 3, 2011).

59. *See* BUREAU OF JUSTICE STATISTICS, SPECIAL REPORT: VIOLENCE AGAINST WOMEN: ESTIMATES FROM THE REDESIGNED SURVEY, NCJ-154338, 3 (1995).

60. Roger T. Weitkamp, *Crimes and Offenses*, 16 GA. ST. U. L. REV. 72, 73 (1999).

61. CAL. PENAL CODE § 273.8 (West 2010).

62. States now recognize that domestic abuse should no longer be presumptively antagonistic to divorce mediation. For years, courts have not availed those accused of domestic abuse with the alternative disposition framework now regularly offered to other domestic disputes and divorce. See Mary Adkins, *Moving Out of the 1990's: An Argument on Updating Protocol on Divorce Mediation in Domestic Abuse Cases*, 22 YALE L. J. & FEMINISM 97 (2010).

63. GA. CODE ANN. § 16-5-20 (2010).

64. Weitkamp, *supra* note 61, at 78.

65. GA. CODE, *supra* note 64.

66. 18 PA. CONS. STAT. § 2711 (2010).

67. Act of October 28, 1998, § 17.16, 1998 N.C. Sess. Laws 212.

68. Gloria F. Taft and Valeree R. Gordon, *Criminal Law (Legislative Survey – North Carolina)*, 21 CAMPBELL L. REV. 353, 353 (Sp. 1999). *See also* Act of October 28, 1998, *supra* note 68.

69. Matthew Shepard and James Byrd, Jr. Hate Crimes Prevention Act, Pub. L. No 111-84, §§ 4701-13, 123 Stat. 2190, 2835-44 (2009); David Jackson, *Obama Signs Hate-Crimes Law Rooted in Crimes of 1998*, USATODAY.com, Oct. 28 2009, http://content.usatoday.com/communities/theoval/post/2009/10/620000629/1 (accessed August 3, 2011); *See also* Anna L. Bessel, *Preventing Hate Crimes Without Restricting Constitutionally Protected Speech: Evaluating the Impact of the Matthew Shepard and James Byrd, Jr. Hate Crimes Prevention on First Amendment Free Speech Rights*, 31 HAMLINE J. PUBL. L. & POL'Y 735 (2010).

70. Matthew Shepard Act, *supra* note 70, §4704(a)(1); Jordan Blair Woods, *Ensuring a Right of Access to the Court for Bias Crime Victims: A Section 5 Defense of the Matthew Shepard Act*, 12 CHAP. L. REV. 389 (2008).

71. For an in-depth discussion, *see* Joseph M. Fernandez, *Bringing Hate Crime into Focus*, 26 HARV. CR-CL L. REV. 261(1991).

72. 18 PA. CONS. STAT. § 2710(c) (2010).

73. CAL. PENAL CODE § 422.6(a) (West 2001). *See also* MD. CODE, PUBLIC SAFETY, § 2-307 (West 2010); FLA. STAT. § 877.19 (2010); IDAHO CODE ANN. §18-7902 (2010); *See also* Fernandez, *supra* note 72, at 267 n.32.

74. *See* 18 U.S.C. §241 (2011). Victims of hate-motivated violence can sue for damages and injunctive relief under 42 U.S.C. §§ 1981–1982, passed as part of the Civil Rights Act of 1866.

75. FEDERAL BUREAU OF INVESTIGATION, TRAINING GUIDE FOR HATE CRIME DATA COLLECTION, UNIFORM CRIME REPORTING 21 (1996).

76. The Hate Crime Statistics Act of 1990, P.L. N. 101-275 (April 23, 1990).

77. Bessel, *supra* note 70, at 750.

78. *See* MD. CODE ANN., CRIM. LAW § 10-301 (West 2009); Eric Lichtblau, *Attacks on Homeless Bring Push to Broaden Laws on Hate Crimes*, N.Y. TIMES, Aug. 8, 2009, at A1.

79. *See* Katherine B. O'Keefe, *Protecting the Homeless Under Vulnerable Victim Sentencing Guidelines: An Alternative to Inclusion in Hate Crime Laws*, 52 WM. & MARY L. REV. 301 (2010).

80. 104 F.3d 76 (5th Cir. 1997).

81. *U.S. v. Bozeman*, 495 F.2d 508, 510 (5th Cir. 1974).

82. *U.S. v. Fulmer*, 108 F.3d 1486, 1491 (1st Cir. 1997).

83. COLO. REV. STAT. § 18-9-124 (2)(a) (2010).

Chapter 6

Sexual Offenses against the Person

KEYWORDS

Consent: Compliance in or approval of what is done or proposed by another; the voluntary agreement or acquiescence by a person of age or with requisite mental capacity who is not under duress or coercion and usually who has knowledge or understanding.

Fornication: Consensual sexual intercourse between a man and especially a single woman who are not married to each other.

Incest: Sexual intercourse between persons so closely related that they are forbidden through law to marry.

Lewd and lascivious behavior: Reflecting or producing sexual desire or behavior especially what is considered indecent or obscene.

Molest: To make annoying sexual advances to; to force physical and usually sexual contact on a child.

Rape: Unlawful sexual activity and sexual intercourse carried out forcibly or under threat of injury against the will usually of a female or with a person who is beneath a certain age or incapable of valid consent because of mental illness, mental deficiency, intoxication, unconsciousness, or deception.

Sexual assault: Sexual contact that is forced upon a person without consent or inflicted upon a person who is incapable of giving consent or who places the assailant in a position of trust.

Sodomy: Oral or anal sexual contact or penetration between persons or of sexual intercourse between a person and an animal.

Statutory rape: Rape consisting of sexual intercourse with a person beneath an age specified by statute.

INTRODUCTION: SEXUAL OFFENSES AGAINST THE PERSON

Few offenses arouse such anger in the hearts and minds of justice professionals as much as the sexual variety. The baseness and volatile nature of these acts really hits home on the streets and in the courthouses. Sexual integrity is intimately bound to personal sanctity and any invasion, without permission and consent, can only be labeled a serious affront. Second, the consequences of unwanted and nonconsensual conduct carry diverse mental, physical, and emotional

consequences. Getting over the stolen television set does not have the baggage problems as rec-
onciling the act of incest or rape. From the communication of sexually transmitted diseases to
the loss of treasured innocence and the resulting emotional scarring, sexual crimes exert a very
heavy price on the victims. Third, uninvited sexual attacks raise serious moral dilemmas for
those impregnated, and are just as likely to foster sexual dysfunction in future relations with others. This is particularly acute in sexual assaults between parties that are known to one another,
whether relative, parent or stepparent, or close family friends. How one sees the world in sexual,
or any other terms, could only be described as negatively and confusedly altered. In this sense,
rape and sexual assaults are more than the motion of criminal agents, and are more aptly typi-
fied as assaults that span lifetimes and generations. These effects cannot be wished or rationalized away. Instead, survival depends on one's capacity to again see temporal and metaphysical
beauty apart from the landscape of sexual criminality; to remember that each recipient of the
sexual onslaught suffers a long and lingering victimization, and to urge the legal system to treat
these very unique victims of crime specially. The Bureau of Justice Statistics in its National Crime
Victimization displays consistent data on the offenses. (See Figure 6.1.[1])

> For a fine overview on the tragedy of sexual offenses in our culture, read and analyze the
> summary of Dr. Dean Kilpatrick of the Medical Center of South Carolina at http://www.
> musc.edu/vawprevention/research/sa.shtml

To say that the law of sexual offense has undergone a dramatic transformation in the last few
decades would be a dramatic understatement. At common law, the crimes were adequately yet
simplistically classified as rape, sodomy (and/or buggery), and fornication, with the tradition of
incest and lewd and lascivious behavior fully intact. Rape was a male against female criminality and sodomy took on a host of definitions from same-sex sexual contact to acts of fellatio
and cunnilingus. Today statutes have been aggressively transformed to reflect the evolution of
sexual practices, perversions, and levels of misconduct never imagined. Most youth and child
case workers laboring in contemporary justice settings will readily confirm the unfortunate
proliferation of sexual decadence heaped upon children and youth. At the same time, the world
witnesses a starkly more active sexuality in our young, a decaying sense of loyalty in marital relationships, and a level of sexual promiscuity that a generation or two ago would have been construed as unaccept-able. There is little doubt that sexual mores have radically changed since the Industrial Revolution and, for some commentators, the change has negatively impacted culture and families and cheapened the perspective of individual sanctity and personal auton-omy.[2] Academic debates, however enticing, do not clean up the muck of sexual crime. The costs are self-evident in human terms. What our task will be is the comprehensive

Rate of Rape and Sexual Assault per 1,000 Age 12 or Older, 2009		
	All	**Female**
Rape/sexual assault	0.5	0.8
Rape	0.3	0.6
Completed	0.1	0.3
Attempted	0.2	0.3
Sexual assault	0.2	0.2
Source: National Crime Victimization Survey.		

Figure 6.1   Rate of rape and sexual assault per 1,000, age 12 or older, 2009.

examination of the standard crimes best termed as sexual, looking at both traditional and evolving statutory standards. In this way, the justice student learns not only where these ideas originated, but where and how these definitions will likely evolve.[3]

RAPE

ELEMENTS

- Sexual intercourse with another person
- Use of force
- Without consent
- Not his spouse
- With intent

The Nature of Force

The use of force by a male upon a female who is not his wife to submit to sexual intercourse; that act of penetration by a penis into a vagina, without consent and with the victim's resistance, summarizes the common law definition of rape. Rape constitutes the forcible imposition of a male person upon an unwilling female partner. Even though this traditional construction has been under continuous scrutiny for its narrow view of partners and victim requirements, the common law tradition instructs and edifies the basis for why our statutes exist in the first place. Reformers of sexual offense law sometimes refuse to see the wisdom in our ancestral traditions, although one can only benefit from this introspection.

Force, for example, remains the critical question in all rape case law and adjudication. Consensual sexual activity signifies a willingness to cooperate and participate, while force implies a lack of will. Sex by force confronts our fundamental sensibilities as to personal and bodily integrity. Without force, rape lacks the seriousness and substantiality to be deemed a high level felony. Without force, a willing agent engages in sexual activity freely and without objection. This is why questions involving date rape, intoxication, and underage sexual conduct are so cumbersome in rape litigation. While force may exist in these contexts, its clarity is muddled by choice, will, and levels of participation. In date rape, part of the series of events that lead to the eventual criminality are consensual, others are not. In statutory rape cases involving young partners, the parties may choose freely and without resistance to engage in sexual intercourse. A female who becomes inebriated, then has little if any recollection of certain sexual conduct, presents a less convincing evidentiary situation for the prosecutor who wants to achieve a rape conviction, but is trumped by the persistent reasonable doubts that may emerge in jurors. In other words, alcohol precipitates the situation. Violent rapists, hidden assaulters, breakers and intruders in the night, lead to the opposite claims. Here, we pristinely see force and the undeniable submission caused by physical attack that subjugates the victim's will.

The relationship with force and consent is firmly grounded in rape law. A lack of consent implies and imputes the force necessary for a rape conviction. Definitionally, rape statutes are attentive to these standards:

§ 11-37-1. Definitions

(2) "Force or coercion" means when the accused does any of the following:
  (i) Uses or threatens to use a weapon, or any article used or fashioned in a manner to lead the victim to reasonably believe it to be a weapon.
  (ii) Overcomes the victim through the application of physical force or physical violence.
  (iii) Coerces the victim to submit by threatening to use force or violence on the victim and the victim reasonably believes that the accused has the present ability to execute these threats.
  (iv) Coerces the victim to submit by threatening to, at some time in the future, murder, inflict serious bodily injury upon or kidnap the victim or any other person and the victim reasonably believes that the accused has the ability to execute this threat.[4]

Within this design, a broad definition is purposeful. What entails force is more than mere physical assault. Modern statutes are mindful that force has many faces. One need not test the inevitability of the injury to understand its ugliness. Rape victims should not be expected to "guess" about the ferocity of the attacker or await the weapon, the foreign or blunt object, or the delineation of potential harms about to be inflicted. At common law, force typically meant the physical and little else. Today, that vision has greatly expanded to recognize a whole host of threatening behavior that the average person fully understands. Sometimes, a victim can reasonably "feel" or sense the urgency of the situation. Other times, the victim will draw calculated conclusions that prudently indicate that resistance is futile and meaningless.

In fact, if rape's very essence grounds itself in a crime of power and violence, feigned or pretensed, consent to sex may, in some cases, be the wisest strategy. Of course, that judgment is cumbersome and difficult for any victim and one the legal system should hesitate to second guess. Few crimes put the victim through the double scrutiny evident in rape and sexual offense. Who would ever challenge a theft, burglary, or arson victim, by way of illustration, with the extraordinary challenge: "Now, did you not really consent to the home being burned or the television being stolen?"

In seemingly endless contexts, the problem of force and consent emerge and reemerge in sexual offense litigation. Too quaint is the demand for physical force alone to meet the element of actus reus; too unsophisticated the impression that resistance has no other face than physical aggression and vocal protest. For most jurisdictions, the issue of force cannot be reconciled in traditional terms.[5]

In its place, the movement is toward proof of compulsion and coercion—a general belief that the will may be overwhelmed in diverse circumstances. To be sure, states like Maine and others hold firm to the idea that compulsion attaches itself to "serious bodily injury" alone.[6] Increasingly, this definition proves unsatisfactory because compulsion includes more than the brutality of assault because it expresses and implies either immediate or gradual circumstances. Compulsion can be possible in cases where the perpetrator is thoroughly silent as to his overall intentions even though his actions typify the fundamental element of rape—sexual intercourse without consent. District Attorney Jennifer Cichetti prosecutes rape cases and readily admits the flaws in the historical definitions of force, consent, and resistance. Her frustration focuses on the antiquated and unreasonable perceptions that have long governed rape law in her jurisdiction. She notes in part:

> Only when the statutory prohibitions against sexual assault are read broadly enough to encompass all denials of consent by victims will these laws protect women. The statutory language regarding

rape in Maine has changed to women's advantage, by including a broader scope of actions and destroying old language, which focused on marital status or social accompaniment. However, it will only fully protect women if it is interpreted as doing so, by according them credibility and respect.[7]

While her zeal to reform the system is certainly admirable, our conceptions of force and consent are not thoroughly misguided. For the most part, these historical definitions attempt to foster credibility and integrity in the legal complaint. Years of experience in various justice offices working with victims and perpetrators paint a picture of human complexity and enormous harm. Linda Fairstein, a former Director of the Manhattan District Attorney's Sex Crimes Unit, offers extraordinary insights in her text, *Sexual Violence: Our War Against Rape*.[8] Sexual offenses are like no other type of criminality, she argued:

> We deal with a thicket of human emotions that twist the healthy around the sick, the vital around the decadent, the creative around the deadly … [I]nstances of sexual abuse, nonviolent crimes quite distinct from other categories of sexual assault, also reveal that the world of human sexuality is extraordinarily complex—and that applying law to that world involves understanding not only of right and wrong, but also of sicknesses and strengths, hope and loss, reason and confusion.[9]

When all is said and done, the rape prosecution challenges the most seasoned practitioners, for this type of litigation drives deep into the emotional and mental psyche of both perpetrator and victim. How one reacts, interprets, and evaluates circumstances widely differs. The face of force and consent eludes capture in many sexual offense cases, while in others the ugliness is impossible to elude.[10]

Visit the Rape, Abuse and Incest National Network at http://www.rainn.org/

The Nature of Consent

Consent implies willingness and lack of objection. Consent represents intellectual assent and emotional willingness to engage in the activity. Consent explicitly relays permission for the sexual conduct engaged in while a lack of consent declares resistance to the same conduct. Consent can only be freely given by those capable of its issuance. Free-willing and consenting beings possess the physical and mental capacity to consent to specific conduct. Thus, persons physically incapacitated, in comas or under the influence of medical drugs that effect consciousness, or those mentally deficient in reasoning and intellectual skills needed for decision making lack the power of consent in any sense. Rape statutes have long recognized these incapacities in the analysis of consent.

(c) A person is deemed incapable of consent if he is:
    (1) Less than 16 years old; or
    (2) Mentally defective; or
    (3) Mentally incapacitated; or
    (4) Physically helpless.[11]

In every other type of case, the team entrusted with proof of sexual offense must muster meaningful evidence of nonconsent. The array of evidence commences with the victim's own account whereby consent is negated. Couple this with corroboration from other witnesses, the reliability of source and story, and the team has its foundation planted. Objective evidence of the force employed and the consent not given is an even higher priority. Hence, the prosecutor hoping to succeed in conviction will search long and hard for evidence of force whether it be in the form of physical injury, damaged genitalia, sexual mutilation, torn clothing, or other signs of physical trauma.[12]

Police investigators are trained repeatedly in the critical collection processes during the early phase of the rape investigation and to develop meaningful relationships with medical and emergency room personnel who fully understand this evidentiary demand.

Consent negates the issue of force because it makes sexual intercourse a volitional act rather than one of terror and power. Consent signifies acceptance of the agent's movement and a willing toleration of what develops in human sexual activity. Consent is the purest and most effective defense to the crime of rape because its proof strikes at the very heart of victimization on the one hand and the mental state of the alleged offender on the other.

The only way around consent for the prosecutorial team is to demonstrate the existence of force and brutality in the rapist. Various forms of objective evidence will prove useful (see Figure 6.2[13]).

Some commentators refer to the other proofs of force and, thereby, a lack of consent in more subjective, internal terms. Nathan Brett's biting examination of consent in rape prosecutions tries to summarize his view of consent as follows:

> Common sense provides a relatively simple answer to these questions: To consent is to give permission; a person acts without consent where no such permission has been obtained. It is this answer that I want to defend in this paper. This view assumes that talk of consent only makes sense in relation to some autonomy right. Giving consent involves autonomously making changes in a prevailing pattern of rights and obligations. It is a limited withdrawal of a right not to be interfered with; and it will make legally permissible actions that would otherwise be subject to criminal and civil penalties. To me, it seems obvious that such a change in the prevailing pattern of rights and obligations can only take place where there is communication between the parties. This means that the question of consent is not just a question about the state of mind or attitude of the complainant. Rather, the matter which should be central to a court's consideration of consent is the question of what was said or done that could be construed as granting permission to do the acts in question.[14]

EVIDENCE OF FORCE OR THREAT OF FORCE

- Victim's resistance efforts (if any).
- Words used by victim to dissuade offender.
- Details concerning victim's submission.
- Evidence regarding victim's fear of offender.
- Evidence regarding victim's fear of environment or situation.
- Any evidence of physical injuries on victim's body.

Figure 6.2   Evidence of force or threat of force. (From Hunter, S. M., B .R. Cew, and J. L. Mills. 1997. *Police response to crimes of sexual assault: A training curriculum.* 2nd ed. East Hartford, CT. Connecticut Sexual Assault Crisis Services, Inc. With permission.)

The measure of consent entails objective and subjective reality, though most would agree that proof of the subjective is a tougher sell. How does one really know what another is thinking? How does a court evaluate a rapist's mens rea? Indeed, every rape defendant conveniently argues a lack of intentionality. This subjective approach weaves its way into issues of consent, previous association, victim willingness, victim history, and other factors. For defense teams, a primordial and recurring task is to implant the subjective difference in the mind of the accused with that of the victimized. One cannot be guilty of a first-degree felony of this magnitude without really intending the consequence alleged. In this world, reasonable doubt has many faces.[15]

If the state's case in chief depends upon a victim who bears no injuries, who gave little or no resistance, and whose verbal objections were not extraordinary, some doubt is inevitable. How much doubt will depend on the holes in the story, so to speak.

Objective reality is a much more dependable measure of the mental state and this can be gleaned from the objective world in which this offense occurred. In other words, the preferable measure is objective reality, e.g., physical injury, torn clothing, words of resistance, actions signifying refusal, objection, screaming out, and fighting off the attack. However, the world of rape and rapists is not so tidy to simply rely on the objective measure, for just as legitimate will be the subjective conclusions we are capable of. In the end, it is the combination of the objective and subjective world that makes defense or prosecution a viable strategy. Proving or disproving consent depends upon how much evidence filters in or out of the record. Reasonable doubt is more likely in cases lacking injury, acquaintance rape, previous sexual history with the offender, and other cumbersome situations involving drugs and alcohol.[16]

The question of consent further mutates as sexual mores are examined and attitudes change. It would be folly to argue that questions of chastity and virginity, for example, weigh as heavily on the mind of contemporary moralists as it did 100 years ago. Staggering rates of promiscuity, the escalation of adultery and premarital sexual activity, and the dramatic rise in sexually transmitted diseases tell a story of escalation, not restraint. Changing sexual perceptions subjectively change victim mindsets whether we accept it or not. Consent has been watered down and elasticized in an age when promiscuity cannot be distinguished from prostitution. The entire idea of consent is buffeted by cultural and social forces that stand less aghast at sexual dalliances and more concerned with scoring as much as possible. There is a changing vision about sexual integrity in our culture and this, undeniably, influences the legal context of consent. There are movements afoot to legalize sexual activities between children and adults, to legalize once frowned upon sexual practices, to legitimize types of sexual behavior once deemed too forceful. An article in the William and Mary University Law Review addressing this changing dynamic represents the radical shift in how sexual activity should be adjudged. In discussing consent in bondage practices, the commentator relays:

> A challenge for gaylaw is to develop a better-articulated line between sadomasochistic fantasies and simply sadistic battering, for same-sex battering is just as pervasive and just as destructive as different-sex battering.[17]

This same article challenges its readers to cast off the prejudiced and allegedly irrational resistance to "man–boy love" as being nothing more than our own repression that causes problems that are worse than the exploitation itself.

An interesting, but not intractable, issue for gaylaw is sex with people under the age of consent. The American gayocracy (Robert Raben's term) has distanced itself from "man–boy love," even while American jurisdictions have progressively lowered the age of consent. What has been missing in the American hysteria about sex with children has been fact-based theorizing about children's sexual development and the effects of sex with older people on that development. On the one hand, substantial evidence shows that adolescent "children" are, in fact, sexual beings for whom experimentation is both natural and healthy. The coming-out literature, the most popular form of gay autobiography, is replete with examples of sexual experimentation by adolescents under the age of 15, Virginia's age of consent. The medical literature systematically supports this impression and raises persistent doubts about American folk efforts to repress adolescent sexuality; as adolescent suicide rates attest, the repression may be a bigger problem than the possible exploitation.[18]

Legal thinkers hopefully will detach themselves from these sorts of social forces and political interests. At the heart of the examination resides proof of sexual violence without consent. The facts and factors surrounding the particular case are sometimes better than others. A life of prostitution bears on the issue of consent whether fair or not. Undoubtedly, a prostitute can be raped. A prostitute has every right to exert control over her own sexual integrity. While this autonomy extends to each person, regardless of their chosen path in life, the evidentiary proof of consent becomes a much more muddled affair in the prosecution of this type of case. Advocates for social movements can conjure up slogans and signs; police and prosecutors must collect and advocate sufficient evidence to deal effectively with questions of consent and denial. Prosecution teams may agree in a factual sense, but are savvy enough to recognize the many dilemmas this type of victim presents in a court of law. Consent, therefore, encompasses more than "No means No" sloganeering. Instead, consent signifies both the subjective state of the victim, the objective state of the evidence collected, and the profile of both victim and offender. Here is where the prosecution team assesses the relative strengths and weaknesses of cases. Here is where cases of rape and sexual assault are won or lost.

The Nature of Resistance

Earlier constructions of rape law also insisted on proof of victim resistance. The terms "earnest" or "utmost" frequently were inserted in case law and codification. Resistance signified the fundamental necessity of proving the nonconsensual nature of the sexual conduct and reality of the force exerted. Without proof of victim resistance, offenders could subjectively impute willingness in the activity. Offenders, to achieve a defensible position, and prosecutors, no matter how politically incorrect it may be, need to prepare for this line of defense. Victims who passively defend are less desirable that those who resist as far as humanly possible. Defense attorneys lay in wait for those who lacked protest even though fear and weaponry may fully justify the silence. Indeed, there are widely differing views of what type of resistance, if any, should be used. (See Figure 6.3 for common advice on the subject.)

Questions of resistance have legal, cultural, and social qualities. Ideally, no sexual offense victim should risk harm or injury during the defense of a sexual offense. Given the already physically dominant position of the rapist, already enraged to lust by the elixir of power and domination, and one sees an extremely uneven match. The reform movement has successfully altered numerous legislative designs by eliminating the resistance requirement altogether.[19] However, nothing precludes defense counsel from mentioning any facts or circumstances dealing with a real or perceived lack of resistance.

Passive Resistance
- Try to calm the attacker. Try to persuade him not to carry out the attack.
- Claim to be sick or pregnant. Tell him you have a sexually transmitted disease. This may intimidate the attacker.
- Try to discourage him. Pretend to faint, cry hysterically, act insane or mentally incapacitated. If you're at your residence, tell the attacker a friend is coming over or that your spouse or roommate will be back soon.

Active Resistance

YELLING—If the attacker is unarmed, you may be able to scare, distract, or injure the person enough to make your escape.
- A yell can surprise or frighten an attacker away if he fears people will come to help. But yelling won't help in isolated or noisy areas. Scream "FIRE," "POLICE," or create a disturbance that will attract attention.

STRUGGLING and FIGHTING BACK
- A forceful struggle also may discourage an attacker, but most will retaliate and have the potential to inflict serious injuries. However, you must not be afraid to hurt an attacker. All kicks and blows must be forceful and should be aimed at vulnerable areas such as the groin, eyes, or instep.

MARTIAL ARTS
- Special self-defense skills, such as judo or karate, are popular. If you are proficient in such techniques, they can be very effective. But proficiency requires practice.

WEAPONS
- Some people carry weapons, such as guns, knives, or spray chemicals, to ward off attackers. Unless you are trained and not afraid to use these weapons, they can be very dangerous. The attacker might be able to turn them against you. Also, some weapons cannot legally be carried, so check with local law enforcement authorities.

Submitting to an Attack
- If you believe you might get hurt defending yourself or if you're afraid to fight back, don't. Sexual assault is still an assault and still a crime, even if you do not have a single cut or bruise. Victims who do not resist should never feel guilty; it is the assailant who committed the crime.
- If attacked, escape.
- If trapped, stay alive.
- If assaulted, memorize details.

Figure 6.3   Advice on resisting a rape.

Date rape advocacy groups passionately plead their cause and for good reason. Yet, their oft heard plea, that "No means No," may be correct and completely defensible; at the same time, it may be unrealistic, for simply saying "No" may not be enough for the prosecutor to prosecute. Slogan may or may not win the day. What is assured is that a prosecution that proves force by a demonstration of physical penetration and other pathology, bruises, injuries, torn clothing, and

CASE 6.1

PEOPLE V. EVANS

22 Cal. App. 4th 1145, 1147-50, 27 Cal. Rptr. 2d 752, 753-54 (1994)

Ms. X testified that in the early morning hours of October 20, 1991, she was alone and asleep in her apartment when she was awakened by a hand over her mouth and a voice telling her not to scream. She found a man on top of her, telling her to spread her legs. The man got "astride" her, fondled her breast, and touched her vaginal area. The man demanded oral copulation or sexual intercourse. Hoping to "get him off his guard," Ms. X agreed to orally copulate the man. He produced a condom and ordered Ms. X to put the condom on him. After she did so, the man checked to see that the door was locked. When he returned, Ms. X jumped up and escaped into the hall, pounding on the walls and screaming.

After Ms. X was admitted to an apartment one floor up from her own, police were summoned. Ms. X gave a telephone description of the man and his clothes. Police arrived at the scene while she was still speaking with the 911 operator. No more than seven minutes after escaping, Ms. X was shown defendant Luther Evans, whom she instantly identified as her attacker. When in her apartment with Officer Ng, he found on the floor of her closet a "key chain coin purse-type of thing," which she told him was not hers. Asked by Officer Ng if a slip had been taken from her apartment, Ms. X checked and found one missing from a rack inside her closet. While at the hospital, she was shown a slip which she identified as hers.

After hearing the screams, the building's assistant manager called 911, dressed, and went to the front door of the building. He saw defendant and two other men just outside the building's front door. Defendant stated that "there had been a rape or attempted rape and that the suspect had run away." While pointing out the direction the "suspect" had fled, defendant was holding up his pants with one hand. The assistant manager saw no one in the direction indicated by defendant. Defendant entered the building, went directly to the victim's apartment (which cannot be seen from the front door), and stated that "this is where it happened," and entered through the closed door without knocking. The assistant manager described defendant as "highly animated," and "babbling," a "whirling dervish" who was "sweating profusely."

When the building manager arrived on the scene, he saw defendant "scurrying around picking up clothing off the floor ... as if he were looking for something" in the hallway near Ms. X's apartment. Carrying an armful of clothing, and repeatedly telling the manager "she asked me to help her," defendant went into Ms. X's apartment. The manager followed and saw defendant roam around "as if he were looking for something," particularly on the floor and near the bed. The manager ordered defendant out of the apartment. Still carrying the armful of clothing, defendant left and rejoined the two men outside the building. Defendant emerged from the building just as Officer Stewart Ng arrived on the scene.

Officer Ng testified that he promptly detained defendant after arriving at the scene and noting that defendant and his clothing were "very close" to the radio description of the assailant. Ng characterized defendant's appearance as "disheveled," which he described as follows: "The belt was undone ... unbuckled, dangling. The pants were only held by the clasp and the zipper was down ... with the shirt tail hanging out the zipper part. The shirt tail in the back hanging out." Ng conducted a pat-search of defendant and found (among other things) two screwdrivers and a knife. Leaving defendant with the just-arrived Officer Yick, Ng met with Ms. X and asked her to look at defendant. After she did so, and identified defendant ("Oh my God, that's him."), defendant was arrested and taken to a police station. During the course of speaking with Ms. X in her apartment, Ng noticed a coin purse on the floor. Ms. X told Ng it was not hers.

Officer Ng then went to the station. After receiving Miranda admonishments from Officer McKay, defendant invoked his right to remain silent. While being booked, defendant asked Ng where his wallet was. As defendant was—at Ng's request—describing the wallet and its contents, Ng realized defendant might be referring to the coin purse found in the victim's apartment. Ng confirmed that defendant had accurately described the contents of that coin purse. Ng showed it to defendant and asked if it belonged to him. Defendant replied that it did.

Officer Patrick Yick testified that he continued the search begun by Officer Ng just after defendant was detained. Among other items found was the slip Ms. X later identified as hers; Yick discovered the slip "stuffed in his [defendant's] pocket." Later that morning, as Yick was escorting defendant to the police station, an unrolled condom fell out of the inside leg of defendant's trousers. Yick searched defendant and found an opened condom package in one of defendant's pants pockets.

Defendant's version of events was that he was collecting cans outside the apartment building when he heard a woman screaming "Rape." Defendant met the assistant manager, walked into the building and into a hallway, where he began picking up clothing strewn on the floor. After the manager ordered him out, defendant left and set the clothes he was carrying down outside the building's entrance. Just then police arrived. Officer Ng grabbed defendant, searched him and removed his change purse, which was taken into the building by police. Defendant was then marched into the building, shown to the victim, and taken to the police station. Once there, Yick did not see an unrolled condom fall out of defendant's pants leg; Yick did, however, take from defendant an unrolled condom still in its package. Defendant denied telling the assistant manager that he had seen a man running down the street. He denied holding up unbuckled pants while doing so. Defendant denied ever being in Ms. X's apartment with her. Defendant was impeached with five prior felony convictions, two for rape, and one each for robbery, burglary, and assault with intent to commit rape.

The jury found defendant guilty as charged of committing first degree burglary (Pen. Code, § 459), assault with intent to commit rape (Pen. Code, § 220), assault with intent to commit oral copulation (Ibid.), and sexual battery (Pen. Code, § 243.4). After finding true two of the five prior serious felony allegations, the trial court sentenced him to state prison for a total term of twelve years.

Questions

1. How does the condom play out in an evidentiary sense? Does it help or hurt the defense?
2. What other physical evidence helps prove guilt by association?
3. Is proof of nonconsent easy or difficult in a case like this?
4. If you were on the jury, how would you find?

the results of a rape kit test, will go much farther than just the word "No." Cute phrases will not meet the evidentiary burden—hard evidence will.

The Nature of Sexual Penetration

Common law tradition emphasized that sexual intercourse was the exclusive actus reus for any rape charge. Under traditional scrutiny, sexual intercourse consists of the insertion or penetration of penis into a female vagina. Penetration, however slight, was part of the order of proof. Ejaculation was not required, but proof of penetration could be easily inferred from the presence of this biological material. Sexual intercourse constituted the act central to rape and these same statutes excluded a wide series of other sexual acts including anal sex, oral sex, use of foreign object for insertion, and the full range of conduct between same sex adults.

§ 18.2-61. Rape

A. If any person has sexual intercourse with a complaining witness, whether or not his or her spouse, or causes a complaining witness, whether or not his or her spouse, to engage in sexual intercourse with any other person and such act is accomplished (i) against the complaining witness's will, by force, threat or intimidation of or against the complaining witness or another person; or (ii) through the use of the complaining witness's mental incapacity or physical helplessness; or (iii) with a child under age 13 as the victim, he or she shall be guilty of rape.[20]

The qualification is not as senseless as so many of its critics charge.

When distinguishing and differentiating a sexual act with potential or actual sexual results, the differences are real in some ways and similar in others. To illustrate, all forced, coercive sexual acts are an affront to human dignity. In addition, few would argue that the mental and emotional costs can be equally weighty. Differences between forced fellatio (oral sex) or analingus (anal sex) and that of conventional sexual intercourse also are obvious. Pregnancy cannot result from these practices, while it is certainly a frequent consequence of the latter. Early drafters, living in an age of noncontraception and legalized abortion, perceived these consequences with a gravity exclusive to sexual intercourse.[21] From a less than enlightened perspective, these same legal thinkers employed a perverse "damaged goods" mentality under the "property" label unfortunately inflicted on women. Put another way, the gravity of the offense was rooted in a puritan context—one that valued virginity and chastity more than our contemporary counterparts. Even today, the question of virginity is one for the woman to make, not her intruder rapist. Taking away one's own sense of destiny is another tragedy of the rapist's design. In this sense, we truly see why so many call rape a crime of power more than sex.[22] Indeed, any theory based on pent up sexual starvation can only be described as comical in the twenty-first century. Feminist scholars, like Catherine MacKinnon, see rape as the inevitable consequence of a male-dominated world and that all women, in one way or the other, are the victims of rape.

> The wrong of rape has proved so difficult to define because the unquestionable starting point has been that rape is defined as distinct from intercourse, while for women it is difficult to distinguish the two under conditions of male dominance.[23]

Katherine Baker's research on gender and rape delivers another dimension in the troublesome crime of rape and its proof.[24] For Baker and other colleagues, male and female perspectives on how the sexual conduct unfolded, are vastly different, so much so that one feels criminalized and the other the satisfied lover.[25] Of recent interest are studies linking the act of rape with biological disposition based on genetic codes in the male species. These biobehavioral explanations prompt even more polarization amongst those who wish to maintain the common law traditions and the reform of the reform.[26]

The Nature of the Marital Exemption and Its Ongoing Challenge

For these reasons, and more, the crime of rape reflects certain values and mores that may or may not be relevant today. Certainly our state legislatures never miss a day inventing a new and improved version of this offense and its elements. When states modify the historical marital exemption, where men are deemed legally incapable of raping spouses, these intentions sweep away centuries of jurisprudence. States like New Jersey[27] and Michigan were early reformers in the world of marital exemption. A bevy have followed and done so with the same good-faith motives. However, is it fair to at least rethink whether husband rapists are of the same genre as the surreptitious stranger who intrudes the domicile. The law must take great pains to qualify and grade these perpetrators and be convincingly certain that proof of criminal intent is on the same page. It seems only fair that a prosecutor be wary of lumping these two agents together. It is downright dangerous to do so automatically. Clearly, an estranged husband with a history of severe violence should not be permitted to hide behind the veil of marital exemption. Contrarily, the term and consequence of first degree rape may be a little severe given a review of the relationship and the facts.

This resistance to political and social thinking is a recurring caveat to those entrusted with the enforcement of the criminal laws.[28] Fads, support groups, activists, and political pressure lobbies fashion law out of impulse more than a reasoned view of how evidence plays out in the courtroom. It may sound attractive, yet still be cumbersome to the legal processes we have come to so heavily depend upon to discern truth in the circumstances. To edify, consider a Texas attempt to retroactively apply a rule of evidence to a defendant who was tried and convicted under different rules. At the original trial, the defendant could not be convicted without the corroboration of the victim's claim. The statute in place at the time of the defendant's trial contained these provisions:

> A conviction is supportable on the uncorroborated testimony of the victim of the sexual offense if the victim informed any person, other than the defendant, of the alleged offense within six months after the date on which the offense is alleged to have occurred. The requirement that the victim inform another person of an alleged offense does not apply if the victim was younger than 14 years of age at the time of the alleged offense.[29]

Subsequent revisions to the law allow a victim under the age of 18 to avoid the corroboration rule. The statute read in part:

> ... informed any person, other than the defendant, of the alleged offense within one year after the date on which the offense is alleged to have occurred. The requirement that the victim inform another person of an alleged offense does not apply if the victim was younger than 18 years of age at the time of the alleged offense.[30]

In reversing the defendant's conviction,[31] the U.S. Supreme Court could not brook the *ex post facto* application of a corroboration rule, no matter how well intentioned.

No justice party is as impacted by rape reform as much as the prosecutor or district attorney. He or she pursues the defendant and protects victims. A case riddled with discontinuity and doubt just makes the task more difficult. In fact, most prosecutors, in a wide series of surveys, believe that a husband can rape a wife, yet do not relish this type of prosecution.[32] Putting reform desires aside, imagine consent in a case of marital rape. The marriage contract, whereby the parties promise a host of things including sexual activity to procreate, some have argued, imputes consent, though this view is not universal. In addition, many abused women do not equate a husband's attempts to have sexual intercourse, without consent, as rape, but as a terrible indicator of abuse: a disregard, physical contempt, and general disrespect for the marital state. Other wives qualify this type of sex as part of the marital obligation.[33] To certain people, the matter of will is irrelevant to the submission of the wife. In fact, a few evangelical, Pentecostal adherents think rejection or refusal is an unjust result for the man and the marriage, though this biblical interpretation is usually wrong. Whether we concur or are aghast at such thinking is not really the point. What is meaningful is how a mindset, no matter how insensible it may appear to the general population, operates in the alleged perpetrator. If rape is unlawful sexual intercourse, without consent or permission, how does the man whose basis for submission is biblical intent to rape? These are exceptionally tough questions that bear directly on the matter of mens rea. The rapist must intend to utilize force to get the sexual intercourse he wants without the permission of the party he attacks. The biblical husband lacks these qualities in full. So, too, the contentious couple that keeps a physical relationship going despite the daily wars and battles that signify a less than tranquil home life. The war of words, the pushes and shoves, may not translate automatically into the world of sexual assault and rape. This caution should not be construed as a universal principle. Data on domestic abuse often paints a troubling picture of escalating violence that can and does take sexual form, although the picture is mixed.[34] Police officers soon learn the strangeness and unpredictability of human relationships. Certainly, not all agree with this commentary, as many legal commentators call for an end to the marital exemption and the historic resistance to prosecuting such cases. Emily Sack urges the "fight to end violence against women."[35] Sacks cannot find a defensible rationale for maintenance of the status quo and that "we dive back into this history and challenge its ongoing hold on the full achievement of equal rights."[36]

The Nature of Gender in Sexual Offenses

Similar dilemmas emerge when the discussion turns to the victim's gender. At common law, the crime of rape was exclusively a female victimization, while today the trend is toward gender neutrality. The motivations for reserving rape to the female gender have arisen from a protectionist mentality, chivalry, a view about chastity and the "damaged goods" mentality, and the possibility of pregnancy. In the pregnancy arena, there is much to be said for the logic of it since men cannot get pregnant. As for damaged goods, the chastity argument tended to be chauvinistic rather than enlightened. The question of chastity seems more aptly, though irrationally, a female issue rather than a male concern. Contemporary legislators have lost all sight of these distinctions.[37]

For example, North Carolina crafts language that is usually termed gender neutral.

§ 14-27.2. First-degree rape

(a) A person is guilty of rape in the first degree if the person engages in vaginal intercourse:
   (1)   With a victim who is a child under the age of 13 years and the defendant is at least 12 years old and is at least four years older than the victim; or

(2)   With another person by force and against the will of the other person, and:
   a.   Employs or displays a dangerous or deadly weapon or an article which the other person reasonably believes to be a dangerous or deadly weapon; or
   b.   Inflicts serious personal injury upon the victim or another person; or
   c.   The person commits the offense aided and abetted by one or more other persons.[38]

In sum, the common law components of the rape offense are an interesting blend of prejudice and wisdom. Rape, without qualification, is a mighty serious offense rationalized under sound logic or historic prejudice. Reformers, in their zeal to expand the protections to more categories of victims, may actually be harming the very victims they hope to protect. For some, the expansions of types of sexual behavior and bodily orifices that qualify, the broadening of the gender classifications and the loosening of the resistance requirements, have done much to heighten the tent's coverage of sexual victims. A well-meaning illustration of this tendency in rape reform law was the successful claim that being "raped" on the job was an "accidental injury" under Workers' Compensation laws in New York.[39] For this fleeting moment, the victim receives a benefit from an unexpected source. But does this approach advance justice? That judges lack the understanding of this offense's seriousness will not be surprising to those who labor in American courtrooms. Judges are on record with decisions that can only be described as sexist and disturbed. Unfortunately, the judiciary, like all other sectors of society, is burdened with its share of the incompetent and unenlightened. Reformers have attacked these decisions head on and with good results. A recent 1st Circuit Court of Appeals decision amazingly held that a rapist's most severe sentence could not take place because rape is not "serious bodily injury" under a federal statute.[40] From rulings like these, the reform movement has its work cut out. And, while reform of arcane and sexist laws is always a good thing, reform should not replace common sense and the evidentiary rigor necessary for convictions. Viewed from another slant, these expansions may be watering down the seriousness of first-degree rape from its historical roots. Rape in the first degree was and still is a very serious offense against the human person. To maintain its seriousness, the justice professional cannot avoid the categorization of not only perpetrators, but also types of victims.

The Nature of the Victim's Character

Historically, defense challenges to a victim's character were central to the litigation strategy. By character, the emphasis was on the sexual reputation of the victim. Such tactics caused added victimization and distracted the jury from its fundamental duties and enveloped the tribunal in a sort of salaciousness that was unhealthy for the legal system. In order to avoid further trauma on the part of the victim, and to assure a fair and just adjudication of the complaint, various state legislatures, as well as the federal system, have instituted rape shield laws that seek to limit character examination. The purpose is to minimize questioning of the complainant relative to sexual background, experiences, and proclivities. So prejudicial is this evidence and so destructive to a complainant that the shield seeks to protect them from systematic abuse. "Rape shield laws, enacted in fifty states and the District of Columbia, limit the use of prior sexual history as a means of undermining the credibility of the victim's testimony."[41]

Undeniably, defense attorneys will use each weapon in the arsenal to disprove the allegation. Past sexual relations, questionable sexual histories, and previous attempts to prosecute an unrelated sexual offense, target the nature of consent and will. No matter how tough the result may be, defense counsel's task is to paint the victim into a corner, and a very unfavorable one at that. During this type of attack, the victim's credibility and believability are repeatedly attacked. Some examples of this line of questioning might include:

- Have you ever had sexual relations with the defendant in this case?
- How many times have you had sexual relations with the accused?
- For what period of time and what was the level and extensiveness of your sexual relations?
- How many sexual partners have you had during your lifetime?
- Have you ever accused another party of a similar or the same crime?
- What types of sexual practices have you engaged in?
- Have you ever become so intoxicated you cannot remember with whom you have sexual relations?
- Have your ever been arrested for prostitution?
- Do you have any communicable sexual diseases?
- Have you ever been cited for fraud, perjury, or other crime relating to honesty?

At first glance, the questions memorialize a second tier of victimization from which rape victims suffer. There is little that is less galling than this type of barrage, the effect of which calls into question your integrity and general credibility. Looked at from the defense slant, these types of questions seem almost imperative. Defense counsel must rightfully use any rational means to undercut the veracity and credibility of the complainant.

From the victim's perspective, this series of inquiries is nothing more than added insult and injury. To the defendant, character scrutiny is another way of challenge, a method of impeachment and a general challenge to the veracity of accuser. The rape shield seeks to balance the interests of the state to prosecute, defense counsel to defend and the sanctity and dignity of the victim. Review the statute below:

§ 3104. Evidence of victim's sexual conduct

(a) GENERAL RULE. —Evidence of specific instances of the alleged victim's past sexual conduct, opinion evidence of the alleged victim's past sexual conduct, and reputation evidence of the alleged victim's past sexual conduct shall not be admissible in prosecutions under this chapter except evidence of the alleged victim's past sexual conduct with the defendant where consent of the alleged victim is at issue and such evidence is otherwise admissible pursuant to the rules of evidence.

(b) EVIDENTIARY PROCEEDINGS. —A defendant who proposes to offer evidence of the alleged victim's past sexual conduct pursuant to subsection (a) shall file a written motion and offer of proof at the time of trial. If, at the time of trial, the court determines that the motion and offer of proof are sufficient on their faces, the court shall order an in camera hearing and shall make findings on the record as to the relevance and admissibility of the proposed evidence pursuant to the standards set forth in subsection (a).[42]

The Federal Rules of Evidence at Rule 609[43] sets a similar protective tone toward the victim. For the past decade or two, the defense challenge has been fast and furious. As the shield works, it forbids the defendant from challenging the victim on the grounds noted above. In general, the shield declares irrelevant the sexual history of the victim, finds impertinent the questions involving chastity or promiscuity, and forbids the usual attack dog tactics that defense attorneys relish during cross-examination. In this sense, defendants are placed at an evidentiary disadvantage when compared to other felonies.[44] Despite this rare disadvantage, the framers of the shield feel that public policy leans in the direction of the victim to the detriment of the accused; a very rare circumstance in the justice system.

This procedural imbalance has not gone unnoticed by criminal constitutionalists who decry the lack of due process afforded the accused and cite specifically the watering down of historic confrontation rights guaranteed under the Sixth Amendment. An accused wants every tactic to raise the specter of reasonable doubt and to examine his or her accusers with every available slant and option. Anything short of this smacks of favoritism and an abridgement of rights. While most of the landscape tends to be pro-victim, in some sectors of the legal community, there is growing recognition that some type of victim examination may be helpful to the jury and the Court. It is one thing to argue the shield and protection for the victim, but quite another when the tribunal cannot weigh and evaluate the credibility and integrity of the complainant. A recent idea promotes the use of expert witnesses to give testimony on the believability and credibility of the victim's presentation—a sort of seal of certainty and genuineness. Exactly how those experts would measure these traits and characteristics is yet to be fully developed, but it is an idea worthy of further examination.[45]

The antidefense sentiment is further evident in recent amendments to the character evidence principles enunciated in the Federal Evidence at Rules 413 and 414.[46] Here, the defendant may be attacked for other sexual offenses than at his present case. Historically, such commentary was considered too prejudicial to see the light of day, but the amendments add on to the traditional exceptions of motive, plan, knowledge, intent, method, and opportunity.

Under Rule 413(a), in a case in which a criminal defendant is accused of a sexual assault crime, "evidence of the defendant's commission of another offense or offenses of sexual assault is admissible, and may be considered for its bearing on any matter to which it is relevant."[47] In other words, in a case in which a defendant is charged with raping a victim, the prosecutor can introduce evidence that the defendant has previously raped someone, in order to prove that the defendant raped the victim in the instant case.[48]

Federal Rule 414 specifically extends these principles to cases of child molestation. "Rule 414(a) ... allows prosecutors accusing a defendant of child molestation to prove the defendant's criminal liability by introducing evidence that the defendant molested children in the past."[49] A host of other reforms regarding children and sexual crimes crop up with great regularity. Efforts to strike down the application of the marital privilege doctrine, where one spouse can invoke a refusal to testify against the other spouse who is abusing family members, including children, appear to be gaining steam. The U.S. District Court for the Western District of Texas "has forged the broadest exception, hold that the marital communications privilege should not apply to statements relating to a crime where the victim is a child, even when the abuse did not occur in the home."[50]

Defense counsel can argue that the admission of this type of evidence is gravely prejudicial to the accused and contrary to the thrust of the federal rules, which generally forbids the admission of relevant evidence "if its probative value is substantially outweighed by the danger of unfair prejudice, confusion of the issues, or misleading the jury, or by considerations of undue delay, waste of time, or needless presentation of cumulative evidence."[51]

STATUTORY RAPE

ELEMENTS

- Sexual intercourse
- Person under the legal age of consent
- Certain number of years older than the complainant
- Not married to each other
- Strict liability as to intent

Long a heated principle in law, statutory rape inflicts a form of strict liability on the perpetrator for what he or she might perceive as consensual sexual activity when by age difference alone the law deems the consent ineffective. The typical mens rea requirements for a major felony are discarded due to the special class and status of the participants. The perpetrator of this offense may wish no harm, have no malevolent motive, or even recognize the criminality of his or her acts. Under the strict liability language of statutory rape statutes, it makes little difference to eventual culpability.

This form of rape is age-specific and depends upon legislative design. Ages of both victim and perpetrator are listed and when a marked age imbalance occurs in the sexual relationship, the law imposes harsh penalties. Thus, if a 24-year-old man engages in sexual relations with a willing, in a factual sense, 15-year-old, the age differential triggers the criminal liability. Review the statute below:

§ 3122.1. Statutory sexual assault

Except as provided in section 3121 (relating to rape), a person commits a felony of the second degree when that person engages in sexual intercourse with a complainant under the age of 16 years and that person is four or more years older than the complainant and the complainant and the person are not married to each other.[52]

Why the severity for this conduct? A driving rationale for the criminalization has long been the prevention of teenage pregnancy. Unfortunately, our statistical data on out-of-wedlock pregnancies shows nothing but escalation.[53] Our society's rejection of the statute's ideal does not negate its merit. There is much that can be said favorably about a nation and a justice model that seeks to keep its youth, our underage children in middle and high schools, from entering into the very weighty world of parenting. Maturity, personal development, and occupational preparation are reasonable conditions precedent to the birth of children in less than normative circumstances. Scholars and policymakers, from Senator Daniel Patrick Moynihan to former Secretary of Education, William Bennett, have already catalogued the grave consequences for this careless approach to procreation.[54] (See Figure 6.4 for teenage pregnancy rates since 1991.[55])

Aside from this stark reality, sexual activity, and the consequences that derive therefrom, has many serious connotations whether physical, emotional, or spiritual in nature. Gone are the days when policymakers can make light of children engaging in very adult behaviors without implication. Statutory rape laws try to address the gravity of this human activity, and to put it in some context that is meaningful for the individual and the collective. Our toleration of continually younger sexual participants cannot reap the rewards of a virtuous nation, nor does it bode well

Age, Race, and Hispanic Origin of Mother	Year						Percent Change			
	2009	2008	2007	2006	2005	1991	2007–2009	2008–2009	2005–2007	1991–2005
10–14 years										
All races and origins[1]	0.5	0.6	0.6	0.6	0.7	1.4	-17	-17	-14	-50
Non–Hispanic white[2]	0.2	0.2	0.2	0.2	0.2	0.5	†	†	†	-60
Non–Hispanic black[2]	1.2	1.4	1.5	1.6	1.7	4.9	-20	-14	-12	-65
American Indian or Alaska Native total[2,3]	0.8	0.9	0.9	0.9	0.9	1.6	-11	-11	†	-44
Asian or Pacific Islander total[2,3]	0.2	0.2	0.2	0.2	0.2	0.8	†	†	†	-75
Hispanic[4]	1.0	1.2	1.2	1.3	1.3	2.4	-17	-17	-8	-46
15–19 years										
All races and origins[1]	39.1	41.5	42.5	41.9	40.5	61.8	-8	-6	5	-34
Non–Hispanic white[2]	25.6	26.7	27.2	26.6	25.9	43.4	-6	-4	5	-40
Non–Hispanic black[2]	59.0	62.8	64.2	63.7	60.9	118.2	-8	-6	5	-48
American Indian or Alaska Native total[2,3]	55.5	58.4	59.3	55	52.7	84.1	-6	-5	13	-37
Asian or Pacific Islander total[2,3]	14.6	16.2	16.9	17	17	27.3	-14	-10	†	-38
Hispanic[4]	70.1	77.5	81.8	83	81.7	104.6	-14	-10	†	-22
15–17 years										
All races and origins[1]	20.1	21.7	22.1	22	21.4	38.6	-9	-7	3	-45
Non–Hispanic white[2]	11.0	11.5	11.8	11.8	11.5	23.6	-7	-4	3	-51
Non–Hispanic black[2]	32.1	34.8	35.8	36.2	34.9	86.1	-10	-8	3	-59
American Indian or Alaska Native total[2,3]	30.6	32.5	31.8	30.7	30.5	51.9	-4	-6	†	-41
Asian or Pacific Islander total[2,3]	7.1	7.9	8.2	8.8	8.2	16.3	-13	-10	†	-50
Hispanic[4]	41.0	46.1	47.9	47.9	48.5	69.2	-14	-11	-1	-30

Figure 6.4   Birth rates for women under 20 years, by age, race, and Hispanic origin of mother: United States, final 1991, 2005–2008, and preliminary 2009, and percent change in rates, 1991–2005, 2005–2007, 2007–2009, 2008–2009, and 2007–2009.   (*continued*)

Age, Race, and Hispanic Origin of Mother	Year							Percent Change		
	2009	2008	2007	2006	2005	1991	2007–2009	2008–2009	2005–2007	1991–2005
18–19 years										
All races and origins[1]	66.2	70.6	73.9	73	69.9	94	–10	–6	6	–26
Non–Hispanic white[2]	46.1	48.5	50.4	49.3	48	70.6	–9	–5	5	–32
Non–Hispanic black[2]	97.5	104.6	109.3	108.4	103	162.2	–11	–7	6	–36
American Indian or Alaska Native total[2,3]	90.5	96.6	101.6	93	87.6	134.2	–11	–6	16	–35
Asian or Pacific Islander total[2,3]	25.7	28.4	29.9	29.5	30.1	42.2	–14	–10	†	–29
Hispanic[4]	114.0	127.2	137.2	139.7	134.6	155.5	–17	–10	2	–13

[1] Includes origin not stated.

[2] Race and Hispanic origin are reported separately on birth certificates. Persons of Hispanic origin may be of any race. Race categories are consistent with the 1977 Office of Management and Budget (OMB) standards. In 2009, 32 states and the District of Columbia reported multiple-race data. The multiple-race data for these states were bridged to the single-race categories of the 1977 OMB standards for comparability with other states; see "Technical Notes." Multiple-race reporting areas vary for 2005–2008; see "Technical Notes."

[3] Data for persons of Hispanic origin are included in the data for each race group according to the mother's reported race; see "Technical Notes."

[4] Includes all persons of Hispanic origin of any race; see "Technical Notes."

Note: † = Difference not statistically significant. Data for 2009 are based on continuous files of records received from the states. Rates per 1,000 women in specified age and race and Hispanic origin group. For information on the relative standard errors of the data and further discussion, see reference 9.

Figure 6.4 (*continued*) Birth rates for women under 20 years, by age, race, and Hispanic origin of mother: United States, final 1991, 2005–2008, and preliminary 2009, and percent change in rates, 1991–2005, 2005–2007, 2008–2009, and 2007–2009.

for the generations of children having children, whose offspring may soon act in even less wise terms. If the law stands for anything, it must have a positive message of some sort. For all its criticism, statutory rape laws are an honorable attempt to protect the young from the predator, and to corral in those who use age differential to cast their net. It is indefensible for a grown person, whether it be former teacher Mary Kay LaTourneau or sadistic predator John Wayne Gacy, to engage in sexual practices with children. It is inexcusable that we allow the power differential to mollify and mitigate consent in the young. If anything, the young are incapable, just as the old and infirm, the ward and retarded, from forging the type of intentional participation that betokens consent. Then, too, should our laws be a reflection of our social practices even when corrupted? Frequently, one hears of the staggering increases in sexual activity amongst the young. Even if only partially accurate, do our legislators look at how the mob acts to craft the law? Do we lower the statutory rape age to 13, as was proposed in New Jersey, because law should reflect the new and very depressing reality?

STORY 6.1

LOWERING THE AGE OF CONSENT

How old is old enough? When does a child become a young adult—12, 14, 18, or 21? Can a 12-year-old make a responsible decision about sexual encounters, alcohol usage, or medical care? There are several factions throughout the United States who would lower or completely abolish the notion of an age of consent or majority. Some of these are organizations of pedophiliacs and homosexuals and some are not. Although the discussion has simmered down somewhat, the question still hangs in the air. Is there a magical date when a child is all of a sudden an adult? Obviously, a major transformation does not take place overnight; the transformation comes from years of parental guidance and correct decision making on the part of the parents and the child. The reasoning behind the age of consent in certain situations is to protect the child from harm when they may be too young to make an intelligent and informed decision.

The age of consent is most controversial when discussing sexual activity. Should 12-year-olds be free to enjoy any sexual encounter they want? Some factions, such as NAMBLA, believe that children 12 years old and younger should be free to enjoy any sexual act they choose, with any partner they choose. These factions state that sexual activity at a young age does not result in any mental damage when done correctly and not criminalized. The other side of the argument is that sexual activity does result in significant psychological trauma for children that lasts the rest of their lives. Children who have been exposed to pornography and sexual maltreatment and abuse end up being drug addicts, criminals, sexually promiscuous, etc.

What age should be the age of consent? Should sexual activity below the age of consent remain illegal? The vast majority of American adults agree with the age of consent, that it should remain 16 or 18 for sexual activity and at 21 for alcohol usage. Teenagers will of course disagree. If the age of consent was abolished, what would be the result?

> For a summary of statutory rape policies in the various states, read http://www.hhs.gov/opa/familyplanning/toolsdocs/statutory_rape_state_laws_lewin.pdf

Or, should the law stand fast or at least stand for something even when its target pays it no heed? Steadfastness may not be the cure, but it certainly is the message that most citizens want their justice system to broadcast. None of us wants children involved in the emotional cauldron of sex and relationships. Some average adults have already shown incapacity in these matters. All of us wish for some level of innocence for our children and we should look to the law to enforce the message of virtue rather than hedonism. In this strange, but admittedly clumsy way, statutory rape law qualifies sex at the right time, and with the right person. Law clerk Elizabeth Hollenberg describes the thicket in which we find ourselves:

> Teenagers are having sex, and a lot of it. This year alone, approximately 10 million teenagers will engage in 126 million acts of sexual intercourse, resulting in about one million pregnancies, 406,000 abortions, 134,000 miscarriages,[56] and approximately half a million live births.[57] These figures have been a source of political debate and social concern since the 1960s, when the "teen sex problem" first gained a place on the national agenda. Since that time, the focus of public discourse has shifted from teenage sex to teenage pregnancy. Teenage pregnancy has come to symbolize a range of pervasive social problems: deepening poverty, escalating drug abuse and gun violence, the failing education system, joblessness, welfare reliance, and the disintegration of the nuclear family.[58] Indeed, public debate over teenage pregnancy is not primarily about the half million children born each year to teenage mothers, but rather about the array of deeply entrenched social problems that teenage mothers have come to represent.[59]

In academic circles, it is now chic to dismiss the protectors of the innocents as a band of religious right lunatics. In its place, the new vision touts the exploratory nature of sexuality and the inevitability of it all. One commentator bemoans our horrid unsophistication when compared to Europe and other continents. Urging that we be guided by "international law" instead of our own hang ups, the author further says that international law focuses "on rehabilitating juvenile defendants and serving the best interests of those victimized by statutory rape."[60] Sexual conduct between the young and the older should be countenanced with a gleeful wisdom without regard for its complexity, emotional dimension, or potential objectification of the human person.

On the other hand, making improvements to statutory rape designs is a laudable exercise, as the "one size fits all" may not work. For example, does a mentally retarded person understand or comprehend the age differentiation standards? If we assume that the mentally retarded defendant is incapable of properly and intelligently assessing the restrictions of sexuality in these age brackets, how can a strict liability finding be applied to this setting?[61]

From another slant, it may be sensible to adjust the severity of the act for the accused and the victim when both are designated minors. Some statutory rape laws punish any perpetrator, even if underage. The intent here is to heap negative reinforcement on the young who decide to engage in sexual activity. Most commentators would describe this policy as a lost cause. The Florida Supreme Court in *B.B. v. State*[62] overturned the conviction of a 16-year-old who had consensual sex with another 16-year-old under this statute:

§ 794.05. Unlawful sexual activity with certain minors

(1) A person 24 years of age or older who engages in sexual activity with a person 16 or 17 years of age commits a felony of the second degree, punishable as provided in s. 775.082, s. 775.083, or s. 775.084. As used in this section, "sexual activity" means oral, anal, or vaginal penetration by, or union with, the sexual organ of another; however, sexual activity does not include an act done for a bona fide medical purpose.[63]

The Court sidestepped the statute by declaring that its content abridged the privacy clause of the First Amendment of the Florida Constitution and effectively mooted any future prosecutions of minors engaged in consensual sexual conduct. "The significance of the B.B. holding is that it essentially creates a privacy right for minors to engage in consensual sexual conduct with other minors. This decision expands privacy rights jurisprudence in Florida, and the B.B. Court's conclusion that the statute was not the least intrusive means to regulate the sexual activity of 16- to 18-year-olds is contrary to Florida precedent. Giving minors the same privacy rights as adults may raise questions in the future concerning the constitutionality of other statutes regulating activities involving minors that may implicate privacy rights."[64]

While the argument appears attractive, is it legally defensible? In the dissenting opinion, Justice Grimes queried:

> ... in holding section 794.05 unconstitutional as applied, the majority appears to be saying that a sixteen-year-old child has a constitutional right to engage in sex with another sixteen-year-old child, though an older person would not have such a right.[65]

As controversial as these types of laws can be, wholesale elimination at the state level does not appear likely. What does occur with some regularity is the grading down of the offense to lower severity. Instead of the class A felony, which brings the harshest penalties, statutory rape is now largely a lower grade of sexual offense.[66]

To be sure, there are no easy answers to these formidable social problems, but critics of the statutory rape laws cannot simply legalize all sexual behavior with any schema of partners and age groups, and not expect negative influences in the culture.

SODOMY/INVOLUNTARY DEVIATE SEXUAL INTERCOURSE

ELEMENTS

- Deviate sexual intercourse: anal and/or oral
- With force
- Without consent
- Same sex or opposite sex activity depending on jurisdiction

Throughout the timeline of Western tradition, acts of sodomy have been criminally defined. The once well-accepted landscape involving sodomy was turned on its head when the U.S. Supreme Court overturned its own precedent, *Bowers v. Hardwick*,[67] by issuing a constitutional protection

CASE 6.2

LAWRENCE V. TEXAS
539 U.S. 558 (2003)

> (*For the entire Opinion, Concurrence, and Dissents, please visit Cornell's Legal Information Institute at* http://www.law.cornell.edu/supct/html/02-102.ZS.html)

The question before the Court is the validity of a Texas statute making it a crime for two persons of the same sex to engage in certain intimate sexual conduct.

In Houston, Texas, officers of the Harris County Police Department were dispatched to a private residence in response to a reported weapons disturbance. They entered an apartment where one of the petitioners, John Geddes Lawrence, resided. The right of the police to enter does not seem to have been questioned. The officers observed Lawrence and another man, Tyron Garner, engaging in a sexual act. The two petitioners were arrested, held in custody overnight, and charged and convicted before a Justice of the Peace.

The complaints described their crime as "deviate sexual intercourse, namely anal sex, with a member of the same sex (man)." The applicable state law is Tex. Penal Code Ann. § 21.06(a) (2003). It provides: "A person commits an offense if he engages in deviate sexual intercourse with another individual of the same sex." The statute defines "[d]eviate sexual intercourse" as follows:

(A) any contact between any part of the genitals of one person and the mouth or anus of another person; or

(B) the penetration of the genitals or the anus of another person with an object. § 21.01(1).

The petitioners exercised their right to a trial de novo in Harris County Criminal Court. They challenged the statute as a violation of the Equal Protection Clause of the Fourteenth Amendment and of a like provision of the Texas Constitution. Tex. Const., Art. 1, § 3a. Those contentions were rejected. The petitioners, having entered a plea of nolo contendere, were each fined $200 and assessed court costs of $141.25.

We granted certiorari to consider:

1. Whether petitioners' criminal convictions under the Texas 'Homosexual Conduct' law—which criminalizes sexual intimacy by same-sex couples, but not identical behavior by different-sex couples—violate the Fourteenth Amendment guarantee of equal protection of the laws.
2. Whether petitioners' criminal convictions for adult consensual sexual intimacy in the home violate their vital interests in liberty and privacy protected by the Due Process Clause of the Fourteenth Amendment.

...

The petitioners were adults at the time of the alleged offense. Their conduct was in private and consensual.

We conclude the case should be resolved by determining whether the petitioners were free as adults to engage in the private conduct in the exercise of their liberty under the Due Process Clause of the Fourteenth Amendment to the Constitution. ...

After Griswold, it was established that the right to make certain decisions regarding sexual conduct extend beyond the marital relationship. In *Eisenstadt v. Baird*, the Court invalidated a law prohibiting the distribution of contraceptives to unmarried persons. The case was decided under the Equal Protection Clause, but with respect to unmarried persons, the Court went on to state the fundamental proposition that the law impaired the exercise of their personal rights. It quoted from the statement of the Court of Appeals finding the law to be in conflict with fundamental human rights, and it followed with this statement of its own:

"It is true that in Griswold the right of privacy in question inhered in the marital relationship. ... If the right of privacy means anything, it is the right of the individual, married or single, to be free from unwarranted governmental intrusion into matters so fundamentally affecting a person as the decision whether to bear or beget a child."

...

In *Carey v. Population Services Int'l*, the Court confronted a New York law forbidding sale or distribution of contraceptive devices to persons under 16 years of age. Although there was no single opinion for the Court, the law was invalidated. Both Eisenstadt and Carey, as well as the holding and rationale in Roe, confirmed that the reasoning of Griswold could not be confined to the protection of rights of married adults. This was the state of the law with respect to some of the most relevant cases when the Court considered *Bowers v. Hardwick*.

The facts in Bowers had some similarities to the instant case. A police officer, whose right to enter seems not to have been in question, observed Hardwick, in his own bedroom, engaging in intimate sexual conduct with another adult male. The conduct was in violation of a Georgia statute making it a criminal offense to engage in sodomy. One difference between the two cases is that the Georgia statute prohibited the conduct whether or not the participants were of the same sex, while the Texas statute, as we have seen, applies only to participants of the same sex. Hardwick was not prosecuted, but he brought an action in federal court to declare the state statute invalid. He alleged he was a practicing homosexual and that the criminal prohibition violated rights guaranteed to him by the Constitution. The Court, in an opinion by Justice White, sustained the Georgia law.

The Court began its substantive discussion in Bowers as follows: "The issue presented is whether the Federal Constitution confers a fundamental right upon homosexuals to engage in sodomy and, hence, invalidates the laws of the many States that still make such conduct illegal and have done so for a very long time." That statement, we now conclude, discloses the Court's own failure to appreciate the extent of the liberty at stake. To say that the issue in Bowers was simply the right to engage in certain sexual conduct demeans the claim the individual put forward, just as it would demean a married couple were it to be said marriage is simply about the right to have sexual intercourse. The laws involved in Bowers and here are, to be sure, statutes that purport to do no more than prohibit a particular sexual act. Their penalties and purposes, though, have more far-reaching consequences, touching upon the most private human conduct, sexual behavior, and in the most private of places, the home. The statutes do seek to control a personal relationship that, whether or not entitled to formal recognition in the law, is within the liberty of persons to choose without being punished as criminals.

This, as a general rule, should counsel against attempts by the State, or a court, to define the meaning of the relationship or to set its boundaries absent injury to a person or abuse of an institution the law protects. It suffices for us to acknowledge that adults may choose to enter upon this relationship in the confines of their homes and their own private lives and still retain their dignity as free persons. When sexuality finds overt expression in intimate conduct with another person, the conduct can be but one element in a personal bond that is more enduring. The liberty protected by the Constitution allows homosexual persons the right to make this choice.

Having misapprehended the claim of liberty there presented to it, and thus stating the claim to be whether there is a fundamental right to engage in consensual sodomy, the Bowers Court said: "Proscriptions against that conduct have ancient roots." In academic writings, and in many of the scholarly amicus briefs filed to assist the Court in this case, there are fundamental criticisms of the historical premises relied upon by the majority and concurring opinions in Bowers. ... We need not enter this debate in the attempt to reach a definitive historical judgment, but the following considerations counsel against adopting the definitive conclusions upon which Bowers placed such reliance.

At the outset it should be noted that there is no longstanding history in this country of laws directed at homosexual conduct as a distinct matter. Beginning in colonial times there were prohibitions of sodomy derived from the English criminal laws passed in the first instance by the Reformation Parliament of 1533. The English prohibition was understood to include relations between men and women as well as relations between men and men. Nineteenth-century commentators similarly read American sodomy, buggery, and crime-against-nature statutes as criminalizing certain relations between men and women and between men and men.

The absence of legal prohibitions focusing on homosexual conduct may be explained in part by noting that according to some scholars the concept of the homosexual as a distinct category of person did not emerge until the late 19th century. Thus early American sodomy laws were not directed at homosexuals as such, but instead sought to prohibit nonprocreative sexual activity more generally. This does not suggest approval of homosexual conduct. It does tend to show that this particular form of conduct was not thought of as a separate category from like conduct between heterosexual persons.

Laws prohibiting sodomy do not seem to have been enforced against consenting adults acting in private. A substantial number of sodomy prosecutions and convictions for which there are surviving records were for predatory acts against those who could not or did not consent, as in the case of a minor or the victim of an assault. As to these, one purpose for the prohibitions was to ensure there would be no lack of coverage if a predator committed a sexual assault that did not constitute rape as defined by the criminal law. Thus the model sodomy indictments presented in a 19th-century treatise addressed the predatory acts of an adult man against a minor girl or minor boy. Instead of targeting relations between consenting adults in private, 19th-century sodomy prosecutions typically involved relations between men and minor girls or minor boys, relations between adults involving force, relations between adults implicating disparity in status, or relations between men and animals.

To the extent that there were any prosecutions for the acts in question, 19th-century evidence rules imposed a burden that would make a conviction more difficult to obtain even taking into account the problems always inherent in prosecuting consensual acts committed in private. Under then-prevailing standards, a man could not be convicted of sodomy based upon testimony of a consenting partner, because the partner was considered an accomplice. A partner's testimony, however, was admissible if he or she had not consented to the act or was a minor, and therefore incapable of consent. The rule may explain in part the infrequency of these prosecutions. In all events that infrequency makes it difficult to say that society approved of a rigorous and systematic punishment of the consensual acts committed in private and by adults. The longstanding criminal prohibition of homosexual sodomy upon which the Bowers decision placed such reliance is as consistent with a general condemnation of nonprocreative sex as it is with an established tradition of prosecuting acts because of their homosexual character.

The policy of punishing consenting adults for private acts was not much discussed in the early legal literature. We can infer that one reason for this was the very private nature of the conduct. Despite the absence of prosecutions, there may have been periods in which there was public criticism of homosexuals as such and an insistence that the criminal laws be enforced to discourage their practices. But, far from possessing "ancient roots," American laws targeting same-sex couples did not develop until the last third of the 20th century. The reported decisions concerning the prosecution of consensual, homosexual sodomy between adults for the years 1880–1995 are not always clear in the details, but a significant number involved conduct in a public place.

It was not until the 1970s that any State singled out same-sex relations for criminal prosecution, and only nine States have done so. Post-Bowers even some of these States did not adhere to the policy of suppressing homosexual conduct. Over the course of the last decades, States with same-sex prohibitions have moved toward abolishing them.

In summary, the historical grounds relied upon in Bowers are more complex than the majority opinion and the concurring opinion by Chief Justice Burger indicate. Their historical premises are not without doubt and, at the very least, are overstated.

It must be acknowledged, of course, that the Court in Bowers was making the broader point that for centuries there have been powerful voices to condemn homosexual conduct as immoral. The condemnation has been shaped by religious beliefs, conceptions of right and acceptable behavior, and respect for the traditional family. For many persons, these are not trivial concerns but profound and deep convictions accepted as ethical and moral principles to which they aspire and which thus determine the course of their lives. These considerations do not answer the question before us, however. The issue is whether the majority may use the power of the State to enforce these views on the whole society through operation of the criminal law. "Our obligation is to define the liberty of all, not to mandate our own moral code."

Chief Justice Burger joined the opinion for the Court in Bowrs and further explained his views as follows: "Decisions of individuals relating to homosexual conduct have been subject to state intervention throughout the history of Western civilization. Condemnation of those practices is firmly rooted in Judeo-Christian moral and ethical standards."

As with Justice White's assumptions about history, scholarship casts some doubt on the sweeping nature of the statement by Chief Justice Burger as it pertains to private homosexual conduct between consenting adults. In all events, we think that our laws and traditions in the past half century are of most relevance here. These references show an emerging awareness that liberty gives substantial protection to adult persons in deciding how to conduct their private lives in matters pertaining to sex. "[H]istory and tradition are the starting point but not in all cases the ending point of the substantive due process inquiry."

This emerging recognition should have been apparent when Bowers was decided. In 1955, the American Law Institute promulgated the Model Penal Code and made clear that it did not recommend or provide for "criminal penalties for consensual sexual relations conducted in private." It justified its decision on three grounds: (1) The prohibitions undermined respect for the law by penalizing conduct many people engaged in; (2) the statutes regulated private conduct not harmful to others; and (3) the laws were arbitrarily enforced and thus invited the danger of blackmail. In 1961 Illinois changed its laws to conform to the Model Penal Code. Other States soon followed.

In Bowers, the Court referred to the fact that before 1961 all 50 States had outlawed sodomy, and that, at the time of the Court's decision, 24 States and the District of Columbia had sodomy laws. Justice Powell pointed out that these prohibitions often were being ignored, however. Georgia, for instance, had not sought to enforce its law for decades.

...

In our own constitutional system the deficiencies in Bowers became even more apparent in the years following its announcement. The 25 States with laws prohibiting the relevant conduct referenced in the Bowers decision are reduced now to 13, of which four enforce their laws only against homosexual conduct. In those States where sodomy is still proscribed, whether for same-sex or heterosexual conduct, there is a pattern of nonenforcement with respect to consenting adults acting in private. The State of Texas admitted in 1994 that as of that date it had not prosecuted anyone under those circumstances.

Two principal cases decided after Bowers cast its holding into even more doubt. In *Planned Parenthood of Southeastern Pa. v. Casey,* the Court reaffirmed the substantive force of the liberty protected by the Due Process Clause. The Casey decision again confirmed that our laws and tradition afford constitutional protection to personal decisions relating to marriage, procreation, contraception, family relationships, child rearing, and education. In explaining the respect the Constitution demands for the autonomy of the person in making these choices, we stated as follows:

"These matters, involving the most intimate and personal choices a person may make in a lifetime, choices central to personal dignity and autonomy, are central to the liberty protected by the Fourteenth Amendment. At the heart of liberty is the right to define one's own concept of existence, of meaning, of the universe, and of the mystery of human life. Beliefs about these matters could not define the attributes of personhood were they formed under compulsion of the State."

Persons in a homosexual relationship may seek autonomy for these purposes, just as heterosexual persons do. The decision in Bowers would deny them this right.

The second post-Bowers case of principal relevance is *Romer v. Evans*. There the Court struck down class-based legislation directed at homosexuals as a violation of the Equal Protection Clause. Romer invalidated an amendment to Colorado's Constitution which named as a solitary class persons who were homosexuals, lesbians, or bisexual either by "orientation, conduct, practices, or relationships," and deprived them of protection under state antidiscrimination laws. We concluded that the provision was "born of animosity toward the class of persons affected" and further that it had no rational relation to a legitimate governmental purpose.

As an alternative argument in this case, counsel for the petitioners and some *amici* contend that Romer provides the basis for declaring the Texas statute invalid under the Equal Protection Clause.

...

Were we to hold the statute invalid under the Equal Protection Clause, some might question whether a prohibition would be valid if drawn differently, say, to prohibit the conduct both between same-sex and different-sex participants.

Equality of treatment and the due process right to demand respect for conduct protected by the substantive guarantee of liberty are linked in important respects, and a decision on the latter point advances both interests. If protected conduct is made criminal and the law which does so remains unexamined for its substantive validity, its stigma might remain even if it were not enforceable as drawn for equal protection reasons. When homosexual conduct is made criminal by the law of the State, that declaration in and of itself is an invitation to subject homosexual persons to discrimination both in the public and in the private spheres. The central holding of Bowers has been brought in question by this case, and it should be addressed. Its continuance as precedent demeans the lives of homosexual persons.

The stigma this criminal statute imposes, moreover, is not trivial. The offense, to be sure, is but a class C misdemeanor, a minor offense in the Texas legal system. Still, it remains a criminal offense with all that imports for the dignity of the persons charged. The petitioners will bear on their record the history of their criminal convictions. Just this Term we rejected various challenges to state laws requiring the registration of sex offenders. We are advised that if Texas convicted an adult for private, consensual homosexual conduct under the statute here in question, the convicted person would come within the registration laws of at least four States were he or she to be subject to their jurisdiction. This underscores the consequential nature of the punishment and the state-sponsored condemnation attendant to the criminal prohibition. Furthermore, the Texas criminal conviction carries with it the other collateral consequences always following a conviction, such as notations on job application forms, to mention but one example.

...

"Our prior cases make two propositions abundantly clear. First, the fact that the governing majority in a State has traditionally viewed a particular practice as immoral is not a sufficient reason for upholding a law prohibiting the practice; neither history nor tradition could save a law prohibiting miscegenation from constitutional attack. Second, individual decisions by married persons, concerning the intimacies of their physical relationship, even when not intended to produce offspring, are a form of 'liberty' protected by the Due Process Clause of the Fourteenth Amendment. Moreover, this protection extends to intimate choices by unmarried as well as married persons."

Justice STEVENS' analysis, in our view, should have been controlling in Bowers and should control here.

The present case does not involve minors. It does not involve persons who might be injured or coerced or who are situated in relationships where consent might not easily be refused. It does not involve public conduct or prostitution. It does not involve whether the government must give formal recognition to any relationship that homosexual persons seek to enter. The case does involve two adults who, with full and mutual consent from each other, engaged in sexual practices common to a homosexual lifestyle. The petitioners are entitled to respect for their private lives. The State cannot demean their existence or control their destiny by making their private sexual conduct a crime. Their right to liberty under the Due Process Clause gives them the full right to engage in their conduct without intervention of the government. "It is a promise of the Constitution that there is a realm of personal liberty which the government may not enter." The Texas statute furthers no legitimate state interest which can justify its intrusion into the personal and private life of the individual.

Had those who drew and ratified the Due Process Clauses of the Fifth Amendment or the Fourteenth Amendment known the components of liberty in its manifold possibilities, they might have been more specific. They did not presume to have this insight. They knew times can blind us to certain truths and later generations can see that laws once thought necessary and proper in fact serve only to oppress. As the Constitution endures, persons in every generation can invoke its principles in their own search for greater freedom.

The judgment of the Court of Appeals for the Texas Fourteenth District is reversed, and the case is remanded for further proceedings not inconsistent with this opinion.

It is so ordered.

Justice SCALIA, with whom THE CHIEF JUSTICE and Justice THOMAS join, dissenting.

...

Most of the rest of today's opinion has no relevance to its actual holding—that the Texas statute "furthers no legitimate state interest which can justify" its application to petitioners under rational-basis review. Though there is discussion of "fundamental proposition[s]," and "fundamental decisions," nowhere does the Court's opinion declare that homosexual sodomy is a "fundamental right" under the Due Process Clause; nor does it subject the Texas law to the standard of review that would be appropriate (strict scrutiny) if homosexual sodomy were a "fundamental right." Thus, while overruling the outcome of Bowers, the Court leaves strangely untouched its central legal conclusion: "[R]espondent would have us announce ... a fundamental right to engage in homosexual sodomy. This we are quite unwilling to do." Instead, the Court simply describes petitioners' conduct as "an exercise of their liberty," which it undoubtedly is, and proceeds to apply an unheard-of form of rational-basis review that will have far-reaching implications beyond this case.

I begin with the Court's surprising readiness to reconsider a decision rendered a mere 17 years ago in *Bowers v. Hardwick*. ...

Today's approach to *stare decisis* invites us to overrule an erroneously decided precedent (including an "intensely divisive" decision) if: (1) its foundations have been "ero[ded]" by subsequent decisions; (2) it has been subject to "substantial and continuing" criticism; and (3) it has not induced "individual or societal reliance" that counsels against overturning. The problem is that Roe itself—which today's majority surely has no disposition to overrule—satisfies these conditions to at least the same degree as Bowers.

(1) A preliminary digressive observation with regard to the first factor: The Court's claim that *Planned Parenthood v. Casey* "casts some doubt" upon the holding in Bowers (or any other case, for that matter) does not withstand analysis. As far as its holding is concerned, Casey provided a less expansive right to abortion than did Roe, which was already on the books when Bowers was decided. And if the Court is referring not to the holding of Casey, but to the dictum of its famed sweet-mystery-of-life passage ... : That "casts some doubt" upon either the totality of our jurisprudence or else (presumably the right answer) nothing at all. I have never heard of a law that attempted to restrict one's "right to define" certain concepts; and if the passage calls into question the government's power to regulate actions based on one's self-defined "concept of existence, etc.," it is the passage that ate the rule of law.

I do not quarrel with the Court's claim that *Romer v. Evans* "eroded" the "foundations" of Bowers' rational-basis holding. But Roe and Casey have been equally "eroded" by *Washington v. Glucksberg*, which held that only fundamental rights, which are "deeply rooted in this Nation's history and tradition" qualify for anything other than rational-basis scrutiny under the doctrine of "substantive due process." Roe and Casey, of course, subjected the restriction of abortion to heightened scrutiny without even attempting to establish that the freedom to abort was rooted in this Nation's tradition.

Bowers, the Court says, has been subject to "substantial and continuing [criticism], disapproving of its reasoning in all respects, not just as to its historical assumptions." Exactly what those nonhistorical criticisms are, and whether the Court even agrees with them, are left unsaid, although the Court does cite two books. Of course, Roe too (and by extension Casey) had been (and still is) subject to unrelenting criticism, including criticism from the two commentators cited by the Court today.

That leaves, to distinguish the rock-solid, unamendable disposition of Roe from the readily overrulable Bowers, only the third factor. "[T]here has been," the Court says, "no individual or societal reliance on Bowers of the sort that could counsel against overturning its holding. ..." It seems to me that the "societal reliance" on the principles confirmed in Bowers and discarded today has been overwhelming. Countless judicial decisions and legislative enactments have relied on the ancient proposition that a governing majority's belief that certain sexual behavior is "immoral and unacceptable" constitutes a rational basis for regulation. We ourselves relied extensively on Bowers when we concluded, in *Barnes v. Glen Theatre, Inc.*, that Indiana's public indecency statute furthered "a substantial government interest in protecting order and morality." State laws against bigamy, same-sex marriage, adult incest, prostitution, masturbation, adultery, fornication, bestiality, and obscenity are likewise sustainable only in light of Bowers' validation of laws based on moral choices.

Every single one of these laws is called into question by today's decision; the Court makes no effort to cabin the scope of its decision to exclude them from its holding. The impossibility of distinguishing homosexuality from other traditional "morals" offenses is precisely why Bowers rejected the rational-basis challenge. "The law," it said, "is constantly based on notions of morality, and if all laws representing essentially moral choices are to be invalidated under the Due Process Clause, the courts will be very busy indeed."

...

Having decided that it need not adhere to *stare decisis*, the Court still must establish that Bowers was wrongly decided and that the Texas statute, as applied to petitioners, is unconstitutional.

Texas Penal Code Ann. § 21.06(a) (2003) undoubtedly imposes constraints on liberty. So do laws prohibiting prostitution, recreational use of heroin, and, for that matter, working more than 60 hours per week in a bakery. But there is no right to "liberty" under the Due Process Clause, though today's opinion repeatedly makes that claim. The Fourteenth Amendment expressly allows States to deprive their citizens of "liberty," so long as "due process of law" is provided:

"No state shall ... deprive any person of life, liberty, or property, without due process of law."

Our opinions applying the doctrine known as "substantive due process" hold that the Due Process Clause prohibits States from infringing fundamental liberty interests, unless the infringement is narrowly tailored to serve a compelling state interest.

We have held repeatedly, in cases the Court today does not overrule, that only fundamental rights qualify for this so-called "heightened scrutiny" protection, that is, rights which are "'deeply rooted in this Nation's history and tradition.'" All other liberty interests may be abridged or abrogated pursuant to a validly enacted state law if that law is rationally related to a legitimate state interest.

Bowers held, first, that criminal prohibitions of homosexual sodomy are not subject to heightened scrutiny because they do not implicate a "fundamental right" under the Due Process Clause. Noting that "[p]roscriptions against that conduct have ancient roots," that "[s]odomy was a criminal offense at common law and was forbidden by the laws of the original 13 States when they ratified the Bill of Rights," and that many States had retained their bans on sodomy, Bowers concluded that a right to engage in homosexual sodomy was not "'deeply rooted in this Nation's history and tradition'".

The Court today does not overrule this holding. Not once does it describe homosexual sodomy as a "fundamental right" or a "fundamental liberty interest," nor does it subject the Texas statute to strict scrutiny. Instead, having failed to establish that the right to homosexual sodomy is "'deeply rooted in this Nation's history and tradition,'" the Court concludes that the application of Texas's statute to petitioners' conduct fails the rational-basis test, and overrules Bowers' holding to the contrary. "The Texas statute furthers no legitimate state interest which can justify its intrusion into the personal and private life of the individual."

...

After discussing the history of antisodomy laws, the Court proclaims that, "it should be noted that there is no longstanding history in this country of laws directed at homosexual conduct as a distinct matter." This observation in no way casts into doubt the "definitive [historical] conclusio[n]," on which Bowers relied: that our Nation has a longstanding history of laws prohibiting sodomy in general—regardless of whether it was performed by same-sex or opposite-sex couples:

"It is obvious to us that neither of these formulations would extend a fundamental right to homosexuals to engage in acts of consensual sodomy. Proscriptions against that conduct have ancient roots. Sodomy was a criminal offense at common law and was forbidden by the laws of the original 13 States when they ratified the Bill of Rights. In 1868, when the Fourteenth Amendment was ratified, all but 5 of the 37 States in the Union had criminal sodomy laws. In fact, until 1961, all 50 States outlawed sodomy, and today, 24 States and the District of Columbia continue to provide criminal penalties for sodomy performed in private and between consenting adults. Against this background, to claim that a right to engage in such conduct is 'deeply rooted in this Nation's history and tradition' or 'implicit in the concept of ordered liberty' is, at best, facetious."

It is (as Bowers recognized) entirely irrelevant whether the laws in our long national tradition criminalizing homosexual sodomy were "directed at homosexual conduct as a distinct matter." Whether homosexual sodomy was prohibited by a law targeted at same-sex sexual relations or by a more general law prohibiting both homosexual and hetero-sexual sodomy, the only relevant point is that it was criminalized—which suffices to establish that homosexual sodomy is not a right "deeply rooted in our Nation's history and tradition." The Court today agrees that homosexual sodomy was criminalized and thus does not dispute the facts on which Bowers actually relied.

...

Realizing that fact, the Court instead says: "[W]e think that our laws and traditions in the past half century are of most relevance here. These references show an emerging awareness that liberty gives substantial protection to adult persons in deciding how to conduct their private lives in matters pertaining to sex." Apart from the fact that such an "emerging awareness" does not establish a "fundamental right," the statement is factually false. States continue to prosecute all sorts of crimes by adults "in matters pertaining to sex": prostitution, adult incest, adultery, obscenity, and child pornography. Sodomy laws, too, have been enforced "in the past half century," in which there have been 134 reported cases involving prosecutions for consensual, adult, homosexual sodomy. In relying, for evidence of an "emerging recognition," upon the American Law Institute's 1955 recommendation not to criminalize "consensual sexual relations conducted in private," the Court ignores the fact that this recommendation was "a point of resistance in most of the states that considered adopting the Model Penal Code."

In any event, an "emerging awareness" is by definition not "deeply rooted in this Nation's history and tradition[s]," as we have said "fundamental right" status requires. Constitutional entitlements do not spring into existence because some States choose to lessen or eliminate criminal sanctions on certain behavior. Much less do they spring into existence, as the Court seems to believe, because foreign nations de-criminalize conduct. The Bowers majority opinion never relied on "values we share with a wider civilization," but rather rejected the claimed right to sodomy on the ground that such a right was not " 'deeply rooted in this Nation's history and tradition.'" Bowers' rational-basis holding is likewise devoid of any reliance on the views of a "wider civilization." The Court's discussion of these foreign views (ignoring, of course, the many countries that have retained criminal prohibitions on sodomy) is therefore meaningless dicta. Dangerous dicta, however, since "this Court ... should not impose foreign moods, fads, or fashions on Americans."

I turn now to the ground on which the Court squarely rests its holding: the contention that there is no rational basis for the law here under attack. This proposition is so out of accord with our jurisprudence—indeed, with the jurisprudence of any society we know—that it requires little discussion.

The Texas statute undeniably seeks to further the belief of its citizens that certain forms of sexual behavior are "immoral and unacceptable," the same interest furthered by criminal laws against fornication, bigamy, adultery, adult incest, bestiality, and obscenity. Bowers held that this was a legitimate state interest. The Court today reaches the opposite conclusion. The Texas statute, it says, "furthers no legitimate state interest which can justify its intrusion into the personal and private life of the individual." The Court embraces instead Justice STEVENS' declaration in his Bowers dissent, that "'the fact that the governing majority in a State has traditionally viewed a particular practice as immoral is not a sufficient reason for upholding a law prohibiting the practice.'" This effectively decrees the end of all morals legislation. If, as the Court asserts, the promotion of majoritarian sexual morality is not even a legitimate state interest, none of the above-mentioned laws can survive rational-basis review.

...

I dissent.

Questions

1. What does the Court mean when it terms homosexuals a class?
2. Does homosexuality have explicit discussion in the Constitution?
3. How does the idea of moral disapproval fit in the Court's reasoning?
4. If the Court construes a targeting of one group over another, would it be reasonable for tax cheats to make a similar claim?
5. How does the Court overrule itself in less than 17 years?
6. What role does morality play in this case, as stated by the Court?
7. In the dissent by Justice Scalia and Justice Thomas, how do they deal with their own precedent of Bowers?
8. In what way does the dissent make Western tradition or morality relevant to its decision making?
9. How does the dissent argue that "conduct" cannot be the basis of some fundamental right?

to consenting adults engaged in consensual same-sex activity. In *Lawrence v. Texas*,[68] the court overturned the Texas law criminalizing consensual sodomy. As a result, code provisions, such as the design below, had to be dramatically eliminated. Pre-*Lawrence*, the mere act of homosexuality was considered criminal. The code provision was unequivocal and was declared unconstitutional by *Lawrence*.

Sec. 21.06. Homosexual conduct

(a) A person commits an offense if he engages in deviate sexual intercourse with another individual of the same sex.[69]

Once the Supreme Court struck down consensual sodomy as being protected under the Fourteenth Amendment, the state shifted to other statutes that dwelt upon the forcible version of a sexual assault. For example, the seriousness of forcible sodomy would be covered under Aggravated Assault, the pertinent provision below:

Sec. 22.021. Aggravated sexual assault

(a) A person commits an offense:
   (1) if the person:
      (A) intentionally or knowingly:
         (i) causes the penetration of the anus or sexual organ of another person by any means, without that person's consent;
         (ii) causes the penetration of the mouth of another person by the sexual organ of the actor, without that person's consent; or
         (iii) causes the sexual organ of another person, without that person's consent, to contact or penetrate the mouth, anus, or sexual organ of another person, including the actor; or
      (B) intentionally or knowingly:
         (i) causes the penetration of the anus or sexual organ of a child by any means;
         (ii) causes the penetration of the mouth of a child by the sexual organ of the actor;
         (iii) causes the sexual organ of a child to contact or penetrate the mouth, anus, or sexual organ of another person, including the actor;
         (iv) causes the anus of a child to contact the mouth, anus, or sexual organ of another person, including the actor; or
         (v) causes the mouth of a child to contact the anus or sexual organ of another person, including the actor.[70]

As if a seismic culture shift, the once universally condemned practice of consensual sodomy had changed overnight.[71] Of course, forcible, violent sodomy will be covered by a host of other sexual offense statutes. Sodomy has meant a whole host of sexual practices including oral sexuality (fellatio and cunnilingus), anal intercourse, and even bestiality.

§ 18.2-67.1. Forcible sodomy

A. An accused shall be guilty of forcible sodomy if he or she engages in cunnilingus, fellatio, analingus, or anal intercourse with a complaining witness whether or not his or her spouse, or causes a complaining witness, whether or not his or her spouse, to engage in such acts with any other person

§ 18.2-67.2. Object sexual penetration; penalty

A. An accused shall be guilty of inanimate or animate object sexual penetration if he or she penetrates the labia majora or anus of a complaining witness, whether or not his or her spouse, other than for a bona fide medical purpose, or causes such complaining witness to so penetrate his or her own body with an object or causes a complaining witness, whether or not his or her spouse, to engage in such acts with any other person or to penetrate, or to be penetrated by, an animal.[72]

The term "deviate" precedes sexual intercourse in most legislative designs because the framers originally saw these practices at odds with vaginal–penal intercourse. These practices were out of the ordinary and in many circles, religious and legal alike, were declared "unnatural" and an abomination of nature itself. Jurisdictions like Rhode Island labeled the offense a Crime Against Nature until 1998.[73] Most learned treatises in the law, from Blackstone to Wigmore, employ similar language. Whether heterosexual or homosexual in practice, the acts were frowned upon. With fire and brimstone, the American sexual morality crept heavily into the lawmaker's pen, and with the same ferocity as was witnessed during the drafting days of adultery and fornication, which were capital offenses. Modernists can't play this type of moralizing and one wonders whether the law has the capacity to dwell on such subjects.

However, after considering the historical roots for the prohibitions, critics can at least appreciate the justifications. Let's assess a few. First, before the more contemporary view that sexual activity can be for pleasure as well as procreation, the West separated pleasure from sex since the former was not only sinful but irrelevant to the act. Procreation was the *a priori* reason for sexual encounters in the confines of marriage. Procreation remains a medical impossibility by and through sodomy. Consider the definition:

> "Deviate sexual intercourse" means sexual intercourse per os or per anus between human beings and any form of sexual intercourse with an animal. The term also includes penetration, however slight, of the genitals or anus of another person with a foreign object for any purpose other than good-faith medical, hygienic, or law enforcement procedures. "Foreign object" includes any physical object not a part of the actor's body.[74]

In no way should we impute that the procreative mission is devoid of pleasure. Given the size of families previous to World War II, one can deduce that children and the pleasure factor go hand in hand. Second, our religious heritage, at point the Judeo-Christian ethic, harshly viewed these practices as outside the mainstream of sexual movement. Whether the Roman Catholic or Orthodox Jew, the Muslim or Evangelical, religious tradition provides a basis for reacting negatively to these practices. Not surprisingly, church and religious leaders throughout the world still grapple with these issues each day—the ordination of gays, the moral legitimacy of homosexual conduct, same-sex marriage, birth control and abortion are a few stones on the giant rock mound of moral dilemmas. The Koran, the Talmud, and the Bible regularly dwell on these topics.[75]

Third, there has been legitimate health risks associated with all sorts of sexual behavior, which by no means is exclusively reserved to any one group or practice. Heterosexual behavior can transmit the 500 or so sexually transmitted diseases (STDs) as fast as any homosexual practice. Previous to these modern conceptions, our culture was not weighed down as heavily with these types of problems. In essence, we condemned the different and the distinct while trying to be a puritanical nation. AIDS, for example, cannot be minimized or downplayed as a health threat and sodomy is one of the avenues of transmission. Prostitution is as well. Indeed, prostitution remits to its customers a rash of every proportion. These facts lead to some very telling health conclusions that the criminal law system needs be cognizant of. Unprotected practices of sodomy, nonregulated places of prostitution, brothels and bathhouses, public rendezvous for stranger sex, and other new age sexual interplay, generate health costs without many positive benefits. Critics charge that references to the "heterosexual" types of statutes are missing the boat and chide those who cannot appreciate what their ultimate aim is—the focus on homosexuals and their selective prosecution.[76]

These arguments are by no means unassailable and, in fact, questions of privacy and personal autonomy weigh in this type of analysis. If the state is the guarantor of human freedom, what role will the state play in the regulation of sexual practices and lifestyles? If one can accept that both heterosexuals and homosexuals engage in many sexual practices at odds with the historic copulation standard voluntarily, does the state want to referee the bedroom and assure that only legitimate sexual practices occur? For the past three decades or so, the legal system has witnessed a generous redrafting of statute when sexual conduct is consensual. Professor Janet Halley traces the repeal phenomena in her insightful work, *Reasoning about Sodomy*.[77] She comments:

> This repeal history has left in place only five statutes targeting same-sex sodomy and not cross-sex sodomy,[78] but eighteen facially neutral statutes. Michigan maintains not only a facially neutral sodomy statute, but also three statutes distinguishing between gay male, lesbian, and heterosexual encounters. The statutes prohibit "gross indecency," a term that may include fellatio, and apply to acts between men, to acts between women, and to acts between a man and a woman. By their terms, these statutes apply to private as well as public conduct. Application of these statutes to consensual activity in the home has been declared a violation of state privacy guidelines in an unpublished lower-court decision.[79]

As here, and across the nation, it is clear that these sexual practices, when consensual, are now subject to some level of privacy protection. Sentimentally, most would concur with this trend for few Americans wish their government to invade the bedroom in an attempt to ferret out sexual behavior between consenting adults. The better policy might be the maintenance of sexual lifestyles that are sustainable and of reasonable duration, that are based on singular devotion and fidelity, and that construct a base on the buttresses of moderation and virtue. However well-intentioned these laws may be, their future will depend on efficacy and moral ardor. To proselytize by and through law simply won't do.

This is primarily the reason the Supreme Court eliminated the consensual sodomy category and exclusively defined the act in violent or forcible terms. Sex is a difficult thing to criminalize in general, though this resistance does not forbid the legislative attempt to curb the practices. Of significant import has been the U.S. Supreme Court's approval of the criminalization of consensual sodomy in the State of Georgia.[80] Here the consensual sodomy statute was attacked on a series of constitutional grounds, from privacy to equal protection and to the allegation that the practice of homosexuality between consenting adults was a fundamental constitutional protection. To strict constructionists of the founding documents, it would be an impossible task finding reference to sexual rights. Chief Justice Burger wrote in the majority that "there is no such thing as a fundamental right to commit homosexual sodomy."[81]

The Court further resisted attempts to throw out what it termed "the nation's history and tradition,"[82] the net effect to "cast aside millennia of moral teaching."[83] That the Court looks to tradition in its thirst to solve this type of problem is undeniable as the majority finds:

> [s]odomy was a criminal offense at common law and was forbidden by laws of the original 13 states when they ratified the Bill of Rights. In 1868, when the Fourteenth Amendment was ratified, all but

5 of the 37 States in the Union had criminal sodomy laws. In fact, until 1961, all 50 States outlawed sodomy, and today, 24 States and the District of Columbia continue to provide criminal penalties for sodomy performed in private and between consenting adults.[84]

Professor Halley calls this argument an "historiographical embarrassment" because "the history of sodomy shows a startling variation in the kinds of physical acts deemed to be sodomitical."[85]

In this very close and heated decision (5-4), the Court mirrors the frustration and division on this very controversial criminal codification. All of these cross-currents were resolved in *Lawrence v. Texas,*[86] which made clear that privacy interests outweighed any compelling argument the state could muster. In the majority opinion, the Court concluded:

The present case does not involve minors. It does not involve persons who might be injured or coerced or who are situated in relationships where consent might not easily be refused. It does not involve public conduct or prostitution. It does not involve whether the government must give formal recognition to any relationship that homosexual persons seek to enter. The case does involve two adults who, with full and mutual consent from each other, engaged in sexual practices common to a homosexual lifestyle. The petitioners are entitled to respect for their private lives. The State cannot demean their existence or control their destiny by making their private sexual conduct a crime. Their right to liberty under the Due Process Clause gives them the full right to engage in their conduct without intervention of the government. "It is a promise of the Constitution that there is a realm of personal liberty which the government may not enter."[87] The Texas statute furthers no legitimate state interest which can justify its intrusion into the personal and private life of the individual.

Had those who drew and ratified the Due Process Clauses of the Fifth Amendment or the Fourteenth Amendment known the components of liberty in its manifold possibilities, they might have been more specific. They did not presume to have this insight. They knew times can blind us to certain truths and later generations can see that laws once thought necessary and proper, in fact, serve only to oppress. As the Constitution endures, persons in every generation can invoke its principles in their own search for greater freedom.[88]

Lawrence, however, is a close case, with a strong and powerful dissent. A close reading of Justice Scalia, as included in Case 6.2, educates the reader on the historical bases for the criminalization.

It seems to me that the "societal reliance" on the principles confirmed in Bowers and discarded today has been overwhelming. Countless judicial decisions and legislative enactments have relied on the ancient proposition that a governing majority's belief that certain sexual behavior is "immoral and unacceptable" constitutes a rational basis for regulation ... We ourselves relied extensively on Bowers when we concluded, ... that Indiana's public indecency statute furthered "a substantial government interest in protecting order and morality,"... State laws against bigamy, same-sex marriage, adult incest, prostitution, masturbation, adultery, fornication, bestiality, and obscenity are likewise sustainable only in light of Bowers' validation of laws based on moral choices. Every single one of these laws is called into question by today's decision; the Court makes no effort to cabin the scope of its decision to exclude them from its holding. ... The impossibility of distinguishing homosexuality from other traditional "morals" offenses is precisely why Bowers rejected the rational-basis challenge. "The law," it said, "is constantly based on notions of morality, and if all laws representing essentially moral choices are to be invalidated under the Due Process Clause, the courts will be very busy indeed"(citations omitted).[89]

NECROPHILIA

ELEMENTS

- Sexual defilement
- Of a corpse
- With intent

At the outer edge of outrage about sexual perversion rests the hideous crime of necrophilia. To the dismay of the normal exists a small band of warped personalities whose sexual gratification is drawn from defiling and sexually desecrating the deceased.[90] The problem, while not common, has been escalating due to the rise of satanic cults. Satanic ritualism, in its more bizarre forms, employs dead animals, blood, and even embalmed and rotting remains of the human species. Also known as "Abuse of a Corpse," the law inflicts penalties on those who desecrate the dead. A code provision from Georgia contains this language:

§ 16-6-7. Necrophilia

(a) A person commits the offense of necrophilia when he performs any sexual act with a dead human body involving the sex organs of the one and the mouth, anus, penis, or vagina of the other.[91]

Even in the age where judgment is frowned upon, necrophilia musters up very little support. "Necrophilia is a psychosexual disorder and is categorized with the group of disorders that comprise the paraphilias, a subtype of psychosexual disorder involving unusual or bizarre fantasies or acts that are necessary for full sexual excitement. In all, there are eight named paraphilias listed in the American Psychiatric Association's *Diagnostic and Statistical Manual of Mental Disorders*, including pedophilia (the act or fantasy of engaging in sexual activity with prepubescent children), exhibitionism (repetitive acts of exposing the genitals for the purpose of achieving sexual excitement), and sexual masochism (sexual arousal attained through being humiliated, bound, beaten, or otherwise made to suffer). In addition to the eight named paraphilias, there is a group of "not otherwise specified" paraphilias, which includes necrophilia along with such disorders as telephone scatologia (obscene phone calls), zoophilia (animals), coprophilia (feces), klismaphilia (enemas), and urophilia (urine)."[92]

In this panoply of "philias," some would argue that the behavior is harmless if not acted upon with aggression. Certain sectors of the psychiatric community have a difficult time labeling any conduct as perverse or criminal in design and can see a place for fantasies and behaviors that do not lead to another's harm. But, one is really hard pressed to see how sexual activity with corpses can be intrinsically a fantasy and not a perversion. Clearly one who seeks the humiliation of others in a sexual context may or may not have difficulties with the psyche, though it would be impossible to paint necrophilia in a positive light for any purpose. The level of self-degradation guarantees the rot of mind and body and augurs a form of mental dementia that is rather unparalleled.

Much to the distress of law enforcement, cemetery owners, mortuary facilities, and hospitals each has ongoing concerns about the potential for defilement. Most states have crafted specialized statutory language to account for this deed and realize that traditional rape and other sexual offense charges will not withstand any defense challenge.[93] Other states entwine the continuous pattern of the defendant's behavior, say murder that evolves into defilement, and reconstruct life to fit the ongoing felony. These jurisdictions resist the artificial defense that the perpetrator waited until the victim died, at his own hand, to commit the rape to avoid the consequences. In Massachusetts, as illustration, a court remarked that "[i]n the circumstances of one continuous event, it does not matter whether the victim's death preceded or followed the sexual attack."[94] Some states lack statutory constructions to hold one accountable for the activity and must rely on other aligned offenses for the prosecution. California, for example, has only recently enacted a necrophilia statute and had in the past mistakenly relied on rape charges as a substitute.[95] The mistake was so profound that a court and jury had little choice but to set free the perpetrators since the victim lacks the requisite intellect and will to be raped. As a matter of law and fact, a deceased lacks the capacity to consent to any practice let alone a sexual one.[96] In *People v. Kelly*, a California decision lays out the unavoidable result:

> It is manifest that the "feelings" of a female cannot be offended nor does the victim suffer "outrage" where she is dead when sexual penetration has occurred. Thus, it appears that the female must be alive at the moment of penetration in order to support a conviction of rape.[97]

From another perspective, a rape charge is no more than a legal and factual impossibility—a defense not lost on parties incorrectly charged.[98] Nor will attempted rape be applicable in these circumstances.[99]

Learn how the *Diagnostic Symptom Manual*, used by psychiatrists, describes necrophilia at http://www.dsm5.org/Documents/Sex%20and%20GID%20Lit%20Reviews/Paraphilias/KAFKA.PARNOS.pdf

---

SEXUAL TRANSMISSION OF HIV

Another evolving issue in sexual offense laws regards the knowing transmission of HIV (human immunodeficiency virus). While civil remedies and actions appear on the legal landscape, the criminalization of the transmission is a recent phenomenon. Most states have yet to address the complex dynamics in criminalizing the behavior, though on the international scene efforts are afoot.[100] Those that do, have a heavy burden when proving the requisite intent because the statutory constructions uniformly insist on a specific intent mens rea. Arkansas has dabbled aggressively in this area of emerging law.

5-14-123. Exposing another person to human immunodeficiency virus

(a) A person with acquired immunodeficiency syndrome or who tests positive for the presence of human immunodeficiency virus antigen or antibodies is infectious to another person through the exchange of a body fluid during sexual intercourse and through the parenteral transfer of blood or a blood product and under these circumstances is a danger to the public.

(b) A person commits the offense of exposing another person to human immunodeficiency virus if the person knows he or she has tested positive for human immunodeficiency virus and exposes another person to human immunodeficiency virus infection through the parenteral transfer of blood or a blood product or engages in sexual penetration with another person without first having informed the other person of the presence of human immunodeficiency virus.

(c) (1) As used in this section, "sexual penetration" means sexual intercourse, cunnilingus, fellatio, anal intercourse, or any other intrusion, however slight, of any part of a person's body or of any object into a genital or anal opening of another person's body.

(2)   However, emission of semen is not required.

(d) Exposing another person to human immunodeficiency virus is a Class A felony.[101]

Throughout this provision, one witnesses the mind that knows and is aware of a condition, has received notice of specific testing, and then fully knowing this condition, exposes another to the viral infection.[102] The statute mentions sexual penetration and blood transfer as the chief basis for exposure and curiously leaves out the shared needle route. Sexual penetration includes literally any orifice of the body without much concern for the likelihood of infection depending upon the orifice. While well intentioned, one can readily discern the various struggles that are likely in this type of litigation. Why would the state seek the serious penalties that result from a conviction without distinguishing the potential for AIDS transmission in the diverse cavities of the body? Does HIV transmit identically during anal intercourse and fellatio? Do objects cause HIV transmission? What objects are we referring to?[103] How does one really know what another knows about their present condition? How does one account for intentional ignorance or the avoidance of testing? Why does notice, telling a willing partner about the condition, negate the offense? Can a party consent to harm? Consent, as a fundamental principle in law, cannot be freely given in conduct that is, in fact, illegal. If HIV transmission violates health laws and criminal provisions, how does a victim willingly waive and consent to that transmission? What will the net effect of this statutory construction be—an increase in testing or the outright avoidance of the lab that announces the tragic news?[104]

For an overview of legislative attempts that seek to thwart the transmission of HIV Aids, visit: http://www.ncvc.org/ncvc/main.aspx?dbName=DocumentViewer&DocumentID=32468#2

Public policy reasons are extraordinarily persuasive and this author does not make light of the noble purposes behind the law. Transmission is a death sentence. Of course, this game of risk and nondisclosure is another by-product of a world that increasingly tolerates sexual promiscuity. Cavalier sexual activity does have its consequences, some being incredibly risky. Many states are framing laws that are keenly intent on criminalizing the transmission.[105] High profile cases involving actor Rock Hudson and NBA star Magic Johnson are instructive for a host of reasons. First, this type of case indicates the terminality of a lifestyle that can reap grave consequences. Second, both cases portray the difficulties inherent in the matter of consent and knowledge. How and when does one know of the virus and is it fair to impute knowledge when a history of multiple partners and promiscuity increases the odds of infection?

How exactly the law will evolve itself is a story in its first chapter. The element of knowledge will be the key to the imposition of any criminal liability. The actor who transmits will be responsible when he or she has "(1) actual knowledge of HIV infection; (2) the presence of symptoms associated with HIV/AIDS; and, (3) actual knowledge that a previous sex partner is infected with HIV."[106]

In our lifetimes, we cannot predict how this trend in criminalization will exactly unfold only that its presence will be markedly felt in the legal system.[107]

INCEST

ELEMENTS

- Sexual intercourse
- With family members
- Based on consanguinity or affinity
- With intent

Sexual intercourse between select bloodlines and familial relations has been universally condemned throughout human history. Incest connotes a sexual offense between those related by marriage, adoption, or genetics. The rationale behind the prohibition is fundamentally twofold. First, the hereditary and genetic consequences from reproduction in and among those interrelated are negative and destructive, and, second, the breach of bond and intimate trust that naturally exist in familial relationships. In this last bastion of the perverse, there are fringe groups holding otherwise. Amazingly, these aberrant thinkers rationalize their way through another thicket of deviance that even the worst of criminal offenders find disagreeable.

Incest constitutes an attack on blood (consanguinity), and relations and status (affinity), and the ramifications from unwanted pregnancy to physical trauma, which are exacerbated by the natural and abiding trust that children have for those who oversee development. From whatever angle the offense is scrutinized, the act and its consequence inexorably alter a person for the remainder of his/her lifetime. Research on sexual abusers, prostitution, and deviant sexual lifestyles usually demonstrates the interplay between incestuous experiences and the lifestyle chosen.[108]

Child case workers, special units dedicated to children and their defense, have witnessed a staggering increase in the reporting and commission of these types of offenses. The situation is especially acute when one considers the collapse of the traditional family, the patterns of multiple marriage, divorce, and transient inhabitants who live with children. Birth children sometimes have no real and meaningful idea who their real father might be if the lifestyle has been inhabited by multiple partners. The sanctity of family and the innocence of children have no assurances in the world of incest.

The key to any successful prosecution of an incest case rests in relationships. The trier of fact will have to be convinced that the victim suffered at the hands of a particular class of person that is prohibited from having sexual relations with that victim. Biological parents and siblings plainly meet the qualification. So do aunts, uncles, and close cousins, usually first and, in some cases, the second cousins, and even more remote degrees of separation. Within the biological sphere, our parties are easy enough to identify. What about stepparents and stepbrothers and sisters? What about grandparents and siblings? Read closely the qualifying parties under the Pennsylvania statute below:

§ 4302. Incest

A person is guilty of incest, a felony of the second degree, if that person knowingly marries or cohabits or has sexual intercourse with an ancestor or descendant, a brother or sister of the whole or half blood, or an uncle, aunt, nephew, or niece of the whole blood. The relationships referred to in this section include blood relationships without regard to legitimacy, and relationship of parent and child by adoption.[109]

Stepchildren are less protected under the Pennsylvania design than they are in Utah. Critics of this liberalization reference the power imbalance and the position of trust that resides in these relationships.[110]

The messages of sexual conduct are confusing enough for a stranger let alone those living in the same domicile. Adoption changes this qualification no matter how artificial it is. Ludicrous is the claimant who argues that the Court's signature on an adoption decree now makes the step-child an untouchable, while previous to its execution the child was fair game. One gets the feeling that the problems of amalgamated and blended families are now so confusing that the law's head is turning like a whirlwind. In addition, the statute is silent as to cousins in any degree—a fact surprising to some. Utah's code provision is more encompassing.

(2) (a) An actor is guilty of incest when, under circumstances not amounting to rape, rape of a child, or aggravated sexual assault, the actor knowingly and intentionally:
   (i)   engages in conduct under Subsection (2)(b)(i), (ii), (iii), or (iv); or
   (ii) provides a human egg or seminal fluid under Subsection (2)(b)(v).
   (b) Conduct referred to under Subsection (2)(a) is:
   (i)   sexual intercourse between the actor and a person the actor knows has kinship to the actor as a related person;
   (ii) the insertion or placement of the provider's seminal fluid into the vagina, cervix, or uterus of a related person by means other than sexual intercourse;
   (iii) providing or making available his seminal fluid for the purpose of insertion or placement of the fluid into the vagina, cervix, or uterus of a related person by means other than sexual intercourse;
   (iv) a woman 18 years of age or older who:
       (A) knowingly allows the insertion of the seminal fluid of a provider into her vagina, cervix, or uterus by means other than sexual intercourse; and
       (B) knows that the seminal fluid is that of a person with whom she has kinship as a related person; or
   (v)   providing the actor's sperm or human egg that is used to conduct *in vitro* fertilization, or any other means of fertilization, with the human egg or sperm of a person who is a related person.
   (c) This Subsection (2) does not prohibit providing a fertilized human egg if the provider of the fertilizing sperm is not a related person regarding the person providing the egg.[111]

Utah also punishes more harshly by designating the offense a felony while Pennsylvania maintains the offense a misdemeanor.[112] "The relationships referred to in this provision include blood relationships without regard to legitimacy, and relationship of parent and child by adoption. "Cohabit" means to live together under the representation or appearance of being married."[113]

A common defense rebuttal claims that incest merges with a simultaneous rape prosecution and that it cannot remain a separate offense in eventual sentencing. Yet any inspection of the rape statute paints a very distinct criminal offense. True, both witness sexual intercourse, as either broadly or narrowly defined. True, both are acts of sexual impermissibility. The distinction rests not in the act, but in the act's target. A charge of incest would not withstand the defense that the victim was unrelated in any sense, and it seems just as compelling to claim that a rape could or could not exist in incest cases. Is it rape when a brother has sexual relations with a sister? It could be rightfully argued that any parent having sexual relations with a child simultaneously rapes and engages in incest since the victim is incapable of consent. A few states have struggled with the differentiation, such as Utah whose language "under circumstances not amounting to a rape," has provided defense strategists with the avenue to challenge one charge or the other. In *Montoya*,[114] the Utah Supreme Court rejected the defense contention that the State was under an affirmative duty to prove the lack of rape or aggravated sexual assault intent before proceeding with the incest charge. Because the state charged both incest and aggravated sexual assault, was it required to disprove one charge to the detriment of the other? Would it have been better for the prosecution team to pick one charge instead of two? It would appear that the two charges are, as the defense put it, repugnant to each other. The defendant's argument fell on deaf ears. The Court remarked:

> The State acted within the bounds of the law by charging aggravated sexual assault and incest in the alternative. Montoya's defense was not prejudiced for lack of notice or ability to prepare a defense. No material facts have been, nor need be, alleged which are inconsistent or contradictory.[115]

While the result can be applauded, is it the correct resolution in a legal sense? If you were a prosecutor, which offense would you have chosen? Dramatic escalation in interfamily offenses should give policymaker, legislators, and community leaders sufficient reason to pause and reflect on how this tragedy can be ameliorated.

Incest, aside from its inherent tragedy, impacts and affects in vastly stronger ways than many other offenses. A wide assortment of support groups are available to incest survivors. Review the list below.

National Children's Advocacy Center
210 Pratt Avenue
Huntsville, AL 35801
Phone: (256) 533-KIDS (256-533-5437)
Fax: (256) 534-6883
www.nationalcac.org

Prevent Child Abuse America
500 South Michigan Avenue, Suite #200
Chicago, IL 60611
Phone: (312) 663-3520
Fax: (312) 939-8962
1-800-244-5373
www.preventchildabuse.org

National Council on Child Abuse & Family Violence
1025 Connecticut Avenue, Suite #1000
Washington, D.C. 20036
Phone: (202) 429-6695
www.nccafv.org

National HIV/AIDS Hotline
Centers for Disease Control and Prevention
1600 Clifton Road
Atlanta, GA 30333
Phone: (404) 498-1515
1-800-311-3435
www.cdc.gov

National Center for Victims of Crime
2000 M Street, NW, Suite 480
Washington, D.C. 20036
Toll-free helpline: 1-800-FYI-CALL
Monday–Friday, 8:30 a.m. to 8:30 p.m. ET
www.ncvc.org

RAINN (Rape, Abuse & Incest National Network)
1-800-656-HOPE
www.rainn.org

Survivors of Incest Anonymous
World Service Office
P.O. Box 190
Benson, MD 21018
Phone: (419) 893-3322
www.siawso.org

ALIGNED OFFENSES INVOLVING CHILDREN

Much to the dismay of the good and virtuous citizenry, sexual abuse of children shows signs of a vigorous escalation. As children become sexually objectified in the mainstream culture, and visual imagery and content of popular media continually impress the normalcy and urgency of sexual activity at younger and younger ages, is it any wonder that sexual abuse rates rise?[16] One tragic offshoot of this objectification is that the distorted imagery makes acceptable conduct that was once dreamed unimaginable in children. (See Figure 6.5 for the rates of never-married teenagers who have had sexual intercourse.[117])

The scandal with former President Bill Clinton manifests the confusion where a significant portion of youth believe, just as he supposedly did, that oral sex is not sex at all, but just something one does that is a harmless sideshow. Another curious result has been the proliferation of predators and even caregivers, such as foster families and adoptive families, who have sufficiently decriminalized sexual activity in the young, at least in their own minds. This mental shift affords the party, who was once described as predator and molester, as just another being with an alternative form of sexual expression. The demise of any sensible morality sees its void filled with amorality or ethical indifference.

There is nothing new in this conversation because justice professionals have known for years how cheap and vacuous sexual activity has become for so many youth. Unfortunately they have learned much of their behavior, from not only the media and culture, but their own caregivers who engage in all sorts of once-condemned behavior. One of the greatest tragedies is the silence, the lack of outrage regarding the sexual molestation of children. Without question, we are witnessing a "numbing and dumbing down of our historical moral outrage."[118] In this jaded, amoral wasteland, one loses the feeling of outrage that should accompany every act of molestation and sexual abuse.

Failure to Protect Child from Abuse

Parents and other caregivers are under an affirmative duty to care for and protect the children that are entrusted to them. Unfortunately, too many families witness the parent who knows of sexual abuse by another family member and takes no action to halt the activity. In sexual cases, the negligence is even more mind-boggling. Researchers identify a long list of potential effects when sexual offenses continue in the domicile, including: "fears, anxiety, phobias, sleep and eating disturbances,

Female	1995	2002	2006-2008
15–19 years of age	49.3%	45.5%	41.6%
15–17 years of age	38.0%	*30.3%	27.7%
18–19 years of age	68.0%	68.8%	59.7%
Male	1995	2002	2006-2008
15–19 years of age	55.2%	*45.7%	42.6%
15–17 years of age	43.1%	*31.3%	28.8%
18–19 years of age	75.4%	*64.3%	65.2%

*Change from 1995 to 2002 is statistically significant at the 5 percent level.

Figure 6.5   Percent of never-married teenagers 15 to 19 years of age who have had intercourse, listed by age and sex: United States, 1995, 2002, and 2006–2008.

CASE 6.3

COMMONWEALTH V. CARDWELL
357 Super. Ct. 38, 515 A. 2d 311, app den 515 Pa Super 573, 527 A. 2d 535 (1986)

During the relevant time period, appellant Julia Cardwell (Julia) lived in a house in Philadelphia in a family unit with her daughter, Alicia, and her husband, Clyde Cardwell (Clyde), Alicia's stepfather. For at least four years, beginning approximately in 1979, Clyde engaged in a pattern of sexual abuse of his stepdaughter Alicia. When Alicia was "about eleven" years old, Clyde began to buy her sexually stimulating clothing. He then began to photograph the child while clothed and in sexually explicit positions. Later, these photographic sessions included taking of photographs of Alicia either totally nude or wearing only stockings and garter belts. It was Clyde's habit to write sexually suggestive notes to Alicia on an almost daily basis.

Alicia testified that Clyde had vaginal intercourse with her on four occasions and on one occasion had attempted anal intercourse. Alicia became pregnant by Clyde twice in 1983 and had abortions both times, the second abortion occurring on October 18, 1983. There was also testimony that Clyde had sex with the child with the use of a vibrator. The last instance of intercourse occurred in 1984.

Alicia testified that she did not tell anyone about any of the sexual abuse until she told her mother after the second abortion. On cross-examination, Alicia admitted that at first she "played a sort of guessing game with [her mother]" and that it was not until some time in November, 1983, that Julia clearly understood that Clyde had been abusing Alicia.

Julia wrote two lengthy letters to Clyde in January and February of 1984, indicating her full knowledge of this abhorrent situation and warning him vaguely that she would not tolerate it. We note that Alicia testified that she and Julia were afraid of Clyde, that Clyde beat up Julia on one occasion, that he threw and broke things in the house, that he had punched a number of holes in the walls of the house, and that he carried a .357 magnum pistol, which he kept on the mantelpiece. In February of 1984, Julia moved some of her and Alicia's clothes to her mother's (Alicia's grandmother's) house. However, both Julia and Alicia remained at home with Clyde. In March 1984, Julia applied for a transfer of Alicia from her school to a school closer to Julia's mother's house. In April 1984, however, Julia's mother's house was demolished by fire, causing the death of Julia's father. The record reveals Julia took no further steps to relieve the situation until Alicia ran away from home on September 14, 1984.

On October 2, 1984, a criminal complaint was sworn against Julia Cardwell, listing Alicia as complainant and charging Julia with violating 18 Pa.C.S.A. § 4304, stating that she: "as parent supervising [Alicia] ... knowingly endangered the welfare of said child by violating a duty of care, protection, and/or support, to wit: defendant was aware that Clyde Cardwell was having sex with complainant and taking Polaroid™ pictures of complainant in various sexually explicit positions without reporting this to authorities. ..."

Julia was tried and convicted in a bench trial in Municipal Court of Philadelphia. She was sentenced to one-year probation and appealed the judgment of sentence to Common

Pleas Court by filing a petition for a writ of certiorari. Judge Ned L. Hirsh of the Philadelphia Court of Common Pleas denied the writ of certiorari on August 13, 1985. This appeal of the order denying the writ of certiorari followed. On appeal, appellant challenges the sufficiency both of the complaint and of the evidence. ...

18 Pa.C.S.A. § 4304, Endangering the welfare of children, provides:

A parent, guardian, or other person supervising the welfare of a child under 18 years of age commits a misdemeanor of the second degree if he knowingly endangers the welfare of the child by violating a duty of care, protection or support.

Appellant alleges that this statute requires a "knowing act" of endangering the welfare of a child, and appellant implies that an omission to act cannot satisfy the statute. We do not agree. The crime of endangering the welfare of a child is a specific intent offense. The intent element required by § 4303 is a knowing violation of a duty of care. We must, therefore, interpret when an accused knowingly violates his or her duty of care.

This court previously discussed the issue of a parent's duty of care in the context of a challenge to the sufficiency of evidence on a conviction for involuntary manslaughter. In *Commonwealth v. Howard*, 265 Pa.Super. 535, 402 A.2d 674 (1979), we upheld the conviction of a mother who failed to protect her child from the physical abuse of the mother's boyfriend, who lived with them. We said in Howard:

" ... an omission to act may create criminal culpability under our Crimes Code even though the law defining the offense, as here, requires an 'act,' where 'a duty to perform the omitted act is otherwise imposed by law.' 18 Pa.C.S.A. § 301(b)(2).

Here, appellant and the victim stood in the relation of parent and child. A parent had the legal duty to protect her child, and the discharge of this duty requires affirmative performance. ...

Appellant's brief suggests that we must negate intent because Julia did "something." Therefore, the question is raised whether acts which are so feeble as to be ineffectual can negate intent. We find they cannot, and reject that argument. The affirmative performance required by § 4304 cannot be met simply by showing any step at all toward preventing harm, however incomplete or ineffectual. An act which will negate intent is not necessarily one which will provide a successful outcome. However, the person charged with the duty of care is required to take steps that are reasonably calculated to achieve success. Otherwise, the meaning of "duty of care" is eviscerated.

We conclude that a parent's duty to protect his or her child requires affirmative performance to prevent harm and that failure to act may mean that the parent "knowingly endangers the welfare of the child." 18 Pa.C.S.A. § 4304.

...

We hold that evidence is sufficient to prove the intent element of the offense of endangering the welfare of a child, 18 Pa.C.S.A. § 4304, when the accused is aware of his or her duty to protect the child; is aware that the child is in circumstances that threaten the child's physical or psychological welfare; and has either failed to act or has taken actions so lame or meager that such actions cannot reasonably be expected to be effective to protect the child's physical or psychological welfare.

Questions

1. Is this a crime of omission or commission?
2. Did defendant have the requisite level of knowledge to be convicted under the statute?
3. How does the principle of legal duty impact the court's decision?
4. What is your impression of the court's initial sentence? Was it wise for the defendant to appeal?

poor self-esteem, depression, self-mutilation, suicide, anger, hostility, aggression, violence, running away, truancy, delinquency, increased vulnerability to revictimization, substance abuse, teenage prostitution, and early pregnancy."[119] In many jurisdictions the attempt to hold the omission accountable can be found under "endangering the welfare of a minor or child" provision or "failure to report" laws.

(a) Offense defined.—A parent, guardian, or other person supervising the welfare of a child under 18 years of age, commits an offense if he knowingly endangers the welfare of the child by violating a duty of care, protection, or support.
(b) Grading.—An offense under this section constitutes a misdemeanor of the first degree. However, where there is a course of conduct of endangering the welfare of a child, the offense constitutes a felony of the third degree.[120]

This codification imposes an affirmative duty on the part of parent or other lawful guardian to report and intervene in sexual or other abuse of children cases.[121] In a world that witnesses parents, addicted and enslaved to drugs, who live as prostitutes, and whose primary means of living income aside from public assistance is drug sales, the abuse should not be surprising.

Child Molestation

Broadly defined, molestation statutes encompass and integrate what traditional rape and sodomy statutes do not. For the most part, these types of laws deal with sexual contact rather than forcible penetration. In fact, the question of will and consent in molestation is irrelevant due to the age of the victim. Molestation laws usually employ the term "sexual contact," a rather all-inclusive depiction of what adults are capable of inflicting on the innocents. These same statutes tend to be very age sensitive and method oriented, and to grade offenses in terms of classification and resulting severity. Pedophiles are the chief target of these laws. Pedophiles are clinically diagnosed as:

> A diagnosed pedophile has (1) an impairment that lasts at least six months, with recurrent and "intense sexually arousing fantasies, sexual urges, or behaviors" that involve sexual activity with a prepubescent child or children (generally 13 years or younger); (2) fantasies, sexual urges, or behaviors [that] cause clinically significant distress or impairment in social, occupational, or other important areas of functioning"; and (3) the impaired person is at least 16 years and at least 5 years older than the child or children.[122]

In general, the younger the child, the more serious the offense will be. Missouri lays out precise definitions:

§ 566.067. Child molestation, first degree, penalties

1. A person commits the crime of child molestation in the first degree if he or she subjects another person who is less than fourteen years of age to sexual contact.
2. Child molestation in the first degree is a class B felony unless:
   (1) The actor has previously been convicted of an offense under this chapter or in the course thereof the actor inflicts serious physical injury, displays a deadly weapon or deadly instrument in a threatening manner, or the offense is committed as part of a ritual or ceremony, in which case the crime is a class A felony.[123]

When compared to sexual intercourse, sexual contact liberally construes any form of sexual behavior between adults and minors.[124] To contact implies penetration and a wide array of other physical touching. To contact could mean no more than an adult male placing his hand on top of genitalia, without insertion or intrusion. Molestation statutes reflect a type of sexual affront that illegally gratifies the pedophile and fondler, the indecent assaulter and exposer. In terms of sheer gravity, the offense of molestation may or may not be less serious than rape in the first degree. On the other hand, the outrage generated by these types of offenses directly connects to the innocence and age of the victims. Pedophiles are held in enormous disdain not only for what they do, but also to whom they do it. "Additionally, pedophilic molestation of children falls into a class of crimes against which society categorically wishes to guard. It is a crime we seek to prevent at all costs. It is true that societies seek to prevent all types of crime."[125]

Here one can readily discern the often confused state that prosecutors find themselves in. What is the appropriate charge? How do these facts fit into the provisions cited? Can a case of forcible molestation be merged into a major sexual offense? What type of offenses are easier to prove and defend?

Analyze the fundamental facts of *Missouri v. Graham*[126] wherein the defendant was charged with sodomy for placing his hand on the genitals of the child victim for periods ranging from 8 to 20 minutes during camping events. The statute in force at the time of the offense defined "deviate sexual intercourse" as:

> any sexual act involving the genitals of one person and the mouth, tongue, hand or anus of another person.[127]

The Court denied the appeal, not because the present language of the statute would have provided a legitimate defense, but because the statute in place at the time of offense included hand to genital contact as a form of deviate sexual intercourse. The Court read the statute to include a claim of sodomy and simultaneously upheld convictions for child molestation since contact was the fundamental element that could be proved. Under Missouri's current statute, a prosecution would not be possible.[128]

So profound are the levels of abuse thrust upon children that state legislators are drafting laws that cover every type of imaginable conduct. Statutes covering the sexual exploitation of children for pornographic purposes have been authored.

§ 13-3553. Sexual exploitation of a minor; evidence; classification

A. A person commits sexual exploitation of a minor by knowingly:
1. Recording, filming, photographing, developing or duplicating any visual depiction in which a minor is engaged in exploitive exhibition or other sexual conduct.

2. Distributing, transporting, exhibiting, receiving, selling, purchasing, electronically transmitting, possessing or exchanging any visual depiction in which a minor is engaged in exploitive exhibition or other sexual conduct.

B. If any visual depiction of sexual exploitation of a minor is admitted into evidence, the court shall seal that evidence at the conclusion of any grand jury proceeding, hearing or trial.[129]

Other legislative designs include the imposition of criminal liability for orchestrating sexual conduct between minors, for filming and videotaping children in sexual activities, for the plying of the young with drug and alcohol in exchange for sexual favors.[130] Distressingly, the extent to which lawmakers refine existing statutes directly correlates to the novel ways in which adults molest and abuse the young. New York law lumps much together under the "endangering" umbrella by criminalizing any conduct that is "injurious to the physical, mental, or moral welfare of a child less than seventeen years old or directs or authorizes such child to engage in an occupation involving a substantial risk of danger to his life or health; or ... he fail[ing] or refus[ing] to exercise reasonable diligence in the control of such child to prevent him from becoming an "abused child," a "neglected child," a "juvenile delinquent," or a "person in need of supervision,"[131]

What most legislators know only too keenly is that the molester's pathology is unlikely to be reformed. Some have even suggested that repeat offenders be castrated due to their inability to alter the basic tendencies. A liberal state like California, reflecting its frustration, has enacted a chemical castration law that, upon second offence, forces the pedophile into a drug maintenance program that allegedly squelches the sex drive. The statute contains these select provisos:

Cal Penal Code 645.

(a) Any person guilty of a first conviction of any offense specified in subdivision (c), where the victim has not attained 13 years of age, may, upon parole, undergo medroxyprogesterone acetate treatment or its chemical equivalent, in addition to any other punishment prescribed for that offense or any other provision of law, at the discretion of the court.

(b) Any person guilty of a second conviction of any offense specified in subdivision (c), where the victim has not attained 13 years of age, shall, upon parole, undergo medroxyprogesterone acetate treatment or its chemical equivalent, in addition to any other punishment prescribed for that offense or any other provision of law. ...

(c) The parolee shall begin medroxyprogesterone acetate treatment one week prior to his or her release from confinement in the state prison or other institution and shall continue treatments until the Department of Corrections demonstrates to the Board of Prison Terms that this treatment is no longer necessary.

(d) If a person voluntarily undergoes a permanent, surgical alternative to hormonal chemical treatment for sex offenders, he or she shall not be subject to this section.[132]

The problem rests not in the drug's effectiveness at muting the drive, it resides in the monitoring once on parole or probation. Is there any effective way to control this situation? Physical castration would resolve the dilemma.

One of the more popularly known attempts to rectify child molestation has been Megan's Law,[133] that controversial requirement that sexual offenders of children report and announce their presence to local justice authorities and the neighboring communities that they inhabit. This represents the zeal of the legal system in trying to curb an avalanche of abuse toward our

---

STORY 6.2

MEGAN'S LAW

In July 1994, 7-year-old Megan Kanka was lured into her neighbor's home, sexually molested, and murdered. On June 9, 1995, 4-year-old My Ly Nghiem was raped and murdered by a man who lived and worked in her building. The murderers of both girls had previously been convicted of child molestation several times, and none of their neighbors knew. The murder of Megan Kanka started a nationwide effort to keep track of released or paroled sexual offenders. On May 17, 1996, almost two years after Megan's murder, President Clinton signed Megan's Law.

Megan's Law requires all states to register individuals convicted of sex crimes against children, and allows states to make private and personal information about sex offenders available to the public. Many states have followed suit and have created their own law regarding sex offender registration and community notification.

For example, New York's law establishes registration and notification provisions and requires the classification of offenders using a three-tiered system. These levels of notification increase as the offender's risk to the community increases. The risk level determines the amount of notification to the public and/or law enforcement agencies. Many states now post their lists online for easy access by the community.

Some opposition from Megan's Law has resulted with people claiming that released sex offenders have paid their dues and that reporting should not be mandatory, that it is a violation of that person's rights. However, parents demanding protection for their children and notification of threats to their children's safety have prevailed.

---

young. Opponents to these types of requirements recite constitutional infringements from privacy intrusions to a lack of due process. Other criticisms mention the "labeling" and nonrehabilitative effects on the former perpetrator. Advocates dismiss these negative characterizations as extreme and radical protectionism for a group unlikely to change or be cured of this heinous malady "ignores the reality of the criminal justice system."[134] Child molesters garner very little empathy in most settings and the recidivism rates for pedophiles provides an adequate backdrop for their skepticism.[135]

Another, even more extreme reaction to the hideousness of child molestation and pedophilia is the enactment of Sexual Predator Laws. Here, the state seeks the civil commitment of a molester because they are threats to individuals and the community at large. Wisconsin, for example, classifies predators as those "who are mentally disordered, sexually violent, and or sexually motivated." Civil commitment after serving time in prison is possible when any of the following definitional standards are met:

(2) "Mental disorder" means a congenital or acquired condition affecting the emotional or volitional capacity that predisposes a person to engage in acts of sexual violence.

(5) "Sexually motivated" means that one of the purposes for an act is for the actor's sexual arousal or gratification.

(6) "Sexually violent offense" means ... any crime specified ... that is determined, in a proceeding under s. 980.05(3)(b), to have been sexually motivated.

CASE 6.4

STATE V. PERROW

231 P. 3d 853 (2010)

The State appeals the trial court's dismissal of its child molestation prosecution against James Martin Perrow based upon the State's violation of Mr. Perrow's attorney–client privilege. The trial court found a detective had wrongfully seized attorney–client writings while executing a search warrant, examined and copied the writings, and delivered the writings to the State's prosecution team before charges were filed. The State contends the trial court abused its discretion in dismissing the charges because (1) the Sixth Amendment right to counsel had not attached when the writings were seized; (2) Mr. Perrow failed to establish the writings were protected by the attorney–client privilege; and (3) Mr. Perrow waived the privilege. We disagree, do not reach Mr. Perrow's cross-appeal challenging the search warrant, and affirm.

The facts mainly derive from the trial court's unchallenged findings of fact following Mr. Perrow's motion to dismiss for violation of the attorney–client privilege. Since the court's findings are unchallenged, they are verities on appeal.

In October 2007, Detective Craig Sloan began investigating Mr. Perrow's alleged sexual abuse of his daughter, A.P. On October 26, Detective Sloan called A.P. and told her he would assist her with obtaining a civil antiharassment protection order against her father. After speaking with A.P., the detective contacted an Okanogan County prosecuting attorney. A civil protection order was issued against Mr. Perrow on November 13. On or about November 14, Detective Sloan called Mr. Perrow and informed him of A.P.'s allegations. Detective Sloan then prepared an affidavit for a search warrant of Mr. Perrow's home.

Mr. Perrow received a copy of the protection order on November 17 and contacted Michael Vannier, an attorney, on or about November 19. Mr. Vannier agreed to represent Mr. Perrow on the civil protection order matter as well as the potential criminal charges. On November 20, Mr. Vannier met with Mr. Perrow and asked him to gather information about A.P.'s allegations and provide him with a "written narrative" of the matters. Mr. Perrow prepared the requested materials for his attorney.

On November 29, Detective Sloan and other law enforcement officers executed a search warrant at Mr. Perrow's home. Detective Sloan seized written materials from Mr. Perrow's residence, including two composition books, some notes, and a yellow note pad. During the search, Mr. Vannier received a phone call from either Mr. Perrow or his wife informing him that Detective Sloan was taking the materials Mr. Perrow had prepared for Mr. Vannier. Mr. Vannier told the caller to tell the officer that the materials were protected by the attorney–client privilege. Mr. Perrow told Detective Sloan that the seized items had been prepared for Mr. Vannier. Detective Sloan removed the items from Mr. Perrow's home and took them to the Okanogan County sheriff's office where he read and analyzed them.

Detective Sloan observed that the documents appeared to have been written after Mr. Perrow was served with the protection order on November 17. He read through the documents page by page and compared them with what Mr. Perrow had said on the phone. Detective Sloan prepared a written analysis of the documents. He forwarded his report and the seized documents to the prosecutor's office.

On December 17, the State charged Mr. Perrow with two counts of child molestation. Mr. Perrow moved to dismiss based on unjustifiable interference of the right to counsel, violation of the attorney–client privilege, and prejudicial governmental misconduct under CrR 8.3(b). He argued that the seized documents were clearly meant for his attorney and that Detective Sloan knew this at the time he seized them.

The court granted Mr. Perrow's motion, concluding Mr. Vannier represented him at the time of the seizure on the civil and the criminal matters and, therefore, the seized items were protected by the attorney–client relationship. It concluded the detective's conduct violated Mr. Perrow's constitutional right to counsel and his right to privileged communication with his attorney under RCW 5.60.060(2)(a). It did not address Mr. Perrow's CrR 8.3(b) argument. Based on Detective Sloan's communication to the prosecutor's office about the contents of the writings, the court concluded suppression was not an adequate remedy and dismissed the charges. The State appealed.

The issue is whether the trial court erred in granting Mr. Perrow's motion to dismiss for constitutional violations of the right to counsel and violation of the attorney–client privilege. We review a trial court's decision to dismiss criminal charges for an abuse of discretion. A trial court abuses its discretion only when its decision is manifestly unreasonable or based on untenable grounds.

The State first contends the trial court abused its discretion dismissing the case because Mr. Perrow's Sixth Amendment right to counsel had not attached when the writings were seized. It argues his right to counsel did not attach until charges were later filed and he failed to establish the writings were protected by the attorney–client privilege under RCW 5.60.060(2)(a). Mr. Perrow responds that the State's arguments are disposed of by the trial court's unchallenged findings establishing he prepared the writings at his counsel's request to obtain legal advice on the very matters under investigation by Detective Sloan. Mr. Perrow argues privilege attachment is immaterial; the relevant inquiry is whether the attorney–client privilege violation was so egregious that dismissal was the sole remedy considering the "conduct is by definition so egregious that prejudice is presumed and dismissal warranted."

Initially, we examine whether the seized writings were privileged attorney–client communications. Washington's attorney–client privilege is found at RCW 5.60.060(2)(a). The privilege applies to communications and advice between an attorney and client and extends to documents that contain a privileged communication. It applies to any information generated by a request for legal advice.

"The attorney–client privilege exists in order to allow the client to communicate freely with an attorney without fear of compulsory discovery." The privilege encourages a client to make a full disclosure to his or her attorney, enabling the attorney to render effective legal assistance. Whether an attorney–client relationship exists is a question of fact. The defendant has the burden of establishing the existence of the attorney–client privilege.

Dietz gives an eight-part test to guide courts in determining if an attorney–client relationship exists: (1) the client must have sought legal advice; (2) from an attorney; (3) the communication was made to obtain legal advice; (4) in confidence; (5) by the client; (6) the client must wish to protect his identity; (7) from disclosure; and (8) the protection must not have been waived.

The State argues Mr. Perrow did not show the seized materials were intended for his attorney; and, even if they were privileged, Mr. Perrow waived the privilege because many of the seized documents were made public record in Mr. Perrow's protection order case. We are not persuaded. The court's unchallenged findings unequivocally establish the seized writings were intended for Mr. Vannier and no evidence shows the materials were used in the protection order proceedings.

The findings establish: (1) prior to the execution of the search warrant on November 28, 2007, Mr. Perrow retained the services of Mr. Vannier, an attorney; (2) Mr. Vannier's representation involved the defense of a civil protection order filed by A.P., as well as representation during the investigative stage of the potential criminal charges that could be filed as a result of A.P.'s allegations; (3) Mr. Perrow was aware of A.P.'s allegations based on his conversation with Detective Sloan on or about November 14, 2007; (4) Mr. Vannier first met with Mr. Perrow on November 20, 2007, after previously speaking with him by telephone and receiving faxed documents concerning the allegations; (5) Mr. Vannier asked Mr. Perrow to provide him with information about A.P. and her allegations; (6) during the November 20, 2007 meeting, Mr. Vannier asked Mr. Perrow to gather additional information and to put that information into writing; (7) Mr. Perrow prepared written materials for his attorney which consisted of a green composition book, a black composition book, miscellaneous notes located in his office, and a yellow note pad; and (8) Mr. Vannier met with Mr. Perrow on November 27, 2007, to review the information and discuss the case.

Based on these findings, the court concluded "[a]n attorney/client relationship had been formed and existed at the time the papers and notebooks were seized on November 28, 2007, inasmuch as defendant sought and received legal assistance from Mr. Vannier on matters related to the civil protection petition filed by A.P. and the active criminal investigation." And, the court concluded Mr. Perrow satisfied the Dietz test because: (1) Mr. Perrow sought specific legal advice; (2) from Mr. Vannier in his capacity as an attorney; (3) the papers and notebooks were prepared and made to obtain legal advice, outline strategy, and prepare a defense; (4) in confidence; (5) by Mr. Perrow; (6) the materials were intended for his attorney; (7) they were not for disclosure; and (8) the desire for protection was not waived.

It follows from the court's conclusions that the writings seized from Mr. Perrow's residence were protected by the attorney–client privilege and the State's seizure of these materials violated that privilege. Given the violation, the next inquiry is whether dismissal was the appropriate remedy. The State contends dismissal is an extraordinary remedy available only when the accused's rights have been materially prejudiced, affecting his right to a fair trial. It argues Mr. Perrow's Sixth Amendment right to counsel had not attached when the writings were seized and he fails to show egregious governmental misconduct justifying dismissal under CrR 8.3(b). Mr. Perrow's responsive arguments are exactly the opposite.

Here, the trial court relied primarily on *State v. Cory*, to support the dismissal. The Cory court analyzed government intrusion into the attorney–client relationship. Mr. Cory met with his attorney to discuss his case in a private jail room where the sheriff had secretly installed a microphone. The trial court excluded the evidence derived from the eavesdropping, but declined to dismiss the case. The Supreme Court dismissed, stating: "There is no way to isolate the prejudice resulting from an eavesdropping activity, such as this. If the prosecution gained information which aided it in the preparation of its case, that information would be as available in the second trial as in the first."

The Cory court noted effective representation requires a defendant to be able to consult with his or her attorney in private.

The State argues Cory is distinguishable because Mr. Perrow's Sixth Amendment right to counsel had not attached at the time of the search and Detective Sloan did not purposely intercept communication between Mr. Perrow and his attorney. We disagree. First, we need not evaluate if the State's conduct violated Mr. Perrow's constitutional rights to counsel because the Cory court observed that in addition to the Sixth Amendment right to counsel, the State's eavesdropping violated the attorney–client communications privilege established in RCW 5.60.060(2).

Considering the State's egregious behavior, Mr. Perrow establishes the seized writings were protected under RCW 5.60.060(2). Under Cory, dismissal is the sole adequate remedy when, like here, the State intercepts privileged communications between an attorney and client. It is not possible to isolate the prejudice resulting from the intrusion.

The State's conduct is analogous to that in Cory. The court's unchallenged findings establish: (1) Mr. Perrow informed Detective Sloan during the search that the written materials were for Mr. Vannier; (2) Detective Sloan nevertheless seized the materials, closely analyzed them, made copies of them, and concluded the information contradicted previous statements made by Mr. Perrow; and (3) Detective Sloan forwarded copies of the documents to the prosecutor's office.

Based on these findings, the court entered conclusions:

Although this Court most assuredly cannot conclude that Det. Sloan consciously undertook to violate defendant's attorney/client privilege, this Court does conclude that the detective's conduct was in violation not only of the constitutional provision assuring the right to counsel, but also of RCW 5.60.060(2)(a), which establishes that communication between an attorney and his client shall be privileged and confidential.

The Court concludes that since the privileged papers, documents, and notebooks were not impounded by Det. Sloan, but were, rather, reviewed and analyzed as to specific content and therefore communicated to the prosecutor's office, suppression is not an adequate remedy.

In sum, we conclude the trial court did not abuse its discretion in dismissing the charges against Mr. Perrow. As in Cory, it is impossible to isolate the prejudice presumed from the attorney–client privilege violation. The resolution of this issue is dispositive of this appeal. Thus, we, like the trial court, do not reach Mr. Perrow's CrR 8.3(b) arguments. Nor, do we address Mr. Perrow's cross-appeal.

Affirmed.

Questions

1. Did the Court deal with the substantive charges of child molestation?
2. What were those charges?
3. Was the defendant found innocent of those charges on factual or legal grounds?
4. What was the basis of his declaration of innocence?
5. Could the Court have resolved this procedural dilemma in any other way other than releasing the defendant?

---

(7) "Sexually violent person" means a person who has been convicted of a sexually violent offense, has been adjudicated delinquent for a sexually violent offense, or has been found not guilty of or not responsible for a sexually violent offense by reason of insanity or mental disease, defect, or illness, and who is dangerous because he or she suffers from a mental disorder that makes it likely that the person will engage in one or more acts of sexual violence.[136]

The tragedy and scandal of priestly molestation of children, admittedly a small minority of priests, has rocked the Catholic Church. The larger betrayal has been in poor leadership in the Church itself. Visit, SNAP, an organization dedicated to discovering these most unfortunate cases at http://www.snapnetwork.org/

The Internet has provided the pedophile and molester with a unique safe haven. In this virtual reality of unknowns and personal shadows, the molester lurks without much chance of detection or possibility of prosecution. Predators on the Web think and say bad thoughts; those inchoate, intellectual steps that cannot be criminalized. For how do we know what the molester and pedophile thinks and when is it thought? Pedophiles in chat rooms likely know not who the target is and the exchange remains virtual; through admittedly perverse fantasy, the law cannot effectively prosecute. The pedophile may not even know whether the contact person is a child in the first place. "Virtually any type of sexual fantasy may be witnessed (or participated in), including explicit rapes and violent encounters. In this environment, where all members of the room are using assumed identities, there is no ability to determine the race, sex, or age of occupants."[137] At whom are these perverse thoughts directed? As much as our disgust may boil over in the examination of these child molesters, the criminal law model resists the punishment of mere thoughts.

This general nervousness should not impact the ability to pose other criminal complaints in the area of solicitation and distribution of pornography or other pandering charges. Free speech and mental freedom surely does not preclude alternative charges for the arrogant and confident pedophile.[138] The primary approach rests in solicitation for the solicitor knows who and what the target is. Just as critically, the solicitor moves from thought to action, taking overt steps to effectuate the fantasy into a meaningful and tragic reality. Florida's *Computer Pornography and Child Exploitation Act of 1986*[139] does an admirable job of balancing the constitutional questions with the criminal ones. As commendably, the provision charts the fine line of thought and action to assure successful prosecutions of predators on the Internet.

New York's defines the process of communication as "transfer" of harmful materials, as if the act was one of commerce rather than thoughts and speech. "The court further concluded that, given the unique nature of the Internet, the only way to avoid inconsistent regulation was to reserve legislative power to Congress. Accordingly, the court held that the New York statute violated the Commerce Clause."[140] The commerce argument minimizes the constitutional defense by redirecting the legal argument to the Commerce Clause of the United States Constitution. In a challenge by the American Libraries Association, the federal appeals court overruled the plan by indicating the state's lack of capacity to regulate in this national area.[141]

At the federal level, various legislative proposals have been rebuffed under free speech and other constitutional theories.[142] In 1998, Congress passed the *Child Online Protection Act*,[143] which punished "knowing" communicators of harmful materials to minors. The statute reads in part:

§ 231. Restriction of access by minors to materials commercially distributed by means of World Wide Web that are harmful to minors

(a) Requirement to restrict access

   (1) Prohibited conduct

      Whoever knowingly and with knowledge of the character of the material, in interstate or foreign commerce by means of the World Wide Web, makes any communication for commercial purposes that is available to any minor and that includes any material that is harmful to minors shall be fined not more than $50,000, imprisoned not more than 6 months, or both.

   (2) Intentional violations

      In addition to the penalties under paragraph (1), whoever intentionally violates such paragraph shall be subject to a fine of not more than $50,000 for each violation. For purposes of this paragraph, each day of violation shall constitute a separate violation.[144]

The American Civil Liberties Union (ACLU) has constitutionally challenged the law on free speech grounds.[145] The debate between constitutionalists who advocate unlimited and unqualified free speech and those wishing to move toward a collective criminalization of Internet predators, remains intense.

Other efforts to formalize protections by restricting the Internet have been only partially successful. In 2000, Congress passed the *Children's Internet Protection Act*.[146]

While mostly applicable to educational settings, such as elementary and secondary schools, the Act has goals:

- Balancing the importance of allowing children to use the Internet with the importance of protecting children from inappropriate material.
- Accessing online educational materials with a minimum level of relevant content being blocked.
- Deciding on the local level how best to protect children from Internet dangers.
- Understanding how to fully utilize Internet protection technology measures.
- Considering a variety of technical, educational, and economic factors when selecting technology protection measures
- Adopting an Internet safety strategy that includes technology, human monitoring, and education.[147]

> Read the Parent's Guide to Internet Safety at http://www.fbi.gov/stats-services/publications/parent-guide/parent-guide

Of greatest necessity will be the recognition that a select class of molester cannot be granted an impenetrable haven and harbor for his own deviancy known as the Internet. The legal system, in weighing the people's right to safety, should be able to ferret out the deranged and the despicable and not employ constitutional plaudits and platitudes to foster untouchability. For this is where the pedophile thrives—in the shadows, without conscience, without guilt, and without eventual consequence.

States have also made enormous inroads as to legislative protections for children and the Internet. Figure 6.6[148] summarizes legislative efforts.

DISCUSSION QUESTIONS

1. Why have rape law reformers called for the elimination of any resistance requirement on the part of victim?
2. How has the reform of rape and sexual assault laws impacted the definitions employed in rape prosecutions?
3. Is there a relationship between force employed and the nature of consent?
4. Explain the exceptions to the Rape Shield statutes.
5. Why have incest rates been rising?
6. Discuss the policy implications behind statutory rape laws.
7. Describe the various ways in which sodomy is defined.
8. Should voluntary sodomy be criminalized or decriminalized?
9. Should sexual offense laws be gender-neutral? Explain the advantages and disadvantages?
10. What does the marital exemption assume?

SUGGESTED READINGS

Aggrawal, A. 2008. *Forensic and medico-legal aspects of sexual crimes and unusual sexual practices.* Boca Raton, FL: CRC Press.

Aggrawal, A. 2010. *Necrophilia: Forensic and medico-legal aspects.* Boca Raton, FL: CRC Press.

Davies, P. 2010. *Gender, crime and victimization.* Thousand Oaks, CA: Sage Publications Ltd.

Denmark, F. L., and M. A. Paludi. 2010. *Victims of sexual assault and abuse [2 vols.]: Resources and responses for individuals and families* (Women's Psychology). Santa Barbara, CA: Praeger Publishers.

Greenfield, L. A. 1997. *Sex offenses and offenders.* Washington, DC: Office of Justice Programs.

Henssonow, S. F., L. M. Surhone, and M. T. Tennoe. 2010. *Sodomy laws in the United States.* Saarbrücken, Germany: Betascript Publishing.

Levesque, R. J. R. 2010. *Child maltreatment and the law: Returning to first principles.* New York: Springer Publishing Company.

McGlynn, C. and V. E. Munro. 2011. *Rethinking rape law: International and comparative perspectives.* London: Cavendish Publishing Ltd.

Russell, D. E. H., and R. M. Bolen. 2000. *The epidemic of rape and child sexual abuse in the United States.* Thousand Oaks, CA: Sage Publications.

Taslitz, A. E. 1999. *Rape and the culture of the courtroom.* New York: New York University Press.

State Laws

STATE	CITATION	APPLIES TO SCHOOLS	APPLIES TO LIBRARIES	SUMMARY
ARIZONA	Ariz. Rev. Stat. Ann. § 34-501 to -502	X	X	Requires public libraries to install software *or* develop policies to prevent minors from gaining access on the Internet to materials harmful to minors. Requires public schools to install computer software that would prevent minors from gaining access to materials harmful to minors.
ARKANSAS	Ark. Code § 6-21-107, § 13-2-103	X	X	Requires school districts to develop a policy and to adopt a system to prevent computer users from accessing materials harmful to minors. Requires public libraries to adopt a policy to prevent minors from gaining access to materials harmful to them.
CALIFORNIA	Cal. Ed. Code § 18030.5		X	Requires public libraries that receive state funds to adopt a policy regarding Internet access by minors.
COLORADO	Colo. Rev. Stat. § 24-90-401 to 404; § 24-90-603; § 22-87-101 to 107	X	X	Requires public schools to adopt and enforce reasonable policies of Internet safety that will protect children from obtaining harmful material. Provides grants to publicly supported libraries, including school libraries, that equip public access computers with filtering software and that have policies to restrict minors from accessing obscene or illegal information. Requires public libraries to adopt a policy of Internet safety for minors that includes the operation of a technology protection measure for computers with Internet access.
DELAWARE	Del. Code tit. 29 § 6601C-6607C		X	Requires public libraries to have acceptable use policies and prohibits the use of library computers or mobile devices to access illegal or obscene materials. The minor's parent or guardian must specify the level of access to the Internet the minor may have.
GEORGIA	Ga. Code § 20-2-324, § 20-5-5	X	X	Requires public schools and public libraries to adopt and enforce reasonable policies of Internet safety that will protect children from access to harmful material. Prohibits a public school or library from receiving state funds unless it implements and enforces the acceptable-use policy.

Figure 6.6   State-level legislative protections for children and the Internet.

(continued)

State Laws (*continued*)

STATE	CITATION	APPLIES TO SCHOOLS	APPLIES TO LIBRARIES	SUMMARY
IDAHO	Idaho Code § 33-132	X		Requires each local school district in the state to adopt and file an Internet use policy with the state superintendent of public instruction. The policy, approved by the local board of trustees, shall require filtering technology that blocks Internet materials that are harmful to minors, establish disciplinary measures for violators, and provide a component of Internet safety to be integrated into the schools instructional program.
IOWA	Iowa Code § 256.57		X	Requires public libraries that apply for and receive state "Enrich Iowa Program" money to have an Internet use policy in place.
KENTUCKY	Ky. Rev. Stat. § 156.675	X	X	Requires the Department of Education to develop regulations to prevent sexually explicit material from being transmitted via education technology systems.
LOUISIANA	La. Rev. Stat. Ann. § 17:100.7	X		Requires schools to adopt policies regarding students' and school employees' access to certain Internet and online sites.
MARYLAND	Md. Code art. 23 § 506.1		X	Requires county–state libraries to adopt policies to prevent minors from obtaining access to obscene materials via the Internet.
MASSACHUSETTS	Mass. Gen. Laws 71 § 93	X		Requires public schools providing computer access to students to have a policy regarding Internet safety measures to protect students from inappropriate subject matter and materials that can be accessed via the Internet.
MICHIGAN	Mich. Comp. Laws § 397.602, § 397.606		X	Requires libraries to use a system to prevent minors from viewing obscene or sexually explicit matter, or to reserve separate terminals exclusively for adults or children so as to prevent minors access to obscene or sexually explicit matter.

MINNESOTA	Minn. Stat. § 134.5	X	Requires public library computers with access to the Internet available for use by children to be equipped to restrict, including by use of available software filtering technology or other effective methods, access to material that is reasonably believed to be obscene or child pornography or material harmful to minors. Also requires public libraries that receive state money to prohibit, including through the use of available software filtering technology or other effective methods, adult access to material that under federal or state law is reasonably believed to be obscene or child pornography.
MISSOURI	Mo. Rev. Stat. §§ 182.825, 182.827	X	X	Requires public school and public libraries with public access computers to either (a) equip the computer with software or a service to restrict minors access to material that is pornographic for minors, or (b) develop a policy that establishes measures to restrict minors from gaining access to such material.
NEW HAMPSHIRE	N.H. Rev. Stat. Ann. § 194:3-d	X		Requires school boards to adopt a policy regarding Internet access for school computers, and establishes liability for violation of the policy.
NEW YORK	N.Y. Ed. Law § 260(12)		X	Requires public libraries to establish policies concerning patron use of computers.
OHIO	ORC § 3314.21 1997 H.B. 215 (uncodified, see Section 76)	X	X	Requires Internet- or computer-based community schools to use a filtering device or install filtering software that protects against Internet access to materials that are obscene or harmful to juveniles. Requires the schools to provide free filtering devices or software to students who work from home. As a condition of funding, requires local libraries to adopt policies to control access to obscene materials.
OKLAHOMA	1996 H.C.R. 1097 (uncodified)	X		Directs all state agencies and educational institutions to keep computer systems free from obscene materials.

Figure 6.6 (continued) State-level legislative protections for children and the Internet.

State Laws (*continued*)

STATE	CITATION	APPLIES TO SCHOOLS	APPLIES TO LIBRARIES	SUMMARY
PENNSYLVANIA	24 P.S. 4604 - 4612	x	X	Requires school boards and publicly-funded libraries to adopt and enforce acceptable use policies for Internet access that include the (1) use of software programs reasonably designed to block access to visual depictions of obscenity, child pornography or material that is harmful to minors; or (2) selection of online servers that block access to visual depictions of obscenity, child pornography or material that is harmful to minors.
SOUTH DAKOTA	S.D. Codified Laws Ann. § 22-24-55 to 59	X		Requires schools to equip computers with filtering software or to adopt policies to restrict minors from access to obscene materials.
SOUTH CAROLINA	S.C. Code Ann. § 10-1-205 to -206	X		Requires publicly funded libraries and public school libraries to adopt policies intended to reduce the ability of the user to access websites displaying obscene material. Also establishes a pilot program to evaluate the use of filtering software in libraries.
TENNESSEE	Tenn. Code § 49-1-221	X		Requires the development of acceptable Internet use policies for public and private schools to protect children from certain online material.
UTAH	Utah Code Ann. § 9-7-215, 9-7-216	X	X	Prohibits a public library from receiving state funds unless the library enforces measures to filter Internet access to certain types of images; allows a public library to block materials that are not specified in this bill; and allows a public library to disable a filter under certain circumstances. Requires local school boards to adopt and enforce a policy to restrict access to Internet or online sites that contain obscene material.

STATE	CITATION			SUMMARY
VIRGINIA	Va. Code § 22.1-70.2, § 42.1-36.1	X	X	Requires public libraries to adopt Internet use policies. Requires public schools to adopt Internet use policies that (1) prohibit transmitting or viewing illegal material on the Internet, (2) prevent access by students to materials the school determines harmful, (3) select technology to filter or block child pornography and obscenity. Requires each school division to post its Internet use policies on its website.

OTHER RELATED STATE LAWS:

STATE	CITATION	SUMMARY
FLORIDA	Fla. Stat. § 257.12 (3)	Encourages public libraries to adopt an Internet safety education program, including the implementation of a computer-based educational program.
LOUISIANA	La. Rev. Stat. § 51:1426	Requires Internet service providers to make available to subscribers who are Louisiana residents a product or service that enables the subscriber to control a child's use of the Internet.
MARYLAND	Md. Code § 14-3701 et seq.	Requires Internet service providers to make parental controls that enable blocking or filtering of websites available to subscribers in the state.
NEVADA	Nev. Rev. Stat. § 603.100 to 603.170	Requires Internet service providers to offer, under certain circumstances, products or services that enable subscribers to regulate and monitor a child's use of the Internet.
TEXAS	Tex. Bus. & Comm. Code §§ 35.101 to 35.103	Requires an interactive computer service provider to place a link to free or shareware filtering software conspicuously on the first accessible web page of the service provider. Establishes a civil penalty of $2,000 for each day the provider fails to comply.
UTAH	Utah Code § 76-10-1231	Requires Internet service providers, upon request by a consumer, to provide in-network filtering or filtering software to prevent transmission of material harmful to minors.

Figure 6.6 (continued) State-level legislative protections for children and the Internet.

ENDNOTES

1. Bureau of Justice Statistics, Rape and Sexual Assault, at http://bjs.ojp.usdoj.gov/index.cfm?ty=tp&tid=317#key_facts (accessed December 7, 2010).
2. Others see the unfolding of sexual activity as a stream of empowerment.
3. MARTIN D. SCHWARTZ, NATIONAL INSTITUTE OF JUSTICE VISITING FELLOWSHIP: POLICE INVESTIGATION OF RAPE-ROADBLOCKS AND SOLUTIONS, NCJ 232667 (2010).
4. R.I. GEN. LAWS § 11-37-1 (2010).
5. Aside from the criminal remedies, rape and other sexual offense victims are not adverse to using the civil courts for an alternative remedy in damages. Money damages for assault and emotional distress can never make whole the harmed party, but serve as some consolation in the tragedy. *See* Paul S. Edelman, *Cruise Line Liability for Sexual Assaults*, N.Y. L.J., July 30, 1999, at 3.
6. *See* ME. REV. STAT. tit. 17-A, § 251(1)(E) (2010).
7. Jennifer S. Cicchetti, *Rape to Gross Sexual Assault: A Statutory History of Sexual Violence Statutes in Maine*, 6 ME. B.J. 146, 146 (May 1991).
8. LINDA FAIRSTEIN, SEXUAL VIOLENCE: OUR WAR AGAINST RAPE (1993).
9. *Id.* at 197.
10. A Maine Supreme Court case affords a keen look into traditional of compulsion when it notes: "As the gravity of the threat diminishes, the situation gradually changes from one where compulsion overwhelms the will of the victim to a situation where she can make a deliberate choice to avoid some alternative evil. The man may threaten to disclose an illicit affair, to foreclose the mortgage on her parents' farm, to cause her to lose her job, or to deprive her of a valued possession. The situation may move into a shadow area between coercion and bargain." Model Penal Code § 207.4, comment (Proposed Official Draft 1955); *see* Model Penal Code § 2213.1 (Proposed Official Draft, 1962). *See also State v. Colson*, 405 A.2d 717 (Me. 1979).
11. ALA. CODE § 13A-6-70 (2010).
12. See MINNESOTA CENTER AGAINST VIOLENCE & ABUSE, UNDERSTANDING SEXUAL VIOLENCE: PROSECUTING ADULT RAPE AND SEXUAL ASSAULT CASES, PARTICIPANT'S BINDER (2001); SHARON HUNTER ET AL., POLICE RESPONSE TO CRIMES OF SEXUAL ASSAULT: A TRAINING CURRICULUM (2nd ed. 1997).
13. SHARON M. HUNTER, BONNIE R. BENTLEY CEWE, & JAMIE L. MILLS, POLICE RESPONSE TO CRIMES OF SEXUAL ASSAULT: A TRAINING CURRICULUM Overhead 3-3 (1997).
14. Nathan Brett, *Sexual Offenses and Consent*, 11 CAN. J. L. & JURIS. 69, 69 (1998).
15. James Faulkner, *Mens Rea in Rape: Morgan and the Inadequacy of Subjectivism or Why No Should Not Mean Yes in the Eyes of the Law*, 18 MELB. U. L. REV. 60 (1991).
16. *See* Brett, *supra* note 14, at 81–82.
17. William N. Eskridge, Jr., *Essay: The Many Faces of Sexual Consent*, 37 WM. & MARY L. REV. 47, 64–65 (1995).
18. *Id.* at 65.
19. *See* for example 18 PA. CONS. STAT. § 3107 (2010).
20. VA. CODE ANN. § 18.2-61 (2010).
21. Charles P. Nemeth, *Character Evidence in Rape Trials in 19th Century New York: Chastity and the Admissibility of Specific Acts*, 6 WOMEN'S RIGHTS L. REP. (1980).
22. *See* SUSAN BROWNMILLER, AGAINST OUR WILL (Ballantine Books, 1993).
23. CATHARINE A. MACKINNON, TOWARD A FEMINIST THEORY OF THE STATE 174 (1989).
24. Katharine K. Baker, *Gender and Race in the Evidence Policy: Text, Context, and the Problem with Rape*, 28 SW. U. L. REV. 297 (1999).
25. *Id.* at 304.
26. *See* Owen D. Jones, *Reconsidering Rape*, NAT. L. J., Feb. 21, 2000, at A21.
27. Charles P. Nemeth, *How New Jersey Prosecutors View the New Sexual Offense Statutes*, N. J. L. J., May 5, 1983.

28. Reformers in the rape movement have been extraordinarily creative in their approach. In *U.S. v. Antonio Morrison*, 529 U. S. 598 (2000), the rape victim sought an alternative remedy to the criminal law alone, namely civil rights protections under the commerce clause, the due process clause of the Fourteenth Amendment and 42 U.S.C. § 13981, which provides a civil remedy for gender-based violence. On both fronts, commerce- and gender-based violence, the Court was unsatisfied. The court ruled that "Section 13981 is also different from these previously upheld remedies in that it applies uniformly through-out the Nation. Congress' findings indicate that the problem of discrimination against the victims of gender-motivated crimes does not exist in all States, or even most States. By contrast, the § 5 remedy upheld in *Katzenbach v. Morgan*, 384 U.S. 641, 16 L.Ed. 2d 828, 86 S.Ct. 1717 (1966), was directed only to the State where the evil found by Congress existed, and in *South Carolina v. Katzenbach*, 383 U.S. 301, 15 L.Ed. 2d 769, 86 S.Ct. 803 (1966), the remedy was directed only to those States in which Congress found that there had been discrimination. For these reasons, we conclude that Congress' power under § 5 does not extend to the enactment of § 13981." *Id.* at 648–49. However, a federal judge who sexually assaulted women in his judicial chambers could be criminally liable under federal law for the deprivation of a constitutional right. See *U.S. v. Lanier*, 520 U.S. 259 (1997).
29. TEX. CRIM. PROC. CODE ANN. § 38.07 (Vernon 1983).
30. TEX. CRIM. PROC. CODE ANN. § 38.07, as amended by Act of May 29, 1993, 73d Leg., Reg. Sess., ch. 900 § 12.01, 1993 Tex. Gen. Laws 3765, 3766, and Act of May 10, 1993, 73d Leg., Reg. Sess., ch. 200, § 1 1993 Tex. Gen. Laws 387, 388.
31. Defendant had repeatedly raped his stepdaughter over a four-year period when she was 12 to 15 years of age.
32. Nemeth, *supra* note 27.
33. Jennifer L. Reichert, *Many Rape Victims Are Children and Adolescents, Survey Finds*, TRIAL, Feb. 1999, at 106.
34. PATRICIA TJADEN & NANCY THOENNES, PREVALENCE, INCIDENCE, AND CONSEQUENCES OF VIOLENCE AGAINST WOMEN: FINDINGS FROM THE NATIONAL VIOLENCE AGAINST WOMEN SURVEY (1998), available at https://www.ncjrs.gov/pdffiles/172837.pdf (accessed August 3, 2011).
35. Emily J. Sack, *Is Domestic Violence a Crime: Intimate Partner Rape as Allegory*, 24 ST. JOHN'S J. L. COMM. 535, 566 (2010).
36. *Id.* at 567.
37. Leslie M. Rose, *The Supreme Court and Gender-Neutral Language: Setting the Standard or Lagging Behind?* 17 DUKE J. GENDER L. & POL'Y 81 (2010); Philip N. S. Rumney, *In Defence of Gender Neutrality within Rape*, 6 SEATTLE J. SOC. JUST. 481(2007); *Cf.* Patricia Novotny, *Rape Victims in the (Gender) Neutral Zone: The Assimilation of Resistance?*, 1 SEATTLE J. SOC. JUST. 743 (2003).
38. N.C. GEN STAT. § 14-27.2 (2010).
39. See Michael A. Riccardi, *Rape Ruled "Accidental Injury" under Workers' Compensation*, N.Y. L.J., Feb. 7, 2000, at 1.
40. In *U.S. v. Rivera*, 83 F.3d 542 (1st Cir. 1996), the court withheld the worst possible sentence because "there was no evidence of any cuts or bruises in her vaginal area." *Id.* at 547.
41. *Eleventh Annual Review of Gender and Sexuality Law: Criminal Law Chapter: Sexual Assault and Evidentiary Matters*, 11 GEO. J. GENDER & L. 191, 196 (2010); *See also* Jamie Goss Dempsey, *Fells v. State: Good Decision on Procedural Grounds, Dangerous Precedent for Future Application of Arkansas's Rape Shield Statute*, 59 ARK. L. REV. 943 (2007).
42. 18 PA. CONS. STAT. § 3104 (2010).
43. Rule 609. Impeachment by Evidence of Conviction of Crime
    (a) General rule.

    For the purpose of attacking the credibility of a witness,

    (1) evidence that a witness other than an accused has been convicted of a crime shall be admit-ted, subject to Rule 403, if the crime was punishable by death or imprisonment in excess of one year under the law under which the witness was convicted, and evidence that an accused has been convicted of such a crime shall be admitted if the court determines that

the probative value of admitting this evidence outweighs its prejudicial effect to the accused; and

(2) evidence that any witness has been convicted of a crime shall be admitted if it involved dishonesty or false statement, regardless of the punishment.

44. *See Olden v. Kentucky*, 488 U.S. 227 (1988), which reversed defendant's conviction on confrontation grounds.

45. Kaarin Long, Caroline Palmer, and Sara G. Thorne, *Current Public Law and Public Policy Issues: Article: A Distinction without a Difference: Why the Minnesota Supreme Court Should Overrule in Precedent Precluding the Admission of Helpful Expert Testimony in Adult Victim Sex Assault Cases*, 31 HAMLINE J. PUB. L. & POL'Y 569 (2010).

46. Rule 413. Evidence of Similar Crimes in Sexual Assault Cases:

(a) In a criminal case in which the defendant is accused of an offense of sexual assault, evidence of the defendant's commission of another offense or offenses of sexual assault is admissible, and may be considered for its bearing on any matter to which it is relevant.

(b) In a case in which the Government intends to offer evidence under this rule, the attorney for the Government shall disclose the evidence to the defendant, including statements of witnesses or a summary of the substance of any testimony that is expected to be offered, at least fifteen days before the scheduled date of trial or at such later time as the court may allow for good cause.

(c) This rule shall not be construed to limit the admission or consideration of evidence under any other rule.

(d) For purposes of this rule and Rule 415, "offense of sexual assault" means a crime under Federal law or the law of a State (as defined in section 513 of title 18, United States Code) that involved:

(1) any conduct proscribed by chapter 109A of title 18, United States Code;

(2) contact, without consent, between any part of the defendant's body or an object and the genitals or anus of another person;

(3) contact, without consent, between the genitals or anus of the defendant and any part of another person's body;

(4) deriving sexual pleasure or gratification from the infliction of death, bodily injury, or physical pain on another person; or

(5) an attempt or conspiracy to engage in conduct described in paragraphs (1)-(4).

Rule 414. Evidence of Similar Crimes in Child Molestation Cases

(a) In a criminal case in which the defendant is accused of an offense of child molestation, evidence of the defendant's commission of another offense or offenses of child molestation is admissible, and may be considered for its bearing on any matter to which it is relevant.

(b) In a case in which the Government intends to offer evidence under this rule, the attorney for the Government shall disclose the evidence to the defendant, including statements of witnesses or a summary of the substance of any testimony that is expected to be offered, at least fifteen days before the scheduled date of trial or at such later time as the court may allow for good cause.

(c) This rule shall not be construed to limit the admission or consideration of evidence under any other rule.

(d) For purposes of this rule and Rule 415, "child" means a person below the age of fourteen, and "offense of child molestation" means a crime under Federal law or the law of a State (as defined in section 513 of title 18, United States Code) that involved:

(1) any conduct proscribed by chapter 109A of title 18, United States Code, that was committed in relation to a child;

(2) any conduct proscribed by chapter 110 of title 18, United States Code;

(3) contact between any part of the defendant's body or an object and the genitals or anus of a child;

(4) contact between the genitals or anus of the defendant and any part of the body of a child;

(5) deriving sexual pleasure or gratification from the infliction of death, bodily injury, or physical pain on a child; or

(6) an attempt or conspiracy to engage in conduct described in paragraphs (1)-(5).

47. *See* FED. R. EVID. 413.

48. Robert F. Thompson III, *Character Evidence and Sex Crimes in the Federal Courts: Recent Developments*, 21 UNIV. LITTLE ROCK ARK. L. REV. 241, 241 (1999).

49. *Id.*

50. *See State v. Myers*, 359 N.W.2d 604, 609-610 (Minn. 1984); *see also* Emily C. Aldridge, *To Catch a Predator or to Save His Marriage: Advocating for an Expansive Child Abuse Exception to the Marital Privileges in Federal Courts*, 78 FORDHAM L. REV. 1761 (2010); Naomi Harlin Goodno, *Protecting "Any Child": The Use of the Confidential-Marital-Communications Privilege in Child-Molestation Cases*, 59 KAN. L. REV. 1 (2010).

51. FED. R. EVID. 403.

52. 18 PA. CONS. STAT. § 3122.1 (2010).

53. For an incisive review of the staggering rates, see Elizabeth Hollenberg, *The Criminalization of Teenage Sex: Statutory Rape and the Politics of Teenage Motherhood*, 10 STAN. L. & POL'Y REV. 267 (1999). *See* Centers for Disease Control, *Report of Final Natality Statistics, 1995*, 45 MONTHLY VITAL STAT. REP. 26, T.2 (1997).

54. WILLIAM J. BENNETT, THE MORAL COMPASS: STORIES FOR A LIFE'S JOURNEY (1996); WILLIAM J. BENNETT, THE BOOK OF VIRTUES (1993); DANIEL PATRICK MOYNIHAN, ON THE LAW OF NATIONS (1992); DANIEL PATRICK MOYNIHAN, MILES TO GO: A PERSONAL HISTORY OF SOCIAL POLICY (1997).

55. Brady E. Hamilton et al., *Births: Preliminary Data for 2009*, NAT'L VITAL STAT. REP., Dec. 21, 2010, available at http://www.cdc.gov/nchs/data/nvsr/nvsr59/nvsr59_03.pdf (accessed August 3, 2011); *see also* a startling complication of current statistical trends in the United States in WILLIAM J. BENNETT, THE INDEX OF LEADING CULTURAL INDICATORS, Chapters 1–3 (1994).

56. Douglas J. Besharov & Karen N. Gardiner, *Truth & Consequences: Teen Sex*, AM. ENTERPRISE, Jan.–Feb. 1993, at 542, 53.

57. Centers for Disease Control, *Report of Final Natality Statistics, 1995*, 45 MONTHLY VITAL STAT. REP. 26, T.2 (1997).

58. See KRISTIN LUKER, DUBIOUS CONCEPTIONS: THE POLITICS OF TEEN PREGNANCY 81 (1996).

59. Elizabeth Hollenberg, *The Criminalization of Teenage Sex: Statutory Rape and the Politics of Teenage Motherhood*, 10 STAN. L. & POL'Y REV. 267, 267 (1999).

60. Lisa Pearlstein, *Walking the Tightrope of Statutory Rape Law: Using International Legal Standards to Serve the Best Interests of Juvenile Offenders and Victims*, 47 AM. CRIM. L. REV. 109, 110 (2010); *see also* Suzanne Meiners-Levy, *Challenging the Prosecution of Young "Sex Offenders": How Developmental Psychology and the Lessons of Roper Should Inform Daily Practice*, 79 TEMP. L. REV. 499 (2006).

61. Elizabeth Nevins-Saunders, *Incomprehensible Crimes: Defendants with Mental Retardation Charged with Statutory Rape*, 85 N.Y.U. L. REV. 1067 (2010).

62. 659 S.2d 256 (Fla. 1995).

63. FLA. STAT. §794.05 (2010).

64. Anthony N. Amelio, *Note: Florida's Statutory Rape Law: A Shield or a Weapon? A Minor's Right of Privacy Under Florida Statutes § 794.05*, 26 STETSON L. REV. 407, 409 (1996).

65. *B.B.*, 659 S.2d at 262.

66. *See* Darryl van Duch, *Judge Posner: Statutory Rape Is Not Always Violent*, 34 NAT. L. J., April 21, 1997, at A7.

67. 478 U.S. 186 (1986).

68. 539 U.S. 558 (2003).

69. TEX. PENAL CODE ANN. § 21.06(a) (West 2003).

70. *Id.* at §22.021.

71. DAVID A. J. RICHARDS, THE SODOMY CASES: BOWERS V. HARDWICK AND LAWRENCE V. TEXAS (2009); *See also* a diatribe about the allegedly brilliant legal scholar, Martha Nussbaum, in: Mary Anne Case, *Honoring the Contributions of Professor Martha Nussbaum to the Scholarship and Practice of Gender and Sexuality: History, Identity & Sexuality: A Lot to Ask: Review Essay of Martha Nussbaum's from Disgust to Humanity: Sexual Orientation and Constitutional Law*, 19 COLUM. J. GENDER & L. 89 (2010).

72. VA. CODE ANN. §§ 18.2-67.1, 67.2 (2010).

73. *See* R.I. GEN. LAW §11-10-1 (since repealed).

74. *See* SUMM. PA. JURIS. §15.40.

75. DONALD P. KOMMERS, JOHN E. FINN & GARY J. JACOBSOHN, AMERICAN CONSTITUTIONAL LAW: ESSAYS, CASES, AND COMPARATIVE NOTES 363 (2009); *See also* William N. Eskridge, Jr., *Sexual and Gender Variation In American Public Law: From Malignant to Benign to Productive*, 57 UCLA L. REV. 1333 (2010).

76. Susan Ayres, *Coming Out: Decision-making in State and Federal Sodomy Cases*, 62 ALB. L. REV. 355 (1998).

77. Janet E. Halley, Reasoning about Sodomy: Act and Identity in and after *Bowers v. Hardwick*, 79 VA. L. REV. 1721 (1993).

78. ARK. CODE ANN. §5-14-122 (2010); KAN. STAT. ANN. §§21-3501, 3505 (2010); MO. REV. STAT. §566.010 (2010); MONT. CODE ANN. §§45-2-101, 45-5-505 (2010); TENN. CODE ANN. §39-13-510 (2010).

79. Halley, *supra* note 77, at 1774–75.

80. *Hardwick v. Bowers*, 478 U.S. 186 (1986).

81. *Id.* at 196.

82. *Id.* at 190.

83. *Id.* at 197.

84. *Id.* at 192-94.

85. Halley, *supra* note 77, at 1753.

86. 539 U.S. 558 (2003).

87. *Planned Parenthood of Southeastern Pa. v. Casey*, 505 U.S. 833, 847 (1992).

88. 539 U.S. at 578-579.

89. *Id.* at 589-590.

90. See *Wisconsin Supreme Court Applies Sexual Assault Statute to Attempted Sexual Intercourse with a Corpse. — State v. Grunke, 752 N.W.2d 769 (Wis. 2008)*, 122 HARV. L. REV. 1780 (2009); Jonathan P. Rosman and Phillip J. Resnick, *Sexual Attraction to Corpses: A Psychiatric Review of Necrophilia*, 17 BULL. AM. ACAD. PSYCHIATRY & L. 153–163 (1989).

91. GA. CODE ANN. § 16-6-7 (2010).

92. Tyler Trent Ochoa and Christine Newman Jones, *Defiling the Dead: Necrophilia and the Law*, 18 WHITTIER L. REV. 539, 540–41 (1997).

93. *See Rogers v. State*, 890 P.2d 959, 959 (Okla. Crim. App. 1995); *Doyle v. State*, 921 P.2d 901, 914 (Nev. 1996); *State v. Holt*, 382 N.W.2d 679, 685 (Wis. 1985); *Lipham v. State*, 362 S.E.2d 840 (Ga. 1988).

94. *Commonwealth v. Waters*, 649 N.E.2d 724, 726 (Mass. 1995). *See Lipham*, 362 S.E.2d.

95. *See* CAL. HEALTH & SAFETY CODE § 7052 (West 2011).

96. *People v. Sellers*, 203 Cal. App. 3d 1042, 1050, 250 Cal. Rptr. 345, 350 (1988); *see also People v. Davis*, 10 Cal. 4th 463, 521 n.20, 41 Cal. Rptr. 2d 826, 858 n.20, 896 P.2d 119, 151 n.20 (1995); *People v. Stanworth*, 11 Cal. 3d 588, 604 n. 15, 114 Cal. Rptr. 250, 262 n. 15, 522 P.2d 1058, 1070 n. 15 (1974).

97. *People v. Kelly*, 1 Cal. 4th 495, 3 Cal. Rptr. 2d 677, 822 P.2d 385 (1992), *quoting People v. Sellers*, 203 Cal. App. 3d 1042, 1050, 250 Cal. Rptr. 345, 350 (1988).

98. *People v. Thompson*, 12 Cal App. 4th 195, 15 Cal. Rptr. 2d 333 (1993).

99. *See* Ochoa and Jones, *supra* note 92.

100. Erin E. Langley and Dominic J. Nardi, Jr., *Eleventh General Issue of Gender and Sexuality Law: Article: The Irony of Outlawing Aids: A Human rights Argument against the Criminalization of HIV Transmission*, 11 GEO. J. GENDER & L. 743 (2010).

101. ARK. CODE ANN. §5-14-123 (a) – (d) (2010).

102. Matthew Weait, *Criminal Law and the Sexual Transmission of HIV: R. v. Dica*, 68 MOD. L. REV. 121–134 (2005).

103. Michael L. Closen, *The Arkansas Criminal HIV Exposure Law: Statutory Issues, Public Policy Concerns, and Constitutional Objections*, ARK. L. NOTES 47 (1993).

104. Some argue that criminalization is inappropriate. *See* Scott Burris and Edwin Cameron, *The Case against Criminalization of HIV Transmission*, 300 J. AM. MED. ASS'N 578–581 (2008).

105. *See* 720 ILL. COMP. STAT. §5/12–16.2 (2010); ARK. CODE ANN. §5-14-123 (2010); IDAHO CODE ANN. §39-608 (1998); MD. CODE ANN., HEALTH-GEN.§ I 18-601.1 (West 2010); MICH. COMP. LAWS §14.15 (5210) (2010); MO. REV. STAT. §191.677 (2010).

106. *Doe v. Johnson*, 817 F. Supp. 1382, 1391-92 (W.D. Mich. 1993).

107. One good thing to report is that prison cases continue a seven-year decline. *See* Press Release, Bureau of Justice Statistics Number of HIV-Positive State and Federal Inmates Continues to Decline Tuesday (April 23, 2008), available at http://www.ojp.usdoj.gov/newsroom/pressreleases/2008/bjs08014.htm (accessed August 3, 2011).

108. Research on sexual abusers, prostitution, and deviant sexual lifestyles usually demonstrates the interplay between incestuous experiences and the lifestyle chosen.

109. 18 PA. CONS. STAT. § 4302 (2010).

110. This is quite the Pandora's Box and tolerance levels contribute to increased activity between non-biological parties. *See* David M. Greenberg et al., *Biological Fathers and Stepfathers Who Molest Their Daughters: Psychological, Phallometric, and Criminal Features*, SEXUAL ABUSE: J. RES.& TREATMENT, Jan. 2005, at 39-46; Alison Adams, *Seen But Not Heard: Child Sexual Abuse, Incest, and the Law in the United States*, 2009 UTAH L. REV. 591(2009).

111. UTAH CODE § 76-7-102 (West 2010).

112. *Id.* at § 76-7-102(2).

113. SUMM. PA. JURIS. § 15.41; *See also* Leigh B. Bienen, *Symposium: Defining Incest*, 92 NW. U. L. REV. 1501 (1998).

114. 910 P.2d 441 (Utah Ct. App. 1996).

115. *Id.* at 446.

116. Eric S. Janus and Emily A. Polachek, *A Crooked Picture: Re-Framing the Problem of Child Sexual Abuse*, 36 WM. MITCHELL L. REV. 142 (2009).

117. J. C. Abma et al., *Teenagers in the United States: Sexual activity, contraceptive use, and childbearing, 2002*, 23 VITAL HEALTH STAT. (2004), available at http://www.cdc.gov/nchs/data/series/sr_23/sr23_024.pdf (accessed August 3, 2011); J.C. Abma et al., *Teenagers in the United States: Sexual activity, contraceptive use, and childbearing, National Survey of Family Growth 2006–2008*, 23 VITAL HEALTH STAT. (2010), available at http://www.cdc.gov/nchs/data/series/sr_23/sr23_030.pdf (accessed August 3, 2011).

118. *See* ROBERT H. BORK, SLOUCHING TOWARDS GOMORRAH (1996); WILLIAM BENNETT, BOOK OF VIRTUES (1993).

119. Frank W. Putnam and Penelope K. Trickett, *Child Sexual Abuse: A Model of Chronic Trauma*, 56 PSYCHIATRY 82, 84 (1993).

120. 18 PA. CONS. STAT. §4304 (2010).

121. Not all cases involve sexual or physical abuse. Constitutional challenges have been lodged against charges that are rooted in the family's decision not to seek medical attention for the child. Certain religious sects are opposed to medical intervention and characterize the state intervention an abridgment of the freedom of religious expression. *See Commonwealth v. Banrhardt*, 497 A.2d 616 (Pa. Super. 1985).

122. Michael W. Sheetz, *Cyberpredators: Police Internet Investigations under Florida Statute 847.0135*, 54 U. MIAMI L. REV. 405, 416-417 (2000) *quoting* DIAGNOSTIC AND STATISTICAL MANUAL OF MENTAL DISORDERS 527–28 (4th ed. 1994).

123. MO. REV. STAT. § 566.067 (2010).

124. S. Bogaerts et al., *Intra- and Extra-Familial Child Molestation as Pathways Building on Parental and Relational Deficits and Personality Disorders (NCJ 231294)*, 54 INT'L J. OFFENDER THERAPY & COMP. CRIMINOLOGY 478-493 (2010); *See also* Danielle A. Harris, *Child Molestation*, in DIFFERENT CRIMES DIFFERENT CRIMINALS: UNDERSTANDING, TREATING AND PREVENTING CRIMINAL BEHAVIOR 83–102, (Doris Layton MacKenzie et al., eds. 2006).

125. Sheetz, *supra* note 122, at 408.

126. No. 56309 (Mo. App. 1999).

127. MO. REV. STAT. §566.010(2) (Supp. 1990).

128. The statute currently reads: "any act involving the genitals of one person and the mouth, tongue, or anus of another person or a sexual act involving the penetration, however slight, of the male or female sex organ or the anus by a finger, instrument or object done for the purpose of arousing or gratifying the sexual desire of any person." *Id.* at § 566.010(1).

129. ARIZ. REV. STAT. ANN. § 13-3553 (2010).

130. Brian E. Oliver, *Three Steps to Reducing Child Molestation by Adolescents*, 31 CHILD ABUSE & NEGLECT 683-689 (2007).

131. N.Y. PENAL LAW § 260.10 (McKinney 2010).

132. CAL. PENAL CODE § 645 (West 2010).

133. Megan Nicole Kanka and Alexandra Nicole Zapp Community Notification Program, Pub. L. No. 109-248 (2006) (codified at 42 U.S.C. § 16921 (2011)).

134. Juliet M. Dupuy, *The Evolution of Wisconsin's Sexual Predator Law*, 79 MARQ. L. REV. 873, 892 (1996). *See* NATHANIEL J. PALLONE, REHABILITATING CRIMINAL SEXUAL PSYCHOPATHS 2 (1990).

135. *See* WIS. STAT. 980.01 (2010); *see also* Dupuy, *supra* note 134, at 874-875.

136. WIS. STAT. § 980.01 (2010).

137. Sheetz, *supra* note 122, at 426–27.

138. *See* Charles P. Nemeth, *Decriminalization in Sexual Offense Cases Involving Children: A Disturbing Trend*, PA. CHILD ADV. (1990).

139. FL. STAT. § 847.0135 (2010).

140. Mark D. Marino, *State's Criminal Statute Proscribing Use of the Internet to Transfer Sexually Explicit Material to Minors Violates the Commerce Clause*, 8 SETON HALL CONS. L.J. 945, 949 (Sum. 98). *See American Libraries Assn v. Pataki*, 969 F. Supp. 160 (S.D.N.Y. 1997).

141. Marino, *supra* note 140, at 950.

142. Congress wisely enacted the Protection of Children from Sexual Predators Act (10 Pub. L. No. 105-314), which requires electronic communication services providers to report the commission of child pornography offenses to authorities; provides the Attorney General with authority to issue administrative subpoenas in child pornography cases; permits forfeiture of the proceeds derived from offenses against children, and of the facilities and instrumentalities used to perpetuate those offenses; gives prosecutors the power to seek pretrial detention of sexual predators; provides federal law enforcement with additional authority to assist States in kidnapping and series murder investigations; creates the Child Abduction and Serial Murder Investigative Resources Center. Otto G. Obermaier and Ronald R. Rossi, *Evaluating the Crime Legislation Passed by the 105th Congress*, N.Y. L. J., Jan. 26, 1999, at 1.

143. 47 U.S.C. § 231 (2010). *See* Jill Jacobson, *Comment: The Child Online Protection Act: Congress's Latest Attempt to Regulate Speech on the Internet*, 40 SANTA CLARA L. REV. 221 (1999).

144. *Id.*

145. *ACLU v. Reno*, 31 F. Supp. 2d 473 (E.D. Pa. 1999). *See* Jacobsen, *supra* note 143.

146. Children's Internet Protection Act (CIPA), Pub. L. No. 106-554 (2000) (codified at 20 U.S.C. §§ 6801, 6777, 9134 (2003); 47 U.S.C. § 254 (2003)).

147. 20 U.S.C. § 9134 (2011).

148. National Conference of State Legislators, Children and the Internet, Laws Relating to Filtering, Blocking and Usage Policies in Schools and Libraries, (2011), available at http://www.ncsl.org/default.aspx?tabid=13491#states (accessed August 3, 2011).

Chapter 7

Crimes against Property

KEYWORDS

Blackmail: Extortion or coercion by often written threats of public exposure, physical harm, or criminal prosecution.

Bribe: A benefit given, promised, or offered in order to influence the judgment or conduct of a person in a position of trust.

Carjacking: Theft by force or intimidation of an auto that has a driver or passenger present.

Embezzle: To convert property entrusted to one's care fraudulently to one's own use.

Extortion: The act or practice of extorting money or other property; the act or practice of extorting by a public official acting under color of office.

Forgery: The act of falsely making, altering, or imitating with intent to defraud.

Fraud: Any act, expression, omission, or concealment calculated to deceive another to his or her disadvantage.

Larceny: The unlawful taking and carrying away of personal property with the intent to deprive the rightful owner of it permanently.

Material: Being of real importance or consequence; being an essential component.

Misrepresentation: An intentionally or sometimes negligently false representation made verbally, by conduct, or sometimes by nondisclosure or concealment and often for the purpose of deceiving, defrauding, or causing another to rely on it detrimentally.

Property: Something that is owned or possessed.

Receiving stolen property: A crime requiring that property be stolen by someone other than the person receiving it; that the person receiving it has actually received the property or aided in concealing it; that the person has knowledge that the property has been stolen; that the person received it with wrongful intent.

Shoplift: To steal displayed goods from a store.

Theft: A criminal taking of the property or services of another without consent.

INTRODUCTION: OFFENSES AGAINST PROPERTY

In a capitalist society, the valuation of property will assuredly lead to distinct levels of criminality. Not only is the valuation tied to self-worth and individual wealth, but also, because of the free market, values tend to rise to higher levels. Americans intensely believe that personal ownership is not a sign of material greed, but much more the ownership of goods and services in a free market environment. Hence, its criminal justice system takes seriously offenses that undermine the rights to ownership. Property can encompass anything of value, from tangible to intangible, from rock hard assets to stocks and bonds, from art artifacts to cash money. At common law, the broad rubric was "larceny." In our more codified life, the idea of theft and its diverse offenses defined has fully blossomed. Larceny/theft covers a wide range of affronts to property ownership, including a purloined personal item to shoplifted item, embezzlement, fraud, forgery, extortion, bribery, and other coercive tactics used to gain property illegally, and they are this chapter's subject matter.

THEFT

ELEMENTS

- Intent to take permanently another's property
- The taking and asportation of property
- Property taken has value
- Without privilege or right

Labeled "larceny" at common law, the crime of theft is a violation of one's possessory right to property. What is mine is mine to protect and cherish, and what is yours, the very same. When looked at this way, it is easy to see why this offense is so often described as an attack against possession. In a free society, possessory rights are both natural and expected. If our society was communitarian, whereby all things were owned as share and share alike, there would be no sense of outrage when thievery occurred. Idyllic as this communitarian approach seems, even these forms of self-governance lay down parameters of individual possession. Theft is just as much a crime in a socialist republic as it is in a democracy, although the opportunities for thievery dramatically rise in materially rich nations. Third world countries have less to own and less to pilfer. Even so, the justice and law enforcement community have done a good job in stemming the tide of property offenses over the past three decades. In addition, community involvement, security systems, and tamper proof technology has helped as well. (See Figure 7.1.[1])

Our task dwells on the many faces of theft and how the criminal law categorizes and defines the basic and specialized elements witnessed in property offenses. Larceny/theft also breaks down in various grades and levels that usually reflect the value of what has been taken and/or the methods employed to unlawfully seize. Simple/petty thefts to grand larceny definitions, which use dollar or other valuations sums to distinguish one offense from the other, are the usual players.

(A.1) FELONY OF THE THIRD DEGREE.— Except as provided in subsection (a), theft constitutes a felony of the third degree if the amount involved exceeds $2,000, or if the property stolen is an automobile, airplane, motorcycle, motorboat or other motor-propelled vehicle, or, in the case of theft, by receiving stolen property, if the receiver is in the business of buying or selling stolen property.

(B) OTHER GRADES.— Theft not within subsection (a) or (a.1) of this section, constitutes a misdemeanor of the first degree, except that if the property was not taken from the person or by threat, or in breach of fiduciary obligation, and:

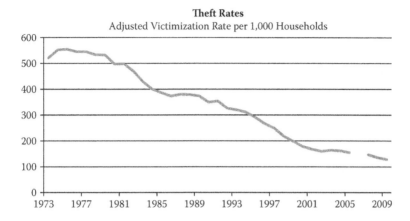

Theft Rates
Adjusted Victimization Rate per 1,000 Households

Figure 7.1 Theft rates per 1,000 households.

(1) the amount involved was $50 or more, but less than $200, the offense constitutes a misdemeanor of the second degree; or
(2) the amount involved was less than $50, the offense constitutes a misdemeanor of the third degree.[2]

A cursory glance at most theft statutes indicates the simplicity of form and content. By way of example, Michigan's statute clearly defines the proscribed conduct:

(1) A person who commits larceny by stealing any of the following property of another person is guilty of a crime as provided in this section:
(a) Money, goods, or chattels.
(b) A bank note, bank bill, bond, promissory note, due bill, bill of exchange or other bill, draft, order, or certificate.
(c) A book of accounts for or concerning money or goods due, to become due, or to be delivered.
(d) A deed or writing containing a conveyance of land or other valuable contract in force.
(e) A receipt, release, or defeasance.
(f) A writ, process, or public record.[3]

For the sake of ease, most legislatures, by emulating the Model Penal Code (MPC) have merged and categorized offenses under the broad heading of "theft" rather than employing the numerous distinctions inherent in larceny law. In addition, they have included many of the once separate offenses, such as embezzlement. Check the local statutes closely in your jurisdiction. This mindset reflects an overall improvement in our understanding of the nature of property interest and its corresponding ownership. Distinctions between types and kinds of property stolen are really artificial inventions that bear little relationship to the severity and gravity of the offense committed. Theft becomes not the unique or specialized form of taking that depends on the type of property purloined, but the unified action of stealing something of value. Theft for the MPC is first and foremost the "unauthorized taking or disposition of movable or immovable property."[4] Forms of theft are further expounded upon throughout the suggested legislative design. Keep the basic elements close to the chest and remember that the accused will be quite capable of emphasizing the subtleties that set them free. Remember these essential issues:

- Was the taking temporary or permanent?
- What type of property was subject to taking?
- What type of value did the property have?
- How far was the property carried away?

The Taking

Inherent in every act of theft is an unlawful acquisition of another's possessory interest.[5] One cannot steal, embezzle, deceive, thieve or pilfer what rightfully belongs to oneself. Aside from this absurdity, it is just as difficult to label a thief as one who possesses a right or claim to specific property higher than the former possessor. In this sense, the actor can only take from another who is more entitled than he or she. The actor dispossesses another without right or privilege and certainly lacks the necessary consent to strip the possessory interest from the victim. Taking, therefore, imputes a "grab" from another—a formal removal from another's possession to one's own sphere of possessory interest. A taking happens not because the accused wishes what another has, but because the actor has embarked on affirmative and well-defined steps to dislodge the former possessor from actual possession. The MPC, matter of fact, characterizes this action as "takes or exercises unauthorized control."[6]

Pennsylvania employs the terms "deprive and obtain" in order to illustrate the many avenues and approaches to the theft.[7] The statute displays an unrivaled sophistication in describing the offense:

(a) Movable property.—A person is guilty of theft if he unlawfully takes, or exercises unlawful control over, movable property of another with intent to deprive him thereof.

(b) Immovable property.—A person is guilty of theft if he unlawfully transfers, or exercises unlawful control over, immovable property of another or any interest therein with intent to benefit himself or another not entitled thereto.[8]

Herein, we see how plainly larceny/theft directs itself to the realm of property alone. Unlike robbery, which involves a taking of things with a corresponding act of force or violence to effectuate the act, larceny/theft lacks such excitement.[9]

Taking goods, services, negotiable instruments, bond certificates, chattels, things and physical objects summarize the crime's focal point. As a result, without the actual taking of things, larceny/theft remains a factual and legal impossibility. In fact, larceny involves little more than the relationship between the unauthorized taker and the thing taken. Even unsuccessful robbery charges can still be actual assaults and batteries because robbery has more nuances than the typical theft. Stated another way, violence against another person need not be over property of any sort, leaving open a host of other charges that might apply in a nonproperty-driven, yet violent occurrence. But, in larceny, what you see is what you get: property desired and property taken.

Due to this firm reality, the "taking," that act or movement to acquire what rightfully belongs to another, is the lynchpin of any alleged theft. The taking need not solely signify the physical removal of property, but entail how property once possessed is now illegally possessed by another. In consolidated theft statute jurisdictions, the point becomes apparent early on. Not only is the thief who grabs the television and gold ring in the statute's domain, but so too the employee who takes by "embezzling" funds or who acquires ownership by "forgery" of a legal document or who gains control over another's property by "fraud and misrepresentation." Each of these cases takes from another without privilege or right. Each case displaces the possessory interest that occurs upon the taking whether it is actual or constructive in design.

As in other felony prosecutions, the type of intent necessary to prove guilt will depend on statutory construction with the more serious versions calling for higher levels while the petty variety needs little mental acuity.[10]

What is indisputable in each and every case of larceny is that the actor desires to take from another and that the taking lacks any real sense of justification or right. A thief knows only too well that their sense of entitlement is faulty, and the target of the take is not their possession but another's. Looked at another way, the alleged thief lacks the requisite intent to be convicted when they believe what they possess is, in fact, theirs for the taking. A mistaken belief that the wallet picked up or the shopping bag put in the cart is, in fact, theirs negates mens rea. The true thief understands the disenfranchisement he or she causes and those who operate under diffuse or mistaken principles cannot be prosecuted.

The accused may be unjustly charged when he or she believes that the former possessor relinquished any claim or right to the property or consented to its delivery or giving to another. In this case, the defendant lacks the necessary intent to take and is devoid of a criminal plan to dispossess another of what belongs to them. Taking is further manifested in the actor's permanent and long-term desire to displace the property of another. Thieves do not borrow, even though they may disingenuously claim so. Thieves steal the goods and services for a lifetime of usage. Hence, a criminal taking is not a temporary displacement or usage, but a permanent intrusion into the property of another.

For many commentators, a larceny charge cannot be upheld if proof regarding the mind behind the taking is not clearly and articulately proffered. Whether by fraud or collusion, whether by deceit and misrepresentation, whether by physical acquisition, each larceny case demands proof of the mind's understanding of the unlawful taking. In sum, the perpetrator cannot take, in any criminal sense, what belongs to another without understanding that said taking lacks regularity and right. Thieves take because the subject matter of the taking is what they lust after. Historically, larceny/theft represents the taking of another's possessory interest and a criminal agent accused of intending this end must be shown to be aware of his or her lack of right to the goods. To take, therefore, calls for more than mere movement, but an accompanying mental state that is culpably aware.

Asportation

Further proof of the meaningfulness of the taking was the decision by the perpetrator to carry away the goods sought. The term "asportation" came to be known as the carrying away component of the larceny case.[11]

Without proof of asportation, no credible jury or judge would ever find an accused guilty of this offense. Asportation evidentially demonstrates much more than a desire to have something of someone else, but the intent to formalize the intent to deprive. When the thief carries away the prize, the larceny has achieved a factual reality that cannot be denied. The criminal need not be successful in working his forlorn deed since the law does require some overt act that proves the unwarranted and unwanted transference of property. Without it, doubt lingers. Without it, prosecutors think long and hard about pursuing the case.

Asportation is effective no matter how slight or insignificant.[12]

CASE 7.1

BRITT V. COMMONWEALTH
667 S.E.2d 763 (Va.2008)

In this appeal from a defendant's conviction for grand larceny, we consider whether the evidence was sufficient to establish that the value of the goods taken was at least $200. Richard L. Britt was convicted in a bench trial in the Circuit Court of the City of Richmond of grand larceny, in violation of Code § 18.2-95, and of statutory burglary, in violation of Code § 18.2-91. Britt's burglary conviction is not before us in this appeal. The circuit court sentenced Britt for the grand larceny conviction to a term of ten years imprisonment, which was suspended in its entirety.

The evidence at trial showed that City of Richmond Police Officer R. Joy Norwood responded to a report of a "break-in" that occurred at the Chamberlayne Food Mart (the store) around 4:00 a.m. one morning. As Norwood approached the store in her police vehicle, she observed that a window in the store had been broken. Norwood also saw various types of packaged tobacco products (collectively, "cigarette packs") on the ground outside the store's front entrance. Immediately thereafter, Norwood noticed two men standing in a parking lot across the street from the store. At that time, Norwood saw one of these men, later identified as Britt's accomplice, holding a black plastic bag. Norwood also observed the other man, later identified as Britt, reaching into the bag in an apparent attempt to retrieve some of its contents.

When the men saw Norwood's police car, they fled. Norwood pursued and ultimately apprehended Britt, who had dropped three sealed cigarette packs during the chase. Police later retrieved these three items and the contents of the black plastic bag.

The storeowner, Sama Azeire, arrived at the store later that morning. He testified that he found some cigarette packs, which were ordinarily located on shelves behind the cash register, on the store floor. However, Azeire did not describe the specific location of those cigarette packs on the floor. Azeire stated that the total retail price of all the cigarette packs retrieved from the store floor and from outside the store was $410.59. This total amount included the retail price of the cigarette packs found in the plastic bag, on Britt's flight trail, and on the floor of the store.

Defense counsel objected to the admission of Azeire's receipts showing the total amount of $410.59. Counsel argued that those receipts did not establish the value of the property taken, because the receipts did not contain separate tabulations distinguishing the value of the cigarette packs found outside the store from those located inside on the store floor. The circuit court overruled the objection and admitted the receipts in evidence.

At the close of the Commonwealth's case, defense counsel made a motion to strike the evidence, which the circuit court denied. Britt did not present evidence on his own behalf. After denying defense counsel's renewed motion to strike, the circuit court found Britt guilty of both grand larceny and burglary.

Britt appealed both his convictions to the Court of Appeals, which denied Britt's petition by order. *Britt v. Commonwealth*, Record No. 0040-07-2 (Oct. 1, 2007). We awarded Britt an appeal from his grand larceny conviction limited to the question whether the evidence presented on the grand larceny charge was sufficient to establish the value of the property taken.

Britt contends that the evidence was insufficient as a matter of law to establish that the value of the stolen property was at least $200. He argues that the Commonwealth's evidence failed to separate the value of the items taken out of the store from the value of the items found inside on the floor. Britt asserts that the record in this case lacks any evidence that he ever seized or moved the cigarette packs found on the store floor. According to Britt, it is equally likely that those items were "inadvertently knocked" from the store shelves during the taking of the items later found outside the store, and that such inadvertent movement does not constitute asportation for purposes of proving a larceny. Thus, Britt argues that the cigarette packs found on the store floor should not have been included in calculating the total value of the stolen property, and that the record before us proves only that he is guilty of petit larceny.

In response, the Commonwealth asserts that the crime of grand larceny was complete the moment the cigarette packs were removed from the store shelf, and that, regardless of their exact location on the floor, the retail price of those items properly was included in the valuation of the property taken. The Commonwealth contends that the circuit court reasonably could have inferred that Britt and his accomplice moved all the cigarette packs from the shelf with the intent to steal them. According to the Commonwealth, the fact that the men ultimately were unsuccessful in removing all the displaced cigarette packs from the store does not affect the value of the property taken. We disagree with the Commonwealth's arguments.

We consider the evidence in the light most favorable to the Commonwealth, the prevailing party in the circuit court; and we accord the Commonwealth the benefit of all reasonable inferences deducible from the evidence. Circumstantial evidence, if convincing, is entitled to the same weight as direct testimony. However, evidence that engenders only a suspicion or probability of guilt is not sufficient to support a conviction.

When a defendant challenges the sufficiency of the evidence, we accord the judgment of a circuit court sitting without a jury the same weight as a jury verdict. We will affirm the circuit court's judgment, unless it is plainly wrong or without evidence to support it. We have defined larceny, a common law crime, as the wrongful or fraudulent taking of another's property without his permission and with the intent to permanently deprive the owner of that property. Grand larceny includes the taking, not from the person of another, of goods having a value of $200 or more.

The monetary amount specified in Code § 18.2-95 is an essential element of the crime of grand larceny, and the Commonwealth bears the burden of proving this element beyond a reasonable doubt. Although proof that stolen items have some value will sustain a conviction for petit larceny, a conviction for grand larceny requires proof that the value of the stolen goods is at least $200. Plainly, the Commonwealth must prove that the goods taken, as distinguished from those not taken, have a value of $200 or more. An item is taken, for purposes of larceny, when a defendant secures dominion or absolute control over the property. The duration of such dominion or absolute control, however, may be very brief or only momentary. The defendant must hold, seize, or grasp the property with his hands or otherwise.

In addition, proof of larceny requires that there be an asportation, or a movement of the seized goods, however slight, coupled with an intent to permanently deprive the owner of those goods. The defendant's intent to steal must exist at the time the seized goods are moved.

Applying these principles, we conclude that the evidence of value in this case was insufficient as a matter of law to establish that element of grand larceny. There was no evidence, circumstantial or otherwise, that Britt or his accomplice seized, grasped, or held the cigarette packs found on the store floor so as to exercise dominion or absolute control over them. In particular, the record is silent regarding the relative distance of those cigarette packs from their original location on the store shelves.

Lacking evidence that Britt or his accomplice exercised dominion or absolute control over the cigarette packs found on the floor, the record also necessarily fails to establish that there was an asportation of those items, that is, movement of the seized items accompanied by the intent to steal. In effect, therefore, the Commonwealth asks us to speculate that Britt and his accomplice tried to remove from the premises the items found on the store floor, but were unsuccessful in doing so, or that the items actually removed from the store had a value of $200 or more. We will not engage in such speculation. We hold that it is impossible to determine from the evidence the cumulative value of the items Britt and his accomplice seized and carried from the store. Because the total amount of $410.59 computed by the store's owner included the value of the cigarette packs found on the store floor and because there was no evidence showing the quantity or value of those items retrieved from the floor, the total amount of $410.59 was not competent evidence of the value of the items removed from the store. Thus, we conclude that the Commonwealth failed to prove that the value of the items taken was $200 or more. In the absence of such evidence, Britt's conviction of grand larceny rests on speculation and cannot stand.

For these reasons, we will reverse the Court of Appeals' judgment and vacate the conviction for grand larceny. We will remand the case to the Court of Appeals with direction that the case be remanded to the circuit court for a new trial on a charge of petit larceny if the Commonwealth be so advised. We do not remand solely for imposition of a new sentence on the lesser offense as we did in *Commonwealth v. South*, 272 Va. 1, 630 S.E.2d 318 (2006), because here, unlike in South, both parties have not consented to that relief.

Reversed and remanded

Questions

1. When the Court considers questions of value, what is its rationale?
2. How is value, at least in this case, related to asportation?
3. What property was the subject matter of the asportation?
4. What is the Court's view of the Commonwealth's proof of asportation?

The Property

Exactly what the target of the theft is predictably affects the charge chosen. The intricacies of property forms directly reflect the level and grade of charge and whether the facts bear out the intelligence of the offenses soon to be prosecuted. For example, embezzlement in the banking environment offers a strange dilemma for traditional larceny analysis. First, do cash dollars from the bank drawer qualify as "property"? Second, how can the embezzler really

CASE 7.2

MANNING V. STATE

166 S.E. 658 (Ga. Sup. 1932)

The Court of Appeals certified to this court the following question: "Section 192 of the Penal Code of 1910 reads as follows: 'If any person who has been entrusted by another with any money, note, bill of exchange, bond, check, draft, order for the payment of money, cotton or other produce, or any other article or thing of value, for the purpose of applying the same for the use or benefit of the owner or person delivering it, shall fraudulently convert the same to his own use, he shall be punished by imprisonment and labor in the penitentiary for not less than one year nor longer than five years.' When this section is properly construed, do the words 'or any other article or thing of value,' as used therein, include or cover real estate?"

Penal Code § 192 is one of a number of sections included in the sixth division, under the title "Crimes Relative to Property." The first article under the sixth division has reference to the crime of robbery, the second to larceny, and the third to "Embezzlement and Fraudulent Conversions." Section 192 falls within article 3, and under the subtitle "Embezzlement and Fraudulent Conversions."

It is insisted by counsel for the State that the offense of "Embezzlement and Fraudulent Conversions" was not known at common law, and was created by statute in this State for the purpose of supplying defects and protection in instances not included under the penal statutes applying to larceny. It has been so declared by this court. In *Robinson v. State*, which was a case of embezzlement, this court, speaking through Mr. Justice Little, said: "This offense was unknown to the common law, and is entirely the creation of statutes both in England and in this country. In its nature, it is near akin to larceny, the difference being, that in order to constitute the latter offense, the property must be taken from the actual or constructive possession of the owner." Crimes falling within the offenses named in the sixth division, third article, of the Code, have sometimes been referred to by this court and the Court of Appeals as larceny after trust.

In 2 Wharton's Criminal Law, 1489, the author states: "Embezzlement covers only cases, which common-law larceny does not include. No inconvenience can arise from the maintenance of this distinction, since it is allowable as well as prudent to join a count for larceny to that for embezzlement."

Bromberger v. U. S. was a case falling under the Federal statute, where a mail carrier was indicted for abstracting a letter and unlawfully taking money therefrom. The indictment was in two counts, one count charging embezzlement and the other larceny. In discussing the indictment with reference to a demurrer, the court said: "It is insisted that there is an irreconcilable repugnancy between the terms 'theft' and 'embezzlement'; that therefore both counts cannot stand, and that acquittal should have been directed on the second one; that the first count is itself defective, because inconsistent and repugnant in charging in the same count a destruction as well as an embezzlement and secretion of the same letter. ... The sufficient answer to all this, however, is that we are dealing not with the common law, but with a specific statute."

It would appear that the codifiers considered all of the offenses under the three articles, and under the sixth division, denominated "Crimes Relative to Property," were related crimes.

Theft, stealing, and fraudulent conversion are very nearly, if not quite, synonymous terms, as used in the Penal Code. Baldwin's Century Edition of *Bouvier's Law Dictionary*, at p. 532, states that an original unlawful taking is, in general, conclusive evidence of conversion. Under our Penal Code, simple larceny is the wrongful and fraudulent taking and carrying away of the goods of another, with intent to steal. In larceny or theft, *animus furandi*, that is, the intent, must be shown to exist; and in these cases there must also exist some degree of asportation, however slight. Where an offense of larceny, or even one so nearly related as that defined in Penal Code § 192, is charged, the element of asportation becomes important.

In *Hagood v. State*, it was held that the words "fraudulent conversion" are synonymous with the words "taking with intent to steal" in case of ordinary larceny. In *Keys v. State*, the court was dealing with a conviction under the Penal Code of 1895, § 194. In the indictment, the offense was designated as "larceny after trust." This court stated that the accused was indicted for that offense, and treated the case as such. Of course, it is a well-known principle that the name given to an offense in an indictment is not conclusive, but that the court will look to the allegations. It is significant that this court did not take occasion to note any error in the name given to the offense. This is merely mentioned as an indication that section 192 defines an offense which, if not in its essence a larceny under our code, is of such near kin that calling it larceny is no substantial misnomer.

In no case, so far as we have been able to discover, has this court ever decided the precise question involved. That question has arisen in extremely few cases in this country.

In *State v. Eno*, it was held that a similar, though not identical statute, did not include fraudulent conversion of land. In that case, it was said: "It is the general holding that neither the common law, nor the statutes of the several States defining the crime of cheating by false pretense, apply to real estate. Under the English law, real property was never the subject either of cheating or of false pretenses. Being incapable of larcenous asportation, it was not regarded as requiring the same protection as personal property. The crime of obtaining money or goods by false pretenses is said to be closely allied to that of larceny, and the common law and statutes defining the crime were undoubtedly designed for the fuller protection of personal property and in aid of the laws against larceny and theft. While the American statutes differ in phraseology, they are in substance copied from the English and are based on the same principle, and have the same object in view."

After all, while it is interesting to note the origin of offenses for "fraudulent conversion" and their relationship to crimes of larceny, we are in fact dealing with a statutory crime. It is a crime not known to the common law, but is a crime of the genus of larceny. It is a crime in dealing with which we must apply the general principles applicable to larceny. Real estate has never been a subject of larceny. "Land being incapable of larcenous asportation, it was not regarded as requiring at the hands of the criminal law the same protection as personalty. Since it could not be carried away and dissipated like chattels, although a man might be deprived of his landed estate by means of fraudulent practices and devices, yet the property was bound to remain stationary and accessible to the reach of the law, and he was relegated to the civil courts for his redress of the wrong. It is there used as an annotation to the text, wherein it is said: "At common law the offense of cheating did not apply to a fraudulent transaction whereby the owner of land was deprived of it; and statutes as to false pretenses do not usually include real property. But there are statutes which are broad enough to include such property or any interest therein." On the other hand, in *State v. Layman*, the contrary view was taken.

In the sixth division of our Penal Code, and included in article 2, which has reference to larceny, are included sections 166 and 167, as follows: "§ 166. Things savoring of the realty, and fixtures. Theft or larceny may be committed of anything which, in the language of the law, savors of the realty, or of any fixture; and the punishment shall be as for a misdemeanor." "§ 167. Detached becomes personalty. Anything detached from the realty becomes personalty instantly on being so detached, and may be the subject matter of larceny, even by the person wrongfully detaching it." These are the only sections in the sixth division of the Penal Code which contain the words "realty." Undoubtedly real estate is a "thing of value," but it is not the kind of thing that can be the subject of "fraudulent conversion" under the Penal Code (1910), § 192.

Questions

1. Under traditional common law principles, asportation is related to what type of property?
2. Why is realty not capable of asportation?
3. How does embezzlement lack the common law elements of larceny?
4. Instead of asportation, the court looks to what?
5. Why is a fixture incapable of asportation?

take what he or she is entitled to possess in the first place. Bank tellers, by nature of their occupations, have a possessory right to hold and dispense cash. The framers of the embezzlement law perceived this conundrum early on. One cannot take what one has the right to hold. And, one cannot steal cash because cash is not the type of property originally envisioned as movable, personal property. Embezzlement represents one of many dilemmas that continue to evolve in larceny analysis. For generations, it was factually and legally impossible to steal services, e.g., restaurant and theatre, or utilities like electric, gas, and cable, or certain agricultural products. The American legal system has continuously reassessed the concept of property and possession in the marketplace. The original larceny framers could never have envisioned computer online services as capable of theft nor would anyone ever have predicted that a government benefit, such as food stamps or prescription benefits, would be larcenable. Originally these forms were not part of the statutory landscape. Even identity is subject to new property definitions.[13]

Even identity is now larcenable in a world of ATMs and credit purchases. Take the U.S. Department of Justice's Identity Theft Quiz at http://www.justice.gov/criminal/fraud/websites/idquiz.html

Figure 7.2   Stolen weapons. (Photo courtesy of B. Kohlhepp, Ross Township Police Department.)

At common law, only certain forms of movable property qualified. Property was relegated to hard goods, what was visibly portable. Today, property encompasses literally any type of valued interest. An enviable construction might be:

"PROPERTY." Anything of value, including real estate, tangible and intangible personal property, contract rights, chooses-in-action and other interests in or claims to wealth, admission or transportation tickets, captured or domestic animals, food and drink, electric or other power (Figure 7.2).[14]

State legislatures constantly grapple with new and emerging property forms that need inclusion in the theft framework. Mentioned already have been utilities, cables, and other services, documentary proof of ownership and computer services. Connecticut separates its degrees of larceny by employing diverse property forms. Its second-degree charge delineates specific dollar thresholds and particular types of property:[15]

Sec. 53a-123. Larceny in the second degree: Class C felony

(a) A person is guilty of larceny in the second degree when he commits larceny, as defined in section 53a-119, and:
    (1) The property consists of a motor vehicle, the value of which exceeds ten thousand dollars,
    (2) the value of the property or service exceeds ten thousand dollars,
    (3) the property, regardless of its nature or value, is taken from the person of another,
    (4) the property is obtained by defrauding a public community, and the value of such property is two thousand dollars or less,

(5) the property, regardless of its nature or value, is obtained by embezzlement, false pretenses or false promise and the victim of such larceny is sixty years of age or older or is blind or physically disabled, as defined in section 1-1f, or

(6) the property, regardless of its value, consists of wire, cable or other equipment used in the provision of telecommunications service and the taking of such property causes an interruption in the provision of emergency telecommunications service.[16]

Sure to happen over the next generation or two will be the emergence of other property forms not presently predicted in the statutory scheme, especially electronic formats. Maybe a more reasoned approach would be to simply look at the question of value and worth. Something subject to theft must have real and meaningful value. In other words, property that is either the real thing or its representation may be equally subject to theft analysis. For example, checks represent a specific value of property in the form of cash, as does a "performance bond representing the insurer's promise to pay."[17] Historically, the check itself would be insufficient to meet the property standard, but under new theft laws it will qualify; so too would food stamp coupons, legal documents, and negotiable instruments. Here, valuation is the centerpiece rather than property format. In the area of services, we discern the same evolution. Services are incapable of tangible grasp when compared to the common law picture. How can one steal labor or restaurant dining or musical performances? The Model Penal Code authors a two-fold designation for what property fits in the theft construct: movable and immovable. It states:

Section 206.1 Theft by unauthorized taking or disposition

(1) Movable Property. A person commits theft if he takes or exercises unauthorized control over movable property of another with the purpose of applying or disposing of it permanently for the benefit of himself or of another not entitled thereto.

(2) Immovable Property. A person commits theft if, having the power to transfer or encumber immovable property of another, he does so without authority and for the benefit of himself or of another not entitled thereto.[18]

Today, the bulk of jurisdictions gather all these formats under the theft tent. Property is, in the end, anything that has value, part of another's interest, which can be obtained and deprived without permission.

Without License or Privilege

Because theft primarily is an offense against another's possessory interest in property, the taking and carrying away must lack any form of justification. The illegality of larceny grounds itself in the unlawfulness of the taking. If a specific right or privilege exists that permits the taking, a prosecutor's office will be hard pressed to file such charges. To be assured that defenses do not shield the alleged actor, clarify the respective rights in the property. Is the victim really a victim in the legal sense? Does either party really have a possessory interest deserving a legal protection? The law does not require that someone have strict evidence of ownership, only a superior possessory claim. This is why the mechanic or construction firm that exerts control over property, by and through a lien, may lack true ownership in the property disputed, yet still maintain a superior claim above even the real and true owner. Banks and other parties with secured interests in an auto or recreational vehicle can defensibly reacquire or repossess property despite protest from the true owner. Repossession specialists are licensed to take property that is clearly not theirs on behalf of a party who can exert the superior possessory interest. In the world of debtors and creditors, mortgagors and mortgagees, pawn shops and loan services, the party with the best and most protected interest in property may not be the buyer. In the complex world of secured transactions and credit liens, we quickly discern that repossession and resale is not larceny, but a legitimate business practice statutorily protected.

Another clarification of the license principle can be deduced from the activities of law enforcement in the Racketeer Influenced and Corrupt Organizations Act (RICO)[19] or civil forfeiture. Police are licensed and privileged to take control of property that they as officers have no personal interest in and are shielded from any liability based on the statutory privilege given to public officers carrying out their duties. The same is true for a sheriff's department that conducts foreclosures and sales on executed and inventoried property. Similarly, private citizens, with lawful aspirations, are given the authority to reclaim improperly taken property. This right and privilege, if timely exercised, permits the reclamation of property by an aggrieved owner.

All of these examples further edify the fundamental notion of how larceny is an unjustified act against a possessory interest.[20] An individual with rights and privileges superior to the present possessor cannot be adjudged guilty of larceny, for it is their supreme position that protects them from the allegation. Indeed a thief who steals from a subsequent thief has victimized the initial wrongdoer because the first thief's initial possessory interest is vastly more original in time than the subsequent wrongdoer.[21] The law will not exonerate the subsequent thief because it presumes that he or she knows little or nothing about the victim. Since larceny confronts our basic idea of what possession is, it makes little difference who the victim is.

These same conclusions apply in various other legal contexts. Property that has been mislaid or lost cannot be the subject of larceny due to its lack of possessory interest. Who will be able to assert the loss? On what basis would the property infraction cause victimization if the party to whom the property belonged could not be discovered? An actor who has no affirmative knowledge that property belongs to Mr. A or Ms. B fails to formulate the requisite intent for larceny. Intentional ignorance and blind awareness will not be tolerated in these cases and, by most statutory accounts, finders of such property are affirmatively obliged to turn in the goods and report the loss. If after a set timeframe no one has rightfully claimed the goods, the finder automatically owns the property. The MPC insists that the finder of lost or mislaid property make reasonable efforts to return the property to its rightful owners. It holds in part:

> (3) Reasonable Measures. In determining what are reasonable measures, account shall be taken of the following factors, among others; the nature and value of the property, the expense and inconvenience of the restoration measures, and the reasonable expectation of compensation to the finder for expense and inconvenience borne by him. The following, among others, are reasonable measures which bar liability under this subsection unless the actor purposely omits other steps which he believes would be more likely to result in restoration:
> (a)   compliance with procedure prescribed by laws relating to the preservation and restoration of lost property; or
> (b)   delivery of the property to law officers for restoration of the owner; or
> (c)   delivery of the property to the occupant of the premises or operator of the vehicle where the property was found for restoration to the owner.[22]

Here under finder's laws, the party collecting is immune to prosecution. Similarly, the same result occurs in cases of abandoned property. It would be incongruous to hold accountable the acquirer of property long known to be abandoned and left behind. For example, an abandoned vehicle, left on a county road for a period of three years, could not be the subject matter of a subsequent larceny charge if the current possessor took innocently and with the understanding that the property was abandoned long ago. The law in every American jurisdiction grants various parties rights and privileges to deal with abandoned vehicles, boats, personal goods, and the like. Landlords whose apartments are strewn with left-behind junk and useless artifacts cannot be held accountable for any larceny when they possess and dispose of the goods, especially after having followed the legislative design on its collection and removal.

Finally, parties with legal rights and obligations to control property on behalf of another are immune to larceny and theft prosecution if they have carried out their responsibilities in good faith. Guardians who account for the funds for incompetent parties, trustees who oversee income and principle on behalf of beneficiaries, and sureties and other guarantors obliged to maintain the integrity of funds are licensed and privileged to utilize said funds without incurring criminal liability. These parties are termed "fiduciaries and are heavily regulated and disciplined in the absence of good faith on behalf of the parties they represent. One of the more telling examples of this growing phenomenon is lawyer misappropriation of client funds, which subjects the lawyer to both disciplinary and criminal penalties. Disbarment occurs when the misappropriation is either negligent or intentional, but criminal liability is usually imposed when the plan of misappropriation is willful."[23]

DEFENSE STRATEGIES

Does the property belong to another?

Which party has the superior legal interest in said property?

Did the accused believe in a specifically enforceable personal interest in property?

Did the accused borrow or intend to use for a limited time?

What type of property was stolen?

Is the property specially covered by other statutes, e.g., retail shoplifting, etc.?

Does the property have any real value?

Did the taker have license or privilege to acquire?

Did the taker carry away?

What type of property was stolen? Is it larcenable?

The costs of theft border on the astronomical. See the FBI's recent analysis of retail theft alone at http://www.fbi.gov/news/stories/2011/january/retail_010311/retail_010311

SPECIAL STATUTORY DESIGNS IN THE LAW OF THEFT

With the fundamental review of theft and larceny covered, it makes perfect sense to assess a variety of legislative responses which build upon this foundation. As noted earlier, larceny matures with both the marketplace of property subject to the illegal taking and the sophistication of the criminal population. The usage of credit cards, by way of illustration, is a modern practice that early lawmakers never foretold, nor could they have predicted the many means to thieve and defraud through the electronic, computerized age we presently live in, nor would it have been possible to anticipate the level of corruption that presently exists. Sadly, our poor boxes in churches, synagogues, and temples are no longer safe havens. For that matter, very little appears off limits to the criminal mind of the new millennium.

As a result of this decline and perverse innovation, legislators constantly need to update the theft statutes on the books. Our attention turns to the some of the more typically seen additions to theft codification.

Theft of Services

For many generations, the common law idea of what property means did not include the value of services rendered.[24] In a service economy, it is natural to witness growth in not only the types of services available to the masses, but to accept that services can be valued. Criminal codes now have either defined their property term to be inclusive or have determined that an additional offense is necessary. The MPC crafts a new offense entitled, "Theft of Labor or Service."

Section 206.7 Theft of labor or services

(1) A person commits theft if he obtains the labor or service of another by deception or intimidation, knowing that the provision of such labor or service is part of the calling or business of the person providing it.

(2) A person commits theft if, having control over the disposition of labor or service of others, to which he is not entitled, he diverts their labor or service to his own benefit or to the benefit of another not entitled thereto.

(3) A person commits theft if he obtains transportation, telephone service, or any service available for hire, without the consent of the person authorized to give consent or by means of deception or intimidation.[25]

In its commentary, the MPC describes this code addition as somewhat revolutionary especially when one considers the traditional rules.

Since the time of recommendation, the states continue to experiment with a host of statutory designs that zero in on all the possibilities for this type of theft. New York has an elaborate template that attempts to cover every imaginable tract. Its coverage makes theft of specific services criminal in these settings:

- Lodgings
- Restaurant services
- Credit cards
- Public transportation
- Telecommunications services
- Telephone access
- Utilities and tampering with utility devices
- Entertainment admission
- Computers and computer services
- Labor for improper cause[26]

Undoubtedly, lawmakers are listening to the constituents who have much at stake in the economic drain, such as pilferage causes. Incredibly, many accused cannot appreciate the illegitimacy of these acts in the same way other thefts unravel. Some defendants view cable or online services as being incapable of theft by being in the airwaves and, thus, naturally free. Utility companies frequently hear defenses, which justify the tapping of electricity and water and will meet up with defendants who take offense with any effort to cut their supplies off. Services don't seem to stir up the same sense of outrage. Yet, the value of services exceeds many tangible goods.

The definition of property is sure to change as the criminal element discovers new and improved methods of thievery. Review the language below and anticipate what needs to be added.

(1) A person is guilty of theft if he intentionally obtains services for himself or for another which he knows are available only for compensation, by deception or threat, by altering or tampering with the public utility meter or measuring device by which such services are delivered or by causing or permitting such altering or tampering, by making or maintaining any unauthorized connection, whether physically, electrically or inductively, to a distribution or transmission line, by attaching or maintaining the attachment of any unauthorized device to any cable, wire or other component of an electric, telephone or cable television system or to a television receiving set connected to a cable television system, by making or maintaining any unauthorized modification or alteration to any device installed by a cable television system, or by false token or other trick or artifice to avoid payment for the service.

Retail Theft

The dramatic rise in shoplifting has prompted legislative bodies to erect new code provisions that deal differently with an obvious act of theft.[28] Under existing larceny laws, the justice system lacked nothing in the way of enforceable charges, but given the severity of the felony larceny, and the extraordinary increase in retail theft, another design minimized the impact. In sum, the multiplicity of the acts caused lawmakers to soften the blow. (See Figure 7.3[29] for Shoplifting Rates from the FBI's Uniform Crime Report.)

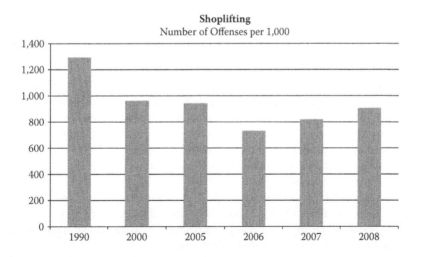

Figure 7.3 Shoplifting offenses per 1,000.

Pressure groups in the commercial marketplace clamored for the new statutes because the judicial system was often reticent to impose any serious penalties or even reach findings of guilt in far too many cases. Inaccurately, many hold that shoplifting lacks the type of criminal spark that ignites the justice system in general. Just as unfortunate is the common perception among many of its perpetrators that the conduct lacks any real gravity and should be ignored.[30] One wonders whether this approach can be morally or legally justified, but the adoption of retail theft statutes patently reflect the political and social reality of the law-making process.

The adoption of retail theft schemes has the unfortunate effect of continuing the decriminalization revolution so evident in the last half of the twentieth century. In place of the hard and fast larceny principles just enunciated, defendants are treated to a much kinder and gentler response upon their prosecution. Most initial offenses are never litigated and generally diverted to alternative disposition. Many convictions eventually are expunged by time or operation of law and others dismissed in exchange for other nonjudicial remedies like community service. So intent is this substituted response that it precludes prosecutors from choosing the general theft felony when the facts lead to the shoplifting conclusion.[31]

Any reasoned examination of retail theft laws make plain their identicality to the fundamental elements appearing in any larceny charge. The taking, or asportation, of a thing of value, without license or privilege is not extinguished from the legislated framework. The only difference rests in the qualification of where the conduct occurs and who becomes the victim. In retail theft, the commercial establishment is the targeted victim. In a way, the retail theft advocate perceives the victimization of the commercial entity as being substantively different than the person. How can big, impersonal, and wealthy businesses really feel the sting of larceny in the same way as an individual? A merchant and a mercantile establishment reaps the benefits and sows the misery such statutes bring to the table. [32] Individuals victimized by larceny always gain greater protections. As arguable as this view may be, it affords some level of justification to the proponent of the difference.

The statutes typically contain the following language:

§ 3929. Retail theft

(a) OFFENSE DEFINED.— A person is guilty of a retail theft if he:
   (1) takes possession of, carries away, transfers or causes to be carried away or transferred, any merchandise displayed, held, stored or offered for sale by any store or other retail mercantile establishment with the intention of depriving the merchant of the possession, use or benefit of such merchandise without paying the full retail value thereof;
   (2) alters, transfers or removes any label, price tag marking, indicia of value or any other markings which aid in determining value affixed to any merchandise displayed, held, stored or offered for sale in a store or other retail mercantile establishment and attempts to purchase such merchandise personally or in consort with another at less than the full retail value with the intention of depriving the merchant of the full retail value of such merchandise;
   (3) transfers any merchandise displayed, held, stored or offered for sale by any store or other retail mercantile establishment from the container in or on which the same shall be displayed to any other container with intent to deprive the merchant of all or some part of the full retail value thereof; or
   (4) under-rings with the intention of depriving the merchant of the full retail value of the merchandise.[33]

DEFENSE STRATEGIES IN RETAIL THEFT

Did the merchant have reasonable suspicion to arrest?
Was the taking intentional or inadvertent?
What was the value of the taking?
Did the mercantile establishment racially target suspects?
Was the property suspected of theft a disputed item?

Auto Theft

Another staggering rise in criminal conduct has been apparent in vehicular theft.[34] Why law-makers have determined the necessity for this distinguished offense in the larceny/theft family is open to interpretation. Others hold that the offense is often done with less than permanent motivations and rather than criminalize the "joy ride" believe we should deal less severely with the unauthorized use of the auto when compared to other property forms. Stereotypically, wild and reckless youths are the main players in this offense, but this picture is only a partial caricature. Every second or so, someone is victimized by the national crisis of auto theft.[35] The sheer numbers of auto theft, just as in shoplifting, has caused the invention of a new law. Rather than the harsh reality of felony theft, the justice system affords the less oppressive misdemeanor under various nomenclatures. Pennsylvania's construction is fairly common:

§ 3928. Unauthorized use of automobiles and other vehicles

(a) OFFENSE DEFINED. —A person is guilty of a misdemeanor of the second degree if he operates the automobile, airplane, motorcycle, motorboat, or other motor-propelled vehicle of another without consent of the owner.
(b) DEFENSE. —It is a defense to prosecution under this section that the actor reasonably believed that the owner would have consented to the operation had he known of it.[36]

A few compelling issues come forth in this analysis, though the concept of permanency in the taking repeatedly challenges the application. Joy rides, as they are affectionately called, are not the stuff of theft, but temporary inconvenience alone. The joy rider never really intends to steal anything, only to borrow for the moment. "The problem has been, and still is, how far can one go on a joy ride without converting the joy ride into a theft."[37] Once again, we see glimmers of the decriminalization tendency in the criminal culture and the creative defense tactics that mitigate the mens rea of this type of offense.

The City of Pittsburgh, Pennsylvania Police Department educates the public about the multiple ways in which auto thievery occurs at http://www.city.pittsburgh.pa.us/bat/html/types_of_car_theft.html

---

Carjacking

Worth mentioning is the far more serious offense of carjacking. To some, the offense directs itself to personal injury and confrontation in place of the property target. There is much truth to this assertion. Carjacking utilizes the instrumentality of a vehicle to escape or abscond from lawful chase or to enable a grander criminal enterprise. The federal law best encapsulates the nature of this offense in its Carjacking Correction Act of 1996, which reads:

Whoever, with the intent to cause death or serious bodily harm [1] takes a motor vehicle that has been transported, shipped, or received in interstate or foreign commerce from the person or presence of another by force and violence or by intimidation, or attempts to do so, shall:

(1) be fined under this title or imprisoned not more than 15 years, or both,
(2) if serious bodily injury (as defined in section 1365 of this title, including any conduct that, if the conduct occurred in the special maritime and territorial jurisdiction of the United States, would violate section 2241 or 2242 of this title) results, be fined under this title or imprisoned not more than 25 years, or both, and
(3) if death results, be fined under this title or imprisoned for any number of years up to life, or both, or sentenced to death.[38]

A cursory reading makes plain that the offender must intend serious harm or death in the taking of the vehicle and that the force component opens up new requirements in the proof of this taking. In *Holloway v. United States*,[39] the US. .Supreme Court closely scrutinized mens rea in the carjacking circumstance. Does the offense require a mental state that specifically and unconditionally intends to inflict death or serious bodily injury, or is the intent one conditionally applied if and only when the owner of the vehicle does not comply? In the latter case a defendant might argue the statute's inapplicability if no force was exerted since the vehicle's owner willingly parted with it. The majority of the Court held that either actual or constructive intent was acceptable under this construction. Justices Scalia and Thomas were none too amused in their dissent, a portion of which highlights the dilemma.

> Indeed, it seems to me much more implausible that Congress would have focused upon the ineffable "conditional intent" that the Court reads into the statute, sending courts and juries off to wander through "would-a, could-a, should-a" land. It is difficult enough to determine a defendant's actual intent; it is infinitely more difficult to determine what the defendant planned to do upon the happening of an event that the defendant hoped would not happen, and that he himself may not have come to focus upon. There will not often be the accomplice's convenient confirmation of conditional intent that exists in the present case. Presumably it will be up to each jury whether to take the carjacker ("your car or your life") at his word. Such a system of justice seems to me so arbitrary that it is difficult to believe Congress intended it. Had Congress meant to cast its carjacking net so broadly, it could have achieved that result—and eliminated the arbitrariness—by defining the crime as "carjacking under threat of death or serious bodily injury." Given the language here, I find it much more plausible that Congress meant to reach—as it said—the carjacker who intended to kill.[40]

Theft by Receiving Stolen Property

The array of theft possibilities continue with those offenders who may not directly steal, but rely on others who do the taking. When a criminal agent receives or takes into possession property he or she knows is suspect, the law construes the receipt to be a criminal theft no different than the initial larceny. To not declare this conduct illegal would open up a world of endless possibilities for our criminal population whose innocence could be shielded by second and third parties. Theft statutes are now wise enough to ferret out those who gain and profit from the larceny done by others. The usual statute mimics the recommendations of the MPC, which contains this language:

Section 206.8 Theft by receiving

(1) In General. A person who receives stolen movable property otherwise than for the purpose of restoring it to the owner commits theft if he knows that it is stolen property or, in the case of a dealer, if he believes that it is probably stolen property.
(2) Receiving Defined. Receiving means:

(a)   acquiring possession, control or title;

(b)   selling or lending on the security of the property;

(c)   retaining or transferring possession, control or title after the actor has information leading him to knowledge or belief, as the case may be, that the property is stolen, without notifying the police.[41]

The statute is unique for many reasons. First the essence of the offense rests in the receipt rather than the real taking. In fact, the novelty of this infraction arises from the receiver who does "not commit the trespassory taking, but instead acquires the property by the voluntary delivery of the original thief."[42]

Equally distinguishable is the varying standards that exist for the dealer/merchant versus the individual who does not commercially operate in the marketplace of goods and services. For the merchants, the law imposes a presumptive awareness about what things are really worth. For the experienced buyer and seller, ignorance of value is a much harder sell than for the novice trans-actor. Without valuation expertise, individuals can be quite unaware about what something is regularly worth, but this economic naiveté cannot give way to forced or feigned ignorance. Consumers do have some sense of what things are worth. A new CD player for $5 triggers suspi-cion in any quarter. For the individual, actual knowledge and awareness are minimally required before any successful prosecution can occur. Jurors will be far less sympathetic to the merchant who knows not his or her own business.

See how this offense's elements are targeted in the recommendation jury instructions and charge for the State of New Jersey at http://www.judiciary.state.nj.us/criminal/charges/theft008.pdf

---

In the final analysis, the trier of fact must weigh the reasonableness of the alleged ignorance of price and value.[43] A person with a checkered past of criminal violations, particularly those of this garden variety, are presumptively knowledgeable. Moreover, the judgment as to individuals will be borne from a reasonable person standard, not the erudite and expert dealer whose commer-cial experience could not be imputed to the every Mary and Joe. Dealers of stolen goods have long and arduous paths littered with past convictions and seedy histrionics. Innocent consumers can only be evaluated in light of the totality of circumstances.

THEFT BY INTIMIDATION (EXTORTION)

Extortion conjures images of loan sharks and other tough characters that lend at exorbitant rates and nearly make impossible any reasonable payback. Part of this picture is on the mark, but extortion covers a great deal of generally unknown territory.[44] Extortion contains additional qualities that relate to force, intimidation, and/or threat to inflict harm. Also known as "black-mail" in some jurisdictions, the end results of this threat are identical to every other class of larceny and theft because a victim relinquishes involuntarily rightful property or some other benefit. In the federal code, drafters have authored a broad and comprehensive set of principles that covers every imaginable form of threat for benefit.

18 USC §1951. Interference with commerce by threats or violence

(a) Whoever in any way or degree obstructs, delays, or affects commerce or the movement of any article or commodity in commerce, by robbery or extortion or attempts or conspires so to do, or commits or threatens physical violence to any person or property in furtherance of a plan or purpose to do anything in violation of this section shall be fined under this title or imprisoned not more than twenty years, or both.

(b) As used in this section—

 (1) The term "robbery" means the unlawful taking or obtaining of personal property from the person or in the presence of another, against his will, by means of actual or threatened force, or violence, or fear of injury, immediate or future, to his person or property, or property in his custody or possession, or the person or property of a relative or member of his family or of anyone in his company at the time of the taking or obtaining.

 (2) The term "extortion" means the obtaining of property from another, with his consent, induced by wrongful use of actual or threatened force, violence, or fear, or under color of official right.

 (3) The term "commerce" means commerce within the District of Columbia, or any Territory or Possession of the United States; all commerce between any point in a State, Territory, Possession, or the District of Columbia and any point outside thereof; all commerce between points within the same State through any place outside such State; and all other commerce over which the United States has jurisdiction.[45]

Getting something is what the blackmailer and extortionist aim at. How their aim is achieved will vary according to target, circumstance, position, occupation, and social strata. Some jurists classify blackmail as the noneconomic form of extortion, though this general finding cannot be relied on. Attorney Stanley Arkin relays a quick historical distinction.

> The etymological roots of "blackmail" date from sixteenth century Scotland. Blackmail was the tribute exacted at the Scottish border by freebooting chiefs "in exchange" for the payer's immunity from pillage. The term has evolved into encompassing the extortion of money or something of value "by the threat of exposure of something criminal or discreditable." The extortionate intimidation exerted is thus one of fear of disclosure of potentially harmful information.[46]

Practitioners quickly notice that things or property are subject to the claim, but so are items with a nontangible benefit. Ohio, for example, labels this secondary classification the "valuable benefit."[47]

An appellate court in Ohio found that a stalker's requests for a young girl's undergarments that was delivered to the offender satisfied the valuable benefit rule cited.[48] Texas affords an even broader definition of the subject matter of extortion, which is "anything of value."[49] New York's statute is quite instructive on how the worlds of blackmail and extortion have merged for the most part. At 155.05, the broad definition is apparent:

> By means of instilling in [another person] a fear that if the property is not so delivered, the actor will … (iv) accuse some person of a crime or cause criminal charges to be instituted against him; or (v) expose a secret or publicize an asserted fact, whether true or false, tending to subject some person to hatred, contempt or ridicule; or … (ix) perform any other act which would not in itself materially benefit the actor but which is calculated to harm another person materially with respect to his health, safety, business, calling, career, financial condition, reputation or personal relationships.[50]

Threats of disclosure of specific facts seem another approach.[51] In this scenario, the black-mailer/extortionist wants something and will use threat of embarrassment, shock and false-hood, defamatory material or inactivity by governmental authority, or aggressive activity by a unionist to achieve the benefit sought. The costs of privacy alone justify the continuing criminal-ization of the offense.[52]

What further separates this type of theft from its counterparts is the intimidation to the party victimized. The criminal agent succeeds because he or she frightens and threatens a person with real and actual harm.[53] One major qualification for this method of taking is that the threat never evolves into actual assault or physical injury. If it did, would robbery be the more appropriate charge? This does not paint a perfectly accurate picture either, for extortion lacks an imminent quality that would be demanded in a robbery prosecution where the offender takes and inflicts force simultaneously. Extortion displays a futuristic tendency. The perpetrator speaks of harm to come down the road if the victim does not cooperate. The layout of the extortion statute cor-roborates these general tendencies.[54]

Section 206.3 Theft by intimidation

A person commits theft if he obtains property of another by means of a threat to:
 (1) inflict physical harm on the person threatened or any other person or on property; or
 (2) subject any person to physical confinement or restraint; or
 (3) commit any criminal offense; or
 (4) accuse any person of a criminal offense; or
 (5) expose any person to hatred, contempt or ridicule; or
 (6) harm the credit or business repute of any person; or
 (7) reveal any secret; or
 (8) take action as an official against anyone or anything, or withhold official action, or cause such action or withholding; or
 (9) bring about or continue a strike, boycott or other collective unofficial action, if the property is not demanded or received for the benefit of the group which he purports to represent; or
 (10) testify or provide information or withhold testimony or information with respect to another's legal claim or defense; or
 (11) inflict any other harm which would not benefit the actor.[55]

For an excellent summary of this offense and aligned crimes, visit Professor Stuart Green, of Louisiana State University at http://faculty.law.lsu.edu/stuartgreen2/Green-extortion.pdf

Loan sharks are one piece of this legislative puzzle. Here, the many dynamics of threat and intimidation, in order to acquire what is not lawfully the demander's, are delineated. The offender may not only threaten bodily harm, but so much more. To be successful, the extortionist will stoop to the lowest forms of conduct including the false and malicious prosecution of cases, the violation of privacy, the exposure of private, intimate matter, or the contemptible effort to destroy individual reputations. Although not strictly defamation, the offender here sells "for-bearance" without justification or right.

A person is guilty of theft if he obtains property of another by threatening to:

(a) inflict bodily injury on anyone or commit any other criminal offense; or
(b) accuse anyone of a criminal offense; or
(c) expose any secret tending to subject any person to hatred, contempt or ridicule, or to impair his credit or business repute; or
(d) take or withhold action as an official, or cause an official to take or withhold action; or
(e) bring about or continue a strike, boycott or other collective unofficial action, if the property is not demanded or received for the benefit of the group in whose interest the actor purports to act; or
(f) testify or provide information or withhold testimony or information with respect to another's legal claim or defense; or
(g) inflict any other harm which would not benefit the actor.[56]

A model state statute is reproduced below:

§ 3923. Theft by extortion

(A) OFFENSE DEFINED. —A person is guilty of theft if he intentionally obtains or withholds property of another by threatening to:
  (1) commit another criminal offense;
  (2) accuse anyone of a criminal offense;
  (3) expose any secret tending to subject any person to hatred, contempt or ridicule;
  (4) take or withhold action as an official, or cause an official to take or withhold action;
  (5) bring about or continue a strike, boycott or other collective unofficial action, if the property is not demanded or received for the benefit of the group in whose interest the actor purports to act;
  (6) testify or provide information or withhold testimony or information with respect to the legal claim or defense of another; or
  (7) inflict any other harm which would not benefit the actor.[57]

At the federal level, the extortion claim curiously combines commerce questions and the use of power and might to gain a benefit. Within the statutory language one now discovers the common law crime of bribery where public officials use their power of office to extract an unlawful benefit of some form.[58] This dramatic expansion of the common law principles prompted the U.S. Supreme Court to grant certiorari in *Evans v. United States*,[59] a case where campaign contributions became the focal point in a zoning case. While no one could dispute some level of impropriety in this case, the opinion dwells upon whether or not the doing of an official act, under color of state law, in exchange for money amounts to extortion. The majority determined that despite the lack of force, threat, or intimidation, the act of giving money produced a particular benefit. Citing the *Federal Extortion Act*,[60] the Court held that this was an act of extortion since it was an inducement. The dissent, authored by Justice Clarence Thomas, queried about the complete and total lack of force or intimidation in these facts. How could extortion exist if the facts do not support the statutory demand that the inducement be coupled by the "wrongful use of actual or threatened force, violence, or fear."[61] The dissenting opinion raises the flag of disbelief by remarking:

> I have no doubt that today's opinion is motivated by noble aims. Political corruption at any level of government is a serious evil, and, from a policy perspective, perhaps one well-suited for federal law

---

CASE 7.3

U.S. V. ARENA
180 F.3d 380 (2nd Cir 1999).

Visit your local county law library, online library, or a law library at a local college or university and obtain the above case. Respond to the following questions.

Questions

1. Do you think the jury and the appellate court correctly interrelated the extortion statute to include the suspected acts?
2. In what sense is this case of interstate commerce?

---

enforcement. But federal judges are not free to devise new crimes to meet the occasion. Chief Justice Marshall's warning is as timely today as ever: "It would be dangerous, indeed, to carry the principle, that a case which is within the reason or mischief of a statute, is within its provisions, so far as to punish a crime not enumerated in the statute, because it is of equal atrocity, or of kindred character, with those which are enumerated."[62] Whatever evils today's opinion may redress, in my view, pale beside those it will engender. "Courts must resist the temptation to stretch criminal statutes in the interest of the long-range preservation of limited and even-handed government."[63] All Americans, including public officials, are entitled to protection from prosecutorial abuse. The facts of this case suggest a depressing erosion of that protection.[64]

Beware of those who mix up the idea of collection activity in a lawful sense, or the initiation or maintenance of a legal action to protect or enforce a particular legal right with the theft by threat. Aggressive pursuit of what rightfully belongs to a legitimate party cannot be equated with the action of an extortionist.

THEFT BY UNAUTHORIZED DISPOSITION (EMBEZZLEMENT)

An actor who embezzles takes without right or justification, though in a significantly different fashion. Each offense scrutinized thus far requires a taking, a carrying away, the specific intent to strip away the possessory interest of another without license or privilege to do so. Embezzlement differs in one particular sense—that of right to possess.[65] Embezzlers are entitled to possess the cash, funds, or other property taken. Their positions are ones of entrustment where the owner grants a license or privilege to the third party to have and to hold. Bank tellers have a possessory right to handle cash since occupational responsibilities demand it. Lawyers hold large sums of money in escrow on behalf of clients, as do money managers and financial consultants, trustees and guardians. These are custodial positions with fiduciary responsibility. Perverting the purpose of the entrustment and converting the funds for other purposes is the hallmark of the theft by unauthorized disposition. When the teller pockets the money, he or she does while in possessory right. The position of trust assigned to role and occupation necessitates this type of possessory interest.[66] Granting this authority to have and possess does not give license and privilege beyond the limited purpose of the occupation. When the embezzler converts another's property, the protection against theft winnows away. When the trustee transfers to his or her own account, theft by embezzlement has occurred.[67]

In short, the embezzlement claim contains all the requisite components of other larcenies except the altered view of possessory interest of another. For that short span of time, the embezzler is the lawful and rightful agent of possession. When diverted to other means and purposes, the embezzler descends down the slippery slope of criminal liability. The MPC promulgates a model statute most states emulate at 206.4.

Section 206.4 Theft by failure to make required disposition of funds received

(1) In General. A person who obtains property upon agreement, or subject to a known legal obligation, to make specified payment or other disposition, whether from such property or its proceeds or from his own property in equivalent amount, commits theft if he deals with the property obtained as his own and fails to make the required payment or disposition, unless the actor proves that his obligation in the transaction was limited to a promise or other duty to be performed in the future without any present duty to reserve property for such performance. The foregoing applies notwithstanding that it may be impossible to identify particular property as belonging to the victim at the time of the actor's failure to make the required payment or disposition.[68]

The confiscation aggressively presumes knowledge on the part of fiduciaries leaving the burden of proving a lack of criminal intent by the defendant in any subsequent prosecution.

PROSECUTORIAL STRATEGIES

What was the subject matter of the taking?
Who was entrusted with possessory interest other than the owner?
How were the funds diverted or converted from the primary purpose?
Has there been a consistent, long-term pattern of taking?
What type of institution did the act occur in?
Is it reasonable to believe the entrusted party knew?

THEFT BY DECEPTION (FRAUD)

Another emerging area of contemporary criminality readily appears in the domain of fraud and misrepresentation. Not content to thieve and take by commonplace means, the criminal element now engages in every type of subterfuge and flimflam artistry. Stealing directly becomes a passé exercise when compared to the intricate fraud and dupe artist. The taking still occurs, as does the carrying away. It is the shell game or possessory relinquishment that so tricks and befuddles victims of this fraudulent form.[69] The myriad of theft by fraud laws could be assessed in one text alone. Suffice it to say, there are as many statutory responses as there are ways to defraud both individuals as well as institutions. In "Theft by False Pretenses," the agent misrepresents in such a way to cause another party to sign over, assign, release, or bequest some property, the ownership of which is usually signified by a legal document. Examples of these illegal transactions may be by pretense, gaining a deed or stock certificate, the title to a vehicle or boat or other documentary proof of ownership interest. At its heart, the offender engaged in false pretenses tricks the victim into the taking by appearing utterly legitimate in the context in which the fraud takes place.

Other manifestations of fraud involve the full panoply of government benefits by false application for welfare, food stamp collusion, and false Medicaid and Social Security filings. Any false statement, which secures the payment of government benefits, constitutes fraudulent practice.[70] In these types of cases, we see the accused attempting to dupe the governmental authority into paying who is not entitled. Fraudulent theft betokens a scheme and other chicanery where the dispensation of the goods, services, or other property happens without full and complete disclosure.

The range of fraudulent theft is further gleaned in the mail and shipping services where corrupt and unconscionable practices of sale, bait and switch, and false and glaring misrepresentation are a regular happenstance.[71] The U.S. Postal Service Inspector Division spends the bulk of its time tracking down criminals who use the mail to enable their fraudulent designs. (See Figure 7.4[72] for a representation of the various types of mail fraud from the U.S. Postal Inspector's Web site.)

The alteration of checks for fraudulent purposes depicts one more nuance in theft by deception.[73] Check offenses in general are statutorily lumped into all types of disconnected categories, although fraud remains a strong choice if the facts warrant.[74] Changing payees and sums due and owed on a series of checks was upheld as fraud in *U.S. v. Laljie*.[75] After altering the checks, the defendant used the mail to deposit the proceeds. Evidence was sufficient to be convicted of mail fraud since the defendant "engaged in a scheme to defraud ... and that scheme was furthered by the use of the mails."[76]

In each of these cases, the offender depends on the victim's seemingly willing participation. Each offense betrays trust by the use of ruse and harlotry. Deception connotes this type of theft very accurately. As the MPC declares:

Figure 7.4   United States Postal Inspection Service Web site.

Section 206.2 Theft by deception

(1) General. A person commits theft if he obtains property of another by means of deception. A person deceives if he purposely:
   (a) creates or reinforces an impression which is false and which he does not believe to be true; or
   (b) prevents another from acquiring information which the actor knows would influence the other party in the transaction; or
   (c) fails to disclose a lien, adverse claim, or other legal impediment to the enjoyment of property being sold or otherwise transferred or encumbered, regardless of the legal validity of the impediment and regardless of any official record disclosing its existence; or
   (d) fails to correct a false impression previously created or reinforced by him; or
   (e) fails to correct a false impression which he knows to be influencing another to whom he stands in a relationship of special trust and confidence.[77]

The centerpiece of every fraud investigation lies in the falsehood and material misrepresentation that manipulates the transference. Without the dupe, the property would remain in the hands of the rightful owner.

> Visit the FDIC Web location that outlines a series of fraudulent conducts involving banks and the financial system at http://www.fdic.gov/consumers/theft.

The fraud expert knows how to gain possessory interest under the guise of a self-righteous plan. In fact, the fraudulent party frequently befriends and impresses the very individuals he or she will subsequently victimize. These same deceivers are fully aware of where the best hunting will be, namely the elderly, the uneducated, the emotionally insecure, and those in search of something more than life presently offers. If P.T. Barnum felt there was a sucker born every minute, the fraud perpetrator feels even more optimistic. The District of Columbia has crafted an enviable statute:

§ 22-3221. Fraud

(a) Fraud in the first degree. —A person commits the offense of fraud in the first degree if that person engages in a scheme or systematic course of conduct with intent to defraud or to obtain property of another by means of a false or fraudulent pretense, representation, or promise and thereby obtains property of another or causes another to lose property.
(b) Fraud in the second degree. —A person commits the offense of fraud in the second degree if that person engages in a scheme or systematic course of conduct with intent to defraud or to obtain property of another by means of a false or fraudulent pretense, representation, or promise.
(c) False promise as to future performance. —Fraud may be committed by means of false promise as to future performance which the accused does not intend to perform or knows will not be performed. An intent or knowledge shall not be established by the fact alone that one such promise was not performed.[78]

Consumer groups and the Office of State Attorney General are always on the lookout for the con personality. Entire investigative divisions are solely dedicated to protecting the public from the serious harm that results from this criminality.

Overzealousness in the area of consumer protection should not frustrate the free markets. It would be difficult, if not impossible, to not discover some level of exaggeration in the marketing of almost any goods or services. Capitalism jades the marketplace with its surreal descriptions of products and services and the reasonable citizen can distinguish puffing and braggadocio from outright falsehood. Most statutes accept a healthy degree of what is termed "puffing" as to value and result in the marketplace. That line between fraud and puff is not always easy to discern. However, the bulk of fraud cases scream injustice once discovered. This is what the fraudulent and collusive individual wants so intensely—to hide in the shadows amongst the innocent hoping no one will discover his or her corrupted ambition.

Fraud offenses relating to credit cards, electronic transfers, identity, and the like are often labeled "economic crimes." See the Memphis Police Department's dedicated Web location to economic crime at http://www.memphispolice.org/Economic%20Crimes.htm.

THEFT BY FORGERY

ELEMENTS

- Writing or some documentary form
- Alteration, modification, and falsification of writing
- With specific intent to defraud another

Closely aligned to theft law, though not perfectly so, is the crime of forgery. If the context of our interpretation is strictly related to how the perpetrator achieves an unlawful gain by taking the property of another by the forged act or instrument, then the parallel is very strong. Both cases display the underlying thrust of the theft, which results in a loss of something of value to the illegal benefit of another. Forgery also may involve the alteration or production of currency. The United States Secret Service, aside from protecting political figures, is entrusted with assuring the integrity of our currency and the investigation of counterfeit funds.

Visit this mission of the Secret Service at http://www.secretservice.gov/know_your_money.shtml

On the other hand, the crime of forgery can be slightly more complicated, particularly as to the element of actus reus. The series of theft and larceny actions delved into thus far possess remarkable similarities, the mental states are generally identical and the acts affirm the notion of a taking. When we analyze forgery, we should be able to identify its extraordinary closeness to fraud. In fact, many jurisdictions combine by definition and grade the fraudulent theft with our long-held belief of exactly what forgery is and what it means. Other jurisdictions view forgery as one of a long line of fraud offenses that differ without historical understanding of basic larceny.[79] Other jurisdictions qualify the type of forgery by the amount and value of the written instrument. Maine, for example, distinguishes first- and second-degree forgery by the instrument's overall valuation. The statute states in part:

§ 703. Forgery

1. A person is guilty of forgery if, with the intent to defraud or deceive another person or government:
    A. The person falsely makes, completes, endorses or alters a written instrument, or knowingly utters or possesses such an instrument. Violation of this paragraph is a Class D crime;
    B. The person causes another, by deception, to sign or execute a written instrument, or utters such an instrument.[80]

Maine also has adopted what it terms "aggravated forgery"[81] to target offenders who are not only con artists, but intend without any reservation to effect the fraud. The line here seems a little fuzzy, the language of the statute is definitely one of specific intent.

§ 702. Aggravated forgery

1. A person is guilty of aggravated forgery if, with intent to defraud or deceive another person or government, he falsely makes, completes, endorses or alters a written instrument, or knowingly utters or possesses such an instrument, and the instrument is:
    A. Part of an issue of money, stamps, securities or other valuable instruments issued by a government or governmental instrumentality;
    B. Part of an issue of stocks, bonds or other instruments representing interests in or claims against an organization or its property;
    C. A will, codicil or other instrument providing for the disposition of property after death;
    D. A public record or an instrument filed or required or authorized by law to be filed in or with a public office or public employee;[82]

Oregon's codification speaks well of its drafters

165.013 Forgery in the first degree

(1) A person commits the crime of forgery in the first degree if the person violates ORS 165.007:
    (a) And the written instrument is or purports to be any of the following:
        (A) Part of an issue of money, securities, postage or revenue stamps, or other valuable instruments issued by a government or governmental agency;
        (B) Part of an issue of stock, bonds or other instruments representing interests in or claims against any property or person;
        (C) A deed, will, codicil, contract or assignment;
        (D) A check for $1,000 or more, a credit card purchase slip for $1,000 or more, or a combination of checks and credit card purchase slips that, in the aggregate, total $1,000 or more, or any other commercial instrument or other document that does or may evidence, create, transfer, alter, terminate or otherwise affect a legal right, interest, obligation or status; or
        (E) A public record;[83]

Here, one appreciates the significance of the legal document as the controlling factor in forgery, that is the will, the revenue stamps, and the stock to name a few examples. The self-executing nature of these documents, meaning their inherent capacity to transfer or stimulate property interests or rights is what the forgery felony is. Oregon has instituted a second-degree offense that descend downwards in importance by listing any written instrument that an Oregon Court of Appeals labeled a check for certain government benefits.[84] Forgery resides in its own territory recognizing that aligned offenses dealing with insurance fraud, unworn falsification to public authorities, check fraud, false identifications, and unauthorized applications for benefits are dealt with by other enactments.

The similarities do not end with fraud, but extend to any documentary ruse that makes possible the illegal transference of an interest in property. Bad checks,[85] misrepresentations that result in seemingly lawful legal documents being turned over to fraudulent parties, and falsified application for the sake of government benefits all qualify. All of these offenses and many others have incorporated the fundamental tenets of the forgery offense, though watch closely the other enactments that supplant or merge the primary offense with a lower variety. In forgery, the actor takes without right or privilege, but utilizes some instrument, some documentary form or altered version thereof to achieve the end sought. The forging party employs an instrumentality to carry out the plot to unlawfully take. Just as critically, the forging party "utters" a representation on that same instrumentality, which causes another to think a legitimate property interest exists when the very opposite is true.

In sum, the criminal agent who forges takes another's valued interest by reliance on a document that falsely represents a material fact or condition. By "material" one means a central feature of the writing's integrity that influences the parties victimized to act in one way or the other. The writing's very power has resulted from the fraudulent activity to alter or modify its content or to offer material misrepresentations in completion or content.

715A.2 Forgery

1. A person is guilty of forgery if, with intent to defraud or injure anyone, or with knowledge that the person is facilitating a fraud or injury to be perpetrated by anyone, the person does any of the following:
   a. Alters a writing of another without the other's permission.
   b. Makes, completes, executes, authenticates, issues, or transfers a writing so that it purports to be the act of another who did not authorize that act, or so that it purports to have been executed at a time or place or in a numbered sequence other than was in fact the case, or so that it purports to be a copy of an original when no such original existed.
   c. Utters a writing which the person knows to be forged in a manner specified in paragraph "a" or "b".
   d. Possesses a writing which the person knows to be forged in a manner specified in paragraph "a" or "b".[86]

The Writing

Using some discernable writing for the fraudulent plan gives legal life to the forgery. Exactly what writing entails has been the subject of endless dialogue in the legal and legislative community. Easily identified are documents that evidence actual ownership in real or personal property and whose alteration would falsely transfer that property interest to another. Deeds, titles to cars and boats, stock and bond certificates, convertible debentures, bearer bonds, commercial papers, secured instruments, judgment notes, credit notes, and other financial instruments satisfy the writing requirement. The modern legislative tendency has been to greatly and generously expand the qualified categories. South Dakota adopts the all-inclusive term "written instrument of any kind."[87] Tennessee does an admirable job of liberally catching many formats conducive to forgery.

"Writing" includes printing or any other method of recording information, money, coins, tokens, stamps, seals, credit cards, badges, trademarks, and symbols of value, right, privilege, or identification.[88]

Within this statutory design, counterfeiting even is permissible since the alteration or the utterance relative to the integrity of money funds meets the criteria.

§ 472. Uttering counterfeit obligations or securities

Whoever, with intent to defraud, passes, utters, publishes, or sells, or attempts to pass, utter, publish, or sell, or with like intent brings into the United States or keeps in possession or conceals any falsely made, forged, counterfeited, or altered obligation or other security of the United States, shall be fined under this title or imprisoned not more than 20 years, or both.

§ 473. Dealing in counterfeit obligations or securities

Whoever buys, sells, exchanges, transfers, receives, or delivers any false, forged, counterfeited, or altered obligation or other security of the United States, with the intent that the same be passed, published, or used as true and genuine, shall be fined under this title or imprisoned not more than 20 years, or both.[89]

See the U.S. Secret Service's Web page on how to recognize counterfeit money at Figure 7.5.[90]

The depth and breadth of forgery coverage quashes any preconceived notions about what these offenses are generally about. Literally any writing that carries with it a binding or legally authoritative power can be the instrument of the forgery. Money orders, traveler's checks, CD passbooks, negotiable commercial paper, or any "certification of interest to any tangible or intangible property"[91] qualifies. To be subject to forgery, the instrument must have some level of authority or value. A paper bag or writing pad has no operative effect beyond its usage and confers no particular rights or privileges upon its owner. Forgery writings are accompanied by certain enforceable rights or interests. In *U.S. v. Johnson*,[92] the unique qualities of forged instruments were described as:

For a writing to be the proper subject of a forgery, it must appear either on its face or from the extrinsic facts to impose a legal liability on another, or to change a legal right or liability to another's prejudice. Writings that are preliminary to the creation of legal rights or liabilities, such as credit applications and credit reference forms, are not subject to forgery.[93]

Critics charge that the expansive interpretation of the term "writing" has had the unexpected effect of turning misdemeanors and other petty offenses into the graver forgery felony.[94] Another passionate challenge to the contemporary vision of what a forgery is relates to double jeopardy claims. Here the defendant urges the court to throw a charge or two out when forgery duplicitously reflects facts that lead to other charges, such as in cases of check fraud, falsified records for benefits, or other fraudulent writing. There is some merit in this contention. If, on the one hand, the government craves the broadest definition possible for what the term "writing" is, it is debatable whether the same government can then stack charges of multiple offenses all arising from the same or closely similar transaction. Often heard from defendants

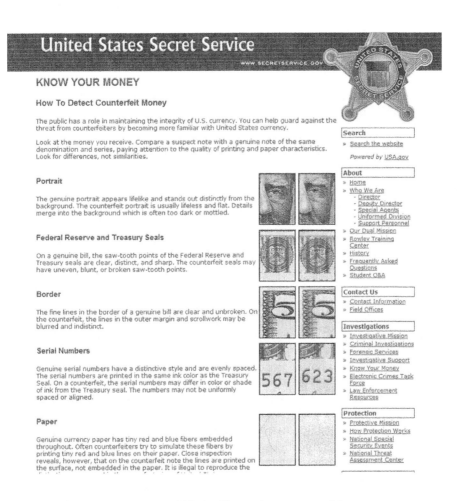

Figure 7.5   United States Secret Service Web site: How to detect counterfeit money.

at sentencing is the unfair infliction of punishment for what to their eyes is one transaction, but to the government is a long series of unrelated acts. Challenges to the habitual offender statutes rest upon the same theory.[95] Claims of double jeopardy fail when the offenses charged contain even the slightest difference in elements or the transactions are divisible. In *State v. Pace*,[96] the defense appeal hallmarked the inequity of not merging insurance fraud with the forgery since the elements were identical. The Court denied the defense request on the rationale that insurance fraud distinctly intends a different end than simple forgery, though one is hard pressed to appreciate the distinction.[97] Distinguishing that line is an exercise fraught with minefields. The Iowa Supreme Court opinion in the *Jacobs*[98] decision weighed this very argument posed as so:

> The defendant contends it is "illogical" to think that the legislature intended to punish him for all of the offenses he committed in connection with each theft. However, we have previously recognized that, by enacting separate statutes, the legislature may address "separate evils" even when the offenses grow out of the same incident.[99]

CASE 7.4

MAINE V. RAY,
741 A.2d 455 (Me. Sup. 1999).

The parties stipulated to the following facts. On December 31, 1997, Ray was stopped for speeding by a Dexter police officer. Rather than giving his real name, Ray told the officer that he was "Kenneth Deschaine" of Waterville. The officer smelled alcohol on Ray's breath and administered field-sobriety tests, which Ray failed. Accordingly, Ray was arrested. Following a breath test, which disclosed a .09% blood alcohol level, the officer issued a Uniform Summons and Complaint using the information supplied by Ray (i.e., that his name was Kenneth Deschaine). The Complaint contained the date of arraignment on the charges. Ray falsely signed that document "Kenneth Deschaine," and the officer gave Ray a copy of the Complaint and released him. The Complaint was then filed in the Newport District Court Clerk's Office. When no one appeared for arraignment, an arrest warrant was issued for Deschaine. Subsequently, the original arresting officer discovered Ray's true identity, and the charge against Deschaine was dismissed. Ray was arrested and charged with operating under the influence, as well as other charges related to the original traffic stop, and with the new charge of aggravated forgery.

Ray waived a jury trial on the aggravated forgery charge and pled guilty to all other charges. He stipulated to the facts relevant to the aggravated forgery charge and moved for a judgment of acquittal on that charge. Following argument from the parties, the court denied the motion for a judgment of acquittal and found Ray guilty of aggravated forgery. This appeal followed.

Ray contends that the trial court erred when it found that, by signing a false name to the Complaint, he had committed aggravated forgery under 17-A M.R.S.A. § 702. The State argues that the plain meaning of "endorse," undefined in the statute, includes the defendant's conduct.

Pursuant to section 702, [a] person is guilty of aggravated forgery if, with intent to defraud or deceive another person or government, he falsely makes, completes, endorses or alters a written instrument ... and the instrument is ... [a] public record or an instrument filed or required or authorized by law to be filed in or with a public office or public employee.

17-A M.R.S.A. § 702(1)(D). "Written instrument" is defined to "include[] any token, coin, stamp, seal, badge, trademark, credit card, absentee ballot application, absentee ballot envelope, or other evidence or symbol of value, right, privilege or identification, and any paper, document, or other written instrument containing written or printed matter or its equivalent." 17-A M.R.S.A. § 701(4) (1983). The statute defines the terms "falsely alters," "falsely completes," and "falsely makes," see 17-A M.R.S.A. § 701(1)-(3) (1983), but does not explicitly define "falsely endorses."

Ray concedes that the Uniform Summons and Complaint is a "public record or an instrument required or authorized to be filed in or with a public office or public employee." 17-A M.R.S.A. § 702(1)(D). The State did not argue that Ray made, completed, or altered the Complaint when he gave the false identifying information and signed it under a false name. Thus, the sole issue before the court was whether Ray "endorsed" the Complaint for purposes of section 702. The court concluded that Ray did falsely endorse a public record or instrument when he signed the Complaint with a false name.

Questions

1. Does Ray's conduct qualify for "aggravated forgery"?
2. What was the written instrument in this case?
3. How does this document have the type of value that forgery speaks of?

Undeniably, the term "writing" and the acts associated with forgery are interpreted as broadly as possible.

Alteration, Modification or Change to a Writing

Within the broad expanse of every forgery statute is the fundamental requirement that change occur within the writing. That change can be the erasure of key and essential terms, the addition or elimination of critical information or the substitution of data. In this way documents are modified or altered from their original state. The forging party has other available avenues of alteration. Misrepresentation satisfies this component too since it is the forger who misrepresents a material fact or condition in said writing. Dishonesty relating to the identity of the writing's author, age, eligibility, address, or other crucial information also qualifies. Tampering with official documents to gain a benefit falls within these parameters as well, though many jurisdictions have enacted offenses lower than or different from the felony of forgery.[100]

Holding out a document as one's own when, in fact, its legal significance relates to another is an indication of a forgery about to unfold. At common law, the proclamation that a document represents an alleged, though false interest, was termed the "utterance." So, an Arizona Court of Appeals held that alteration of vehicle VIN numbers was properly within the scope of a forgery prosecution.[101] Change can be the utterance. Some jurisdictions retain the requirement of utterance or have even promulgated offenses that directly deal with utterance cases alone.[102] So close are the terms and conditions of forgery to the uttering offense that the Court found the defendant had been aggrieved because of the "unreasonable multiplication of charges."[103] The affirmative step of changing the writing includes many connotations. The Pennsylvania statute lists comprehensively:

§ 4101. Forgery

(a) OFFENSE DEFINED. —A person is guilty of forgery if, with intent to defraud or injure anyone, or with knowledge that he is facilitating a fraud or injury to be perpetrated by anyone, the actor:

(1) alters any writing of another without his authority;

(2) makes, completes, executes, authenticates, issues or transfers any writing so that it purports to be the act of another who did not authorize that act, or to have been executed at a time or place or in a numbered sequence other than was in fact the case, or to be a copy of an original when no such original existed; or

(3)   utters any writing which he knows to be forged in a manner specified in paragraphs (1) or (2) of this subsection.[104]

Hence, the author of the forgery engages the instrument itself and those who rely on its content. Utterance facilitates the fraud of forgery because without an overt act, the actor merely doodles on the document. Alteration without implementation is incapable of leaping beyond the preparatory step, which is insufficient for the imposition of criminal liability. To utter is to proclaim the legitimacy of writing when its proponent knows of its falsity.

An utterance tells the world to rely on its content when the uttered knows its unreliability and when the forger passes "a forged document off as genuine to obtain money, etc., or completing or purporting to have a writing for which he does not have authority."[105]

The concept of utterance gives fruition to the fraudulent design and purpose and communicates the corrupted motive.

Specific Intent to Defraud

Careless mistake or minor technical errors will not meet the forgery threshold because the forger sets out to alter and modify what is materially critical to the writing's purpose. Changing deeds means changing eventual owners. Falsely applying for pecuniary benefit under an assumed or fictitious name bespeaks the presumptuousness of the forger—one who wants to fool his audience and be enriched in the process. Forgery lacks any sense of negligence or accident. Forgery, by its dark and unannounced design, schemes against others and hopes to fool the innocent. Forgery, when compared to other felonies, lacks mitigation and provocation, mental disease or defect, and, in its place, emboldens the brazen sham where intent shines brightly and the offender tricks without reservation. Forgery "requires as an element of the offense an intent to defraud, which may be inferred from the doing of the wrongful, fraudulent, or illegal acts, which, in their necessary results, naturally produce loss or injury."[106] The majority of states mention this intentionality, such as South Dakota:

22-39-36. Forgery defined

Felony. Any person who, with intent to defraud, falsely makes, completes, or alters a written instrument of any kind, or passes such an instrument is guilty of forgery.[107]

Courts and jurors need to closely examine the alleged instrument subject to the forgery and deduce the intent in the making. A transmitted and altered Western Union money order was construed as conclusive evidence of the intent to defraud in *State v. Goodroad*.[108] A stolen credit card usage at a premier hotel cannot be explained away as a simple mistake or error, but is more aptly described as forgery in *Zanders v. D.C.*[109] In these and a host of other cases, courts are empowered to infer intent from the acts themselves, especially when no plausible explanation exists otherwise.

PROSECUTORIAL STRATEGY

That the party who forged stood to gain some benefit.
That the writing contained some level of value or authority.
That the facts can be only explained in light of a fraudulent purpose.
That the alteration involved a material item in the writing.
That the defendant's action were concealed.

BRIBERY

ELEMENTS

- Confers or accepts payment or other economic benefit for official action
- Communicated to public officials or political parties
- For commercial or contractual purposes

Bribery has long been labeled an offense against the public administration of justice. Some type of official action had to be sought and a corresponding offer with value had to be communicated to achieve its elements. Bribery, simply put, is money or other benefit for specific favors. Whether a fee for a judgment, an under-the-table cash handout for a favorable zoning finding, or grant of some benefit other than cash, the offender wants a quid pro quo for the exchange. Bribery, if tolerated, corrodes public trust in government and judicial operations and stains and sullies the integrity of institutions that citizens expect will be on the up and up.[110] To the cynical, payment in the right amount can buy just about any result from government agents. To the idealist, one hopes that our public officers, judges, senators, and administrative heads will be able to withstand the temptations that go hand-in-hand with the power inherent in their positions. Judicial interpretation of the term "public official" has not been restrictive and includes not only politicians, but school board members as well as jurors deliberating at trial.[111] At first glance, the inclusion of jurors in the mix of roles qualifying for bribery seems a stretch, but the 5th Circuit for the United States Court of Appeals outlines with insight why:

> Examining the role of a juror in our criminal justice system, some of these indicia of high-level responsibility are present. Although a juror does not alone possess final decision-making authority over the guilt or innocence of a criminal defendant, he does maintain the essentially absolute power to force a mistrial. His discretion in this respect is virtually unchecked and, depending on the case, any result in the squander of substantial amounts of precious time and money in the form of both judicial and prosecutorial resources. Moreover, each juror is in a very potent position to influence the verdict ... More profound than any of these considerations, however, is the tremendous responsibility every juror has with respect to the criminal justice system as a whole. The critical importance of neutral, law-respecting juries to our legal system cannot be gainsaid.[112]

Judges, prosecutorial staff, and other court personnel also are part of the class of public officials whose influence and power base can be corrupted. One of the chief reasons judges should maintain personal and professional distance from the Bar and the political machine is the avoidance of the bribery dilemma.[113] Bribery fosters a mentality of corruption that if left unchecked becomes rampant. Political commentators have said for years that communist bloc nations, especially the former Soviet Union, were so riddled with corruption that it became normative and the exclusive way of doing business. Bribery can flourish in any governmental form. Stories from New York's Tammany Hall at the turn of the past century, and Bayou politics in Louisiana show all the glaring negatives of government gone astray.

Bribery statutes attempt to keep our leaders and the offices entrusted to them on the straight and narrow and to block passage for those on the outside who see this corruption as opportunity. Organized crime has known for years how lucrative the money-for-favor game can be. One of the major frustrations of law enforcement in targeting out corrupt officials is their seeming legitimacy in some contexts and their hidden corruption in the next. Consider California's attempt to codify.

> 92. Every person who gives or offers to give a bribe to any judicial officer, juror, referee, arbitrator, or umpire, or to any person who may be authorized by law to hear or determine any question or controversy, with intent to influence his vote, opinion, or decision upon any matter or question which is or may be brought before him for decision, is punishable by imprisonment in the state prison for two, three, or four years.[114]

Fuzzy, too, has become the line between legitimate political contributions and undue influence through bribery. Politicians who assert a lack of political pressure from heavy-handed donors can't expect us to take them too seriously. Whether we like it or not, money talks.

It would be unfair to label the frequently criticized political landscape as one riddled with bribery, but it would be just as ludicrous to not believe that economic transfer does not generate favors. Federal regulators have tried to "freshen up" what mostly amounts to a special interest, monied system, by passage of automatic disclosure rules, reporting of sums and amounts, and restrictions and limitation on amounts that can be given. Certainly the breath of fresh air these requirements bring have done some to restore the public's confidence in the political process. Despite these good faith attempts, the public at large is generally not fond of its political system nor the officials who reside within it. In an imperfect world, the justice system does what it can to minimize the inevitable corruption that money brings into the system.

Benefit for Favor

Frequently litigated on appeal is the issue of whether or not a benefit was given for a particular favor. What types of benefits are tradable? Clearly cash and other instruments that represent immediate commercial value qualify. What other benefits, and what other favors? In the illegal relationships that develop between bribing offeror and accepting offeree, investigators must be able to identify how an exchange takes place beyond the cash in a bag. Some examples might include:

- To vote or abstain from a vote
- To rule or not rule in a legal case
- To advance or dismiss a legal action
- To dismiss with justification or right a legal claim
- To award or not award a contract for services
- To do or not do an action in exchange for contribution
- To misplace a police report or other official document
- To issue governmental or legal opinions that favor the bribe
- To pay for the public official to look the other way.

By no means is the list exhaustive, but instructive on the diverse ways that nonmoney benefits can drive the bribery marketplace. As in contract law, anything of value, relative to public action, can qualify for the consideration necessary for the bribery.

Commercial Bribery

Of more recent enactment have been provisions that forbid commercial bribery. Instead of targeting politicians, these statutes look for an allegedly free market environment where money bribes

BRIBERY IS BOTH A STATE AND FEDERAL CRIME

Review the federal statute at 18 U.S.C. § 201 and then compare with Pennsylvania Statute at Title 18, §4701.

18 U.S.C. §201. Bribery of public officials and witnesses

(b) Whoever—

(1) directly or indirectly, corruptly gives, offers or promises anything of value to any public official or person who has been selected to be a public official, or offers or promises any public official or any person who has been selected to be a public official to give anything of value to any other person or entity, with intent:

   (A) to influence any official act; or

   (B) to influence such public official or person who has been selected to be a public official to commit or aid in committing, or collude in, or allow, any fraud, or make opportunity for the commission of any fraud, on the United States; or

   (C) to induce such public official or such person who has been selected to be a public official to do or omit to do any act in violation of the lawful duty of such official or person;

(2) being a public official or person selected to be a public official, directly or indirectly, corruptly demands, seeks, receives, accepts, or agrees to receive or accept anything of value personally or for any other person or entity, in return for:

   (A) being influenced in the performance of any official act;

   (B) being influenced to commit or aid in committing, or to collude in, or allow, any fraud, or make opportunity for the commission of any fraud, on the United States; or

   (C) being induced to do or omit to do any act in violation of the official duty of such official or person;

(3) directly or indirectly, corruptly gives, offers, or promises anything of value to any person, or offers or promises such person to give anything of value to any other person or entity, with intent to influence the testimony under oath or affirmation of such first-mentioned person as a witness upon a trial, hearing, or other proceeding, before any court, any committee of either House or both Houses of Congress, or any agency, commission, or officer authorized by the laws of the United States to hear evidence or take testimony, or with intent to influence such person to absent himself therefrom;

(4) directly or indirectly, corruptly demands, seeks, receives, accepts, or agrees to receive or accept anything of value personally or for any other person or entity in return for being influenced in testimony under oath or affirmation as a witness upon any such trial, hearing, or other proceeding, or in return for absenting himself therefrom; shall be fined under this title or not more than three times the monetary equivalent of the thing of value, whichever is greater, or

imprisoned for not more than fifteen years, or both, and may be disqualified from holding any office of honor, trust, or profit under the United States.

(c) Whoever—
  (1) otherwise than as provided by law for the proper discharge of official duty:
    (A) directly or indirectly gives, offers, or promises anything of value to any public official, former public official, or person selected to be a public official, for or because of any official act performed or to be performed by such public official, former public official, or person selected to be a public official; or
    (B) being a public official, former public official, or person selected to be a public official, otherwise than as provided by law for the proper discharge of official duty, directly or indirectly demands, seeks, receives, accepts, or agrees to receive or accept anything of value personally for or because of any official act performed or to be performed by such official or person;
  (2) directly or indirectly, gives, offers, or promises anything of value to any person, for or because of the testimony under oath or affirmation given or to be given by such person as a witness upon a trial, hearing, or other proceeding, before any court, any committee of either House or both Houses of Congress, or any agency, commission, or officer authorized by the laws of the United States to hear evidence or take testimony, or for or because of such person's absence therefrom;
  (3) directly or indirectly, demands, seeks, receives, accepts, or agrees to receive or accept anything of value personally for or because of the testimony under oath or affirmation given or to be given by such person as a witness upon any such trial, hearing, or other proceeding, or for or because of such person's absence therefrom; shall be fined under this title or imprisoned for not more than two years, or both.

18 Pa. Cons. Stat. § 4701. Bribery in official and political matters

(a) OFFENSES DEFINED.—A person is guilty of bribery, a felony of the third degree, if he offers, confers or agrees to confer upon another, or solicits, accepts or agrees to accept from another:
  (1) any pecuniary benefit as consideration for the decision, opinion, recommendation, vote or other exercise of discretion as a public servant, party official or voter by the recipient;
  (2) any benefit as consideration for the decision, vote, recommendation or other exercise of official discretion by the recipient in a judicial, administrative or legislative proceeding; or
  (3) any benefit as consideration for a violation of a known legal duty as public servant or party official.

Questions

1. What are the operative words of exchange for favors in both statutes?
2. How does the Pennsylvania statute describe benefits that are nonmonetary?
3. What does Pennsylvania mean by a lack of defense even based on lack of qualification?

CASE 7.5

COMMONWEALTH V. LEWIS
452 A.2d 13 (Pa. Super. 1982).

On August 25, 1980, appellee, Albert E. Lewis, III, was arrested and charged with four counts of corrupt organizations, 113 counts of commercial bribery and breach of duty to act disinterestedly and 113 counts of tampering with records or identification. Similar charges were also brought against one George Ardrey, an employee of North American Car Corporation, who had allegedly awarded his company's contracts to Lewis in return for kickbacks from the income that a trucking company owned by Lewis would earn from those contracts. Mr. Ardrey was tried and acquitted of all charges. Thereafter, appellee filed a pretrial motion to dismiss the charges against him on grounds of collateral estoppel. Following a hearing on the motion to dismiss, the lower court granted appellee's motion and issued an order on May 4, 1981, dismissing all of the aforesaid counts. The Commonwealth filed a timely appeal to this court. We reverse.

The illegal payments alleged to have been made by Mr. Lewis to Mr. Ardrey are identical in days and dates to those charges for which Mr. Ardrey was tried and acquitted in March, 1981. Mr. Ardrey had not been charged with tampering with records or identification. However, a conviction of appellee on these counts would also depend on the existence or nonexistence of the alleged bribery scheme.

Appellee contends that, because of Mr. Ardrey's acquittal, the Commonwealth is precluded from relitigating the factual issue of whether or not the bribery scheme existed and whether or not payments were made since those same issues were adversely determined against the Commonwealth in the first trial. "[C]ollateral estoppel is issue preclusion. It seeks to prevent relitigation of a finally litigated issue in a subsequent proceeding between the same parties whether the same or different evidence is to be introduced." The requirement of mutuality of estoppel, or identity of parties, has been eroded by judicial decisions. The lower court cited *Blonder-Tongue v. University of Illinois Foundation*; *Oldham v. Pritchett*; and *Parklane Hosiery Co. v. Shore*, in holding that mutuality was not a prerequisite to appellee's use of collateral estoppel in this case. The Pennsylvania courts have also made exceptions to the technical requirement of mutuality where collateral estoppel or *res judicata* (claim preclusion) are sought to be invoked.

The lower court relied extensively on *Commonwealth v. Hude & Klinger* where two defendants were charged with perjury for allegedly lying on the witness stand in earlier jury trials in which they both had been acquitted. The Supreme Court held that the credibility of these defendants had already been decided when they denied committing the offenses for which they were charged and the juries chose to believe these denials. In its analysis of Hude & Klinger, the Pennsylvania high Court relied on *Ashe v. Swenson*, where the United States Supreme Court held that collateral estoppel is part of the Fifth Amendment's guarantee against double jeopardy and is applicable to the states through the Fourteenth Amendment. In the instant case, the lower court felt that collateral estoppel was applicable since the issue of giving or accepting bribes is substantially identical in both the Ardrey case and the Lewis case, and because the Commonwealth had a full and fair opportunity to litigate the issues in the earlier case before a final judgment on the merits was entered. At the May 4, 1981 hearing on appellee's motion to dismiss, the assistant district attorney assigned to both the Ardrey and Lewis cases testified that the two key witnesses who testified in the Ardrey case would also be the chief witnesses in the Commonwealth's case against Mr. Lewis.

The comparison between Hude & Klinger and the situation we are now presented with is appealing, but there is an important distinction between the two cases with which the lower court did not come to terms. Hude & Klinger involved later prosecutions of the same parties, not, as is presented instantly, prosecution of different parties arising out of the same transaction or occurrence. Although the lower court cited cases which make exceptions to the mutuality rule, those cases are all on the civil side. This appeal is based solely on the question of whether or not the doctrine of nonmutual collateral estoppel should be extended to criminal prosecutions, a question of first impression for the Pennsylvania courts.

The United States Supreme Court was recently confronted with this precise issue in a case whose facts are strikingly similar to the instant case. In *Standefer v. United States*, the United States Supreme Court refused to extend the doctrine of nonmutual collateral estoppel to criminal prosecutions. Standefer was indicted on four counts of making gifts to an agent of the Internal Revenue Service in violation of 18 U.S.C.A. § 201(f), and on five counts of aiding and abetting a revenue officer in accepting compensation in addition to that authorized by law, in violation of 26 U.S.C.A.§ 7214(a)(2) and 18 U.S.C.A. § 2. Prior to the filing of these indictments, the I.R.S. agent was acquitted of some of the violations for which Standefer was accused of aiding and abetting. For this reason, Standefer filed a motion to dismiss the counts charging him with aiding and abetting those offenses which the I.R.S. agent had been acquitted of. The Court, in distinguishing between civil cases and criminal cases, stated:

"This, however, is a criminal case, presenting considerations different than those in Blonder-Tongue or Parklane Hosiery. First, in a criminal case, the Government is often without the kind of 'full and fair opportunity to litigate' that is a prerequisite of estoppel. Several aspects of our criminal law make this so: the prosecution's discovery rights in criminal cases are limited, both by rules of court and constitutional privileges; it is prohibited from being granted a directed verdict or from obtaining a judgment notwithstanding the verdict no matter how clear the evidence in support of guilt; it cannot secure a new trial on the ground that an acquittal was plainly contrary to the weight of the evidence; and it cannot secure appellate review where a defendant has been acquitted.

...

The application of nonmutual estoppel in criminal cases is also complicated by the existence of rules of evidence and exclusion unique to our criminal law. It is frequently true in criminal cases that evidence inadmissible against one defendant is admissible against another. The exclusionary rule, for example, may bar the Government from introducing evidence against one defendant because that evidence was obtained in violation of his constitutional rights. And the suppression of that evidence may result in an acquittal. The same evidence, however, may be admissible against other parties to the crime 'whose rights were (not) violated.' (citations omitted). In such circumstances, where evidentiary rules prevent the Government from presenting all its proof in the first case, application of nonmutual estoppel would be plainly unwarranted.

...

Finally, this case involves an ingredient not precise in either Blonder-Tongue or Parklane Hosiery: the important federal interest in the enforcement of the criminal law. Blonder-Tongue and Parklane Hosiery were disputes over private rights between private litigants. In such cases, no significant harm flows from enforcing a rule that affords a litigant only one full and fair opportunity to litigate an issue, and there is no sound reason for burdening the court with repetitive litigation.

...

In short, this criminal case involves 'competing policy considerations' that outweigh the economy concerns that undergird the estoppel doctrine. "

Appellee argues that the Standefer case is inapposite to the case at bar because no evidence was suppressed nor excluded in the case of *Commonwealth v. Ardrey*, there was no evidence admissible against one defendant that was admissible against another, the weight of the evidence in the case of *Commonwealth v. Ardrey* was not in favor of the Commonwealth, and because the Commonwealth elected to try the case of *Commonwealth v. Ardrey* before the case of *Commonwealth v. Lewis*. Although these circumstances are not insignificant, we remain pursuaded [*sic*] by the policy considerations that influenced a unanimous Supreme Court to limit nonmutual collateral estoppel to civil cases. In Standefer, as to two specific payments, the I.R.S. agent tried in the earlier case was convicted of receiving something of value "because of any official act performed ... by him," but was acquitted of receiving "any fee, compensation, or award ... for the performance of any duty." The Supreme Court could not explain these seemingly irreconcilable determinations and found this inconsistency to be reason, in itself, for not giving preclusive effect to the earlier acquittal. The Court stated that "this case does no more than manifest the simple, if discomforting, reality that 'different juries may reach different results under any criminal statute. This is one of the consequences we accept under our jury system.'"

Although a jury acquitted Mr. Ardrey of accepting any bribes, it is not inconceivable that another jury may convict appellee of paying bribes. We hold that the Commonwealth's interest in enforcing the criminal laws of this state outweighs the policies underlying the doctrine of collateral estoppel.

Reversed and remanded for trial.

Questions

1. Point out the public bribery case. Be specific about the particular charges.
2. Point out the commercial bribery case. Be specific about the particular acts.
3. Since the commercial bribery case involved two companies, one company defendant was acquitted? Which one? What impact?
4. Is the government estopped from charging the other defendant with commercial bribery when the other defendant is acquitted? Estoppel means that it would be unfair to impute criminal responsibility when other conduct was deemed lawful. Explain the dilemma.

force the award of contracts, cause exclusive purchase/buy agreements, and generate kickbacks to and from union officials.[115] At its worst, commercial bribery distorts the marketplace because it thwarts competition, favors a select few, and drives up prices in the economy.[116] Some states further qualify the criminality by insisting that the commercial bribery take place within a fiduciary relationship, an agent for a principal, a fiduciary or guardian capacity or other trustee. The MPC has taken an aggressive stance on the fiduciary role, which it believes includes lawyers, bank officers, and accountants, and anyone else capable of violating the fiduciary relationship.[117]

> Discover how business executives get caught up in the world of favor and bribery at: http://www.fbi.gov/news/stories/2010/january/fcpa_012610

Another version might emphasize the charlatan who collects money or other favors even when not authorized to negotiate on behalf of his or her employer. Disgruntled or corrupted employees who act in ways that are "contrary to the interests of their employers,"[118] such as skimming from receivables, gaining kickbacks for the award of contractual goods and services, referrals in exchange for cash payments, and inflated goods prices for continued work and referral, are usually under the umbrella of commercial bribery. The Pennsylvania Supreme Court stated that "the purpose of [Pennsylvania's commercial bribery statute] is to require an agent, employee, or servant to possess an undivided duty of loyalty to his principal."[119] This is consistent with the Pennsylvania legislature's Official Comment associated with § 4108, which states that the statutes purpose is to criminalize bribery in "relationships where a duty of fidelity is owed." This duty of loyalty is breached only when an employee acts contrary to the interest of his employer."[120]

Fundamentally, bribery subverts the free will of the parties in both the governmental and market sectors since the agenda of benefit for favor hides in the background. Increasingly, legislatures construe the bribery action as extending far beyond the political sphere and into the many worlds where money and power inhabit decision making.

DISCUSSION QUESTIONS

1. Asportation in larceny can be best defined as what?
2. Can a larceny occur when the subject of the theft lacks value?
3. Can a party licensed or privileged to handle property be guilty of its theft?
4. Why is larceny referred to as a possessory rather than an ownership offense?
5. Discuss the difference between retail theft and traditional larceny.
6. In a receiving stolen property case, what level of knowledge proves awareness of the value of the stolen goods?
7. Contrast embezzlement with the historical definition of larceny.
8. What types of misrepresentations are required in fraud cases?
9. Explain the "writing" requirement in forgery.
10. How does commercial bribery differ from ordinary bribery?

SUGGESTED READINGS

Albanese, J. S. 2009. *Combating piracy: Intellectual property theft and fraud*. Piscataway, NJ: Transaction Publishers.

Braswell, M. C., J. T. Fish, and L. S. Miller. 2010. *Crime scene investigation*, 2nd ed. Scotch Plains, NJ: Anderson Publishers.

Clarke, R. V., and M. G. Maxfield. 2004. *Understanding and preventing car theft* (Crime Prevention Studies V.17). Monsey, NY: Criminal Justice Press.

Klaus, P. 1999. *Carjackings in the United States, 1992–96*. Washington, D.C.: Bureau of Justice Statistics.

McBrewster, J., F. P. Miller, and A. F. Vandome. 2009. *Credit card fraud: Theft, fraud, credit card, identity theft, basis point, England, chargeback insurance, credit card hijacking, financial crimes, friendly fraud*. Beau Bassin, Mauritius: Alphascript Publishing.

Office for Victims of Crime. 2000. *Victims of fraud and economic crime: Results and recommendations*. Washington, D.C.: Office of Justice Programs.

O'Shea, E. 2011. *Bribery and corruption: Law and practice*. Bristol, U.K.: Jordan Publishing.

Rand, M. R. 1994. *Carjacking: National crime victimization survey*. Washington, D.C.: Bureau of Justice Statistics.

ENDNOTES

1. BUREAU OF JUSTICE STATISTICS, NATIONAL CRIME VICTIMIZATION SURVEY (NCVS) (2008), available at http://bjs.ojp.usdoj.gov/content/glance/theft.cfm (accessed August 3, 2011).
2. 18 PA. CONS. STAT. § 3903 (2010).
3. MICH. COMP. LAWS § 750.356 (2010).
4. Model Penal Code § 206.1 (Proposed Office Draft 1962).
5. *See* TODD KEISTER, THEFTS OF AND FROM CARS ON RESIDENTIAL STREETS AND DRIVEWAYS (COPS, U.S. Dep't Just., Problem-Oriented Guides for Police, Problem-Specific Guides Series, No. 46, 2007).
6. MPC, *supra* note 4.
7. 18 PA. CONS. STAT. § 3901 (2010).
8. *Id.* at § 3921.
9. Larceny and robbery codifications are closer than originally thought upon close inspection. In *Connecticut v. Wright*, 716 A.2d 870 (Conn. Sup. Ct. 1998), a defendant's appeal creatively rested on a novel theory—that larceny in the second degree could not have a more serious punishment than robbery in the third degree. The apparent inconsistency served as the basis for some level of unconstitutionality in the sentence imposed and proof, according to this defendant that the statute was irrational in design. As enticing as the argument first appears, the Supreme Court of Connecticut dismissed it by construing third-degree robbery a less serious offense in select cases. The Court interestingly held: "In our view ... larceny from the person is a more serious offense than simple robbery ... each crime is an aggravated form of larceny. The differentiating factor is the nature of the aggravating characteristic of each offense. "A person is guilty of larceny ... from the person when he commits larceny ... and the property, regardless of its nature or value, is taken from the person of another." (CONN. GEN. STAT. § 53a-123) In contrast, a person is guilty of simple robbery ... "when, in the course of committing a larceny, he uses or threatens the immediate use of physical force upon another person ... which aids in the commission of the larceny." (CONN. GEN. STAT. §53a-133) ... The distinguishing characteristic of larceny from the person is that the property is taken from the person of the victim; the distinguishing characteristic of simple robbery is that force or the threat of immediate force is used to facilitate the taking—whether the property is taken from the person or not." *Wright*, 716 A.2d at 877-78.
10. What the defendant's mental state is in larceny cases bears directly on the type of larceny offenses chosen by the District Attorney. What if the Defendant desired to take only $500 worth of appliances but mistakenly took cash and other items that ballooned the value of the take? What type of intent controls? That of simple or grand larceny? Or what if the defendant's scheme to defraud was discovered, which in turn minimize the potential losses that the aggrieved parties would have incurred? How do we measure intent in these cases? James Gibson, the Attorney-Advisor to the U.S. Sentencing

Commission addresses the question smartly. "By ignoring actual loss when intended loss is higher, the rule sentences inchoate crimes as harshly as completed crimes, even though the criminal law normally recognizes a substantive distinction between the two. By ignoring intended loss when actual loss is higher, the rule wrongly ignores the less serious mens rea of the defendant who, but for a fortuitous apprehension, would have given the victims some value for their money." James Gibson, *How Much Should Mind Matter? Mens Rea in Theft and Fraud Sentencing*, Fed. Sentencing Rep., Nov-Dec 1997, at 136, 137.

11. *See* Matthew Ross Lippman, Contemporary Criminal Law: Concepts, Cases, and Controversies 448 (2009).
12. *Manning v. State*, 166 S.E. 658 (Ga. Sup. 1932).
13. Bi-National Working Group On Cross-Border Mass Marketing Fraud, Identity-Related Crime: A Threat Assessment: A Report to the Attorney General of the United States and the Minister of Public Safety of Canada (2010), available at http://www.justice.gov/criminal/fraud/documents/reports/2010/11-01-10mass-market-fraud.pdf (accessed August 3, 2011).
14. 18 Pa. Cons. Stat. § 3901(2) (2010).
15. For an interesting comparison with Islamic law, *see* Hisham M. Ramadan, *Larceny Offenses in Islamic Law*, 2006 Mich. St. L. Rev. 1609 (2006).
16. Conn. Gen. Stat. 53a-123(a) (2010).
17. Summ. Pa. Jur. § 27.4.
18. Model Penal Code § 206.1(1) & (2) (Proposed Official Draft 1962).
19. 18 U.S.C. §§ 1961-1968 (2011).
20. Kathleen F. Brickey, *The Jurisprudence of Larceny: An Historical Inquiry and Interest Analysis*, 33 Vand. L. Rev. 1101 (1980).
21. *State v. Craycraft*, 152 N.C. App. 211 (2002).
22. Model Penal Code § 206.5 at (3) Proposed Official Draft 1962).
23. For an interesting story of a Brooklyn New York prosecutor caught stealing an office paralegal's wallet (party's funds for her own personal purposes), *see* Daniel Wise, *No Indictment of Prosecutor in Theft Case*, N.Y.L.J., Oct. 5, 1999, at 1. Fiduciaries are expected to act in the best interest of the party for which they are responsible. In *People v. Cain*, 605 N.W.2d 28, (Mich. App. 1999), the Michigan Court of Appeals upheld the conviction of a guardian who manipulated an agreement from a feeble, elderly person and then proceeded to use the incompetent alleged license and privilege as guardian to gain access to the incompetent party's funds to which the Court retorted: "Additionally... the evidence that her spending habits became more liberal after she had access ... was relevant to prove asportation. Although this evidence was circumstantial, it was relevant to demonstrate that Cain took and carried away {the Ward's} money, which was necessary to prove larceny." *Cain*, 605 N.W.2d at 45.
24. Rita J. Verga, *An Advocate's Toolkit: Using Criminal Theft of Service Laws to Enforce Workers' Right to Be Paid*, 8 N.Y. City L. Rev. 283 (2005).
25. Model Penal Code § 206.7 (Proposed Official Draft 1962).
26. N.Y. Penal. Law § 165.15 (McKinney 2010). *See also* Abraham Abramovsky, *Theft of Services: Current State of the Law*, 216 N.Y.L.J., Oct. 31, 1996, at 3.
27. 18 Pa. Cons. Stat. §3926(2) (1994) (amended 1995).
28. Charles P. Nemeth, Private Security and the Investigative Process 233-255 (3rd ed. 2010).
29. U.S. Department of Justice, Federal Bureau of Investigation, Crime in the United States, available at http://www.fbi.gov/about-us/cjis/ucr/crime-in-the-u.s./2009/clus2009 (accessed August 3, 2011).
30. *See* Nemeth, *supra* note 28, at 234.
31. *See* Summ. Pa. Jur. § 27.108.
32. *See* 18 Pa. Cons. Stat. § 3929 (f) (2001).
33. *Id.* at § 3929.
34. Doug Shepard, *Attacking Auto Theft in Washington State: The Redmond Initiative*, Police Chief, April 2009, at 124,127,129.

35. Michael R. Rand, *Carjacking-Crime Data Brief*, NCJ-147002 (1994), available at http://www.ncjrs.gov/pdffiles1/Digitization/147002NCJRS.pdf (accessed August 3, 2011). In 2009, there were 794,616 reported motor vehicle thefts, down 14 percent from the 1990 figure of 1,635,907. U.S. DEPARTMENT OF JUSTICE, FEDERAL BUREAU OF INVESTIGATION, CRIME IN THE UNITED STATES, Table 1 available at http://www2.fbi.gov/ucr/cius2009/data/table_01.html (accessed August 3, 2011).

36. 18 PA. CONS. STAT. § 3928 (2010).

37. *Id.* at § 3928, at comment.

38. 18 U.S.C. § 2119 (2010).

39. 526 U.S. 1 (1998).

40. *Id.* at 20. *See* also *Jones v. U.S.*, 526 U.S. 227 (1998), which highlights the interplay between robbery and carjacking statutes and the constitutional dilemmas associated with dual prosecutions of such similar offenses.

41. Model Penal Code § 206.8 (Proposed Official Draft 1962).

42. *Id.* at § 206.8, at comment.

43. Stuart P. Green, *Thieving and Receiving: Overcriminalizing the Possession of Stolen Property*, NEW CRIM. L. REV. (forthcoming 2011).

44. A new slant at odds with the caricature of the loan shark is the applicability of extortion to corrupt police officials. In *U.S. v. Murphy*, 193 F.3d 1 (1999), a corrupt police officer falsified warrants and search documents, then colluded with defense attorneys to extort money from falsely accused defendants. In *U.S. v. Benny Smith*, 198 F.3d 377 (1999), two police officers actually became lenders and enforcers in a sophisticated scheme that was highly embarrassing for law enforcement.

45. 18 U.S.C. § 1951 (2010).

46. Stanley S. Arkin, *Blackmail and the Practice of Law*, N.Y. L. J., Feb. 7, 1995, at 3, 4.

47. OHIO REV. CODE ANN. § 2905.11 (West 2010).

48. *Ohio v. Evans*, 1999 Ohio App. 2181 (1999).

49. TEX. PENAL CODE ANN. §§ 31.02, 31.03 (West 2011).

50. N.Y. PENAL LAW §155.05 (McKinney 2010).

51. Ken Levy, *The Solution to the Real Blackmail Paradox: The Common Link between Blackmail and Other Criminal Threats*, 39 CONN. L. REV. 1051 (2007).

52. For a bizarre look at decriminalization and the obtuse justifications for the plan, *see* Mitchell N. Bermann, *The Evidentiary Theory of Blackmail: Taking Motives Seriously*, 65 UNIV. CHI. L. REV. 795 (1998).

53. As in assault and robbery, the reaction must be reasonably related to the threat made. Would it be reasonable to conclude that defendant meant to offer threat when he uttered the following? "Mr. Curren testified appellant told him "I'm gonna cut you[r] f***ing throat."... "I know the vehicle your daughter drives. I'll get the little b****, her little tight ass. I'll rape her. I'll f*** her. ... I'll run her off the road. I'll kill her." Appellant also made threats against Mr. Curren's wife telling Mr. Curren ... he would "slip in some night when she's working late" and "f*** her," "f*** her real good." "I'll wait till you're all home asleep some night in your house and I'll burn you[r] house up. I'll blow you up. I'll get you all." *Ohio v. Dal Balbridge*, Case No. 1997 CA 00577 (Ct. App. Ohio. 5th App. D. 1998) quoting Trial Transcript at 29-30.

54. 18 PA. CONS. STAT. § 3923, at comment (2010).

55. Model Penal Code §206.3 (Proposed Official Draft 1962).

56. *Id.* at §223.4.

57. 18 PA. CONS. STAT. § 3923, at comment (2010).

58. *See* 18 U.S.C. §1952 (2010).

59. 504 U.S. 255 (1992).

60. 18 U.S.C. § 1951 (2010).

61. *Id.* at § 1951(b)(2).

62. *U.S. v. Wiltberger*, 5 Wheat. 96.

63. *U.S. v. Mazzei*, 521 F.2d 639,656 (3rd Cir. 1975) (en banc).

64. *Evans*, 504 U.S. at 293.

65. Ella A. McCown, *Embezzlement—A White Collar Crime: A Review of Federal and Supreme Court Cases during Economically Challenging Eras*, PROCEEDINGS OF ASBBS ANNUAL CONFERENCE, Feb. 2010, at 69.

66. Lawyers who mingle and utilize funds of clients misrepresent the status of a case to be able to gain access to funds, are not only potentially liable in a criminal sense, but sure to be disciplined by licensing authority. *See* In re David M. Druten, No. 82,952 (Kan., July 9, 1999).
67. PAUL SHAW & JACK BOLOGNA, PREVENTING CORPORATE EMBEZZLEMENT (2000).
68. Model Penal Code § 206.4 (Proposed Official Draft 1962).
69. Civil remedies abound and reside side-by-side for various fraudulent activities. Law enforcement and the legal system employ both depending upon circumstance. *See D'Ambrosio v. Collonade*, 71 A.2d 356 (1998) and *Goldsmith v. Tapper*, No. 98-CV-520 (D.C. App. 2000) as representative examples.
70. In Arkansas, the theft by fraud in Medicaid offering must show that the applicant "purposely makes or causes to be made a false statement or representation of a material fact in any application for any benefit or payment under the Arkansas Medicaid Program." ARK. CODE ANN. § 5-55-111(1) (Repl. 1997). *See Blackwell v. State*, 1 S.W.3d 399 (Ark.1999).
71. Fraudulent activities frequently combine more than one type of fraud. As an example, the defrauder uses the mails to collect funds then relies on the banking industry to hide the proceeds of the scheme that constitute bank fraud. *See Napoli v. U.S.*, 179 F.3d 1 (1998).
72. U.S. Postal Inspection Service Web site, Mail Fraud Schemes, at https://postalinspectors.uspis.gov/investigations/MailFraud/fraudschemes/FraudSchemes.aspx (accessed August 3, 2011).
73. For the federal response to bank fraud, *see* 18 U.S.C. § 1344 (2010).
74. *See* Federal Trade Commission, Facts for Consumers—Giving the Bounce to Counterfeit Check Scams, at http://www.ftc.gov/bcp/edu/pubs/consumer/credit/cre40.shtm (accessed August 3, 2011).
75. *U.S. v. Laljie*, 184 F.3d 180 (1999).
76. *Id.* at 188, *see also* 18 U.S.C. § 1341 (2011).
77. Model Penal Code § 206.2 (Proposed Official Draft 1962).
78. D.C. CODE § 22-3221 (2010).
79. The power of forgery to impeach and undermine credibility of a defendant is quite remarkable. A series of recent cases allow the reference to these types of other offenses when the defendant puts his or her character in issue because forgery says everything about the opposite of credibility. Rule 404 of the Federal Rules of Evidence has been interpreted to allow evidence of other forgery offenses to prove motive, identity, and the absence of mistake, accident, and the existence of intent. See the South Carolina decision, *State v. Brooks*, 515 S.E.2d 764 (S.C. App. 1999).
80. ME. REV. STAT. tit. 17-A §703 (2010).
81. *Id.* at §702.
82. *Id.* at §702(1).
83. OR. REV. STAT. § 165.013 (2010).
84. The Court was careful to restrict forgery cases to exclusive types of documentation by relaying: "for those cases in which the writing is ... an issue of money, securities or other government issued instruments ... The legislature apparently recognized a logical and crucial difference in ... inherently valuable instruments versus checks under $750, and it thereby fashioned the severity of the penalty for forgery to reflect that difference." *State v. Tarrence*, 985 P.2d 225, 229 (Or. App. 1999).
85. For a case involving false signature cards upon opening a bank account, *see U.S. v. Sherman*, 52 M.J. 856 (U.S. Army Court of Crim. App. 2000).
86. IOWA CODE § 715A.2 (2010).
87. S.D. CODIFIED LAWS § 22-39-36 (2001).
88. TENN. CODE ANN. § 39-14-114(b)(2) (2010).
89. 18 U.S.C. §§ 472, 473 (2010).
90. U.S. Secret Service, How to Detect Counterfeit Money, at http://www.secretservice.gov/money_detect.shtml (accessed August 3, 2011).
91. S.D. CODIFIED LAWS § 22-38-41 (2011).
92. No. NMCM 97 01777 (N.M. Ct. Crim. App. 1998).
93. *Id.* at 4 .
94. *See* 36 AM JUR 2D FORGERY § 24 (1999), *U.S. v. Sherman*, 52 M.J. 856 (A. Ct. Crim. App. 2000).
95. *Iowa v. Miller*, 590 N.W.2d 724 (1999).
96. 523 S.E.2d 466 (S.C. 1999).

97. The Court remarked: "Pace's conviction for forgery required proof that she falsely made a writing or instrument, which is not an element of insurance fraud. Conversely, to obtain a conviction for insurance fraud, the State had to prove Pace intended to obtain an undeserved economic benefit, i.e., Unisun's insurance payment, which is not required to prove a forgery. Because each offense contains at least one element, which must be proven by an additional fact that the other does not require, the trial court correctly held that Pace's conviction on both counts does not violate double jeopardy." *Pace*, 523 S.E.2d at 471.

98. No. 323/98-1638 (Iowa, 2000).

99. *Id.* at 22.

100. 18 PA. CONS. STAT. § 4103 (2010).

101. *Arizona v. Thompson*, 981 P.2d 595 (Ariz.1999). ARIZ. REV. STAT. ANN. § 13-2002 (2000).

102. The crime of "making and uttering bad checks" was the subject matter of an appeal in *U.S. v. Kirby*, No. NMCM 99 00108 (N.M. Ct. Crim. App. 1999).

103. *Id.* at 6.

104. 18 PA. CONS. STAT. § 4101(a) (2010).

105. Id. at § 4101, at comment.

106. 36 SUMM. PA. JUR. § 25.6.

107. S.D. CODIFIED LAWS § 22-39-36 (2001).

108. 521 N.W.2d 433 (1994).

109. 678 A.2d 556 (D.C. 1996).

110. Kim-Kwang Raymond Choo, *Challenges in Dealing with Politically Exposed Persons*, TRENDS & ISSUES CRIME & CRIM. JUST., Feb. 2010.

111. *Snell v. U.S.*, 152 F.3d 345 (5th Cir. 1998).

112. *Id.* at 347.

113. The line between professional courtesy and corruption is sometimes very fine. In *U.S. v. Frega*, 179 F.3d 793 (9th Cir. 1999), defendant appealed on this very basis and targeting these instructions, which the court subsequently upheld: "Even though giving a judge something of value may be inappropriate or a violation of the ethical rules ... such an act is not done corruptly so as to constitute a bribery offense unless [it] is intended at the time it is given to affect a specific action the judge officially will take in a case before him, or may take in a case that may be brought before him. A gift or favor bestowed on a judge solely out of friendship, to promote good will, or for motive wholly unrelated to influence over official action does not violate the bribery statutes." *Id.* at 807.

114. CAL. PENAL CODE § 92 (West 2010).

115. For a classic case of a business paying union officials money for certain favors, *see Brogan v. U.S.*, 522 U.S. 398 (1998), where the Supreme Court's Justice Scalia writes a fascinating opinion on how the statute must bind rather than bend to common opinion (*lex communis*) and other shenanigans.

116. Jeffrey J. Ansley et al., *Commercial Bribery and the New International Norms*, 2 BLOOMBERG L. REP. - WHITE COLLAR CRIME REP. (2009); *see also* D. Bruce Johnsen, *The Ethics of 'Commercial Bribery': Integrative Social Contract Theory Meets Transaction Cost Economics*, 88 J. BUS. ETHICS (2009).

117. 18 PA. CONS. STAT. §4108 (2010).

118. *U.S. v. Parise*, 159 F.3d 790, 804 (dissent, Garth, Cir. Judge) (3rd Cir. 1998). Almost two dozen states now have such provisions. *See* ALA. CODE §13A-11-120 (2010); CONN. GEN. STAT. § 53A-160 (2010); MISS. CODE ANN. §97-9-10 (West 2010); 18 PA. CONS. STAT. § 4108 (2010); S.C. CODE ANN. § 16-17-540 (2009).

119. *State v. Bellis*, 399 A.2d 397, 400 (Pa. 1979).

120. *Parise, supra* note 118, at 805.

Chapter 8

Crimes against Habitation

KEYWORDS

Arson: The act or crime of willfully, wrongfully, and unjustifiably setting property on fire, often for the purpose of committing fraud.

Break: To open another's real property by force or without privilege for entry, often used in the phrase break and enter.

Burglary: The act of breaking and entering an inhabited structure especially at night with intent to commit a felony; the act of entering or remaining unlawfully in a building with intent to commit a crime.

Criminal (malicious) mischief: The act or offense of intentionally damaging or destroying another's property.

Criminal trespass: Trespass to property that is forbidden by statute and punishable as a crime as distinguished from trespass that creates a cause of action for damages.

Curtilage: The area surrounding and associated with a home.

Domicile: The place where an individual has a fixed and permanent home for legal purposes.

Habitation: A dwelling place.

Intrusion: The act of wrongfully entering upon, seizing, or taking possession of the property of another.

Vandalism: The willful or malicious destruction or defacement of property.

INTRODUCTION

The criminal law has long condemned attacks against the habitation. Habitat should have some sense of security. The domicile, the place of residence, can be the criminal's target and the systematic response will vary according to the injury inflicted. From the severity of arson to the misdemeanant mentality of the vandal, the law's condemnation of habitation offenses signifies the view that a home is one's castle. Assaults on the domicile occur on many fronts. In arson, the offender destroys with the ferocity of fire and incendiary explosion. It is also known as a personal offense because arson can achieve two ends: the destruction of real property and personal harm and injury, including death. Burglary depicts the serious intrusion into the sanctity of home and residential tranquility. Burglary destroys a home's integrity by stripping away the sense of security that each habitant wants and desires. Within the home, the burglar engages in felonious conduct. Trespass represents the unwarranted intrusion into personal space by physical invasion and uninvited nuisance. Vandals and other misdemeanants disavow the notion of ownership and display disrespect for individual and community. In sum, every offense involving habitation either causes physical damage to the habitat or undermines the serenity and security that a resident surely expects and deserves.

BURGLARY

ELEMENTS

- Breaking and entering
- A domicile or other qualified structure
- With intent to commit a felony therein

In criminal law analysis, both the experienced and inexperienced interpreter and practitioner will soon come to respect the complexities of this action. Part of its mystique relates to its own misconception. The average person portrays the offense as exclusively property-oriented—the burglar breaks in and enters solely for the purpose of theft. While there is some traditional legal support for this position, this narrow conception inaccurately describes the crime because the purpose of the breaking is directed toward the commission of any felony within the premises. One can steal, but also rob and rape within the domicile.

Another aspect that prompts so much confusion involves the dual intents that accompany the typical burglary prosecution. Initially, the perpetrator intends to break and enter a domicile or other qualified structure. At the same time, this perpetrator must intend some other felony as part of the master plan of invasion. Which intent controls? Are both intents needed? Or does each have the same weight? What if the prosecution fails to prove one type of intent? In this sense, burglary is often labeled a crime of dual intents.[1]

Add to this the incredibly creative and energized defenses posed by the accused in the criminal courtroom and you have a recipe for befuddlement. Despite these complexities, the basic elements of burglary are quite consistent among most American jurisdictions.

The Breaking and Entry

What causes the general citizenry to be so outraged at the act of burglary is its invasiveness. Few acts in the criminal arena, outside of personal offenses, raise such alarm and for good cause. A few jurisdictions have divided up the burglary elements into distinct offenses. For example, Arkansas categorizes and defines the distinct offense of "Breaking or Entering."

(a) A person commits the offense of breaking or entering if for the purpose of committing a theft or felony he or she breaks or enters into any:
  (1) Building, structure, or vehicle;
  (2) Vault, safe, cash register, safety deposit box, or money depository;
  (3) Money vending machine, coin-operated amusement machine, vending machine, or product dispenser;

CASE 8.1

PEOPLE V. REYES

76 A.3d 864 (N.Y. App. 2010)

The deliberating jury sent a note in relation to the second-degree burglary count for "clarification of intent—How does the age of the victim impact on intent?" In response, the court stated that it would tell the jury: "The answer to their intent question is if he intended to go into the building with a person and intended to have physical contact with that person, the age does not matter. In essence, he's stuck with the age."

Defense counsel objected, "No. No. No. No," and requested that the court reread its original instruction on that subject: "I'm asking for the readback of just the burglary with just the intent because in order to commit a crime, in a burglary situation, I believe that he has to know the age of the person when he goes in. He doesn't have to know the age of the person to commit the underlying crimes of the sex[ual] abuse. But, in order to have an intent to commit a crime inside, burglary in the second degree [he does]. And you are guaranteeing a conviction."

The court responded by saying "It's not. And once again, if there is a conviction—as you now predict—this is the first point on appeal, I gather."

Because the trial court ruled on defense counsel's objection, the court demonstrated "that [it] specifically confronted and resolved this issue. Under these circumstances, ... preservation was adequate."

However, the court declined to reread its instruction and instead delivered a more specific instruction. Counsel "did not specify why the charge as given was inadequate. Thus, while there was preservation as to the court's refusal to charge in accordance with defendant's request, there was no preservation with respect to error in the [intent] charge as given." Because the jury had already expressed its inability to understand the original instructions, it was appropriate for the court to provide more than the simple readback counsel had requested. While counsel raised a specific issue regarding defendant's intent, he never requested anything but a rereading of the original charge and made no objection to the supplemental charge the court actually delivered until he made his postverdict motion, which had no preservation effect. This Court recently found a lack of preservation in *People v. Hesterbay* when defense counsel only asked the court to reread the elements of the crimes in response to the jury's note. The Court of Appeals recently reiterated its warnings to the defense bar about the importance of specifying objections sufficiently to "alert the trial court to the argument now being advanced." Accordingly, by only asking for a rereading of the original charge on intent in the second-degree burglary charge, defendant's present claim that the supplemental instruction was incorrect or prejudicially misleading is unpreserved and we decline to review it in the interest of justice.

As an alternative holding, we also reject defendant's present claim on the merits. Defendant argues that his commission of strict liability offense of third-degree sexual abuse was not sufficient to satisfy the specific element of burglary that he "intended" to commit a crime when he entered the building. However, as the trial court correctly explained in its supplemental charge:

"How does the age of victim impact on intent? If the jury determines that a person intentionally went into a building for the purposes of having some sexual contact with an underaged person, even if the accused did not know the age of the underaged person, it would not matter.

"The intent—the intent that the law would focus on under those circumstances are the intent to have sexual contact.

"And the law says that a person is responsible for the age of a person with whom they have sexual interaction of any sort, notwithstanding the fact that the actor—supposed actor[—] did not know the actual age, even if the person who was the supposed victim informed the person of a different age than what the person actually was."

The crimes of which the jury convicted defendant were endangering the welfare of a child and four counts of sexual abuse in the third degree. The convictions are all strict liability crimes, in which, for the sexual abuse, the victim's lack of consent was based on the victim's incapacity because of age (Penal Law § 130.55 ["A person is guilty of sexual abuse in the third degree when he or she subjects another person to sexual contact without the latter's consent"]; Penal Law § 130.05 [3] [a] ["A person is deemed incapable of consent when he or she is — less than seventeen years old"]). And, Penal Law § 260.10 (1) states: "A person is guilty of endangering the welfare of a child when ... [h]e knowingly acts in a manner likely to be injurious to the physical, mental, or moral welfare of a child less than seventeen years old."

At the trial, the People established that the victim was 14 years old and defendant was 32 years old. Because these misdemeanors do not require a specific intent, can their violation satisfy the intent required for a second-degree burglary conviction?

Penal Law § 140.25 (2) states: "A person is guilty of burglary in the second degree when he knowingly enters or remains unlawfully in a building with intent to commit a crime therein, and when ... [t]he building is a dwelling."

Matter of *Gormley v. New York State Ethics Commn.* [*sic*] is instructive. In discussing the Penal Law definitions of "knowingly" and "intentionally" to construe Public Officers Law § 73, the Court noted the definitions revolve around a conscious objective to engage in conduct as opposed to a conscious objective to violate a statute (id. at 427). Thus, Penal Law § 15.05 (1) states: "'Intentionally.' A person acts intentionally with respect to a result or to conduct described by a statute defining an offense when his conscious objective is to cause such result or to engage in such conduct" (emphasis added).

Here, the trial court correctly charged the jury that all the People had to prove was that defendant entered the building intending to have sexual contact with the victim. The People did not have to prove that defendant intended to commit a crime or that he knew the victim's age or that she was under 17, as that was irrelevant to the intention necessary for the jury to find defendant committed burglary in the second degree.

This analysis is similar to the reasoning utilized in convictions for attempt. A defendant may intend to commit a particular act, but does not complete the act because of legal impossibility. Even though the crime itself may not require intent because it is a strict liability crime, the defendant may be convicted of the attempt. For instance, in a conviction for attempted rape in the second degree, the court reasoned that defendant could be convicted for attempting to have sex with a police officer who posed as a 13-year-old girl over the Internet. The "core conduct" was "[e]ngaging in sexual intercourse with a person who does not give, or is incapable of giving, consent"; the victim's age was an additional circumstance that made the conduct felonious. Likewise, the "core conduct" proscribed in the second-degree burglary statute is knowingly entering a residential building with intent to have sexual contact without consent.

Questions

1. In what way does the Court deal with two differing intents?
2. Why does the defendant argue that his intent cannot be demonstrated and, therefore, he cannot be convicted of burglary?
3. How does the Court describe away the "age" question?
4. What does the defendant hope to accomplish by arguing "strict liability?"
5. Which of these two offenses can be strict liability?
6. Does the defendant win the argument on strict liability? Why or why not?

(4)   Coin telephone or coin booth;
(5)   Fare box on a bus; or
(6)   Other similar container, apparatus, or equipment.
(b) It constitutes a separate offense under this section for the breaking or entering into of each separate:
(1)   Building, structure, or vehicle;
(2)   Vault, safe, cash register, safety deposit box, or money depository;
(3)   Money vending machine, coin-operated amusement machine, vending machine, or product dispenser;
(4)   Coin telephone or coin booth;
(5)   Fare box on a bus; or
(6)   Other similar container, apparatus, or equipment.
(c) Breaking or entering is a Class D. Felony.[2]

Upon close inspection, the statute represents a catchall provision for many offenses that ironically include the burglary charge. The range of actions and degrees of severity, however, is vastly different than traditional burglary.

In some jurisdictions, there have been drops in the overall numbers of burglary. Visit Maryland's data center for a representative overview at http://www.goccp.maryland.gov/msac/crime-statistics.php

The target of the break and enter usually is the private home or residence of the prospective victim. If there is anything sacrosanct in the world, it should be the place we call home, that locus where protection is rightly expected, that interior domain that should be free from unwanted intrusion. All of us sense the assault of residential intrusion when hearing noises that are unexplained in our homes and houses, and when people violate what space we are

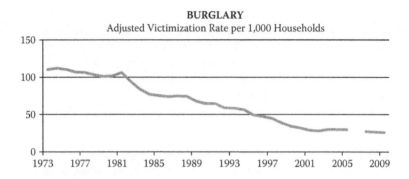

Figure 8.1   Burglary: Adjusted victimization rate per 1,000 households.

fortunate to possess. If a man or woman's home is their castle, they can properly be outraged when invasion occurs. Indeed select sentencing guidelines view the act with such gravity that a life sentence for its commission has been held appropriate when violence accompanies the burglary.[3]

On a national level, the offense has been heading to lower numbers over the past three decades. (See Figure 8.1.[4])

Whether burglary represents the level of gravity to constitute a "violent felony" for purposes of federal sentencing has been keenly debated.[5] For defendants, the designation "violent" aggravates their circumstances when it comes to penalties. In *Taylor v. U.S.*,[6] the U.S. Supreme Court pretty much labeled burglary an act of either actual or potential violence. A burglar knows full well the implications of his conduct because "he is prepared to use violence if necessary to carry out his plans or to escape."[7] The act of the burglar lacks any regularity for it is unlicensed, unwanted, and startling. The burglar lacks consent for entry and knows it. The party victimized by the intrusion knows the intent only after experiencing the dramatic effects that the crime causes.

Breaking

At common law, the offender had to have broken something in order to gain an entrance. In that way, the breaking signified the lack of consent so inherent in the offense of burglary; without some physical evidence of destruction, the case had to be demonstrated by other means however undestructive it might be—the lifting of a screen or the loosening of a screw. The broken pane of glass, the jimmied door, the torn or ripped screen or door jamb easily manifest an unwelcome intruder and a corresponding lack of consent. To be sure, there are a myriad of burglaries each day where nothing physical to the premises occurs. The accused may simply leave his or her mark or impress a footprint with a unique trademark.[8] Crossing the plane of permissible usage is a better way of looking at the breaking component because the term implies not only a breaking of certain physical barriers, but also the infringement on personal space in the domicile. Breaking also signified the destruction of tranquility in the domicile, a rather artificial, but well-intentioned effort to determine culpability. Modern-day statutes have for the most part eliminated the requirement of breaking in order "to avoid such illogical distinctions as that drawn between the raising of a closed window and that of a partially opened window."[9] Pennsylvania, for example, has eliminated the term from its statutory construction by defining burglary as:

A person is guilty of burglary if he enters a building or occupied structure, or separately secured or occupied portion thereof, with intent to commit a crime therein, unless the premises are at the time open to the public or the actor is licensed or privileged to enter.[10]

Besides these physical connotations of breaking things to get inside the domicile or other qualified structure, the breaking element infers a right or claim to be at a particular place at a particular time. One cannot burglarize a place of employment if the agent merely goes to work, with full and unbridled permission to be on the premises, and then subsequently formulates a criminal intent to commit a felony therein. A breaking, in any sense of the term, cannot occur when one has a right, privilege, or license to be on the premises. The agent may yet commit another offense at his or her place of employment, but if legitimately employed, the employer will have a tough time proving a lack of right to be there in the first place. In short, the term "breaking" has physical and metaphysical qualities. The perpetrator who gains access stealthily in the middle of the night, without right or privilege, is a far different character from the party who has a right to be on the premises in the first place. There is, in this latter case, no breaking in a figurative sense because no right or claim of privacy or privilege has been abridged. Of course, an agent's right or privilege may lapse or be revoked. The employee who surreptitiously accesses a place of employment after his shift and hours are over, now perpetrates the crime of burglary if his or her intent is to commit a felony therein.

These same principles equally apply in public buildings like bars and restaurants, train and bus stations, and other public venues. Breaking cannot occur during normal business hours because these facilities are widely and generously open to the public at large. This reality does not preclude the criminal actor from engaging in all sorts of criminality within these facilities. Nevertheless, a charge of burglary would be inappropriate given the lack of breaking.

Even in public facilities, such as hotels and restaurants, the "open to the public" argument only goes so far. Hotel occupants can expect that their rooms be off limits to the wandering public. A recent New Hampshire case illustrates how a defense team attempted, though unsuccessfully, to negate the lack of right or privilege. In *State of New Hampshire v. Flynn,*[11] the accused claimed that the hotel was a public facility and, therefore, the entry noncriminal in design. Although this argument lacks merit, defense strategy next turns to the claim that the evidence in the record could not have proved an entry since it is exclusively circumstantial. Here, the Supreme Court rejected the claim by noting that possession of a wedding band, wallet, and other personal artifacts, while circumstantial, were sufficient to support the finding. Simple possession of stolen items from a burglary location has been held sufficient to prove the intent to burglary despite a lack of direct proof.[12]

Breaking additionally implies that any entry gained by subterfuge or trickery will suffice in the burglary prosecution. From this perspective, the true nature of the breaking element can be deduced. While physical destruction qualifies, so will the deceptive intrusion or unlicensed trespass. Therefore, breaking encompasses physical intrusions resulting from physical violence to some portion of the domicile or in the absence of this obvious evidence, unauthorized access, without privilege or right, or as a result of trickery, collusion, or deception. See Figure 8.2 and Figure 8.3 for representations of a burglary point of entry and the aftermath of the intrusion.

Entry
Closely aligned to the breaking component in a burglary case is the requirement of entry. The discussion here entails more than academic distinctions. While it is fair to impute a purpose to a breaking (why else would one break except to enter), this sole conclusion does not cover all the

Figure 8.2   Point of entry. (Photo courtesy of B. Kohlhepp, Ross Township Police Department.)

possibilities. Breaking may occur for random or vandalistic purposes. A rock through a window or door may be nothing more than the malicious destruction of property. Beyond this explanation, and a host of other rationales, successful burglary adjudication will tie the breaking into the entry—a fact that must be offered for any real chance of victory. The offender breaks to enter, almost as if the words melded together in this way: "breaking in." Put another way, these elements are not strange bedfellows, but compatible companions.

Figure 8.3   The aftermath of a burglary. (Photo courtesy of B. Kohlhepp, Ross Township Police Department.)

Without entry, the burglary remains a factual and legal impossibility. State codifications fully understand the importance of the element of entry. Tennessee, as an illustration, employs the term repeatedly in its construction.

(a) A person commits burglary who, without the effective consent of the property owner:
  (1) Enters a building other than a habitation (or any portion thereof) not open to the public, with intent to commit a felony, theft or assault;
  (2) Remains concealed, with the intent to commit a felony, theft or assault, in a building;
  (3) Enters a building and commits or attempts to commit a felony, theft or assault; or
  (4) Enters any freight or passenger car, automobile, truck, trailer, boat, airplane or other motor vehicle with intent to commit a felony, theft or assault or commits or attempts to commit a felony, theft or assault.[13]

New Hampshire follows similar suit by delineating in this way:

A person is guilty of burglary if he enters a building or occupied structure, or separately secured or occupied section thereof, with purpose to commit a crime therein, unless the premises are at the time open to the public or the actor is licensed or privileged to enter. It is an affirmative defense to prosecution for burglary that the building or structure was abandoned.[14]

Entry takes the offender toward the aim of the burglary effort and gives life to the unseemly plan about to unfold. In some jurisdictions, the entry need not be very significant and the "element of entry is satisfied if any part of the intruder's body enters the structure."[15]

In general, courts have liberally construed the notion of entry and usually find that any force or exertion that gains access to the domicile or other structure suffices.[16] As in the case of breaking, entry analysis must inevitably dwell on ultimate end or purpose of the entry in order to constitute a burglary. One who enters without license or privilege, but lacks the requisite intent to commit a felony therein, fails as burglar, but succeeds as a trespasser. It is important to keep the offender's mindset and intentionality close to the vest as we seek to decipher plan and purpose.

Time of Day

The severity of burglary has long been tied to the likely time of its commission. While burglary takes place at just about any time, the historical prohibition against this offense was grounded in its surreptitiousness. The burglar stalking into the night may be inaccurate in every case, but crime statistics do quantify the regularity of the night intruder. Naturally, the seriousness of the offense was tied to timing because night offenses strike at our very notions of safety and security in the domicile. As a result of this view, burglary was once an exclusively nighttime offense. In fact, one could not be convicted without proof of the time of day element.

Today, this requirement has largely been modified. In many jurisdictions, the degree or grade of burglary still depends on its timing. The worst offense was defined in the night while the lower gradations of burglary were reserved for the daytime. North Dakota reserves first-degree status for night burglaries alone.

Burglary as a class B felony is:
  a. The offense is committed at night and is knowingly perpetrated in the dwelling of another; or
Otherwise burglary is a class C felony.[17]

(See Figure 8.4[18] for statistics regarding burglaries that occur during the day versus night.)

Time of day certainly serves as an aggravating factor when questions of charge and gradation are considered by prosecutorial staff and just as likely to be weighed at the time of sentencing.

Similarly, legislatures grade the burglary offense by factors that evidence violence. In Maine, first-degree burglary occurs when firearms are employed during the burglary's commission.[19] Class B burglary includes variations on this theme by using the term "dangerous weapons" as opposed to the firearm.[20]

Domicile or Other Qualified Structure

That burglary historically has been associated with private and personal residences is well established. As noted earlier, the level of distaste for the criminal act is largely the result of the boldness of the intrusion into the inner sanctum known as "home." There is much to be said about maintaining this distinction between domicile and commercial or other establishments. However, the distinction has long been foremost on legislative framers minds, whose primary approach has been to expand the classifications that qualify for the burglary charge. Statutory designs are replete with new and ever emerging categories of structures that allow the burglary charge. From boats to autos, from sheds to garages, from stores to commercial warehouses, legislatures liberally include these and a myriad of other designations.

Iowa's criminal code defines structures in many distinct ways and the gravity of the offense may depend on how it is defined as well as whether it is occupied or not. Visit http://coolice.legis.state.ia.us/cool-ice/default.asp?category=billinfo&service=iowacode&ga=83&input=713

For generations, only the primary residential structure could qualify for inclusion while other secondary and aligned buildings were considered disconnected, thereby disqualifying the burglary charge. The theory of "curtilage" subsumed adjoining properties so that they might be considered as part of the whole, e.g., greenhouses, garages, tool sheds, and springhouses. While technically these structures were not lived in, their overall usage so intimately tied them to the main structure that they were deemed an essential part of the primary structure. Minnesota refers to these facilities as "appurtenant property."[21] Litigation regarding what is in or out of curtilage reached legendary proportions during the nineteenth century, though this question is now fairly settled.[22] The State of Washington uses the term "building"[23] as does Minnesota.[24] Other jurisdictions have attempted to retain these traditional underpinnings by redefining the term "domicile" to "occupied structure." In other words, if it can be lived in, for whatever period and under whatever conditions, it qualifies.[25] Commercial establishments have generally been the recipient of legislative largesse as politicians spread the benefits of their crime policies to the largest amount of constituents.[26]

The Intents of Burglary

The clear complication that burglary causes in mens rea analysis appears early during fact-finding and legal analysis. Even trial courts get lost in the mystery.[27] How will the prosecutor show the

	Total[a]	Residence (dwelling)			Nonresidence (store, office, etc.)		
		Night	Day	Unknown	Night	Day	Unknown
1976	100%	22%	25%	16%	23%	5%	9%
1977	100	23	26	16	21	5	9
1978	100	22	26	16	20	6	10
1979	100	21	26	16	21	6	10
1980	100	21	28	17	18	5	10
1981	100	22	29	17	18	5	9
1982	100	22	27	16	19	6	10
1983	100	23	26	18	18	6	10
1984	100	22	27	18	17	6	10
1985	100	21	27	18	17	6	10
1986	100	22	28	18	17	6	10
1987	100	21	28	18	16	6	10
1988	100	21	29	18	16	7	10
1989	100	20	28	17	16	8	10
1990	100	21	29	16	16	8	9
1991	100	21	28	17	16	8	10
1992	100	21	29	16	16	9	9
1993	100	21	29	16	16	8	10
1994	100	20	30	17	15	9	9
1995	100	20	29	17	14	9	10
1996	100	20	28	19	15	8	11
1997	100	19	28	19	15	8	11
1998	100	19	29	19	14	8	11
1999	100	19	29	18	14	9	11
2000	100	19	30	16	15	11	10
2001	100	19	30	16	15	11	10
2002	100	19	31	15	14	11	9
2003	100	19	31	16	14	10	10
2004	100	19	31	16	14	10	10
2005	100	19	31	16	14	10	10
2006	100	19	32	15	14	11	9
2007	100	19	34	15	14	10	8
2008	100	20	36	14	12	10	7
2009	100	20	37	15	12	9	7

Figure 8.4 Percent distribution of burglaries known to police, by place and time of occurrence (United States, 1976–2009).   (*continued*)

ᵃBecause of rounding, percents may not add to total.

Note: These data were compiled by the Federal Bureau of Investigation through the Uniform Crime Reporting (UCR) Program. On a monthly basis, law enforcement agencies (police, sheriffs, and state police) report the number of offenses that become known to them in the following crime categories: murder and nonnegligent manslaughter, forcible rape, robbery, aggravated assault, burglary, larceny-theft, motor vehicle theft, and arson. A count of these crimes is taken from records of all complaints of crime received by law enforcement agencies from victims or other sources and/or from officers who discovered the offenses. Whenever complaints of crime are determined through investigation to be unfounded or false, they are eliminated from an agency's count (Source. 2009, About Crime in the U.S., Methodology). In trend tables "constructed" or "adapted" by SOURCEBOOK staff from *Crime in the United States,* the data are from the first year in which the data are reported. It should be noted that the number of agencies reporting and the populations represented vary from year to year. Also, the percent distributions are based on offense reports for which the FBI received detailed information from local law enforcement agencies and exclude jurisdictions for which the FBI generated estimated offense totals. For data on the estimated total number of offenses occurring in the United States for each Part I offense, see table 3.106.2009. For information on States supplying incomplete data for selected years, see Appendix 3.

Source: U.S. Department of Justice, Federal Bureau of Investigation, *Crime in the United States, 1976,* p. 159, Table 18; *1977,* p. 159, Table 18; *1978,* p. 174, Table 18; *1979,* p. 176, Table 18; *1980,* p. 179, Table 18; *1981,* p. 150, Table 17; *1982,* p. 155, Table 17; *1983,* p. 158, Table 17; *1984,* p. 151, Table 18; *1985,* p. 153, Table 18; *1986,* p. 153, Table 18; *1987,* p. 152, Table 18; *1988,* p. 156, Table 18; *1989,* p. 160, Table 18; *1990,* p. 162, Table 18; *1991,* p. 201, Table 23; *1992,* p. 205, Table 23; *1993,* p. 205, Table 23; *1994,* p. 205, Table 23; 1995, p. 196, Table 23; *1996,* p. 202, Table 23; *1997,* p. 210, Table 23; *1998,* p. 197, Table 23; *1999,* p. 199, Table 23; *2000,* p. 204, Table 23; *2001,* p. 218, Table 23; *2002,* p. 217, Table 23; *2003,* p. 252, Table 23; *2004,* p. 259, Table 23 (Washington. D.C.: USGPO); *2005,* Table 23 [Online]. Available: http://www2.fbi.gov/ucr/05cius/data/table 23.html [Oct. 13, 2006]; *2006,* Table 23 [Online]. Available: http://www2.fbi.gov/ucr/cius2006/data/table 23.html [Oct. 24, 2007]; *2007,* Table 23 [Online]. Available: http://www2.fbi.gov/ucr/cius2007/data/table 23.html [Jan. 21, 2009]; *2008,* Table 23 [Online]. Available: http://www2.fbi.gov/ucr/cius2008/data/table 23.html [Dec. 29, 2009]; *2009,* Table 23 [Online], Available: http://www2.fbi.gov/ucr/cius2009/data/table 23.html [Oct. 18, 2010]. Table constructed by SOURCEBOOK staff.

Figure 8.4 *(continued)* Percent distribution of burglaries known to police, by place and time of occurrence (United States, 1976–2009).

intentionality of the offender? Will it be possible to convict the accused when demonstrating the intent to commit a felony without the intent to enter? Or is the intent to enter satisfactory without proof of the intent to commit a felony? If burglary constitutes intent to commit a felony, what if the prosecution fails to prove the requisite state of intent of the underlying crime? Will the burglary charge be dismissed because of an unsuccessful felony prosecution? None of these queries provides confident answers because how and what a defendant thinks in the typical criminal case calls for subjective and objective analysis. Objectively, we can only know select facts. Subjectively, we can only infer and deduce from these objective facts what a defendant knows. Rarely do investigative teams discover proof of mental purpose. Almost always, defendants proclaim their innocence. In this very imprecise science, the justice system struggles to discern whether defendant wanted or willed the result. In burglary cases, the prosecution team seems to have two burdens instead of one.

Admittedly, these burdens are not that onerous especially when one considers how the facts so often lead to the crime in question. Crimes in the domicile do not happen in a vacuum, but are the results of conscious choice. Defendants can be shown to have connected the dots, so to speak.

At the same time, defense attorneys can be expected to launch vigorous defenses that bifurcate or separate the dual intents. The benefits of this type of confusion are self-evident and reasonable doubts as to one charge or the other can evolve rather quickly.

At the heart of any prosecution or defense is the demonstration of purposeful entry with knowing or willed design to commit a felony therein. The intent to commit a felony is contemporaneous to the decision to enter. It is even arguable that an offender who enters with no criminal plan, but then subsequently develops his or her enterprise while within the domicile, cannot be properly charged with burglary. In this circumstance, the burglary gives way to the independently grounded felony. At the other end of the spectrum, it is equally arguable that a defendant who plans intently and with clarity his or her criminal scheme, enters the building, then fails in the criminal conduct due to extenuating circumstance, is, in fact, still the burglar. Consumption of the criminality does not make the burglar—intent to enter with a simultaneous intent to commit a felony does. Readily obvious are the permutations and differing defense slants that are sure to come from the mouths of those awaiting trial. Given this complexity, prosecutors sometimes wisely opt out of the burglary charge in favor of focusing on the underlying felony. The consequences of losing one charge because one form of intent is muddled are sometimes too great. From another angle, it may be more sensible to skip burglary all together if there is any chance that the defendant will succeed in the felony prosecution. Rather than coming up empty handed, DAs sometimes choose lesser offenses, such as criminal trespass because the felony intent will not emerge. Prosecutorial staff should be cognizant of the existence of select exclusions as to felonious conduct. Some states, such as South Dakota, expressly exclude retail theft and shoplifting from their burglary elements.[28]

Defendants will vigorously argue that the facts before the tribunal and jury are not two crimes, but one, and that it is inconsistent with due process and double jeopardy principles to be prosecuted with an offense that really resides in the other. In other words, intent to rape should be restricted to the crime of rape alone and efforts to charge burglary simultaneously are fundamentally unfair. This is why the crime of burglary is sometimes said to be an act that merges other acts, yet still retains the power to charge twice. Naturally defendants want one charge instead of two and frequently appeal the injustice based on a theory of "merger." As examples, kidnapping and burglary are really one offense, as is theft and burglary.

So tenacious have these arguments been that state legislatures have adopted "antimerger statutes," which assure two punishments for two differing acts. The State of Washington's antimerger statute protects the traditional picture of burglary:

> Every person who, in the commission of a burglary shall commit any other crime, may be punished therefore as well as for the burglary, and may be punished for each crime separately.[29]

In Washington and other states, the legislature is perfectly entitled to merge or not offenses it deems fit. However, in the absence of said merger, courts generally hold that the offenses and their requisite intents are independent of one another. The Supreme Court of Washington affirmed this basic tendency in 1999 declaring:

> The merger doctrine arises only when a defendant has been found guilty of multiple charges, and the court then asks if the Legislature intended only one punishment for the multiple conviction. It will only apply where the Legislature has clearly indicated it intended the offenses to merge. The plain language of RCW 9A.52.050 expresses the intent of the Legislature that "any other crime" committed in the commission of a burglary would not merge with the offense of first-degree burglary when

a defendant is convicted of both. In this instance, the "other crime" is assault. The statute does not evidence a contrary intent.[30]

Critical to any understanding of burglary is the underlying purpose of the intrusion. A conviction for burglary depends on another felonious act for its own viability. Review the Case 8.2 synopsis and then respond to the questions that follow.

Given the seriousness of the offense, and the corresponding drop in its overall numbers, there are some preventative steps that appear to be effective. The Center for Problem-Oriented Policing delineates some excellent suggestions for minimizing the burglary offense in your community (see Figure 8.5[31]).

CASE 8.2

TENNESSEE V. SWANSON

No. E1998-00041-CCA-R3-CD (Cr. App. Ten. 2000).

During the time period between January 1994 and June 1996, 19 women reported that their purses had been stolen from vehicles parked in recreational areas near Signal Mountain. Law enforcement officials received information that a red or orange truck having wooden panels was used by the perpetrator. While on patrol near the area of the thefts, Officer Greg Hill of the Signal Mountain Police Department received information that a man driving the suspected truck had just stolen a purse from a parked car. Officer Hill then saw the truck and began pursuit. When he activated his emergency lights, the driver refused to stop. Officer Hill placed a call to the fire department and the officers were able to stop the truck by blocking its path with a fire engine. The defendant was the driver of the truck. Officer Hill, a K-9 officer, approached the truck with his dog. The dog alerted. A search yielded two purses which had been stolen in the area, one of which contained narcotics.

After his arrest, the defendant admitted to stealing the 19 purses. He explained that he had been diagnosed as a "sex addict" and that he took the purses in order to satisfy his sexual desires and fantasies. The defendant informed the officers that he would "masturbate to these [stolen] purses." He revealed that he had begun the practice of looking into girls' purses while in high school. With the defendant's cooperation, officers located 31 stolen purses in the defendant's possession, only 19 of which had been reported as missing. In addition to the purses, the officers found a large box containing items, such as drivers' licenses, diaries, and photographs. The defendant explained that he did not keep all of the purses that he had stolen because he lost sexual interest in them, but decided to keep the contents of the purses because he believed he had a "personal relationship" with the female victims and their families. He said that he used the cash from the purses and kept the remainder of the contents. Officers were able to identify a total of 65 victims from the materials the defendant kept in his possession.

At the sentencing hearing, it was established that the defendant, age 30, had been married since 1994. The couple had no children together. The defendant's first marriage, which ended in divorce in 1993, produced one son, age three at the time of the defendant's arrest. The child resides with his mother and the defendant regularly provides support of $50.00

per week. After completing high school, the defendant enrolled in courses at Chattanooga State Community College where he has studied mathematics and maintained a high grade point average. He has a good employment record, including work as a teachers' aide at the community college, as a substitute teacher for the Hamilton County School System in 1995 and 1996, and as a woodworker at a cabinet shop. The defendant has a variety of health problems, which include depression, anxiety, obesity, back pain, cluster headaches, and cardiomegaly (enlarged heart). He has one prior offense, a misdemeanor assault conviction in 1993.

The defendant claimed that he had a "sex and love addiction." He explained that he "created these fantasy relationships that weren't real" and that his low self-esteem causes him to seek out unhealthy relationships. He contended that he had been making significant progress with a 12-step program designed to combat his problems. He apologized to his family and the victims of the crimes. The defendant's wife and father both testified that they were unaware of his "sexual addiction" at any time before his arrest.

Several women whose purses had been stolen by the defendant also testified at the sentencing hearing. None, however, were victims of the 19 burglaries or the four thefts to which the defendant pled guilty. Each of the women expressed the feeling that she had been violated by the defendant. They were particularly concerned about the defendant obtaining their personal information, which included their addresses, social security numbers, and photographs. The women also testified that their children were afraid that the defendant might attempt to break into their homes. At least one of the purses the defendant had stolen contained keys to the victim's home. Each of the women testified to the inconveniences of canceling credit cards, dealing with stolen checks, and replacing drivers' licenses and social security cards. They also testified as to the value of their stolen property and the break-in damage to their vehicles. The women testified that all of their personal belongings had been returned to them, with the exception of any cash.

The only information relating to the actual victims of the crimes for which the defendant was convicted is contained in two victim impact statements. In the section marked "Victim's Property Loss," Mary Seay, one of the burglary victims, wrote the following: "Van side window smashed—$150.00, I think. Purse and contents stolen. A year later, I got everything back except the money, about $20.00. Locks on doors to house changed—$60.00. My husband did this himself, cost him his time, inconvenience." Jennifer Scoggins, a burglary and misdemeanor theft victim, reported that her stolen purse had an estimated value of $40.00. The presentence report indicates that the investigating officer mailed victim impact statement forms to six additional victims, but none of these forms were returned to the officer.

Questions

1. Are the crimes charged serious enough to support the burglary conviction?
2. Is the defense of sexual addiction convincing enough to minimize or mitigate mens rea?
3. How could you argue the doctrine of merger in these facts?
4. Do these facts and findings alter how you perceive burglary as an offense or is it consistent with your long-held views?

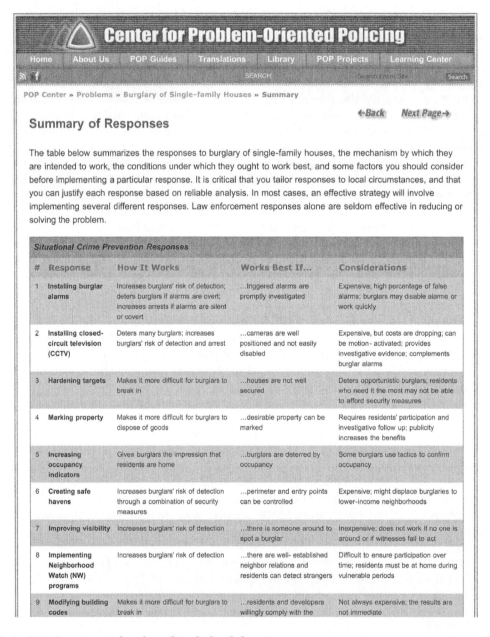

Figure 8.5   Responses to burglary of single-family houses.

CRIMINAL TRESPASS

ELEMENTS

- Intent to enter (break into)
- Without license or privilege
- In a qualified structure

The similarities between the charge of burglary and trespass can be gleaned from statutory comparisons. In fact, the language of competing statutes can be eerily close. Check out the example from Pennsylvania:

§ 3503. Criminal trespass

(a) BUILDINGS AND OCCUPIED STRUCTURES. —
    (1) A person commits an offense if, knowing that he is not licensed or privileged to do so, he:
        (i)   enters, gains entry by subterfuge or surreptitiously remains in any building or occupied structure or separately secured or occupied portion thereof; or
        (ii) breaks into any building or occupied structure or separately secured or occupied portion thereof.[32]

Language like "break into," "without license or privilege," or "surreptitiously" identically appear in burglary and trespass laws. What this demonstrates is the central focus of both offenses: intrusion. In either offense, the perpetrator enters into unlicensed space without permission or consent. The crux of the difference lies in the underlying motivation for why the intrusion occurs in the first place. In burglary, the intent to engage in felonious conduct drives the actor. Not so in trespass because the motive rests in intrusion alone. Defense tactics often relate to double jeopardy claims where the merger theory crops up again. Here, the defendant argues there is really no difference between burglary and trespass, which in turn restricts dual prosecutions.[33] The trespasser's horizon is limited to the intrusion and not much more.

The law fully recognizes a wide variety of grades and degrees of trespass activity, from felonious to summary violations, and the justice practitioner needs to look closely at the language of the statute. Repetitive trespassers, commonly known as "defiant," may suffer differing consequences because of their intractability.[34]

Entry

At the center of every trespass case is the entry and intrusion. Difficult would be the trespass case without someone entering or invading premises. How else could it be done? In the civil realm, trespass retains the possibility of nuisance as a form of trespass, such as fence or partition construction on another's land or the diversion of some natural force onto a neighbor's property. In the criminal realm, we reference only the actor entering into a qualified structure whether it is a domicile or other occupied structure.

Entry implies illegality rather than invitation. Hence, public places that welcome customers or travelers, abandoned structures that lack possessory interest, cannot be entered illegally. Entry, just as witnessed in burglary, should either be actual,[35] whereby the intruder breaks into or gains access by deceit or misrepresentation. In the latter case, courts construe the entry as constructively illegal. The Model Penal Code (MPC) lays out lucid meaning for what it means to enter or intrude by trespass:

§ 206.53 Criminal Trespass

(2) Definitions. To intrude means to enter or remain without consent express or implied of the person entitled to exclude or of another lawful occupant. Warning means notice that the person entitled to exclude does not consent to intrusion; it may be given by written or oral communication to the actor or by posting notices in a manner prescribed by law or reasonably likely to come to the attention of intruders.[36]

While the entry addresses the actus reus of trespass, the mental motivation of trespass involves a little more.

Intent as to License or Privilege

Trespassers lack the right to be within a structure because they are not welcome or invited by the owner/occupant. To be accountable for trespass, the conviction must rest on an evidentiary basis that manifests not only the entry, but also the full awareness of a lack of privilege or right. This type of knowledge targets the mental state of the trespasser whose activity is driven by more than the mere thrill of entry.[37]

Trespass roots its improper purposes in a knowing being, well aware that his or her presence is not permissible. The mens rea element inexorably winds its way back to the offender's own conception of permissibility of presence and whether or not the criminal actor is on notice of his lack of invitation. This mental state assumes the trespasser is consciously aware of his or her lack of welcome. Despite this clear state of mind, the trespasser proceeds with the criminal design. When compared to burglary, the proof of intention rests in a very narrow framework, which centers its attention on a lack of privileged presence.

Another approach in the proof of this crime's intent is the search for motivation. It may not be enough to show that the criminal agent lacks permission to be present. Why do trespassers trespass at all? What are the motivations? Review the checklist in Figure 8.6. Which of these would explain the mental state of the trespass offender?

Notice signs placed conspicuously by the owners of land or other property anticipate the potential defenses related to lack of knowledge, but are conclusive proof that the accused was

Traits of Trespassers	Yes	No
Violation of a protection from abuse or other protective order		
Stalking or other harassment		
Intent to commit a felony		
Burglary		
Co-tenants in apartment complex		
Airport visitor		
Mall shopper		

Figure 8.6 Traits of trespassers.

aware. Jurisdictions like Tennessee set out particular defenses to a charge of trespass in the statute, all of which depict a mens rea that is lacking for purposes of prosecution. The provision states in part:

39-14-405. Criminal trespass

(a) A person commits criminal trespass if the person enters or remains on property, or any portion of property, without the consent of the owner. Consent may be inferred in the case of property that is used for commercial activity available to the general public or, in the case of other property, when the owner has communicated the owner's intent that the property be open to the general public.[38]

Qualified Structure

Trespass statutes liberally define the focus of the trespass to include just about any structure. In addition to the domicile, legislative designs include any occupied structure, commercial establishments, or other structure capable of being occupied. Vehicles and boats also have been inserted into statutory language. Nebraska has drafted a well-rounded statute that lists "any building or occupied structure, or any separately secured occupied portion thereof."[39] The MPC goes even farther by including a "mine, wharf, or other structure."[40]

DEFENSE STRATEGIES

Has the property been abandoned?
Did the owner consent to presence?
Are the alleged restrictions legal?
Was the accused put on notice?
Did the accused have a proprietary interest in property?
Was the entry a breaking?

ARSON

ELEMENTS

- A qualified structure
- An act that constitutes burning, destruction by fire, explosion, or incendiary urge
- Specific intent

Motive and Intent

The plague of arson impacts communities in diverse ways, from economic costs to loss of limb and life. Communities in decline are regular targets of arsonists because property valuation and an inability to sell prompt the criminality. While the arsonist who burns the devalued property due to declining value and the hopelessness of sale, others see arson as a potential profit or treasure due to the receipt of insurance proceeds. The motivations for this crime are indeed diverse.[41]

While arson is a specific intent crime, proof of motive helps understand the mens rea component. Why would burning occur? What drives the firesetter? Accident or mistake will never be a satisfactory basis for proving intent, for this sort of felony expects a nefarious purpose. The crime calls for corrupt motives, such as:

- Economic gain from insurance proceeds
- Economic gain by halting losses on a distressed property
- Homicide and personal injury infliction
- Fire as a means of intimidation
- Fire as a sign of vengeance and jealousy
- Fire as senseless destruction
- Fire as sexual stimulation

In each of these categories, the motive is suspect. The arson for profit character wants the money. He or she sees economic advantage to the criminality. Review the Arson for Profit Interview Questionnaire in Figure 8.7[42] for further insight.

The Nature of Fire

Arson's unequivocal requirements for damage resulting from fire have been longstanding. While the offense is generally identified with fire and fire alone as the agent of destruction, under modern codifications that damage can result from explosions, incendiaries, and other combustible materials. Under common law tradition, fire means what is says. Fire burns and damages property in ways not witnessed in other crimes. Despite all this common sense, even the common law crew saw fire from varied perspectives and eventually expanded the damage definition to include smoke singeing or charring. "If there is the slightest burning of any part of the house, the offense is complete, though the fire may be put out or may go out by itself. There need not even be a blaze, but mere charring is sufficient."[43]

Fire naturally included the burn and charring of flame and incendiary power. The red glow coupled with blue and orange hues manifests the type of intensity needed. However, this view narrowly interprets how fire goes about its business. To be sure, fire spreads and attacks with a ferocity that impresses, though this is only one side of the story. Fire smolders and simmers, it chars and blisters, it smokes and glows, and generally combusts in ways well beyond the usual description. Fire also has the predictable energy to cause other natural forces to erupt whether through explosion, melting, and/or foundational collapse. Anyone who has ever witnessed a fully engulfed building will marvel at the force and domination inherent in fire (Figure 8.8).

Older statutes were rather one dimensional on how the arsonist acted. Language like "sets fire to" and "burns" was the start and end point for the early constructionist. The Model Penal Code's provision added the use of explosives to the mix and for its time was a shocking shift from the status quo. The MPC held:

(1) A person is guilty of arson, a felony of the second degree, if he starts a fire or causes an explosion with the purpose of:
   (a) destroying a building or occupied structure of another; or
   (b) destroying or damaging any property, whether his own or another's, to collect insurance for such loss. It shall be an affirmative defense to prosecution under this paragraph that the actor's conduct did not recklessly endanger any building or occupied structure of another or place any other person in danger of death or bodily injury.[44]

Questions to Ask the Target
- Tell me in your own words what you know about this fire.
- When did you first hear of the arson? Who told you?
- Where were you and what were you doing before, during, and after the arson? Who was with you?
- Do you know who committed the arson?
- Do you have any knowledge of any previous fire at the building?
- Do you have any knowledge of any previous incidents of any kind and at any location owned or rented by the owner/occupant of the building?
- Do you know of any recent changes in insurance coverage?
- Do you know the owner of the arson property? Describe your relationship to the owner?
- Do you have any financial interest in the burned property?

Questions to Ask the Owner:
- Tell me in your own words what you know about this fire.
- How long have your owned the burned property?
- What was the purchase price?
- What was the total amount of the mortgage?
- What is your insurance company? Agent/Broker? Public adjuster?
- How much insurance do you carry?
- Is there more than one policy on this property? On its contents? On rental or business interruption?
- Have you increased your insurance coverage on the property in the past year? If so, why and at whose suggestion?
- Have you ever received an insurance cancellation notice on this property?
- Where were you at the time of the fire?
- When did you first hear of the arson? Who told you?
- When were you last in the building?
- Was the building secured? If so, in what manner?
- Who else has access to or keys to the building?
- Who was the last person to leave the building?
- Do you have any knowledge that the sprinkler system and/or burglar alarm system was on and working?
- Indicate the name and address of all lien holders.
- What is the amount of each lien?
- What was the value of the inventory on hand immediately prior to the fire?
- Can you provide documentation for the value cited in the previous question?
- Was any inventory removed from the premises prior to the fire? Where did it go? Why was it removed?
- Was any inventory removed from the premises after the fire?
- List the inventory removed and its value.
- Did you set the fire or cause it to be set?
- Do you know who set it?

Figure 8.7   Arson for Profit Interview Questionnaire.

Proof of Fire Checklist

1. Are there signs of accelerants?
2. Are there signs of explosives?
3. Are there signs of trailers (items that assist the spreading of fire, such as clothing, bedding, curtains) from one point to another?
4. Can a comparison be made between the normal course and conduct of a fire versus its most intense point? (Often signs of the origination point.)
5. Are there any residues indicating incendiary devices?
6. What was the status of doors and windows?
7. Can a fire pattern be discerned?
8. What is the status and condition of closets?
9. Are hard floors, such as concrete, stone, or tile, more intensely burned in some spots than others? (Look for spalling, which causes the cracking and flaking of cement.)
10. Was the location abandoned or lived in?
11. What was the thermostat setting?
12. What was the condition of the oil burner?
13. What is the wattage of light bulbs?
14. Were electrical conductors overloaded?
15. Were there significant amounts of extension cords?
16. Were items of value and significant expense recently removed from the building?
17. In a multifloored building, can you distinguish the pattern and trial of fire?
18. Are there any witnesses?
19. Is there any photographic evidence?
20. Has physical evidence been cared for to assure the chain of custody?

Figure 8.8   Proof of Fire Checklist.

Coupling burning with exploding marked the beginning of an aggressive trek that spreads a wider net on qualifying behavior. Fire may be the centerpiece although, with modern chemistry, the offender now employs substances that accelerate fire and destruction. It is a bigger question than matches and newspaper, for arsonists have become adept in the interplay between the chemistry of fire and the chemicals to urge spread and hide evidence (Figure 8.9). "Arson prosecutions often depend on the state showing the presence of a chemical accelerant at the scene of a fire."[45]

Visit the ATF's Web location to discover how the agency's arson responsibilities kick in when explosives are utilized, at http://www.atf.gov.

In the end, modern laws appreciate fully the use of explosives and other accelerant as change agents for fire itself. A fire coupled with untraceable chemical substances increase the likelihood of the defendant's actions being undetected. The sophistication of the arson game has made it difficult to not only prosecute but apprehend (Figure 8.10).

Figure 8.9   The aftermath of arson. (Photo courtesy of B. Kohlhepp, Ross Township Police Department.)

Figure 8.10   Axel, Minnesota's first accelerant-detection (arson) dog, with his handler, Eddie Hustad. (Photo courtesy of Eddie Hustad, Inferno Kennels.)

CASE 8.3

PEOPLE V. BEAGLE
6 Cal. 3d 441, 492 P.2d 1 (1972).

Defendant Harvey Lynn Beagle II was convicted by a jury of one count of attempted arson (Pen. Code, § 451a) and one count of arson (Pen. Code, § 448a). A prior conviction of having issued a check without sufficient funds (Pen. Code, § 476a) was charged and admitted, but the judgment reflects no disposition of the allegation. Defendant was sentenced to the state prison for the term prescribed by law.

Although we reject all of the many contentions presented by defendant on appeal from the judgment, we nevertheless conclude, *inter alia*, that a trial judge must exercise his discretion to prevent impeachment of a witness by the introduction of evidence of a prior felony conviction when the probative value of such evidence is substantially outweighed by the risk of undue prejudice. (See Evid. Code, § 352.)

The charges stem from fires independently originating in buildings housing neighboring business establishments, Rudy's Keg, a bar, and north of the bar, Lewin's Furniture Store. Both buildings were located on Vineland Avenue in North Hollywood. Other commercial enterprises are also situated on Vineland south from Rudy's Keg. Behind such establishments are open areas and areas occupied by other structures, including a building in which defendant maintained an apartment.

On May 25, 1969, Rudolph Oravsky, owner of Rudy's Keg, ordered defendant to leave the premises when defendant became intoxicated and obnoxious while a patron in the bar. Defendant attempted to induce another patron to leave with him and when met with a refusal, defendant stated: "Well, come on and go with me anyway. I want to go into Los Angeles and hire a Mexican to firebomb this place for $25.00." This conversation was overheard by a third person.

During the early afternoon of July 1, Oravsky was present in a barbershop adjacent to Rudy's Keg and defendant approached and asked if he could have a drink at the bar. Oravsky replied: "Definitely not ... this is permanent." Defendant, who was obviously disappointed, responded: "Well, okay," and left the barbershop. About 9 p.m. of that same day while Oravsky was in the bar, he heard a noise which sounded to him like the explosion of a large firecracker. He went out through the parking lot to an alley in the rear and was able to see a fire on the roof of the building housing his bar. He climbed to the roof with a water hose and succeeded in extinguishing two small fires. There he discovered and removed a Pepsi-Cola bottle containing a small amount of gasoline and a wick. During the period of time Oravsky was at the rear and on the roof of the building, he noticed nothing unusual at Lewin's, but he did see defendant's car parked near his apartment.

Oravsky returned to his bar and placed a telephone call to the police. Shortly thereafter he telephoned the police a second time and, during this call, Mr. Duffy, who had entered the bar during the interval between the two calls, noticed the lights of a car as it appeared to turn into the alley and stop. The car, similar to defendant's vehicle, proceeded slowly down the alley and then disappeared behind Lewin's. Both men went into the parking area and Oravsky then observed for the first time that a wooden door facing the alley on the Lewin's building was aflame. He also noticed that defendant's car was no longer in the area. Oravsky called the fire department as Duffy attempted without success to extinguish the flames. Oravsky smelled gasoline at the scene of the fire at Lewin's building and Duffy testified that the fire burned as if it had been ignited by the use of gasoline. The blaze caused approximately $100,000 in damages to Lewin's before it was extinguished.

A fire department arson investigator attributed the fire at Rudy's Keg to the ignition of a flammable liquid placed on the roof of the building. He could find no natural or accidental cause for the fire at Lewin's, but a full and conclusive investigation was precluded by reason of the extensive damage.

About 10 p.m. on the evening of the fires, Officer Jones went to defendant's apartment. He was admitted by defendant's wife who told him that her husband had left the apartment two to three hours earlier. While there, Jones saw a cap from a gasoline can. Approximately five minutes after Jones arrived at the apartment, defendant returned home. His hands smelled of gasoline as did stains on his shoes and pants. Defendant told the officer that he worked at a service station and thereafter had been to a bar for a few beers. Jones arrested defendant and found a number of books of paper matches in his pockets.

After defendant had been removed to a police vehicle, an officer in defendant's presence conducted a field test for the flammability of the liquid in the bottle recovered from the roof by Oravsky. The officer poured out a small quantity of the contents and held a match to it. The liquid ignited rapidly. At this point defendant stated: "You can't arrest me for arson because the bottle didn't break." Prior to this statement, the police in dependent's presence had made no mention of the discovery of the bottle nor had they questioned defendant as to either fire.

Defendant testified that on the day of the fires he had had an "early morning" medical appointment and "had taken off work for this at 12:00 noon." Afterwards he went to the Big H, a cocktail lounge, where he consumed a few beers. He returned home about 2 p.m. and later during the afternoon he went to the barbershop to have his hair cut. About 4:30 p.m. he returned to the Big H cocktail lounge and thereafter went to a service station to work during a shift change. Around 6:30 p.m. he returned home with a can of gasoline and a ladder as he planned to do some painting. He poured some of the gasoline into a cardboard carton prior to softening his paint brushes. As the carton began to leak he emptied the gasoline contained therein into a drain and directed his wife to return the ladder and the remaining gasoline to the service station. About 8 p.m. defendant drove his car "across the street" to the Big H and there he consumed several more beers. While at the Big H, he unsuccessfully attempted to telephone his home and, becoming worried, decided to return home. There were fire engines in the vicinity and Vineland was blocked off. He parked his car at a nearby market and walked to his apartment where he was placed under arrest for arson. He admitted that he had been ejected from Rudy's Keg earlier in the year and that he saw the bottle in the possession of the police officers.

Defendant's wife testified, corroborating, and contradicting defendant's testimony in certain particulars. She corroborated generally the frustrated attempt at painting but gave testimony inconsistent with defendant's as to the approximate time of his departure from the apartment.

Questions

1. What was the accelerant employed by the defendant?
2. How would the prior charges involving bad checks be relevant in a case of arson?
3. Was the evidence sufficient to prove agency as to arson?
4. How effective is the defense, "the bottle did not break"?

The effects of fire also are part of a codified mix moving well beyond the actual burning and including secondary effect, such as blistering, charring, peeling, and melting. Cosmetic discoloration will probably not suffice nor will minor smoke damage. Even so, courts have not been shy about jury instructions that favor the more flexible definition (Figure 8.11).

Offenders have developed techniques to mask the starting point with ingenuity and hard to detect deceit. For example, picking places where fires are sometimes common is the regular choice for the arsonist looking for a cover-up. Boilers, water heaters, coffee makers, stoves, and space heaters are just a few of the examples (Figure 8.12).

The sum and substance of it all has caused the legal system and the legislative process to not only continue its aggressive approach toward statutory construction, but also extend its efforts in the funding of specialists that can detect arson. (See the worksheet in Figure 8.13[46] that targets the intent of the agent.)

Arson is sometimes employed as a means of cover-up to hide other crimes, such as murder. Once an uncommon event, cases of domestic dispute have tragically ended in this type of grotesque payback.[47] Vengeance, rage, hatred, and even racially or religiously motivated arson are

Figure 8.11   Is the point of origin of the fire evident? (Photo courtesy of B. Kohlhepp, Ross Township Police Department.)

Figure 8.12 ATF agents at work.

other distorted motivations for arson.[48] The rash of Southern church burnings signify a very unwelcome trend. Just as perverse are the pyro-sexual actors that achieve sexual gratification from arson activities. These types of arsonists are often caught in the crowd as the fires rage. Each of these motivators fulfills malevolent intentionality of arson.

> For another investigatory questionnaire in arson crime, see http://www.nlada.org/ Defender/forensics/for_lib/Documents/1144352140.14/arsonquestionairreScene%2520Sur vey%2520final%2520version.pdf

The Meaning of "Structure"

Over the past 100 years, the meaning and idea of qualifying structure has been liberally extended beyond the domicile. Historically, the offense directed itself to a residence or home dwelling and that dwelling had to be of another party rather than the arsonist's own home. Thus, a homeowner had every right to burn his or her home down without fear of arson charges, though other charges of house burning or fraud might apply. This "another" element did not mandate actual ownership of the victimized party, only a rightful possessory interest in the property. Hence, the tenant in possession can be victimized in the same way as the homeowner. Even temporary guests will have standing to make a claim in an arson prosecution. Landlords are in a legal and equitable position to be complainants because the property is personally owned and leased to another.

The "domicile of another" requirement remained fairly well entrenched until portions of larger estates were destroyed, such as servants' quarters, garages, tool sheds, and other secondary structures (labeled "curtilage"). The definitions began to expand to include curtilage in the

Assets:

Value of stock: _____

Value of fixtures: _____

Accounts receivable: _____

    Percent past due: _____   Percent factored: _____

Loans receivable: _____

    Loaned to: _____   Terms: _____

Stocks: _____

Bonds: _____

Other tangible assets: _____

Bank balance: _____   Name of bank: _____

Total assets: _____

Liabilities:

Accounts payable: _____   Percent past due: _____

Loans payable (total due): _____   Original amount: _____

    Date issued: _____   Terms: _____

    Payable to: _____

Rent/mortages (total due): _____   Original amount: _____

    Date issued: _____   Terms: _____

    Payable to: _____

Taxes due: _____

    Federal withholding: _____

    Other federal taxes: _____

    State withholding: _____

    Other state taxes: _____

    City/county taxes: _____

Obtain all bank accounts and most recent statements, if available.

Other financial information, if applicable:

Monthly payroll: _____   No. of employees: _____

List of employees, including name, address and phone numbers.

Operating costs:

    Commissions: _____

    Heat, electric, phone: _____

    Monthly business volume: _____

    Orders on hand: _____

    Recent cancellations: _____

If incorporated:

Name of all officers, date of incorporation, name of incorporating attorney.

Figure 8.13   Property owner questionnaire.

CASE 8.4

STATE V. LOLLIS

343 S.C. 580, 541 S.E.2d 254 (2001).

On February 19, 1998, at 9:05 a.m., the Liberty Fire Department responded to a fire at Lollis' mobile home. Later that day, the South Carolina Law Enforcement Division ("SLED") Arson Hotline received an anonymous tip concerning the fire. David Tafaoa ("Agent Tafaoa"), a SLED arson investigator, investigated the tip and opined the fire was intentionally set.

Agent Tafaoa's investigation revealed there were two areas of fire origination, the kitchen stove and another unconnected fire in the hallway. At the kitchen stove origination site, some type of paper product was rolled and placed between the skillet and the electric coil of the stove, and the eye of the skillet was turned to "high." Agent Tafaoa was further convinced the fire was intentionally set because many personal items were missing from the mobile home. For example, there were nails and screws in the walls, but there was nothing hanging on them or located on the floor beneath them. Also, a gun rack and a soft gun case were found in the master bedroom, but neither contained a gun. Furthermore, there was nothing in the night stand drawers, there was only one pair of shoes in the closet, and there was no VCR, even though a VCR cable and a few tapes were found in the mobile home.

On the day of the fire, Lollis' common law wife, Tammy Burgess ("Burgess"), confessed in a statement to Agent Tafaoa that she was depressed about her husband's financial condition and intentionally started the fire by leaving a pan of grease on a hot eye of the stove. Burgess admitted Lollis was unaware of her plans to burn their home. She further confessed she took most of their valuables and placed them in a storage room they rented five days prior to the fire. According to Agent Tafaoa, Burgess burned the mobile home so the insurance company would pay the mortgage, their largest debt.

Lollis denies he had any involvement with the fire. He claims he never asked, encouraged, or aided Burgess in the burning of their home. According to Lollis, he had no reason to burn his home because it was being extensively remodeled when the fire occurred. Lollis claims he placed his personal items in the storage room on the day of the fire because he did not want his valuables ruined by drywall dust while he remodeled his home.

The State offered no evidence of Lollis' alleged financial trouble. On cross examination, the State's witness from the finance company testified Lollis was current on his mortgage payment at the time of the fire. Lollis also testified he was current on his accounts to Commercial Credit, Friendly Loans, State Farm Insurance, and Macy's Credit.

Lollis had an outstanding mortgage at the time of the fire. In October 1997, Lollis financed his home in order to pay for carpeting, delinquent taxes, and other matters. Because Lollis did not have homeowner's insurance, the finance company required that insurance be placed on the home in order to cover its mortgage. After the fire, the insurance company fully paid Lollis' mortgage. However, Lollis did not receive any money for his personalty destroyed in the fire because the items were not insured.

Agent Tafaoa was convinced Lollis conspired with his wife to commit arson because Lollis possessed the key to the storage room, which contained many of their valuable personal items, when he accompanied Burgess to the law enforcement center. Lollis was arrested a week after the fire and charged with second-degree arson.

On July 23, 1998, Lollis was convicted of second-degree arson and sentenced to six years incarceration. The Court of Appeals affirmed the decision of the trial court.

Questions

1. Why would a mobile home not historically have qualified as a domicile?
2. How does the state prove motive and criminal intent?
3. Why are the contents in the storage room important?
4. What if the fire commenced in the storage area, would it qualify as an arson structure?

statutory coverage. "In the definition of arson, the 'house' or 'dwelling house' includes and protects all outhouses, as the barn, stable, kitchen, and smokehouse, which are within the curtilage or common enclosure, and which are commonly used in connection with the dwelling proper."[49] Curtilage was originally qualified by whether the owner could possibly sleep or stay over in the building, but this distinction was soon lost as the appended facilities were considered essential to the primary residence. All of these distinctions aside, as exceptions multiplied, the rigid concept of "dwelling" was replaced by "occupied structure."

The term "occupied structure" includes the commercial world and its establishments and in the definition even though these locations were not usual living quarters, legislators extended the logic of arson to places where death or serious injury could occur. The distinction seemed too artificial to maintain, especially when one considers the growth of the commercial economy and the potential for harm. From this point forward, the list of structures grew even faster, so much so that the distinctions may have lost their punch. Examine the following state code:

"OCCUPIED STRUCTURE." Any structure, vehicle or place adapted for overnight accommodation of persons or for carrying on business therein, whether or not a person is actually present. If a building or structure is divided into separately occupied units, any unit not occupied by the actor is an occupied structure of another.[50]

The term "any structure" casts off any remaining loyalty to the common law concept and opens the door for literally any plausible place where someone can inhabit. Would a homeless person's cardboard box qualify under this loose language?[51]

The MPC charges forward with even more categories of structure that will qualify for the arson charge. Sounding like a travel agent, the MPC lists *ad seriatim*:

"Occupied structure" includes a ship, trailer, sleeping car, airplane, or other vehicle, structure or place adapted for overnight accommodation of persons or for carrying on business therein, whether or not a person is actually present.[52]

CRIMINAL MISCHIEF

ELEMENTS

- General intent
- Damages tangible property or
- Causes another pecuniary loss

The lines between arson and criminal mischief, and other lower-level destruction of property offenses, can overlap. Most commentators perceive arson as primarily an offense against real property while criminal conduct in the form of mischief and vandalism takes aim at personal property. For the most part, this contrast holds up, but read closely the code text for crossover. Arson calls for specific intent proof, while mischief and aligned crimes carry far less stringent intentionality requirements.

Read about former Steelers kicker Jeff Reed and his charges for behavior. Reed was eventually fined for other summary offenses, and traded as well. http://www.pittsburghlive.com/x/pittsburghtrib/sports/steelers/s_611755.html

The criminal agent in the mischief may employ identical methods, fire with fire, yet the target will be completely nonidentical. Review the criminal mischief statute below and respond to these questions.

The broad coverage of mischief laws throughout the United States afford prosecutors wide discretion in charges related to high levels of property destruction. The level of the offense's severity will depend on many factors including amount of damage, property subjected to destruction, and the extensiveness of the act. Note, too, that the act of criminal mischief may be inflicted on both real and personal property, if it's not fire-based, because arson would preempt and merge that lesser charge. Spray painting, breaking windows, and other ruination on real property would qualify for prosecution.

VANDALISM

Vandalism represents a serious problem for the general public and the insurance industry that repairs the damage. Any effort to characterize the activity as "kid's stuff" is misplaced and misguided. Some portion of our populace is bound to legitimate this type of conduct as a rite of passage of teenage hooliganism, but for those who suffer its direct impact, the excuse and minimization is offensive. Vandalism statistics paint a depressing picture. (See Figure 8.14[53] for an overview of the past 10 years of available statistics.)

The main thrust of law enforcement has been directed to the protection of commercial and institutional facilities that have the most to lose. Vandalism has the predictable and uncanny

18 Pa. Cons. Stat. (2001)

§ **3304. Criminal mischief**

(a) OFFENSE DEFINED.— A person is guilty of criminal mischief if he:

1. damages tangible property of another intentionally, recklessly, or by negligence in the employment of fire, explosives, or other dangerous means listed in section 3302(a) of this title (relating to causing or risking catastrophe);
2. intentionally or recklessly tampers with tangible property of another so as to endanger person or property;
3. intentionally or recklessly causes another to suffer pecuniary loss by deception or threat;
4. intentionally defaces or otherwise damages tangible public property or tangible property of another with graffiti by use of any aerosol spray paint can, broad-tipped indelible marker, or similar marking device.

Questions

1. Aside from fire and explosive, what other methods of damage qualify?
2. What word or term in the statute leaves open the possibility that the perpetrator had little idea what he or she was doing?
3. Give an example as to how mischief would cause another party to suffer a pecuniary loss?

ability to drive communities and business districts into a downward spiral that is usually not reversible. Therefore, business, community, and law enforcement have teamed together to combat this scourge.[54] Efforts in the area of graffiti, litter and waste, broken windows and doors, seem small in the isolated case, but large when the full measure of multiple acts are counted. Some jurisdictions have erected "institutional vandalism" statutes that focus on the anchors of communities, such as churches, businesses, and community centers.

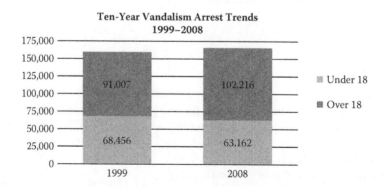

Figure 8.14   Ten-year vandalism arrest trends: 1999–2008.

§ 3307. Institutional vandalism

(a) OFFENSES DEFINED.— A person commits the offense of institutional vandalism if he knowingly desecrates, as defined in section 5509 (relating to desecration or sale of venerated objects), vandalizes, defaces or otherwise damages:

    (1) any church, synagogue or other facility or place used for religious worship or other religious purposes;

    (2) any cemetery, mortuary or other facility used for the purpose of burial or memorializing the dead;

    (3) any school, educational facility, community center, municipal building, courthouse facility, State or local government building or vehicle or juvenile detention center;

    (4) the grounds adjacent to and owned or occupied by any facility set forth in paragraph (1), (2) or (3); or

    (5) any personal property located in any facility set forth in this subsection.

        (a.1)   ILLEGAL POSSESSION.— A person commits the offense of institutional vandalism if, with intent to violate subsection (a), the person carries an aerosol spray paint can, broad-tipped indelible marker, or similar marking device onto property identified in subsection (a).[55]

With the dramatic rise in cemetery attacks, vandalism fits well into any plan to halt the desecration of hallowed ground. Special state and federal laws also have been enacted that deal with religious institutions and agricultural facilities. Remember that vandalism of a church or synagogue, depending upon its content, can easily evolve into a qualified hate crime that brings far greater penalties.

DISCUSSION QUESTIONS

1. Explain how burglary's common law requirements have been altered.
2. How has the definition of domicile been extended?
3. Why is burglary referred to as a dual intent crime?
4. In what way is time of day still relevant in burglary cases?
5. Trespass differs from burglary in what specific ways?
6. Aside from fire and burning, arson damage also can be in what other forms?
7. How does arson parallel burglary's liberalization of the domicile requirement?
8. Does motive prove intention in arson cases?
9. Differentiate criminal mischief from arson.
10. Why do some argue that vandalism is a form of artistic expression?

SUGGESTED READINGS

Almirall, J. R. 2004. *Analysis and interpretation of fire scene evidence.* Boca Raton, FL: CRC Press.

Arnold, J. V., et al. 1984. *Search and seizure and the fire/arson investigator.* National Criminal Justice Reference Service NCJ Number 93545.

Bouquard, T. J. 2004. *Arson investigation: The step-by-step procedure.* Springfield, IL: Charles C Thomas Publisher, Ltd.

Card, R., and J. English. 2011. *Police law,* 12th ed. New York: Oxford University Press.

Casagrande, G., et al. 1990. *Vandalism is not funny*. Wilkes-Barre, PA: Karol Video.

Curtin, L., et al. 2001. *Developing crime reduction plans: Some examples from the reducing burglary initiative*. London: Great Britain Home Office.

Decker, J. F., and B. L. Ottley. 2009. *Arson law and prosecution*. Durham, NC: Carolina Academic Press.

Geason, S., and P. R. Wilson. 1990. *Preventing graffiti and vandalism*. Canberra, Australia: Australian Institute of Criminology.

Loveless, J. 2010. Complete criminal law: Text, cases, and materials, 2nd ed. New York: Oxford University Press.

Prins, H. 1995. Adult fire-raising: Law and psychology. *Psychology, Crime and Law* 1 (June): 271–281.

Reid, S. T. 2011. *Crime and criminology*, 13th ed. New York: Oxford University Press.

Tonry, M. 2009. *The Oxford handbook of crime and public policy*. New York: Oxford University Press.

ENDNOTES

1. *See People v. Booth*, 201 Cal. App. 3d 1499 (1988); *see also* LARRY K. GAINES & ROGER LEROY MILLER, CRIMINAL JUSTICE IN ACTION 112 (2008).
2. ARK. CODE ANN. §5-39-202 (2011). *See also* David A. Bailey, *When Did Shoplifting a Can of Tuna Become a Felony? A Critical Examination of Arkansas's Breaking and Entering Statute*, 63 ARK. L. REV. 269 (2010); JEFFERY T. WALKER ET AL., FREE TO BURGLARIZE: THE AFFECTS OF PRETRIAL AND PREINCARCERATION RELEASE OF BURGLARS IN BURGLARY ACTIVITY, available at http://www.pretrial.org/Docs/Documents/ BurglaryReport.pdf (accessed August 3, 2011).
3. *State v. Anderson*, 583 N.W.2d 151 (S.D. Sup. 1998).
4. BUREAU OF JUSTICE STATISTICS, NATIONAL CRIME VICTIMIZATION SURVEY (NCVS) (2008), available at http://bjs.ojp.usdoj.gov/content/glance/burg.cfm (accessed August 3, 2011).
5. *See* Douglas A. Passon, *Attempted Burglary as a "Violent Felony" under the Armed Career Criminal Act: Avoiding a "Serious Potential Risk" of Confusion in the Wake of Taylor v. United States*, 73 WASH. U. L. QUART. 1649 (1995).
6. 495 U.S. 575 (1990).
7. *Id.* at 588.
8. *North Dakota v. Strutz*, 606 N.W.2d 886 (N.D. 2000).
9. SUMM. PA. JUR. § 24.5.
10. 18 PA. CONS. STAT. § 3502(a) (2010).
11. 744 A.2d 1131 (N.H. 1999).
12. In the matter of the Welfare of T.M.M., Child, C6-98-2306 (Minn. App. 1999).
13. TENN. CODE ANN. § 39-14-402(a)-(d) (2010).
14. N.H. REV. STAT. ANN. § 635:1(I) (2010).
15. SUMM. PA. JUR. § 24.8.
16. *See* JOHN M. SCHEB & JOHN M. SHEB II, CRIMINAL LAW AND PROCEDURE (1994).
17. N.D. CENT. CODE § 12.1-22-02 (2010).
18. SOURCEBOOK OF CRIMINAL JUSTICE STATISTICS Table 3.145 (Kathleen Maguire ed., 2009), available at http://www.albany.edu/sourcebook/pdf/t31452009.pdf (accessed August 3, 2011).
19. ME. REV. STAT. tit.17-A, § 401 (2011).
20. *Id.* at § 401(1)(B)(3).
21. MINN. STAT. § 609.582(1)(c) (2009).
22. *See* HERBERT THORNDIKE TIFFANY, THE LAW OF REAL PROPERTY AND OTHER INTERESTS IN LAND (1970).
23. WASH. REV. CODE § 9A.52.020 (1) (2011).
24. MINN. STAT., *supra* note 21.
25. 18 PA. CONS. STAT. § 3501 (2010).

26. *See U.S. v. Murillo-Lopez*, 444 F.3d 337, 339 (5th Cir.2006); *U.S. v. Gomez-Guerra*, 485 F.3d 301 (5th Cir. 2007).

27. An erroneous jury instruction was very apparent in a trial court in Maine where the judge told the jury that the culpable mental state for burglary was: "knowing that he was not licensed to commit a crime, and knowing that he was not licensed to be there." *Maine v. Child*, 743 A.2d 230, 232 (Me. 1999). The corrected instruction, though, according to the Supreme Court of Maine should have been: "a person is guilty of burglary if he enters a structure knowing that he is not licensed or privileged to do so with the intent to commit a crime therein." *Id.*

28. S.D. CODIFIED LAWS §22-32-1 (2011).

29. WASH. REV. CODE § 9A.52.020 (2011). *See State v. Sweet*, 980 P.2d 1223 (Wash. 1999).

30. *Sweet*, 980 P.2d at 1230.

31. DEBORAH LAMM WEISEL, CENTER FOR PROBLEM ORIENTED POLICING GUIDE NO. 18, BURGLARY OF SINGLE-FAMILY HOUSES 4 (2002), available at http://www.popcenter.org/problems/burglary_home/ summary (accessed August 3, 2011).

32. 18 PA. CONS. STAT. § 3503 (2010).

33. See the language of Supreme Court of New Hampshire in *State v. Anderson*, 714 A.2d 227, 228 (N.H. 1998).

34. ARIZ. REV. STAT. ANN. §§13-1502, 13-1503, 13-1504 (2011).

35. For an excellent case on proof of entry, see the opinion of the Nebraska Supreme Court in *State v. Davis*, No. A-94-1056 (Neb. App. 1995).

36. Model Penal Code § 206.53 at 2 (Proposed Official Draft 1962).

37. For an interesting case on whether a privileged party, namely a lover once living in the house, can trespass within, *see State v. Thurston*, 969 A.2d 906 (Me. 2009); *see also* Meghan E. Magoon, *Accessing Justice in Hard Times: Lessons from the Field and Looking to the Future: Case Note: State v. Thurston: An Examination of Self-Defense, Assault, and Trespass in Relation to Domestic Violence*, 62 ME. L. REV. 717 (2010).

38. TENN. CODE ANN. § 39-14-405 (2010).

39. NEB. REV. STAT. § 28-520 (2010).

40. Model Penal Code § 206.53, at comment (1)(a) (Proposed Official Draft 1962).

41. MATTHEW ROSS LIPPMAN, CONTEMPORARY CRIMINAL LAW: CONCEPTS, CASES, AND CONTROVERSIES 434 (2009); *see also* Joseph A. Davis & Kelli M. Lauber, *Criminal Behavioral Assessment of Arsonists, Pyromaniacs, and Multiple Firesetters: The Burning Question*, J. CONTEMP. CRIM. JUST., Aug. 1999, at 273-290.

42. 2 U.S. DEPARTMENT OF JUSTICE, ENFORCEMENT MANUAL: APPROACHES FOR COMBATING ARSON-FOR-PROFIT SCHEMES App. IV (1979).

43. WILLIAM L. CLARK & WILLIAM L. MARSHALL, A TREATISE ON THE LAW OF CRIMES §13.12 at 1014 (6th ed. 1958). *See also* 4 SIR WILLIAM BLACKSTONE, COMMENTARIES 222 (2001); *People v. Haggerty*, 46 Cal. 354; *Woolsey v. State*, 30 Tex. App. 346, 17 S. 546.

44. Model Penal Code § 220.1(1)(a) & (b) (Proposed Official Draft 1962).

45. Bruce L. Ottley, *Beyond the Crime Laboratory: The Admissibility of Unconfirmed Forensic Evidence in Arson Cases*, 36 N.E. J. CRIM. & CIV. CON. 263, 266 (2010).

46. ENFORCEMENT MANUAL, supra note 42, at 257-58.

47. *Steckel v. Delaware*, 711 A.2d 5 (De. 1998).

48. *People v. Beagle*, 492 P.2d 1 (Cal. 1972).

49. CLARK & MARSHALL, *supra* note 43, at § 13.09, at 1011. *See also State v. Warren*, 33 Me. 30 (Me. 1851); *State v. Meservie*, 118 A. 482 (Me. 1922); *People v. Taylor*, 2 Mich. 250 (Mich. 1851).

50. 18 PA. CONS. STAT. § 3301(j)(1) (2010).

51. *State v. Merolle*, No. 1 CA-CR 08-0458 (Az. App. 2010).

52. Model Penal Code § 220.1(4) (Proposed Official Draft 1962). *See also* JOHN R. HALL JR., U.S. ARSON TRENDS AND PATTERNS (2000); Office of Criminal Justice Programs, *Increasingly Comfortable About Arson*, 2 OCJP RESEARCH UPDATE 1 (1990).

53. UNITED STATES DEPARTMENT OF JUSTICE, FEDERAL BUREAU OF INVESTIGATION, CRIME IN THE UNITED STATES, 2008, Table 32, (2009), available at http://www2.fbi.gov/ucr/cius2008/data/table_32.html (accessed August 3, 2011).

54. CHARLES P. NEMETH & K.C. POULIN, PRIVATE SECURITY AND PUBLIC SAFETY: A COMMUNITY-BASED APPROACH (2005).

55. 18 PA. CONS. STAT. §3307(a) (2010).

Chapter 9

Offenses Contrary to the Public Morality

KEYWORDS

Annulment: A declaration by a court that a marriage is invalid.

Bigamy: The crime of marrying someone while still legally married to someone else.

Divorce: The dissolution of a valid marriage granted on specified statutory grounds arising after the marriage.

Driving under the influence: The offense of operating a motor vehicle while intoxicated by drugs or alcohol.

Intoxicated: To excite or stupefy by alcohol or a drug to the point where physical and mental control is diminished.

Obscene: Extremely or deeply offensive according to contemporary community standards of morality or decency.

Polygamy: The offense of having several and specifically more than two spouses at one time.

Pornography: Material that depicts erotic behavior and is intended to cause sexual excitement.

Possession: The act, fact, or condition of having control of something; control over a controlled substance or other contraband.

Prostitution: The act or practice of engaging in sexual activity indiscriminately for money.

INTRODUCTION: THE INTERSECTION OF LAW AND MORALITY

Over the last generation or so, the debate on the interplay between morality and criminal laws has severely eroded. Two schools emerge: those who consider law without moral inquiry and those that seek to unify law with a corresponding morality. In either case, each school seeks some level of certitude in matters of moral action, though it is clear that the former school dwells a bit more on that relationship to law, because one can have morality displaced from law altogether if a culture so chooses. However, critics of this approach charge that stripping away all moral reasoning from legal analysis is a short route to ruin, as the law, in and of itself, is not self-justifying. The law cannot and does not always make clear what human behaviors are right or wrong. For most of the American experience, we have seen more of the mixture than the secular approach so evident today. And so, somewhere the legal system must make plain what is acceptable in human action and what is not, because what the legislatures tells us is primarily a relative exercise. Those seeking the integration of morality and law hope to bind timeless moral principles to legal enactments to assure their correctness. Certain conduct insults our moral equilibrium and an unwillingness to condemn what is universally agreed upon as immoral conduct leads to civic anarchy. A nation without moral clarity squanders its legacy. To solely enact laws without consideration of moral ramifications is to advance a sterile moral preoccupation with everything but the good or bad of a given law. According to others, the opening up of strictures and rigid conduct formulas frees individuals and nations from the enslavement of convention.

This alleged freedom, "free love" or "free to be you or me," is the modern manifesto for those who wish to do whatever they wish to do. This mindset has led to extraordinary difficulties for the adherents of the new model. Freedom is more than doing or not doing. Freedom, as Aristotle told us, resides in pure and unadulterated happiness where sensual behavior becomes the least necessary for fulfillment.[1] A life of comprehension and contemplation will lead to the happiest life, rather than the frat house existence so often emulated by the young. Sex, drugs, and rock and roll are only temporary forms of fulfillment and cannot be expected to be a self-renewing source of freedom. In fact, these ephemeral pleasures often become a source of tyranny for those that cannot control the intake. For the classical mind, to be free is to not need. To the modernist, freedom is to have without restriction. In the end, we should be seeking criminal laws and moral parameters that allow homo sapiens to grow and flourish in the sciences and arts, in personal development, and the highest level of happiness possible. This is why a moral regimen is so essential to any legal system. It is not enough to say that a law has been enacted, but that enacted law advances moral and spiritual development in the human person. Hence, morality, that judgment about the good and bad of human activity, cannot be severed from legal thinking, neither can the law cut or hack itself away from these considerations. What one wants, craves, or desires may be exactly the thing the human person does not need in any quantity. Some people lust for drugs, crave pedophilic sex, cannot function without the influence of alcohol, cannot survive without sexual aberration because they are convinced these activities promote freedom when, in fact, enslavement occurs. Pope John Paul II's admonition that teenage sex, promiscuity, pornography, and disproportionate sexual lust represents the shackles of moral and physical bondage, rather than freedom in any sense, seems curious at best. Freedom can never be experienced by those enslaved to the passions.[2] Therefore, it is crucial that the criminal law thinker appreciates the moral implications of conduct and how it advances or undermines the human species. Morality forces the legal thinker to assess the value of human conduct in light of individual and communal development. Morality looks for the costs and benefits of certain human behavior. Thus, if drugs were to be legalized, on what moral ground would the argument be made? If efficiency is central to the argument, how do those particular savings comport with a moral framework? If there are costs, precisely what will these be: health, familial, mental, and emotional problems, etc.? What costs will the society, as a collective, suffer with the legalization of drugs? For those simply depending upon the content and text of the law alone, there would be little moral scrutiny as drug legalization should expect. Strict textualism accepts the language of the law as its own power, its own legitimization without much moral inquiry. In contrast, the proponent of morality and law raises questions beyond the text—pressing questions that should be evaluated before supporting a particular course of conduct. Morality also reflects or images what the community consensus might be on a specific topic. The term "morality," from its Latin derivative "mos," meaning "a custom of many, the habits of most," goes well beyond text because it seeks to lay out the general moral agreement on a type of conduct.

Morality serves as the foundation for legal enactment. Laws cannot deliver a morality based on promulgation alone. When the debate turns to criminal conduct, one must always know why the act should be prohibited; not solely because the legislature says so, but because the offense offends our moral sensibilities. Morality, from whatever source, whether religious or humanistic, provides a measure for the discussion.

Some criminal behavior tends to be evaluated in moral terms more than others. This chapter will evaluate how crime and morality intersects in these offenses:

- Prostitution
- Drugs
- Bigamy and polygamy
- Obscenity

PROSTITUTION

ELEMENTS

- Sexual activity for hire
- Work within an unauthorized house of prostitution
- Promote the acts of prostitution (pimping)
- Patronization of prostitutes
- Living off prostitution

The question of whether prostitution should be legalized is long standing.[3] That prostitution is often described as the world's oldest profession is frequently cited as a basis for why the practice should be legalized. As is regularly the case, proponents for any legalization justify the change argument by scanning the level of participation. A morality built on majoritarian rule is lacking in moral rigor and may fail to realize that popular desire cannot be the measure of the right or wrong in law.[4]

Find out about the children who are increasingly parts of the world of prostitution at: http://www.unh.edu/ccrc/

As for prostitution, every American jurisdiction forbids the commerce of sex for money (except for a few legalized counties in Nevada) and expends considerable funds to eradicate the practices in neighborhoods and communities. Analyze the statute below:

§ 5902. Prostitution and related offenses

(a) PROSTITUTION.— A person is guilty of prostitution if he or she:
   (1) is an inmate of a house of prostitution or otherwise engages in sexual activity as a business; or
   (2) loiters in or within view of any public place for the purpose of being hired to engage in sexual activity.[5]

Why has the justice and legal system concluded that this conduct is worthy of criminalization?[6]

Any discussion about the merits must consider all aspects of the practice. What are the merits of decriminalization? Divisions of opinion on this offense are marked. Survey the strengths and weaknesses for legalization and criminalization.

REASONS FOR CRIMINALIZATION

- Promotes communicable disease transmission
- Promotes sexual conduct outside stable relationships
- Promotes divorce and corresponding distrust
- Promotes sexual dysfunction in stable relationships
- Promotes adultery
- Promotes a desensitized view of sexual conduct
- Promotes a desensitized view of women
- Promotes the objectification of woman
- Promotes drug usage among participants
- Promotes physical and mental abuse
- Promotes neighborhood decline
- Promotes and feeds into mental disorders
- Promotes unrealistic sexual expectations of partners
- Promotes aberrant role models for the young
- Promotes hedonism and self-gratification
- Promotes drug trafficking
- Promotes sexual violence in serial killers
- Promotes the pornography industry
- Promotes out of wedlock births
- Promotes abandonment of religious and virtuous principles
- Promotes the demise and ruin of the prostitute
- Promotes suicide
- Promotes family breakdown
- Promotes unrealistic economic expectations
- Promotes depression
- Promotes abusive attitudes in men

Law enforcement has long known the distressing impact that prostitution plays in the community and that the average resident has little tolerance for the side show and circus these activities bring to their respective neighborhoods. This is not a problem that is specific to the United States.[7] The breakdown of neighborhoods, the view of prostitutes as "lesser" people, and the stigma attached to their activities is a worldwide argument against the legalization of prostitution. "In Holland's toleration zones, women are still complaining that the police do not take attacks against sex workers seriously. In West Germany and Nevada, legalized brothels have increased police powers and institutionalized pimping by the State, making it harder for women to keep their earning or to bargain to determine their working conditions. To avoid arrest, prostitute women in Hamburg must register with the police, have compulsory health checks, and carry a health pass. A police record makes it harder for women to leave prostitution."[8]

The arguments that favor prostitution tend to be individualized and utilitarian. Some theorists question "the universal assumption that all sex workers are 'victims' instead emphasizing the heterogeneity of commercial sex work exchanges and the complex nexus of desire and power inherent in all sexual relations. These critics have questioned the possibility of identifying and criminalizing a single, uniform institution of prostitution."[9] At center will be the recognition that law enforcement resources are better spent elsewhere in our violent crime centers. Others argue that governmental authorities, if it regulated the practice, would reap enormous economic rewards for its treasury. A host of other favorable arguments is contained in the list below.

REASONS AGAINST CRIMINALIZATION

- Promotes wiser use of justice agency expenditures
- Promotes free choice
- Promotes empowerment over self and body according to certain feminist schools
- Promotes a freeing up of the mind and body from the shackles of sexual repression
- Promotes the idea that the practice will always be with us
- Promotes law enforcement activity in victimless crimes
- Promotes tax revenues
- Promotes state-run and sanctioned facilities that provides good jobs
- Promotes, if state run, cleaner environments and less sexually transmitted diseases (STDs)
- Promotes individual expression rather than collective moral oppression
- Promotes the availability of sexual products and services

From a libertarian perspective, the state is meddling in personal affairs and overstepping its police power. Here is a place, it is argued, for less governmental influence, although those having to live and labor amongst the prostitution class will find such freedoms have consequences.

After consideration of both sides, which position roots itself in sounder thinking? Which position grounds itself in the moral domain? The legalization proponent argues in a very sterile and unrealistic world, as if the human agent operates as a detached, calculating machine who can withstand the debilitating effects of being prostituted. How personally empowering is the acceptance of this conduct? And, how rewarding must all this be in strictly emotional and spiritual terms? Plenty of money flows into the coffers of these anguished souls each day, but at what cost? If economic empowerment exclusively paved the way to human happiness, then why are so many rich performers and athletes in such personal turmoil? Why does the world see so much depression and mental and personal emptiness that cannot be cured by materialism?

If viewing the human species in strictly material/legal terms, we are bound to come up short for human life has a moral dimension. Acts of the prostitute cannot be stripped away from the essence of the actor. In the end, the gas chamber attendants at the Nazi death camps, who in some cases processed the deaths of 10,000 people a day, cannot bifurcate job and role from their own soul. A man or a woman is, in fact, the sum of many parts—jobs being one, and an extremely superficial component at that.

Studies on prostitutes, whether in legalized Amsterdam or nonlegal New York City, foretell similar ends, ones which tend toward the negative. A few sectors of the feminist movement have aligned themselves with the decriminalization community. Not surprisingly, much of the feminist critique of the justice model is rooted in the system's inherent bias and male dominance. Radical feminism breathes new life into the old debate about the morality of prostitution. Professors Balos and Fellows catalog these conflicting views in their comprehensive work, *A*

Matter of Prostitution: Becoming Respectable. A portion of their analysis cites legalization's most lofty ambition: The change in attitudes toward sex and women.

Prostitution reformers generally fall into two groups: those who believe that prostitution provides a livelihood for women and seek to improve the conditions of their work, and those who seek the eventual elimination of prostitution through antiviolence laws. The first group approaches prostitution through a rights-based framework that identifies a woman in prostitution as a worker who deserves fair compensation and safe working conditions. They seek to decriminalize prostitution, to unionize women in prostitution, and to counteract the stigma of prostitution by portraying it to the public as dignified work and a sophisticated business. This rights-based agenda directly challenges the taint of degeneracy that is traditionally associated with prostitution; it is a claim for respectability.[10]

Neither Balos or Fellows derives much comfort from this type of Pollyanna thinking for it further solidifies the lack of equality as they construe the world around them. How objectification could lead to liberation and respectability puzzles. They continue:

> Currently, the prevailing legal and social view of prostitution is that it is a victimless crime of immoral conduct that can be tolerated as long as it does not disrupt business districts or quiet neighborhoods. Our society, in its literature, science, performing arts, advertising, and media, simultaneously romanticizes and demonizes a woman who is engaged in prostitution. Society constructs her as a powerful entrepreneur in the marketplace exercising her autonomy, as well as an immoral repository for disease and corruption. Both these constructions immunize the purchaser of sex from serious legal scrutiny. It is this popular conception of prostitution that makes it both a potent marker of the boundary between degeneracy and respectability and a practice of inequality.[11]

Other proponents typify prostitution as a form of economic empowerment. University of Chicago Law Professor Marsha Nussbaum finds little difference amongst jobs because each job leads to economic reward. The subject matter of the work escapes her scrutiny since a prostitute is really no different than the "Perdue chicken factory worker who plucks feathers from nearly frozen birds; a domestic servant who works for wealthy families; a nightclub singer who often sings songs requested by customers; and philosophy professors who get paid for lecturing and writing."[12]

Another slant from the fringe calls for the abolishment of legality and state run control, not because the conduct has any shortfall on the moral end, but because legalization negatively impacts the entrepreneurial nature of the endeavor. In arguing against legalized brothels, Nina Lopez-Jones, a member of the English Collective of Prostitutes states:

> Only the abolition of the prostitution laws can remove the stigma attached to the prostitution level, and succeed in disentangling crimes of nuisance and offensive behavior from consenting sex. Abolishing the laws would end the need for red light areas as women would be able to advertise in contact magazines and work from premises without risking arrest or eviction. Only then will women have the legal power to insist on protection from both health services and the police.[13]

Recent efforts to shame the patron has had mixed reviews.[14]

In the growing area of human trafficking for sex, the greatest tragedy involves children.[15] All across the world, children are induced, kidnapped, and then trafficked as if a good or service. Prostitution legislation seeks to enhance the penalties for these offenses, and to impute knowledge of their victim's age and innocence.

CASE 9.1

LUTZ V. U.S.
434 A.2d 442 (D.C. App. 1981).

The trial court, after a bench trial, found appellant, Annabelle L. Lutz, guilty of sexual solicitation. D.C. Code 1973, § 22-2701. Appellant argues that the trial court erred in denying her motion for judgment of acquittal based on her theory that a constitutional right of privacy protects solicitation for prostitution in a private area between two consenting adults. We hold that the constitutional right of privacy does not protect commercial sexual solicitation. Accordingly, we affirm.

On the evening of May 1, 1980, Officers Miller Millard Smith, Jr., and William H. Buss, members of the vice unit of the Metropolitan Police Department, checked into adjoining rooms in the Embassy Row Hotel, in order to investigate complaints about outcall massage services working in the hotels. Officer Smith telephoned an outcall massage service and arranged for a female to come to his room. Later that evening, appellant arrived. According to Officer Smith, he asked appellant how much various sexual services would cost. Appellant replied that the fee quoted over the phone was just for a nude massage and that sexual acts would cost more. After discussing the prices of explicit sexual acts, Officer Smith placed appellant under arrest. At the time of this transaction, Officer Buss, in the adjoining hotel room, overheard the conversation. Officer Buss corroborated Officer Smith's testimony at trial.

At the close of the government's case, appellant moved for judgment of acquittal, arguing that a constitutional right of privacy protects solicitation in a private hotel room for consensual sexual conduct. Following submission of memoranda on the subject, the trial court denied the motion. In so ruling, the court took notice of the fact that massage services engage in public advertisements through cards and the phone book, adding that "the history of massage parlors, certainly, is that massage parlors, for the most part, are fronts for prostitution."

Following the trial court's denial of the motion, appellant testified in her own defense. She stated that she had received a call from an escort service to go to the hotel "for the purpose of massage, only." She described her discussion with Officer Smith as "almost a one-way conversation"; Officer Smith had done virtually all the talking. She stated that Officer Smith had inquired about various sexual services. After she refused to perform them, Officer Smith placed her under arrest.

The defense rested and renewed its motion for judgment of acquittal. The trial court again denied the motion, finding appellant guilty of sexual solicitation. Appellant filed a "Motion For Reconsideration Or, In The Alternative, For A New Trial," which the trial court denied. The court sentenced appellant to a fine of $200.00 or ten days in prison. Appellant paid the fine and filed this appeal.

The sexual solicitation statute, D.C. Code 1973, § 22-2701, is not limited by its terms to public solicitations.

D.C. Code 1973, § 22-2701 provides:

Prostitution — Inviting for purposes of, prohibited.

It shall not be lawful for any person to invite, entice, persuade, or to address for the purpose of inviting, enticing, or persuading any person or persons sixteen years of age or over in the District of Columbia, for the purpose of prostitution, or any other immoral or lewd purpose, under a penalty of not more than $250 or imprisonment for not more than ninety days, or both.

Congress, in fact, expressly removed the public element of the crime when it amended the statute in 1953. On its face, therefore, the statute does not protect sexual solicitations in private places.

Citing *Rittenour v. District of Columbia*, D.C. App., 163 A.2d 558 (1960), appellant contends that a constitutional right of privacy protects solicitation for prostitution in a private area between two consenting adults. In Rittenour, this court held that a related provision prohibiting "lewd, obscene, or indecent" acts (and proposals for such acts), D.C. Code 1973, § 22-1112(a), did not apply to homosexual acts committed in private between consenting persons. See Rittenour, supra at 559. The court did so as a matter of statutory interpretation, even though Congress had amended this statute — as it had amended § 22-2701 — to remove the requirement of an act in public. ...

In any context, whether an individual has a constitutionally protected right to privacy depends on both the conduct at issue and the place where that conduct occurs. One does not necessarily have a protectable privacy interest, for example, when committing a typically private act in a public place; "a man and woman locked in a sexual embrace at high noon in Times Square" cannot invoke a right to privacy. *Paris Adult Theatre I v. Slaton*, 413 U.S. 49, 67, 37 L. Ed. 2d 446, 93 S. Ct. 2628 (1973). On the other hand, certain sexual activities that the law can prohibit in public may be protected in the home. Certain personal decisions and intimate relationships, moreover, are so worthy of protection that the right to privacy reaches beyond the home to other private places. For example, "the constitutionally protected privacy of family, marriage, motherhood, procreation, and child rearing ... extends to the doctor's office, the hospital, the hotel room, or as otherwise required to safeguard the right to intimacy involved."

The question here is whether commercial sexual solicitation in a hotel room warrants constitutional protection on privacy grounds against government intrusion.

We conclude that there is no fundamental right to privacy for commercial sexual solicitation. Although the Supreme Court has recognized the First Amendment right of an individual to possess — without commercial intent — obscene material in his or her home, see Stanley, supra at 559, the Court has distinguished this right from the asserted right of an entrepreneur to engage in "commercialized obscenity." Paris Adult Theatre I, supra at 64. The Court has concluded that "the States have a legitimate interest in regulating commerce in obscene material. ..." Id. at 69; see id. at 57-64.

Similarly, although the Supreme Court has recognized that the constitutional right to privacy for certain intimate conduct extends beyond the home to a hotel room, this right does not extend to protection for commercial sexual solicitation. Commercial sex does not concern an intimate relationship of the sort heretofore deemed worthy of constitutional protection. Nor has the Court in the least suggested that an individual's right to make the fundamental personal "decision whether or not to bear or beget a child," should extend to a constitutionally protected right to sell the use of one's body for sexual purposes.

Accordingly, the trial court properly denied appellant's motion for judgment of acquittal.

Questions

1. How does the defendant define and argue about sexual privacy?
2. What expectation of privacy does a John really have?
3. Why have the majority of American jurisdictions not taken this approach?
4. What risks are there in this type of program?

Visit the University of Rhode Island's Factbook on Prostitution at: http://www.uri.edu/artsci/wms/hughes/factbook.htm

DRUGS AND CONTROLLED SUBSTANCES

DRUG LAWS PRIMARILY FALL INTO THREE CATEGORIES:

- Possession
- Delivery and distribution
- Possession of paraphernalia

Drug abuse pervades literally every aspect of modern life. While addiction cannot be punishable, the use and abuse of drugs to sustain the conviction is.[16] These same statutory designs rely on a Controlled Substances list published by the federal government in consultation with federal and state law enforcement agencies that categorizes those substances that cannot be used, manufactured, sold, or distributed.[17]

A sample from the Controlled Substances Act[18] is reproduced below:

§ 801. Congressional findings and declarations: Controlled substances
The Congress makes the following findings and declarations:

(1) Many of the drugs included within this title have a useful and legitimate medical purpose and are necessary to maintain the health and general welfare of the American people.
(2) The illegal importation, manufacture, distribution, and possession and improper use of controlled substances have a substantial and detrimental effect on the health and general welfare of the American people.
(3) A major portion of the traffic in controlled substances flows through interstate and foreign commerce. Incidents of the traffic, which are not an integral part of the interstate or foreign flow, such as manufacture, local distribution, and possession, nonetheless have a substantial and direct effect upon interstate commerce because—
(A) after manufacture, many controlled substances are transported in interstate commerce,

(B)   controlled substances distributed locally usually have been transported in inter-state commerce immediately before their distribution, and

(C)   controlled substances possessed commonly flow through interstate commerce immediately prior to such possession.[19]

Drug provisions further differentiate according to amounts possessed by weight or sold, and value of transaction, or whether one is a dealer/distributor. A typical drug offense statute follows:

§ 780-113. Prohibited acts; penalties

(a)   The following acts and the causing thereof within the Commonwealth are hereby prohibited:

(1)   The manufacture, sale or delivery, holding, offering for sale, or possession of any con-trolled substance, other drug, device or cosmetic that is adulterated or misbranded.

(2)   The adulteration or misbranding of any controlled substance, other drug, device or cosmetic. ...

(8)   Selling, dispensing, disposing of or causing to be sold, dispensed or disposed of, or keeping in possession, control or custody, or concealing any controlled substance, other drug, device or cosmetic or any container of any drug, device or cosmetic with knowledge that the trademark, trade name or other identifying mark, imprint or symbol of another, or any likeness of any of the foregoing, has been placed thereon in a manner prohibited … .

(9)   Making, selling, disposing of or causing to be made, sold, or disposed of, or keeping in possession, control or custody, or concealing with intent to defraud, any punch, die, plate, stone or other thing designed to print, imprint or reproduce the trade-mark, trade name or other identifying mark, imprint or symbol of another or any likeness of any of the foregoing upon any controlled substance, other drug, device or cosmetic or container thereof.

(10)   The sale at retail of a nonproprietary drug except by a registered pharmacist in a licensed pharmacy or by a practitioner.

(11)   The operation of a drug manufacturing, distributing or retailing establishment, except by registered pharmacists in a licensed pharmacy, without conforming with such standards respecting sanitation, materials, equipment and supplies as the sec-retary, after consultation with the board, may establish by regulation for the protec-tion of the public health and safety.[20]

The problem of illegal drugs in American society has been told and retold. The sheer magnitude of the users and the resources necessary to carry out any rational "war" in its usage cannot be fully measured. The Uniform Crime Reports catalogs both the offenses and expenditures of state and local law enforcement, prosecutorial staffs, and federal agencies, such as the DEA (the Drug Enforcement Agency) and the FBI. (See Figure 9.1[21] for staffing expenditures from 1972 to 2005.)

More alarming has been not only the marked increase in usage, but the ages participating. Less than 20 years ago, drugs like heroin and cocaine were not flowing in middle schools. Today these same schools serve as staging areas for an escalation that generates enormous social, men-tal, and medical costs. It is popular to speak of the justice model's war on drugs, and in each election, particularly the presidential ones, we hear of the next plan or program that will end the scourge. Washington has a Drug Czar and a massive bureaucracy to halt the onslaught. The picture painted by the police sector, the schools, and those who study trends deliver few positive signs of the curtailment. New programs proliferate in every jurisdiction. New laws are engineered

**DEA Staffing and Appropriations
FY 1972–2005 (All Sources)**

Year	Total Employees	Special Agents	Support Staff	Budget ($ in Millions)
1972	2,775	1,470	1,305	65.2
1973	2,898	1,470	1,428	74.9
1974	4,075	2,231	1,844	116.2
1975	4,286	2,135	2,151	140.9
1976	4,337	2,141	2,196	161.1
1977	4,439	2,141	2,298	172.8
1978	4,440	2,054	2,386	192.3
1979	4,288	1,984	2,304	200.4
1980	4,149	1,941	2,208	206.7
1981	4,167	1,964	2,203	219.5
1982	4,013	1,896	2,117	244.1
1983	4,013	1,896	2,117	283.9
1984	4,093	1,963	2,130	326.6
1985	4,936	2,234	2,702	362.4
1986	4,925	2,440	2,485	393.5
1987	5,710	2,879	2,831	773.6
1988	5,740	2,899	2,841	522.9
1989	5,926	2,969	2,957	597.9
1990	6,274	3,191	3,083	653.5
1991	7,096	3,615	3,481	875.0
1992	7,264	3,696	3,568	910.0
1993	7,266	3,518	3,748	921.0
1994	7,049	3,611	3,438	970.0
1995	7,389	3,889	3,500	1,001.0
1996	7,369	3,708	3,661	1,050.0
1997	7,872	3,969	3,903	1,238.0
1998	8,452	4,214	4,238	1,384.0
1999	9,046	4,527	4,519	1,477.0
2000	9,141	4,566	4,575	1,586.6
2001	9,209	4,601	4,608	1,697.4
2002	9,388	4,625	4,763	1,799.5
2003	9,725	4,841	4,884	1,891.9
2004	10,564	5,194	5,370	2,040.0
2005	10,893	5,296	5,597	2,142.0

Figure 9.1   DEA staffing and appropriations: FY 1972–2005.   *(continued)*

DEA Staffing and Appropriations (*continued*)
FY 1972–2005 (All Sources)

Year	Total Employees	Special Agents	Support Staff	Budget ($ in Millions)
2006	10,891	5,320	5,571	2,264.0
2007	10,759	5,235	5,524	2,346.0
2008	10,774	5,223	5,551	2,494.0
2009	10,784	5,233	5,551	2,602.0

Note: Enacted amounts may include rescissions, if applicable.

Figure 9.1   (*continued*) DEA staffing and appropriations: FY 1972–2005.

to tackle another facet of this unceasing dilemma. New sentencing schemes, such as New York's, have delivered exceptionally harsh results for the distributor and manufacturer, but someone always steps in to fill the managerial and delivery void.[22] Even the list of controlled substances grows by the moment, and users experiment and discern other ways to be taken to higher levels than reality itself. Who would have ever envisioned that products like mouthwash, oven cleaner, and nail polish would provide highly successful means to achieve the perennial "high."

The Controlled Substances list is incapable of keeping up with the inventiveness displayed by users. The recent rash of Ecstasy use in the high schools paints a troubling picture of abuse.

Special teams and units are devised, entire agencies dedicate their work to the elimination of this plague, and community leaders, religious leaders, and medical professionals relay the story of harm and addiction. In a word, the justice system appears incapable of stunting the growth of both supply and users. Former Attorney General of the United States Nicholas de Katzenbach recently delivered these sobering insights:

> Unfortunately, relatively few of those convicted—and this is no fault of law enforcement—are the big drug dealers, and almost all of them in the drug economy can be easily replaced in the distribution scheme because of the enormous amounts of money involved. Relatively few are also convicted of crimes of violence. Some are themselves addicts convicted of unlawful possession. Some are not addicts, just young people doing foolish experiments. Most are serving quite long mandatory sentences. I think a rational approach would at least consider some alternatives to long-term incarceration, such as more community service, supervised probation, parole, treatment, and so forth. All, I believe, are cheaper.
>
> Success and failure, and this is important, should really be monitored with the understanding that failures will occur, so we have some idea of what works and some idea of what does not work, and under what circumstances. We should not expect perfection. Just aiming at any kind of cost-effective improvement ought to be politically popular. Treatment, well, that is not any kind of magic bullet either. Getting rid of addiction is tough and you can expect frequent failures and relapses. But, even a modest rate of success is quite cost-effective. And any reduction in demand is important.[23]

To be sure, it is easy to speak of our incapacities in the area of drug enforcement. The system works hard and with good intent and its sacrifices and bravery are well documented. And, some things work better than others. Experience tells us that punishment, especially the harshest of varieties, appears less effective than expected. New York's much vaunted mandatory minimum drug laws, adopted more than 25 years ago, have been repeatedly attacked by those who see

STORY 9.1

w w w . d r u g a b u s e . g o v

ional Institute on Drug Abuse • National Institutes of Health • U.S. Department of Health & Human Services

MDMA (Ecstasy)

MDMA (3,4-methylenedioxymethamphet-amine) is a synthetic, psychoactive drug that is chemically similar to the stimulant methamphetamine and the hallucinogen mescaline. MDMA produces feelings of increased energy, euphoria, emotional warmth, and distortions in time, perception, and tactile experiences.

How Is MDMA Abused?

MDMA is taken orally, usually as a capsule or tablet. It was initially popular among Caucasian adolescents and young adults in the nightclub scene or at weekend-long dance parties known as raves. More recently, the profile of the typical MDMA user has changed, with the drug now affecting a broader range of ethnic groups. MDMA is also popular among urban gay males—some report using MDMA as part of a multiple-drug experience that includes marijuana, cocaine, methamphetamine, ketamine, sildenafil (Viagra), and other legal and illegal substances.

How Does MDMA Affect the Brain?

MDMA exerts its primary effects in the brain on neurons that use the chemical (or neurotransmitter) serotonin to communicate with other neurons. The serotonin system plays an important role in regulating mood, aggression, sexual activity, sleep, and sensitivity to pain. MDMA binds to the serotonin transporter, which is responsible for removing serotonin from the synapse (or space between adjacent neurons) to terminate the signal between neurons; thus MDMA increases and prolongs the serotonin signal. MDMA also enters the serotonergic neurons via the transporter (because MDMA resembles serotonin in chemical structure) where it causes excessive release of serotonin from the neurons. MDMA has similar effects on another neurotransmitter—norepinephrine, which can cause increases in heart rate and blood pressure. MDMA also releases dopamine, but to a much lesser extent.

MDMA can produce confusion, depression, sleep problems, drug craving, and severe anxiety. These problems can occur soon after taking the drug or, sometimes, even days or weeks after taking MDMA. In addition, chronic users of MDMA perform more poorly than nonusers on certain types of cognitive or memory tasks, although some of these effects may be due to the use of other drugs in combination with MDMA. Research in animals indicates that MDMA can be harmful to the brain—one study in nonhuman primates

STORY 9.1 (*continued*)

ww.drugabuse.gov
onal Institute on Drug Abuse • National Institutes of Health • U.S. Department of Health & Human Services

showed that exposure to MDMA for only 4 days caused damage to serotonin nerve terminals that was still evident 6 to 7 years later.[1] Although similar neurotoxicity has not been shown definitively in humans, the wealth of animal research indicating MDMA's damaging properties strongly suggests that MDMA is not a safe drug for human consumption.

Addictive Potential

For some people, MDMA can be addictive.[2] A survey of young adult and adolescent MDMA users found that 43 percent of those who reported ecstasy use met the accepted diagnostic criteria for dependence, as evidenced by continued use despite knowledge of physical or psychological harm, withdrawal effects, and tolerance (or diminished response).[3] These results are consistent with those from similar studies in other countries that suggest a high rate of MDMA dependence among users.[4] MDMA abstinence-associated withdrawal symptoms include fatigue, loss of appetite, depressed feelings, and trouble concentrating.[2]

What Other Adverse Effects Does MDMA Have on Health?

MDMA can also be dangerous to overall health and, on rare occasions, lethal. MDMA can have many of the same physical effects as other stimulants, such as cocaine

and amphetamines. These include increases in heart rate and blood pressure—which present risks of particular concern for people with circulatory problems or heart disease—and other symptoms such as muscle tension, involuntary teeth clenching, nausea, blurred vision, faintness, and chills or sweating.

In high doses, MDMA can interfere with the body's ability to regulate temperature. On rare but unpredictable occasions, this can lead to a sharp increase in body temperature (hyperthermia), which can result in liver, kidney, cardiovascular system failure, or death. MDMA can interfere with its own metabolism (breakdown within the body); therefore, potentially harmful levels can be reached by repeated MDMA administration within short periods of time. Other drugs that are chemically similar to MDMA, such as MDA (methylenedioxyamphetamine, the parent drug of MDMA) and PMA (paramethoxyamphetamine, associated with fatalities in the United States and Australia),[5] are sometimes sold as ecstasy. These drugs can be neurotoxic or create additional health risks to the user. Furthermore, ecstasy tablets may contain other substances, such as ephedrine (a stimulant); dextromethorphan (DXM, a cough suppressant); ketamine (an anesthetic used mostly by veterinarians); caffeine; cocaine; and methamphetamine. Although

STORY 9.1 (*continued*)

INFOFACTS
www.drugabuse.gov
National Institute on Drug Abuse ● National Institutes of Health ● U.S. Department of Health & Human Services

the combination of MDMA with one or more of these drugs may be inherently dangerous, users who also combine these with additional substances such as marijuana and alcohol may be putting themselves at even higher risk for adverse health effects.

What Treatment Options Exist?

There are no specific treatments for MDMA abuse and addiction. The most effective treatments for drug abuse and addiction in general are cognitive-behavioral interventions that are designed to help modify the patient's thinking, expectancies, and behaviors related to their drug use and to increase skills in coping with life stressors. Drug abuse recovery support groups may also be effective in combination with behavioral interventions to support long-term, drug-free recovery. There are currently no pharmacological treatments for addiction to MDMA.

How Widespread Is MDMA Abuse?

Monitoring the Future Survey[†]

After sharp declines in ecstasy use since its peak in 2000/2001, current and past-year use of MDMA has risen among 8th

and 10th graders. This follows several years of decreases in the perceived risk and disapproval of using MDMA.

Use of MDMA by Students 2010 Monitoring the Future Survey			
	8th Grade	10th Grade	12th Grade
Lifetime[††]	3.3%	6.4%	7.3%
Past Year	2.4%	4.7%	4.5%
Past Month	1.1%	1.9%	1.4%

National Survey on Drug Use and Health (NSDUH)[†††]

In 2009, an estimated 760,000 people (0.3 percent of the population) in the United States aged 12 or older used MDMA in the month prior to being surveyed. Lifetime use increased significantly among individuals aged 12 years or older, from 4.3 percent (10.2 million) in 2002 to 5.7 percent (14.2 million) in 2009; however, past-year use of ecstasy decreased from 1.3 percent to 1.1 percent during the same period. Approximately 1.1 million Americans used ecstasy for the first time in 2009, which is a significant increase from the 894,000 first-time users reported in 2008.

STORY 9.1 (*continued*)

INFOFACTS

ww.drugabuse.gov

onal Institute on Drug Abuse • National Institutes of Health • U.S. Department of Health & Human Services

Other Information Sources

For more information on MDMA, please visit **www.clubdrugs.org** and **www. teens.drugabuse.gov.**

For street terms searchable by drug name, cost and quantities, drug trade, and drug use, visit **www.whitehousedrugpolicy. gov/streetterms/default.asp.**

Data Sources

[†] These data are from the 2010 Monitoring the Future survey, funded by the National Institute on Drug Abuse, National Institutes of Health, Department of Health and Human Services, and conducted annually by the University of Michigan's Institute for Social Research. The survey has tracked 12th-graders' illicit drug use and related attitudes since 1975; in 1991, 8th- and 10th-graders were added to the study. The latest data are on line at www.drugabuse.gov.

[††] "Lifetime" refers to use at least once during a respondent's lifetime. "Past year" refers to use at least once during the year preceding an individual's response to the survey. "Past month" refers to use at least once during the 30 days preceding an individual's response to the survey.

[†††] NSDUH (formerly known as the National Household Survey on Drug Abuse) is an annual survey of Americans aged 12 and older conducted by the Substance Abuse and Mental Health Services Administration, Department of Health and Human Services. This survey is available on line at www.samhsa.gov and can be ordered by phone from NIDA at 877–643–2644.

References

[1] Ricaurte GA and McCann UD. Experimental studies on 3,4-methylenedioxymethamphetamine (MDMA, "ecstasy") and its potential to damage brain serotonin neurons. *Neurotox Res* 3(1):85–99, 2001.

[2] Stone AL, Storr CL, and Anthony JC. Evidence for a hallucinogen dependence syndrome developing soon after onset of hallucinogen use during adolescence. *Int J Methods Psychiatr Res* 15:116–130, 2006.

[3] Cottler LB, Womack SB, Compton WM, Ben-Abdallah A. Ecstasy abuse and dependence among adolescents and young adults: Applicability and reliability of DSM-IV criteria. *Human Psychopharmacol* 16:599–606, 2001.

[4] Leung KS, Cottler LB. Ecstasy and other club drugs: A review of recent epidemiological studies. *Curr Opin Psychiatry* 21:234–241, 2008.

[5] Kraner JC, McCoy DJ, Evans MA, Evans LE, Sweeney BJ. Fatalities caused by the MDMA-related drug paramethoxyamphetamine (PMA). *J Anal Toxicol* 25(7):645–648, 2001.

NIDA NATIONAL INSTITUTE ON DRUG ABUSE

National Institutes of Health – U.S. Department of Health and Human Services

This material may be used or reproduced without permission from NIDA. Citation of the source is appreciated.

scant change in drug usage.[24] What can be said with certainty is that New York's incarceration numbers have reached meteoric levels. "The Correctional Association of New York has pointed up the bizarre disparities in treatment of drug offenders and violent criminals. One murderer of a little girl received a minimum sentence of 6⅓ to 19 years; another, heavily dependent upon cocaine, received 8⅓ to 25. And, the young man who strangled his girlfriend in Central park copped 5 to 15 years. On the other hand, a welfare mother who received $2,500 for carrying four ounces of cocaine to help provide for her four children is still serving her mandatory sentence of 15 years to life."[25]

With jails spilling over with drug users, some suffering from extraordinarily tough penalties, especially when compared to severity of other felonious activity, a reexamination of the drug war's policy is mandatory. The amount of funds expended in the drug war can only be described as staggering. (See Figure 9.2[26].)

There are sound reasons to maintain some aspects of the policing and correctional models, suggests David Shultz:

> Seeking to discourage illegal drug use, as well as confining criminal activity surrounding the marketing of illegal drugs, is what is referred to as the "drug problem" in the United States. The basis for opposing the use of drugs generally rests on one of two grounds. First, there is the moral claim that drug use is inherently immoral or bad because it alters the mind, debases human nature, or reduces the capacity for autonomy. The second claim for opposing the use of drugs is social, arguing that the use of drugs and drug-related activity produces certain social costs in terms of deaths, black marketing, and crime. Another variant of this claim is that drug use diminishes social productivity by sustaining bad work habits, or by generating other social costs including increased healthcare costs. For example, there is good data to suggest that illegal drug use led to increased crime and public health problems. According to FBI Uniform Crime Reports, total state and local drug arrests have increased from 558,601 in 1979,[27] to 1,154,046 in 1988.[28] Additionally, estimates show that there are 20,000 premature deaths annually due to illegal drug use, although tobacco and alcohol use account for 400,000 and 100,000 premature deaths, respectively.[29]

Abandoning the law enforcement model would be a drastic error, but not coupling it with novel and innovative approaches would be unwise. Another aspect to the difficulty in forging an effective strategy is the lack of consensus on the drug war. The varieties of views on this topic are quite extraordinary.

First, a segment of the citizenry believes the matter to be more personal when compared to other crimes. Drug usage also has been labeled a matter of choice rather than a coerced or forced criminality. As a result, certain antagonists to the war on drugs see the tactics as invasive and unnecessary. Second, another segment of the population cynically disbelieves drug information disseminated by public authorities. Clinical tests contradict unsubstantiated claims of injury and harm; the serious effects warned of have not panned out. Politicians and governmental agencies lack a uniform approach to the problem and communicate mixed messages to the general public. Third, the generation following World War II engaged in more personal experimentation than had previously been witnessed. For the past 50 years, a vocal minority of the current generation has yet to discover the criminal quality of drug usage. Fourth, mainstream academics and nonprofit lobby groups advocate for legalization and tend toward prolegalization. Groups like NORML (National Organization for the Reform of Marijuana Laws) use slick and convincing tactics to persuade others that marijuana should not be criminalized.

FUNCTIONS	FY 2002 Final	FY 2003 Final	FY 2004 Final	FY 2005 Final	FY 2006 Final	FY 2007 Final	FY 2008 Final	FY 2009 Final	FY 2010 Enacted	FY 2011 Requested
Demand Reduction										
Drug Abuse Treatment	2,358.3	2,387.7	2,545.5	2,556.9	2,470.4	2,465.1	2,647.2	2,747.3	3,092.3	3,208.3
Treatment Research	547.8	611.4	607.2	621.2	600.3	600.8	608.0	814.7	653.2	674.2
Total Treatment	2,906.1	2,999.1	3,152.7	3,178.1	3,070.7	3,065.9	3,255.2	3,561.9	3,745.5	3,882.5
Drug Abuse Prevention	1,642.5	1,567.2	1,557.3	1,544.0	1,465.4	1,423.4	1,334.7	1,358.0	1,090.2	1,279.8
Prevention Research	367.4	382.9	412.4	422.0	411.5	413.4	415.6	496.7	424.1	437.9
Total Prevention	2,009.9	1,950.1	1,969.7	1,966.0	1,876.9	1,836.8	1,750.3	1,854.7	1,514.3	1,717.7
Total Demand Reduction	**4,916.0**	**4,949.2**	**5,122.4**	**5,144.1**	**4,947.6**	**4,902.7**	**5,005.5**	**5,416.6**	**5,259.9**	**5,600.2**
Percentage	45.6%	44.1%	42.7%	40.2%	37.6%	35.4%	37.7%	35.5%	35.0%	36.0%
Supply Reduction										
Domestic Law Enforcement	2,867.2	3,018.3	3,189.8	3,318.1	3,475.0	3,715.3	3,544.8	3,869.4	3,843.5	3,917.3
Interdiction	1,913.7	2,147.5	2,534.1	2,928.7	3,287.0	3,175.9	2,901.4	3,910.2	3,640.1	3,727.0
International	1,084.5	1,105.1	1,159.3	1,393.3	1,434.5	2,050.2	1,824.6	2,082.2	2,288.0	2,308.1
Total Supply Reduction	**5,865.4**	**6,270.9**	**6,883.2**	**7,640.1**	**8,196.5**	**8,941.4**	**8,270.8**	**9,861.8**	**9,771.6**	**9,952.4**
Percentage	54.4%	55.9%	57.3%	59.8%	62.4%	64.6%	62.3%	64.5%	65.0%	64.0%
TOTALS	**10,781.4**	**11,220.1**	**12,005.6**	**12,784.2**	**13,144.1**	**13,844.1**	**13,276.3**	**15,278.4**	**15,031.5**	**15,552.5**

Detail may not add due to rounding.

Figure 9.2   Historical drug control funding by function: FY 2002–FY 2010 (budget authority in millions).

STORY 9.2

NORML FOUNDATION

Educating America about Marijuana and Marijuana Policy

The NORML Foundation, a sister organization to NORML, is a nonprofit foundation established in 1997 to better educate the public about marijuana and marijuana policy options, and to assist victims of the current laws. Read the NORML Foundation mission statement (en Español). Headed by Executive Director Allen F. St. Pierre, the NORML Foundation maintains a professional staff and shares office space with NORML in Washington, D.C.

The NORML Foundation has been qualified as a 501(c)(3) tax-exempt foundation by the Internal Revenue Service, and donations to the foundation are tax deductible.

The NORML Foundation sponsors public advertising campaigns designed to inform the public about the costs of marijuana prohibition and the benefits of alternative policies; distributes a weekly press release to the national media and citizen activists focusing on recent developments pertaining to marijuana research and policy; publishes a regular newsletter; provides legal assistance and support to victims of the current marijuana laws; undertakes relevant research; and hosts, with NORML, an informative Web site and an annual conference.

NORML Web site at http://norml.org/index.cfm?Group_ID=3380 (updated: July 22, 2005).

Medical professionals have also touted the medicinal benefits of certain drugs and urge immediate legalization for regular consumer access. The proliferation of drugs in the medical community enhances acceptability as well. Commonly, medical professionals are either on the forefront of recommending liberalization of the criminal principles or themselves have, due to their proximity, become involved in the drug culture. Unfortunately, the stress of the job and the ready access to drugs are an ongoing temptation for medical professionals.[30]

Visit NORML's Interactive Web location that traces and tracks drug law changes particularly for marijuana at http://norml.org/index.cfm?Group_ID=4516

Marijuana usage for medical purposes has made successful inroads in a variety of American jurisdictions over the past decade.[31] California's medical exception law was struck down by the U.S. Supreme Court in 2001, but Senate Bill 420 was signed into law in October 2003 and took effect on January 1, 2004, permitting its usage.[32]

Find out about Oregon's Medical Marijuana exception at http://www.oregon.gov/DHS/ph/ommp/

The confusion about drugs and illegality is further fostered by some cultural pressures and shifts. If drugs promise anything, it is pleasure, however false it might be. It is the power of drugs

---

CASE 9.2

U.S. V. OAKLAND CANNABIS BUYERS COOPERATIVE ET AL.

No. 00151 (9th Cir. 2001)

In November 1996, California voters enacted an initiative measure entitled the Compassionate Use Act of 1996. Attempting [t]o ensure that seriously ill Californians have the right to obtain and use marijuana for medical purposes, Cal. Health & Safety Code Ann. 11362.5 (West Supp. 2001), the statute creates an exception to California laws prohibiting the possession and cultivation of marijuana. These prohibitions no longer apply to a patient or his primary caregiver who possesses or cultivates marijuana for the patients medical purposes upon the recommendation or approval of a physician. Ibid. In the wake of this voter initiative, several groups organized medical cannabis dispensaries to meet the needs of qualified patients. *United States v. Cannabis Cultivators Club*, 5 F.Supp. 2d 1086, 1092 (ND Cal. 1998). Respondent Oakland Cannabis Buyers Cooperative is one of these groups.

The Cooperative is a not-for-profit organization that operates in downtown Oakland. A physician serves as medical director, and registered nurses staff the Cooperative during business hours. To become a member, a patient must provide a written statement from a treating physician assenting to marijuana therapy and must submit to a screening interview. If accepted as a member, the patient receives an identification card entitling him to obtain marijuana from the Cooperative.

In January 1998, the United States sued the Cooperative and its executive director, respondent Jeffrey Jones (together, the Cooperative), in the United States District Court for the Northern District of California. Seeking to enjoin the Cooperative from distributing and manufacturing marijuana,[1] the United States argued that, whether or not the Cooperatives activities are legal under California law, they violate federal law. Specifically, the Government argued that the Cooperative violated the Controlled Substances Acts prohibitions on distributing, manufacturing, and possessing with the intent to distribute or manufacture a controlled substance. 21 U.S.C. 841(a). Concluding that the Government had established a probability of success on the merits, the District Court granted a preliminary injunction. App. to Pet. for Cert. 39a40a, 5 F.Supp. 2d, at 1105.

The Cooperative did not appeal the injunction, but instead openly violated it by distributing marijuana to numerous persons, App. to Pet. for Cert. at 21a23a. To terminate these violations, the Government initiated contempt proceedings. In defense, the Cooperative contended that any distributions were medically necessary. Marijuana is the only drug, according to the Cooperative, that can alleviate the severe pain and other debilitating symptoms of the Cooperatives patients. Id., at 29a. The District Court rejected this defense, however, after determining there was insufficient evidence that each recipient of marijuana was in actual danger of imminent harm without the drug. Id., at 29a32a. The District Court found the Cooperative in contempt and, at the Governments request, modified the preliminary injunction to empower the United States Marshal to seize the Cooperatives premises. Id., at 37a. Although recognizing that human suffering could result, the District Court reasoned that a courts equitable powers [do] not permit it to ignore federal law. Ibid.

Three days later, the District Court summarily rejected a motion by the Cooperative to modify the injunction to permit distributions that are medically necessary.

The Cooperative appealed both the contempt order and the denial of the Cooperatives motion to modify. Before the Court of Appeals for the Ninth Circuit decided the case; however, the Cooperative voluntarily purged its contempt by promising the District Court that it would comply with the initial preliminary injunction. Consequently, the Court of Appeals determined that the appeal of the contempt order was moot. 190 F.3d 1109, 11121113 (1999).

The denial of the Cooperatives motion to modify the injunction, however, presented a live controversy that was appealable under 28 U.S.C. 1292(a)(1). Reaching the merits of this issue, the Court of Appeals reversed and remanded. According to the Court of Appeals, the medical necessity defense was a legally cognizable defense that likely would apply in the circumstances. 190 F.3d, at 1114. Moreover, the Court of Appeals reasoned, the District Court erroneously believed that it had no discretion to issue an injunction that was more limited in scope than the Controlled Substances Act itself. Id., at 11141115. Because, according to the Court of Appeals, district courts retain broad equitable discretion to fashion injunctive relief, the District Court could have, and should have, weighed the public interest and considered factors such as the serious harm in depriving patients of marijuana. Ibid. Remanding the case, the Court of Appeals instructed the District Court to consider the criteria for a medical necessity exemption, and, should it modify the injunction, to set forth those criteria in the modification order. Id., at 1115.

Following these instructions, the District Court granted the Cooperatives motion to modify the injunction to incorporate a medical necessity defense.

The United States petitioned for certiorari to review the Court of Appeals decision that medical necessity is a legally cognizable defense to violations of the Controlled Substances Act. Because the decision raises significant questions as to the ability of the United States to enforce the Nations drug laws, we granted certiorari. 531 U.S. 1010 (2000).

The Controlled Substances Act provides that, [e]xcept as authorized by this subchapter, it shall be unlawful for any person knowingly or intentionally to manufacture, distribute, or dispense, or possess with intent to manufacture, distribute, or dispense, a controlled substance. 21 U.S.C. 841(a)(1). The subchapter, in turn, establishes exceptions. For marijuana (and other drugs that have been classified as schedule I controlled substances), there is but one express exception, and it is available only for Government-approved research projects, 823(f). Not conducting such a project, the Cooperative cannot, and indeed does not, claim this statutory exemption.

The Cooperative contends, however, that notwithstanding the apparently absolute language of 841(a), the statute is subject to additional, implied exceptions, one of which is medical necessity. According to the Cooperative, because necessity was a defense at common law, medical necessity should be read into the Controlled Substances Act. We disagree.

Questions

1. Describe the California exemption for medical usage of marijuana.
2. Who has the power to authorize the exemption?
3. Is there any potential for abuse in the Act?

STORY 9.3

THE DEA AND THE WAR ON DRUGS

The history of federal drug law enforcement traces back to before the turn of the century, when the federal government began instituting gradual restrictions and controls on newly discovered "wonder drugs," such as heroin and cocaine. Over the next half-century, America would continue to grapple with the negative affects of drugs on society. Multiple government agencies would be charged with monitoring and enforcing the drug laws of the United States. Over the past several decades, the federal government's role in fighting the war against drugs has increased. As the organizations dealing in

Figure 9.3 Glassine envelopes of heroin and OxyContin, 40 and 80 mg. (Photo courtesy of B. Kohlhepp, Ross Township Police Department.)

drugs have grown larger and more sophisticated, so, too, has America's commitment and ability to combat these groups throughout the country and around the world.

On July 1, 1973, President Richard Nixon created the Drug Enforcement Administration (DEA) by merging its predecessor agency, the Bureau of Narcotics and Dangerous Drugs (BNDD) with various law enforcement and intelligence gathering agencies. DEA has been charged with the responsibility of enforcing the nation's federal drug laws and works closely with local, state, federal, and international law enforcement organizations to identify, target, and bring to justice the most significant drug traffickers in the world.

Today, the DEA has grown to an agency of over 9,000 dedicated employees with over 4,500 Special Agents located in communities across the United States and in countries around the world. In order to meet the challenges posed by sophisticated international drug trafficking organizations, the DEA has developed state-of-the-art investigative tools and techniques that are used in 22 field divisions, offices in over 50 foreign countries, and in high-tech laboratories around the nation.

The DEA's continuing commitment is to serve America by providing the very best federal drug law enforcement assistance to communities besieged by drugs and to partner with members of the international community in targeting the highest levels of drug mafias. DEA Web site: http://www.usdoj.gov/dea/deamuseum/home.htm

to deliver immense physical exhilaration and alteration that makes the fix so attractive. A portion of the public needs and wants this pleasure at any cost. And, herein resides the greatest tragedy, the false sense of happiness delivered by the drug while the body suffers under its effects. Pleasure, so often confused with meaningful happiness, can never really come about from a life of drugs. Drugs, most clinicians will say, mask happiness and deliver a temporary substitute that eventually turns ugly. Finally, the lust for drugs in contemporary times says much about the overall quality of modern life. What is this emptiness that drugs seek to fill in? For a few moments, the drugs deliver a form of artificial happiness, although this is transitory. Drug users who become addicted clearly suffer from a ravaging physical slavery, but the larger problem lies in their own conception of existence and life itself. No criminal justice model can cure this type of emptiness. The heroin addict who inserts needles into his penis to find a vein suitable has trudged downward into a human abyss that law cannot elevate. Put another way, the tragedy is first and foremost a spiritual one, where life becomes meaningless. Addicts who neglect their children, sell their children for sex, walk the streets and engage in every sort of perversion to get the money to support the habit have little regard for any law that outlaws the conduct. They are living in another dimension. While this commentary cannot be quantified in a statistical sense, justice practitioners understand that a life of drugs is a world spiraling downward.

In this sense, the problem cannot be tackled by the predictable law enforcement approach. In fact, to edify, the great success stories in the treatment of drugs are often the spiritual ones where the abuser is reborn in more ways than one. Transformation from this lifestyle is a tall order that summons up enviable courage, a supportive family and most importantly, a reason to believe that happiness lies elsewhere.

Legalization as Solution

Accepting the difficulty of the situation has led some legal thinkers to find merit in the legalization of these practices. The idea attracts so many followers because when one honestly examines the results of the "war," the call for retreat makes more sense. From another perspective, if our social and human problems are already evident, what will occur when drugs filter into the culture without restriction? Will dependency rates rise? Will children be better cared for as their addictive parents receive the steady stream of free and legal stuff? Will the nation be more or less virtuous because of our acquiescence to the inevitable?

Weigh the pros and cons of this dilemma.

Pros for Legalization

Realistic recognition of drug problem
An intelligent use of justice expenditures
Better use of justice personnel on more serious offenses
Guards personal freedom and constitutional protections
Replaces penological approach with rehabilitative and clinical model
Allows recreational use of low-harm drugs

Cons against Legalization

Admission of law enforcement failure
Wasted past expenditures
Promotes message of pleasure and hedonism
Promotes lack of self-discipline
Generates medical costs of dependency
Effects worker productivity and economic expansion
Causes rising rates of dependency
Fosters social problems and dysfunction
Contributes to familial breakdown
Negatively influences the national character

One can pinpoint merit in both positions, but exactly how legalization would play out in the national psyche has yet to be determined. We have no experience with wholesale toleration of a social problem of this scope and size. If history tells us anything, drugs, legalized or not, rots the conscience and character of the nation and its citizens. Empires are built by the virtuous and strong, not the enslaved and tortured.

Special Response: Drug Courts

One way the justice system has addressed the dramatic rise in drug cases is by the implementation of new Drug Courts.

> Visit the National Drug Court Resource Center at: http://www.ndcrc.org/

These courts mix penology with mental and physical care regimens that treat the addicted person. Most would agree that it makes little sense to incarcerate small drug users or clinically dependent people attempting to get lives in order.[33] Drug Courts have greater discretion in the handling and disposition of these offenders.[34]

BIGAMY AND POLYGAMY

ELEMENTS

BIGAMY

- A married person
- Intends to marry another despite another marriage
- Carries out a subsequent marriage

POLYGAMY

- Open, consensual practice of multiple marital partners

The fact that bigamy exists in any sector of modern America is quite surprising. With staggering rates of divorce, a growing tendency to cohabit without the benefit of marriage and a developing, but very general, resistance to marriage as an institution would seem to make the practice moot. Granting that all these social observations are true, bigamy still occurs. Bigamy, the often hidden and nondisclosed practice of being married simultaneously to more than one spouse, does exist, but secretly. By contrast, polygamy constitutes an open and notorious multiple partnering in marriage where the parties consent to the practice.

Why the aversion to multiple marriage partners? Why does the justice system criminalize the practice? Is the practice a sign of moral defect or perversion? Is there biblical and even religious precedent for the practice? Does bigamy and polygamy really harm others? Does the government's interference in the practice represent an invasion of privacy, an intrusion into the private affairs of its citizens in a free society? Does government interference infringe upon religious expression? Can the government effectively control the practice?

STORY 9.4

THE EVOLUTION OF DRUG COURTS

A drug court can be defined as "a special court given the responsibility to handle cases involving drug-addicted offenders through an extensive supervision and treatment program." (National Association of Drug Court Professionals, 2001)

Drug court participants undergo long-term treatment and counseling, sanctions, incentives, and frequent court appearances. Successful completion of the treatment program results in dismissal of the charges, reduced or set aside sentences, lesser penalties, or a combination of these. Most importantly, graduating participants gain the necessary tools to rebuild their lives.

Because the problem of drugs and crime is much too broad for any single agency to tackle alone, drug courts rely upon the daily communication and cooperation of judges, court personnel, probation, and treatment providers. (National Strategy for the Co-Funding of Coordinated Drug Court Systems, 1994)

Drug courts vary somewhat from one jurisdiction to another in terms of structure, scope, and target populations, but they all share three primary goals: (1) to reduce recidivism, (2) to reduce substance abuse among participants, and (3) to rehabilitate participants.

Achieving these goals requires a special organizational structure. Specifically, the drug court model includes the following key components:

- Incorporating drug testing into case processing.
- Creating a nonadversarial relationship between the defendant and the court.
- Identifying defendants in need of treatment and referring them to treatment as soon as possible after arrest.
- Providing access to a continuum of treatment and rehabilitation services.
- Monitoring abstinence through frequent, mandatory drug testing.
- Establishing a coordinated strategy to govern drug court responses to participants' compliance.
- Maintaining judicial interaction with each drug court participant.
- Monitoring and evaluating program goals and gauging their effectiveness.
- Continuing interdisciplinary education to promote effective drug court planning, implementation, and operations.
- Forging partnerships among drug courts, public agencies, and community-based organizations to generate local support and enhance drug court effectiveness. (*Defining Drug Courts: The Key Components,* 1997)

The first drug court was implemented in 1989 in Miami, Florida, when Judge Herbert M. Klein, troubled by the disabling effects that drug offenses were wreaking upon Dade County courts, became determined to "solve the problem of larger numbers of people on drugs." (*Miami's Drug Court: A Different Approach,* 1993) The court became a model program for the Nation.

Indeed, the outbreak of drug courts in recent years has been extraordinary. (*The Rebirth of Rehabilitation: Promise and Perils of Drug Courts,* 2000) By December 2000, nearly 600 drug courts were operating in all 50 States, the District of Columbia, Puerto Rico, Guam, and two Federal Districts. Another 456 drug court programs were in the planning stages. (Drug Court Clearinghouse and Technical Assistance Project)

An important force behind the drug court movement was the Violent Crime Control and Law Enforcement Act of 1994, which called for Federal support for planning, implementing, and enhancing drug courts for nonviolent drug offenders. Between 1995 and 1997, the U.S. Department of Justice, Office of Justice Programs, through its Drug Courts Program Office (DCPO), provided $56 million in funding to drug courts. Additionally, the fervent support of national leaders raised the status of drug courts. Their support, and the acknowledgement that (1) substance abuse is a major contributing factor to crime and social problems, and (2) traditional criminal justice system policies were having little impact on substance abuse, suggest that "drug courts will play an increasingly visible role in the nation's response to drug-related crime." (*Research on Drug Courts: A Critical Review*, 1998)

The drug court model has paved the way for the latest criminal justice innovation-therapeutic jurisprudence. A number of jurisdictions are developing special dockets, modeled after the drug court format. Courts and judges have become more receptive to new approaches, resulting in a proliferation of problem-solving courts including DUI courts, domestic violence courts, mental health courts, and reentry courts.

The Drug Courts Program Office was established to administer the drug court grant program and to provide financial and technical assistance, training, related programmatic guidance, and leadership. DCPO offers grants to jurisdictions to plan, implement, or enhance drug courts. In conjunction with the National Institute of Justice, DCPO conducts comparative evaluations of drug court programs to identify the most effective program elements and designs to combat drug abuse and crime.

National Criminal Justice Reference Service, http://www.ncjrs.org/drug_courts/drug_courts.html

For most of the nation's history, there has been little disagreement on the conduct's illegality. When groups or historical movements assert the right to maintain or resurrect the practice, this tolerance or silence evolves into outright condemnation. The history of the Mormon faith in America follows this dilemma up to the present. While the Mormon Church unilaterally condemns the practices of polygamy and bigamy, certain radical sects, outside the church, still maintain its legitimacy (Figure 9.4).

In addition, cultural differences also lead to a silent toleration in certain ethnic sectors of the American experience. Parts of the Arab world accept some polygamous practices in concept, though not necessarily in practice. The point that must be remembered is that culture sometimes influences the criminal law template in ways that cannot be fully explained. More recent commentary tends to see historic objections to the practice as "red herrings"[35] that confuse the real reason for our objections. This passion for moralizing and a side stepping of arguments regarding decriminalization really misses the point, so says Professor Adrienne Davis.

{F}ew scholars have considered polygamy on its own and engaged in detail the regulatory challenges it must pose to our current family law system. Even those who have considered polygamy explicitly from a bargaining perspective ... Seem to assume it is merely dyadic marriage multiplied.[36]

FBI TEN MOST WANTED FUGITIVE

UNLAWFUL FLIGHT TO AVOID PROSECUTION - SEXUAL CONDUCT WITH A MINOR, CONSPIRACY TO COMMIT SEXUAL CONDUCT WITH A MINOR; RAPE AS AN ACCOMPLICE

WARREN STEED JEFFS

DESCRIPTION

Date of Birth:	December 3, 1955	**Hair:**	Brown
Place of Birth:	San Francisco, California	**Eyes:**	Brown
Height:	6'3" to 6'4"	**Complexion:**	Light
Weight:	150 to 155 pounds	**Sex:**	Male
Build:	Slim	**Race:**	White
Occupations:	Private School Teacher, Accountant	**Nationality:**	American
Scars and Marks:	None known		

Remarks: Warren Jeffs is the leader of a polygamous sect known as the Fundamentalist Latter Day Saints (FLDS) and is considered a "prophet" by his estimated 10,000 followers. Jeffs has ties to the following areas: Utah; Arizona; Texas; Colorado; South Dakota; British Columbia, Canada; and Quintana Roo, Mexico. Additionally, Jeffs may travel with a number of loyal and armed bodyguards. He may also wear glasses.

CAUTION

WARREN STEED JEFFS, THE LEADER OF A POLYGAMOUS SECT, IS WANTED FOR THE ALLEGED SEXUAL ASSAULT ON A MINOR IN 2002. HE IS ALSO WANTED FOR ONE COUNT OF CONSPIRACY TO COMMIT SEXUAL CONDUCT WITH A MINOR IN 2002. THE ALLEGED OFFENSES TOOK PLACE IN THE VICINITY OF COLORADO CITY, ARIZONA. ADDITIONALLY, JEFFS IS WANTED FOR RAPE AS AN ACCOMPLICE IN UTAH.

CONSIDERED ARMED AND DANGEROUS

IF YOU HAVE ANY INFORMATION CONCERNING THIS PERSON, PLEASE CONTACT YOUR LOCAL FBI OFFICE OR THE NEAREST U.S. EMBASSY OR CONSULATE.

REWARD

The FBI is offering a reward of up to $100,000 for information leading directly to the arrest of Warren Steed Jeffs.

www.fbi.gov

May 2006

Figure 9.4 Warren Steed Jeffs, a polygamist leader of the Fundamentalist Church of Jesus Christ of Latter Day Saints, was convicted in 2007 of being an accomplice to rape for forcing a 14-year-old girl to marry her 19-year-old cousin.

Those who object are painted as the less tolerant and understanding class. Professor Davis cannot understand why the state "continues to privilege certain intimate relationship{s} at the expense of others."[37] For those who challenge the moral sensibility of polygamy, the objections are not merely political positions or conclusions reached in a power struggle, but heartfelt moral judgments consistent with a host of moral traditions. If convenience is not enough, other commentators claim that the condemnation of polygamy rests in race arguments. Columbia University Professor Martha M. Ertman poses this line of reasoning:

> But race is also at the center of antipolygamy laws, in a way that forces us to rethink the ban in itself. Many Americans, from the highest levels of government to political cartoonists, view the Mormons' political treason as part of a larger, even more sinister offense that I call race treason.[38]

Since the condemnation of polygamy is seldom applied to black, Arabic, or other cultures, Professor Ertman posits that "white supremacist values"[39] are to blame for the ban. Reasonable minds may disagree this argument seems a bit far-fetched.

Assuming these diverse positions, weigh the pros and cons of bigamy and polygamy.

Pro

Increased rates of childbirth
Multiple means of caring for larger family units
Enhanced sexual partnering
Respect for personal integrity and privacy
Respect for religious expression

Con

Undermines traditional family unit
Undermines estate, trust, and intestacy laws
Confusion of role models
Objectification of women (since the predominance of cases are one man/multiple women)
Transmission of communicable diseases
Promotes dishonesty in relationships

Bigamy, due to its surreptitious nature, its lack of disclosure, has little, if any support. Informally, it is a safe bet the justice system has an undetected caseload. Think about the number of separated partners whose formal divorce records have yet to be processed who enter into subsequent marriage relationships. Technically, these parties practice bigamy. What if the former spouse marries another under the mistaken belief that the former spouse was deceased? In these cases, the party lacks the specific intent to commit bigamy and most statutory designs recognize this exception. What about a party who never formally married though due to long periods of cohabitation qualifies for the common law marriage declaration? If common law marriage is recognized, then bigamy can be charged.

What is the impact of an annulment and a marriage subsequently contracted? Does a marriage lawfully in existence at the time of the act of bigamy, which subsequently is adjudged

CASE 9.3

MURPHY V. RAMSEY
114 U.S. 15 (1885)

The wrong complained of in each case by the respective plaintiffs is "that the defendants, and each of them, intending to wrongfully deprive the plaintiff of the elective franchise in said territory, willfully and maliciously, by the acts and in the manner aforesaid, refused the plaintiff registration, as a voter, at the said registration commenced on the second Monday of September, 1882, and deprived the plaintiff of the right to vote at the election held in said territory on the seventh day of November, 1882, and at all elections under said registration."

The acts which, it is alleged, were done by the five defendants, as a board of commissioners or canvassers, under the law of March 22, 1882, and which contributed to the wrong, and constituted part of it, are that they prescribed as a condition of registration an unauthorized oath, set out in the complaint, in a rule promulgated by them for the government of the registration officers; and that the deputy registration officer having, in obedience to such rule, "acting under the directions of the other defendants," willfully and maliciously refused to receive the affidavit tendered by the plaintiff, in lieu of that prescribed by the rule of the board, and to register the plaintiff; and that the county registration officer, on appeal, having refused to order otherwise, the board of commissioners also refused to reverse and correct these rulings, and to direct the registration of the plaintiffs, respectively, but affirmed and approved the same.

But an examination of the ninth section of the act of March 22, 1882, providing for the appointment and prescribing the duties and powers of that board, shows that they have no functions whatever in respect to the registration of voters, except the appointment of officers in place of those previously authorized, whose offices are by that section of the law declared to be vacant; and the persons appointed to succeed them are not subject to the direction and control of the board, but are required, until other provision be made by the legislative assembly of the territory, to perform all the duties relating to the registration of voters, "under the existing laws of the United States and of said territory." The board are not authorized to prescribe rules for governing them in the performance of these duties, much less to prescribe any qualifications for voters as a condition of registration. The statutory powers of the board are limited to the appointment of the registration and election officers, authorized to act in the first instance under the law until provision is made by the territorial legislature for the appointment of their successors, and to the canvass of the returns and the issue of certificates of election "to those persons who, being eligible for such election, shall appear to have been lawfully elected." The proviso in the section does, indeed, declare "that said board of five persons shall not exclude any person otherwise eligible to vote from the polls on account of any opinion such person may entertain but, in the absence of any general and express power over the subject of declaring the qualification of voters, it is not a just inference, from the words of this proviso, that it was intended to admit by implication the existence of any authority in the board to exclude from registration, or the right to vote, any person whatever, or in any manner to define and declare what the qualifications of a voter shall be. The prohibition against excluding any person from the polls, for the reason assigned, must be construed, with the additional injunction, "nor shall they refuse to count any such vote on account of the opinion of the person casting it on the subject of bigamy or polygamy," to apply to the action of the board in canvassing the returns of elections, made to them by the officers holding such elections; or, if it includes more, it is to be taken as the announcement of a general principle to govern all officers concerned in the registration of in canvassing the returns of elections," ...

In the case in which Mary Ann M. Pratt is plaintiff, she clearly excludes herself from the disqualifications of the act. She alleges in her complaint "that she is not, and never has been, a bigamist or a polygamist; that she is the widow of Orson Pratt, Sr., who died prior to the twenty-second day of March, 1882, after a continuous residence in said territory of more than thirty years, and that since the death of her said husband she has not cohabited with any man." The same is true in reference to the allegations of the complaint in the case in which Mildred E. Randall and her husband are plaintiffs. They are, "that the plaintiff Mildred E. Randall, for more than three years last past, has been and is the wife of the plaintiff Alfred Randall, who is, and prior to March 22, 1882, was, a native-born citizen of the United States of America; that she has not, on or since March 22, 1882, cohabited with any bigamist, polygamist, or with any man cohabiting with more than one woman; that she is not a bigamist or polygamist, and never has been a bigamist or polygamist, and has not in any way violated the act of congress entitled 'An act to amend section 5352 of the Revised Statutes of the United States in reference to bigamy, and for other purposes,' approved March 22, 1882. The requirements of the eighth section of the act, in reference to a woman claiming the right to vote, are that she does not, at the time she offers to register, cohabit with a polygamist, bigamist, or person cohabiting with more than one woman; and it is sufficient if the complaint denies the disqualification in the language of the act. These requirements are fully met in the two cases just referred to.

The case of Ellen C. Clawson is different. In the complaint, filed by herself and her husband, it is alleged that she "is not, and never has been, a bigamist or polygamist, and is not cohabiting, and never has cohabited, with any man except her husband, the co-plaintiff herein, to whom she was lawfully married more than fifteen years ago, and of whom she is the first and lawful wife; that the plaintiff Hiram B. Clawson has not married, or entered into any marriage contract or relation with any woman within the last six years, and has continuously and openly resided in the city of Salt Lake, in said territory of Utah, for more than twenty years last past." It is quite consistent with these statements that the husband of the female plaintiff was, at the time she claimed registration, a bigamist or a polygamist, or that he was then cohabiting with more than one woman; and that she was cohabiting with him at the same time. She would be, on either supposition, expressly disqualified from voting by the eighth section of the act of March 22, 1882, and she does not negative the fact. It cannot, therefore, be inferred that she was a lawfully qualified voter.

The cases of Murphy and Barlow are alike in substance. In Murphy's case, the allegations are "that he has not, since more than three years prior to March 22, 1882, married or entered into any marriage contract or relation with any woman, or in anywise violated the act of congress, approved July 1, 1862, defining and providing for the punishment of bigamy in the territories, ... and has not violated any of the provisions of the act of congress, approved March 22, 1882, etc., ... and that he has not, on or since the twenty-second day of March, 1882, cohabited with more than one woman, and has never been charged with or accused or convicted of bigamy or polygamy, or cohabiting with more than one woman, in any court or before any officer or tribunal." In Barlow's case, the statement on one point is stronger. It is "that he has not, on or since the first day of July, 1862, married or entered into any marriage contract or relation with any woman, or in anywise violate the act of congress, approved July 1, 1862, defining and providing for the punishment of bigamy in the territories." That is to say, that, although he may have married a second wife, it was before any law existed in the territory prohibiting it, and, therefore, it could not have been a criminal offense when committed.

But in both cases the complaints omit the allegation, that, at the time the plaintiffs respectively claimed to be registered as voters, they were not each either a bigamist or a polygamist. It is admitted that the use of these very terms in the complaint is not necessary, if the disqualifications lawfully implied by them are otherwise substantially denied. That such is their case is maintained by the appellants. The words "bigamist" and "polygamist" evidently are not used in this statute in the sense of describing those who entertain the opinion that bigamy and polygamy ought to be tolerated as a practice, not inconsistent with the good order of society, the welfare of the race, and a true code of morality, if such there be; because, in the proviso in the ninth section of the act, it is expressly declared that no person shall be excluded from the polls, or be denied his vote, on account of any opinion on the subject. It is argued that they cannot be understood as meaning those who, prior to the passage of the act of March 22, 1882, had contracted a bigamous or polygamous marriage, either in violation of an existing law, such as that of July 1, 1862, or before the enactment of any law forbidding it; for to do so would give to the statute a retrospective effect, and by thus depriving citizens of civil rights merely on account of past offenses, or on account of acts which, when committed, were not offenses, would make it an *ex post facto* law, and therefore void. And the conclusion is declared to be necessary, that the words polygamist and bigamist, as used in the eighth section of the act, can mean only such persons as, having violated the first section of the act, are guilty of polygamy; that is, "every person who has a husband or wife living, who, in a territory or other place over which the United States have exclusive jurisdiction, hereafter marries another, whether married or single, and any man who hereafter simultaneously or on the same day marries more than one woman, in a territory or other place over which the United States have exclusive jurisdiction."

Questions

1. Which Amendment in the United States Constitution may provide a defense to the practice of bigamy and polygamy? Explain why.
2. Does the Court argue the case from a strictly legal perspective or depend on historical tradition and moral custom in reaching its conclusion?
3. What type of pattern of multiple marriages occurred in this case: open or nondisclosed?

void, provide a legitimate line of defense? What about the effect of a divorce? What impact does separation have upon a charge of bigamy?

Most statutes address these and other issues relative to the intent to commit bigamy.

§ 4301. Bigamy

(a)   BIGAMY. —A married person is guilty of bigamy, a misdemeanor of the second degree, if he contracts or purports to contract another marriage, unless at the time of the subsequent marriage:
   (1)   the actor believes that the prior spouse is dead;
   (2)   the actor and the prior spouse have been living apart for two consecutive years throughout which the prior spouse was not known by the actor to be alive; or
   (3)   a court has entered a judgment purporting to terminate or annul any prior disqualifying marriage, and the actor does not know that judgment to be invalid.

(b)   OTHER PARTY TO BIGAMOUS MARRIAGE. —A person is guilty of bigamy if he contracts or purports to contract marriage with another knowing that the other is thereby committing bigamy.[40]

Honest, good faith mistakes about the formality of a pled divorce, or a reasonable belief that an annulment decree had been entered, serve as acceptable defenses to the mens rea element. "The thought is that a person with any sophistication in law may be uncertain as to the validity of a foreign divorce. It seems harsh to subject him to a criminal bigamy prosecution, especially since the questionable divorce may be that of his second spouse from another person."[41]

Long-term and inexplicable abandonment by a spouse also affords a reasonable defense since the remarrying party assumes the death or abandonment relationship.[42]

Read the basis for the ACLU's objection to Utah's bigamy and polygamy laws at: http://www.acluutah.org/bigamystatute.htm

---

OBSCENITY

ELEMENTS

- Sale, production, distribution of obscene materials
- With knowledge and intent
- Which violates the community standard

In a world obsessed with free speech and the unrestricted communication of ideas, obscene materials have always had more protection than artistically deserved. Much of our obscenity tradition is grounded in a Victorian, almost puritanical ethos that displayed little toleration for open and published sexual content. Our present culture rests in a very different place. The image of a pornographic descent can be seen everywhere and even with children. The National Center for Missing and Exploited Children reported that nearly 19 percent of child pornographers have pictures of children younger than three years old, while 39 percent less than six, and 83 percent possessing material depicting children 12 years or younger.[43] Gone are the days when partial nudity was not tolerated or when texts, pictures, or movies were scathingly condemned because of sexual explicitness. A visit to the local beach would stand our nineteenth-century predecessors on their heads, and visual media, including television and the Internet, accelerate the ongoing slide into an overly expressive, tolerant, and coarsening world.[44] Violence alone floods the airways in ways once unimaginable according to the Center for Media and Public Affairs. (See Figure 9.5[45] for a tally of 24 hours of television.)

Day by day, the criminalization of sexual exhibition, nudity, pornography, and lewdness becomes less imaginable. For civil libertarians and free speech purists, this state of affairs should not be labeled as a descent into oblivion, but more accurately a trek toward freedom of expression and sexual liberty. Loosening ourselves from the puritanical shackles of guilt and conscience, they say, is a welcome evolution. To others, like the American Civil Liberties Union (ACLU), the government restriction on the production and dissemination of any form of expression exacts too heavy a toll on freedom itself. It is rare to find any material that would be objectionable to an organization in the vein of the ACLU. So "liberating" are its speech policies that the organization would have difficulty supporting a prosecution for the possession of a pedophile's manual of instruction.

Pluralistically, a diverse culture like the United States will always have a troubling time with these types of restrictions. Despite this natural liberality, there are some expressions that no culture should tolerate and, for that reason alone, obscenity laws are necessary. The law of obscenity suggests a viable, though admittedly imperfect set of parameters.

The Nature of Obscenity

Obscenity can be defined from a wide array of contexts: spiritual, religious, moral, feminist, constitutional and legal, as well as the artistic and the cultural. Too often pornography is offered up as obscenity's defining moment, yet pornography cannot envision, in every case, what is obscene, nor can pornography be declared, in all cases, offensive, nor can it be controlled by law in every setting. Pornography can descend into the illegality of obscenity, but need not. We live with pornographic expression in many settings, from the mainstream magazine stands, cable

Act	Number of Scenes	Percentage of Total
Serious assaults (without guns)	389	20
Gunplay	362	18
Isolated punches	273	14
Pushing, dragging	272	14
Menacing threat with a weapon	226	11
Slaps	128	6
Deliberate destruction of property	95	5
Simple assault	73	4
All other types of violence	28	1

Figure 9.5 Violent acts on television in a 24-hour period. (From William J. Bennett. 1994. *The Index of Leading Cultural Indicators*. Colorado Springs, CO: Waterbrook Press, p. 104.)

systems, video stores on the local corner, and even art museums. A hundred years ago, the line between pornography and obscenity would be indiscernible. Presently "pornographic material is a subset of all material that is obscene, that is, material that because of its extreme 'hardcore' content is not protected under the First Amendment. Pornographic material might be described as portraying erotic behavior designed to cause sexual excitement. The proponents of further regulation of sexually explicit material would argue that, in addition, pornography causes harm. Nonetheless, even though such material may be offensive, there is no agreement that it is any more harmful than material within the protected zone of the First Amendment."[46]

Obscenity, as compared to pornography, takes on more of the legal dynamic in its definition. Obscenity is the designated crime that may subsume select pornographic materials, but it is an elusive concept because the threshold for tolerance and the outrage it generates varies community by community. Obscenity defies universal definition. Or does it? Are there not forms of communication, which in all cases should be declared obscene? Consider these:

- Necrophilia: Sexual activities with the dead
- Pedophilia: Sexual activities with children
- Incest: Sexual activities with offspring
- Rape and snuff media: Promotes the rape of and brutal violence toward a victim
- Bestiality: Sexual activity with animals
- Violent materials/extreme violence targeted at minors[47]

Do these behaviors qualify under the obscenity heading? Are free speech rights superior to the separatism of these "speech forms"? Should these expressions be tolerated? Is the American cultural outlook so dissipated that it cannot come to terms with condemnation on some expression? And, should our efforts be more vigilant when it comes to minors? *David-Kidd Booksellers, Inc. v. McWherter*[48] attempted to restrict materials of "excess violence" to minors. The Court struck down the relevant statute for vagueness, which held that "a person or portion of the human body, which depicts ... Excess violence, or sadomasochistic abuse and which is harmful to minors ... exceed common limits of custom and candor."[49] Similarly in *Bookfriends v. Taft*,[50] the court declared the following Ohio law overly broad and vague:

A. display, description, or representation in lurid detail of the violent physical torture, dismemberment, destruction, or death of a human being ... that tends to glorify or glamorize the activity.[51]

Efforts to codify the crime are evident in the state and federal systems with special controls over Internet and cyberspace providers as it involves children.[52] Criminal sanctions involving obscenity, while tougher than it used to be, have fortunately not been abrogated. See the following statute.

§ 5903. Obscene and other sexual materials and performances

(a) Offenses defined.—No person, knowing the obscene character of the materials or performances involved, shall:
  1. display or cause or permit the display of any explicit sexual materials as defined in subsection (c) in or on any window, showcase, newsstand, display rack, billboard, display board, viewing screen, motion picture screen, marquee, or similar place in such manner that the display is visible from any public street, highway, sidewalk, transportation facility, or other public thoroughfare, or in any business or commer-

cial establishment where minors, as a part of the general public or otherwise, are or will probably be exposed to view all or any part of such materials;

2. sell, lend, distribute, exhibit, give away or show any obscene materials to any person 18 years of age or older or offer to sell, lend, distribute, transmit, exhibit or give away or show, or have in his possession with intent to sell, lend, distribute, transmit, exhibit or give away or show any obscene materials to any person 18 years of age or older, or knowingly advertise any obscene materials in any manner;

3. design, copy, draw, photograph, print, utter, publish or in any manner manufacture or prepare any obscene materials;

4. write, print, publish, utter or cause to be written, printed, published or uttered any advertisement or notice of any kind giving information, directly or indirectly, stating or purporting to state where, how, from whom, or by what means any obscene materials can be purchased, obtained or had;

5. produce, present, or direct any obscene performance or participate in a portion thereof that is obscene or that contributes to its obscenity;

6. hire, employ, use, or permit any minor child to do or assist in doing any act or thing mentioned in this subsection;

7. knowingly take or deliver in any manner any obscene material into a State correctional institution, county prison, regional prison facility, or any other type of correctional facility;

8. possess any obscene material while such person is an inmate of any State correctional institution, county prison, regional prison facility, or any other type of correctional facility; or

9. knowingly permit any obscene material to enter any State correctional institution, county prison, regional prison facility, or any other type of correctional facility if such person is a prison guard or other employee of any correctional facility described in this paragraph.

(a.1) Dissemination of explicit sexual material via an electronic communication.—No person, knowing the content of the advertisement to be explicit sexual materials as defined in subsection (c)(1) and (2), shall transmit or cause to be transmitted an unsolicited advertisement in an electronic communication as defined in section 5702 (relating to definitions) to one or more persons within this Commonwealth that contains explicit sexual materials as defined in subsection (c)(1) and (2) without including in the advertisement the term "ADV-ADULT" at the beginning of the subject line of the advertisement. ...

(c) Dissemination to minors.—No person shall knowingly disseminate by sale, loan, or otherwise explicit sexual materials to a minor. "Explicit sexual materials," as used in this subsection, means materials which are obscene or:

1. any picture, photograph, drawing, sculpture, motion picture film, videotape, or similar visual representation or image of a person or portion of the human body, which depicts nudity, sexual conduct, or sadomasochistic abuse and which is harmful to minors; or

2. any book, pamphlet, magazine, printed matter however reproduced, or sound recording, which contains any matter enumerated in paragraph (1), or explicit and detailed verbal descriptions or narrative accounts of sexual excitement, sexual conduct, or sadomasochistic abuse and which, taken as a whole, is harmful to minors.

CASE 9.4

UNITED STATES V. BROXMEYER
616 F. 3d 120 (2ⁿᵈ Cir. 2010)

Todd Broxmeyer, convicted in the United States District Court for the Northern District of New York (McAvoy, J.), challenges the sufficiency of the evidence to support his convictions for [i] production of child pornography ... He also raises an as-applied challenge to the statute criminalizing the production of child pornography.

Broxmeyer, a 37-year-old field hockey coach, entered into a sexual relationship (legal under state law) with a 17-year-old player. The two counts alleging production of child pornography are premised on two photos (one per count) that the girl took of herself. He was found to have induced her to produce them; but while there is evidence that he encouraged her to take photographs of that kind, and that she took several with his encouragement, there is no evidence that he encouraged her to take the two photos specified in the two counts of conviction.

...

Broxmeyer was for some years a field hockey coach to girls 14 to 18 years old. During this career, Broxmeyer engaged in sexual relationships with several of his players, some of whom were younger than 18. These relationships involved both physical acts and "sexting" (defined here to mean the exchange of sexually explicit text messages, including photographs, via cell phone).

In September 2008, Broxmeyer was convicted by a jury on all counts of a five-count indictment, of which Counts One, Two, and Four are at issue on this appeal:

Counts One and Two: Production of child pornography, in violation of 18 U.S.C. § 2251(a);

Count Three: Attempted production of child pornography, in violation of 18 U.S.C. § 2251(a), (e);

Count Five: Possession of child pornography, in violation of 18 U.S.C. § 2252A(a)(5)(B).

...

Broxmeyer met A.W. in 2005, while he was coaching at a field hockey camp in New England. Over the next few years, and through her senior year in high school, A.W. attended Broxmeyer's practices at field hockey camps across Pennsylvania, New Jersey, and New York.

Beginning in the spring of 2007 (and continuing until his arrest in December 2007), Broxmeyer and A.W.—who was then 17—began a consensual sexual relationship, legal under New York's statutory rape law. The two engaged in sexting as well as physical sex.

They exchanged images as follows. They used their cell phones to take pictures of themselves engaged in sexual acts with each other. Broxmeyer texted A.W. a picture of his arousal. Broxmeyer texted A.W. sexually explicit pictures of other field hockey players, including one of several girls in their underwear, who were arranged in a pyramid. Broxmeyer showed A.W. several sexually explicit pictures of field hockey players that he had saved to an Internet photo album. He challenged A.W. to acquire naked pictures of other field hockey players, and A.W. obliged. A.W. also texted Broxmeyer explicit photos of herself. Broxmeyer never expressly asked A.W. to send him pictures of herself, but he did tell her that he liked them and that she was doing something nice by sending them to him.

Counts One and Two relate to two photos—one per Count—that A.W. took of herself and texted to Broxmeyer. The first ("Photo 1") shows A.W. from the neck down, naked, touching her private parts. The second ("Photo 2") shows A.W. using a handheld showerhead to spray water between her legs. But, there is no evidence as to when the two photos at issue were taken, i.e., produced, or how or whether their production fits into the series of other communications and exchanges.

The federal statute criminalizing the production of child pornography, 18 U.S.C. § 2251(a), provides:

Any person who employs, uses, persuades, induces, entices, or coerces any minor to engage in ... any sexually explicit conduct for the purpose of producing any visual depiction of such conduct ... shall be punished ... if such person knows or has reason to know that such visual depiction will be transported or transmitted using any means or facility of interstate or foreign commerce or in or affecting interstate or foreign commerce ... if that visual depiction was produced or transmitted using materials that have been mailed, shipped, or transported in or affecting interstate or foreign commerce by any means. ...

Section 2251(a) applies only to the actual production of child pornography; other statutes—not charged in this case—proscribe distribution. To secure a conviction under § 2251(a), the government must prove beyond a reasonable doubt that: "(1) the victim was less than 18 years old; (2) the defendant used, employed, persuaded, induced, enticed, or coerced the minor to take part in sexually explicit conduct for the purpose of producing a visual depiction of that conduct; and (3) the visual depiction was produced using materials that had been transported in interstate or foreign commerce." *United States v. Malloy*, 568 F.3d 166, 169 (4th Cir.2009).

Broxmeyer does not contest the sufficiency of proof as to the first and third elements: A.W. was 17 when she took Photos 1 and 2; and the cell phone she used to take them was made in South Korea. His challenge is to the sufficiency of the evidence on the second element.

...

The decisive question here is whether the prosecution proved beyond a reasonable doubt that Broxmeyer persuaded, induced, or enticed A.W. to take Photos 1 and 2. The terms "persuade," "induce," and "entice" are not defined in § 2251(a), but they are "words of common usage that have plain and ordinary meanings," *United States v. Gagliardi*, 506 F.3d 140, 147 (2d Cir.2007), ...

These are words of causation; the statute punishes the cause when it brings about the effect. Sequence is therefore critical. The facts of this case require us to belabor the obvious: Broxmeyer could only persuade, induce, or entice A.W. to take Photos 1 and 2 if his persuasion, inducement, or enticement came before she took them. Broxmeyer's counsel failed to present this argument to the district court and conceded at oral argument that he raised it for the first time in his reply brief on appeal. Generally speaking, such arguments are deemed forfeited. However, because "manifest injustice" would result if we were to invoke that rule here, see McCarthy, 406 F.3d at 186-87, we go to the merits of this contention.

All that the record shows on this sequencing point is that A.W. turned 17 in January 2007; she took Photos 1 and 2 when she was 17; and she began a sexual relationship with Broxmeyer in the spring of 2007. There is nothing to tie Broxmeyer to Photos 1 and 2 except that he received them when she transmitted them. His receipt may or may not have violated § 2252—but that statute was not charged in the indictment. As to the production of Photos 1 and 2—which is charged—there is no evidence that Broxmeyer inspired it. For all the record evidence shows, Photos 1 and 2 could have been taken in the early part of 2007, for an audience other than Broxmeyer, or for A.W. alone; or during the preliminary stage of their encounter when she was flirting with him on a basis not yet reciprocated; or later in 2007, while in the course of her sexual relationship with Broxmeyer. Photos 1 and 2 were taken in one of these three periods, but as to when—and whether they were taken before or after he solicited photos of her—one can only guess.

The government adduced no evidence on this point. At trial, the government questioned A.W. at length (she was a government witness, at least nominally); but she was not asked when in the sequence of events she took Photos 1 and 2. The jury was left to speculate or guess.

As to sequence, the government fudged. It adduced evidence that during the sexual relationship: Broxmeyer took explicit photographs of the couple having sex; he challenged A.W. to take naked pictures of other field hockey players; A.W. and Broxmeyer took sexually explicit pictures of themselves and sent them to one another while sexting; Broxmeyer told A.W. that he thought the naked pictures A.W. sent of herself were "nice" and "hot"; and Broxmeyer made A.W. feel as though she "did something right" by sending him naked pictures (either of her or other girls; that is unclear). The government also relies heavily on A.W.'s testimony that there were approximately 15 pictures "taken during the entire time that [she] and Todd Broxmeyer engaged in any kind of sexual act." Gov't App. at 53. But none of this evidence is specific to Photos 1 and 2. Some of the evidence reflects encouragement or incitement by Broxmeyer that was presumably proscribed by § 2251(a); but there is no evidence that Photos 1 and 2 were among those taken at his behest.

...

To the extent the district court concluded that the jury could infer that A.W. took Photos 1 and 2 at Broxmeyer's prodding, no such inference was available: The government presented no evidence bearing on when Photos 1 and 2 were taken. In a footnote to its decision and order denying Broxmeyer's post-verdict motion, the district court observed that "[t]here was testimony at trial that [Broxmeyer] took photographs while engaging in sexual acts with A.W." Def.'s App. at 147. This is true, but irrelevant. Neither Photo 1 nor Photo 2 showed Broxmeyer at all. Presumably there is a reason the government did not premise the § 2251(a) counts on the photographs that Broxmeyer took of him and A.W. having sex; but for present purposes, all that matters is that it did not do so. Whether Broxmeyer took photographs of A.W. having sex (or, indeed, took sexually explicit photographs of other under-18 girls) has no bearing on the sole decisive issue of whether he persuaded, induced, or enticed A.W. to produce Photos 1 and 2. The district court also cited evidence that Broxmeyer persuaded, induced, or enticed A.W. "to send sexually explicit pictures of herself to him." Def.'s App. at 147 (emphasis added). As we have explained, however, § 2251(a) applies only to the production of child pornography. Distribution is proscribed by § 2252, which was not charged. Accordingly, a § 2251(a) conviction cannot be premised on the fact that Broxmeyer persuaded, induced, or enticed A.W. to send him her pornographic self-portraits.

For these reasons, we hold that the government adduced insufficient evidence on which to sustain a conviction under 18 U.S.C. § 2251(a); accordingly, we reverse the convictions on Counts One and Two. In light of this holding, Broxmeyer's as-applied commerce clause challenge to § 2251(a) has no further bearing on the outcome of this case.

Questions

1. In the matter of child pornography, what Acts or laws were charged?
2. Explain what the defendant actually did in this case that relates to these laws.
3. What did the Court hold regarding the counts relating to child pornography?
4. What is your opinion of this holding?

(d) Admitting minor to show.—It shall be unlawful for any person knowingly to exhibit for monetary consideration to a minor or knowingly to sell to a minor an admission ticket or pass or knowingly to admit a minor for a monetary consideration to premises whereon there is exhibited, a motion picture show or other presentation or performance, which, in whole or in part, depicts nudity, sexual conduct, or sadomasochistic abuse and which is harmful to minors, except that the foregoing shall not apply to any minor accompanied by his parent.[53]

The Value and Quality of the Expression

Whether something can be declared obscene depends upon a host of variables according to case law from the nation's highest court. The 1973 decision, *Miller v. California*,[54] has become the cornerstone for the measure of what is obscene. Here, the Court addressed a series of qualitative concerns about these expressive forms that lack merit in a reasonable context when:

(a) whether the average person, applying contemporary community standards, would find that the work, taken as a whole, appeals to the prurient interest;

(b) whether the work depicts or describes, in a patently offensive way, sexual conduct specifically defined by the applicable state law; and

(c) whether the work, taken as a whole, lacks serious literary, artistic, political, or scientific value.[55]

The key provision relative to quality is at part c, which scans the horizon for some literary, political, scientific, or artistic merit in the presentation. At first glance, this qualification seems fair enough. On closer inspection, the standard suffers from some nebulousness since twenty-first

STORY 9.5

ROBERT MAPPLETHORPE

Robert Mapplethorpe was an American photographer whose critically acclaimed work was known to sometimes display pornographic content. Other works included photos of flowers and nudes as well as portraits of celebrities. Born in Queens, New York, and educated at the Pratt Institute of Art, he studied painting, drawing, sculpture, and photography. He had his first one-man show in 1976. In 1977, he exhibited pictures of homosexual men in sexual acts or with sadomasochistic paraphernalia. Despite their erotic or pornographic subject matter, Mapplethorpe's work was critically acclaimed. Mapplethorpe had exhibitions at the Corcoran Gallery, Washington, D.C. (1978), the Musée National d'Art Moderne in Paris (1983), and the Whitney Museum in New York (1988). A planned exhibit at the Corcoran was cancelled because the content was thought to be pornographic and displaying it jeopardized the gallery's federal funding. When his works were shown in Cincinnati, the director of the Contemporary Arts Center was arrested on obscenity charges. Mapplethorpe died from AIDS in 1986.

"Mapplethorpe, Robert," Microsoft® Encarta® Online Encyclopedia 2001
http://encarta.msn.com © 1997–2001 Microsoft Corporation. All rights reserved.

century artistic forms often achieve this ignoble status. Television has long been critiqued as a cultural wasteland. A review of listings corroborates the deprivation so obvious in art, science, and politics. Does this mean it is obscene? No, because the standard insists on a qualitative finding on additional bases. Does the expression have any meaningful purpose beyond titillation and solely appealing to prurient purposes? Does the depiction and portrayal appeal to baser instincts, to sexual gratuity without purpose, which conjures up sexual stimuli in a depraved way? Does the form of expression present itself in a patently offensive way that offends the ordinary sensibilities of the average citizen? Case law looks to the level of offensiveness the expression exhibits to determine quality. Does the depiction of a child in sexually provocative settings offend the average person or should the pictorial display be more aptly labeled artistic freedom? Or is it a continuing slide toward deviant tolerance, or a "culture desensitized to pedophilia."[56]

The judgment of quality rests in how the average person reacts to artistic expression, not the extreme zealot who takes offense at materials that may be disagreeable yet acceptable in a pluralistic sense. And, the Miller decision seems to comprehend this lack of uniformity. The Miller standard has been attacked for its lack of precision in the matter of content and definition and for its clear abandonment of any attempt to nationalize the standard for obscenity. Supporters of the decision appreciate the wisdom of a Court unwilling to regulate for each community from a central vantage point and applaud the Court's willingness to allow differing perspectives to flourish state-by-state and community-by-community. "In Miller, the Court did not establish a comprehensive and definite standard by which to determine what expression is obscene and thus subject to regulation. Given the difficulty defining obscenity, the Court could have decided that no person or institution can determine what is improper, and thus set down no guidelines, thereby permitting any type of consensual sexual expression. Instead, the Court, in trying to define obscenity, essentially set out general guidelines that permit local institutions to determine

---

CASE 9.5

FLYNT V. OHIO

407 N.E 2d 15 (Ohio 1980).

Visit your local law library or go online. Retrieve the above case and answer the following questions.

Questions

1. What type of content was determined obscene by the local prosecutor's office?
2. What is your opinion of the content? Would you criminalize?
3. Do the citizens of Cincinnati have the right to ban these types of publications?

---

what is proper sexual expression."[57] In *Pope v. Illinois*,[58] the Supreme Court continued its community bases evaluation of value and quality, by declaring,

> [T]he proper inquiry is not whether an ordinary member of any given community would find serious literary, artistic, political, or scientific value in allegedly obscene material, but whether a reasonable person would find such value in the material, taken as a whole.[59]

Community Standard of Obscenity

The variability in obscenity determinations is a direct result of Miller and its progeny.[60] Obscenity cannot be interpreted in any universal way, but looks to individualized judgments rooted in community settings. In other words, obscenity in Missouri will predictably vary from the Times Square, New York City perspective. Some places are more accustomed to sexual explicitness than others. Even despite this general conclusion on relative community toleration for obscenity, does the Internet or virtual world need another test. "Computer technologies allow individuals to create unique communities of people with no geographical boundaries."[61] As a result, some have argued for a distinct test for Internet obscenity and argue that "users of the Internet should comprise the community for a national community standards test."[62] In *Ashcroft v. ACLU*,[63] the United States Supreme Court, when considering the constitutionality of the Child Online Privacy Act (COPA)[64] was overbroad in its particular applications due to the lack of a geographic boundary.[65]

Read the provisions of COPA at: http://epic.org/free_speech/censorship/copa.html

---

The relativity of community views can cause difficulty for the legal interpreter. The mere existence of material in a particular community is not prima facie evidence of community consensus or agreement.[66]

The Internet, cyberspace, and the virtual world are global by design, yet house large purveyors of pornography—some of which would be objected to as obscene. In the virtual world, what community standard applies? If it is too difficult to measure, should surveys and opinions polls be utilized as some have suggested?[67] Or might some expert take the stand to precisely define whether a particular expression is indeed compatible with a particular community?[68] Tennessee courts, by way of edification, have upheld the regulation of BBS Adult Swinger services under its existing obscenity laws.[69] That an alternative result may occur in another community setting is highly probable. Nude dancing, explicit sexual performances, lap dance parlors and studios, and the full panoply of sexual entertainment find a welcome mat in some places and barred doors in others. Morality in Media, a nonprofit lobby group that often files *amicus curiae* briefs in obscenity appeals, adopts the conservative view when reading the Miller community standard. It wants the court to honestly appraise the content of sexual exhibition. Can the community find any worth or merit in the depiction from the qualitative standards enunciated by court precedent. Where is the art? What science is involved? What cultural contribution can be discovered in the expression? In doing so, Morality in Media links the expression to the standards promulgated.

First Amendment values should not be invoked in the instant case by merely linking the words "dancing" and "nude." It is the nudity that customers pay pruriently to watch, not the dancing. If the "erotic" dance is the assumed expressive element, as the Court below presumed, then pasties and a G-string will not interfere with the dance, though it could interfere with the profits of those who pander the nudity. As this Court has so often concluded, prurience is not a serious value and, in fact, pandering to prurience is the evidentiary proof that the claimed value is not serious.[70] This Court recognized that he who pruriently looks at pornography, like he who watches strippers bare their body parts on stage, "looks for titillation, not for saving intellectual content."[71]

Liberal constitutionalists cringe at the regulation of speech and tend to infer that the First Amendment condemns any restriction.[72] However, our constitutional legacy holds that speech is not an unlimited right and carries with it responsibilities at the individual and collective levels. Artistic speech cannot be protected at the same level as political discourse. Nor is it sensible to argue that this nation's Founders ever envisioned the level of decadency in speech witnessed in contemporary settings. Sexual content can make no claim to absolute expression without restriction and it is perfectly appropriate for government to "regulate the content of constitutionally protected speech in order to promote a compelling interest if it chooses the least restrictive means to further the articulated interest."[73] The U.S. Attorney General under the Clinton Administration, Janet Reno, posited this very argument to uphold the Communications Decency Act[74] that attempts to regulate Internet distribution of obscene materials to children. A portion of the act is reproduced below:

> Whoever ... (A) uses an interactive computer service to send to a specific person or persons under 18 years of age, or (B) uses any interactive computer service to display in a manner available to a person under 18 years of age, any comment request, suggestion, proposal, image, or other communication that, in context, depicts or describes, in terms patently offensive as measured by contemporary community standards, sexual or excretory activities or organs, regardless of whether the user of such service placed the call or initiated the communication ... shall be fined under Title 18, or imprisoned not more than two years, or both.[75]

Not surprisingly, antagonists to this type of regulation term the enactment as a free speech infringement without justification that will chill speech in the community.

Forgotten by those opposed to the Act is the target of its protection—children. "Our Nation's duty to protect children from harm and equip them for the future, has been recognized as a paramount obligation. With respect to the "dissemination of material which

CASE 9.6

U.S. V. MICHAEL WILLIAMS

553 U. S. 285 (2008)

Section 2252A(a)(3)(B) of Title 18, United States Code, criminalizes, in certain specified circumstances, the pandering or solicitation of child pornography. This case presents the question whether that statute is overbroad under the First Amendment or impermissibly vague under the Due Process Clause of the Fifth Amendment.

...

Section 503 of the Act amended 18 U.S.C. § 2252A to add a new pandering and solicitation provision, relevant portions of which now read as follows:

(a) Any person who
   (3) knowingly ...
      (B) advertises, promotes, presents, distributes, or solicits through the mails, or in interstate or foreign commerce by any means, including by computer, any material or purported material in a manner that reflects the belief, or that is intended to cause another to believe, that the material or purported material is, or contains
        (i) an obscene visual depiction of a minor engaging in sexually explicit conduct; or
        (ii) a visual depiction of an actual minor engaging in sexually explicit conduct, ... shall be punished as provided in subsection (b). § 2252A(a)(3)(B) (2000 ed., Supp. V).

Section 2256(2)(A) defines "sexually explicit conduct" as actual or simulated
   (i) sexual intercourse, including genital-genital, oral-genital, anal-genital, or oral-anal, whether between persons of the same or opposite sex;
   (ii) bestiality;
   (iii) masturbation;
   (iv) sadistic or masochistic abuse; or
   (v) lascivious exhibition of the genitals or pubic area of any person.

Violation of § 2252A(a)(3)(B) incurs a minimum sentence of five years imprisonment and a maximum of 20 years. 18 U.S.C. § 2252A(b)(1).

...

The following facts appear in the opinion of the Eleventh Circuit. On April 26, 2004, respondent Michael Williams, using a sexually explicit screen name, signed into a public Internet chat room. A Secret Service agent had also signed into the chat room under the moniker "Lisa n Miami." The agent noticed that Williams had posted a message that read: "Dad of toddler has 'good' pics of her an [sic] me for swap of your toddler pics, or live cam." The agent struck up a conversation with Williams, leading to an electronic exchange of nonpornographic pictures of children. (The agent's picture was, in fact, a doctored photograph of an adult.) Soon thereafter, Williams messaged that he had photographs of men molesting his four-year-old daughter. Suspicious that "Lisa n Miami" was a law-enforcement agent, before proceeding further Williams demanded that the agent produce additional pictures. When he did not, Williams posted the following public message in the chat room: "HERE ROOM; I CAN PUT UPLINK CUZ IM FOR REAL—SHE CANT." Appended to this declaration was a hyperlink that, when clicked, led to seven pictures of actual children, aged approximately 5 to 15, engaging in sexually explicit conduct and displaying their genitals. The Secret Service then obtained a search warrant for Williams's home, where agents seized two hard drives containing at least 22 images of real children engaged in sexually explicit conduct, some of it sadomasochistic.

Williams was charged with one count of pandering child pornography under § 2252A(a)(3)(B) and one count of possessing child pornography under § 2252A(a)(5)(B). He pleaded guilty to both counts, but reserved the right to challenge the constitutionality of the pandering conviction. The District Court rejected his challenge, and imposed concurrent 60-month prison terms on the two counts and a statutory assessment of $100 for each count, see 18 U.S.C. § 3013. The United States Court of Appeals for the Eleventh Circuit reversed the pandering conviction, holding that the statute was both overbroad and impermissibly vague.

We granted certiorari.

II

A

According to our First Amendment overbreadth doctrine, a statute is facially invalid if it prohibits a substantial amount of protected speech. ... In order to maintain an appropriate balance, we have vigorously enforced the requirement that a statute's overbreadth be substantial, not only in an absolute sense, but also relative to the statute's plainly legitimate sweep. Invalidation for overbreadth is "strong medicine" that is not to be "casually employed."

The first step in overbreadth analysis is to construe the challenged statute; it is impossible to determine whether a statute reaches too far without first knowing what the statute covers. Generally speaking, § 2252A(a)(3)(B) prohibits offers to provide and requests to obtain child pornography. The statute does not require the actual existence of child pornography. ... Rather than targeting the underlying material, this statute bans the collateral speech that introduces such material into the child pornography distribution network. Thus, an Internet user who solicits child pornography from an undercover agent violates the statute, even if the officer possesses no child pornography. Likewise, a person who advertises virtual child pornography as depicting actual children also falls within the reach of the statute.

The statute's definition of the material or purported material that may not be pandered or solicited precisely tracks the material held constitutionally proscribable in Ferber and Miller: obscene material depicting (actual or virtual) children engaged in sexually explicit conduct, and any other material depicting actual children engaged in sexually explicit conduct.

A number of features of the statute are important to our analysis:

First, the statute includes a scienter requirement. The first word of § 2252A(a)(3)—"knowingly"—applies to both of the immediately following subdivisions, both the previously existing § 2252A(a)(3)(A) and the new § 2252A(A)(3)(B) at issue here. We think that the best reading of the term in context is that it applies to every element of the two provisions. This is not a case where grammar or structure enables the challenged provision or some of its parts to be read apart from the "knowingly" requirement. Here "knowingly" introduces the challenged provision itself, making clear that it applies to that provision in its entirety; and there is no grammatical barrier to reading it that way.

Second, the statute's string of operative verbs—"advertises, promotes, presents, distributes, or solicits"—is reasonably read to have a transactional connotation. That is to say, the statute penalizes speech that accompanies or seeks to induce a transfer of child pornography—via reproduction or physical delivery—from one person to another. ...

To be clear, our conclusion that all the words in this list relate to transactions is not to say that they relate to commercial transactions. One could certainly "distribute" child pornography without expecting payment in return. Indeed, in much Internet file sharing of child pornography each participant makes his files available for free to other participants, as Williams did in this case. ... To run afoul of the statute, the speech need only accompany or seek to induce the transfer of child pornography from one person to another.

Third, the phrase "in a manner that reflects the belief" includes both subjective and objective components. "[A] manner that reflects the belief" ... suggests that the defendant must actually have held the subjective "belief" that the material or purported material was child pornography. Thus, a misdescription that leads the listener to believe the defendant is offering child pornography when the defendant in fact does not believe the material is child pornography, does not violate this prong of the statute. (It may, however, violate the "manner ... that is intended to cause another to believe" prong if the misdescription is intentional.) There is also an objective component ... The statement or action must objectively manifest a belief that the material is child pornography; a mere belief, without an accompanying statement or action that would lead a reasonable person to understand that the defendant holds that belief, is insufficient.

Fourth, the other key phrase, "in a manner ... that is intended to cause another to believe," contains only a subjective element: The defendant must "intend" that the listener believe the material to be child pornography, and must select a manner of "advertising, promoting, presenting, distributing, or soliciting" the material that he thinks will engender that belief, whether or not a reasonable person would think the same. ...

Fifth, the definition of "sexually explicit conduct" (the visual depiction of which, engaged in by an actual minor, is covered by the Act's pandering and soliciting prohibition even when it is not obscene). ... "Sexually explicit conduct" connotes actual depiction of the sex act rather than merely the suggestion that it is occurring. And "simulated" sexual intercourse is not sexual intercourse that is merely suggested, but rather sexual intercourse that is explicitly portrayed, even though (through camera tricks or otherwise) it may not actually have occurred. The portrayal must cause a reasonable viewer to believe that the actors actually engaged in that conduct on camera. Critically, unlike in Free Speech Coalition, § 2252A(a)(3)(B)(ii)'s requirement of a "visual depiction of an actual minor" makes clear that, although the sexual intercourse may be simulated, it must involve actual children (unless it is obscene). This change eliminates any possibility that virtual child pornography or sex between youthful-looking adult actors might be covered by the term "simulated sexual intercourse."

B

We now turn to whether the statute, as we have construed it, criminalizes a substantial amount of protected expressive activity.

Offers to engage in illegal transactions are categorically excluded from First Amendment protection. One would think that this principle resolves the present case, since the statute criminalizes only offers to provide or requests to obtain contraband child obscenity and child pornography involving actual children, both of which are proscribed, and the proscription of which is constitutional. The Eleventh Circuit, however, believed that the exclusion of First Amendment protection extended only to commercial offers to provide or receive contraband: "Because [the statute] is not limited to commercial speech, but extends also to noncommercial promotion, presentation, distribution, and solicitation, we must subject the content-based restriction of the PROTECT Act pandering provision to strict scrutiny. ..."

This mistakes the rationale for the categorical exclusion. It is based not on the less privileged First Amendment status of commercial speech, but on the principle that offers to give or receive what it is unlawful to possess have no social value and thus, like obscenity, enjoy no First Amendment protection. Many long established criminal proscriptions, such as laws against conspiracy, incitement, and solicitation, criminalize speech (commercial or not) that is intended to induce or commence illegal activities. Offers to provide or requests to obtain unlawful material, whether as part of a commercial exchange or not, are similarly undeserving of First Amendment protection. It would be an odd constitutional principle that permitted the government to prohibit offers to sell illegal drugs, but not offers to give them away for free.

We replied: "Whatever the merits of this contention may be in other contexts, it is unpersuasive in this case. Discrimination in employment is not only commercial activity, it is illegal commercial activity. ... We have no doubt that a newspaper constitutionally could be forbidden to publish a want ad proposing a sale of narcotics or soliciting prostitutes." The import of this response is that noncommercial proposals to engage in illegal activity have no greater protection than commercial proposals to do so.

To be sure, there remains an important distinction between a proposal to engage in illegal activity and the abstract advocacy of illegality. The Act before us does not prohibit advocacy of child pornography, but only offers to provide or requests to obtain it. There is no doubt that this prohibition falls well within constitutional bounds. The constitutional defect we found in the pandering provision at issue in Free Speech Coalition was that it went beyond pandering to prohibit possession of material that could not otherwise be proscribed.

In sum, we hold that offers to provide or requests to obtain child pornography are categorically excluded from the First Amendment. Since the Eleventh Circuit erroneously concluded otherwise, it applied strict scrutiny to § 2252A(a)(3)(B), lodging three fatal objections. We address these objections because they could be recast as arguments that Congress has gone beyond the categorical exception.

The Eleventh Circuit believed it a constitutional difficulty that no child pornography need exist to trigger the statute. In its view, the fact that the statute could punish a "braggart, exaggerator, or outright liar" rendered it unconstitutional. That seems to us a strange constitutional calculus. Although we have held that the government can ban both fraudulent offers and offers to provide illegal products, the Eleventh Circuit would forbid the government from punishing fraudulent offers to provide illegal products. We see no logic in that position; if anything, such statements are doubly excluded from the First Amendment.

The Eleventh Circuit held that under Brandenburg, the "noncommercial, noninciteful promotion of illegal child pornography" is protected, and § 2252A(a)(3)(B) therefore overreaches by criminalizing the promotion of child pornography. As we have discussed earlier, however, the term "promotes" does not refer to abstract advocacy, such as the statement "I believe that child pornography should be legal" or even "I encourage you to obtain child pornography." It refers to the recommendation of a particular piece of purported child pornography with the intent of initiating a transfer.

The Eleventh Circuit found "particularly objectionable" the fact that the "reflects the belief" prong of the statute could ensnare a person who mistakenly believes that material is child pornography. This objection has two conceptually distinct parts. First, the Eleventh Circuit thought that it would be unconstitutional to punish someone for mistakenly distributing virtual child pornography as real child pornography. We disagree. Offers to deal in illegal products or otherwise engage in illegal activity do not acquire First Amendment protection when the offeror is mistaken about the factual predicate of his offer. The pandering and solicitation made unlawful by the Act are sorts of inchoate crimes—acts looking toward the commission of another crime, the delivery of child pornography. As with other inchoate crimes—attempt and conspiracy, for example—impossibility of completing the crime because the facts were not as the defendant believed is not a defense. "All courts are in agreement that what is usually referred to as 'factual impossibility' is no defense to a charge of attempt."

Under this heading the Eleventh Circuit also thought that the statute could apply to someone who subjectively believes that an innocuous picture of a child is "lascivious." That is not so. The defendant must believe that the picture contains certain material, and that material in fact (and not merely in his estimation) must meet the statutory definition. Where the material at issue is a harmless picture of a child in a bathtub and the defendant, knowing that material, erroneously believes that it constitutes a "lascivious exhibition of the genitals," the statute has no application.

Williams and amici raise other objections, which demonstrate nothing so forcefully as the tendency of our overbreadth doctrine to summon forth an endless stream of fanciful hypotheticals. Williams argues, for example, that a person who offers nonpornographic photographs of young girls to a pedophile could be punished under the statute if the pedophile secretly expects that the pictures will contain child pornography.

That hypothetical does not implicate the statute because the offeror does not hold the belief or intend the recipient to believe that the material is child pornography.

...

Finally, the dissent accuses us of silently overruling our prior decisions in Ferber and Free Speech Coalition. According to the dissent, Congress has made an end run around the First Amendment's protection of virtual child pornography by prohibiting proposals to transact in such images rather than prohibiting the images themselves. But, an offer to provide or request to receive virtual child pornography is not prohibited by the statute. A crime is committed only when the speaker believes or intends the listener to believe that the subject of the proposed transaction depicts real children. It is simply not true that this means "a protected category of expression [will] inevitably be suppressed,". Simulated child pornography will be as available as ever, so long as it is offered and sought as such, and not as real child pornography. The dissent would require an exception from the statute's prohibition when, unbeknownst to one or both of the parties to the proposal, the completed transaction would not have been unlawful because it is (we have said) protected by the First Amendment. We fail to see what First Amendment interest would be served by drawing a distinction between two defendants who attempt to acquire contraband, one of whom happens to be mistaken about the contraband nature of what he would acquire. Is Congress prohibited from punishing those who attempt to acquire what they believe to be national security documents, but which are actually fakes? To ask is to answer. There is no First Amendment exception from the general principle of criminal law that a person attempting to commit a crime need not be exonerated because he has a mistaken view of the facts.

III

As an alternative ground for facial invalidation, the Eleventh Circuit held that § 2252A(a)(3)(B) is void for vagueness. Vagueness doctrine is an outgrowth not of the First Amendment, but of the Due Process Clause of the Fifth Amendment. A conviction fails to comport with due process if the statute under which it is obtained fails to provide a person of ordinary intelligence fair notice of what is prohibited, or is so standardless that it authorizes or encourages seriously discriminatory enforcement. Although ordinarily "[a] plaintiff who engages in some conduct that is clearly proscribed cannot complain of the vagueness of the law as applied to the conduct of others," we have relaxed that requirement in the First Amendment context, permitting plaintiffs to argue that a statute is overbroad because it is unclear whether it regulates a substantial amount of protected speech.

The Eleventh Circuit believed that the phrases "'in a manner that reflects the belief'" and "'in a manner ... that is intended to cause another to believe'" are "so vague and standardless as to what may not be said that the public is left with no objective measure to which behavior can be conformed." The court gave two examples. First, an email claiming to contain photograph attachments and including a message that says " little Janie in the bath—hubba, hubba!'" According to the Eleventh Circuit, given that the statute does not require the actual existence of illegal material, the Government would have "virtually unbounded discretion" to deem such a statement in violation of the "'reflects the belief'" prong. The court's second example was an e-mail entitled "'Good pics of kids in bed'" with a photograph attachment of toddlers in pajamas asleep in their beds. The court described three hypothetical senders: a proud grandparent, a "chronic forwarder of cute photos with racy tongue-in-cheek subject lines," and a child molester who seeks to trade the photographs for more graphic material. According to the Eleventh Circuit, because the "manner" in which the photographs are sent is the same in each case, and because the identity of the sender and the content of the photographs are irrelevant under the statute, all three senders could arguably be prosecuted for pandering.

We think that neither of these hypotheticals, without further facts, would enable a reasonable juror to find, beyond a reasonable doubt, that the speaker believed and spoke in a manner that reflected the belief, or spoke in a manner intended to cause another to believe, that the pictures displayed actual children engaged in "sexually explicit conduct" as defined in the Act. The prosecutions would be thrown out at the threshold.

But the Eleventh Circuit's error is more fundamental than merely its selection of unproblematic hypotheticals. Its basic mistake lies in the belief that the mere fact that close cases can be envisioned renders a statute vague. That is not so. Close cases can be imagined under virtually any statute. The problem that poses is addressed, not by the doctrine of vagueness, but by the requirement of proof beyond a reasonable doubt.

What renders a statute vague is not the possibility that it will sometimes be difficult to determine whether the incriminating fact it establishes has been proved; but rather the indeterminacy of precisely what that fact is. ...

There is no such indeterminacy here. The statute requires that the defendant hold, and make a statement that reflects, the belief that the material is child pornography; or that he communicate in a manner intended to cause another so to believe. Those are clear questions of fact. ... Thus, the Eleventh Circuit's contention that § 2252A(a)(3)(B) gives law enforcement officials "virtually unfettered discretion" has no merit. No more here than in the case of laws against fraud, conspiracy, or solicitation.

...

Child pornography harms and debases the most defenseless of our citizens. Both the State and Federal Governments have sought to suppress it for many years, only to find it proliferating through the new medium of the Internet. This Court held unconstitutional Congress's previous attempt to meet this new threat, and Congress responded with a carefully crafted attempt to eliminate the First Amendment problems we identified. As far as the provision at issue in this case is concerned, that effort was successful.

The judgment of the Eleventh Circuit is reversed.

Questions

1. The majority seems to say there is a long line of cases on obscenity determinations. Is this true?
2. Why was this action held constitutional?
3. Is it fair to say that the Supreme Court has actually made some aspects of child pornography constitutionally protected speech?
4. Whose mind should be measured when determining who wanted child pornography?

CASE 9.7

U.S. V. KNOX

977 F.2d 815 (3rd Cir. 1992).

We now turn to the merits of the case on remand. The Protection of Children Against Sexual Exploitation Act of 1977, as subsequently amended, criminalizes knowingly receiving through the mail visual depictions of a minor engaged in sexually explicit conduct and knowingly possessing three or more videotapes which contain a visual depiction of a minor engaging in sexually explicit conduct. 18 U.S.C. § 2252(a)(2), (4). "Sexually explicit conduct" for purposes of both of these offenses is defined to include the "lascivious exhibition of the genitals or pubic area." Id. § 2256(2)(E). In our prior opinion, we held that the statute contains no nudity requirement because the above quoted statutory phrase refers to a "lascivious exhibition," not a nude or naked exhibition. *U.S. v. Knox*, 977 F.2d 815, 820 (3rd Cir. 1992). Our review of the relevant legislative history revealed that Knox had not met his burden of demonstrating that Congress clearly intended the statute only to proscribe nude or partially nude displays of the genitals or pubic area. *US. v. Knox*, 977 F.2d 815, 820-21 (3rd Cir. 1992). Because the meaning of the statutory phrase "lascivious exhibition" under 18 U.S.C. § 2256(2)(E) poses a pure question of law, our review is plenary. *United States v. Brown*, 862 F.2d 1033, 1036 (3d Cir. 1988).

Defendant Knox continues to assert that the genitals or pubic area must be unclad or nude, and fully exposed to the camera, before an exhibition may occur. Several amici parties, including the amici Members of Congress, support our prior statutory interpretation that no nudity is required. The government contends that the pictorial representation of the genitals or pubic area, covered only by underwear, a bikini bathing suit, a leotard, or other abbreviated attire, constitutes a lascivious exhibition if (1) those body parts are at least somewhat visible in the videotapes, and (2) the minors were engaged in conduct that can be judged "lascivious." ...

Thus, we conclude that a "lascivious exhibition of the genitals or pubic area" of a minor necessarily requires only that the material depict some "sexually explicit conduct" by the minor subject, which appeals to the lascivious interest of the intended audience. Applying this standard in the present case, it is readily apparent that the tapes in evidence violate the statute. In several sequences, the minor subjects, clad only in very tight leotards, panties, or bathing suits, were shown specifically spreading or extending their legs to make their genital and pubic region entirely visible to the viewer. In some of these poses, the child subject was shown dancing or gyrating in a fashion indicative of adult sexual relations. Nearly all of these scenes were shot in an outdoor playground or park setting where children are normally found. Although none of these factors is alone dispositive, the totality of these factors lead us to conclude that the minor subjects were engaged in conduct—namely, the exhibition of their genitals or pubic area—which would appeal to the lascivious interest of an audience of pedophiles.

Questions

1. Define the term lascivious.
2. Can lascivious materials be obscene?
3. What type of conduct does the Court construe as qualifying?
4. Can you think of any other legitimate, artistic, or scientific purpose for these materials?
5. To whom are these materials directed?
6. What punishment is appropriate for those who distribute these types of materials?

shows children engaged in sexual conduct, regardless of whether such material is obscene"... "the prevention of sexual exploitation and abuse of children constitutes a government objective of surpassing importance."[76] Of course, here the indecent images, messages and communication have not necessarily been produced with the involvement of children. The threat to children from such indecent materials lies, not in its making, but in its immediacy and its ubiquity."[77]

The sense of communal acceptance and outrage centers the debate on whether materials can be properly labeled obscene or not. Is a crucifix photographed in a Teflon container filled with human urine so offensive that the justice system should intervene?[78] What about human excrement cast all over images of Mary, the Christian mother of Jesus Christ? Obscenity patently offends the average and very reasonable person's sensibilities and makes no contribution to the greater glory of art or science. What about an art display that has shrunken human heads, derived from corpses, the origin unknown, or a human head adorned with earrings of human fetuses at the ¾ stage of gestation and growth?[79] Is this obscene? Critics of sexual exposition perceive these depictions as an affront to women, human objectification that socializes and entrenches male dominance and promotes sexual hostility and crimes against women. Law Professor Catherine A. MacKinnon's *Only Words*, advocates this line of reasoning:

> Words and images are how people are placed in hierarchies, how social stratification is made to seem inevitable and right, how feelings of inferiority and superiority are engendered, and how indifference to violence against those on the bottom is rationalized and normalized.[80]

Oddly enough, MacKinnon's feminist approach tends to be at the liberal frontier rather than the usual conservative call for censorship and governmental control. So passionate are her arguments concerning the regulation of obscenity that she, like her unchecked and unrestrained anticensorship and free speech counterparts, seems to leave little room for contrary viewpoint.

DRIVING UNDER THE INFLUENCE/DRIVING WHILE INTOXICATED

ELEMENTS

- Operation (physical control) of a qualified vehicle
- With a blood alcohol as defined by statute (.08–.010%)

If the criminal law has been revolutionized in any one area over the past few decades, it has been in the area of alcohol detection during vehicular operation. From a social perspective, a dramatic shift has taken place, a change in opinion that can only be described as remarkable. Less than 30 years ago, the use of alcohol while driving a car was not part of the criminal imagination. Ingesting beer, while cruising on the open road, conjured up images of freedom and entertainment rather than grave criminality. For that matter, there has been an extraordinary evolution in our way of thinking about alcohol in general. As with smoking, the nation now understands the various impacts alcoholic beverages have on life, and in a completely different manner than a generation or two ago. Alcohol is not just fun and games nor is driving under the influence. The mix of alcohol and automobiles is a volatile one that causes incredible carnage on the highways and byways and is directly responsible for loss of life and property damage.

A similar carnage and human toll could be described when dealing with those operating vehicles under the influence of drugs. While most states do not treat the drug offender in the same way as the alcohol offender, that reality is changing fast.[81] Presently, there are 16 states that have Driving Under the Influence of drug laws.[82] (See Figure 9.6[83] for some facts relating to the monetary cost of driving under the influence.)

What has occurred is the slow but sure criminalization of conduct once considered harmless and social. Historically, driving under the influence was tolerated and handled informally or, if prosecuted, was given the proverbial "slap on the wrist." Most cases were unreported and handled by officers outside the systematic processes in place today. Others were diverted by and through other means, such as infraction fines, community service, or licensure penalties. The problem, while real, was not fundamentally a criminal one, but better termed a social dilemma or behavioral error. DUI was not even codified as a crime and its perpetrators were far more likely to be given a ride home by the empathetic police officer rather than receive a charge sheet at arraignment. The scale and gravity of this social problem turned crime tells a powerful story of how perceptions and public opinion alter the criminal law process. The law, for all its shortcomings, displays a fairly dynamic quality in responding to the clamors for change. Strangely enough, DUI cases sometimes see harsher sentences than other felonies with more dreadful victimization.

Operating a motor vehicle under the influence of alcohol is worthy of our condemnation, but to what degree? The seriousness of the offense, the malice and the depraved indifference in the acts appear less compelling than a host of other felonious conduct, yet our attention seems unceasingly riveted on the assorted evil effects the conduct delivers. Special interest groups, like MADD, GLAD, and SADD have demonized the act to such a degree that penalties and justice responses seems disproportionate. Task forces are established, and avant garde approaches to search and seizure in the form of checkpoints and roadblocks are established despite constitutional infirmities.[84] Media campaigns run endlessly, mandatory sentencing schemes are implemented, special police units whose singular target is the driver under the influence are erected, all seem to withstand criticism and legal challenge (Figure 9.7).

So popular are efforts to regulate and curtail driving under the influence that people accept these exceptional measures to affect the underlying and truly honorable goal of minimizing the harm caused by these behaviors.

Is the justice system better served when it expends sizeable dollar sums to eradicate this problem? Can the expenditures be justified in light of how victims may be shortchanged on resources? When compared to other criminal offenses, does this infraction really deserve the aggressive allotment of personnel and expenditure? Are these programs effective in treating the social problems the law seeks to cure? In the final analysis, should our jails be filled up with

- Alcohol-related crashes cost society $45 billion, yet this conservative estimate does not include pain, suffering, and lost quality of life. These indirect costs raise the alcohol-related crash figure to a staggering $116 billion in 1993.
- Alcohol-related fatal injuries accounted for 45 percent of all fatal injury costs: 26 percent of the nonfatal injury costs were alcohol-related.
- Medical costs for 1993 traffic crash injuries were approximately $22 billion and the alcohol-related portion is estimated to have been $7 billion.
- The cost for each injured survivor of an alcohol-related crash averages $67,000, including $6,000 in healthcare costs and $13,000 in lost productivity.
- Crashes involving BAC positive drivers under 21 cost society $21 billion, including $1.2 billion in medical spending. 18 percent of their crash costs result from alcohol-involved crashes.
- Over 25 percent of the first-year medical costs for persons hospitalized as a result of a crash are paid by tax dollars, about two-thirds through Medicaid and one-third through Medicare.
- Alcohol-related crashes cost society $.95 per drink or $1.90 per ounce of alcohol consumed. This figure includes drinks consumed at home.
- Crash costs are $5.82 per mile driven while drunk. This includes $2.87 to people other than the drunk driver. By comparison, crash costs are $.11 per mile driven while sober.
- In 1993, medical care for alcohol-related injury and illness cost at least $28.5 billion. That's $.48 per ounce of alcohol consumed.
- Alcohol-related crashes account for 12 percent of auto insurance payments in 1993, a decline from 26 percent in 1990.
- The consequences of excessive drinking extend beyond crashes. Overall, excessive drinking costs people, other than the drinkers, $135 billion annually. Of this alcohol-attributable amount, $51 billion is due to crashes, $60 billion is due to other violence, and the remainder to chronic illness and other alcohol-abuse problems.
- A drunk driving crash costs innocent victims $26,000. Comparable crime costs per victim: assault, $19,000; robbery, $13,000; motor vehicle theft, $4,000. Yet, the drunk driving crash is only one of the crimes that is often not a felony for the first offense.

Figure 9.6   Costs of alcohol-related crashes.

two-time offenders who could only be said to have had the potential to harm another when in actuality no party was harmed at all?

While the seriousness of the DUI/DWI is undeniable, a pause in the action may be worth posing. Take a breath and think the dilemma through. The criminal law model serves the interest of the common good and does so by the allocation of resources for specific conducts that if left unchecked cause incredible harm for both individuals and the community. Comparatively, is DUI the great Satan when considered side-by-side with rape and sexual abuse of children, murder and arson, spousal abuse and pedophilia? Does it make good public policy for so much time, energy, and resources to be directed in this corner of the world? What was once adjudged noncriminal conduct that so often saw the informal structures of diversion in the justice model at work, has now been demonized to the point of insensibility. Is this our gravest criminality? At

Figure 9.7   DUI checkpoint. (Photo courtesy of B. Kohlhepp, Ross Township Police Department.)

least, could we not consider another approach? In the end, our outrage and umbrage reaches its mighty peak when the drunken driver kills or harms another. This is as it should be. Forgetting about the other criminal remedies, negligent homicide, assault, reckless endangerment, or others, only serves to narrow our range of options or to obsessively and slavishly dwell on the few contained in the DUI/DWI construct. This approach may be the most inane of all.

Proof of DUI/DWI

Aside from the political debates about the severity and efficacy of DUI/DWI statutes, the meaning and content of the respective code provisions is pretty straightforward. State legislatures set out the general parameters of what it means to operate a motor vehicle and attach blood alcohol or repository measure of alcohol vapor as indicators of intoxication. This common understanding often neglects that no measure of alcohol whether by blood, urine, or respiratory value, is really mandatory. Police officers are still entitled to make their cases using a host of other means including:

- Observation
- Behavior of the defendant including speech, emotional state, and cognitive qualities
- Agility and physical testing
- Memory tests
- Patterns of driving
- Evidence of alcohol
- Breath, vomitus, and other signs of elimination

Hence, mechanical instruments that measure vapor, the intoxilyzer and intoximeter, have unfortunately become the chief means to proof or disproof in a DUI case (Figure 9.8). In fact, many jurisdictions consider the requisite reading from the machine as prima facie evidence of the offense. In essence, the newer statutes impose "strict liability upon anyone whose blood

Figure 9.8   DUI intoxication test. (Photo courtesy of B. Kohlhepp, Ross Township Police Department.)

alcohol level is determined to be over" a certain percentage.[85] Older methods, such as those listed above, are still available, but usually as corroborative evidence forms. No one can be forced to submit to these extraction methods, though legislatures have devised punishment mechanisms for those who do not cooperate, in the form of sanctions and lost driving and license privileges.[86] The predictable Fifth Amendment challenges to the evidence, based on self-incrimination principles, usually fail because the evidence is primarily of the nontestimonial variety to which the self-incrimination protection does not extend. When DUI charges rest side-by–side other felony conduct, defendants will try to merge the constitutional protections of the other felony with the DUI claim. It rarely works because Courts hold firm and fast to the public safety policy rationale for the limitation of these questionable rights.[87]

More intrusive and expensive extraction methods that measure alcohol in the urine and blood also have fallen in disfavor when compared to the machines like the breathalyzer. The machines that measure vapor content have been specifically incorporated into the new statutory models. These devices easily and very economically provide accurate and fast readings on content that either put the defendant in or out of the statute's coverage. A typical example of the DUI/DWI provision might be:

(a) It is unlawful for any person to drive or to be in physical control of any automobile or other motor driven vehicle on any of the public roads and highways of the state, or on any streets or alleys, or while on the premises of any shopping center, trailer park or any apartment house complex, or any other premises that is generally frequented by the public at large, while:

(1) Under the influence of any intoxicant, marijuana, controlled substance, drug, substance affecting the central nervous system or combination thereof that impairs the driver's ability to safely operate a motor vehicle by depriving the driver of the clearness of mind and control of himself which he would otherwise possess; or

---

CASE 9.8

FELGATE V. ARKANSAS
974 S.W.2d 479 (Ark. App. 1998).

Appellant John Felgate was convicted in a bench trial of DWI and failing to submit to a Breathalyzer test. As a result of his convictions, he was fined $1,000.00, and his driver's license was suspended for six months. Mr. Felgate now appeals from his DWI conviction, arguing that there was insufficient evidence to support the verdict.

The test for determining the sufficiency of the evidence is whether the verdict is supported by substantial evidence, direct or circumstantial. *Thomas v. State*, 312 Ark. 158, 847 S.W.2d 695 (1993). Substantial evidence is evidence forceful enough to compel a conclusion one way or the other beyond suspicion or conjecture. *Lukach v. State*, 310 Ark. 119, 835 S.W.2d 852 (1992). In determining the sufficiency of the evidence, we review the proof in the light most favorable to the appellee, considering only that evidence which tends to support the verdict. *Brown v. State*, 309 Ark. 503, 832 S.W.2d 477 (1992).

Officer Robert Stanley Jones testified first on behalf of the State. He stated that, at about 2:00 a.m. on November 22, 1996, he met Mr. Felgate's Jeep on an Arkadelphia street and noticed that a headlight was out. Officer Jones turned around, pursued the Jeep, and after following it for a short while he decided to make a stop. Prior to the stop, Officer Jones did not observe erratic driving, although he did notice that the Jeep crossed the center line a couple of times.

When the stop was made, Officer Jones informed Mr. Felgate that one of his headlights was not working, at which time Mr. Felgate raised the hood of his Jeep and attempted to correct the problem by adjusting some loose wiring. Officer Jones noticed that Mr. Felgate smelled of alcohol and was unsteady on his feet, but did not ask him if he had been drinking. Shortly thereafter, Officer Richie Smith arrived at the scene, and Officer Jones noticed that, while he was questioning Mr. Felgate's girlfriend, Officer Smith was subjecting Mr. Felgate to field sobriety tests. Based on Officer Smith's observations, Mr. Felgate was placed under arrest and transported to the police station.

Officer Smith testified that, while at the scene of the arrest, he asked Mr. Felgate if he had been drinking, and Mr. Felgate replied that he had had one mixed drink. According to Officer Smith, he administered three sobriety tests before making the decision to arrest Mr. Felgate on suspicion of DWI. While at the police station, Officer Smith advised Mr. Felgate of his rights regarding the administration of a Breathalyzer test, and Mr. Felgate refused to take the test after being asked to do so.

Kim Bryan, Mr. Felgate's girlfriend, testified that she was riding in the passenger's seat of Mr. Felgate's Jeep during this incident. According to her testimony, she arrived at his fraternity house at about midnight, and the couple proceeded to eat at the Waffle House sometime thereafter. She acknowledged that she had been drinking beer, but maintained that she was unaware that Mr. Felgate had been drinking at all.

Mr. Felgate's roommate at the fraternity house also testified on Mr. Felgate's behalf. He stated that he saw Mr. Felgate mix one screwdriver on the night in question, and that he was certain that this was the only drink that Mr. Felgate could have consumed while he was at the fraternity house before driving to the Waffle House. Mr. Felgate testified on his own behalf, and he also indicated that he consumed just one drink on the night of his arrest. He estimated that the drink probably contained less than two ounces of vodka, and explained that he refused to take the Breathalyzer test because it was his understanding that "if you drink one drink, ... you are going to fail it anyway."

For reversal, Mr. Felgate contends that his DWI conviction was not supported by substantial evidence. Pursuant to Ark. Code Ann. § 5-65-103(a) (Repl. 1997), it is unlawful for any person who is intoxicated to operate a motor vehicle. "Intoxicated" is defined by Ark. Code Ann. § 5-65-102(1) (Repl. 1997), which provides:

> (1) "Intoxicated" means influenced or affected by the ingestion of alcohol, a controlled substance, any intoxicant, or any combination thereof, to such a degree that the driver's reactions, motor skills, and judgment are substantially altered and the driver, therefore, constitutes a clear and substantial danger of physical injury or death to himself and other motorists or pedestrians[.]

Mr. Felgate submits that, in the case at bar, there was no evidence produced to demonstrate that his actual driving skills were impaired or that his driving created a substantial danger to himself or others.

In support of his argument, Mr. Felgate notes that Officer Jones admitted that, prior to the stop, nothing led him to believe that the driver of the Jeep posed a danger to others on the highway. Moreover, although Officer Jones executed the stop of Mr. Felgate's vehicle, he did not ask whether Mr. Felgate had been drinking and did not make the decision to have him arrested. Officer Jones's testimony regarding Mr. Felgate's driving was corroborated by Mr. Felgate's girlfriend, who testified that he was not driving erratically before the stop, and that he appeared to be normal.

Mr. Felgate also argues that Officer Smith's testimony was inconclusive because, although he stated that the three sobriety tests led him to believe that Mr. Felgate was intoxicated, he could not remember specifics about the tests. Officer Smith's explanation for failing to give more specific testimony was that the incident occurred a long time ago and that he had since thrown away his field notes.

Finally, Mr. Felgate contends that the trial court erred in stating that his failure to submit to the Breathalyzer test had a "great impact" on how it decided the case. Mr. Felgate points out that, at the time of his arrest, he was only twenty years old and could have been successfully prosecuted under Ark. Code Ann. § 5-65-303 (Repl. 1997) if he had registered only .02% on a Breathalyzer test. He submits that one drink might have resulted in such a reading, and therefore argues that his refusal to take the test offered little to prove that he had committed DWI, the offense with which he was charged. Mr. Felgate further notes that, during the time that he was arrested and refused the Breathalyzer test, there was no evidence that he exhibited glassy eyes, slurred speech, or staggering.

We find that there was substantial evidence to support Mr. Felgate's DWI conviction. At the scene of the arrest, both police officers smelled alcohol on Mr. Felgate's breath, and Mr. Felgate admitted that he had consumed alcohol on the evening at issue. Although Officer Smith could not recall the specifics regarding the sobriety tests, he indicated that he administered the horizontal-gaze-nystagmus test, ABC's test, and finger-to-nose test, and that Mr. Felgate failed all three. Moreover, it was Officer Smith's recollection that the vehicle smelled of alcohol, and that it appeared that a drink had been spilled on the interior and partially disposed of on the ground outside of the Jeep. Finally, there was evidence that Mr. Felgate crossed the center line prior to the stop and was unsteady on his feet after being stopped by Officer Jones.

Mr. Felgate argues that the trial court erred in placing great weight on his refusal to submit to a Breathalyzer test during its deliberation of his guilt, because that fact does not prove any element of the offense of DWI. Furthermore, he argues that his reluctance to be tested was because he could have been found guilty of violating Ark. Code Ann. § 5-65-303 (DUI) if the test reflected a blood-alcohol level of as much as .02%. First, we note that refusal to be tested is admissible evidence on the issue of intoxication because it may indicate the defendant's fear of the results of the test and consciousness of guilt. *Medlock v. State*, 332 Ark. 106, 964 S.W.2d 196 (1998); *Spicer v. State*, 32 Ark. App. 209, 799 S.W.2d 562 (1990). As to Mr. Felgate's argument that he refused the Breathalyzer test because of his concern about DUI exposure rather than DWI, we recognize that, because Mr. Felgate was 20 years of age at the time, it is conceivable that part of his motive for refusing the test was to avoid any positive blood-alcohol reading at all. However, his abstract does not reflect that he made this argument before the trial court. Therefore, we cannot now consider the argument as it is being raised for the first time on appeal. *Harris v. State*, 320 Ark. 677, 899 S.W.2d 459 (1995). Notwithstanding his failure to make this argument before the trial court, we note that in *Hill v. State*, 366 So. 2d 318 (Ala. 1989), which was cited with approval in *Medlock v. State*, supra, and *Spicer v. State*, supra, the Alabama Supreme Court addressed an analogous contention as follows:

Any circumstance tending to show the refusal was conditioned upon factors other than consciousness of guilt may properly be considered by the jury in determining the weight to attach to the refusal. Therefore, the evidence of Hill's refusal to submit to a chemical test for intoxication was relevant and properly admitted. Whether his refusal was due to the desire for consultation with his physician or attorney or to the fear of bodily harm, rather than consciousness of guilt, was best determined by the jury. *Hill v. State*, 366 So. 2d at 321. Similarly, whether Mr. Felgate's refusal to submit to a chemical test for intoxication was due to a consciousness of guilt of DWI, or whether it was out of fear of conviction for DUI, was a matter for the court sitting as fact-finder to weigh and determine.

We conclude that the evidence before the trial court constituted substantial evidence to support Mr. Felgate's conviction for DWI.

Questions

1. Was Felgate convicted by a mechanical device?
2. Did Felgate appeal based on the results of the mechanical device?
3. What evidence was utilized to determine defendant's guilt?
4. Was the evidence sufficient?

(2)   The alcohol concentration in the person's blood or breath is eight-hundredths of one percent (.08 %) or more.[88]

Within this framework, the legislature pinpoints the key elements in each DUI/DWI charge. First, a driver exerts "physical control" over a motor vehicle. Second, that driver operates the vehicle under the influence of some substance, namely a drug or alcohol intoxicant. Third, the level of chemical influence on the operator, as measured in blood, meets or exceeds.

A closer look at how these standard clauses play out in the judicial arena is now in order.

Elements of the Offense

Motor Vehicle

DWI statutes narrowly include vehicles capable of operation by an intoxicated operator whose blood content exceeds a stated limit. In ordinary parlance, a vehicle means auto or truck. In legal nomenclature, the term "vehicle" encompasses a larger audience and may include but not be limited to snowmobile, boat, ATV or other off-road vehicle, and bicycle — even horse-drawn vehicles have been offered up as part of the vehicular definition.[89] A more expansive statutory interpretation is prone to designate once unthinkable items into the vehicle category and given the tone of this reform movement, it is a safe bet more are on the way.

Physical Control

The majority of statutes mandate that the operator be in physical control of the qualifying vehicle in order to be liable. To control could only mean drive under usual circumstances, but under these charged ones, control is more a matter of symbolism than fact. To control a vehicle infers the driving of same and orchestrating a series of movements that can only occur because the controller dictates that result. California employs the term "drive a vehicle," which exquisitely hits the mark.

(a)   It is unlawful for any person who is under the influence of any alcoholic beverage or drug, or under the combined influence of any alcoholic beverage and drug, to drive a vehicle.

(b)   It is unlawful for any person who has 0.08 percent or more, by weight, of alcohol in his or her blood to drive a vehicle.

(c)   It is unlawful for any person who is addicted to the use of any drug to drive a vehicle.[90]

Problems arise when the word "drive" is replaced by "actual physical control," such as in the Arizona design reproduced below:

A.   It is unlawful for a person to drive or be in actual physical control of a vehicle in this state under any of the following circumstances:

1.   While under the influence of intoxicating liquor, any drug, a vapor releasing substance containing a toxic substance or any combination of liquor, drugs or vapor releasing substances if the person is impaired to the slightest degree.

2.   If the person has an alcohol concentration of 0.08 or more within two hours of driving or being in actual physical control of the vehicle and the alcohol concentration results from alcohol consumed either before or while driving or being in actual physical control of the vehicle.

3.   While there is any drug defined in § 13-3401 or its metabolite in the person's body.

CASE 9.9

COMMONWEALTH V. ENGLISH

53 D&C 2d 668 (Pa Comm. Warren County 1979)

Defendant was arrested on two charges of violation of The Vehicle Code, operating a motor vehicle while under the influence of intoxicating liquor in violation of section 1037 and failure to stop and identify himself after being involved in an accident involving damage to personal property under section 10279d).

Subsequent to his arrest and preliminary hearing, defendant filed an application to quash the criminal complaint and transcript of the justice of the peace and for dismissal of the charge of operating a motor vehicle while under the influence of intoxicating liquor.

Defendant bases his position on the undisputed facts that at the time the arresting officer arrived at the scene, his motor vehicle was stuck in a ditch and defendant was approaching it from his home when the officer first sighted him. After interrogation, the officer placed defendant under arrest for driving under the influence. The Commonwealth acknowledges the officer did not observe defendant driving his vehicle and was summoned to the scene by a third party who suffered damage to her children's toy and flower pot when defendant drove or skidded off the road and did damage to these two articles and left without identifying himself and subsequently become lodged in the ditch.

Section 1204 of The Vehicle Code permits arrests on view when the offense is designated a felony or a misdemeanor or, in cases causing or contributing to an accident, resulting in injury or death to any person. The Commonwealth argues it need not show the arresting officer actually observed the defendant operating his vehicle in order to make the arrest in this case. The Commonwealth's reasoning is, in order to do so would place too heavy a burden upon it.

We have found no cases sustaining the Commonwealth's position nor has it submitted any. Certainly, the section under which the charge was made does not contain any such language or inference. Although, admittedly a short period of time transpired between the ditching of the vehicle and when the officer arrived, which, from the testimony appears to be less than one hour, still, an arrest cannot be made on suspicion or surmise as a "view arrest." This is especially so where defendant, although he admitted he was drinking after the ditching of the vehicle, denied he was drinking when he operated it into the ditch and denied he made any confession of doing so. To permit this type of an arrest under these circumstances would certainly open the door to permitting arrest on speculation, surmise, conjecture and hearsay.

Questions

1. Where did the arresting officer apprehend the accused?
2. What impact does this location have upon the state's ability to charge DUI?
3. If the conviction had been upheld, arrests could then be justified, according to this court, upon what grounds?

4. If the vehicle is a commercial motor vehicle that requires a person to obtain a commercial driver license as defined in § 28-3001 and the person has an alcohol concentration of 0.04 or more.[91]

What is physical control? Asleep at the wheel in a parking lot? Stopped and parked on the side of an interstate highway? Sitting on top of the roof of a vehicle? Laying in the backseat of a vehicle while the keys are locked in the trunk? Initially these case examples seem easy enough to answer in a factual sense. In a legal sense, each of these scenarios represents control.

Think about these critical issues when assessing the issue of control:

- Driver in close proximity to vehicle and potential for operation
- Driver has keys on person
- Driver may temporarily stop
- Driver renews driving without sufficient time to minimize alcohol effects
- Driver has not relinquished control

Amount of Intoxication

Jurisdictions rely on machine devices in their codifications to compute acceptable and unacceptable limits. A rough sketch might be:

- .08–.10 percent equals a presumption of intoxication[92]
- .04–.07 percent is inconclusive either as intoxication or nonintoxication
- .03 percent or less is indicative of nonintoxication[93]

At the lower numbers, the presumptions shifts to nonintoxication, while at the higher numbers, the reverse is true. In the middle of this computational design, the deduction is unpersuasive either way. Certainly police officers avoid tackling the middle case unless other corroborative evidence, such as traffic infractions and harm caused, would eliminate the ambiguity.

Arizona's statute explains how presumptions work at either end of the spectrum.

G. In a trial, action, or proceeding for a violation of this section or section 28-1383 other than a trial, action, or proceeding involving driving or being in actual physical control of a commercial vehicle, the defendant's alcohol concentration within two hours of the time of driving or being in actual physical control as shown by analysis of the defendant's blood, breath, or other bodily substance gives rise to the following presumptions:
1. If there was at that time 0.05 or less alcohol concentration in the defendant's blood, breath, or other bodily substance, it may be presumed that the defendant was not under the influence of intoxicating liquor.
2. If there was at that time in excess of 0.05 but less than 0.10 alcohol concentration in the defendant's blood, breath, or other bodily substance, that fact shall not give rise to a presumption that the defendant was or was not under the influence of intoxicating liquor, but that fact may be considered with other competent evidence in determining the guilt or innocence of the defendant.
3. If there was at that time 0.10 or more alcohol concentration in the defendant's blood, breath, or other bodily substance, it may be presumed that the defendant was under the influence of intoxicating liquor.[94]

How meaningful are these numerical findings? Does science back up the conclusion of intoxication? Are the machines utilized capable of delivering accurate results? The answer here is yes and no. (See Figure 9.9 for a common chart regarding body weight, alcohol consumption and average BAC.)

Yes, because alcohol content in the human body is measurable biologically and seriologically. Yes, because machinery has been reliably engineered that can perform the testing. Yes, because medical science is clearly capable of running laboratory tests to measure content. No, because the methodologies and the deductive bases for computing intoxication are not infallible. Common sense tells us that some portion of the populace operate vehicles quite normally within the ranges of supposed intoxication, while others cannot walk a straight line in the inconclusive zone or even in the lower numbers where intoxication cannot be presumed. Some people cannot hold alcohol in any amount where others seem, at least from our own weak observational powers, unfazed. Add the variables of timing, alcohol type, body weight and size, health and fitness of the drinker, duration of drinking, experience and tolerance levels of alcohol, and scientific certitude is a thing of the past. The passage of time, or the complete absence of time to process the effects of alcohol, educates most observers on the transient reliability of readings. What is true at arrest may not be so at the stationhouse or vice versa. Criminal codifications understand that time alters readings and, as a result, set windows of time to measure, for example, two hours.[95] Other factors directly impact the accuracy of findings and should give legal thinkers pause about their infallibility. It also is abundantly clear that drivers whose levels exceed the stated intoxication measures may be legally intoxicated, but factually in complete control. It may be equally probative that the .05 candidate could not stand erect yet still be declared nonintoxicated. For this reason alone, the test has the capacity for arbitrariness and unreliability. In general, the test

Body Weight	Drinks											
	1	2	3	4	5	6	7	8	9	10	11	12
100 lbs	.038	.075	.113	.150	.188	.225	.263	.300	.338	.375	.413	.450
110 lbs	.034	.066	.103	.137	.172	.207	.241	.275	.309	.344	.379	.412
120 lbs	.031	.063	.094	.125	.156	.188	.219	.250	.281	.313	.344	.375
130 lbs	.029	.058	.087	.116	.145	.174	.203	.232	.261	.290	.320	.348
140 lbs	.027	.054	.080	.107	.134	.161	.188	.214	.241	.268	.295	.321
150 lbs	.025	.050	.075	.100	.125	.151	.176	.201	.226	.251	.276	.301
160 lbs	.023	.047	.070	.094	.177	.141	.164	.188	.211	.234	.258	.281
170 lbs	.022	.045	.066	.088	.110	.132	.155	.178	.200	.221	.244	.265
180 lbs	.021	.042	.063	.083	.104	.125	.146	.167	.188	.208	.229	.250
190 lbs	.020	.040	.059	.079	.099	.119	.138	.158	.179	.198	.217	.237
200 lbs	.019	.038	.056	.075	.094	.113	.131	.150	.169	.188	.206	.225
210 lbs	.018	.036	.053	.071	.090	.107	.125	.143	.161	.179	.197	.215
220 lbs	.017	.034	.051	.068	.085	.102	.119	.136	.153	.170	.188	.205
230 lbs	.016	.032	.049	.065	.081	.098	.115	.130	.147	.163	.180	.196
240 lbs	.016	.031	.047	.063	.078	.094	.109	.125	.141	.156	.172	.188

Figure 9.9   Alcohol influence chart.

attempts depend upon the average person's profile and while applying its provisions, does some injustice in select cases.

The shortcomings in mechanical testing seem to have escaped most state legislators because the passage of new laws with even lower or less stringent requirements, continues unabated. Lower levels, enhanced penalties, and stronger provisions relating to juveniles and repeat offenders are a few of the many novel approaches. Multiple offenders receive special treatment because the recidivism level of intoxicants accounts for a sizeable portion of the criminal justice processing. Review Kentucky's attempt to track the repeaters:

(5) Any person who violates the provisions of paragraph (a), (b), (c), or (d) of subsection (1) of this section shall:

    (a)   For the first offense within a five (5) year period, be fined not less than two hundred dollars ($200) nor more than five hundred dollars ($500), or be imprisoned in the county jail for not less than forty-eight (48) hours nor more than thirty (30) days, or both. Following sentencing, the defendant may apply to the judge for permission to enter a community labor program for not less than forty-eight (48) hours nor more than thirty (30) days in lieu of fine or imprisonment, or both. If any of the aggravating circumstances listed in subsection (11) of this section are present while the person was operating or in physical control of a motor vehicle, the mandatory minimum term of imprisonment shall be four (4) days, which term shall not be suspended, probated, conditionally discharged, or subject to any other form of early release.

    (b)   For the second offense within a five (5) year period, be fined not less than three hundred fifty dollars ($350) nor more than five hundred dollars ($500) and shall be imprisoned in the county jail for not less than seven (7) days nor more than six (6) months and, in addition to fine and imprisonment, may be sentenced to community labor for not less than ten (10) days nor more than six (6) months. If any of the aggravating circumstances listed in subsection (11) of this section are present, the mandatory minimum term of imprisonment shall be fourteen (14) days, which term shall not be suspended, probated, conditionally discharged, or subject to any other form of early release.

    (c)   For a third offense within a five (5) year period, be fined not less than five hundred dollars ($500) nor more than one thousand dollars ($1,000) and shall be imprisoned in the county jail for not less than thirty (30) days nor more than twelve (12) months and may, in addition to fine and imprisonment, be sentenced to community labor for not less than ten (10) days nor more than twelve (12) months. If any of the aggravating circumstances listed in subsection (11) of this section are present, the mandatory minimum term of imprisonment shall be sixty (60) days, which term shall not be suspended, probated, conditionally discharged, or subject to any other form of early release.

    (d)   For a fourth or subsequent offense within a five (5) year period, be guilty of a Class D felony. If any of the aggravating circumstances listed in subsection (11) of this section are present, the mandatory minimum term of imprisonment shall be two hundred forty (240) days, which term shall not be suspended, probated, conditionally discharged, or subject to any other form of release.

    (e)   For purposes of this subsection, prior offenses shall include all convictions in this state, and any other state or jurisdiction, for operating or being in control of a motor vehicle while under the influence of alcohol or other substances that impair one's driving ability, or any combination of alcohol and such substances, or while having an unlawful alcohol concentration, or driving while intoxicated, but shall not include convictions for violating subsection (1)(e) of this section. A court shall receive as proof of a prior conviction a copy of that conviction, certified by the court ordering the conviction.[96]

In sum, however well-meaning these laws claim to be, there is something fundamentally unsettling about content and construction. Few would disagree that the human costs associated with alcohol abuse are almost incalculable. Few would deny that the society has a critical problem with which to contend. The troubles lie not in intentions but in methodology. If intoxication need be demonstrated, it cannot be a strict, and often overly reliant, almost lazy mechanical approach we have become so accustomed to. With so much at stake, in light of the increasing criminalization of the conduct, the system owes its accused a fair playing field, a reliable science, and due process that casts convictions in constitutional armor.

The power and force of the DUI/DWI presumption causes fits for the defense strategist. How does one refute a machine? How can the internal workings of the intoxilyzer be subject to cross-examination and confrontation? The danger and the beauty of machines, depending on which side of the aisle you sit, rest in silent science. It is easy enough to cross examine Officer X who conducts field sobriety tests. This is a thinking and breathing being subject to all the typical frailties unique to testimonial capacity. Machines cannot be assailed in the same way. As a result, defense tactics in DUI cases are markedly different than other criminal litigation.[97]

DEFENSE STRATEGIES

MECHANICAL

- Age and condition of machine
- Machine service record
- Machine repair and calibration record
- Reliability of machine model
- Timing of tests

OPERATOR

- Experience of the operator
- Certification of the operator
- Licensure of the operator
- Training of the operator
- Supervision of the operator

FIELD TESTING

- Fair and impartial process
- Corroboration by witness or videotape
- Alternative explanation for behavior
- Demeanor of officer[98]

CONSTITUTIONAL CHALLENGES

- Basis for stop and detention
- Probable cause basis
- Explanation of rights
- Implications of testing refusal explanation
- Conduct of officer

DISCUSSION QUESTIONS

1. Offenses against the public morality imply more than personal choice. How so?
2. Describe the best arguments in favor of prostitution legalization.
3. Argue against the legalization of drugs.
4. Why is bigamy considered a more hidden offense than polygamy?
5. Why is pornography not necessarily obscene in a legal sense?
6. What areas of the media will most severely be tested by the proliferation of obscene materials?
7. How does the question of obscenity comport with free speech protections?
8. By which standard is obscenity measured?
9. Why have Drug Courts been instituted?
10. Has the enactment of DUI/DWI laws been effective in curbing the behavior?

SUGGESTED READINGS

Albanese, J. S. 1996. *Looking for a new approach to an old problem: The future of obscenity and pornography.* Upper Saddle River, NJ: Prentice Hall.

Bensinger, G. J. 2001. Trafficking of women and girls. *Crime & Justice International* 17 (October/November): 11–13.

Brumbaugh, J. M. 1991. *Assault, rape, bigamy, and related offenses.* New York: Foundation Press.

Cauduro, A., A. DiNicola, M. Lombardi, and P. Ruspini. 2010. *Prostitution and human trafficking: Focus on clients.* New York: Springer Publishing Company.

Feinberg, J. 1988. *Harmless wrong: The moral limits of criminal law.* New York: Oxford University Press.

Flowers, R. B. 2011. *Prostitution in the digital age: Selling sex from the suite to the street.* Santa Barbara, CA: Praeger Publishers.

Giobbe, E. 1991. *Prostitution: Buying the right to rape.* New York: Garland.

Goode, E. 2011. *Drugs in American society*, 8th ed. New York: McGraw-Hill Humanities/Social Sciences/ Languages Publishers.

Herring, J. 2010. *Criminal law: Text, cases, and materials*, 4th ed. New York: Oxford University Press.

Levinthal, C. F. 2011. *Drugs, society and criminal Justice*, 3rd ed. Lebanon, IN: Prentice Hall.

Moffitt, A., et al. 1998. *Drug precipice: Illicit drugs, organized crime, fallacies of legalization, worsening problems, solutions.* Portland, OR: International Specialized Book Services.

National Center for Missing and Exploited Children. 1992. *Female juvenile prostitution: Problem and response.* Washington, D.C.: National Institute of Justice.

National District Attorney's Association. 1993. *Prosecutor's perspective: Drunk driving.* Washington, D.C.: National Institute of Justice.

ENDNOTES

1. *See* ARISTOTLE, NICHOMACHEAN ETHICS (Joe Sachs trans., 2002).
2. *See* POPE JOHN PAUL II, VERITATIS SPLENDOR, Papal Encyclical delivered in Rome (Aug. 6, 1993).
3. For a thorough analysis of the proprostitution arguments, *see* Jocelyn Eskow, *Eleventh Annual Review of Gender and Sexuality Law: Criminal Chapter: Prostitution and Sex Work,* 11 GEO. J. GENDER & L. 163 (2010).
4. PROSTITUTION AND PORNOGRAPHY: PHILOSOPHICAL DEBATE ABOUT THE SEX INDUSTRY (Jessica Spector ed., 2006).
5. 18 PA. CONS. STAT. § 5902 (2010).
6. For one thing, prostitution has become a product, a commercial marketplace that traffics human beings, not only in the states, but internationally. *See* MARY FINN ET AL., EVALUATION OF THE DEMONSTRATION PROJECT TO ADDRESS COMMERCIAL SEXUAL EXPLOITATION OF CHILDREN IN ATLANTA-FULTON COUNTY (2009), available at http://www.ncjrs.gov/pdffiles1/nij/grants/226610.pdf (accessed August 3, 2011).
7. Those who sell their own children to collect the proceeds for drugs are guilty of endangering the welfare of a minor as well as prostitution. *See* a contrary view that exists in England in Gavin Dingwall, *Comment: Expanding the Definition of Prostitution,* 61 J. CRIM. L. 435 (1997).
8. Nina Lopez-Jones, *Legalizing Brothels,* 142 NEW L. J. 594, 594 (1992).
9. Eskow, *supra* note 3, at 186.
10. Beverly Balos & Mary Louise Fellows, *A Matter of Prostitution: Becoming Respectable,* 74 N.Y.U. L. REV. 1220, 1291-92 (1999). *See* Laurie Shrage, *Should Feminists Oppose Prostitution?,* 99 ETHICS 347 (1989); LAURIE SHRAGE, MORAL DILEMMAS OF FEMINISM: PROSTITUTION, ADULTERY, AND ABORTION (1994); SHEILA JEFFRIES, THE IDEA OF PROSTITUTION (1997).
11. Balos & Fellows, *supra* note 10, at 1301-02.
12. M.A. Stapleton, *Legalize Prostitution, Erase Stigma, Prof Argues,* CHI. DAILY L. BULL., Ap. 25, 1997, at 3, 3. *See also* MAGGIE O'NEILL, PROSTITUTION AND FEMINISM: TOWARDS A POLITICS OF FEELING (2001).
13. Lopez-Jones, *supra* note 8, at 595.
14. *See* Courtney Guyton Persons, *Sex in the Sunlight: The Effectiveness, Efficiency, Constitutionality, and Advisability of Publishing Names and Pictures of Prostitutes' Patrons,* 49 VAND. L. REV. 1525 (1996).
15. *U.S. v. Brooks,* 510 F.3d 1186 (2010); *See also* 18 U.S.C. §§1591(a), 2423(a) (2010).
16. The U.S. Supreme Court in its Powell and Robinson decisions forbade the criminalization of the addictive status. *See Robinson v. California,* 414 U.S. 417 (1974) and *Powell v. Texas,* 392 U.S. 514 (1968).
17. For an excellent overview of how the Controlled Substances Act and its provisions work, *see* John A. Gilbert, Jr., *DEA Regulation of Controlled Substances and Listed Chemicals,* 65 FOOD DRUG L. J. 623 (2010).
18. Controlled Substances Act, 21 U.S.C. § 801 (2011).
19. *Id.*
20. 35 PA. CONS. STAT. § 780-113 (2010).
21. U.S. Drug Enforcement Administration, DEA Staffing and Budget, DEA Staffing and Appropriations, FY 1972-2005, available at http://www.justice.gov/dea/agency/staffing.htm (accessed August 3, 2011).
22. The Uniform Crime Reports do catalog the offenses in staggering numbers and dollar sums expended.
23. Nicholas de Katzenbach, *A Rational Discussion of Current Drug Laws,* 25 FORDHAM URB. L.J. 443, 446 (1998).
24. "The figures clearly show why something must be done. Since May 1973, when the penalties took effect, the prison population of New York State has grown from 13,000 to nearly 70,000, while the total number of illegal substance abusers in communities throughout the state has remained relatively constant at an estimated 300,000." Harvard Hollenberg, *Drug Laws Went Wrong 25 Years Ago,* NAT. L.J., June 1, 1998, at A21, A21.
25. *Id.*
26. OFFICE OF THE PRESIDENT, NATIONAL DRUG CONTROL STRATEGY: FY 2011 BUDGET SUMMARY Table 3 (2011), available at http://www.whitehousedrugpolicy.gov/publications/policy/11budget/fy11budget.pdf (accessed August 3, 2011).

27. FEDERAL BUREAU OF INVESTIGATION, UNIFORM CRIME REPORTS, AND ADMINISTRATIVE OFFICE OF THE US COURT, reprinted in DAEDALUS, Summer 1992, at 262.

28. *Id.*

29. David Schultz, *Rethinking Drug Criminalization Policies*, 25 TEX. TECH. L. REV. 151, 153-54 (1993). *See also* Peter Reuter, *Hawles Ascendant: The Punitive Trend of American Drug Policy*, DAEDALUS, Summer 1992, at 15, 33.

30. Doctors have come under substantial criticism for the special status granted them under sentencing schemes and the interpretation of the controlled substances act. Are they any different than a street pusher who sells controlled substances while they illegally prescribe? *See* Sharon B. Roberts, *All "Pushers" Are Not Created Equal! The Inequities of Sanctions for Physicians Who Inappropriately "Prescribe" Controlled Substances*, 23 NOVA L. REV. 881 (1999).

31. For example, Oregon has amended its laws. See *Oregon Medical Marijuana Act*, OR. REV. STAT. §§475.300-475.346 (2007).

32. CAL. HEALTH & SAFETY CODE, §§ 11362.7 – 11362.83 (West 2010). For a full state-by-state comparison of these laws, see National Public Radio's interactive map at: http://www.npr.org/templates/story/story.php?storyId=12613748 (accessed August 3, 2011).

33. A study of New York City's fast track court seems to indicate very little difference in rates of recidivism or cure. *See* Steven Belenko, Jeffrey A. Fagan & Tamara Dumanovsky, *The Effects of Legal Sanctions on Recidivism in Special Drug Courts*, 17 JUSTICE SYS. J. 53 (1994).

34. BUREAU OF JUSTICE ASSISTANCE, DEFINING DRUG COURTS: THE KEY COMPONENTS, NCJ 205621 (2004); for a summary of Drug Courts throughout the nation, *see* BJA Drug Court Clearinghouse, American University, State list of all Drug Courts, July 14, 2009, available at http://www1.spa.american.edu/justice/documents/2150.pdf (accessed August 3, 2011).

35. Adrienne D. Davis, *Regulating Polygamy: Intimacy, Default Rates and Bargaining for Equality*, 110 COLUM. L. REV. 1955, 1958 (2010).

36. *Id.* at 1959.

37. *Id.* at 1962.

38. Martha M. Ertman, *Race Treason: The Untold Story of America's Ban on Polygamy*, 19 COLUM. J. GENDER & L. 287 (2010).

39. *Id.* at 289.

40. 18 PA. CONS. STAT. § 4301 (2010).

41. SUMM. PA. JUR. 2d § 10:3 at 268. *See also* TOLL, PA. CRIMES CODE ANN. § 4301.

42. *See* MARTIN WEINSTEIN, SUMMARY OF AMERICAN LAW 169–170 (1988).

43. Deleting Commercial Pornography Sites from the Internet: The U.S. Financial Industry's Efforts to Combat This Problem: Hearing before the Subcomm. on Oversight and Investigations of the H. Comm. on Energy and Commerce, 109th Cong. 29 (2006) (statement of Ernie Allen, president and chief executive officer, National Center for Missing and Exploited Children), available at http://frwebgate.access.gpo.gov/cgi-bin/getdoc.cgi?dbname=109_house_hearings&docid=f: 31467.pdf (accessed February 27, 2009); National Center for Missing and Exploited Children, National Mandate and Mission, http://www.missingkids.com/missingkids/servlet/PageServlet?   LanguageCountry=en_US&PageId=1866 (accessed March 21, 2010); Benjamin A. Mains, *Virtual Child Pornography, Pandering, and the First Amendment: How Developments in Technology and Shifting First Amendment Jurisprudence Have Affected the Criminalization of Child Pornography*, 37 HASTINGS CONST. L. Q. 809 (2010).

44. For an interesting discussion of antipornography organizations still battling other forces, see Stephen Bates, *Father Hill and Fanny Hill: An Activist's Group's Crusade to Remake Obscenity Law*, 8 FIRST AMEND. L. REV. 217 (2010).

45. WILLIAM J. BENNETT, THE INDEX OF LEADING CULTURAL INDICATORS 104 (1994).

46. Tim Bakken, *Liberty, Obscenity, and Majoritarian Institutions: Who Determines the Value of Expression?* 16 GLENDALE L. REV. 1, 7 (1998).

47. *See* Joel Timmer, *Violence as Obscenity: Offensiveness and the First Amendment*, 15 COMM. L & POL'Y 25 (2010); Lorraine M. Buerger, *Comment: The Safe Games Illinois Act: Can Curbs on Violent Video Games Survive Constitutional Challenges?* 37 LOY. U. CHI. L.J. 617 (2006); Clay Calvert and Robert D. Richards, *Mediated Images of Violence and the First Amendment: From Video Games to the Evening News*, 57 ME.

L. REV. 91 (2005); Eric C. Chaffee, *Sailing toward Safe Harbor Hours: The Constitutionality of Regulating Television Violence*, 39 U. MICH. J. L. REFORM 1 (2005); Faith M. Sparr, *The FCC's Report on Regulating Broadcast Violence: Is the Medium the Message?*, 28 LOY. L. A. ENT. L. REV. 1 (2007/2008).

48. 866 S.W.2d 520 (Tenn. 1993).

49. TENN. CODE ANN. §39-17-901 (4) (1991).

50. 223 F. Supp. 2d 932 (S. D. Ohio 2002).

51. OHIO REV. CODE ANN. § 2907.31(D)(1) (West 2002).

52. *See* 18 U.S.C. § 2251 (2010); 47 U.S.C. § 223(d) (2010); Communications Decency Act of 1996, Pub. L. No. 104-104, 502, 110 Stat. 133 (1996). *See also Alexander v. U.S.*, 509 U.S. 544 (1993); *Knox v. U.S.* 510 U.S. 939 (1993); *Crawford v. Lungren*, 96 F.3d 380 (9th Cir. 1996), cert. denied, 519 U.S. 820 (1996); *Amatel v. Reno*, 156 F.3d 192 (D.C. Cir. 1998); and *ACLU v. Reno*, 929 F. Supp. 824 (E.D. Pa. 1996).

53. 18 PA. CONS. STAT. § 5903 (2010). *See also* Mains, *supra* note 43.

54. 413 U.S. 15 (1973).

55. *Id.* at 24

56. Mains, *supra* note 43, at 814.

57. Bakken, *supra* note 46, at 6.

58. 481 U.S. 497 (1987).

59. *Id.* at 500.

60. Miller, 413 U.S.; *see also Paris Adult Theatre I v. Slaton*, 413 U.S. 49 (1973).

61. Sarah Kagan, *Obscenity on the Internet: Nationalizing the Standard to Protect Individual Rights*, 38 HASTINGS CONST. L. Q. 233, 244 (2010).

62. *Id.* at 247.

63. 535 U.S. 564 (2002).

64. 47 U.S.C §231(e)(6) (1994).

65. *See U.S. v. Kilbride*, 584 F.3d 1240 (9th Cir. 2009), which has called for a national test.

66. See *U.S. v. Kilbride*, 507 F. Supp. 2d 1051 (D. Ariz. 2007).

67. Shannon Creasy, *Defending against a Charge of Obscenity in the Internet Age: How Google Searches Can Illuminate Miller's "Contemporary Community Standards,"* 26 GA. ST. U. L. REV. 1029, 1045(2010); *See also* Jonathan P. Wentz, *Ashcroft v. ACLU: The Context and Economic Implications of Burdened Access to Online Sexual Speech*, 17 GEO. MASON U. CIV. RTS. L. J. 477 (2007).

68. See *Belleville v. Family Video Movie Club, Inc.*, 744 N.E.2d 322 (Ill. App. Ct. 2001).

69. *U.S. v. Thomas*, 74 F.3d 701 (6th Cir. 1996). *See* David C. Yunick, *Computers and the Criminal Law*, 34 CRIM. L. BULL. 448 (1998).

70. *Ginzburg v. U.S.*, 383 U.S. 463, 467-68 (1966); *Hamling v. U.S.*, 418 U.S. 87, 130 (1974); *Splawn v. California*, 341 U.S. 595, 597-98 (1977); *Pinkus v. U.S.*, 436 U.S. 293, 303-04 (1978).

71. *Erie, Pa. v. PAP's A.M.*, No. 98-1161, 1998 U.S. Briefs 116,1 Aug. 4, 1999, Brief of Morality in Media, Inc., at 21.

72. In general, there seems a growing sector of toleration and acceptance in a perverse sense. Punishments tend to be weak and soft. Child molesters and pornographers cannot even be subject to lifetime probationary status when the recidivism rate is so utterly high. *See Peek v. Peek*, 195 P.3d 641 (Ariz. 2008); *see also* Ahron D. Cohen, *The Arizona Supreme Court Review: Non-Death Penalty Violent Criminal Law: A Discussion of Arizona Supreme Court 2008–2009*, 42 ARIZ. ST. L. J. 623 (2010).

73. *Sable Communications v. FCC*, 492 U.S. 115, 126 (1989).

74. The Communications Decency Act of 1996, Title V of the Telecommunications Act of 1996. Pub. L. No. 104-104, 110 Stat. 56 (104th Cong., 2nd Sess, Feb. 6, 1996) (Codified at 47 U.S.C. §223).

75. 47 U.S.C. §223(d) (2010)

76. *New York v. Ferber*, 458 U.S. 747, 753, 758 (1982).

77. *Reno v. ACLU*, No. 96-511, 1996 U.S. Briefs 511, Jan. 21, 1997. Brief Amicus curiae of the Family Life Project of the American Center for Law & Justice, at 14.

78. See the inflammatory works of Robert Maplethorpe.

79. *See* M. Childs, *Outraging Public Decency: The Offence of Offensiveness*, 1991 PUBLIC L. 10 (1991).

80. CATHARINE A. MACKINNON, ONLY WORDS 31 (1993).

81. Matthew C. Rappold, *Evidence of Inactive Drug Metabolites in DUI Cases: Using a Proximate Analysis to Fill the Evidentiary Gap between Prior Drug Use and Driving under the Influence*, 32 U. ARK. LITTLE ROCK L. REV. 535 (2010).

82. ARIZ. REV. STAT. ANN. § 28-1381(A)(3) (2006); DEL. CODE ANN. tit. 21 § 4177(a)(6) (2006); GA. CODE ANN. § 40-6-391(a)(6) (2007); 625 ILL. COMP. STAT. 5/11-501(a)(6) (2007); IND. CODE § 9-30-5-1(1)(c) (2007); IOWA CODE § 321J.2(1)(c) (2007); MICH. COMP. LAWS § 257.625(8) (2007); MINN. STAT. § 169A.20(1)(7) (2007); N.C. GEN. STAT. § 20-138.1(a)(3) (2007); 75 PA. CONS. STAT. § 3802(d) (2007); R.I. GEN. LAWS § 31-27-2(b)(2) (2005); UTAH CODE ANN. § 41-6a-517(2) (West 2007); WIS. STAT. § 346.63(1)(a) (2006); NEV. REV. STAT. § 484.379 (2007); OHIO REV. CODE ANN. § 4511.19(A)(1)(j) (West 2007); VA. CODE ANN. § 18.2-266 (2007).

83. TED R. MILLER ET AL., VICTIM COSTS AND CONSEQUENCES: A NEW LOOK, Research Report, (1996); Ted R. Miller et al., *Highway and Crash Costs in the U.S. by Victim Age, Driver Age, Restraint Use, and Blood Alcohol Level*, Association for the Advancement of Automotive Medicine, 40th Annual Proceedings (1996).

84. *Michigan Dept. of State Police v. Sitz*, 496 U.S. 444 (1990); *Delaware v. Prouse*, 440 U.S. 648 (1979).

85. PENNSYLVANIA BAR INSTITUTE, DRIVING UNDER THE INFLUENCE 84 (1996).

86. *See Mekos v. Miller*, No. 25817 (W.Va. 1999). The Mekos decision emphasizes the power of administrative agencies like Departments of Motor Vehicle to suspend or cancel license and driving privileges due to the legislature's delegatory powers.

87. *See Justice v. Kentucky*, 987 S.W.2d 306 (Ky. 1998).

88. TENN. CODE ANN. § 55-10-401 (2010).

89. *See* SUMM. PA. JURIS. at 393.

90. CAL. VEHICLE CODE § 23152 (West 2011).

91. ARIZ. REV. STAT. ANN. § 28-1381(A) (2011).

92. The trend to .08 appears irreversible. See CAL. VEHICLE CODE § 25153(b) (West 2011).

93. States like California set out even lower limits for commercial operators, as low as .04 being an unlawful amount: CAL. VEHICLE CODE § 25153(d) (West 2011). Kentucky goes to greater numerical depths when it comes to juveniles, *see* KY. REV. STAT. ANN. § 189A.010(e) (West 2011).

94. ARIZ. REV. STAT. ANN. § 28-1381(G) (2010).

95. See 75 PA. CONS. STAT. § 3802 (2011).

96. KY. REV. STAT. ANN. § 189A.010(5) a-e (West 2010).

97. *See People v. Sainz*, 74 Cal. App. 4th 565, 88 Cal. Rptr. 2d 203 (1999). Not surprisingly, defendants who are convicted of multiple offenses in addition to DUI, want the softer penalties usually assigned to DUI offenses. So, if an assault occurs as a result of the DUI collision, defendant cannot hide behind the less prohibitive DUI when the penalty for assault would apply.

98. *See Tennessee v. Jarnagin*, No. E1998-00892-CCA-R8-CD (Ten. App. 2000) where OFFICER'S methods of testing and fairness during the process were vigorously raised on an appeal from a DUI conviction, but to no avail.

Chapter 10

Inchoate Offenses

KEYWORDS

Attempt: The crime of having the intent to commit and taking action in an effort to commit a crime that fails or is prevented.

Capacity: An individual's ability or aptitude; mental ability as it relates to responsibility for the commission of a crime.

Confiscate: To seize without compensation as forfeited to the public treasury.

Conspiracy: An agreement between two or more people to commit an act prohibited by law or to commit a lawful act by means prohibited by law.

Inchoate: Of or relating to a crime that consists of acts that are preliminary to another crime and that are in themselves criminal.

Overt act: An outward act that is done in furtherance of a conspiracy, of treason, or of the crime of attempt and that is a required element of such crimes for conviction even if it is legal in itself.

Racketeering: The extortion of money or advantage by threat or force; a pattern of illegal activity that is carried out in furtherance of an enterprise that is owned or controlled by those engaged in such activity.

Solicit: To ask, induce, advise, or command to do something and to commit a crime.

INTRODUCTION: THE NATURE OF AN INCHOATE OFFENSE

For the most part, the study of criminal law will primarily be consumed with proof of two critical elements: first, proof of the action that causes the harm; second, proof of the actor's mental state when committing the offense. American substantive criminal law heralds this type of evidentiary rigor and, at its base, uses these dual proofs as safeguard and protection against a government that alleges crimes without any material protections. The American experience places the heaviest of burdens on the prosecution and allows its defendant to stand mute before the tribunal, not requiring any affirmative step in the defense of charges and forbidding the presumption that a defendant who does not testify is guilty because of silence. For all our shortcomings, this nation affords defendants unrivaled protections in both a constitutional and statutory sense and holds back the might of a government that, if left unchecked, would trample rights without reservation. The tough evidentiary burdens placed on the prosecution in almost every criminal case are glowing testimony to this strength in American republicanism. In short, a prosecutor must prove both the act and the mind or prove nothing at all.[1]

As in all legal analysis, there are a few exceptions to this basic proposition. First, strict liability offenses, which will often be discussed in this text, waive the traditional expectation of mens rea due to strong public policy rationales. Certain types of governmental infractions, petty offenses, and others of little consequence seem less intent on the dual mode of proof.

In this chapter, we witness the preparatory and very incomplete offenses that still rise to the level of criminality. The term "inchoate" means "incomplete" and "unfulfilled" and is relevant to those crimes that are preparatory in nature. Inchoate offenses possess some of the qualities of traditional criminal infractions, but never all of them. They tend to be mentally complete, but substantially incomplete. Thus, a person who engages in conspiracy plans and plots a criminal design with another person or persons, and by this conspiratorial plan, which has yet to reach fruition, a finding of guilt in conspiracy is possible. Therefore, a conspirator intends to commit a crime, and may take a small, overt, though utterly incomplete step toward that commission, although this act will never be sufficient enough to meet the element known as actus reus. Once the conspirator plans and then does, he or she is both conspirator and criminal perpetrator of the offense in question. If he or she never does, taking only partial steps to the culmination of the criminal event, a charge of conspiracy is all that remains.[2] This depiction manifests fully the meaning of inchoate. Other inchoate offenses include: solicitation, enticement and criminal encouragement, and criminal attempts.

SOLICITATION

ELEMENTS

- Solicitation of another
- To commit a felony
- With intent

A person indicted on a charge of solicitation never reached the endgame of the request or enticement. In this sense, solicitation is purely inchoate because the solicitor entreats others, but never carries out the desire for which he/she wished. The basis for the system's aversion to the crime rests in its manipulative quality—getting others to do the dirty work.[3]

The central crux of solicitation is the asking not the doing, because the criminal solicitor knows full well the request might possibly or actually generate the illegal subject matter of the request.[4]

The Model Penal Code (MPC) has an enviable construction that incorporates the elements necessary for a finding of guilt.

> A person is guilty of solicitation to commit a crime if with the purpose of promoting or facilitating its commission he commands, encourages, or requests another person to engage in specific conduct which would constitute such crime or an attempt to commit such crime or which would establish his complicity in its commission or attempted commission.[5]

Words like "promoting, facilitating, commands, and encourages" paint the weasel's portrait—the human agent who glories when others offend or when the requesting party lacks the mettle to

---

CASE 10.1

PEOPLE V. BURT

288 P.2d 503 (Cal.1955).

Visit your local law library or go online to retrieve the above case and answer the following questions.

Questions

1. What was the solicited conduct?
2. Did the solicited party ever carry out the request?
3. What would be the best defense?
4. Was the offense a misdemeanor because it related to prostitution? If so, how did the solicitation charge eventually stick?

---

do his or her own bidding.[6] This is the profile of an inciter and manipulator of others. Even when the solicited party rejects the request, the requester will be held accountable. In this context, one can appreciate the truly incomplete nature of solicitation because the offense is rooted in the asking not the doing. "The solicitation constitutes a substantive crime in itself, and not an abortive attempt to perpetrate the crime solicited. It falls short of an attempt, in the legal sense, to commit the offense solicited."[7]

When the solicitation evolves into a more active role, though still short of actual commission, the criminal agent also may be convicted under attempt statutes.

Other characteristics of the crime of solicitation include:

- The solicitation focuses on felonious activity.
- Solicitation is personal to the solicitor.
- Solicitation preys on the weak and criminally inclined.
- Solicitation may cause an innocent person to unwittingly engage in crime.

For some excellent examples of solicitation and other inchoate offenses, see the training module prepared by the State of New Mexico at: http://www.dps.state.nm.us/training/legal/documents/Attempt_Accessory_Conspiracy.pdf

---

CRIMINAL ATTEMPTS

The vagaries of criminal attempts test even the most seasoned scholars of criminal law. That courts and legislatures assess the standards applicable to attempts in diverse ways should be no real surprise. Attempted crimes, a major inchoate category, are so close to fruition, but yet interrupted. In an attempt case, the actor intends clearly to commit an underlying felony and expresses no reservations about this purpose, nor does this same actor utilize other people to affect these desires.[8] The attempt criminal acts on a higher level than simple intention by driving toward the commission of a goal—the actual crime. The criminals, Robert Wagner argues, "simply by luck, have not committed the underlying crime, but who are indistinguishable in blameworthiness from those who have succeeded."[9] Here, the criminal gets close, but something intervenes, whether an act of God or police intervention. Something foils the plan as it unfolds. A typical construction of a criminal attempt statute might be:

(a) Definition of attempt.—A person commits an attempt when, with intent to commit a specific crime, he does any act which constitutes a substantial step toward the commission of that crime.

(b) Impossibility.—It shall not be a defense to a charge of attempt that because of a misapprehension of the circumstances it would have been impossible for the accused to commit the crime attempted.[10]

Criminal attempts go farther down the preparatory schema than the solicitation, for the attempting criminal plans and plots, then commits an act that moves closer to the ultimate goal.[11]

Like a fox ready to spring on a rooster, attempted crimes leap beyond expectancy into the realm of actuality. In each case of attempt, these legal standards need to be addressed:

- The attempt directs itself to a specific crime (felony).
- The criminal actor intends to commit the crime.
- The criminal actor is unable to commit the crime.
- The criminal actor was capable and ready to commit the crime.
- The criminal actor has taken the substantial and overt step towards commission.

Type of Intent

The mens rea of attempts are not rooted in attempt. In other words, the intending party does not say: "I intend to attempt and I hope I succeed." The intentionality should be anchored in a felony that is the aim of the attempter. The agent attempts not the attempt, but the underlying criminality where he or she will eventually come up short. This crucial distinction leads to the harsh conclusion that attempted murderers, rapists, arsonists, and other ilk are just as despicable as those who reach their final destination. The lines between the successfully carried out crime and the unaccomplished or foiled are pretty proximate. This is why the punishments are largely the same and the law construes the attempted act to be synonymous with the actual act. From this angle, the level of intentionality is equally grave to that of the completed offender, though the attempted offense is distinguishable on elemental grounds.

Overt or Substantial Step

To carry out the intended consequence, the attempting party needs to do more than ruminate about what he or she intends. The prosecution would be hard pressed to indict any party for the content of the mind alone.[12] As a result, both at common law and by statutory authority, an additional requirement must be met before a conclusive finding in favor of attempt can be drawn. That step or act is often termed "overt" or "substantial," which means the criminal moved toward the commission of the offense in some specific way and by some identifiable action. The thorny challenge in defining a "substantial" step has been the subject of endless litigation.[13] Clark and Marshall describe this stepping into the external world as an "outward manifestation" of

CASE 10.2

PEOPLE V. BERGER
280 P.2d 136 (Cal. 1955).

Defendant appeals from a judgment convicting him of an attempt to commit an abortion and from the order of the trial court denying his motion for a new trial. Appellant was indicted jointly with Inez L. Burns. The indictment contained several counts, but it was agreed that the prosecution would proceed on count 2 charging an attempt to commit abortion; appellant and his counsel waived a jury trial and stipulated to submit the charge to the trial judge on the testimony given before the grand jury.

The evidence may be summarized as follows: Adrienne Scheuplein, an investigator for the district attorney, went to the office of appellant, a licensed physician. She introduced herself as Kathryn Phillips and told appellant that she was pregnant and that she had come to him for the same reason as the young woman who had referred her to him. He directed her to go to a laboratory for a test to establish pregnancy. She was later informed by telephone that the test was positive and requested to call again at appellant's office. When she went to his office the second time, the codefendant Burns was there. Appellant told Mrs. Scheuplein that it was difficult to do anything about her problem and asked if the operation could be performed at the place where she was staying. It was subsequently arranged that the operation should be performed at Mrs. Scheuplein's home. Appellant told Mrs. Scheuplein that a suitcase would be delivered at her home and that the person who would perform the operation would get in touch with her and he gave her specific instructions on preparing herself for surgery. The suitcase was delivered that night and the following morning Inez Burns arrived.

Mrs. Burns went to the kitchen and began making arrangements for the operation. The suitcase containing the surgical instruments was brought into the kitchen, the instruments were wrapped in towels and placed on the stove in pans of water to boil. A sheet was placed over the window to conceal it from the view of any person outside. Mrs. Burns placed cotton, jars of pitocin, ergotrate, metsol, and ammonia and a large roll of gauze on a side table. Mrs. Scheuplein paid Mrs. Burns $525 in marked money. These activities occupied about 45 minutes during which Mrs. Burns talked of her past activities and reassured Mrs. Scheuplein about the pending operation. When the water in the pans containing the instruments was starting to boil, Mrs. Scheuplein went upstairs, supposedly to disrobe, and the police arrived and arrested Mrs. Burns. Mrs. Burns admitted that she was there for the purpose of performing an abortion. Other details of evidence connecting appellant with these activities need not be stated since no claim is made that, if Mrs. Burns was guilty of the crime charged, the appellant could not under the evidence be found guilty also. ...

Penal Code, section 274, defines the crime of abortion as follows: "Every person who provides, supplies, or administers to any woman, or procures any woman to take any medicine, drug or substance, or uses or employs any instrument or other means whatever, with intent thereby to procure the miscarriage of such woman, unless the same is necessary to preserve her life, is punishable by imprisonment in the state prison not less than two nor more than five years."

It is appellant's position that this section itself makes an attempt to procure a miscarriage the substantive offense and hence Penal Code, section 664, which only applies "where no provision is made by law for the punishment of such attempts," is not applicable. Tersely, appellant argues that there can be no such crime as an attempt to attempt. The argument is one of semantics rather than logic. The Legislature could have made the actual inducement of a miscarriage the substantive offense, in which event the acts prohibited by Penal Code, section 274, would have constituted an attempt (in which case other preceding acts might also be sufficient to constitute an attempt). But the Legislature has chosen to make those acts performed with intent to procure a miscarriage the substantive offense and no logical reason appears why the attempt to commit that substantive offense does not fall within the definition of Penal Code, section 664. To apply the sections to this particular case: "Every person ... who uses or employs any instrument ... with intent thereby to procure" a miscarriage is guilty of the substantive offense. No good reason appears why any person who attempts "to use or employ any instrument" with the same intent is not guilty of an attempt under Penal Code, section 664. While this question has apparently not been suggested before, it is significant that the courts have held that a person may be guilty of an attempt to commit an abortion as that crime is defined in Penal Code, section 274.

Appellant points out that the black letter heading of section 275, Penal Code, which prohibits similar acts by a pregnant woman herself reads: "Submitting to an attempt to produce miscarriage." The offense is not the same, but even if it were, while the black letter headings of sections of the code may be looked to in case of ambiguity they are not conclusive. We are satisfied that where, as here, the Legislature makes certain acts a complete substantive offense the attempt to commit those acts falls under Penal Code section 664.

The more serious question is whether the acts performed by Mrs. Burns amounted to no more than mere preparation. The cases make clear that mere preparation to commit a crime does not constitute an attempt to commit it, but the drawing of the line between mere preparation and attempt in close cases is not an easy task. ...

The rule was thus stated in *People v. Fiegelman*, 33 Cal.App.2d 100, 105 [91 P.2d 156]: "Whenever the design of a person to commit a crime is clearly shown, slight acts done in furtherance of that design will constitute an attempt, and the courts should not destroy the practical and commonsense administration of the law with subtleties as to what constitutes preparation and what constitutes an act done toward the commission of a crime."

It may be added that even where the intent is clearly proved: "In order to establish an attempt, it must appear that the defendant ... did a direct, unequivocal act toward that end; preparation alone is not enough, and some appreciable fragment of the crime must have been accomplished." (*People v. Gallardo*, supra, 41 Cal.2d 57, 66.) ...

On the other hand, in *People v. Reed*, supra, 128 Cal.App.2d 499, while the intended abortee was not yet on the operating table, the defendant took a speculum from the sterilizer and ran cold water over it. He was arrested at that moment. The court concluded that this was sufficient to constitute an attempt saying (p. 502): "Here defendant started to use the means to procure a miscarriage."

In the case before us, the acts performed by appellant's confederate were one step removed from those in the Reed case. Appellant had placed the instruments in pans on the stove for the purpose of sterilizing them in boiling water, and the problem presented is, the intent with which this act was done being clearly and unequivocally established, did this amount to a mere preparation, or was it a first step in the commission of the intended crime itself and thus sufficient to constitute an attempt? ...

In *People v. Gibson*, 94 Cal.App.2d 468 [210 P.2d 747], defendant took a ladder in the nighttime with intent to burglarize some building in the locality. He had not yet selected the building to be burglarized when he was apprehended. The court affirmed a conviction of attempt to commit burglary since the intent was clearly proved by defendant's admissions. The court said (p. 470): "It is not necessary that the overt act proved should have been the ultimate step toward the consummation of the design. It is sufficient if it was 'the first or some subsequent step in a direct movement towards the commission of the offense after the preparations are made.'" ...

It is a matter of common knowledge that the sterilization of the instruments to be used in a surgical operation is the first step taken in the performance of the operation in modern surgical procedure. In a case where the intent was not clearly established, the boiling of surgical instruments might be too equivocal an act to be held to constitute an attempt, but we have concluded that, since the intent with which this act was done in this case is established beyond any doubt, the boiling of the surgical instruments under the reasoning of the authorities cited was an act done toward the commission of the crime and hence sufficient to support the judgment.

Questions

1. What offense was targeted by the defendant?
2. What overt or substantial step was taken by the defendant?
3. How did the Court rule?
4. Would that ruling be upheld today?

the offender's mind.[14] Overt acts traverse beyond the mental faculties of the accused and offer a glimpse of the intentionality by the actor's actual movement. Overt acts jump out of the internal, intellectual workings of the actor and afford some picture of how mind and human action coalesce. The Model Penal Code delivers a cogent series of illustrations that might meet the threshold of substantiality at 5.01, subsection 2.

Conduct shall not be held to constitute a substantial step under Subsection (1)(c) of this Section unless it is strongly corroborative of the actor's criminal purpose. Without negating the sufficiency of other conduct, the following, if strongly corroborative of the actor's criminal purpose, shall not be held insufficient as a matter of law:

(a) lying in wait, searching for or following the contemplated victim of the crime;
(b) enticing or seeking to entice the contemplated victim of the crime to go to the place contemplated for its commission;
(c) reconnoitering the place contemplated for the commission of the crime;
(d) unlawful entry of a structure, vehicle or enclosure in which it is contemplated that the crime will be committed;

   (e)   possession of materials to be employed in the commission of the crime, which are specially
         designed for such unlawful use which can serve no lawful purpose of the actor under the
         circumstances;
   (f)   possession, collection or fabrication of materials to be employed in the commission of the
         crime, at or near the place contemplated for its commission, where such possession, collec-
         tion or fabrication serves no lawful purpose of the actor under the circumstances;
   (g)   soliciting an innocent agent to engage in conduct constituting an element of the crime.[15]

The examples of lying in wait, entering and reconnoitering, possession and collection of criminal's tools, intelligently lead the fact finder to the sensible conclusion that a felony is moving
toward its actuality.[16] When burglars' tools and safecracking materials are purchased, it is reasonable to deduce a substantial step in the movement toward the felony. The task at hand is to
identify acts that advance the criminal agency.

Review the Lexis/Nexis Capsule summary in the law of attempts at: http://www.lexisnexis.
com/lawschool/study/outlines/html/crim/crim20.htm

The closer the attempter gets to actual commission, the easier the proof. Rutgers Professor
Douglas Husak sees the overt act and substantial step requirement as a sort of insurance or guarantee that the system can rely on, a sort of security blanket whereby we are sure the defendant is
an actual doer and not simply a thinker. "In other words, we need some principled basis for the act
requirement here and elsewhere in the criminal law."[17] However, these are, at times, very fuzzy cases.
Exactly when the idea moves into the actionable realm is not always easy to tell. At times, prosecutorial zeal finds the connection between act and attempt a bit too quickly. Less sophisticated defendants, without the resources to challenge each charge can be flooded with attempt claims that are
tenuous at best. Consider the *Commonwealth v. White*[18] decision at Case 10.3.

While injustice occurs on occasion in the law of attempts, the justice system needs a tool to
combat those that plan, who act, and yet falter as they near the finish line of a completed act. In a
way, there is no other reasonable alternative to this technique of adjudication. Some have argued
that it is better to forget these types of cases and reserve our resources on those crimes that are
accomplished rather than those we can only infer or predict might happen. People can and do
have changes of heart, and that power to abandon the enterprise, even after the substantial step
has been imprinted, may be undermined by too much fervor in the battle over the attempt.[19] Our
system of justice has enough on its plate presently and a retreat from this type of case might be
intelligent discretion. Prosecutors need be prepared for the diverse defense strategies in attempt
cases.

Capacity and Impossibility

To be guilty of an attempt requires the capacity to commit the target felony. If the felony intended
cannot be legally or factually carried out, then the agent does not possess the requisite capacity
to carry out the deed.[20]

Tied closely to capacity is the concept of impossibility, from a factual and legal sense.
Attempt prosecutions fail when a defendant astutely asserts that the target offense could not
be carried out, so it is of little importance whether the attempt is followed through or not. Not
all arguments involving capacity and impossibility work. A defendant who attempts to steal

CASE 10.3

COMMONWEALTH V. WHITE

335 A.2d 436 (Pa. Super. 1975).

The appellant, George White, was found guilty in a nonjury trial of conduct, which corrupted or tended to corrupt the morals of a minor, attempted indecent assault, and terroristic threats. He was acquitted on indictments charging attempted rape and attempted statutory rape.

Post-trial motions were argued and denied, whereupon the appellant was sentenced to three years psychiatric probation for the offense of corrupting the morals of a minor. A concurrent sentence of two years psychiatric probation was imposed on the conviction of attempted indecent assault. Sentence was suspended on the bill charging terroristic threats. This appeal followed.

At trial, the complainant, Walesca Rodriquez, an eight-year-old girl, testified that in July of 1973, she was playing outside her home located in Philadelphia, when a man, who she later identified as the appellant, came over to her and placed his hand over her mouth and shined a flashlight on her face. The child further testified that the appellant carried her to the back of an abandoned house located on the same block as her own home. Once inside, the appellant told the girl he was going to grab her. The child then testified that the appellant held her against a wall by her shoulders and proceeded to pull her skirt up approximately six inches when she suddenly saw a neighbor, Edwin Negron, passing a window. The child called out to Mr. Negron that the appellant wanted to kill her. At this point, the appellant left the child alone and fled the house with Mr. Negron unsuccessfully giving chase. The appellant testified that on the night of the incident, he was using his flashlight in search of his dog in the vicinity of the abandoned house. Appellant further testified that as he was leaving the old house Mr. Negron confronted him and asked him what he was doing. When Mr. Negron advanced toward him, the appellant fled. The appellant also testified that he never touched the complainant, nor was she with him when he entered the old house. The appellant called four witnesses to testify in his behalf. In essence, these witnesses testified to the effect that the defendant told them he was going to look for his dog on the night in question.

With respect to his conviction for attempted indecent assault, appellant contends that in the first instance, the evidence was insufficient to constitute the crime and, in any event, since he was specifically indicted for indecent assault he could not be convicted of attempted indecent assault. We do not agree with either contention.

The recently enacted Pennsylvania Crimes Code, Act of December 6, 1972, P.L. 1482, No. 334, § 1, eff. June 6, 1973, 18 Pa. C.S. § 101 et seq., controls the disposition of this appeal since the alleged offenses occurred subsequent to June 6, 1973. The crime of indecent assault is defined in § 3126 of Title 18 as follows: "A person who has indecent contact with another not his spouse, or causes such other person to have indecent contact with him is guilty of indecent assault, a misdemeanor of the second degree, if: (1) he knows that the contact is offensive to the other person; ..." "Indecent contact" is defined as: "Any touching of the sexual or other intimate parts of the person for the purpose of arousing or gratifying sexual desire, in either person." 18 Pa. C.S. § 3101 (1973). An accused is guilty of attempt when, "with intent to commit a specific crime, he does any act which constitutes a substantial step toward the commission of that crime." 18 Pa. C.S. § 901 (1973). Application of the above statutes to the facts at bar, i.e., the appellant's act of carrying the complainant to the back of an abandoned house; holding her shoulders, threatening to grab her, and lifting her skirt up approximately six inches, all of which occurred against the complainant's will, demonstrates that the appellant had the requisite intent to commit, at the minimum, an indecent assault and, furthermore, had taken substantial steps towards the completion of the reprehensible act. Appellant concedes that under the Act of June 24, 1939, P.L. 872, § 1107, 18 P.S. § 5107, a conviction for an attempt upon an indictment charging a substantive crime would have been proper. Appellant argues, however, that since 18 P.S. § 5107 has been repealed by the new Crimes Code, his conviction for attempted indecent assault cannot stand. We reject this argument for several reasons. Initially, appellant's argument fails because 18 Pa. C.S. § 905 specifically provides, *inter alia*, that the punishment for attempt shall be of the same grade and degree as the most serious offense which is attempted. In addition, neither the Crimes Code nor the Pennsylvania Rules of Criminal Procedure contain any provision requiring a conviction of the substantive offense, as distinguished from the attempt, when the indictment charges the actual offense. Furthermore, when appellant was convicted of attempted indecent assault, he was necessarily convicted of a crime which is an integral part of the substantive crime of indecent assault, since the consummated act of indecent assault cannot exist without first the attempt to commit an indecent assault. Therefore, appellant could not seriously claim that he was caught by surprise, insomuch as his defense against the charge of indecent assault also constituted a defense against the attempt to commit such an act. For all of the foregoing reasons we hold that the appellant was properly convicted of attempted indecent assault. Appellant next maintains that his conduct did not constitute the crime of corrupting or tending to corrupt the morals of a minor. The relevant statute, 18 Pa. C.S. § 3125, provides in pertinent part: "(a) Whoever, being of the age of 18 years and upwards, by any act corrupts or tends to corrupt the morals of any child under the age of 18 years, or who aids, abets, entices or encourages any such child in the commission of any crime, or who knowingly assists or encourages such child in violating his or her parole or any order of court, is guilty of a misdemeanor of the second degree." Parenthetically, we note at the outset that this section re-enacts verbatim the prior statute, which prohibited conduct that corrupted or tended to corrupt the morals of a minor, with the exception of the degree of punishment prescribed.

Questions

1. What felony does the court say the defendant attempts?
2. Do these facts lead to that conclusion?
3. While the conduct of defendant is despicable, does the court analyze the law of attempts correctly?
4. How would you have ruled?

a wallet when none exists on that person cannot claim the impossibility of theft as a defense. A justice model that provides a defense because of altered or changed circumstances would be continuously hoodwinked when things turned out differently than the defendant intended them.[21] Impossibility is gauged from the mind of the offender under reasonable circumstances, not from the victim's perspective. Thus, if the accused believed his gun was filled with ammunition and capable of inflicting the critical wound, providing a window into the defendant's objective intentionality, even though the weapon cannot factually produce the injury sought, the attempt should be sustained.[22] Using objective reality again, the threat to kill with a spaghetti noodle cannot be factually or legally plausible and a party believing that a spaghetti noodle can kill is short on the intellectual capacity to formulate the required intent for the attempt. No matter how many swings the offender takes, his victim will not succumb to fatal injuries. If the means are adequate to inflict the desired injury, and the offender believes them to be adequate, the end result will not alter the intent to commit the felony by attempt. Factual impossibility cases will vary according to fact and circumstance and must be evaluated in light of the reasonable person standard.

Questions involving legal impossibility are sprinkled throughout the lore of American jurisprudence. Most jurisdictions retain some aspects of the defense, though most center the focus on the objective mind of the defendant. If the defendant believes in the criminality of his or her deed, no further inspection is necessary. Evaluate these cases:

Case A: The accused appeals a conviction of attempted murder when he later discovers the victim was already deceased.

Case B: The accused sets out to rape a particular female only to have consent to intercourse given.

Case C: The accused is charged with receiving stolen property when the property, in fact, was not stolen.

Case D: The accused sells colored liquid that looks like whiskey to federal agents.

In each of the above cases, the dilemma of legal impossibility emerges, for murder on a corpse is legally impossible as is consensual sexual intercourse being designated rape.[23] The doctrine of legal impossibility bars convictions for the offense in normal circumstances let alone attempted ones. It seems somewhat unjust to exonerate those directly charged while convicting attempt defendants because of their own internal operations. It would not be appropriate to assign guilt and retroactively impose a conviction for an attempt of an offense that had not been codified or enacted by the legislative process, or for an offense since repealed for which the accused was not aware.

In general, the world of attempts is accurately typed as gray and ambiguous because its chief evidentiary form resides internally in the actor's mind. It is he or she alone who truly knows the content of intention. While it is always acceptable for our system of adjudication to infer and deduce from actions what an actor intends, the lack of proximity to the targeted felony presents a thornier and more cumbersome picture in the law of attempts. The "substantial step" drives us closer though the distance between potential desire and actual criminality remains formidable.

CONSPIRACY

ELEMENTS

- An agreement or plan to commit a criminal offense
- By two of more parties
- An overt act
- With intent to agree and intent to commit a crime

Frequently termed the mental crime, conspiracy is the illegal plan and agreement between two or more parties to implement a crime. Conspiracy needs conspirators. Conspirators or co-conspirators, whose allegiance and relationship is meshed by the illicit agreement to carry out a felonious plan, form the core of this inchoate offense.[24] Unlike attempts, a conviction rests on dual intents: first, the intent to illegally confederate and, second, the intent to do something unlawful.[25] The harder issue will always relate to the agreement because the crux of conspiracy is the plan, the collective agreement, and the illegal confederation of parties dedicated to an amorphous concept known as crime. All that need be shown is the parties' mutual intent to engage in crime, the attempts thereto, or its solicitation. What crime really does not matter? The Model Penal Code provision is widely imitated.

> A person is guilty of conspiracy with another person or persons to commit a crime if with the purpose of promoting or facilitating its commission he:
>
> (a) agrees with such other person or persons that they or one or more of them will engage in conduct which constitutes such crime or an attempt or solicitation to commit such crime; or
> (b) agrees to aid such other person or persons in the planning or commission of such crime or of an attempt or solicitation to commit such crime.[26]

Aside from the obvious mental musings in the codification, the statute does insist that some type of overt act take place, which confirms the mental wishes of the conspirators. The MPC, like most other statutory authority, leaves the door open on how overt the act should be and it clearly need not be as substantial as the step that is standard in attempts.

The attack on the conspiracy offense has been persistent and for good cause. Former Justice Jackson of the U.S. Supreme Court displayed no affection for how this type of law works in the legal marketplace. In *Krulewitch v. United States*,[27] his biting comments provoke some level of examination.

The modern crime of conspiracy is so vague that it almost defies definition. Despite certain elementary and essential elements, it is a chameleon and takes on characteristics from the crime it is paired with. It is always "predominantly mental in composition" because it consists primarily of a meeting of minds and an intent.

The crime comes down to use wrapped in vague but unpleasant connotations. It sounds historical undertones of treachery, secret plotting and violence on a scale that menaces social stability and the security of the state itself.[28]

In a more favorable light, conspiracy laws deliver many benefits to the community and the justice system as a whole. First and foremost, the systematic reaction can be characterized as early intervention since the plan will be thwarted. Second, conspiracy produces a regular windfall of plea bargaining and shared information. Before detection, criminals like to talk and share experiences toward the plan and crime to unfold. Once caught, the actors scurry like rats on a sinking ocean liner, delivering up information against their cohorts that assures a higher rate of convictions. Third, the evidentiary demands of conspiracy are somewhat light when compared to other full-blown felonies. Proving the agreement and the general intent to engage in some level of criminality is not a hard sell with the majority of defendants. Conspiracy provides a welcome breather and a stronger suit to those prosecuting. Fourth, conspiracy has an uncanny ability to generate leads. Granted the plea power is impressive; on top of this is the added benefit that one story leads to another. Criminals flock like birds in many areas and their stories interlock and interrelate more than most people realize. Conspiracy prosecutions open the secret chambers of the underworld.[29]

Weighing the strengths and weaknesses of this offense, the justice model stands more to lose without it than with it. For an example of a state conspiracy statute, see below.

§ 105.15. Conspiracy in the second degree

A person is guilty of conspiracy in the second degree when, with intent that conduct constituting a class A felony be performed, he agrees with one or more persons to engage in or cause the performance of such conduct.

§ 105.20. Conspiracy; pleading and proof; necessity of overt act

A person shall not be convicted of conspiracy unless an overt act is alleged and proved to have been committed by one of the conspirators in furtherance of the conspiracy.[30]

Federal criminal conspiracy, when compared to state versions, covers similar yet distinct coverage areas. The U.S. Code stresses the governmental nature of the act by requiring a conspiratorial plan to "commit any offense against the United States" or an act to "defraud the United States" or violate "a civil or criminal federal law."[31] Hence, the emphasis is similar to state requirements of plan, agreement, and overt act, although the goals for federal conspiracy are critically important for the law's applicability.

Some overlap on the fraud side, as well as certain regulatory violations, cause a civil consideration of conspiracy. Civil conspiracy assumes that an agreement exists, not for crimes per se, but other personal harm, such as fraudulent banking or weaponry sales across multiple state lines. The Civil Conspiracy rests in the agreement as well as the residencies of the defendants themselves. Hence, a resident of one state, who plans and plots with other defendants in other jurisdictions, gives a basis for conspiracy both as to subject matter and the residencies themselves.[32] This is distinctly different than criminal conspiracy.

The Agreement

At the heart of every conspiracy claim is the unity of mind and purpose evident in the parties who come to the table. When a band of thugs cannot concur on an agenda, the conspiracy is absent. If these same undesirables argue heatedly and disjointedly about separate and individual interests, walking away from the same table with no cohesive purpose, a conspiracy is undeveloped. The essence of conspiracy is the Agreement, the meeting of criminal minds to engage in criminal activity. This can only be affirmed by an evidentiary record that not only shows discussion and debate, but eventual consensus.

CASE 10.4

MITCHELL V. MARYLAND
363 Md. 130 (Md. App. 2001)

Petitioner's convictions arose from a shooting that occurred on September 5, 1997. During that morning, the victim, Eddy Arias, received three pages on his pager and, in response to each, left his apartment to use the telephone, as there was no telephone in the apartment. As he reentered his apartment building after responding to the third page, he was attacked by two men at the bottom of the internal stairway, each armed with a handgun and each with a stocking mask over his face. Mr. Arias managed to break free and began to run up the stairs to his apartment, when he was shot in the back by one of the men. For purposes of this appeal, we take as a given that petitioner was one of the two men but that it was the other one, Gregory Ellis, who fired the shot. The State's theory was that the assailants' intent was to kill Mr. Arias and not simply to rob him.

Petitioner was charged in a multicount indictment with a variety of offenses, including a count that was treated as charging conspiracy to commit first degree murder and one that more clearly charged conspiracy to commit second degree murder. At the end of the State's case, a judgment of acquittal was entered on the counts charging attempted first degree murder, conspiracy to commit first degree murder, and possession of a firearm by a convicted felon. Petitioner was convicted, however, of attempted second degree murder, first degree assault, conspiracy to commit second degree murder, conspiracy to commit first degree assault, and use of a handgun in the commission of a felony. Several of the convictions, among them the two for conspiracy, were merged, but petitioner was sentenced to a total of 46 years in prison, including 13 years for conspiracy to commit second degree murder.

Notwithstanding his failure to mount any jurisdictional challenge in the trial court to the count charging conspiracy to commit second degree murder or to object to the court's instruction to the jury on that count, petitioner claimed in the Court of Special Appeals that there was no such crime in Maryland. He argued there, as he argues here, that establishment of a conspiracy to commit murder necessarily establishes the element of premeditation that would make any murder emanating from the conspiracy first degree murder. It is not legally possible, he claims, for a person to conspire to commit a nonpremeditated murder.

Regarding the argument as effectively challenging the jurisdiction of the trial court to render a judgment on the count, the Court of Special Appeals determined that it was one that could be raised initially on appeal and therefore addressed it. See *Williams v. State*, 302 Md. 787, 791-92, 490 A.2d 1277, 1279 (1985); *Lane v. State*, 348 Md. 272, 278, 703 A.2d 180, 183 (1997). The court found no merit in the argument, however, notwithstanding its view that the argument was "appealing on the surface" and "superficially seductive." Mitchell, supra, 132 Md. App. at 338, 353, 752 A.2d at 667, 676. Rather, the court concluded that it was legally and factually possible for a person to conspire to commit an unpremeditated murder. Its theory was that an agreement to kill a person could be arrived at "virtually instantaneously with the commission (or attempt) of that crime" and thus, despite its spontaneity, suffice to constitute a conspiracy but, because of its spontaneity, not suffice to constitute premeditation. Id. at 354, 752 A.2d at 676. Accordingly, in that circumstance (and perhaps in others that the court indicated might exist but did not attempt to define), it was legally possible to conspire to commit a nonpremeditated second degree murder. Id. On that premise, and relying on decisions to that effect in *United States v. Croft*, 124 F.3d 1109 (9th Cir. 1997) and *United States v. Chagra*, 807 F.2d 398 (5th Cir. 1986), cert. denied, 484 U.S. 832, 108 S. Ct. 106, 98

L. Ed. 2d 66 (1987), it affirmed the challenged conviction.

Questions

1. Why was the Court's opinion on Murder 2, Murder 1, and Conspiracy to Murder so complicated?
2. Can one conspire to kill, nonpremeditatively, and be guilty of Conspiracy to Murder?
3. What does the Court mean when it says the defense argument is "superficially seductive"?

On the other end of the spectrum, unanimity of purpose is readily discernable in the meeting of an organized crime family whose agenda (Figure 10.1a and Figure 10.1b), admittedly obtuse and vague in content, dwells upon how to advance the family business.[33]

Visit the FBI's excellent web location on Organized Crime at http://www.fbi.gov/about-us/investigate/organizedcrime/organized_crime

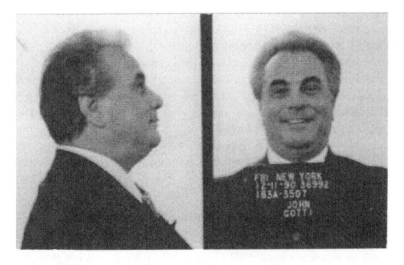

Figure 10.1a   John Gotti. (Courtesy FBI.)

Figure 10.1b   Charlie (Lucky) Luciano. (Courtesy FBI.)

By blood and affinity, by common criminal purpose and desire, the agreement exists among some of the participants. That mental agreement need not be reduced to contractual form, only a consensus or concurrence of ideas that will eventually take shape in a criminal form. "When two agree to carry it into effect, the very plot is an act in itself, and the act of each of the parties, promise against promise, *actus contra actum*, capable of being enforced if lawful, punishable if for a criminal object or for the use of criminal means."[34]

Agreement is further demonstrated by the showing of a purpose for the assembly. To agree requires proof of the content of the agreement. The end sought by the agreement, whether sale of drugs or prostitution, cements the agreement. If the purpose is clear, so is the agreement because "knowledge of that objective and conscious assistance may justify an inference of such purpose."[35]

The Overt Act

Conspiracy charges cannot be leveled at those who merely agree to engage in criminal conduct. If this was the foundation of the offense, police would be little more than thought police trying to ferret out people with wicked ideas. Undoubtedly not a day goes by whereby groups of people mix and converse about what they are going to do, some of it illegal, the rest involving the humdrum conservation of everyday life. Conspiracy claims are not satisfied by words alone and under common law as well as contemporary statutes, an additional requirement is posed—that of the overt act. An overt act is a conscious and open behavior that relates to the criminal plan and an act that furthers the collective agreement. The word "overt" means externally demonstrable rather than covert, which is unseen and internal to the actor accused of conspiracy. Pennsylvania defines the act as so:

> (e) Overt act. —No person may be convicted of conspiracy to commit a crime unless an overt act in pursuant of such conspiracy is alleged and proved to have been done by him or by a person with whom he conspired.[36]

The overt action mirrors the agreement because it furthers the illegal plan. So, in a robbery case, the purchase of weaponry subsequently used in a bank heist could qualify for the overt act.

CASE 10.5

PEOPLE V. RUSSO

No. S088368. (Cal. App. 2001)

In California, a conviction for conspiracy requires proof that at least one of the conspirators committed an overt act in furtherance of the conspiracy. We granted review to decide whether the jury must unanimously agree on a specific overt act. We conclude the jury need not agree on a specific overt act as long as it unanimously finds beyond a reasonable doubt that some conspirator committed an overt act in furtherance of the conspiracy.

On the night of July 14, 1994 (all dates are to the year 1994), a Fresno County deputy sheriff found David Russo's body, dead from a gunshot wound to the back of the head, wrapped inside a sleeping bag in the backseat of David's car in a remote rural location. David's wife, defendant Susan Lee Russo (hereafter defendant), and codefendants Bobby Morris and Jason Andrews were tried together for conspiring to murder and murdering him. The prosecution presented evidence that defendant knew she would receive over $200,000 in the event of David's death from his employer, the United States Navy. Circumstantial evidence, including a comparison of bloodstains found in the bedroom of the Russo house in Riverdale with bloodstains found near the body, indicated that David had been killed in that bedroom. Other evidence showed that David had possessed a nine-millimeter Beretta handgun.

Defendant told the police the following: She let some people into her house around 1:00 a.m. on July 14, and after that she saw David's nine-millimeter Beretta gun. She had given the gun to someone on July 12. She told the people who had entered her house that her husband was asleep and they should keep their voices down. The people were making hand signals. Someone shot David with his own gun. The shot was muffled and occurred while she was checking on one of her children. After the shot, she saw her husband lying on the bed and the other persons still in the bedroom. The gun was wrapped in a towel. She picked up the gun and handed it to one of the others. She and the others then wrapped David's head in a garbage bag and his body in sleeping bags, tied ropes around the body, and put it into David's car. The others talked about a meeting place and then left. She was told the car would be "torched." She later cleaned up the bedroom.

Defendant admitted that she had previously talked about her husband's killing and that "outside people" would be hired to do it. She had the impression it would be done that night. Defendant knew that David was insured. She had planned to buy a house and pay bills with the insurance proceeds. Regarding the killing, she said, "It was just an easy out. It was stupid."

Travis Hayes testified that on July 13, in defendant's presence, Andrews solicited him to kill David. Andrews had a nine-millimeter handgun strapped to his side. Defendant told Hayes she could get him whatever money he wanted. Hayes said he would consider it. Defendant and Andrews gave Hayes $100. Later, Hayes told Andrews he could not go through with the crime. Two days after that, Andrews told Hayes that David had already been killed and asked Hayes to burn David's car. Hayes did not do so.

James Plantz testified that a few days before David's death, Morris asked him if he or anyone he knew would kill someone for $100. Morris said he would help, but the other person would have to do the actual killing. Plantz refused to help Morris. The day before the killing,

Morris made statements to Plantz indicating involvement in the plan to kill David. Later that day, Andrews told Plantz that he had hired someone to do a killing for $100, but that the person had backed out. The next day, Morris told Plantz that Andrews had killed the intended victim by shooting him. Morris took out a nine-millimeter pistol, ejected a spent casing from it, and said, "Oh, there it is."

Morris testified on his own behalf. He said that Andrews had talked to him about killing David, but Morris thought the proposal was "bullshit." He never intended to help Andrews kill David. The night of the killing, defendant asked him to come to the Russo home in order, he assumed, to pick up some drugs. At the house, Andrews handed him a gun and told him he could have $100 if he killed David. Morris declined and returned the gun to Andrews. Andrews then took the gun, wrapped it in a towel as a silencer, and entered David's room with defendant. Morris heard a muffled shot. He then helped Andrews and defendant dispose of David's body and the gun. He felt he had to because his fingerprints were on the gun.

Andrews also testified on his own behalf. He said he had become sexually involved with defendant before David's death. She had talked about possibly divorcing David but never about killing him. Before the killing, defendant gave him some of David's guns, including the nine-millimeter handgun. She told him David wanted the guns out of the house before someone used them in the house. The evening of the killing, defendant asked him to come to her home and drop off some drugs. He and Morris went to the Russo home shortly after midnight and gave defendant some drugs. Morris asked where David was. Defendant told him he was in a back room. Morris disappeared down the hall and Andrews heard a gunshot. Morris then came out of David's room and pointed the nine-millimeter gun at Andrews. Morris told Andrews and defendant to help dispose of the body. Andrews did not think defendant was involved in the shooting. She never asked Andrews to kill David.

Questions

1. Do both defendants in the conspiracy take an overt act?
2. Describe the prime "overt act."
3. In a case of multiple defendants, why is the Court satisfied with a minimum of one overt act? Do you agree?

In a rape case, entry into the house of the victim overtly manifests the will of the conspirator, and, in a drug sale, visitation to a crack house, where the neighborhood reputation precludes visits for any other sensible reason, overtly discloses the conspirator's mind at the agreement table.

Liberally interpreted and the bane to criminal defendants, conspiracy law serves many legitimate purposes.

Special Case: RICO

An offshoot of conspiracy is the daunting federal legislation popularly known as the Racketeer Influenced and Corrupt Organizations Act (RICO)[37] that penalizes individuals for mere membership in a collective enterprise that engages in criminality. It is a touchy subject in many quarters because, while the Act was passed originally to fight organized crime families, its evolution has startled both civil libertarians and moral protesters. The Act's recent usage to weaken abortion protest groups and military militia associations has generated significant criticism.[38]

> Read about the diverse strategies to combat organized crime including the RICO statute in the U.S. Attorneys' Manual at: http://www.justice.gov/usao/eousa/foia_reading_room/usam/title9/110mcrm.htm

Originally, RICO, focused on the Mafioso and crime syndicates by penalizing mere association. As time went forward, RICO was strengthened to allow the federal government to confiscate the proceeds of illegality and the beneficial fruits of a corrupt lifestyle.[39] This confiscation included houses and cars, personal property, cash and bank accounts when no other reasonable explanation for the largesse could be provided. In this way, the government could denude and strip away the economic power base that allowed the criminal enterprise to flourish and continue.

The RICO has incredible teeth.

§ 1962. Prohibited activities

(a) It shall be unlawful for any person who has received any income derived, directly or indirectly, from a pattern of racketeering activity or through collection of an unlawful debt in which such person has participated as a principal within the meaning of section 2, title 18, United States Code, to use or invest, directly or indirectly, any part of such income, or the proceeds of such income, in acquisition of any interest in, or the establishment or operation of, any enterprise which is engaged in, or the activities of which affect, interstate or foreign commerce. A purchase of securities on the open market for purposes of investment, and without the intention of controlling or participating in the control of the issuer, or of assisting another to do so, shall not be unlawful under this subsection if the securities of the issuer held by the purchaser, the members of his immediate family, and his or their accomplices in any pattern or racketeering activity or the collection of an unlawful debt after such purchase do not amount in the aggregate to one percent of the outstanding securities of any one class, and do not confer, either in law or in fact, the power to elect one or more directors of the issuer.

(b) It shall be unlawful for any person through a pattern of racketeering activity or through collection of an unlawful debt to acquire or maintain, directly or indirectly, any interest in or control of any enterprise which is engaged in, or the activities of which affect, interstate or foreign commerce.

(c) It shall be unlawful for any person employed by or associated with any enterprise engaged in, or the activities of which affect, interstate or foreign commerce, to conduct or participate, directly or indirectly, in the conduct of such enterprise's affairs through a pattern of racketeering activity or collection of unlawful debt.

(d) It shall be unlawful for any person to conspire to violate any of the provisions of subsection (a), (b), or (c) of this section.[40]

STORY 10.1

NATIONAL ORGANIZATION FOR WOMEN, INC. V. SCHEIDLER
(547 U.S. 9 (2006); 537 U.S. 393 (2003); 510 U.S. 249 (1994))

In 1986, NOW initiated the suit on behalf of abortion providers in Delaware and Wisconsin that were subjected to clinic blockades by Operation Rescue, Pro-Life Action League, and other antiabortion groups. The RICO Act was established in 1970 as a tool against organized crime that punishes "enterprises" that engage in a "pattern of racketeering." While the Seventh Circuit Court of Appeals held that the law applies only to activities that are motivated by economic gain, NOW argued that RICO is applicable on the grounds that unlawful actions constituted a nationwide conspiracy to eliminate access to abortion by using extortion and intimidation to drive the clinics out of business.

In a unanimous ruling, the Supreme Court overturned the Circuit Court decision, allowing the lawsuit to proceed using RICO as its basis. The court held that RICO can be used in the absence of an economic motive, and that the term "enterprise" can include any individual or group of individuals, partnership, corporation, association, or other legal entity. While the court did not address the possible First Amendment ramifications of the broadened scope of RICO, Justice Souter noted in a concurring opinion that the court was not barring First Amendment challenges to RICO in particular cases.

In 1997, NOW was certified to represent the class of women seeking reproductive healthcare. After a seven-week trial, the jury concluded that the petitioners committed 117 violations of RICO. The case was appealed to the Seventh Circuit again where the lower court's decision was affirmed.

The Supreme Court, in its 2003 decision on the appeal, ruled that although the actions being considered may have been coercive, but were not indicative of extortion because the defendants did not gain property from their victims. Coercion is not covered by RICO.

The case again returned to the Seventh Circuit where the class asked for four violations of the Hobbs Act to be addressed. The appeals court attempted a remand, but defendants appealed to the Supreme Court.

After review, the Supreme Court handed down a unanimous (8-0) decision in favor of Scheidler on February 28, 2006. The Court held that the Hobbs Act did not cover violence unrelated to robbery or extortion and that Congress' 1994 passage of FACE indicated that Congress did not intend RICO to apply to civil actions.

RICO's sweeping power to confiscate has been termed by some as excessive governmental intrusion.[41] The reason RICO falls under the inchoate category is its ability to inflict punishment even without direct proof of a particular criminal act. The membership in the organized crime operation suffices to support the conviction. Just as in conspiracy, the party may plan, take a small step but never complete the deed, or, as in attempts where the defendant never succeeds or the solicitation where the requester never performs the act, RICO defendants are found guilty by association alone. RICO is a formidable weapon against the underworld, but its extension into political groups and protest organizations may be an improper application.

CASE 10.6

H. J. INC. V. NORTHWESTERN BELL TELEPHONE CO.
492 U.S. 229 (1989)

Syllabus: The Racketeer Influenced and Corrupt Organizations Act (RICO), 18 U.S.C. §§ 1961–1968, which is Title IX of the Organized Crime Control Act of 1970 (OCCA), imposes criminal and civil liability upon persons who engage in certain "prohibited activities," each of which is defined to include, as a necessary element, proof of a "pattern of racketeering activity," § 1962. "Racketeering activity" means "any act or threat involving" specified state-law crimes, any "act" indictable under specified federal statutes, and certain federal "offenses." § 1961(1). A "pattern" requires "at least two acts of racketeering activity" within a 10-year period. § 1961(5). Petitioners, customers of respondent Northwestern Bell, filed a civil action in the District Court against Northwestern Bell and other respondents, including members of the Minnesota Public Utilities Commission (MPUC) — which is responsible for determining Northwestern Bell's rates — seeking an injunction and treble damages. They raised four separate claims under §§ 1962(a), (b), (c), and (d), based on factual allegations that between 1980 and 1986, Northwestern Bell made various cash and in-kind payments to MPUC members, and thereby influenced them to approve rates for the company in excess of a fair and reasonable amount. The District Court dismissed the complaint, under Federal Rule of Civil Procedure 12(b)(6), for failure to state a claim upon which relief could be granted, on the ground that each of the fraudulent acts alleged was "committed in furtherance of a single scheme to influence MPUC commissioners" rather than multiple illegal schemes. The Court of Appeals affirmed, confirming that under its precedent, a single scheme is insufficient to establish a pattern of racketeering activity.

Held:

1. In order to prove a pattern of racketeering activity, a plaintiff or prosecutor must show at least two racketeering predicates that are related and that amount to, or threaten the likelihood of, continued criminal activity. Proof of neither relationship nor continuity requires a showing that the racketeering predicates were committed in furtherance of multiple criminal schemes.

(a) Section 1961(5) states that at least two racketeering predicates committed within a 10-year period are necessary to establish a RICO pattern, but implies that two acts may not be sufficient. Section 1961(5) thus assumes that there is something to a pattern beyond merely the number of predicates involved. In normal usage, the word "pattern" would also be taken to require not simply a multiplicity of predicates, but rather predicates arranged or ordered by reason of the relationship they bear to each other or to some external organizing principle. The text of RICO fails to identify the forms of relationship or external principles to be used to determine whether predicates fall into a pattern. RICO's legislative history, however, establishes that Congress intended that to prove a "pattern of racketeering activity" a plaintiff or prosecutor must show both "relationship" and "continuity" — that the racketeering predicates are related, and that they either constitute or threaten long-term criminal activity.

(b)   Relationship and continuity are two distinct requirements, though their proof will often overlap. RICO's notion of relationship is no more constrained than that used in Title X of OCCA, under which "criminal conduct forms a pattern if it embraces criminal acts that have the same or similar purposes, results, participants, victims, or methods of commission, or otherwise are interrelated by distinguishing characteristics and are not isolated events." 18 U.S.C. § 3575(e). Continuity of racketeering activity likewise may be demonstrated in a variety of ways. Continuity is centrally a temporal concept, and may be either closed- or open-ended. A party alleging a RICO violation may demonstrate continuity over a closed period by proving a series of related predicates extending over a substantial period of time. Otherwise, it must be shown that the predicates establish a threat of long-term racketeering activity — for example, because the predicates themselves involve a distinct threat of such activity; because they are part of the regular way of doing business for an ongoing entity such as a criminal association or legitimate business; or because they are a regular means of conducting or participating in an ongoing RICO enterprise. Although proof of multiple criminal schemes may be relevant to this inquiry into continuity, it is not the only way to show continuity. Adopting the Court of Appeals' multiple scheme test would bring a rigidity to the methods of proving a pattern not present in the idea of "continuity" itself, and it would introduce a concept — the "scheme" — that does not appear in RICO's language or legislative history.

(c)   Neither RICO's language nor its legislative history supports a rule that a defendant's racketeering activities form a pattern only if they are characteristic of organized crime. No such restriction appears in RICO's text. Nor is there any language suggesting that RICO's scope should be limited to acts of an association rather than an individual acting alone. Moreover, Congress' approach in RICO can be contrasted with its decision to enact explicit limitations to organized crime in other statutes. E. g., Omnibus Crime Control and Safe Streets Act of 1968, § 601(b). The argument that RICO's broad language should be read restrictively to be congruous with RICO's purpose to eradicate organized crime is rejected: The legislative history shows Congress had no such restriction in mind.

2. The Court of Appeals erred in affirming the District Court's dismissal of petitioners' complaint for failure to allege facts sufficient to demonstrate a "pattern of racketeering activity." Consistent with the allegations in their complaint, petitioners may be able to prove that the multiple predicates alleged satisfy the requirements of continuity and relationship and hence satisfy RICO's pattern of racketeering element.

Questions

1. What is RICO's definition of pattern?
2. Does RICO exclusively relate to organized crime activities?
3. Describe the alleged "racketeering" activity.
4. Do you agree with the Court's judgment of Northwestern Bell?

Review the factual summary of a recent FBI arrest under RICO principles. Discuss whether this is an appropriate application of RICO. Visit: http://sandiego.fbi.gov/dojpressrel/pressrel08/sd_010408.htm

DISCUSSION QUESTIONS

1. Why does the justice system prosecute inchoate offenses?
2. What influence does the "incompleteness" of these offenses have upon juror thinking?
3. How does one solicit others to commit crimes?
4. Does a criminal attempt result in the same criminal responsibility as the actual perpetrator?
5. A criminal attempt needs more than mere ideas. What else?
6. Conspiracy is labeled the "mental" crime. Why?
7. Why does factual impossibility make an attempt a charge not worth making?
8. Describe the "overt act" requirement in conspiracy.
9. What is the relationship between conspiracy and RICO?
10. Can one conspire individually?

SUGGESTED READINGS

Abrams, N., S. S. Beale, and S. R. Klein. 2009. *Federal criminal law and its enforcement,* 5th ed. Eagan, MN: West Law School Publishers.

Ashworth, A. 1988. Criminal attempts and the role of resulting harm under the code, and in the common law. *Rutgers Law Journal* 19 (Spring): 725–772.

Borman, P. D., P. Henning, J. H. Israel, and E. S. Podgor. 2009. *White collar crime: Law and practice,* 3rd ed. Eagan, MN: West Law School Publishers.

Cromwell, P. 2009. *In their own words—Criminals on crime,* 5th ed. New York: Oxford University Press.

DiMarino, F. J. and C. Roberson. 2011. *An introduction to corporate and white collar crime.* Boca Raton, FL: CRC Press.

Grovsten, C. H., and R. E. Mcgowan. 2011. *Forfeiture, conspiracy, venue: Federal crime law.* Hauppauge, NY: Nova Science Publishers Inc.

LaFave, W. R. 2010. Principles of criminal law, 2nd ed. Eagan, MN: West Law School Publishers.

McSorley, J. F. 1996. *Portable guide to federal conspiracy law: Developing strategies for criminal and civil cases.* Washington, DC: American Bar Association.

RICO: The crime of being a criminal, Parts I and II." *Columbia Law Review* 87 (May): 661–764.

Sann, M. and G. Niemann. 1991. Australian criminal law: Attempts. *Criminal Law Forum* 2 (Spring): 511–567.

Shavell, S. 1990. Deterrence and punishment of attempts. *Journal of Legal Studies* 19 (June): 435–466.

Wright, R. S. 2010. *The law of criminal conspiracies and agreements.* Charleston, SC: Nabu Press.

Yaffe, G. 2010. *Attempts—Trying and attempted crimes.* New York: Oxford University Press.

ENDNOTES

1. JEROME HALL, GENERAL PRINCIPLES OF CRIMINAL LAW 569 (2005).

2. Inchoate offenses get even more confusing when dealing with diverse parties. *See* Stuart P. Green, *Moral Ambiguity in White Collar Criminal Law*, 18 NOTRE DAME J. L. ETHICS & PUB. POL'Y 501 (2004).

3. MATTHEW ROSS LIPPMAN, CONTEMPORARY CRIMINAL LAW: CONCEPTS, CASES, AND CONTROVERSIES (2009).

4. Thomas J. Miceli, *Criminal Solicitation, Entrapment, and the Enforcement of Law*, 27 INT'L REV. L. & ECON. 258-268 (2007).

5. Model Penal Code § 5.02 (Proposed Official Draft 1962).

6. On the civil side of law, there is also potential liability that arises from fraudulent inducement of unfair solicitation. *See* Jeffrey R. Doty, *Inducement or Solicitation?: Competition Interpretations of the "Underlying Illegality" Test in the Wake of Roommates.com*, 6 SHIDLER J. L. COM & TECH 125 (2010).

7. *State v. Blechman*, 50 A.2d 152, 154 (1946) *citing Rex v. Higins*, 2 East 5 (1801). *See also People v. Burt*, 288 P.2d 503 (Cal. 1955).

8. R. A. DUFF, CRIMINAL ATTEMPTS (1997); *See also* Thomas Bittner, *Punishment for Criminal Attempts: A Legal Perspective on the Problem of Moral Luck*, 38 CAN. J. PHIL. 51 (2008).

9. Robert E. Wagner, *A Few Good Laws: Why Federal Criminal Law Needs a General Attempt Provision and How Military Law Can Provide One*, 70 U. CIN. L. REV. 1043, 1052 (2010).

10. 18 PA. CONS. STAT. § 901(a) & (b) (2010).

11. KENNETH ADAMS, FELONS WHO ATTEMPT TO PURCHASE GUNS: A STUDY OF PRIOR AND SUBSEQUENT CRIMINAL INVOLVEMENTS, NCJ 194051 (2002), available at http://www.ncjrs.gov/pdffiles1/nij/grants/194051.pdf (accessed August 3, 2011).

12. LIPPMAN, *supra* note 3, at 180.

13. *See Com. v. Adams*, 385 A.2d 525 (Pa. Super. 1970); *Com. v. Hankins*, 460 A.2d 346 (Pa. Super. 1983); *Com. v. Gilliam*, 417 A.2d 1203 (Pa. Super. 1980); *Glover v. Com.*, 86 Va. 382 (1889); *People v. Miller*, 42 P.2d 308 (Cal. 1935); *Hyde v. U.S.*, 225 U.S. 347 (1911).

14. WILLIAM L. CLARK & WILLIAM L. MARSHALL, A TREATISE ON THE LAW OF CRIMES §4.06 at 235 (6th ed. 1958).

15. MODEL PENAL CODE § 5.01(2) (Proposed Official Draft 1962).

16. JOHN M. SCHEB & JOHN M. SCHEB II, CRIMINAL LAW 92 (5th ed. 2008).

17. Douglas Husak, Book Review: *Attempts and the Philosophical Foundations of Criminal Liability: R. A. Duff, Criminal Attempts*, 8 CRIM. L. F. 293, 306 (1997).

18. 335 A.2d 436 (Pa. Super. 1975).

19. *See* DUFF, *supra* note 8.

20. RONALD J. BACIGAL, CRIMINAL LAW AND PROCEDURE: AN OVERVIEW 42 (2008).

21. Arnold N. Enker, *Impossibility in Criminal Attempts—Legality and the Legal Process*, 53 MINN. L. REV. 665 (1968-1969).

22. *See* 1 FRANCIS WHARTON, WHARTON'S CRIMINAL LAW § 183 (Charles E. Torcia ed., 15th ed. 1993). *See also* CLARK & MARSHALL, *supra* note 14, at § 4.12.

23. *See Collins v. City of Rockford*, 113 S.E. 735 (Va. 1922); *Foster v. Comm.*, 31 S.E. 503 (Va. 1898); *Hunt v. State*, 169 S.W. 773 (Ark. 1914); *Territory v. Keyes*, 38 N.W. 440 (Dakota. Terr. 1888); *People v. Gardner*, 38 N.E. 1003 (N.Y. 1894); *People v. Jaffe*, 78 N.E. 169 (N.Y. 1906); *U.S. v. Fox*, 95 U.S. 670 (1877).

24. *See* 4 SIR WILLIAM BLACKSTONE, COMMENTARIES §136 (1941); PROSSER AND KEETON ON THE LAW OF TORTS § 65 (W. Page Keeton ed., 1984); for a full view of Federal Criminal Conspiracy practice, *see* ALI RESTATEMENT OF THE LAW, TORTS 2d §§ 485, 491 (1979); *See also* ANNE LANGER & JONATHAN PARNES, FEDERAL CRIMINAL CONSPIRACY, NCJ 223451 (2008).

25. Paul Marcus, *Conspiracy—The Criminal Agreement in Theory and in Practice*, 65 GEO. L. J. 925–969 (1977).

26. Model Penal Code § 5.03 (Proposed Official Draft 1962).

27. 336 U.S. 440 (1949).

28. *Krulewitch v. U.S.*, 336 U.S. 440, 445 (1949).

29. PETER GILLIES, THE LAW OF CRIMINAL CONSPIRACY (1990).

30. N.Y. PENAL LAW §§ 105.15, 105.20 (McKinney 2010).

31. 18 U.S.C. §371 (2006); *see also* Benjamin L. Dooling and Melissa A. Lalli, *Federal Criminal Conspiracy*, 47 AM. CRIM. L. REV. 561 (2010).

32. McKay Cunningham, *Alabama Mississippi: Attributing One Party's Contacts with the Forum State: Conspiracy Jurisdiction in Alabama*, 71 ALA. LAW. 304 (2010).

33. Organized crime has moved to international levels. *See* U.S. DEPT. OF JUSTICE, OVERVIEW OF THE LAW ENFORCEMENT STRATEGY TO COMBAT INTERNATIONAL ORGANIZED CRIME (2008), available at http://www.justice.gov/criminal/icitap/pr/2008/04-23-08combat-intl-crime-overview.pdf (accessed August 3, 2011).

34. *State v. Carbone*, 91 A.2d 571, 574 (N.J. 1952).

35. Model Penal Code § 5.02, at comments, at 107 (Tent. Draft No. 10, 1960).

36. 18 PA. CONS. STAT. § 903(e) (2010).

37. 18 U.S.C. §§ 1961-1968 (2010).

38. *See NOW v. Scheidler*, 547 U.S. 9 (2006); 537 U.S. 393 (2003); 510 U.S. 249 (1994).

39. From the NRA to Pro-Life Groups, the complaints against misuse are growing. Even the Business Community has its reservations. *See* Barry B. Direnfeld & Melanie Carr, *Government Abuse of Rico Law Threatens Business Civil Liberties*, LEGAL BACKGROUNDER, Feb. 9, 2001, available at http://www.wlf.org/upload/020901LBDirenfeld.pdf (accessed August 3, 2011).

40. 18 U.S.C. § 1962 (2011).

41. *See* Gerard E. Lynch, *A Conceptual, Practical, and Political Guide to RICO Reform*, 43 VAND. L. REV. 769 (1990); *see also* John S. Baker, Jr., *Reforming Corporations through Threats of Federal Prosecution*, 89 CORNELL L. REV. 310 (2004).

Chapter 11

Criminal Defenses

KEYWORDS

Affirmative defense: A defense that does not deny the truth of the allegations against the defendant, but gives some other reason why the defendant cannot be held liable.

ALI substantial capacity test: A test used in many jurisdictions when considering an insanity defense that relieves a defendant of criminal responsibility if at the time of the crime as a result of mental disease or defect the defendant lacked the capacity to appreciate the wrongfulness of his or her conduct or to conform the conduct to the requirements of the law.

Coercion: The use of express or implied threats of violence or reprisal or other intimidating behavior that puts a person in immediate fear of the consequences in order to compel that person to act against his or her will.

Consent: A defense claiming that the victim consented to an alleged crime.

Constructive force: The use of threats or intimidation for the purpose of gaining control over or preventing resistance from another; force that is considered justified under the law and does not create criminal or tort liability.

Defense: The theory or ground that forms the basis for a defendant's opposition to an allegation in a complaint or to a charge in a charging instrument.

Duress: Wrongful and unlawful compulsion that induces a person to act against his or her will.

Durham rule: From *Durham v. United States*, 214 F.2d 862 (1954), a case heard by the District of Columbia Court of Appeals that established the rule that holds, in order to find a defendant not guilty by reason of insanity, the defendant's criminal act must be the product of a mental disease or defect.

Entrapment: The affirmative defense of having been entrapped by a government agent.

Guilty but mentally ill: A verdict available in some jurisdictions in cases involving an insanity defense in which the defendant is found guilty but is committed to a mental hospital rather than sent to prison if an examination shows a need for psychiatric treatment.

Insanity: Unsoundness of mind or lack of the ability to understand that prevents one from having the mental capacity required by law that releases one from criminal responsibility.

Irresistible impulse: A test used in some jurisdictions when considering an insanity defense that involves a determination of whether an impulse to commit a criminal act was irresistible due to mental disease or defect regardless of whether the defendant knew right from wrong.

Justification: A legally sufficient reason or cause for an act that would otherwise be criminal or tortuous; the affirmative defense of having a legally sufficient justification.

M'Naghten test: Common law test of criminal responsibility that stated a person was not responsible for criminal acts if as a result of a mental disease or defect he did not understand what he did or that it was wrong.

Mental defect: An abnormal mental condition that may be of a more fixed nature than a mental disease.

Mental disease: An abnormal mental condition that interferes with mental or emotional processes and internal behavioral control and that is not manifest only in repeated criminal or antisocial conduct.

Miranda rights: From *Miranda v. Arizona*, the 1966 U.S. Supreme Court ruling establishing the rights that an arresting officer must advise the person being arrested.

Mistake of fact: A criminal defense that attempts to eliminate culpability on the ground that the defendant operated from an unintentional misunderstanding of fact rather than from a criminal purpose.

Mistake of law: A criminal defense alleging a mistake involving the misunderstanding or incorrect application of law in regard to an act, contract, transaction, determination, or state of affairs.

Not guilty by reason of insanity: A plea by a criminal defendant who intends to raise an insanity defense.

Presumption: An inference as to the existence of a fact not certainly known that the law requires to be drawn from the known or proven existence of some other fact.

Reasonable force: Lawful force that is reasonably necessary to accomplish a particular end.

Self-defense: The use of force to defend oneself; an affirmative defense alleging that the defendant used force necessarily to protect himself or herself because of a reasonable belief that the other party intended to inflict great bodily harm or death.

(Unnecessary) unlawful force: Force that is not justified under the law and, therefore, is considered a tort or crime or both.

INTRODUCTION: DEFENDING CRIMINAL ACTIONS

As the excursion into the criminal law reaches its final stages, the text would be remiss if it did not address the "defense" to the fundamental elements discussed in each and every offense. The term "defense" means just what it says—that tactic that makes a party nonresponsible, defensible, not necessarily from the factual reality of the crimes charged, but defensible, exonerative of the offense in either a factual or legal sense. A defense differs from a mitigating factor in one prime sense, the fact that successful defenses set perpetrators free or sentence them to alternative disposition, such as mental health placement, while mitigators have the potential to reduce the level of impending culpability. Revisit the murder/manslaughter discussion. Defenses work when directed to the structural components of any crime, pinpointing a lack of act, of causation or mental state sufficient to assign responsibility. The legally insane person will be incapable of formulating the type of intent necessary for conviction, as will the comatose party who could not carry out any criminal design due to nonexistent will, a lack of intentionality, and an incapable body. These examples edify the power and strength of defenses that exonerate and liberate the defendant.

Defense practice deals with both substantive questions that relate to criminal agency, self-defense, misidentification, and other misguided judgments that emanate from the justice system in regard to an improperly targeted defendant, and just as pressingly, the procedural angle whereby the defendant dwells upon mistakes and errors in processing, an issue fully apart from the question of real innocence. Those who claim procedural defenses may or may not be innocent in a legal sense. Some defendants will be innocent strictly for procedural reasons, but guilty as sin for factual and substantive ones. Hence, a murder charge may never be successfully prosecuted, not because the defendant was not the trigger man or because the evidence in a substantive sense suffers from inadequacy, but because the procedural errors abridge guaranteed liberties or statutory rights. The whole concept behind the Miranda doctrine, as a telling illustration, whereby police officers must advise even wily and learned defendants of categorized rights during periods of custodial interrogation, rests on these strange principles. Violations of Miranda can lead guilty people, in a purely procedural sense, to freedom. This superiority of procedural defenses over substantive responsibility causes major friction in all corners of the justice model. Citizen victims as well as prosecutors are not happy about the abolition of personal guilt in favor of some procedural guarantee. Cops and prison officials are equally disturbed, but for those on the front lines of criminal defense, the price of this type of freedom is surely worth the preservation of the guarantees to the accused. From a defense perspective, the procedural challenges are correctly characterized as checks and balances on the justice system itself.

Find out about the National Criminal Defense Lawyers Association at: http://www.nacdl.org/public.nsf/freeform/publicwelcome?opendocument

---

From this domain, one clearly appreciates how defense practice rests on two major prongs: (1) factual or substantive claims, and (2) on the procedural bases that involve constitutional and statutory rights. The latter coverage properly belongs in the analysis of criminal procedure rather than substantive criminal law. Whether the defendant has suitable and effective counsel is only peripherally germane to the structural issue of innocence or guilt though this query pertains to the quality of the accused's due process. In this distinction, we see the text's final aim: to provide a simple overview of those substantive defenses that directly address the mens rea or actus reus element in the questioned offense. Was the defendant capable of formulating the type of intent necessary for culpability? Was the defendant a free willing, volitional being who understood the nature of the act? Did the defendant do something that the complaining party consented to? Was the defendant tricked or entrapped into committing an offense ordinarily not on his/her agenda? Was force, duress, or coercion employed to prompt a usually unwilling defendant to engage in crime? Could the act charged be characterized as justifiable? Could the defendant have been justified in exerting force or other violent means to protect self and property? Did the defendant suffer from some sort of mental defect or disease that made it unlikely that the accused could have intellectualized and willed the charged action? In each of these inquiries, we discover the substantive rather than the procedural defense, that factor which affects the ability of a prosecution team to prove the requisite mind and movement for criminal agency.

Only these types of defenses will be weighed and evaluated, not out of lack of respect for the power of the procedural defense, but out of a recognition of the work's primary aim—that journey in the content of criminal law and its enactments.

CRIMINAL DEFENSES: DEFENSE OF SELF AND PROPERTY

ESSENTIAL ISSUES

- Force must be proportionate to that of attacker
- Review notice and retreat requirements
- Deadly force may have special standards
- Alternative means of resolution
- Deadly force in property protection not justified
- Period of reclamation

The law permits defenses based on urgency and the preservation of life and property. In the case of self, every person has the undeniable right to self-protection and defense when significant bodily injury and/or death can occur. Innocent parties need not be inactive, nonresponsive parties when in physical jeopardy. Self-defense has long been recognized as a legitimate defense involving harm to person. Defense of property, whether domicile or other tangible goods, is another defense rooted in the theory of justification and necessity. In each of these instances, what appears to be criminal conduct becomes justifiable. In this setting, the defendant may perform the actus reus, but will be acutely short on the type of intentionality needed for the criminal mens rea.

The basic premise upon which this right to defend self and property rests is justification. In the justifiable homicide case, the party kills but acts out of necessity. Within the sphere of necessity inhabits the doctrine of justification. Pennsylvania does an admirable job of laying out the tenets of justification at Section 503 of the Crimes Code.

(a) General rule.—Conduct which the actor believes to be necessary to avoid a harm or evil to himself or to another is justifiable if:
   (1) the harm or evil sought to be avoided by such conduct is greater than that sought to be prevented by the law defining the offense charged;
   (2) neither this title nor other law defining the offense provides exceptions or defenses dealing with the specific situation involved; and
   (3) a legislative purpose to exclude the justification claimed does not otherwise plainly appear.
(b) Choice of evils.—When the actor was reckless or negligent in bringing about the situation requiring a choice of harms or evils or in appraising the necessity for his conduct, the justification afforded by this section is unavailable in a prosecution for any offense for which recklessness or negligence, as the case may be, suffices to establish culpability.[1]

In justification, the actor must search for a basis to act and react proportionately. Criminals who pluck themselves into dangerous, criminally driven situations are forbidden the claim of

CASE 11.1

SANDERS V. INDIANA

704 N.W 2d 119 (1999)

On July 7, 1996, Sanders and his friend Rick Booker attended a quinceanera, a coming-out party, for Evita Rodriguez at the Marion Armory. Shortly after his arrival, Sanders fought with another guest, Steve Cunningham, near a door leading to an outside stairway. After Cunningham got away, Sanders walked quickly down the stairs. When he looked back toward the top of the stairs, Sanders saw Jose Rodriguez, Sr., the decedent's brother, put a knife to the neck of his friend Booker. Sanders pulled a gun from his waistband. Jose Rodriguez, Sr., released Booker. Ruben Rodriguez started down the stairs, and Sanders shot him twice. Ruben Rodriguez bled to death from a gunshot wound to the chest. Although Ruben Rodriguez had a knife that night, it is unclear whether he was brandishing it at the time he was shot.

Another guest, Jose Perez, testified that he heard the gunshots shortly after he arrived at the quinceanera with his brother. He began to look for his wife, who had driven separately. When he did not find his wife at her table or at her car, he went to his brother's vehicle and got his gun. He testified that someone shot at him from the passenger side of a small white car, hitting a toe on his right foot. He returned fire. Sanders left the party in the passenger seat of a white Hyundai driven by Rick Booker.

The State charged Sanders with the murder of Ruben Rodriguez, the battery of Jose Perez, and possession of a handgun without a license. It sought enhancement of the handgun charge based on Sander's prior conviction for carrying a handgun without a license.

At trial, the judge refused to give Sanders' tendered instructions on reckless homicide and criminal recklessness because there was no evidence of recklessness, and because a theory of recklessness was inconsistent with Sanders' claim of self-defense.

The jury convicted Sanders of battery and possession of a handgun without a license, but it was unable to reach a decision about the murder charge. The court set the murder charge for retrial and directed that trial on the enhancement take place immediately after the murder retrial.

At the second trial, the judge denied Sanders' motion *in limine* to exclude evidence on the battery of Jose Perez. Sanders again tendered an instruction on reckless homicide, which the court again refused. This time, the trial judge did not state a reason for refusing the instruction, and defense counsel did not object to the court's refusal of that particular instruction.

The second jury convicted Sanders of murder and the enhancement on the handgun charge. The court imposed concurrent sentences as follows: sixty-five years for the murder, eight years for the battery, and eight years for the possession of a handgun without a license (including the enhancement). ...

Sanders claims that the State did not adequately rebut his claim of self-defense and that there was thus insufficient evidence to support his murder conviction.

The standard of review for a challenge to the sufficiency of evidence to rebut a claim of self-defense is the same as the standard for any sufficiency of the evidence challenge. We neither reweigh the evidence nor judge the credibility of witnesses. Instead, we consider the evidence most favorable to the verdict and draw all reasonable inferences drawn therefrom. *Birdsong v. State*, 685 N.E.2d 42 (Ind. 1997). If the evidence and inferences provide substantial evidence of probative value to support the verdict, we affirm. Id.

"A claim of self-defense in a homicide prosecution requires, among other things, that ... the defendant had a reasonable fear of death or great bodily harm." *Brooks v. State*, 683 N.E.2d 574, 577 (Ind. 1977). Once a defendant in a homicide prosecution claims self-defense, the burden shifts to the state to rebut that claim. Birdsong, 685 N.E.2d at 45. "It is only necessary for the State to disprove one of the elements of self-defense beyond a reasonable doubt for the defendant's claim to fail." *Jordan v. State*, 656 N.E.2d 816, 817 (Ind. 1995).

Although some of the trial evidence suggested that the murder victim was advancing aggressively toward Sanders with a knife, the evidence most favorable to the verdict suggests otherwise. At least one witness testified that the victim was unarmed; another testified that prior to the shooting, the victim was at the top of the stairs asking Sanders to leave the party; another testified that the victim did begin to descend the stairs, but did so nonaggressively; another testified that the victim had not advanced toward Sanders at all. We believe this evidence successfully rebuts Sanders' claim of self-defense. We will not, therefore, disturb the jury's verdict. ...

Sanders claims that during the second trial the trial court improperly admitted evidence of the battery shooting of Perez.

Sanders argues that the evidence of the battery was inadmissible at the second murder trial because he committed the battery minutes after the charged crime, and the *res gestae* doctrine, which he claims is the controlling law, is used to admit evidence of misconduct occurring before the charged crime. (Appellant's Br. at 48.) We have held, however, that the *res gestae* doctrine did not survive the adoption of the Indiana Rules of Evidence, and that an evidentiary argument must instead be analyzed by reference to those Rules. *Swanson v. State*, 666 N.E.2d 397 (Ind. 1996). The applicable rule, Indiana Rule of Evidence 404(b), discusses the admissibility of "other crimes, wrongs, or acts," (emphasis added), thereby bringing within its scope all "bad acts," not simply prior misconduct.

Rule 404(b) provides that, although evidence of other misconduct may not be admitted for the purpose of proving that the defendant acted in conformity with a certain character trait it may be admissible for other purposes, such as proof of motive or intent. Evid.R. 404(b). Rule 404(b) "is designed to prevent the jury from assessing a defendant's present guilt on the basis of his past propensities. ..." *Hicks v. State*, 690 N.E.2d 215, 218 (Ind. 1997).

Our analysis of admissibility under Rule 404(b) necessarily incorporates the relevancy test of Rule 401 and the balancing test of Rule 403. Id. at 221. First, "the court must determine that the evidence of other crimes, wrongs, or acts is relevant to a matter at issue other than the defendant's propensity to commit the charged act; and [second,] the court must balance the probative value of the evidence against its prejudicial effect pursuant to Rule 403." Id.

Relevance is broadly defined as probative value, and the trial court has wide discretion in ruling on the relevance of proffered evidence. Id. at 220. The battery evidence in this case was not offered to prove propensity to act in conformity with a character trait for violence, but rather was offered for the "other purpose" of proving Sanders' intent by negating his claim of self-defense. Because the battery evidence makes Sanders' claim of self-defense less likely by indicating his intent to harm the victim, the relevancy test of Rule 401 is satisfied.

Relevant evidence is admissible, Evid.R. 402, unless its probative value is substantially outweighed by the danger of unfair prejudice, Evid.R. 403. "We review this balancing act by the trial court under an abuse of discretion standard." Hicks, 690 N.E.2d at 223. The trial court is again afforded wide latitude to weigh probative value against prejudicial effect. *Bacher v. State*, 686 N.E.2d 791, 799 (Ind. 1997).

The paradigm of evidence inadmissible under Rule 404(b) "is a crime committed on another day in another place, evidence whose only apparent purpose is to prove the defendant is a person who commits crimes." Swanson, 666 N.E.2d at 398. The evidence at issue here is not of that nature. The battery occurred moments after and just steps away from the murder. The evidence caused no unfair prejudice to Sanders, but instead provided highly probative evidence of his intent to harm. We hold that the trial court properly exercised its discretion.

Questions

1. What charge was lodged against the defendant?
2. How does his argument about battery affect the charge of murder?
3. If the facts were true and the appeals court was satisfied, would his use of the gun been proportionate?

justification, but innocent and well-meaning parties can deservedly raise the defense. Nor can a citizen employ force against a law enforcement officer carrying out their lawful duties even when the arrest or confinement is unjustified. This type of self-defense cannot be tolerated because the benefit of the doubt must be given the law enforcement community carrying out its duties. Police are not perfect, but they are deserving of our deference even when wrong.

The right of self-defense is not absolute and while much of its content can be derived from common law tradition, statutory law governs as well. Check local and statewide codes to determine the extent and the limitations of this popular defense. Before acting, ensure that the defense applies. For example, does your jurisdiction call for "retreat" from a dangerous situation if alternative means of escape exist? What does the statutory framework indicate regarding how much force is permissible? What type of weaponry? What would be the effect of a prior conviction, a parole violation, or an illegally possessed firearm on the right to self-defense? How much force can be employed in the defense of property and material possessions? Do the levels of permissible defense vary according to location? Is there a reclamation period in the case of goods? What is proportionate force? Can self-defense be employed in the defense of third parties? When can deadly force be utilized?

A general summary of the more oft-seen principles follows.

Self-Defense/Defense of Others

Exerting force to protect self and others similarly situated is a tricky business. The law generally permits the defender rights in proportion to those exerted. Thus, self-defense analysis always looks to proportionality first. By proportionality, we mean the means employed to withstand the attack matches the force of the attacker. Proportionality does not imply identicality of means, only of effect of the force used to repel. Therefore, a knife-wielding assailant can be met with a gun because the knife and gun harken equal potential for injury. One looks to the potential harm for determining the suitability of the defense chosen. A fist cannot justify a machine gun nor would a pen knife the rocket launcher. Figure the proportional and self-defense will withstand subsequent challenges for excessive reactions.

The Model Penal Code (MPC) refers to this equation as what is "immediately necessary" to counter the onslaught. In most statutory designs, deadly force is frowned upon except in necessitous cases. The MPC confirms this view:

(2) Limitations on Justifying the Necessity for Use of Force
(b)   The use of deadly force is not justifiable under this Section unless the actor believes that such force is necessary to protect himself against death, serious bodily harm, kidnapping or sexual intercourse compelled by force or threat; nor is it justifiable if:
(i)   the actor, with the purpose of causing death or serious bodily harm, provoked the use of force ...
(ii)   the actor knows that he can avoid the necessity of using such force with complete safety by retreating or by surrendering possession of a thing ...[2]

Cases involving battered spouses tragically touch upon many aspects of the self-defense claims. Women who kill their husbands or lovers in fits of rage or reaction are often headline stories.[3]

The "burning bed case," the execution-style murder while sleeping, and other unfortunate reactions to abuse are multiplying in number and severity. How the self-defense claim fits neatly in these domestic situations has been an ongoing issue, particularly in those cases where the woman victim simmers over many years with rage and fear; has spent years being the target of physical, mental, and sexual abuse; and has been frustrated in securing any reasonable remedy from an already beleaguered justice system. In some circles, the condition is labeled Battered Woman's Syndrome and, while not universally accepted as a form of self-defense, the claim works to mitigate the intentionality of force exerted. By no means are these situations easy cases to prosecute or defend.[4]

For some courts, the syndrome's scientific credibility is still unsatisfactory because the bulk of scientific community has yet to endorse this psychological state. In more traditional jurisdictions, the admission of expert testimony is governed by the Frye doctrine.[5] On the other hand, some jurisdictions operate under the Daubert test,[6] which allows admission of less than fully accepted scientific theories, unlike Frye with its more rigid view of scientific acceptability. Others believe that the evidence legitimates a corrosive and repetitive pattern of behavior that leads to a form of self-defense when the offender is the most defenseless. The trend appears otherwise with new laws being adopted, such as in Ohio, whose legislature recently revised its law.

The general assembly hereby declares that it recognizes both of the following, in relation to the "battered woman syndrome:"

(1) that the battered woman syndrome is a matter of commonly accepted scientific knowledge;
(2) that the subject matter and details of the syndrome are not within the general understanding or experience of a person who is a member of the general populace and are not within the field of common knowledge.

CASE 11.2

STATE V. RILEY

No. 23998 (W.Va. 1997)

Appellant Betty Olivia Riley appeals her second degree murder conviction in Cabell County, contending that she had been abused by the victim and that she should have been permitted to more fully develop the battered woman's syndrome as a defense. ... Having reviewed the record, briefs, and arguments of counsel, we conclude that the lower court committed no reversible error and affirm its decision.

On October 5, 1994, Jack Brown telephoned emergency services and indicated that the Appellant had shot and wounded him. When the police arrived at the Huntington, West Virginia, residence, the Appellant was lying on the floor in front of Mr. Brown, who was seated in a chair with one gunshot wound. A .25 caliber semiautomatic handgun, later determined to be the murder weapon, was found approximately one foot from the Appellant's hand. The officers informed the Appellant of her Miranda rights, and she thereafter admitted that she had shot Mr. Brown, indicating a history of domestic violence. Mr. Brown died as a result of the gunshot wound.

On May 11, 1995, the Appellant was charged with first degree murder by a single count indictment issued by the Cabell County Grand Jury. Subsequent to a March 1996 trial, the Appellant was found guilty of second degree murder and was sentenced to thirty-two years in prison. On appeal to this Court, the Appellant identifies four specific issues of alleged error, and asserts that the evidence was insufficient to support the verdict. The Appellant's assignments of error include: refusal of the lower court to allow the Appellant to fully develop testimony and evidence concerning the battered spouse syndrome; ...

Based upon our review of the transcript, we find that the Appellant's opportunity to introduce battered woman's syndrome testimony, including instances of prior abuse, was not unreasonably or erroneously limited.

At trial, the Appellant testified regarding the history of abuse, and informed the jury that shortly before the shooting, Mr. Brown had slapped her in the face while they were standing on the porch of their apartment. The Appellant also testified that after she had gone inside to lie down with her cat, Mr. Brown entered the room and repeatedly threw the cat across the room. Testimony was also introduced concerning the Appellant's initial statements immediately after the police arrived at the scene. The Appellant stated, "I'm tired of him beating me," and she repeatedly said, "domestic abuse, domestic abuse." She told the police, "I don't know how many times that I shot, I was just tired—wanted him to stop hitting me."

The Appellant also testified that she had experienced psychiatric problems since a 1961 suicide attempt. She testified that Mr. Brown was "nasty" and resorted to verbal abuse "so bad you would be afraid that he might use his fist on you." While she characterized the abuse as "infrequent," she did relate an incident in which Mr. Brown had thrown a knife into the wall near her head, "close enough that it bothered me."

The Appellant's treating psychiatrist from 1993 to 1994, Dr. Jack Dodd, testified that the Appellant suffered bipolar disorder, is alcohol dependent, and has been hospitalized on at least three occasions for treatment of her mental illness. A psychologist employed by Dr. Dodd, Ms. Maria Stallo-Leppla, testified that Mr. Brown's action in throwing the cat across could have prompted a psychotic episode in the Appellant.

Dr. Joseph Wyatt, the Appellant's expert psychologist, also diagnosed the Appellant as suffering from bipolar disorder and opined that "it was more likely than not that she could not conform her actions to the requirements of the law ..." because of the psychotic episode at the time of the shooting. Dr. Wyatt also testified regarding the Appellant's history of mental illness, and instances of physical and emotional abuse. Dr. Wyatt characterized the Appellant as "a classic battered spouse," explaining that she had been abused by Mr. Brown and her former husband of twenty-nine years.

In addition to the evidence summarized above, the Appellant also sought to introduce further evidence regarding the nature of prior abusive behavior. That evidence, if ruled admissible, would have consisted of testimony by four individuals: Mr. William Congleton, regarding an incident wherein Mr. Brown allegedly brandished a gun upon Mr. Congleton; Officer Tim Goheen, the officer investigating that allegation; Mr. Mark Dillon, the Appellant's son-in law, regarding the prior abuse; and Mrs. Donna Dillon, the Appellant's daughter, regarding her mother's relationship with her late father. The Appellant also asserts that the testimony of Dr. Wyatt was improperly limited.

The lower court refused to admit the testimony of Mrs. Donna Dillon regarding the abuse suffered by the Appellant at the hands of her former husband, Mrs. Dillon's father, because this testimony would have been cumulative. The Appellant and her experts had already presented testimony regarding this abuse. With regard to Mr. Mark Dillon, the Appellant's son-in-law, the Appellant attempted to introduce testimony of Mr. Dillon regarding instances in which the Appellant had contacted Mr. Dillon requesting assistance. The lower court never ruled on the admissibility of Mr. Dillon's testimony; the court simply sustained the prosecution's objection when hearsay evidence regarding statements allegedly made by the Appellant to Mr. Dillon began to emerge. Subsequent to the lower court's decision to sustain the objection, Appellant's counsel abandoned that particular line of questioning.

With regard to Mr. Congleton and Officer Tim Goheen's testimony concerning the brandishing incident, we have only required the admission of offered evidence of violent acts against third parties where self-defense is relied upon "and there is evidence showing or tending to show, that the deceased was at the time of the killing, making a murderous attack upon the defendant." Syl. Pt. 2, in part, *State v. Louk*, 171 W. Va. 639, 301 S.E.2d 596 (1983). In syllabus point one of *State v. Collins*, 154 W.Va. 771, 180 S.E.2d 54 (1971), this Court held:

> When in a prosecution for murder, the defendant relies upon self-defense to excuse the homicide and the evidence does not show or tend to show that the defendant was acting in self-defense when he shot and killed the deceased, the defendant will not be permitted to prove that the deceased was of dangerous, violent, and quarrelsome character or reputation.

See *State v. Smith*, 198 W.Va. 441, 481 S.E.2d 747 (1996).

The Appellant also contends that the testimony of Dr. Wyatt regarding the battered woman's syndrome and the relevant underlying facts from within the Appellant's history of abuse was improperly limited. We have consistently held that an expert is permitted to explain in detail the factual basis for his opinion. *State v. Duell*, 175 W. Va. 233, 332 S.E.2d 246 (1985). As the questioning of Dr. Wyatt began to encompass particular instances of abuse, the prosecution raised the concern that such hearsay evidence should be admissible only for a limited purpose. The lower court sustained the prosecution's objection and Dr. Wyatt subsequently testified concerning the general nature of the comments by the Appellant regarding her relationship with Mr. Brown. Thus, the lower court did not preclude Dr. Wyatt from testifying regarding the factual underpinnings of his conclusions. The court simply noted that any hearsay evidence which was encompassed therein was being introduced only for the limited purpose of allowing Dr. Wyatt to educate the jury regarding the foundations for his medical conclusions. This same type of exchange transpired regarding medical records, and the lower court noted that such hearsay evidence could not be used as direct evidence of Mr. Brown's abusive behavior, but could be used to build the foundation for Dr. Wyatt's conclusions.

We have consistently maintained that rulings on the admissibility of evidence are largely within the sound discretion of a trial court. In syllabus point two of *State v. Franklin*, 191 W. Va. 727, 448 S.E.2d 158 (1994), we explained:

> "'The action of a trial court in admitting or excluding evidence in the exercise of its discretion will not be disturbed by the appellate court unless it appears that such action amounts to an abuse of discretion.' Syllabus Point 10, *State v. Huffman*, 141 W.Va. 55, 87 S.E.2d 541 (1955)." Syl. pt. 4, *State v. Ashcraft*, 172 W.Va. 640, 309 S.E.2d 600 (1983).
>
> "[E]videntiary decisions of a trial court are entitled to substantial deference." *McDougal v. McCammon*, 193 W.Va. 229, 235 n.5, 455 S.E.2d 788, 794 n.5 (1995).

We have previously permitted introduction of evidence regarding the battered spouse syndrome, and the lower court in the present case admitted substantial evidence on this issue offered by the Appellant. In syllabus point five of *State v. Steele*, 178 W. Va. 330, 359 S.E.2d 558 (1987), for instance, we held that "[e]xpert testimony can be utilized to explain the psychological basis for the battered woman's syndrome and to offer an opinion that the defendant meets the requisite profile of the syndrome." See footnote 66. Conferring the right of introduction of evidence upon a defendant, however, does not translate into authority to engage in an unlimited foray into the issue. The court still possesses the right to limit the testimony; when it becomes duplicative, the court may refuse to accept additional witnesses. Rule 403 of the West Virginia Rules of Evidence provides:

> Although relevant, evidence may be excluded if its probative value is substantially outweighed by the danger of unfair prejudice, confusion of the issues, or misleading the jury, or by considerations of undue delay, waste of time, or needless presentation of cumulative evidence.

See *State v. Ludwick*, 197 W.Va. 70, 475 S.E.2d 70 (1996); *State v. Brown*, 179 W.Va. 681, 371 S.E.2d 609 (1988).

The lower court in the present case exercised its right to limit testimony in that manner. We find no clear error in the lower court's decisions regarding admissibility of evidence, and we therefore affirm those decisions. ...

The Appellant asserts that the verdict of guilty of second-degree murder is contrary to the weight of the evidence. The Appellant appears to believe that her introduction of evidence regarding her mental illness and evidence regarding the battered spouse syndrome should have combined to prohibit of verdict of guilty on the second-degree murder charge.

The Appellant made a valiant effort to convince the jury that her mental trauma rendered her incapable of conforming her actions to the requirements of the law. However, the State presented evidence, through the testimony of Dr. Ralph Smith, an expert in forensic psychiatry, that the Appellant may have "some exaggeration of symptoms and problems." Although Dr. Smith diagnosed the Appellant as suffering from major depression, as well as dependent personality disorder, he rejected to notion that she displayed symptoms of battered spouse syndrome and dispelled the suggestion that she was psychotic when she shot Mr. Brown.

In syllabus point three of *State v. Williams*, 198 W.Va. 274, 480 S.E.2d 162 (1996), we specified:

> "A criminal defendant challenging the sufficiency of the evidence to support a conviction takes on a heavy burden. An appellate court must review all the evidence, whether direct or circumstantial, in the light most favorable to the prosecution and must credit all inferences and credibility assessments that the jury might have drawn in favor of the prosecution. The evidence need not be inconsistent with every conclusion save that of guilt so long as the jury can find guilt beyond a reasonable doubt. Credibility determinations are for a jury and not an appellate court. Finally, a jury verdict should be set aside only when the record contains no evidence, regardless of how it is weighed, from which the jury could find guilt beyond a reasonable doubt. To the extent that our prior cases are inconsistent, they are expressly overruled." Syl. pt. 3, *State v. Guthrie*, 194 W.Va. 657, 461 S.E.2d 163 (1995).

When viewing the evidence in the manner mandated above, we find that the jury could have discounted the testimony of the Appellant and her witnesses and could have concluded beyond a reasonable doubt that the Appellant was sane when she shot Mr. Brown.

Questions

1. Explain the role of expert witness in this case.
2. Do you find the testimony credible?
3. What about the testimony of the accused?
4. Do you see any liberalization of this type of evidence in the Court's reasoning?

(B)   ... the person may introduce expert testimony of the "battered woman syndrome" and expert testimony that the person suffered from that syndrome as evidence to establish the requisite belief of an imminent danger of death or great bodily harm that is necessary, as an element of the affirmative defense, to justify the person's use of the force in question.[7]

Another facet of the self-defense claim relates to the reasonableness of the defender's beliefs.[8] By which party do we measure the reasonableness of the reaction—that of the attacker or the defender? Objectively, self-defense analysis evaluates the conduct of the assailant and, like all other forms of evidence, can impute, infer, and draw conclusions from the assailant's conduct.

Past association, former criminal records and histories, reputation of the assailant, and the context in which the attack takes place can assist the trier in making this troubling determination. In the final analysis, the decision to defend rests in the subjective and objective mindset of the defender for it is he or she that reacts to the attack not the naysayers and Monday morning quarterbacks who critique the improper course of conduct when it is safe to do so. Police officers face this dilemma daily. Was the defendant pulling a gun? Was it a gun or other weapon? Did the officer defend against the correct party? Split-second decisions are sometimes not right and the public appears unwilling to accept error in these cases. Yet, given the intensity of these moments, it seems reasonable to be flexibly tolerant in the close call. Perceptions differ based on individual circumstances and, because of this, stories will differ about what is justifiable. The tribunal looks at whether the reaction would be the reaction of most people—the "reasonable person"—under similar circumstances.[9] (See Figure 11.1[10] for citizen complaints about police use of force.)

The reasonable person's reaction will vary according to facts and conditions under which the parties labor and cannot be packaged into a compact formula. Police, like other individuals, evaluate circumstances in immediate rather than reflective settings.

Learn about the National Institute of Justice's recommendations on the varied uses of force, charted in a continuum at http://www.ojp.usdoj.gov/nij/topics/law-enforcement/officer-safety/use-of-force/continuum.htm

---

Conduct that justifies self-defense takes many forms, such as:

(1) an aggressor unjustifiably threatens harm to the actor; and
(2) the actor engages in conduct harmful to the aggressor;
    (a) when and to the extent necessary for self-protection
    (b) that is reasonable in relation to the harm threatened.[11]

The type of force employed to protect life and limb may appear reasonable during the occurrence, though time may alter that view. See the recommendations on the employment of deadly force at Figure 11.2.[12]

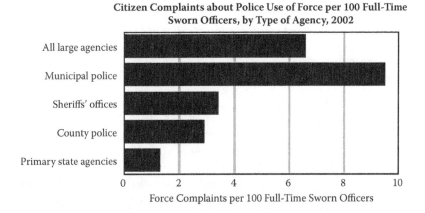

Figure 11.1   Citizen complaints about police use of force.

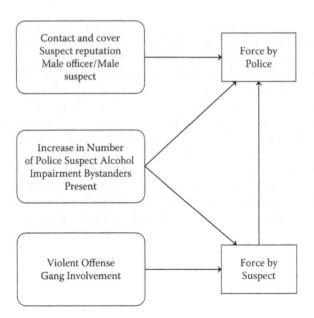

Figure 11.2   Recommendations on the employment of deadly force.

Be mindful that the defense may not be available when alternative means of escape or other avenues of resolution are possible. Retreat sounds like weak-kneed acquiescence, but should be construed more favorably as wise discretion. Self-defense is a dangerous business best left to professional people who understand the intricacies of force and its execution. If police have trouble in select cases, then the layperson cannot be expected to handle the many nuances associated with the application of force. Despite the novelty of these situations, the layperson is empowered to engage the attacker in ways consistent with proportionality and equal reaction.

Defense of Others

The identical principles enunciated for protection of self apply when protecting others. The reaction must be reasonable, proportionate, and justified. The party coming to the aid of another must objectively believe that the force is necessary for the protection of another in a defenseless position.

Review the state code provision.

(A) GENERAL RULE.— The use of force upon or toward the person of another is justifiable to protect a third person when:
   (1) the actor would be justified under section 505 of this title (relating to use of force in self-protection) in using such force to protect himself against the injury he believes to be threatened to the person whom he seeks to protect;
   (2) under the circumstances as the actor believes them to be, the person whom he seeks to protect would be justified in using such protective force; and
   (3) the actor believes that his intervention is necessary for the protection of such other person.[13]

CASE 11.3

LANEY V. U.S.

294 F.2d 414

Visit your local law library, obtain the above case, and answer the following questions.

Questions

1. Describe the facts that led up to the confrontation.
2. Which type of force did the assailant employ?
3. Was the defendant's response proportionate to the force used against him?
4. What does the Court suggest as an alternative means?

The varied nuances of this defense were covered in Chapter 4 (Crimes against the Person: Homicide).

Defense of Property

In no instance is deadly or severe force permissible in the defense of material possessions, though some might argue that defense of the domicile serves as the singular exception. Because a home is a primary domain where families have every right to the highest expectation of privacy and security, defense of the abode may permit even deadly force. Some jurisdictions may require retreat as an alternative. Check with the local jurisdiction to determine the many requirements and qualifications for the defense of home.[14] The Model Penal Code lays out some specific requirements for the use of force in the protection of the domicile.

(1) Use of Force Justifiable for Protection of Property. Subject to the provisions of this Section and of Section 3.09, the use of force upon or toward the person of another is justifiable when the actor believes that such force is immediately necessary:
(a) to prevent or terminate an unlawful entry or other trespass upon land or a trespass against or the unlawful carrying away of tangible, movable property, provided that such land or movable property is, or is believed by the actor to be, in his possession or in the possession of another person for whose protection he acts.[15]

As the property interest becomes less personal than a domicile, the toleration for deadly force melts away completely. Even strong physical force is frowned upon. Material goods can never be equated with the value of human life and limb. On the other hand, property owners need not sit idly by as the thief or the marauder purloins what rightfully belongs to another. Victims can object in more than verbal ways. The level and type of physical objection will depend on the circumstances and the timing of it all. Unlawful entry and trespass provide the defender with the widest latitude. All property may be defended, if reasonable in scope and design, and in select cases may even be reclaimed by the victim of theft. A push or shove, a fight to regain ownership, may even be permissible and will depend upon the behavior of the taker. In fact, reentry on a thief's place of residence to regain property is perfectly legitimate. Reclamation, within the stated statutory periods, is a right. Most codifications embrace the power of the aggrieved party to ask first, and then if unsuccessful, move to alternative means, including force. See the sample statute below:

§ 507. Use of force for the protection of property

(A) USE OF FORCE JUSTIFIABLE FOR PROTECTION OF PROPERTY.— The use of force upon or toward the person of another is justifiable when the actor believes that such force is immediately necessary:

(1) to prevent or terminate an unlawful entry or other trespass upon land or a trespass against or the unlawful carrying away of tangible movable property, if such land or movable property is, or is believed by the actor to be, in his possession or in the possession of another person for whose protection he acts; or

(2) to effect an entry or reentry upon land or to retake tangible movable property, if:

(i) the actor believes that he or the person by whose authority he acts or a person from whom he or such other person derives title was unlawfully dispossessed of such land or movable property and is entitled to possession; and

(ii) (A) the force is used immediately or on fresh pursuit after such dispossession; or (B) the actor believes that the person against whom he uses force has no claim of right to the possession of the property and, in the case of land, the circumstances, as the actor believes them to be, are of such urgency that it would be an exceptional hardship to postpone the entry or reentry until a court order is obtained.[16]

The steps taken should be immediate and in fresh pursuit and reasonable in light of the totality of the circumstances.

LEGAL INSANITY

One of this nation's greatest hallmarks is the belief that those afflicted with demonstrable mental disease and defect, which is directly correlated to the criminality itself, should not be held accountable. In the certifiably insane, in those suffering from congenital and neurological deformity, the element of mens rea cannot take hold as it does in other offenders. A thinking being, a free willing and free choosing moral agent is less likely under these conditions. A hallmark of Western jurisprudence is its insistence on culpability being tied to mental acuity and competency. To be sure, the public tends to the skeptical in these matters given the many charades the system has witnessed in the last century. Despite this, even the most hardened prosecutors know an insane person, in some cases by casual observation and in others by report and assessment that strike at the very heart of what it means to be a rational being. Some defendants do qualify. Even in the Middle Ages, official authorities hesitated in the condemnation and execution of those who appeared mentally disturbed. Known as the "wild beast" theory, the justice system had empathy for those whose mental faculties were clearly in severe disorder and whose awareness and relationship with reality genuinely suspect.[17] Foaming at the mouth, speaking with spirits, suffering from extraordinary delusions occurred then as it does now, and a short visit to any state mental hospital confirms the tragedy of mental illness and, even more importantly, its substantiality.

The declaration that an accused suffers from a form of insanity is often associated with legal defense strategy. Stereotypically, the public believes that any defendant laden with a mental disease or defect can avail themselves of this way of getting out of being responsible, but the reality of insanity pleas and adjudications is a very different matter. First, the claim rarely sees the light of day in a courtroom due to its stringent and cumbersome requirements. Less than 1 percent of American criminals file the pleas and notice of insanity and even fewer succeed in the argument.[18] Next, questions of legal insanity vastly contrast with the medico-psychiatric perspective. For example, a finding of psychiatric conditions in no way guarantees a correlation and connection to a finding of legal insanity. In this way, there really are two forms of insanity: factual and legal. It is the latter category the defendant pleads. Only by the declaration of legal insanity can the defendant escape adjudication and eventual judgment. The distinction is not artificial since the law already understands that some portion of the criminal population will suffer from some type of psycho-psychiatric disorder. Most clinical studies on criminal lifestyles verify that criminal pathology is the product of many forces including addictions, obsessions, alienations, antisocial behaviors, and troubled family life. Your run of the mill criminal can always find a psychiatrist who can diagnose some disorder. To allow these general conditions to be an absolute defense in criminal cases would generate not only enormous controversy, but injustice. Legal insanity, therefore, is very narrowly defined and construed. The finding accepts the reality of a mental disease or defect then moves to an intimate correlation that makes it substantially difficult for that defendant to know right from wrong, or to understand or appreciate the criminality of the act in question, or to engage in criminal conduct because of the disorder itself. As a result, legal insanity causes a blindness of understanding in the criminal agent, an inability to know the right and wrong of the conduct chosen, or difficulty weighing and evaluating the moral, ethical, and legal dimensions of criminal conduct. The insanity defense demands that the defendant respond to two primary questions:

1. Does the accused understand the act to be criminal (good or bad/right from wrong)?
2. Does the offender suffer from some mental disease or defect that directly correlates to this inability to appreciate the fundamental illegality engaged in?

At its heart, the insanity defense forces the evaluator to discern a connection between the illness offered, as impetus, and offense itself. One standard cannot live without the other. Hence, there are millions of mentally disturbed individuals suffering from all sorts of pathologies, from schizophrenia to obsessive paranoia, who are not criminals and who live out life legitimately. Others are crazy infrequently and unpredictably and when this sporadic pathology exists, the defendant will have a tough job of differentiating just when all the neurological marbles worked and when they were scrambled. An accused can even be off-center on a host of behaviors that might not be related to the questioned criminality, but as lucid as a blue sky on the criminal enterprise chosen. Neat categorizations and stereotypes simply do not wash in the law of insanity.[19]

Most jurisdictions have limits on the types of pathology that can be posed. Almost universally, the statutory designs on insanity preclude the defense based on alcohol and drug abuse or addiction. These types of personal and social problems are deemed "antisocial" and inapplicable in the insanity debate. These conditions, however, still play a role in specific intent defenses or as mitigators in charges of murder.[20]

The January 2011 Tucson tragedy involving 19 victims, including a critically wounded U.S. Congresswoman Gabrielle Giffords, has already generated talk of the insanity defense. Under even the most liberal of interpretations, it will be difficult for Jared Lee Loughner to escape

Figure 11.3   Jared Lee Loughner.

his own sense of knowledge, his own clear, unequivocal plan of action, and his premeditated, directed aim at innocent people (Figure 11.3).

His mental state, while confused and bizarrely irrational, has not reached the incapacity to understand the criminality of his acts. His YouTube.com postings are circumstantially indicative of his warped mental processes, but not exculpatory (Figure 11.4).

To be legally insane, the burden is not only narrow, it is extremely heavy. The insane individual acts without the necessary intellectual faculties needed to meet the mens rea standard. In sum, the insane defendant "had not sufficient reason to be able to judge the consequences of this act, or was so far deprived of volition or self-control by the overwhelming violence and mental disease that he was not capable of voluntary action and, therefore, was not able to choose the right and avoid the wrong, he was not responsible for any act committed while in this condition."[21]

The sequence of the insanity plea as defense might go like this:

- Give notice of intent to plea insanity well ahead of trial.[22]
- Demonstrate a clear and clinically deniable mental disease or disorder.
- Employ expert opinion to connect the diagnosis with the criminal conduct.
- Demonstrate that the mental disease or defect interfered with intellectual assent and understanding as to the quality of the offense.

After all of this, and with no assurance of believability, will a defendant be in a position to raise the defense? The defense's uphill battle results partly from the justice model's general presumption that its accused are sane. The burden to overcome that presumption rests exclusively on the defendant seeking to benefit from its use. Even if the defendant succeeds in a finding of legal insanity, freedom is not automatic because institutionalization until "cured" is the plan of remediation. Psychiatric institutions are not always glamorous places even when compared to maximum security prisons. Within a stated timeline, the "institution will submit a report to the

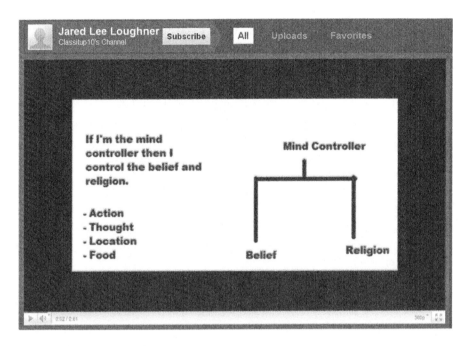

Figure 11.4   Jared Lee Loughner's YouTube page.

court, the results being considered at a hearing within 30 days. The defendant, of course, has the right to be present at the hearing. If the court finds the defendant still should be confined, it shall extend the restriction for no more than one year."[23] (See Figure 11.5 for a sample of a motion to determine competency.)

Legal insanity should not be confused with questions of legal competency either, though the principles sometimes intersect. A finding of incompetency finds that a defendant or other civil party lacks the capacity to understand the nature of the proceedings. Mental state may make incongruous any formal trial or hearings. The grotesque case of racial and ethnic hatred of Richard Baumhammers in Pittsburgh, Pennsylvania, dwells on competency and insanity as it progresses through the courts.

Baumhammers' mental faculties are scary to even the most seasoned veterans of the insanity and incompetency wars. The sheer magnitude of his offenses gives pause, to cause one to not only question his mental faculty in general, but his overall competency to understand the world around him. Baumhammer alleged that due to a host of pathologies, he could not intelligently and rationally participate in his own defense and as a result was incompetent. The argument fell on deaf ears and his sentence of death says much about the community outrage but even more about the failure of defense strategy.[24]

The criteria that should be used to determine competency includes the defendant's capacity to:

- Appreciate the charges against him.
- Appreciate the range and nature of possible penalties that may be imposed in the proceedings against him.
- Understand the adversary nature of the legal process.
- Disclose to counsel facts pertinent to the legal process.
- Manifest appropriate courtroom behavior.

MOTION TO DETERMINE COMPETENCY

Pursuant to (list statute), counsel for the Defendant, (list defendant's name), asks this Court to order a competency examination to determine if he currently has the ability to consult with counsel with a reasonable degree of rational understanding and if he has a rational and factual understanding of the pending proceeding against him. He makes this request for the following reasons:

1. On July 31, 2001 the state arrested (name of defendant) for (list charge(s)).
2. At the time of his arrest, (explain mental condition of defendant).
3. (Explain any other facts, by incident, that support the request.)
4. (List any prior history of commitment or mental health care that effects the decision to grant the motion.)

Based on the above listed reasons, counsel for the defendant in good faith respectfully asks this Court to appoint appropriate mental health experts to examine the defendant to determine his competency to stand trial.

Figure 11.5 Motion to determine competency.

- Testify relevantly.
- Any other factors deemed relevant.

Incompetency is usually a procedural condition that can and does change in most cases. Today's incompetency is tomorrow's understanding. The evidentiary exactitude for offering this claim is far less stringent than the insanity defense because the ultimate results are distinct. In incompetency, we delay till we understand. In insanity, if agreed, we release or commit pending a cure.

Three Tests of Insanity

Insanity law breaks down into three primary approaches. All three require a diagnosis, a finding of some sort of mental disease or defect. All three insist on a correlation between the condition and the offense charged. All three distinguish medical insanity from legal insanity. What separates the tests is language and causation. In the M'Naghten test,[25] the language of right and wrong, good and bad and its respective appreciation, connotes a moral quality thoroughly absent in the Durham rule.[26] In Durham, the offender has the diagnosis, but expert testimony must deduce, without reservation or other explanation, that the crime is the direct "product" of the mental disease or defect. Lastly, in the American Law Institute's (ALI) test, the diagnosis must lead to a confused understanding about the moral qualities of human action—a condition the ALI labels "substantial understanding."[27] While the differences are subtle and at times difficult to distinguish, the consequences for defendants will vary dramatically depending on the jurisdictional test.

M'Naghten Test
Still the law in the majority of American jurisdictions, the M'Naghten rule was named after the defendant Daniel M'Naghten.[28] Under M'Naghten, a person is insane if:

1. He had a mental infirmity, disease, or defect at the time he committed the wrongful act.
2. And, because of that condition;
   a. He did not know what he did or its consequences, or
   b. Although he knew what he was doing and its consequences, he did not know what he was doing was wrong.[29]

Popularly known as the right and wrong test, the M'Naghten rule assesses the accused internal moral compass. It is an objective examination of a very subjective decision that hopes to decipher the good and bad in human activity.[30] Most of us are quite capable of seeing this type of light, and have been endowed naturally and raised appropriately, to be able to declare: "This conduct is bad and this good!" When a defendant's moral barometer functions improperly, the content and quality of the acts chosen is at best amoral. To lack conscience, personal regret, or empathy with evil conduct, paints the picture of a killer without remorse, the rapist with justification, and the hijacker answering to a higher calling. Insane defendants, at least bona fide ones, truly are incapable of this moral differentiation. Like it or not, the world witnesses criminals who are so morally impoverished that choices and conclusions are glaringly separate from any moral code. Juvenile case workers can tell stories by the boatload of the new and emerging class of juvenile offender whose moral indifference frightens. A quick watch of Stanley Kubrick's *A Clockwork Orange* (1971) sends this reality home fast. Amoral, vacuous, cold-blooded, unsympathetic, and chillingly evil describe only parts of the story.

M'Naghten stands for more than moral weakness and indifference because this condition must be connected to the degradation of reason itself. Here, the criminal agent's intellect cannot see the full dimensions of human activity, which includes factual motion, right and privilege, and proper and improper choices. The M'Naghten defendant is only part thinking and more mover than moral deliberator. M'Naghten needs no psychiatric diagnosis, in a formal sense, to play out its interpretation of the law of insanity, but requires a disease of the mind, of knowledge and reasoning itself that makes the human player incapable of understanding the complete dimensions of the conduct in question. The M'Naghten man or woman is conscienceless and dark, blankly resisting judgment and moral outrage the rational person would surely assign.

From this rooftop, one can appreciate the modern psychiatric frustration with this test. Rather than spouting off clinical diagnosis, the M'Naghten rule evaluates the moral dynamics of the human choice. Psychiatrists want explanations and therapeutic modalities while M'Naghten only searches for the man or woman who is incapable of making moral judgments. In an age where questions of right and wrong, good and bad, and judgment seem out of kilter, M'Naghten is a theological and metaphysical throwback to when conduct was evaluated in light of its inherency. M'Naghten, could not be bogged down in compulsions and obsessions, impulses, irresistible and spontaneous, because its frame of reference rests in the objective mind of the offender. Surely the world is plagued by those who are fully aware that certain conduct is grossly unacceptable, yet due to some psychodynamic are incapable of personal control. The term "irresistible impulse" was an early attempt to overturn the M'Naghten rule because individuals, we are told by the psychiatric community, may know right from wrong, good from bad, yet still not be able to control the participation in the conduct. In the world of obsessions, -philias, and delusions, human agents can still moralize in correct, intellectual terms, but still cannot resist the temptation and attraction. For M'Naghten critics, a new test addressing the complexities of human operations had to be adopted.

The Durham rule would open the door to change.

The Durham Test

Only a few American jurisdictions recognize the principles of insanity law enunciated in *Durham v. United States*.[31] New Hampshire, the home state for the case, afforded a slightly varied approach that had been typical in the courtrooms throughout the nineteenth and early twentieth century. In Durham, the defendant argued that the disease or defect that he labored under made it impossible for him to adhere to conduct he morally understood as wrong. Despite his moral discernment, he was driven by what came to be known as the "irresistible impulse." In it, morally knowing defendants cannot resist the pull of the impulse. In this world, the free agent is replaced by external and internal conditions that motivate despite reason. In the place of human reason and free choice, experts describe criminals who cannot control conduct because of some pathology. Using psychiatric determinants rather than human intellect to assign responsibility, the Durham Court went full tilt against the moralizing of M'Naghten.

The science of psychiatry now recognizes that a man is an integrated personality and that reason, which is only one element in that personality, is not the sole determinant of his conduct. The right–wrong test, which considers knowledge or reason alone, therefore, is an inadequate guide to the mental responsibility for criminal behavior.

The fundamental objection to the right–wrong test, however, is not that criminal irresponsibility is made to rest on inadequate, invalid, or indeterminable symptom or manifestation, but that it is made to rest upon any particular symptom.[32]

The Court makes no apologies for its disdain of M'Naghten when it remarks:

> We find that as an exclusive criterion the right–wrong test is inadequate in that (a) it does not take sufficient account of psychic realities and scientific knowledge, and (b) it is based upon one symptom and so cannot validly be applied in all circumstances. We find that the "irresistible impulse" test is also inadequate in that it gives no recognition to mental illness characterized by brooding and reflection and so relegates acts caused by such illness to the application of the inadequate right–wrong test. We conclude a broader test should be adopted.[33]

In order to reach this type of conclusion on irresistibility and other psychic disorders, Durham energetically called for the use of expert opinion that would be capable of correlating these complex findings to particular criminal conduct. Thus, psychiatrists were elevated to far more prominent positions in the litigation arena than previously witnessed because it was the psychiatric community that was exclusively capable of issuing assessments on the types of conduct that lead to irresistible compulsion. A man who knows right and wrong could not be excused on moral grounds, but the neutral judgment of a medical clinician might be comfortable doing so.

In Durham, the shift from personal responsibility to external and internal forces accelerates because of the psychiatric community. In Durham, the psychiatrist becomes the expert who labels the crime a "product," an offshoot of the diagnosis. Because A has paranoia, A does B and cannot resist even when the moral qualities of the act are self-evident. When compared to M'Naghten, the contrast is dramatic. In M'Naghten, the human agent knows and is accountable. In Durham, he knows but can't control and cannot be held accountable.

Durham has borne an unceasing wave of criticism for its rigidity. When it looks for crime as a "product," it assumes a great deal. First, mental disease is far from any quantifiable or mathematic science where A = B. Mental illness is more complicated than the diagnosis matched to the offense. Human personalities and intellects operate under multiple dynamics at any given time and it seems almost too idealistic to conclude this form of equation as reliable science.

Second, Durham grants the psychiatric community unbridled powers previously unseen, and marches into uncharted and extremely nebulous territory with a confidence unjustified. Asking a psychiatrist to rule in an equational way may be a bit much, not only for the role of psychiatrist, but also for a justice system that allegedly relies on its courts and juries to deliver verdicts and findings. To grant the expert such unrestrained authority can only supplant the jury function and debase the fact-finding process. From either the defense or prosecution perspective, no witness should carry opinion to this level of exactitude. Durham's product analysis is packed too tight for the administration for justice.

ALI Test (American Law Institute)

Dissatisfaction with insanity laws in general led the think tank, the American Law Institute (ALI), to come up with its suggested guidelines on how states should model insanity laws. ALI attempts to rectify the problems inherent in both M'Naghten and Durham by advancing some new propositions.[34] The American Law Institute's Commentary section makes clear its disagreeability with what has happened with the state of insanity law. The ALI wanted to revolutionize the definitions and the practice.

> The traditional M'Naghten rule resolves the problem solely in regard to the capacity of the individual to know what he is doing and to know that it was wrong. Absent these minimal elements of rationality, condemnation, and punishment are obviously both unjust and futile ... [T]he attacks on the M'Naghten rule as an inept definition of insanity or as an arbitrary definition in terms of special symptoms are entirely misconceived. The rationale of the position is that these are cases for individuals to be deterred. Moreover, the category defined by the rules is so extreme that to the ordinary man the exculpation of the person it encompasses bespeaks no weakness in the law.[35]

To its credit, ALI attempts to define mental disease or defect, but the substance of exactly what the disease or defect is eludes the interpreter.

Section 4.01 Mental disease or defect excluding responsibility

(1) A person is not responsible for criminal conduct if at the time of such conduct as a result of mental disease or defect he lacks substantial capacity either to appreciate the criminality of his conduct or to conform his conduct to the requirements of law.
(2) The terms "mental disease or defect" do not include an abnormality manifested only by repeated criminal or otherwise antisocial conduct.[36]

Discover the insanity defense from a psychiatric perspective. Visit http://www.psychiatry.us/articledetail.php?ID=44&CID=3

The language takes on a very distinct tone from the Durham model. Specifically, the test ties the disease or defect to the criminal agent's understanding of the crime in question, but does in a curious way. By using the phrase, "substantial capacity," the ALI adopts a less mathematical approach. The door is open to those who know, whose crimes were the direct cause of the disease or the defect, and to those who were messed up enough that they really did not appreciate all the nuances of what the criminal conduct was. The defendant may know the wrongfulness, may be able to withstand some portion of the compulsion yet still could be innocent by reason of insanity because the pathology is so disturbed. Durham rejected those who understood part

CASE 11.4

U.S. V. MASSA

804 F.2d 1020 (8th Cir. 1986).

On April 28, 1983, James Massa was convicted on a forty-three-count indictment arising out of the massive swindle of the Stix & Company brokerage firm and was sentenced to twenty years in prison. This Court affirmed that conviction. *United States v. Massa*, 740 F.2d 629 (8th Cir. 1984). Massa now appeals a decision of the district court denying his motion for a new trial on the basis of newly discovered evidence and denying his motion for reduction of sentence. The issues presented for review include whether the district court erred in denying a new trial: (1) on the basis of a psychiatrist's report; (2) on the basis of alleged evidence that prosecution witness Jerry Maeras committed perjury; (3) on the basis of the government's alleged suppression of evidence impeaching Maeras; and (4) on the basis of false and misleading inferences raised by the government during the trial. Massa also claims the district court abused its discretion in denying his motion for reduction of sentence and in denying his request for a hearing on both motions. For the reasons set forth below, we affirm in part and remand for an evidentiary hearing. ...

Massa argues that psychiatric treatment, subsequent to trial, has revealed that he did not knowingly participate in the scheme to defraud Stix, and, therefore, he is entitled to a new trial. This argument is supported by an affidavit of Dr. R. Eugene Holeman, which essentially states that because Massa idolized Brimberry, he lapsed into "magical thinking" which prevented him from seeing "the big picture," that is, from knowing that he and Brimberry were engaged in an embezzlement scheme:

The [non-criminal] explanation for his behavior lies in the compulsive part of his personality. * * * One compulsive symptom has been to escape into relationships with men whom he saw as stronger, smarter, or wealthier than himself. He idealizes them and allows them to take advantage of him. He sees these individuals as bigger than life, as an answer to his chronic feelings of inadequacy. To maintain this magical view his conscious mind does not see what is obvious to others about this kind of person. * * * In the therapy process, we have seen a series of these relationships, beginning in adolescence and continuing into the relationship with Mr. Brimberry. Each had the same compulsive characteristic, but Mr. Massa was unable to see the "big picture." * * * The relationship with Mr. Brimberry was the most extreme of these relationships — following Brimberry's grandiosity, accepting his lies and distortions and ultimately meeting with his unconscious needs for self-destruction.

The district court determined that Holeman's affidavit did not entitle Massa to a new trial because "the factual circumstances supporting Dr. Holeman's affidavit were certainly known to both defendant and his family well before the trial of this action," and, therefore, the court could not infer diligence on the part of the movant to discover this evidence before trial. We cannot agree with the court's reasoning on this point. Although the factual details underlying Holeman's affidavit were known to Massa prior to trial, he did not know that an expert would opine that those details of his life had so affected his mental state as to render him incapable of committing the crimes with which he was charged. Indeed, Holeman formed this opinion only after counseling Massa for over eighteen months.

Thus, the question becomes whether the jury probably would have acquitted Massa had it been privy to Holeman's report. We answer this question in the negative. As we noted in *United States v. Lewellyn*, 723 F.2d 615, 616 (8th Cir. 1983), this Circuit has adopted the American Law Institute (ALI) insanity test:

(1) A defendant is insane * * * if, at the time of the alleged criminal conduct, as a result of mental disease or defect he lacks substantial capacity either to appreciate the wrongfulness of his conduct or to conform his conduct to the requirements of law.
(2) As used in this Article, the terms "mental disease or defect" do not include any abnormality manifested only by repeated criminal or otherwise antisocial conduct. Model Penal Code § 4.01 (Final Draft 1962). Id. (citations omitted).

We are not convinced by Holeman's affidavit, and we do not think it could have convinced a jury that Massa lacked the capacity either to appreciate the wrongfulness of his conduct or to conform his conduct to the law.

Holeman describes Massa as a dependent person who seeks and finds comfort in relationships with strong men and then subordinates his desires and values to the wishes of the stronger man. While in no way intending to diminish Massa's psychological problems, we cannot see how a jury would excuse Massa based on this diagnosis. A dependent, weak-willed personality is not unique to Massa, and it is certainly not an excuse for criminal behavior recognized by law.

There is, however, another aspect to this matter and that is whether the trial court might have given Massa a lesser sentence had he been aware of Massa's condition as defined in the psychiatric report and as further developed at a hearing.

The rule is that district courts need not always hold hearings on disputed matters of fact arising from post-trial motions. *United States v. Abou-Saada*, 785 F.2d 1, 6 (1st Cir. 1986). Ordinarily, these motions are decided on the basis of affidavits without a hearing, although there may be exceptional circumstances in which an oral hearing should be granted. *United States v. Bednar*, 776 F.2d 236, 239 (8th Cir. 1985).

We think that this case falls in that category as far as the sentence is concerned. We, therefore, remand to the district court with directions to that court to grant Massa a hearing in order to develop the psychiatric evidence. At that hearing, Holeman may be called as a witness to elaborate on his affidavit, and if Holeman does testify, the government should be given an opportunity to cross-examine him.

Thereafter, the district court should decide whether it will reduce Massa's sentence in light of the evidence established at the hearing. If an appeal is taken from the district court, it shall be referred to the panel in this case for final disposition.

Questions

1. What was the defendant's magical thinking? Did this type of thinking qualify under ALI?
2. What did the defendant mean when he said that consideration of these conditions may have resulted in an acquittal?
3. How did the court resolve the question procedurally and substantively?

of the conduct's wrongfulness while M'Naghten closed the door on anyone who understood any portion of the illegality and immorality. ALI opens the gates a little wider by claiming the psychiatric state is neither mathematical nor exclusively rational, but a mix of all of these and more. The psychiatric community could not have been happier with the result since, as in Durham, it will depend on the expertise of those trained in the psychiatric domain.

Those unhappy with the result are proponents of free will and choice, and those resistant to the continuing dilution of the legal processes by the social and psychiatric sciences whose mission, while laudable, may not always compliment the legal model. Psychiatrists under the ALI can always find an argument that lends itself to the theory of substantial appreciation. Our system's decriminalization tendency, replacing personal responsibility with phobias and diseases of explanation, has been spurred on by the open-ended ALI approach. Instead of legal evidence, judgments of emotional disorder and clinical diagnoses rule the roost. In ALI, the psychiatrist runs the show since the system's other players are incapable of issuing these types of findings. For some, the courthouse has abdicated its powers to those untrained in the practice and analysis of law.[37]

At the end of the day, the ALI has delivered little on what it promised especially since the legal system continues to be mired in the imprecision and incongruity of an insanity defense that, at times, makes M'Naghten look all the better.

Guilty But Mentally Ill

The level of dissatisfaction over the insanity defense has generated some innovative approaches in the assignment of criminal responsibility—none more novel than the plea or conviction: guilty but mentally ill.[38] Delaware and Pennsylvania, to name a couple of states, have reached an accommodation with which its public, the correctional community, and police and prosecutors can rest easy.

Given the rampancy of mental health issues confronting our criminal courts, an emerging trend toward establishing Mental Health Courts as substitute forums for mentally ill defendants has become a reality in some jurisdictions. Discover this new form of criminal processing at http://www.mentalhealthamerica.net/go/position-statements/53

While the plea or finding recognizes the mental disease or defect, said declaration will not free the defendant of his or her ultimate responsibility. The plea has both support and criticism, but, as in all political accommodation, attempting to rectify the injustice of bad insanity law, the compromise may be better than the bedrock principle.

§ 314. Guilty but mentally ill

(a) GENERAL RULE.— A person who timely offers a defense of insanity in accordance with the Rules of Criminal Procedure may be found "guilty but mentally ill" at trial if the trier of facts finds, beyond a reasonable doubt, that the person is guilty of an offense, was mentally ill at the time of the commission of the offense, and was not legally insane at the time of the commission of the offense.

(b) PLEA OF GUILTY BUT MENTALLY ILL.— A person who waives his right to trial may plead guilty but mentally ill. No plea of guilty but mentally ill may be accepted by the trial judge until he has examined all reports prepared pursuant to the Rules of

CASE 11.5

ROSS V. DELAWARE

768 A.2d 471 (De. Sup. 2001)

This 6th day of February 2001, upon consideration of the briefs of the parties, it appears that:

(1) The appellant, Jarnell M. Ross ("Ross"), was convicted by a Superior Court jury of attempted murder first degree, reckless endangering first degree, terroristic threatening, theft and related firearms offenses. The charges arose out of Ross's shooting of a female acquaintance following a dispute over a third party. At trial, Ross contended that he acted under extreme emotional distress and raised the defense of "guilty but mentally ill."

(2) In this appeal, Ross alleges three claims of error: (i) an allegedly incorrect jury instruction concerning a "guilty but mentally ill" verdict; (ii) an allegedly incorrect jury instruction concerning his defense of extreme emotional distress; and (iii) the trial court's ruling denying admissibility to certain hearsay evidence concerning violent acts between Ross and the victim. We find no merit to any of these claims and accordingly affirm.

(3) With respect to Ross's claims directed to the trial court's instructions to the jury, we note that Ross made no objection at trial to the instructions at issue. Accordingly, in the absence of such an objection, our review of these claims is under a plain error standard. Under the plain error standard of review, the error complained of must be so clearly prejudicial to substantial rights as to jeopardize the fairness and integrity of the trial process.

(4) To determine the legal sufficiency of the instruction, this Court need not find perfection, but rather, when viewed in its entirety, the instruction must "enable the jury to intelligently perform its duty in returning a verdict." A trial court's charge to the jury will not serve as grounds for reversible error if it is "reasonably informative and not misleading, judged by common practices and standards of verbal communication." Flamer, 490 A.2d at 128 (quoting *Baker v. Reid*, Del. Supr., 44 Del. 112, 57 A.2d 103, 109 (1947)). "To assure a fair and impartial trial, a jury must be adequately informed by the Court, not only regarding the State's burden of proof beyond a reasonable doubt to support a conviction, but also in respect to all the essential elements of the offense." *Taylor v. State*, Del. Supr., 464 A.2d 897, 899 (1983). Thus, plain error may consist of the failure to instruct the jury on the necessary elements of the crime.

(5) Ross argues that the guilty but mentally ill instruction was plain error for two reasons. First, he claims it did not include the word "willpower" in its definition of "psychiatric disorder." Second, Ross complains that the court's instruction distinguishing between "guilty but mentally insane" and "not guilty by reason of insanity" omitted the sentence "or who, due to a psychiatric disorder, lacks sufficient willpower to choose whether to do a particular act or refrain from doing it."

The "willpower" language is not required for a finding of guilty but mentally ill. 11 Del. C. § 401(b) provides three possible bases for such a finding. First, where "a defendant suffered from a psychiatric disorder which substantially disturbed such person's thinking, feeling or behavior." *Aizupitis v. State*, Del. Supr., 699 A.2d 1092, 1096 (1997). Because the statute uses "and/or," the second basis is when "a defendant suffered from [an ongoing] psychiatric disorder which substantially disturbed such person's thinking, feeling or behavior and ... such psychiatric disorder left such person with insufficient willpower to choose whether the person would do the act or refrain from doing it." Id. Finally, a person can be guilty but mentally ill when a "psychiatric disorder left such person with insufficient willpower to choose whether the person would do the act or refrain from doing it." Id. A person can be guilty but mentally insane upon establishing that he or she is within the first category only, "psychiatric disorder which substantially disturbed behavior[.]" In Sanders, this Court held that the language dealing with a defendant's willpower is redundant, and was included in § 401(b) to make it clear that the volitional test had been eliminated from the absolute defense of insanity and that defendants who would have been acquitted under the prior statute must now be found "guilty but mentally ill." Id.

(6) In this case, the trial judge not only read to the jury the statute containing the willpower language, but also instructed the jurors to render a "guilty but mentally insane" verdict if they determined "[Defendant] suffered from a psychiatric disorder which either substantially disturbed his thinking, feeling, or behavior, and/or left [him] with insufficient willpower to choose whether he would do the act or refrain from doing the act, although physically capable to refrain from doing it." Even if the "willpower" language does comprise an alternative method of determining "guilty but mentally insane," the jury instruction was adequate since the jury was instructed as to the relevance of Ross's willpower. When the instruction is viewed in its entirety, the single word, which Ross argues was omitted, is insignificant. The jury received a correct statement of law. While a second or third use of the word "willpower" may have added greater emphasis, the law requires only that the jury be informed of the essential elements. That standard is satisfied here and there is no basis for a finding of error.

(7) Ross next contends that the jury instruction for "extreme emotional distress" was plain error because it misled the jury by requiring them to first find him guilty of murder, then to consider the mitigating circumstances. While the State must prove all elements of the crime beyond reasonable doubt, the mitigating circumstances of extreme emotional distress must be proved by Ross by a preponderance of the evidence. That burden is made explicit in 11 Del. C. § 641. The defendant, in effect, admitted that he intended to kill when he raised an affirmative defense and it is not illogical for the instructions on attempted murder and its elements to precede the instruction on affirmative defenses. The rather lengthy instruction given by the trial court on extreme emotional distress is accurate and complete and does not rise to the level of plain error.

(8) Finally, we reject Ross's contention that the trial court erred in not permitting him to present the testimony of witnesses who would testify about the victim's acts of violence on prior occasions. The court did permit evidence of such conduct to be presented, in hearsay form, through the testimony of a psychologist who testified for the defense. Ross did not claim that the victim was violent toward him on the night of the offense and the relevancy of prior conduct is questionable at best. In any event, the trial court exercised its discretion under D.R.E. 403(b) in excluding such evidence and we conclude that the court did not abuse its discretion in so ruling.

Questions

1. What impact does the question of willpower have upon the court's eventual finding?
2. What two burdens of proof exist in this case?
3. Why are there two?
4. Which is the more difficult to demonstrate?

Criminal Procedure, has held a hearing on the sole issue of the defendant's mental illness at which either party may present evidence and is satisfied that the defendant was mentally ill at the time of the offense to which the plea is entered. If the trial judge refuses to accept a plea of guilty but mentally ill, the defendant shall be permitted to withdraw his plea. A defendant whose plea is not accepted by the court shall be entitled to a jury trial, except that if a defendant subsequently waives his right to a jury trial, the judge who presided at the hearing on mental illness shall not preside at the trial.[39]

For an interesting study on guilty but mentally ill, see Case 11.5.

ENTRAPMENT

ESSENTIAL ISSUES

- Predisposition of the accused
- Level and type of law enforcement involvement
- Sense of fair play and justice in the solicitation
- Objective or subjective mind of accused and officers

Law enforcement's active solicitation of criminal activity, if overly aggressive, can be deemed entrapment when the level of encouragement and solicitation exceeds ordinary boundaries. Enabling crime is an improper law enforcement action. Causing crime when it would otherwise not occur undermines public trust.[40] Entrapment exonerates a defendant who would not ordinarily engage in a criminal purpose or plan, but the idea for the crime was planted and encouraged by public law enforcement.[41] In entrapment cases, the defendant argues that law enforcement encouragement goes well beyond the typical undercover operation and nurtures an unwitting and once unwilling innocent party into a criminal design made only possible by overly solicitous law enforcement. It is excessive inducement prompted by overzealous police officers.

The burden of proof in the entrapment defense rests exclusively with the defendant. The defense is often witnessed in cases involving drugs, prostitution, and distribution of obscene materials.[42] Nearly every American jurisdiction has some version mirroring that of the Model Penal Code.

Section 2.13 Entrapment

(1) A public law enforcement official or a person acting in cooperation with such an official perpetrates an entrapment if for the purpose of obtaining evidence of the commission of an offense, he induces or encourages another person to engage in conduct constituting such offense by either:

    (a)   making knowingly false representations designed to induce the belief that such conduct is not prohibited; or

    (b)   employing methods of persuasion or inducement which create a substantial risk that such an offense will be committed by persons other than those who are ready to commit it.[43]

Justice operatives who encourage and nourish the criminal plan step beyond usual investigative bounds. The entrapped party is so overly influenced by law enforcement that the actor has no real claim to an independent mens rea. In the end, the police provide the plan and the motivation.[44]

The portrait of an unwitting, easily influenced criminal perpetrator seems implausible in a world rampant with crime. In addition, it is difficult to believe the level of naiveté being argued

---

CASE 11.6

JACOBSON V. U.S.

503 U.S. 540 (1992)

Obtain the following case from an online legal database and answer the following questions.

Questions

1. What evidence did the defendant provide that demonstrates his version of entrapment?
2. Did the defendant already possess these inclinations to the type of material possessed?
3. How does the court resolve defendant's appeal?
4. What does the dissent reply to the majority finding?

CASE 11.7

GREENE V. U.S.
454 F.2d 783 (1971)

Mike A. Thomas, John Becker, and Earl D. Greene were jointly indicted, tried, and convicted on charges involving possession of unregistered distilling apparatus, sale without stamp of distilled spirits, and conspiracy. The three took separate appeals which we consolidated for argument and disposition. While these appeals were pending, defendant Greene was murdered. As to his appeal it is, therefore, appropriate to remand with directions to vacate the judgment and dismiss the indictment. We reverse the convictions of Thomas and Becker for the reasons stated below.

In September, 1962, Jack Courtney, a special investigator with the Alcohol and Tobacco Tax Division of the United States Treasury Department, assumed the role of an undercover agent in an effort to penetrate what he believed to be an organization which was selling bootleg whiskey. Posing as a gangster or member of the "syndicate," he was, on September 5, 1962, introduced to defendants Thomas and Becker by Gerald Brown, an informer for the Oakland Police department. The events which thereafter unfolded reveal almost unbelievable naiveté on the part of defendants in accepting Courtney as a representative of the "syndicate." More important, however, they disclose wholly impermissible participation by the Government, through its regularly employed agent, Courtney, in a project to manufacture, sell and distribute bootleg whiskey.

Courtney held himself out to Thomas and Becker as a gangster because he had received information through a police informer that Thomas and Becker were attempting to locate a "syndicate" connection to purchase large quantities of moonshine whiskey. During the course of their September 5, 1962, meeting, Thomas and Becker told Courtney that they had sold nontax paid alcohol to the public prior to meeting Courtney, but indicated that they preferred one buyer. They also told Courtney that if he wanted to deal with them he would have to be able to take delivery of one hundred to two hundred gallons of bootleg whiskey a week. Courtney told them he was in a position to accept whatever they could produce.

Later that same evening Becker took Courtney to his home in Oakland and gave Courtney a sample of Becker's and Thomas' bootleg whiskey. Becker and Thomas at that time described their then-existing still set-up to Courtney. During Courtney's 1962 association with Thomas and Becker, and in order to play the part of a gangster, Courtney showed Thomas and Becker strip stamps, displayed labels in the back of his car, and told them he had a bottling plant as part of the syndicate operation.

On September 10, 1962, Courtney purchased eight gallons of illegal distilled spirits from Becker and Thomas. As a result of Courtney's activities, government agents, in October 1962, located and raided a still on Thomas' property near Sacramento. In early 1963, Thomas and Becker pleaded guilty to charges similar to those alleged in the instant indictment. Both were sentenced to six months in jail and were released from custody in November, 1963.

In late 1962, while the 1962 case was pending and Becker was free on bail, Courtney initiated telephone contact with Becker concerning further relationship between them. Courtney's purpose was to determine whether his undercover identity had been compromised. During the telephone call, Becker manifested a lack of awareness of Courtney's true identity.

Courtney had no further contact with Thomas or Becker until, in December, 1963, he received a letter from Becker, quoted in the margin. The telephone call referred to in the letter was Courtney's 1962 call to Becker, mentioned above.

After receiving the December, 1963 letter, Courtney telephoned Becker and arranged to meet Thomas and Becker at the Hyatt House in San Jose, on February 8, 1964. At the meeting, Courtney continued his role as a big-time gangster. He talked to Thomas and Becker as if the three were partners, offered financial assistance so that Becker could bribe his probation officer, and offered to buy all the alcohol they could produce.

Thomas and Becker informed Courtney at that meeting that they intended to go back into the bootlegging business, that Thomas would be in charge of the still operation, and that they wished Courtney to check periodically with Becker to ascertain their progress. However, they also stated that they had no still at that time.

The meeting lasted seven or eight hours on February 8th, during which time Courtney took Becker and Thomas out to dinner, and continued on February 9th. On the 9th, by the end of the meeting, Thomas and Becker were saying that they would get into production within ninety days.

However, when the three next met, at the Hilton Inn, San Bruno, on May 27, 1964, Thomas and Becker indicated that they were having difficulty getting into operation. At this time Courtney, in an effort to spur production of bootleg whiskey, told Thomas and Becker, "the boss is on my back." On October 22, 1964, some eight months after they had said they would be in production in ninety days, Becker and Thomas made their first delivery of bootleg alcohol to Courtney since their conviction in 1962. The shipment consisted of ten gallons, for which Courtney paid one hundred dollars.

Shortly after this first small delivery, flooding in Northern California apparently disrupted the defendants' still operations. However, they did manage, after another delay of more than four months, to make a thirty-five gallon delivery to Courtney for four hundred and fifty dollars, on March 3, 1965.

Thereafter, there was a fifteen-month delay before the third and final shipment of illicit spirits was made. On June 4, 1966, sixty gallons of alcohol was delivered to a government agent in Sacramento, for which Courtney paid Becker seven hundred and eighty dollars. Immediately thereafter, Courtney arrested Becker and the still site near Ceres, California was raided, thus bringing the undercover role of Courtney to an end.

During the protracted intervals between the three deliveries, there were several other meetings and extensive additional contracts among the individuals involved. Of the thirty-two letters, telephone calls and telegrams between Courtney and either Thomas or Becker, or both, between December 16, 1963 and June 4, 1966, twenty-two were initiated by Courtney.

Courtney also looked for a new distillery site for defendants at their request, going so far as to arrange for the use of a ranch near Sparks, Nevada, which he showed to Thomas and Becker in 1965. After some deliberation, they decided not to use that site.

In addition, Courtney, at one time or another during the two and one-half year period involved, offered to have a still apparatus sent from the East if that of the defendants was unsatisfactory, offered to furnish a still operator (known as a "monkey"), and told Thomas and Becker that he thought he could obtain plastic containers for them. Also, after some discussion, Courtney in 1966 made available to Thomas and Becker, at wholesale prices, two thousand pounds of sugar for use in their bootleg operations. It is undisputed that, during the extended period relevant to the charged offenses, the defendants sold illicit spirits only to the Government, through its undercover agent Courtney.

At the trial, Courtney testified that his dealings with the defendants had been protracted and extensive because of the Government's goal of finding the still and shutting it down, and because of the defendants' caution and unwillingness to disclose the details and location of their operation. Thomas and Becker, on the other hand, argued that while they talked in grandiose terms of criminal activity to impress the "syndicate man," they were reluctant to act and might never have produced any bootleg alcohol without the prodding of Courtney. To support this argument, they stressed Courtney's additional testimony that although he, as an experienced law officer, knew they were stalling him, he kept on in order to get them to sell him some liquor.

Questions

1. Describe the conduct of police officers in this case.
2. Describe the criminal background of the party alleging entrapment.
3. Was law enforcement too entangled with defendant to cause an offense that otherwise would not have happened?

by defendants whose backgrounds are rarely innocent. How believable is this argument? Part of entrapment's longstanding problem has been on its focus. In other words, what is the measure of inducement or manipulation? Do we look to the officers' intentionality to discern motivation? Do we evaluate, in objective terms, the types and degrees of influence and mental manipulation of the justice sector, hoping to decipher acceptable levels or zones of police conduct? Or do we assess the historical record of the offender and scan his or her predisposition to criminality in the first instance? In this last case, we subjectively hope to determine what a defendant was or was not capable of. How are we to believe any of it?

To be sure, an offender with no history of crime and with a pristine personal reputation is more likely the subject of entrapment than an Olympian rap sheet holder; the predisposition to offending is only too obvious. At other times, the inducement is too much for the average person to resist and forebear. Consider Case 11.8.

COERCION/DURESS

ESSENTIAL ISSUES

- Level of coercion/duress
- Reasonableness of reaction
- Ability to withstand the duress
- An unwilling participant

CASE 11.8

COMMONWEALTH V. THOMPSON
484 A.2d 159 (1984)

Beginning on May 1, 1980, state police Trooper Lucinda Hammond became involved in an undercover investigation of appellant, a 46-year-old black male who was married and living with his wife and mentally retarded daughter in Carlisle. At the time this investigation began, he was a ten-year veteran of the Carlisle Borough Police Force. Trooper Hammond was a young, blonde, white female who apparently was very attractive.

The undercover officer came to Carlisle on May 2, May 9, May 12, May 16, May 22, May 23, May 28, June 5, June 6, June 12, June 19, and June 25 of 1980 in an attempt to make contact with appellant. Although Trooper Hammond was unable to establish any direct communication with appellant, he did wave to her on May 22 and May 28. Her purpose in making contact with appellant on all these occasions was to determine if he would provide her with drugs.

Trooper Hammond's first "face-to-face" contact with appellant was on July 10, 1980, at the square in Carlisle. He was on duty and she approached him with a question about a false temporary driver's license which apparently was used as a pretext for starting a conversation. She testified that at the time her hair was long and straight and she wore mid-thigh, cut-off shorts and a short-sleeved jersey. During the conversation which ensued, the two began talking about "partying" and having a good time. Appellant discussed with Hammond his purported use of marijuana and she let him know that she "partied" and "got high." He then told her he would be able to get drugs for her.

The second encounter between appellant and Hammond occurred on August 8, 1980, when she again walked up to him while he was on duty. She was again dressed in cut-offs and a jersey. There was a brief conversation, but no mention of drugs. Sometime after this meeting, Hammond began to telephone appellant at his place of work, the Carlisle Police Station. These calls continued over the course of the investigation, totaling at least eight to ten in all. Appellant never contacted Hammond and she never provided him with a means of doing so.

The third direct contact between them occurred on September 3, 1980, when she again walked up to him while he was working. She wore a blouse that was open in the back and shoulders, as well as her by now standard cut-offs. Appellant recognized her immediately and started a friendly conversation, which included a discussion of drugs and getting high. He tried to get her to meet him after work at a tavern called the Oliver Plunkett, but she declined and instead arranged to meet him the next night at another tavern called Yancy's.

As had been arranged, they met and had drinks together at Yancy's on September 4. It was their fourth meeting and first date. Again the discussion turned to partying and getting high. Appellant stated to Hammond that he kept marijuana in his locker at work which he would seize during drug arrests and then use himself. This appears to have been mere braggadocio. She asked if he was going to get some of this marijuana and he said no. He repeatedly, on that evening and throughout the investigation, indicated to her that he wanted her to trust him, that he might be a policeman, but he liked fun too. He assured her that he was not trying to set her up.

The fifth direct contact occurred on September 29, after she had called him at the police station. They met again at Yancy's for a date, and she then asked him to obtain some marijuana for her personal use or "maybe make a little money on the side." (N.T., Trial at 28). He responded by again trying to get her to go to the Oliver Plunkett after hours with him, telling her she could get some marijuana if she would go with him. She declined to do so and left Yancy's.

The next and sixth personal contact did not occur until December 17, 1980. She had talked to him, however, on October 23 and 24, and, in another telephone conversation on November 25, had "point blank" asked him if he could make a deal for some drugs. On November 26 and December 3, she traveled to Carlisle looking for appellant but could not find him. At the December 17 meeting, when he was on duty, she again asked him about getting drugs. As before, he wanted her to meet him after midnight and she would not do so.

She met with him briefly on January 6, 1982, and arranged to meet him at Yancy's the next day. During that date at Yancy's, she began directly indicating to him that he "wasn't coming across" with any drugs. (N.T. Trial at 88). Possibly as early as October or November, but certainly by this date, she began chiding him, telling him he was "all talk" and never produced anything for her. She began to question appellant's ability to obtain drugs for her. He stated he would get some for her if she'd meet him again the next night. They did meet the following night, January 8, 1981, in a furniture store parking lot at the M. J. Carlisle Mall. On this eighth meeting between the two, she got into his car only to find he had no drugs. He indicated he would get them later in the evening, so they went to the Hamilton Lounge together. When she indicated to him she was interested in getting something for herself for later that night, he made no moves to get any drugs, despite having earlier mentioned his "connection" was in the Oliver Plunkett right across the street. Instead, he questioned her about her social life. Before she left, she asked about paying for the drugs, but he assured her the drugs would not cost her anything.

It is clear from the testimony that on or about December 1980 or January 1981, they were kissing at the end of their dates or meetings, either at her car or while in his car. They were often seen together in public in Carlisle, and appellant would put his arm around her and introduce her to his friends. She concluded from his conduct that he was possibly interested in a romantic or sexual relationship, although he always treated her respectfully. However, she never offered and he never requested sexual relations.

The telephone calls and meetings continued, with Hammond constantly requesting drugs and appellant just as consistently failing to provide them. She would insinuate that he couldn't get any drugs, while he again assured her no payment would be necessary for any drugs he produced. Appellant kept up his entreaties, asking her to meet him after midnight and once to stay overnight, all of which she declined. On one occasion, she mentioned she felt ill and appellant offered to get her a motel room. Around this time, he also started suggesting to Hammond that she move to Carlisle.

Eventually, she arranged a meeting with him on the evening of March 23 at the Hamilton Lounge. She testified on direct examination that:

A After he made these statements about being able to take care of me as far as drugs were concerned, seeing how this was something I had heard from him on several occasions before I just really didn't take it that seriously. And I just said to him, well, you know, you are all talk. I have heard this before. And that's all I ever hear is just talk.

And he said, "well, I am going to show you that I am on the level here." He said "I am going to get a dime bag of grass this evening." And while I was talking with him another individual entered the bar. ...

Q. The codefendant in this case?

A. That's correct.

Q. Go ahead, what happened next?

A. And shortly afterwards [appellant] called over to Mr. Coleman. And he took a $10.00 bill out of his pocket and put it on the bar. And he said to Mr. Coleman, "I want you to get me a dime bag of grass."

(N.T. Trial at 12).

Appellant thereafter obtained 4.5 grams of marijuana from his friend, a Mr. Coleman, and gave it to Hammond. Appellant and Hammond then left the bar and went to his car where he rolled some marijuana cigarettes with papers supplied by Hammond. She offered to pay for the marijuana, but he refused to accept any money.

The final meeting during the investigation was on April 11, 1981, at the Hamilton Lounge. This date had been pre-arranged by Hammond by phone. Appellant asked her how the marijuana was and whether she had any left. She replied that since it was such a little amount, there was no more left. He then talked of obtaining more drugs for her, but never produced any. The meeting ended after the two of them drove around Carlisle looking at apartments as appellant continued to talk about her moving there. Eventually, appellant offered to pay one-half of her rent if she moved to Carlisle.

Questions

1. What was the background of the defendant?
2. What methods did law enforcement use?
3. Are these methods a basis for the entrapment defense?
4. How would you decide the case?

Another defense that delves into the element of intentionality is coercion/duress. Duress against a defendant forces the defendant to do things he or she ordinarily would not do. It is also an affirmative defense that must be raised by the defendant in advance of the litigation. Duress "is an affirmative defense that the actor engaged in the conduct charged to constitute an offense because he was coerced to do so by the use of, or a threat to use, unlawful force against his person or the person of another, which a person of reasonable firmness in his situation would have been unable to resist."[45] To argue effectively, its proponent will have to demonstrate a lack of alternatives in the choice of conduct. Here, the defendant is compelled to act against his or her will and coerced into criminal conduct.[46]

CASE 11.9

JACKSON V. MARYLAND
358 Md. 612 (Md. App. 2000).

After a nonjury trial, petitioner was convicted of first degree felony murder, robbery with a deadly weapon, and several lesser included offenses, for which she was sentenced to life imprisonment. The victim was 73-year old Claude Bowlin, whom the 24-year old petitioner claimed as a friend. Bowlin, a widower who lived alone, frequently gave petitioner money to support her cocaine addiction. Petitioner visited Mr. Bowlin on a weekly basis, to get money for drugs and to perform sexual favors for him. Petitioner was also involved in a romantic relationship with Corey Williams, a co-defendant tried separately. At trial, the State offered substantial evidence to show that, on the evening of August 17, 1997, pursuant to a common scheme between petitioner and Williams to steal from Bowlin, petitioner went to Bowlin's home, that she and Bowlin retired to Bowlin's bedroom where they undressed and engaged in sexual acts, that while Bowlin was so distracted, Williams entered the house, came up to the bedroom, and repeatedly bashed Bowlin in the head with a ceramic beer stein, that either Williams or petitioner gagged Bowlin with a shirt sleeve, that Williams then stole a VCR and a CD player, that petitioner and Williams left together, that petitioner sold the items taken by Williams, and that petitioner and Williams used the proceeds to buy more drugs.

Bowlin died from a combination of the blunt blows and cuts to the head and asphyxia, the latter caused by the gag stuffed into his mouth and across his face. At trial, petitioner essentially conceded that she agreed to distract Bowlin so that Williams could enter the house undetected and steal items therefrom, but she maintained that she had no intent to harm Bowlin. She claimed that she was surprised when Williams appeared in the bedroom and began beating Bowlin. She denied being the one who gagged Bowlin, though she admitted that she got a towel and put it over Bowlin's face in order to stop the bleeding or clean up the blood. In arguing for acquittal, she asserted that (1) there was no evidence that she killed Bowlin, (2) she acted under duress from Williams, (3) the murder was essentially a frolic of Williams and not in furtherance of anything she planned, (4) there was no evidence of a robbery, and (5) to the extent the State relied upon a burglary as the underlying felony, there was insufficient evidence of a breaking. The court rejected all of those arguments and found that Williams, in consort with petitioner, did commit a burglary by opening a closed door to enter the house for the purpose of stealing, that there was also a robbery with a deadly weapon, and that there was no duress.

Petitioner promptly filed a motion for new trial, raising all of the arguments made at trial and, ... claimed that the murder was not really in furtherance of the alleged burglary but was a crime of passion committed entirely by Williams. The court delayed consideration of that motion, and, concomitantly, of sentencing petitioner until the completion of Williams's trial, which occurred in May, 1998. At a hearing conducted on July 16, 1998, at which the State reminded the court of evidence showing that Mr. Bowlin's drawers had been ransacked and items in the room moved around, indicating a search for money and thus an intended theft, the court rejected all of petitioner's arguments. In the course of doing so, it noted that Mr. Bowlin died not just from the blows administered by Williams but also from asphyxiation, and, although it had made no finding on the matter when announcing its verdict, declared that "she's the one that stuck the gag in his mouth because she didn't want the noise." The court concluded that "this is as clearly a murder committed in the furtherance of a felony as I think you can possibly have." ...

On November 10, 1998, while both her appeal and that of Williams were pending in the Court of Special Appeals, petitioner filed another motion for new trial, based on newly discovered evidence. The newly discovered evidence was a handwritten note from Williams, dated September 23, 1998, admitting that he gagged Bowlin, that petitioner "had nothing to do with the gagging of Mr. Claude Bowlin," and that he was "willing to take the stand and [admit] my guilt." That statement, she averred, constituted newly discovered evidence because it was not in existence prior to September, 1998. She asked, as relief, that the court order a new trial, that it re-sentence petitioner, and that it schedule the matter "for an immediate hearing."

The State, in response, characterized the "admission" made by Williams after his own conviction and sentencing as merely "an attempt at gallantry" not sufficient to constitute newly discovered evidence that would have a substantial likelihood of changing the outcome of the trial.

Questions

1. How can the cocaine addict argue compulsion effectively?
2. Is a past history of violence and threat relevant to questions of duress? Does it work in this case?
3. Does the existence of another felonious plan bear on coercion or duress?

However, duress and coercion are not the stuff for the weak and fainthearted, but measured by the reasonableness of the reaction to the coerced circumstances. Some statutes refer to this as a "reasonable firmness."[47] Thus, when a Mafia hit man instructs that a delivery of drugs should occur or yourself or your relatives will suffer the consequences, duress exists. It could be argued that escape from a juvenile facility where harm occurred with regularity might be a coercive environment. While not synonymous with brain washing, the element of mind control flows through duress analysis because the defense admits the wrongdoing, but justifies the action by the impossibility of any other course of conduct.

MISTAKE/IGNORANCE OF LAW

ESSENTIAL ISSUES

- Objective lack of knowledge
- Character and record of defendant
- Application to specific intent crimes
- Presumption of knowledge and notice

One who acts without a true or full understanding of the illegality of the act can always defend under a theory of mistake or ignorance. Raising the defense provides meager assurance of success because these types of defenses are so capable of artificial invention. How can one prove or disprove that this particular defendant in these specific circumstances was unaware of the unlawfulness of conduct or that this defendant thought the once illegal conduct had been decriminalized? Then, too, the defendant may have misinterpreted or misapplied the very principles once correctly interpreted, or operated in reliance on the judgment of others, such as a judicial finding or holding, whose interpretation had been previously trustworthy. Mistakes and ignorance can be in good faith, but the proof thereof is just one more example of dabbling in the subjective mind for proof thereof. In general, the law resists ignorance in the forms of: "I did not know" or "I was not aware of this!" And, is equally hesitant to endorse: "I thought that act was legal but the other not!"

Read and assess the LEXIS/NEXIS summary on Mistake of Law at http://www.lexisnexis.com/lawschool/study/outlines/html/crim/crim18.htm

Consider criminal registration laws that punish offenders who fail to report to local authorities upon visitation, or sex offenders under Megan's law provisions, or firearm registration rules and ordinances, as pertinent examples. Is it reasonable to expect that released offenders know of these requirements?[48] Given the passage of time involving these acts, it is fair to impute knowledge. However, the pace of legal enactments is sometimes so fast that citizenry has a hard time keeping up. Yesterday's tax shelter is now today's tax fraud, or fishing or oystering that was once a right of the landowner, now needs the license, to name just a few examples.

As for sex offenders, the knowledge barrier continues to erode. The Jacob Wetterling Crimes Against Children and Sexually Violent Offender Registration Program Act[49] enacted in 1994, provides a financial incentive for states to establish registration programs for persons who have been convicted of certain sex crimes. Megan's Law amends the Wetterling Act regarding the disclosure of information collected by state sex offender registration programs. The law gives states broad discretion in determining the parameters of notification about offenders, the circumstances, and about which offenders under which they are made.[50]

Clearly the public favors the imposition of criminal liability on sexual offenders, especially pedophiles, and appears ready to accept a strict liability finding of guilt for those who did not comply.[51] Ignorance of the requirements does not save the day in these facts.

§ 2.04. Ignorance or mistake

(1) Ignorance or mistake as to a matter of fact or law is a defense if:
    (a) the ignorance or mistake negatives the purpose, knowledge, belief, recklessness or negligence required to establish a material element of the offense; or
    (b) the law provides that the state of mind established by such ignorance or mistake constitutes a defense.
(2) Although ignorance or mistake would otherwise afford a defense to the offense charged, the defense is not available if the defendant would be guilty of another offense had the situation been as he supposed. In such case, however, the ignorance or mistake of the defendant shall reduce the grade and degree of the offense of which he may be convicted to those of the offense of which he would be guilty had the situation been as he supposed.

(3) A belief that conduct does not legally constitute an offense is a defense to a prosecution for that offense based upon such conduct when:

    (a) the statute or other enactment defining the offense is not known to the actor and has not been published or otherwise reasonably made available prior to the conduct alleged; or

    (b) he acts in reasonable reliance upon an official statement of the law, afterward determined to be invalid or erroneous, contained in (i) a statute or other enactment; (ii) a judicial decision, opinion or judgment; (iii) an administrative order or grant of permission; or (iv) an official interpretation of the public officer or body charged by law with responsibility for the interpretation, administration or enforcement of the law defining the offense.

(4) The defendant must prove a defense arising under Subsection (3) of this Section by a preponderance of evidence.[52]

Generally, the law is more tolerant of this defense in lower level crimes and misdemeanors. Higher level crimes, with specific intent requirements, are much tougher forums for ignorance and mistake arguments. Everyone knows murder is murder and rape is rape. For specific intent crimes, the prosecution's evidence can be challenged because complete ignorance bespeaks a mind incapable of such certitude. Knowingly and willfully cannot comport to represent the ignorant and mistaken mind although those that are reckless or depraved, provoked and passionate will not garner the protection this defense provides. In short, abject ignorance and a misguided interpretation relay a mens rea in the type of turmoil specific intent offenses could not fathom.

At common law, the preference was straightforward since *ignorantia legis neminem excusat* (ignorance of the law excuses no one) was a rudimentary tenet.[53] This same tradition presumed that every citizen was on notice of a law's promulgation or rootedness in historical terms. Contemporary legislative designs mirror this presumption in many definitional sections to the crime codification holding that the state presumes knowledge and awareness of the enactment. Public policy reasons alone mandate the rule of imputed awareness or understanding because to hold contrarily would open the door to disingenuous defenses. Every defendant can be ignorant or mistaken if need be.

Clark and Marshall keenly convey this message:

> But there is a double aspect lurking in case precedent: (a) ignorance of law, and (b) mistake of law. Defending on grounds of an alleged unawareness (a) that certain behavior is proscribed and punishable is unlike asserting, in good faith, reliance upon competent, though erroneous (b), legal advice. The first collides with expediency and public policy while the second phase (b) has been allowed as a defense.[54]

The folly of presumed knowledge can be taken to extremes, and it is a safe bet that most courts will entertain the defense in specific intent circumstances. If, in fact, the defendant knows nothing of the infraction charged, it is imprudent to charge specific intentionality. On the other hand, it is fair to deduce from the circumstances, from the history of the defendant, and the sophistication of the players a suspicion about the sincerity of mistake or ignorance as it involves law.

MISTAKE/IGNORANCE OF FACT

ESSENTIAL ISSUES

- Good faith mistake on part of accused
- Lack of knowledge about material fact or condition
- Mistake relates to a specific intent offense

When the mistake or ignorance relates to a particular fact or condition involved in the criminality, and that fact is crucial to the offense charged, courts and statutes are more amenable to the defense than the mistake of law claim.[55] In this setting, the defendant cannot be held to a notice or presumptive knowledge standard about the content of the law and, in the bulk of cases, the factual impression held, however incorrect it might be, is one of first instance. Defendants who believe that a piece of property belongs to them, this belief being flawed, may employ the mistake defense in a charge of larceny/theft. As long as the belief held is reasonable and excusable under the average person standard, courts should be willing to entertain the defense of mistake or ignorance of a fact.

Thus, the killing of another can be defended on the theory that the accused thought the moving party was a deer or other game. These mistakes of fact center the focus on the central elements in homicide—the unlawful killing of another without license or right. The errant hunter acts and operates under mistaken beliefs not the willful desire to kill another.

Specific intent crimes are ripe for the defense since the prosecution is obliged to demonstrate that the criminal agent wished and willed a particular end. The stray bullet from the hunter's rifle tells us nothing about this form of intentionality and factually concludes otherwise. "The general rule that ignorance or nonnegligent mistake of fact is a defense, was well settled at common law. It follows necessarily from the principle that an act is not a crime unless there is a criminal intent."[56] In strict liability or general intent offense, the defense has minimal effectuality. As the MPC holds, the defense is best suited to the realm of the specific intending.

(1) Ignorance or mistake as to a matter of fact or law is a defense if:
  (a) the ignorance or mistake negatives the purpose, knowledge, belief, recklessness or negligence required to establish a material element of the offense; or
  (b) the law provides that the state of mind established by such ignorance or mistake constitutes a defense.[57]

In these cases, the mistake negates the intent as long as the claim is reasonably based in light of the circumstances. The mistake must be honestly and convincingly based on facts and parties. Bigamy and polygamy cases often witness the defense strategy. See Case 11.10 as an example.

CASE 11.10

COMMONWEALTH V. KENNY LOPEZ
433 Mass. 722 (2001)

The defendant, Kenny Lopez, was convicted on two indictments charging rape and one indictment charging indecent assault and battery on a person over the age of fourteen years. We granted his application for direct appellate review. The defendant claims error in the judge's refusal to give a mistake of fact instruction to the jury. He asks us to recognize a defendant's honest and reasonable belief as to a complainant's consent as a defense to the crime of rape, and to reverse his convictions and grant him a new trial. Based on the record presented, we decline to do so, and affirm the convictions.

1. Background. We summarize facts that the jury could have found. On May 8, 1998, the victim, a seventeen year old girl, was living in a foster home in Springfield. At approximately 3 P.M., she started walking to a restaurant where she had planned to meet her biological mother. On the way, she encountered the defendant. He introduced himself, asked where she was going, and offered to walk with her. The victim met her mother and introduced the defendant as her friend. The defendant said that he lived in the same foster home as the victim and that "they knew each other from school." Sometime later, the defendant left to make a telephone call. When the victim left the restaurant, the defendant was waiting outside and offered to walk her home. She agreed.

The two walked to a park across the street from the victim's foster home and talked for approximately twenty to thirty minutes. The victim's foster sisters were within earshot, and the victim feared that she would be caught violating her foster mother's rules against bringing "a guy near the house." The defendant suggested that they take a walk in the woods nearby. At one point, deep in the woods, the victim said that she wanted to go home. The defendant said, "Trust me," and assured her that nothing would happen and that he would not hurt her. The defendant led the victim down a path to a secluded area.

The defendant asked the victim why she was so distant and said that he wanted to start a relationship with her. She said that she did not want to "get into any relationship." The defendant began making sexual innuendos to which the victim did not respond. He grabbed her by her wrist and began kissing her on the lips. She pulled away and said, "No, I don't want to do this." The defendant then told the victim that if she "had sex with him, [she] would love him more." She repeated, "No, I don't want to. I don't want to do this." He raised her shirt and touched her breasts. She immediately pulled her shirt down and pushed him away.

The defendant then pushed the victim against a slate slab, unbuttoned her pants, and pulled them down. Using his legs to pin down her legs, he produced a condom and asked her to put it on him. The victim said, "No." The defendant put the condom on and told the victim that he wanted her to put his penis inside her. She said, "No." He then raped her, and she began to cry. A few minutes later, the victim made a "jerking move" to her left. The defendant became angry, turned her around, pushed her face into the slate, and raped her again. The treating physician described the bruising to the victim's knees as "significant." The physician opined that there had been "excessive force and trauma to the [vaginal] area" based on his observation that there was "a lot of swelling" in her external vaginal area and her hymen had been torn and was "still oozing." The doctor noted that in his experience it was "fairly rare" to see that much swelling and trauma.

The defendant told the victim that she "would get in a lot of trouble" if she said anything. He then grabbed her by the arm, kissed her, and said, "I'll see you later." The victim went home and showered. She told her foster mother, who immediately dialed 911. The victim cried hysterically as she spoke to the 911 operator.

The defendant's version of the encounter was diametrically opposed to that of the victim. He testified that the victim had been a willing and active partner in consensual sexual intercourse. Specifically, the defendant claimed that the victim initiated intimate activity, and never once told him to stop. Additionally, the defendant testified that the victim invited him to a party that evening so that he could meet her friends. The defendant further claimed that when he told her that he would be unable to attend, the victim appeared "mildly upset."

Before the jury retired, defense counsel requested a mistake of fact instruction as to consent. The judge declined to give the instruction, saying that, based "both on the law, as well as on the facts, that instruction is not warranted." Because the defendant's theory at trial was that the victim actually consented and not that the defendant was "confused, misled, or mistaken" as to the victim's willingness to engage in sexual intercourse, the judge concluded that the ultimate question for the jury was simply whether they believed the victim's or the defendant's version of the encounter. The decision not to give the instruction provides the basis for this appeal.

2. Mistake of fact instruction. The defendant claims that the judge erred in failing to give his proposed mistake of fact instruction. The defendant, however, was not entitled to this instruction. In *Commonwealth v. Ascolillo*, we held that the defendant was not entitled to a mistake of fact instruction, and declined to adopt a rule that "in order to establish the crime of rape, the Commonwealth must prove in every case not only that the defendant intended intercourse but also that he did not act pursuant to an honest and reasonable belief that the victim consented." Neither the plain language of our rape statute nor this court's decisions prior to the Ascolillo decision warrant a different result.

A fundamental tenet of criminal law is that culpability requires a showing that the prohibited conduct (actus reus) was committed with the concomitant mental state (mens rea) prescribed for the offense. The mistake of fact "defense" is available where the mistake negates the existence of a mental state essential to a material element of the offense. In determining whether the defendant's honest and reasonable belief as to the victim's consent would relieve him of culpability, it is necessary to review the required elements of the crime of rape.

At common law, rape was defined as "the carnal knowledge of a woman forcibly and against her will." Since 1642, rape has been proscribed by statute in this Commonwealth. While there have been several revisions to this statute, the definition and the required elements of the crime have remained essentially unchanged since its original enactment. The current rape statute, G. L. c. 265, s. 22 (b), provides in pertinent part:

> "Whoever has sexual intercourse or unnatural sexual intercourse with a person and compels such person to submit by force and against his will, or compels such person to submit by

threat of bodily injury, shall be punished by imprisonment in the state prison for not more than twenty years."

This statute follows the common-law definition of rape, and requires the Commonwealth to prove beyond a reasonable doubt that the defendant committed (1) sexual intercourse (2) by force or threat of force and against the will of the victim.

As to the first element, there has been very little disagreement. Sexual intercourse is defined as penetration of the victim, regardless of degree. The second element has proven to be more complicated. We have construed the element, "by force and against his will," as truly encompassing two separate elements each of which must independently be satisfied. Therefore, the Commonwealth must demonstrate beyond a reasonable doubt that the defendant committed sexual intercourse (1) by means of physical force; nonphysical, constructive force; or threats of bodily harm, either explicit or implicit; and (2) at the time of penetration, there was no consent.

Although the Commonwealth must prove lack of consent, the "elements necessary for rape do not require that the defendant intend the intercourse be without consent." Historically, the relevant inquiry has been limited to consent in fact, and no mens rea or knowledge as to the lack of consent has ever been required.

A mistake of fact as to consent, therefore, has very little application to our rape statute. Because G. L. c. 265, s. 22, does not require proof of a defendant's knowledge of the victim's lack of consent or intent to engage in nonconsensual intercourse as a material element of the offense, a mistake as to that consent cannot, therefore, negate a mental state required for commission of the prohibited conduct. Any perception (reasonable, honest, or otherwise) of the defendant as to the victim's consent is consequently not relevant to a rape prosecution.

This is not to say, contrary to the defendant's suggestion, that the absence of any mens rea as to the consent element transforms rape into a strict liability crime. It does not.

Rape, at common law and pursuant to G. L. c. 265, s. 22, is a general intent crime, and proof that a defendant intended sexual intercourse by force coupled with proof that the victim did not in fact consent is sufficient to maintain a conviction.

Other jurisdictions have held that a mistake of fact instruction is necessary to prevent injustice. New Jersey, for instance, does not require the force necessary for rape to be anything more than what is needed to accomplish penetration. Thus, an instruction as to a defendant's honest and reasonable belief as to consent is available in New Jersey to mitigate the undesirable and unforeseen consequences that may flow from this construction. By contrast, in this Commonwealth, unless the putative victim has been rendered incapable of consent, the prosecution must prove that the defendant compelled the victim's submission by use of physical force; nonphysical, constructive force; or threat of force. Proof of the element of force, therefore, should negate any possible mistake as to consent.

We also have concerns that the mistake of fact defense would tend to eviscerate the long-standing rule in this Commonwealth that victims need not use any force to resist an attack. A shift in focus from the victim's to the defendant's state of mind might require victims to use physical force in order to communicate an unqualified lack of consent to defeat any honest and reasonable belief as to consent. The mistake of fact defense is incompatible with the evolution of our jurisprudence with respect to the crime of rape.

We are cognizant that our interpretation is not shared by the majority of other jurisdictions. States that recognize a mistake of fact as to consent generally have done so by legislation. Some State statutes expressly require a showing of a defendant's intent as to nonconsent. Alaska, for example, requires proof of a culpable state of mind. "Lack of consent is a 'surrounding circumstance' which under the Revised Code, requires a complementary mental state as well as conduct to constitute a crime." Because no specific mental state is mentioned in Alaska's statute governing sexual assault in the first degree, the State "must prove that the defendant acted 'recklessly' regarding his putative victim's lack of consent." So understood, an honest and reasonable mistake as to consent would negate the culpability requirement attached to the element of consent.

The New Jersey statute defines sexual assault (rape) as "any act of sexual penetration engaged in by the defendant without the affirmative and freely-given permission of the victim to the specific act of penetration." A defendant, by claiming that he had permission to engage in sexual intercourse, places his state of mind directly in issue.

The jury must then determine "whether the defendant's belief that the alleged victim had freely given affirmative permission was reasonable." The mistake of fact "defense" has been recognized by judicial decision in some States. In 1975, the Supreme Court of California became the first State court to recognize a mistake of fact defense in rape cases. Although the court did not make a specific determination that intent was required as to the element of consent, it did conclude that, "if a defendant entertains a reasonable and bona fide belief that a prosecutrix [sic] voluntarily consented ... to engage in sexual intercourse, it is apparent he does not possess the wrongful intent that is a prerequisite under Penal Code section 20 to a conviction of ... rape by means of force or threat." Thus, the intent required is an intent to engage in nonconsensual sexual intercourse, and the State must prove that a defendant intentionally engaged in intercourse and was at least negligent regarding consent.

Other State courts have employed a variety of different constructions in adopting the mistake of fact defense. "We arrive at that result, however, not on the basis of our penal code provision relating to a mistake of fact ... but on the ground that whether a complainant should be found to have consented depends upon how her behavior would have been viewed by a reasonable person under the surrounding circumstances"

However, the minority of States sharing our view is significant "whether the defendant intended to commit the offense[s] without the victim's consent is not relevant, the critical question being whether the victim did, in fact, consent. This involves her mental state, not the defendant's" "[D]efendant's awareness of a putative sexual abuse victim's lack of consent is not an element of third-degree sexual abuse. ... [I]t follows from this premise that a defendant's mistake of fact as to that consent would not negate an element of the offense" "The legislature, by carefully defining the sex offenses in the criminal code, and by making no reference to a culpable state of mind for rape, clearly indicated that rape compelled by force or threat requires no culpable state of mind." "The crux of the offense of rape is force and lack of [the] victim's consent. ... When one individual uses force or the threat thereof to have sexual relations with a person ... and without the person's consent he has committed the crime of rape" This case does not persuade us that we should recognize a mistake of fact as to consent as a defense to rape in all cases. Whether such a defense might, in some circumstances, be appropriate is a difficult question that we may consider on a future case where a defendant's claim of reasonable mistake of fact is at least arguably supported by the evidence. This is not such a case.

Questions

1. What does the Court mean when it indicates that mistake of fact is not really a pure defense?
2. In what way does the defendant try to demonstrate the mistake in these facts?
3. Has the Court permitted proof of guilt under a strict liability framework?
4. What is your view of this holding?
5. Would you agree that defendants are losing even more due process protections under a ruling such as this, or are they gaining more?

CONSENT

ESSENTIAL ISSUES

- Capacity to consent
- Willingness to consent
- Public policy restrictions

In rape cases, the issue of consent weaves its way into the typical defense strategy. Consent negates the force and violence; consent implies a willing partner rather than a victim. Consent is prima facie proof of a victim's willingness to a particular act rather than to victimhood.[58] The same conclusion is reached when dealing with the consent defense in theft cases. When consent is proved, the defendant shows that the owner of said property willingly agreed to part with that property. In an assault of battery case, a boxer entering the ring will have a difficult time arguing the lack of consent. The boxer freely chooses his own fate, his own injury if these occur, and, by his participation, negates any claim of intended crime. Sexual offenses probably edify the dynamics of consent more than any other crimes. A closer look at this setting follows.

DEFENSE STRATEGIES ON CONSENT AND RAPE

Victim knew the assailant.
Victim had previous sexual relations with the accused.[59]
Victim once had a long-term relationship with the accused: marriage, cohabitation, or engagement.
Victim had a checkered criminal past including sexual pandering and prostitution.
Victim has a history of rape complaints.
Victim has a previous history of fraudulent rape complaints.

Victim initiated contact with accused.

Victim maintained contact with the accused.

Victim failed to notify authorities in a timely way.

Victim's story is inconsistent.

In each of these approaches, defense counsel challenges the innocent victim status with the willing participant. While these events are rare in the world of sexual offenses, the fact that defense attorneys stress the consent avenue of explanation edifies the power of this defense approach. Consent statutes emphasize the obvious, namely that consent be given by those capable, that consent must be mutual, and that certain types of activities, due to their inherent legality, cannot be consented to. See Pennsylvania's version.

(a) GENERAL RULE.—The consent of the victim to conduct charged to constitute an offense or to the result thereof is a defense if such consent negatives an element of the offense or precludes the infliction of the harm or evil sought to be prevented by the law defining the offense.

(b) CONSENT TO BODILY INJURY.—When conduct is charged to constitute an offense because it causes or threatens bodily injury, consent to such conduct or to the infliction of such injury is a defense if:

   (1) the conduct and the injury are reasonably foreseeable hazards of joint participation in a lawful athletic contest or competitive sport; or

   (2) the consent establishes a justification for the conduct under Chapter 5 of this title (relating to general principles of justification).

(c) INEFFECTIVE CONSENT.—Unless otherwise provided by this title or by the law defining the offense, assent does not constitute consent if:

   (1) it is given by a person who is legally incapacitated to authorize the conduct charged to constitute the offense;

   (2) it is given by a person who by reason of youth, mental disease or defect or intoxication is manifestly unable or known by the actor to be unable to make a reasonable judgment as to the nature or harmfulness of the conduct charged to constitute the offense;

   (3) it is given by a person whose improvident consent is sought to be prevented by the law defining the offense; or

   (4) it is induced by force, duress or deception of a kind sought to be prevented by the law defining the offense.[60]

This provision stresses the essential features in the defense. First, consent can only be given by one capable of its issuance. The feeble minded, the physically infirm, and the young and infant do not have the requisite competency to consent. Hence, the consent of a young girl in a statutory rape case is ineffectual due to age and the full measure of reason. Second, the statutory rape case also edifies how public policy influences the debate on certain conduct. Underage sexual intercourse, aside from being a rigid example of the strict liability doctrine, silences the victim's own choice and will. The implications of sexual conduct at a young age is thought so pressing that its avoidance is worth the negation of the consent defense. Third, the law fully recognizes that consent need be consensual in the fullest sense of the word and that any assent gained by trickery, fraud, duress, or coercion will not be consent as popularly defined.

CASE 11.11

STATE V. WIDMAIER
724 A.2d 214 (N.J. 1999)

This appeal primarily requires us to determine what constitutes a refusal to take a breath-alyzer test. When defendant John Widmaier was arrested for driving while intoxicated, the arresting police officer asked him to take a breathalyzer test and informed him that his right to consult with an attorney did not apply to the taking of breath samples. Defendant responded to the officer's request by saying only that he wanted to place a telephone call to his attorney. After the police officer again instructed defendant that his right to consult with an attorney did not apply to the taking of breath samples, defendant agreed to submit to a breathalyzer test, but requested that his attorney be present "for calibration purposes." The officer determined that defendant's response constituted a refusal to take the test. Defendant was convicted of driving while intoxicated, but acquitted of the charge of refusing to take a breathalyzer test. The primary issue before us is whether, in so responding, defendant "refused" to submit to the breathalyzer test within the meaning of N.J.S.A. 39:4-50.4a and in contravention of N.J.S.A. 39:4-50.2. We also address whether the double jeopardy clause of the federal and state constitutions bars the State from appealing defendant's acquittal of the refusal charge.

At 3:04 a.m. on July 14, 1996, police officer Wayne Walker of the Little Egg Harbor Township Police Department was on duty in a marked patrol car, waiting to make a right-hand turn from Parkertown Drive onto the southbound lane of Route 9. After defendant, who was driving south on Route 9, passed Parkertown Drive, Walker made a right-hand turn onto Route 9 and proceeded on that road a few hundred yards behind defendant's vehicle.

Walker observed defendant negotiate a tight curve, at which time defendant's left front and rear tires crossed the center line of Route 9 into the northbound lane. Walker testi-fied that the area was well illuminated and that he did not observe any traffic or obstacles that might have interfered with defendant's ability to maintain his lane. Walker contin-ued to follow defendant's vehicle on Route 9 and observed defendant again cross the cen-ter line. Defendant continued south on Route 9 until, without using his turn indicator lights, he abruptly made a sharp left turn onto Great Bay Boulevard in Tuckerton Borough. Defendant then traveled eastbound on Great Bay Boulevard and made a right turn onto Radio Road. In maneuvering that turn, defendant cut the wheel hard, and his vehicle began to skid toward the guardrail. After defendant appeared to have regained control of the car, his tires lost traction. Again, defendant was able to straighten the vehicle out of the skid. At that point, Walker activated his overhead lights. Defendant pulled over to the side of the road, turned off his engine, and through the open sunroof placed his keys on top of his car.

As Walker approached defendant's vehicle, he smelled alcohol. Walker requested that defendant produce his driver's license, registration, and insurance card. The officer observed defendant fumble as he searched through his wallet for the requested documents; he was able to produce only his driver's license and registration. Asked whether he had had anything to drink that evening, defendant responded in the negative. Defendant spoke in a slow, slurred whisper, his face was flushed, and his eyes were red and watery. Defendant staggered as he complied with the officer's request to step out of his car and walk to the rear of his vehicle. Although the ground surface was flat macadam, defendant stood with his feet wide apart in order to maintain his balance. Defendant assumed a rigid posture but periodically swayed from side to side. Asked by the officer if he had any injuries, defendant replied that he had diabetes.

The officer requested that defendant perform two field sobriety tests. Defendant was unable to perform the first test, which required him to stand for thirty seconds with his feet together, his hands down by his side, his head tilted back, and his eyes closed. Defendant did not perform the second test because he said he did not understand Walker's instructions; Walker had asked defendant to stand on one leg and count up to thirty.

Defendant was arrested for driving while intoxicated, in violation of N.J.S.A. 39:4-50, and was informed of his Miranda rights as he was placed in the back of Walker's patrol car. Although the rear passenger compartment of the patrol car was separated from the driver's area by plexiglass, Walker noticed that an odor of alcohol was emanating from the passenger compartment.

Defendant was taken to the Little Egg Harbor Township police headquarters. At headquarters, defendant's handcuffs were removed, and defendant was placed in a holding area. Walker then turned on the breathalyzer to warm it up, inserted a video tape into the video camera, and had defendant sit within the camera's view. When the breathalyzer was ready and the camera was filming, Walker read aloud paragraphs one through ten of the "standard statement" prepared by the Director of the Division of Motor Vehicles pursuant to N.J.S.A. 39:4-50.2(e):

1. You have been arrested for operating a motor vehicle while under the influence of intoxicating liquor or drugs or with blood alcohol concentration of 0.10% or more.
2. You are required by law to submit to the taking of samples of your breath for the purpose of making chemical tests to determine the content of alcohol in your blood.
3. A record of the taking of the samples, including the date, time, and results, will be made. Upon your request, a copy of that record will be made available to you.
4. Any warnings previously given to you concerning your right to remain silent and your right to consult with an attorney do not apply to the taking of breath samples and do not give you the right to refuse to give, or to delay giving, samples of your breath for the purposes of making chemical tests to determine the content of alcohol in your blood. You have no legal right to have an attorney, physician, or anyone else present, for the purpose of taking breath samples.
5. After you have provided samples of your breath for chemical testing, you have the right to have a person or physician of your own selection, and at your own expense, take independent samples and conduct independent chemical tests of your breath, urine, or blood.
6. If you refuse to provide samples of your breath you will be issued a separate summons for this refusal.
7. According to N.J.S.A. 39:4-50.4a, if a court of law finds you guilty of refusing to submit to chemical tests of your breath, then your license to operate a motor vehicle

will be revoked for a period of six months. If your refusal conviction is in connection with a second offense under this statute, your license to operate a motor vehicle will be revoked for a period of two years. If your refusal conviction is in connection with a third or subsequent offense under this statute, your license to operate a motor vehicle will be revoked for a period of ten years. The Court will also fine you a sum of between [sic] $250 and $500 for your refusal conviction.

8. Any license suspension or revocation for refusal conviction will be independent of any license suspension or revocation imposed for any related offense.

9. If you are convicted of refusing to submit to chemical tests of your breath, you will be referred by the Court to an Intoxicated Driver Resource Center and you will be required to satisfy the requirements of that center in the same manner as if you had been convicted of a violation of N.J.S.A. 39:4-50, or you will be subject to penalties for your failure to do so.

10. I repeat, you are required by law to submit to the taking of samples of your breath for the purpose of making chemical tests to determine the content of alcohol in your blood. Now, will you submit to the samples of your breath?

Defendant's reply to the above-quoted statement was, "Sir, I would like you to call Francis Xavier Moore, my attorney."

The instructions accompanying the standard statement indicate that if the person remains silent, states that he has the right to remain silent, or says he wishes to consult an attorney, physician, or other person, the police officer shall read the following additional statement:

"I have previously informed you that the warnings given to you concerning your right to remain silent and your right to consult with an attorney do not apply to the taking of breath samples and do not give you a right to refuse to give, or delay giving, samples of your breath for the purpose of making chemical tests to determine the content of alcohol in your blood. If you (1) do not respond to my question about submitting breath samples; or (2) tell me that you refuse to answer this question because you have a right to remain silent or first wish to consult with an attorney, physician or any other person; or (3) tell me that you will not submit breath samples because you have a right to remain silent or first wish to consult with an attorney, physician, or any other person, then you will be issued a separate summons charging you with refusing to submit to the taking of samples of your breath for the purpose of making chemical tests to determine the content of alcohol in your blood. Once again, I ask you, will you submit to giving samples of your breath?"

Walker read the above statement to defendant, who responded by saying, "I agree to the samples of my breath, but I would like my attorney present for calibration purposes." Walker again informed defendant that he did not have the right to have his attorney present for the breathalyzer test. Defendant remained silent, and Walker did not offer the breathalyzer mouthpiece to defendant. Walker again informed defendant of his Miranda rights, and defendant responded simply by saying that he understood. Walker asked defendant to perform physical coordination tests, and defendant refused to do so. Walker then issued defendant summonses for driving while under the influence of alcohol (DWI), failure to maintain a lane, and refusal to submit to a breathalyzer test, in contravention of N.J.S.A. 39:4-50, N.J.S.A. 39:4-88(b), and N.J.S.A. 39:4-50.2, respectively.

At trial, the Municipal Court merged the charge of failure to maintain a lane into the DWI charge and found defendant guilty of DWI. For that offense, defendant was assessed fines, penalties, and court costs in addition to mandatory attendance for twelve hours at the Intoxicated Driver Resource Center (IDRC) and revocation of his driving privileges for six months. With regard to the refusal charge, however, the court was not satisfied that defendant had refused to submit to a breathalyzer test. The court determined that defendant's statement, "I agree to the samples of my breath, but I would like my attorney present for calibration purposes," was not a refusal.

Questions

1. What was the name of the law that dealt with consent?
2. What was the infraction that the legislature felt compelling enough to waive the consent requirement?
3. What is the difference between unequivocal consent and conditional assent?

Find out how experienced criminal defense attorneys defend sexual offenders on theories of consent at http://publicdefender.mt.gov/training/09/lackofconsent/DefendingConsentRape.pdf

Implied Consent

In the area of DUI/DWI prosecution, the law of implied consent has caused much consternation in academic and legal circles.[61] By applying for the driver's license, it is argued that one impliedly consents to be subject to a breathalyzer test upon request. Failure to cooperate can result in loss of license and fines or other sanctions. Since driving is referenced as a privilege, the legislature deems the danger of drunk driving so substantial that traditional protections are waived in the area of consent and self-incrimination.[62] When the suspected driver refuses to test, the law punishes those who otherwise, in any other type of case, would have the right to reject the request or those who would exercise free will and choice as consent law demands. The law of implied consent substitutes the actor's assent with that of the state's implication that the driver agrees.[63] While few would object to the fervor and good intentions of those addressing the enormous harm caused by drunk drivers, the elimination of free choice and the usual understanding of what consent means in a criminal case may be too high a price to pay.

Most states follow similar regimens in the matter of DUI/DWI. Visit the Kentucky model at http://transportation.ky.gov/drlic/dui/dui_laws.htm

DISCUSSION QUESTIONS

1. What types of individuals are unlikely candidates for entrapment?
2. What level of force is permissible in property offenses?
3. Explain the doctrine of reclamation.
4. What level of force is authorized in protection of self?
5. Which insanity test is termed "moral" and judgmental?
6. Which insanity test employs the term "appreciates"? What does the word refer to?
7. Why have various states passed the guilty but mentally ill plea?
8. Discuss the plausibility of the ignorance of the law defense.
9. How would a sports injury case involve the consent defense?
10. Give a case where real coercion exists.

SUGGESTED READINGS

Arrigo, B. A., and M. C. Bardwell. 2000. Law, psychology, and competency to stand trial: Problems with and implications for high-profile cases. *Criminal Justice and Policy Review* 11 (March): 16–43.

Bartlett, P., P. Fennell, L. Gostin, R, D, Mackay, and J. McHale. 2010. *Principles of mental health law and policy.* New York: Oxford University Press.

Bonnie, R. J., J. C. Jeffries, Jr., and P. W. Low. 2008. *A case study in the insanity defense—The trial of John W. Hinckley, Jr.,* 3rd ed. Eagan, MN: West Law School Publishers.

Cheng, E. K., D. L. Faigman, M. J. Saks, and J. Sanders. 2008. *Modern scientific evidence: Forensics,* 2008 Student ed. Eagan, MN: West Law School Publishers.

Ewing, C. P. 2008. Insanity: Murder, madness, and the law. New York: Oxford University Press.

Gorr, M. 2000. Duress and culpability. *Criminal Justice Ethics* 19 (Summer/Fall): 3–16.

Gronberg, K. 2010. *Police guide for responding to people with mental illness* (Criminal Justice, Law Enforcement and Corrections). Hauppauge, NY: Nova Science Publishers Inc.

Hubble, G. 1999. Self-defense and domestic violence: A reply to Bradfield. *Psychiatry, Psychology and Law* 6 (1999): 51–66.

Jones, R. 2010. *Mental capacity act manual.* London: Sweet & Maxwell.

Klein, G. C. 2010. *Law and the disordered: An explanation in mental health, law, and politics.* Lanham, MD: University Press of America.

Marcus, P. 1995. Presenting, back from the (almost) dead, the entrapment defense. *Florida Law Review* 47 (April): 205–245.

Rai, A., R. Reisner, and C. Slobogin. 2008. *Law and the mental health system: Civil and criminal aspects,* 5th ed. Eagan, MN: West Law School Publishers.

Wallace, H. 1994. Battered woman syndrome: Self-defense and duress as mandatory defenses? *Police Journal* 67 (April–June): 133–139.

ENDNOTES

1. 18 Pa. Cons. Stat. § 503 (2011).
2. Model Penal Code § 3.04(2) (Proposed Official Draft 1962).
3. Cara Cookson, *Confronting Our Fear: Legislating beyond Battered Woman Syndrome and the Law of Self-Defense in Vermont,* 34 Vt. L. Rev. 415 (2009), available at http://lawreview.vermontlaw.edu/articles/v34/2/cookson.pdf (accessed August 3, 2011).

4. *See* Hugh Breyer, *The Battered Woman Syndrome and the Admissibility of Expert Testimony*, 28 CRIM. L. BULL. 99 (1991); note: *The Admissibility of Expert Testimony on the Battered Woman Syndrome in Support of a Claim of Self-Defense*, 15 CONN. L. REV. 121, 128 (1982); *People v. Torres*, 128 N.Y. 129, 488 N.Y.S.2d 358 (1985).

5. *Frye v. U.S.*, 293 F. 1013 (D.C. Cir. 1923) established a longstanding test on expert admissibility is slow to accept these sorts of defenses. *See also* CHARLES P. NEMETH, LAW AND EVIDENCE: A PRIMER FOR CRIMINAL JUSTICE, CRIMINOLOGY, LAW, AND LEGAL STUDIES 200-206 (2nd ed. 2011).

6. 509 U.S. 579 (1993). *See also* NEMETH, *supra* note 5, at 201–206.

7. OHIO REV. CODE ANN. § 2901.06 (West 2010).

8. *See* Russell L. Christopher, *Mistake of Fact in the Objective Theory of Justification: Do Two Rights Make Two Wrongs Make Two Rights ...?*, 85 J. CRIM. L. & CRIMINOLOGY 295 (1994); Douglas N. Husak, *Justifications and the Criminal Liability of Accessories*, 80 J. CRIM L. & CRIMINOLOGY 491, (1989); Kent Greenawalt, *The Perplexing Borders of Justification and Excuse*, 84 COLUM. L. REV. 1897 (1984); George P. Fletcher, *The Right and the Reasonable*, 98 HARV. L. REV. 949 (1985).

9. MATTHEW J. HICKMAN, CITIZEN COMPLAINTS ABOUT POLICE USE OF FORCE, BJS SPECIAL REPORT, NCJ 210296 (June 2006), available at http://bjs.ojp.usdoj.gov/content/pub/pdf/ccpuf.pdf (accessed August 3, 2011); MICHAEL R. SMITH ET AL., MULTI-METHOD EVALUATION OF POLICE USE OF FORCE OUTCOMES, EXECUTIVE SUMMARY, NCJ 231177 (2010), available at http://www.ncjrs.gov/pdffiles1/nij/grants/231177.pdf (accessed August 3, 2011); INT'L ASSOC. OF CHIEFS OF POLICE, POLICE USE OF FORCE IN AMERICA, NCJ 197636 (2001).

10. HICKMAN, *supra* note 9, at 1.

11. 2 PAUL H. ROBINSON, CRIMINAL LAW DEFENSES, §3-3, Model Codifications, app. A (1984).

12. National Institute of Justice, *Understanding Use of Force by and against Police*, Nov. 1996, at 1.

13. 18 PA. CONS. STAT. § 506 (2010).

14. *Id.* at § 507.

15. Model Penal Code § 3.06 (Proposed Official Draft 1962).

16. 18 PA. CONS. STAT. § 507(a) (2010).

17. WILLIAM L. CLARK & WILLIAM L. MARSHALL, A TREATISE ON THE LAW OF CRIMES § 6.01 at 380 (6th ed. 1958); *See also* Arnolds' Case, 16 How St. Tr. 764 (1724).

18. CHARLES P. NEMETH & DAVID A. DAVIS, FLORIDA CRIMINAL LAW (1996).

19. Russell D. Covey, *Criminal Madness: Cultural Iconography and Insanity*, 61 STAN. L. REV. 1375 (2009); DAVID E. AARONSON & RITA J. SIMON, THE INSANITY DEFENSE: A CRITICAL ASSESSMENT OF LAW AND POLICY IN THE POST-HINCKLEY ERA (1988); CHARLES PATRICK EWING, INSANITY: MURDER, MADNESS, AND THE LAW (2008).

20. Model Penal Code § 2.08 (Proposed Official Draft 1962).

21. *State v. Noble*, 384 P.2d 504, 508 (Mont.1963).

22. *See* NEMETH & DAVIS, *supra* note 18, at 283.

23. *Id.* at 275.

24. *Com. v. Baumhammers*, 960 A.2d 59 (Pa. 2008).

25. The Case of Daniel M'Naghten, 8 Eng. Rep. 718.

26. *Durham v. United States*, 214 F.2d 862 (1954).

27. Model Penal Code § 2.08 (Proposed Official Draft 1962).

28. An entire text is dedicated to the impact of this case, *see* DONALD JAMES WEST & ALEXANDER WALK, DANIEL MCNAUGHTON: HIS TRIAL AND THE AFTERMATH (1977).

29. *M'Naghten*, 8 Eng. Rep. at 718.

30. John K. McHenry, *The Judicial Evolution of Ohio's Insanity Defense*, 13 U. DAYTON L. REV. 49 (1987-1988).

31. 214 F.2d 862 (1954).

32. *Id.* at 871–875.

33. *Id.*

34. Christopher J. Lockey and Joseph D. Bloom, *The Evolution of the American Law Institute Test for Insanity in Oregon: Focus on Diagnosis*, 35 J. AM. ACAD. PSYCHIATRY L. 325-329 (2007); *See also* IRVING B. WEINER & ALLEN K. HESS, THE HANDBOOK OF FORENSIC PSYCHOLOGY 378 (2006).

35. Model Penal Code § 401, comment at 156 (Proposed Official Draft 1962).

36. *Id.* at § 401.

37. "I have great respect for the profession of psychiatry. Vast areas of information have been made available through its efforts ... Yet, there are compelling reasons for not blindly following the opinions of experts on controlling issues of fact ... When the experts have made available their knowledge to aid the jury or the Court in reaching a conclusion, their function is completed. The opinions and judgments or inferences of experts ... are not necessarily conclusive on the trier of the facts and may be disregarded when, in the light of the facts adduced, such judgments, opinions or inferences do not appear valid. The jury, in determining the probative effect to be given to expert testimony, is not to disregard its own experience and knowledge and its collective conscience." *U.S. v. Pollard*, 171 F. Supp. 474, set aside 282 F.2d 450, mandate clarified 285 F.2d 81 (Eastern Mich. 1959).

38. JOHN S. GOLDKAMP & CHERYL IRONS-GUYNN, EMERGING JUDICIAL STRATEGIES FOR THE MENTALLY ILL IN THE CRIMINAL CASELOAD: MENTAL HEALTH COURTS IN FORT LAUDERDALE, SEATTLE, SAN BERNARDINO, AND ANCHORAGE, NCJ 182504 (2000), available at http://www.ncjrs.gov/pdffiles1/bja/182504.pdf (accessed August 3, 2011); *See also* Ira Mickenberg, *A Pleasant Surprise: The Guilty But Mentally Ill Verdict Has Both Succeeded in Its Own Right and Successfully Preserved the Traditional Role of the Insanity Defense*, 55 U. CIN. L. REV. 943 (1987); C.A. Palmer & M. Hazelrigg, *The Guilty But Mentally Ill Verdict: A Review and Conceptual Analysis of Intent and Impact*, 28 J. AM. ACAD. PSYCHIATRY L. 47-54 (2000).

39. 18 PA. CONS. STAT. § 314 (2010).

40. Barbara H. Zaitzow, *Empowerment Not Entrapment: Providing Opportunities for Incarcerated Women to Move Beyond "Doing Time,"* 3 JUST. POL'Y J. 1-24 2006; *see also* Rolando V. del Carmen, Jeffery T. Walker, *Entrapment, in* BRIEFS OF 100 LEADING CASES IN LAW ENFORCEMENT 185-192 (1991).

41. *See Sorrells v. U.S.*, 287 U.S. 435 (1932).

42. *See Jacobson v. U.S.*, 503 U.S. 540 (1992).

43. Model Penal Code § 2.13 (Proposed Official Draft 1962).

44. *Greene v. U.S.*, 454 F.2d 783 (1971).

45. Model Penal Code § 2.09 (Proposed Official Draft 1962). *See also* Lawrence Newman and Lawrence Weitzer, *Duress, Free Will and the Criminal Law*, 30 S. CAL. L. REV. 313 (1956–1957); THOMAS J. GARDNER & TERRY M. ANDERSON, CRIMINAL LAW 134 (2008).

46. *See* Peter Westen and James Mangiafico, *The Criminal Defense of Duress: A Justification, Not an Excuse—And Why It Matters*, 6 BUFF. CRIM. L. REV. 833 (2003). http://wings.buffalo.edu/law/bclc/bclrarticles/6/2/westen.pdf (accessed August 3, 2011)

47. 18 PA. CONS. STAT. § 309 (2010).

48. FBI National Sex Offender Registry Information Page, at http://www.fbi.gov/hq/cid/cac/registry.htm (accessed March 22, 2011). The FBI's Crimes against Children Unit coordinates the development and implementation of the National Sex Offenders Registry (NSOR). The Pam Lychner Sexual Offender Tracking and Identification Act of 1996 (Lychner Act), requires the Attorney General to establish a national database at the FBI to track the whereabouts and movements of certain convicted sex offenders under Title 42 of the United States Code Section 14072. The National Crime Information Center (NCIC) enables the NSOR to retain the offender's current registered address and dates of registration, conviction, and residence. The Lychner Act also created a new federal statute making it a criminal offense for a registered sex offender to move to another state and knowingly fail to notify the FBI and authorities in the new state of residence.

49. 42 U.S.C. § 14071 (2010).

50. *See* FBI National Sex Offender Registry Information Page at http://www.fbi.gov/hq/cid/cac/registry.htm (accessed August 3, 2011).

51. Assaf Hamdani, *Mens Rea and the Cost of Ignorance*, 93 VA. L. REV. 415 (2007), available at http://www.virginialawreview.org/content/pdfs/93/415.pdf (accessed August 3, 2011); *see also* Michelle Oberman, *Girls in the Master's House: Of Protection, Patriarchy and the Potential for Using the Master's Tools to Reconfigure Statutory Rape Law*, 50 DEPAUL L. REV. 799 (2001).

52. Model Penal Code § 2.04 (Proposed Official Draft 1962).

53. *See* 1 Hale, Pleas of the Crown 42; 1 Hawkins, Pleas of the Crown 5; *State v. Boyett*, 10 Ired L. (32 NC) 336, 343; JOHN AUSTIN, LECTURES ON JURISPRUDENCE § 669 (1875).

54. CLARK & MARSHALL, *supra* note 17, at § 5.12 at 336.
55. Mistake of fact as to age in a statutory rape charge no defense in *State v. Browning*, 177 N.C. App. 487, 492-94 (2006).
56. CLARK & MARSHALL, *supra* note 17, at §5.11 at 323.
57. Model Penal Code § 2.04 (Proposed Official Draft 1962).
58. *See* Dennis J. Baker, *The Moral Limits of Consent as a Defense in the Criminal Law*, 12 NEW CRIM. L. REV. 93 (2009).
59. *See* NEMETH, *supra* note 5, at 20–21.
60. 18 PA. CONS. STAT. § 311 (2010).
61. For a full review, state-by-state, of the DUI/DWI laws, read the Insurance Institute of Highway Safety's summary at http://www.iihs.org/laws/dui.aspx (accessed August 3, 2011).
62. *See* James C. Sheil, *Criminal Law-Implied Consent—Anything Less Than Unconditional Assent to Request to Submit to Breathalyzer Test Constitutes a Refusal—State v. Widmaier*, 157 N.J. 475, 724 A.2d 214 (1999), 29 SETON HALL L. REV. 1688 (1999).
63. *See State v. Widmaier*, 724 A.2d 214 (N.J. 1999).

Appendix

1. To know that God exists (Ex. 20:2; Deut. 5:6)
2. Not to entertain the idea that there is any god but the Eternal (Ex. 20:3)
3. Not to blaspheme (Ex. 22:27; in Christian texts, Ex. 22:28), the penalty for which is death (Lev. 24:16)
4. To hallow God's name (Lev. 22:32)
5. Not to profane God's name (Lev. 22:32)
6. To know that God is One, a complete Unity (Deut. 6:4)
7. To love God (Deut. 6:5)
8. To fear Him reverently (Deut. 6:13; 10:20)
9. Not to put the word of God to the test (Deut. 6:16)
10. To imitate His good and upright ways (Deut. 28:9)
11. To honor the old and the wise (Lev. 19:32)
12. To learn Torah and to teach it (Deut. 6:7)
13. To cleave to those who know Him (Deut. 10:20)
14. Not to add to the commandments of the Torah, whether in the Written Law or in its interpretation received by tradition (Deut. 13:1)
15. Not to take away from the commandments of the Torah (Deut. 13:1)
16. That every person shall write a scroll of the Torah for himself (Deut. 31:19)
17. To circumcise the male offspring (Gen. 17:12; Lev. 12:3)
18. To put tzitzit on the corners of clothing (Num. 15:38)
19. To bind tefillin on the head (Deut. 6:8)
20. To bind tefillin on the arm (Deut. 6:8)
21. To affix the mezuzah to the doorposts and gates of your house (Deut. 6:9)
22. To pray to God (Ex. 23:25; Deut. 6:13)
23. To read the Shema in the morning and at night (Deut. 6:7).
24. To recite grace after meals (Deut. 8:10)
25. Not to lay down a stone for worship (Lev. 26:1)
26. To love all human beings who are of the covenant (Lev. 19:18)
27. Not to stand by idly when a human life is in danger (Lev. 19:16)
28. Not to wrong any one in speech (Lev. 25:17)
29. Not to carry tales (Lev. 19:16)
30. Not to cherish hatred in one's heart (Lev. 19:17)
31. Not to take revenge (Lev. 19:18)
32. Not to bear a grudge (Lev. 19:18)
33. Not to put any Jew to shame (Lev. 19:17)
34. Not to curse any other Israelite (Lev. 19:14)
35. Not to give occasion to the simple-minded to stumble on the road (Lev. 19:14)
36. To rebuke the sinner (Lev. 19:17)
37. To relieve a neighbor of his burden and help to unload his beast (Ex. 23:5)
38. To assist in replacing the load upon a neighbor's beast (Deut. 22:4)
39. Not to leave a beast, that has fallen down beneath its burden, unaided (Deut. 22:4)
40. Not to afflict an orphan or a widow (Ex. 22:21)
41. Not to reap the entire field (Lev. 19:9; Lev. 23:22)
42. To leave the unreaped corner of the field or orchard for the poor (Lev. 19:9)
43. Not to gather gleanings (the ears that have fallen to the ground while reaping) (Lev. 19:9)
44. To leave the gleanings for the poor (Lev. 19:9)
45. Not to gather ol'loth (the imperfect clusters) of the vineyard (Lev. 19:10)
46. To leave ol'loth (the imperfect clusters) of the vineyard for the poor (Lev. 19:10; Deut. 24:21)
47. Not to gather the peret (grapes) that have fallen to the ground (Lev. 19:10)
48. To leave peret (the single grapes) of the vineyard for the poor (Lev. 19:10)
49. Not to return to take a forgotten sheaf (Deut. 24:19)
50. To leave the forgotten sheaves for the poor (Deut. 24:19-20)
51. Not to refrain from maintaining a poor man and giving him what he needs (Deut. 15:7)
52. To give charity according to one's means (Deut. 15:11)
53. To love the stranger (Deut. 10:19)
54. Not to wrong the stranger in speech (Ex. 22:20)
55. Not to wrong the stranger in buying or selling (Ex. 22:20)
56. Not to intermarry with gentiles (Deut. 7:3)
57. To exact the debt of an alien (Deut. 15:3)

(continued)

APPENDIX (*continued*)

58. To lend to an alien at interest (Deut. 23:21)
59. To honor father and mother (Ex. 20:12)
60. Not to smite a father or a mother (Ex. 21:15)
61. Not to curse a father or mother (Ex. 21:17)
62. To reverently fear father and mother (Lev. 19:3)
63. To be fruitful and multiply (Gen. 1:28)
64. That a eunuch shall not marry a daughter of Israel (Deut. 23:2)
65. That a mamzer shall not marry the daughter of a Jew (Deut. 23:3)
66. That an Ammonite or Moabite shall never marry the daughter of an Israelite (Deut. 23:4)
67. Not to exclude a descendant of Esau from the community of Israel for three generations (Deut. 23:8-9)
68. Not to exclude an Egyptian from the community of Israel for three generations (Deut. 23:8-9)
69. That there shall be no harlot (in Israel); that is, that there shall be no intercourse with a woman, without previous marriage with a deed of marriage and formal declaration of marriage (Deut. 23:18)
70. To take a wife by kiddushin, the sacrament of marriage (Deut. 24:1)
71. That the newly married husband shall (be free) for one year to rejoice with his wife (Deut. 24:5)
72. That a bridegroom shall be exempt for a whole year from taking part in any public labor, such as military service, guarding the wall and similar duties (Deut. 24:5)
73. Not to withhold food, clothing or conjugal rights from a wife (Ex. 21:10)
74. That the woman suspected of adultery shall be dealt with as prescribed in the Torah (Num. 5:30)
75. That one who defames his wife's honor (by falsely accusing her of unchastity before marriage) must live with her all his lifetime (Deut. 22:19)
76. That a man may not divorce his wife concerning whom he has published an evil report (about her unchastity before marriage) (Deut. 22:19)
77. To divorce by a formal written document (Deut. 24:1)
78. That one who divorced his wife shall not remarry her, if after the divorce she had been married to another man (Deut. 24:4)
79. That a widow whose husband died childless must not be married to anyone but her deceased husband's brother (Deut. 25:5)
80. To marry the widow of a brother who has died childless (Deut. 25:5).
81. That the widow formally release the brother-in-law (if he refuses to marry her) (Deut. 25:7-9)
82. Not to indulge in familiarities with relatives, such as kissing, embracing, winking, skipping, which may lead to incest (Lev. 18:6)
83. Not to commit incest with one's mother (Lev. 18:7)
84. Not to commit sodomy with one's father (Lev. 18:7)
85. Not to commit incest with one's father's wife (Lev. 18:8)
86. Not to commit incest with one's sister (Lev. 18:9)
87. Not to commit incest with one's father's wife's daughter (Lev. 18:9)
88. Not to commit incest with one's son's daughter (Lev. 18:10)
89. Not to commit incest with one's daughter's daughter (Lev. 18:10)
90. Not to commit incest with one's daughter (this is not explicitly in the Torah but is inferred from other explicit commands that would include it)
91. Not to commit incest with one's fathers sister (Lev. 18:12)
92. Not to commit incest with one's mother's sister (Lev. 18:13)
93. Not to commit incest with one's father's brothers wife (Lev. 18:14)
94. Not to commit sodomy with one's father's brother (Lev. 18:14)
95. Not to commit incest with he's son's wife (Lev. 18:15)
96. Not to commit incest with one's brother's wife (Lev. 18:16)
97. Not to commit incest with one's wife's daughter (Lev. 18:17)
98. Not to commit incest with the daughter of one's wife's son (Lev. 18:17)

(*continued*)

APPENDIX (*continued*)

99. Not to commit incest with the daughter of one's wife's daughter (Lev. 18:17)

100. Not to commit incest with one's wife's sister (Lev. 18:18)

101. Not to have intercourse with a woman, in her menstrual period (Lev. 18:19)

102. Not to have intercourse with another man's wife (Lev. 18:20)

103. Not to commit sodomy with a male (Lev. 18:22)

104. Not to have intercourse with a beast (Lev. 18:23)

105. That a woman shall not have intercourse with a beast (Lev. 18:23)

106. Not to castrate the male of any species; neither a man, nor a domestic or wild beast, nor a fowl (Lev. 22:24)

107. That the new month shall be solemnly proclaimed as holy, and the months and years shall be calculated by the Supreme Court only (Ex. 12:2)

108. Not to travel on Shabbat outside the limits of one's place of residence (Ex. 16:29)

109. To sanctify Shabbat (Ex. 20:8)

110. Not to do work on Shabbat (Ex. 20:10)

111. To rest on Shabbat (Ex. 23:12; 34:21)

112. To celebrate the festivals [Passover, Shavu'ot and Sukkot] (Ex. 23:14)

113. To rejoice on the festivals (Deut. 16:14)

114. To appear in the Sanctuary on the festivals (Deut. 16:16)

115. To remove chametz on the Eve of Passover (Ex. 12:15)

116. To rest on the first day of Passover (Ex. 12:16; Lev. 23:7)

117. Not to do work on the first day of Passover (Ex. 12:16; Lev. 23:6-7)

118. To rest on the seventh day of Passover (Ex. 12:16; Lev. 23:8)

119. Not to do work on the seventh day of Passover (Ex. 12:16; Lev. 23:8)

120. To eat matzah on the first night of Passover (Ex. 12:18).

121. That no chametz be in the Israelite's possession during Passover (Ex. 12:19)

122. Not to eat any food containing chametz on Passover (Ex. 12:20)

123. Not to eat chametz on Passover (Ex. 13:3).

124. That chametz shall not be seen in an Israelite's home during Passover (Ex. 13:7)

125. To discuss the departure from Egypt on the first night of Passover (Ex. 13:8)

126. Not to eat chametz after mid-day on the fourteenth of Nissan (Deut. 16:3)

127. To count forty-nine days from the time of the cutting of the Omer (first sheaves of the barley harvest) (Lev. 23:15)

128. To rest on Shavu'ot (Lev. 23:21).

129. Not to do work on the Shavu'ot (Lev. 23:21).

130. To rest on Rosh Hashanah (Lev. 23:24).

131. Not to do work on Rosh Hashanah (Lev. 23:25).

132. To hear the sound of the shofar on Rosh Hashanah (Num. 29:1)

133. To fast on Yom Kippur (Lev. 23:27).

134. Not to eat or drink on Yom Kippur (Lev. 23:29).

135. Not to do work on Yom Kippur (Lev. 23:31).

136. To rest on the Yom Kippur (Lev. 23:32).

137. To rest on the first day of Sukkot (Lev. 23:35).

138. Not to do work on the first day of Sukkot (Lev. 23:35).

139. To rest on the eighth day of Sukkot (Shemini Atzeret) (Lev. 23:36)

140. Not to do work on the eighth day of Sukkot (Shemini Atzeret) (Lev. 23:36)

141. To take during Sukkot a palm branch and the other three plants (Lev. 23:40)

142. To dwell in booths seven days during Sukkot (Lev. 23:42).

143. To examine the marks in cattle (so as to distinguish the clean from the unclean) (Lev. 11:2).

144. Not to eat the flesh of unclean beasts (Lev. 11:4).

145. To examine the marks in fishes (so as to distinguish the clean from the unclean) (Lev. 11:9).

146. Not to eat unclean fish (Lev. 11:11).

147. To examine the marks in fowl, so as to distinguish the clean from the unclean (Deut. 14:11).

148. Not to eat unclean fowl (Lev. 11:13).

149. To examine the marks in locusts, so as to distinguish the clean from the unclean (Lev. 11:21).

150. Not to eat a worm found in fruit (Lev. 11:41).

151. Not to eat of things that creep upon the earth (Lev. 11:41-42).

152. Not to eat any vermin of the earth (Lev. 11:44).

(*continued*)

APPENDIX (*continued*)

153. Not to eat things that swarm in the water (Lev. 11:43 and 46).
154. Not to eat of winged insects (Deut. 14:19).
155. Not to eat the flesh of a beast that is terefah (lit torn) (Ex. 22:30).
156. Not to eat the flesh of a beast that died of itself (Deut. 14:21).
157. To slay cattle, deer and fowl according to the laws of shechitah if their flesh is to be eaten (Deut. 12:21).
158. Not to eat a limb removed from a living beast (Deut. 12:23).
159. Not to slaughter an animal and its young on the same day (Lev. 22:28).
160. Not to take the mother-bird with the young (Deut. 22:6).
161. To set the mother-bird free when taking the nest (Deut. 22:6-7).
162. Not to eat the flesh of an ox that was condemned to be stoned (Ex. 21:28).
163. Not to boil meat with milk (Ex. 23:19).
164. Not to eat flesh with milk (Ex. 34:26).
165. Not to eat the of the thigh-vein which shrank (Gen. 32:33)
166. Not to eat chelev (tallow-fat) (Lev. 7:23).
167. Not to eat blood (Lev. 7:26).
168. To cover the blood of undomesticated animals and of fowl that have been killed (Lev. 17:13).
169. Not to eat or drink like a glutton or a drunkard (Lev. 19:26; Deut. 21:20)
170. Not to do wrong in buying or selling (Lev. 25:14).
171. Not to make a loan to an Israelite on interest (Lev. 25:37).
172. Not to borrow on interest (Deut. 23:20)
173. Not to take part in any usurious transaction between borrower and lender, neither as a surety, nor as a witness, nor as a writer of the bond for them (Ex. 22:24).
174. To lend to a poor person (Ex. 22:24)
175. Not to demand from a poor man repayment of his debt, when the creditor knows that he cannot pay, nor press him (Ex. 22:24).
176. Not to take in pledge utensils used in preparing food (Deut. 24:6).
177. Not to exact a pledge from a debtor by force (Deut. 24:10).
178. Not to keep the pledge from its owner at the time when he needs it (Deut. 24:12)
179. To return a pledge to its owner (Deut. 24:13).
180. Not to take a pledge from a widow (Deut. 24:17)
181. Not to commit fraud in measuring (Lev. 19:35).
182. To ensure that scales and weights are correct (Lev. 19:36).
183. Not to possess inaccurate measures and weights (Deut. 25:13-14).
184. Not to delay payment of a hired man's wages (Lev. 19:13)
185. That the hired laborer shall be permitted to eat of the produce he is reaping (Deut. 23:25-26).
186. That the hired laborer shall not take more than he can eat (Deut. 23:25)
187. That a hired laborer shall not eat produce that is not being harvested (Deut. 23:26)
188. To pay wages to the hired man at the due time (Deut. 24:15)
189. To deal judicially with the Hebrew bondman in accordance with the laws appertaining to him (Ex. 21:2-6)
190. Not to compel the Hebrew servant to do the work of a slave (Lev. 25:39)
191. Not to sell a Hebrew servant as a slave (Lev. 25:42).
192. Not to treat a Hebrew servant rigorously (Lev. 25:43).
193. Not to permit a gentile to treat harshly a Hebrew bondman sold to him (Lev. 25:53)
194. Not to send away a Hebrew bondman servant empty handed, when he is freed from service (Deut. 15:13)
195. To bestow liberal gifts upon the Hebrew bondsman (at the end of his term of service), and the same should be done to a Hebrew bondwoman (Deut. 15:14)
196. To redeem a Hebrew maid-servant (Ex. 21:8).
197. Not to sell a Hebrew maid-servant to another person (Ex. 21:8)
198. To espouse a Hebrew maid-servant (Ex. 21:8-9).
199. To keep the Canaanite slave forever (Lev. 25:46).
200. Not to surrender a slave, who has fled to the land of Israel, to his owner who lives outside Palestine (Deut. 23:16).
201. Not to wrong such a slave (Deut. 23:17)

(*continued*)

APPENDIX (*continued*)

202. Not to muzzle a beast, while it is working in produce which it can eat and enjoy (Deut. 25:4).
203. That a man should fulfill whatever he has uttered (Deut. 23:24).
204. Not to swear needlessly (Ex. 20:7)
205. Not to violate an oath or swear falsely (Lev. 19:12)
206. To decide in cases of annulment of vows, according to the rules set forth in the Torah (Num. 30:2-17)
207. Not to break a vow (Num. 30:3)
208. To swear by His name truly (Deut. 10:20)
209. Not to delay in fulfilling vows or bringing vowed or free-will offerings (Deut. 23:22).
210. To let the land lie fallow in the Sabbatical year (Ex. 23:11; Lev. 25:2)
211. To cease from tilling the land in the Sabbatical year (Ex. 23:11) (Lev. 25:2)
212. Not to till the ground in the Sabbatical year (Lev. 25:4).
213. Not to do any work on the trees in the Sabbatical year (Lev. 25:4)
214. Not to reap the aftermath that grows in the Sabbatical year, in the same way as it is reaped in other years (Lev. 25:5).
215. Not to gather the fruit of the tree in the Sabbatical year in the same way as it is gathered in other years (Lev. 25:5).
216. To sound the Ram's horn in the Sabbatical year (Lev. 25:9).
217. To release debts in the seventh year (Deut. 15:2).
218. Not to demand return of a loan after the Sabbatical year has passed (Deut. 15:2)
219. Not to refrain from making a loan to a poor man, because of the release of loans in the Sabbatical year (Deut. 15:9).
220. To assemble the people to hear the Torah at the close of the seventh year (Deut. 31:12)
221. To count the years of the Jubilee by years and by cycles of seven years (Lev. 25:8).
222. To keep the Jubilee year holy by resting and letting the land lie fallow (Lev. 25:10).
223. Not to cultivate the soil nor do any work on the trees, in the Jubilee Year (Lev. 25:11)
224. Not to reap the aftermath of the field that grew of itself in the Jubilee Year, in the same way as in other years (Lev. 25:11)
225. Not to gather the fruit of the tree in the Jubilee Year, in the same way as in other years (Lev. 25:11).
226. To grant redemption to the land in the Jubilee year (Lev. 25:24)
227. To appoint judges and officers in every community of Israel (Deut. 16:18)
228. Not to appoint as a judge, a person who is not well versed in the laws of the Torah, even if he is expert in other branches of knowledge (Deut. 1:17).
229. To adjudicate cases of purchase and sale (Lev. 25:14)
230. To judge cases of liability of a paid depositary (Ex. 22:9).
231. To adjudicate cases of loss for which a gratuitous borrower is liable (Ex. 22:13-14)
232. To adjudicate cases of inheritances (Num. 27:8-11)
233. To judge cases of damage caused by an uncovered pit (Ex. 21:33-34)
234. To judge cases of injuries caused by beasts (Ex. 21:35-36).
235. To adjudicate cases of damage caused by trespass of cattle (Ex. 22:4)
236. To adjudicate cases of damage caused by fire (Ex. 22:5)
237. To adjudicate cases of damage caused by a gratuitous depositary (Ex. 22:6-7)
238. To adjudicate other cases between a plaintiff and a defendant (Ex. 22:8)
239. Not to curse a judge (Ex. 22:27)
240. That one who possesses evidence shall testify in Court (Lev. 5:1)
241. Not to testify falsely (Ex. 20:13)
242. That a witness, who has testified in a capital case, shall not lay down the law in that particular case (Num. 35:30)
243. That a transgressor shall not testify (Ex. 23:1)
244. That the court shall not accept the testimony of a close relative of the defendant in matters of capital punishment (Deut. 24:16)
245. Not to hear one of the parties to a suit in the absence of the other party (Ex. 23:1)
246. To examine witnesses thoroughly (Deut. 13:15)
247. Not to decide a case on the evidence of a single witness (Deut. 19:15)

(*continued*)

APPENDIX (*continued*)

248. To give the decision according to the majority, when there is a difference of opinion among the members of the Sanhedrin as to matters of law (Ex. 23:2)
249. Not to decide, in capital cases, according to the view of the majority, when those who are for condemnation exceed by one only, those who are for acquittal (Ex. 23:2)
250. That, in capital cases, one who had argued for acquittal, shall not later on argue for condemnation (Ex. 23:2)
251. To treat parties in a litigation with equal impartiality (Lev. 19:15)
252. Not to render iniquitous decisions (Lev. 19:15)
253. Not to favor a great man when trying a case (Lev. 19:15)
254. Not to take a bribe (Ex. 23:8)
255. Not to be afraid of a bad man, when trying a case (Deut. 1:17)
256. Not to be moved in trying a case, by the poverty of one of the parties (Ex. 23:3; Lev. 19:15)
257. Not to pervert the judgment of strangers or orphans (Deut. 24:17)
258. Not to pervert the judgment of a sinner (a person poor in fulfillment of commandments) (Ex. 23:6)
259. Not to render a decision on one's personal opinion, but only on the evidence of two witnesses, who saw what actually occurred (Ex. 23:7)
260. Not to execute one guilty of a capital offense, before he has stood his trial (Num. 35:12)
261. To accept the rulings of every Supreme Court in Israel (Deut. 17:11)
262. Not to rebel against the orders of the Court (Deut. 17:11)
263. To make a parapet for your roof (Deut. 22:8)
264. Not to leave something that might cause hurt (Deut. 22:8)
265. To save the pursued even at the cost of the life of the pursuer (Deut. 25:12)
266. Not to spare a pursuer, but he is to be slain before he reaches the pursued and slays the latter, or uncovers his nakedness (Deut. 25:12)
267. Not to sell a field in the land of Israel in perpetuity (Lev. 25:23)
268. Not to change the character of the open land (about the cities of) the Levites or of their fields; not to sell it in perpetuity, but it may be redeemed at any time (Lev. 25:34)
269. That houses sold within a walled city may be redeemed within a year (Lev. 25:29)
270. Not to remove landmarks (property boundaries) (Deut. 19:14)
271. Not to swear falsely in denial of another's property rights (Lev. 19:11)
272. Not to deny falsely another's property rights (Lev. 19:11)
273. Never to settle in the land of Egypt (Deut. 17:16)
274. Not to steal personal property (Lev. 19:11)
275. To restore that which one took by robbery (Lev. 5:23)
276. To return lost property (Deut. 22:1)
277. Not to pretend not to have seen lost property, to avoid the obligation to return it (Deut. 22:3)
278. Not to slay an innocent person (Ex. 20:13).
279. Not to kidnap any person of Israel (Ex. 20:13)
280. Not to rob by violence (Lev. 19:13)
281. Not to defraud (Lev. 19:13)
282. Not to covet what belongs to another (Ex. 20:14)
283. Not to crave something that belongs to another (Deut. 5:18)
284. Not to indulge in evil thoughts and sights (Num. 15:39)
285. That the Court shall pass sentence of death by decapitation with the sword (Ex. 21:20; Lev. 26:25)
286. That the Court shall pass sentence of death by strangulation (Lev. 20:10)
287. That the Court shall pass sentence of death by burning with fire (Lev. 20:14)
288. That the Court shall pass sentence of death by stoning (Deut. 22:24)
289. To hang the dead body of one who has incurred that penalty (Deut. 21:22)
290. That the dead body of an executed criminal shall not remain hanging on the tree over night (Deut. 21:23)
291. To inter the executed on the day of execution (Deut. 21:23)
292. Not to accept ransom from a murderer (Num. 35:31)

(*continued*)

APPENDIX (*continued*)

293. To exile one who committed accidental homicide (Num. 35:25)
294. To establish six cities of refuge (for those who committed accidental homicide) (Deut. 19:3)
295. Not to accept ransom from an accidental homicide, so as to relieve him from exile (Num. 35:32)
296. To decapitate the heifer in the manner prescribed (in expiation of a murder on the road, the perpetrator of which remained undiscovered) (Deut. 21:4)
297. Not to plow nor sow the rough valley (in which a heifer's neck was broken) (Deut. 21:4)
298. To adjudge a thief to pay compensation or (in certain cases) suffer death (Ex. 21:16; Ex. 21:37; Ex. 22:1)
299. That he who inflicts a bodily injury shall pay monetary compensation (Ex. 21:18-19)
300. To impose a penalty of fifty shekels upon the seducer (of an unbetrothed virgin) and enforce the other rules in connection with the case (Ex. 22:15-16)
301. That the violator (of an unbetrothed virgin) shall marry her (Deut. 22:28-29)
302. That one who has raped a damsel and has then (in accordance with the law) married her, may not divorce her (Deut. 22:29)
303. Not to inflict punishment on Shabbat (Ex. 35:3) (because some punishments were inflicted by fire).
304. To punish the wicked by the infliction of stripes (Deut. 25:2)
305. Not to exceed the statutory number of stripes laid on one who has incurred that punishment (Deut. 25:3) (and by implication, not to strike anyone)
306. Not to spare the offender, in imposing the prescribed penalties on one who has caused damage (Deut. 19:13)
307. To do unto false witnesses as they had purposed to do (to the accused) (Deut. 19:19)
308. Not to punish any one who has committed an offense under duress (Deut. 22:26)
309. To heed the call of every prophet in each generation, provided that he neither adds to, nor takes away from the Torah (Deut. 18:15)
310. Not to prophesy falsely (Deut. 18:20)
311. Not to refrain from putting a false prophet to death nor to be in fear of him (Deut. 18:22)
312. Not to make a graven image; neither to make it oneself nor to have it made by others (Ex. 20:4) (CCN9).
313. Not to make any figures for ornament, even if they are not worshipped (Ex. 20:20)
314. Not to make idols even for others (Ex. 34:17; Lev. 19:4)
315. Not to use the ornament of any object of idolatrous worship (Deut. 7:25)
316. Not to make use of an idol or its accessory objects, offerings, or libations (Deut. 7:26).
317. Not to drink wine of idolaters (Deut. 32:38).
318. Not to worship an idol in the way in which it is usually worshipped (Ex. 20:5)
319. Not to bow down to an idol, even if that is not its mode of worship (Ex. 20:5)
320. Not to prophesy in the name of an idol (Ex. 23:13; Deut. 18:20)
321. Not to hearken to one who prophesies in the name of an idol (Deut. 13:4)
322. Not to lead the children of Israel astray to idolatry (Ex. 23:13)
323. Not to entice an Israelite to idolatry (Deut. 13:12)
324. To destroy idolatry and its appurtenances (Deut. 12:2-3)
325. Not to love the enticer to idolatry (Deut. 13:9)
326. Not to give up hating the enticer to idolatry (Deut. 13:9)
327. Not to save the enticer from capital punishment, but to stand by at his execution (Deut. 13:9)
328. A person whom he attempted to entice to idolatry shall not urge pleas for the acquittal of the enticer (Deut. 13:9)
329. A person whom he attempted to entice shall not refrain from giving evidence of the enticer's guilt, if he has such evidence (Deut. 13:9)
330. Not to swear by an idol to its worshipers, nor cause them to swear by it (Ex. 23:13)
331. Not to turn one's attention to idolatry (Lev. 19:4)
332. Not to adopt the institutions of idolaters nor their customs (Lev. 18:3; Lev. 20:23)

(*continued*)

APPENDIX (*continued*)

333. Not to pass a child through the fire to Molech (Lev. 18:21)
334. Not to suffer any one practicing witchcraft to live (Ex. 22:17)
335. Not to practice onein (observing times or seasons as favorable or unfavorable, using astrology) (Lev. 19:26)
336. Not to practice nachesh (doing things based on signs and portents; using charms and incantations) (Lev. 19:26)
337. Not to consult ovoth (ghosts) (Lev. 19:31)
338. Not to consult yid'onim (wizards) (Lev. 19:31)
339. Not to practice kisuf (magic using herbs, stones and objects that people use) (Deut. 18:10)
340. Not to practice kessem (a general term for magical practices) (Deut. 18:10)
341. Not to practice the art of a chover chaver (casting spells over snakes and scorpions) (Deut. 18:11)
342. Not to enquire of an ob (a ghost) (Deut. 18:11)
343. Not to seek the maytim (dead) (Deut. 18:11)
344. Not to enquire of a yid'oni (wizard) (Deut. 18:11)
345. Not to remove the entire beard, like the idolaters (Lev. 19:27)
346. Not to round the corners of the head, as the idolatrous priests do (Lev. 19:27)
347. Not to cut oneself or make incisions in one's flesh in grief, like the idolaters (Lev. 19:28; Deut. 14:1)
348. Not to tattoo the body like the idolaters (Lev. 19:28)
349. Not to make a bald spot for the dead (Deut. 14:1)
350. Not to plant a tree for worship (Deut. 16:21)
351. Not to set up a pillar (for worship) (Deut. 16:22)
352. Not to show favor to idolaters (Deut. 7:2)
353. Not to make a covenant with the seven (Canaanite, idolatrous) nations (Ex. 23:32; Deut. 7:2)
354. Not to settle idolaters in our land (Ex. 23:33)
355. To slay the inhabitants of a city that has become idolatrous and burn that city (Deut. 13:16-17)
356. Not to rebuild a city that has been led astray to idolatry (Deut. 13:17)
357. Not to make use of the property of city that has been so led astray (Deut. 13:18)
358. Not to cross-breed cattle of different species (Lev. 19:19)
359. Not to sow different kinds of seed together in one field (Lev. 19:19)
360. Not to eat the fruit of a tree for three years from the time it was planted (Lev. 19:23).
361. That the fruit of fruit-bearing trees in the fourth year of their planting shall be sacred like the second tithe and eaten in Jerusalem (Lev. 19:24)
362. Not to sow grain or herbs in a vineyard (Deut. 22:9)
363. Not to eat the produce of diverse seeds sown in a vineyard (Deut. 22:9)
364. Not to work with beasts of different species, yoked together (Deut. 22:10)
365. That a man shall not wear women's clothing (Deut. 22:5)
366. That a woman should not wear men's clothing (Deut. 22:5)
367. Not to wear garments made of wool and linen mixed together (Deut. 22:11)
368. To redeem the firstborn human male (Ex. 13:13; Ex. 34:20; Num. 18:15).
369. To redeem the firstling of an ass (Ex. 13:13; Ex. 34:20)
370. To break the neck of the firstling of an ass if it is not redeemed (Ex. 13:13; Ex. 34:20)
371. Not to redeem the firstling of a clean beast (Num. 18:17)
372. That the kohanim shall put on priestly vestments for the service (Ex. 28:2) S
373. Not to tear the High Kohein's robe (Ex. 28:32).
374. That the kohein shall not enter the Sanctuary at all times (i. e. , at times when he is not performing service) (Lev. 16:2).
375. That the ordinary kohein shall not defile himself by contact with any dead, other than immediate relatives (Lev. 21:1-3).
376. That the kohanim defile themselves for their deceased relatives (by attending their burial), and mourn for them like other Israelites, who are commanded to mourn for their relatives (Lev. 21:3).

(*continued*)

APPENDIX (*continued*)

377. That a kohein who had an immersion during the day (to cleanse him from his uncleanness) shall not serve in the Sanctuary until after sunset (Lev. 21:6).
378. That a kohein shall not marry a divorced woman (Lev. 21:7) S.
379. That a kohein shall not marry a harlot (Lev. 21:7) S.
380. That a kohein shall not marry a profaned woman (Lev. 21:7).
381. To show honor to a kohein, and to give him precedence in all things that are holy (Lev. 21:8).
382. That a High Kohein shall not defile himself with any dead, even if they are relatives (Lev. 21:11).
383. That a High Kohein shall not go (under the same roof) with a dead body (Lev. 21:11).
384. That the High Kohein shall marry a virgin (Lev. 21:13).
385. That the High Kohein shall not marry a widow (Lev. 21:14).
386. That the High Kohein shall not cohabit with a widow, even without marriage, because he profanes her (Lev. 21:15).
387. That a person with a physical blemish shall not serve (in the Sanctuary) (Lev. 21:17)
388. That a kohein with a temporary blemish shall not serve there (Lev. 21:21)
389. That a person with a physical blemish shall not enter the Sanctuary further than the altar (Lev. 21:23)
390. That a kohein who is unclean shall not serve (in the Sanctuary) (Lev. 22:2-3).
391. To send the unclean out of the Camp of the Shechinah, that is, out of the Sanctuary (Num. 5:2)
392. That a kohein who is unclean shall not enter the courtyard (Num. 5:2-3).
393. That the kohanim shall bless Israel (Num. 6:23).
394. To set apart a portion of the dough for the kohein (Num. 15:20).
395. That the Levites shall not occupy themselves with the service that belongs to the kohanim, nor the kohanim with that belonging to the Levites (Num. 18:3).
396. That one not a descendant of Aaron in the male line shall not serve (in the Sanctuary) (Num. 18:4-7)
397. That the Levite shall serve in the Sanctuary (Num. 18:23).
398. To give the Levites cities to dwell in, these to serve also as cities of refuge (Num. 35:2).
399. That none of the tribe of Levi shall take any portion of territory in the land (of Israel) (Deut. 18:1).
400. That none of the tribe of Levi shall take any share of the spoil (at the conquest of the Promised Land) (Deut. 18:1).
401. That the kohanim shall serve in the Sanctuary in divisions, but on festivals, they all serve together (Deut. 18:6-8).
402. That an uncircumcised person shall not eat of the t'rumah (heave offering), and the same applies to other holy things. (Ex. 12:44-45 and Lev. 22:10)
403. Not to alter the order of separating the t'rumah and the tithes; the separation be in the order first-fruits at the beginning, then the t'rumah, then the first tithe, and last the second tithe (Ex. 22:28)
404. To give half a shekel every year (to the Sanctuary for provision of the public sacrifices) (Ex. 30:13)
405. That a kohein who is unclean shall not eat of the t'rumah (Lev. 22:3-4).
406. That a person who is not a kohein or the wife or unmarried daughter of a kohein shall not eat of the t'rumah (Lev. 22:10).
407. That a sojourner with a kohein or his hired servant shall not eat of the t'rumah (Lev. 22:10).
408. Not to eat tevel (something from which the t'rumah and tithe have not yet been separated) (Lev. 22:15)
409. To set apart the tithe of the produce (one tenth of the produce after taking out t'rumah) for the Levites (Lev. 27:30; Num. 18:24).
410. To tithe cattle (Lev. 27:32)
411. Not to sell the tithe of the heard (Lev. 27:32-33)
412. That the Levites shall set apart a tenth of the tithes, which they had received from the Israelites, and give it to the kohanim (called the t'rumah of the tithe) (Num. 18:26).
413. Not to eat the second tithe of cereals outside Jerusalem (Deut. 12:17)

(*continued*)

APPENDIX (*continued*)

414. Not to consume the second tithe of the vintage outside of Jerusalem (Deut. 12:17)
415. Not to consume the second tithe of the oil outside of Jerusalem (Deut. 12:17)
416. Not to forsake the Levites (Deut. 12:19); but their gifts (dues) should be given to them, so that they might rejoice therewith on each and every festival.
417. To set apart the second tithe in the first, second, fourth and fifth years of the sabbatical cycle to be eaten by its owner in Jerusalem (Deut. 14:22)
418. To set apart the second tithe in the third and sixth year of the sabbatical cycle for the poor (Deut. 14:28-29)
419. To give the kohein the due portions of the carcass of cattle (Deut. 18:3).
420. To give the first of the fleece to the kohein (Deut. 18:4).
421. To set apart t'rumah g'dolah (the great heave-offering, that is, a small portion of the grain, wine and oil) for the kohein (Deut. 18:4).
422. Not to expend the proceeds of the second tithe on anything but food and drink (Deut. 26:14)
423. Not to eat the Second Tithe, even in Jerusalem, in a state of uncleanness, until the tithe had been redeemed (Deut. 26:14)
424. Not to eat the Second Tithe, when mourning (Deut. 26:14)
425. To make the declaration, when bringing the second tithe to the Sanctuary (Deut. 26:13)
426. Not to build an altar of hewn stone (Ex. 20:22)
427. Not to mount the altar by steps (Ex. 20:23)
428. To build the Sanctuary (Ex. 25:8)
429. Not to remove the staves from the Ark (Ex. 25:15)
430. To set the showbread and the frankincense before the L-rd every Shabbat (Ex. 25:30)
431. To kindle lights in the Sanctuary (Ex. 27:21)
432. That the breastplate shall not be loosened from the ephod (Ex. 28:28)
433. To offer up incense twice daily (Ex. 30:7)
434. Not to offer strange incense nor any sacrifice upon the golden altar (Ex. 30:9)
435. That the kohein shall wash his hands and feet at the time of service (Ex. 30:19).
436. To prepare the oil of anointment and anoint high kohanim and kings with it (Ex. 30:31).
437. Not to compound oil for lay use after the formula of the anointing oil (Ex. 30:32-33)
438. Not to anoint a stranger with the anointing oil (Ex. 30:32)
439. Not to compound anything after the formula of the incense (Ex. 30:37)
440. That he who, in error, makes unlawful use of sacred things, shall make restitution of the value of his trespass and add a fifth (Lev. 5:16)
441. To remove the ashes from the altar (Lev. 6:3)
442. To keep fire always burning on the altar of the burnt-offering (Lev. 6:6)
443. Not to extinguish the fire on the altar (Lev. 6:6)
444. That a kohein shall not enter the Sanctuary with disheveled hair (Lev. 10:6).
445. That a kohein shall not enter the Sanctuary with torn garments (Lev. 10:6).
446. That the kohein shall not leave the Courtyard of the Sanctuary, during service (Lev. 10:7).
447. That an intoxicated person shall not enter the Sanctuary nor give decisions in matters of the Law (Lev. 10:9-11)
448. To revere the Sanctuary (Lev. 19:30) (today, this applies to synagogues).
449. That when the Ark is carried, it should be carried on the shoulder (Num. 7:9)
450. To observe the second Passover (Num. 9:11)
451. To eat the flesh of the Paschal lamb on it, with unleavened bread and bitter herbs (Num. 9:11)
452. Not to leave any flesh of the Paschal lamb brought on the second Passover until the morning (Num. 9:12)
453. Not to break a bone of the Paschal lamb brought on the second Passover (Num. 9:12)
454. To sound the trumpets at the offering of sacrifices and in times of trouble (Num. 10:9-10)
455. To watch over the edifice continually (Num. 18:2)
456. Not to allow the Sanctuary to remain unwatched (Num. 18:5)
457. That an offering shall be brought by one who has in error committed a trespass against sacred things, or robbed, or lain carnally with a bond-maid betrothed to a man, or

(*continued*)

APPENDIX (*continued*)

denied what was deposited with him and swore falsely to support his denial. This is called a guilt-offering for a known trespass.

458. Not to destroy anything of the Sanctuary, of synagogues, or of houses of study, nor erase the holy names (of G-d); nor may sacred scriptures be destroyed (Deut. 12:2-4) To sanctify the firstling of clean cattle and offer it up (Ex. 13:2; Deut. 15:19)

459. To slay the Paschal lamb (Ex. 12:6)

460. To eat the flesh of the Paschal sacrifice on the night of the fifteenth of Nissan (Ex. 12:8)

461. Not to eat the flesh of the Paschal lamb raw or sodden (Ex. 12:9)

462. Not to leave any portion of the flesh of the Paschal sacrifice until the morning unconsumed (Ex. 12:10)

463. Not to give the flesh of the Paschal lamb to an Israelite who had become an apostate (Ex. 12:43)

464. Not to give flesh of the Paschal lamb to a stranger who lives among you to eat (Ex. 12:45)

465. Not to take any of the flesh of the Paschal lamb from the company's place of assembly (Ex. 12:46)

466. Not to break a bone of the Paschal lamb (Ex. 12:46)

467. That the uncircumcised shall not eat of the flesh of the Paschal lamb (Ex. 12:48)

468. Not to slaughter the Paschal lamb while there is chametz in the home (Ex. 23:18; Ex. 24:25)

469. Not to leave the part of the Paschal lamb that should be burnt on the altar until the morning, when it will no longer be fit to be burnt (Ex. 23:18; Ex. 24:25)

470. Not to go up to the Sanctuary for the festival without bringing an offering (Ex. 23:15)

471. To bring the first fruits to the Sanctuary (Ex. 23:19)

472. That the flesh of a sin-offering and guilt-offering shall be eaten (Ex. 29:33)

473. That one not of the seed of Aaron, shall not eat the flesh of the holy sacrifices (Ex. 29:33)

474. To observe the procedure of the burnt-offering (Lev. 1:3).

475. To observe the procedure of the meal-offering (Lev. 2:1)

476. Not to offer up leaven or honey (Lev. 2:11)

477. That every sacrifice be salted (Lev. 2:13)

478. Not to offer up any offering unsalted (Lev. 2:13)

479. That the Court of Judgment shall offer up a sacrifice if they have erred in a judicial pronouncement (Lev. 4:13)

480. That an individual shall bring a sin-offering if he has sinned in error by committing a transgression, the conscious violation of which is punished with excision (Lev. 4:27-28).

481. To offer a sacrifice of varying value in accordance with one's means (Lev. 5:7)

482. Not to sever completely the head of a fowl brought as a sin-offering (Lev. 5:8)

483. Not to put olive oil in a sin-offering made of flour (Lev. 5:11)

484. Not to put frankincense on a sin-offering made of flour (Lev. 5:11)

485. That an individual shall bring an offering if he is in doubt as to whether he has committed a sin for which one has to bring a sin-offering. This is called a guilt-offering for doubtful sins (Lev. 5:17-19).

486. That the remainder of the meal offerings shall be eaten (Lev. 6:9)

487. Not to allow the remainder of the meal offerings to become leavened (Lev. 6:10)

488. That the High Kohein shall offer a meal offering daily (Lev. 6:13)

489. Not to eat of the meal offering brought by the kohanim (Lev. 6:16)

490. To observe the procedure of the sin-offering (Lev. 6:18).

491. Not to eat of the flesh of sin offerings, the blood of which is brought within the Sanctuary and sprinkled towards the Veil (Lev. 6:23)

492. To observe the procedure of the guilt-offering (Lev. 7:1).

493. To observe the procedure of the peace-offering (Lev. 7:11).

494. To burn meat of the holy sacrifice that has remained over (Lev. 7:17)

495. Not to eat of sacrifices that are eaten beyond the appointed time for eating them (Lev. 7:18) The penalty is excision

(*continued*)

APPENDIX (continued)

496. Not to eat of holy things that have become unclean (Lev. 7:19)

497. To burn meat of the holy sacrifice that has become unclean (Lev. 7:19)

498. That a person who is unclean shall not eat of things that are holy (Lev. 7:20)

499. A kohein's daughter who profaned herself shall not eat of the holy things, neither of the heave offering nor of the breast, nor of the shoulder of peace offerings (Lev. 10:14, Lev. 22:12).

500. That a woman after childbirth shall bring an offering when she is clean (Lev. 12:6).

501. That the leper shall bring a sacrifice after he is cleansed (Lev. 14:10)

502. That a man having an issue shall bring a sacrifice after he is cleansed of his issue (Lev. 15:13-15)

503. That a woman having an issue shall bring a sacrifice after she is cleansed of her issue (Lev. 15:28-30)

504. To observe, on Yom Kippur, the service appointed for that day, regarding the sacrifice, confessions, sending away of the scapegoat, etc. (Lev. 16:3-34)

505. Not to slaughter beasts set apart for sacrifices outside (the Sanctuary) (Lev. 17:3-4)

506. Not to eat flesh of a sacrifice that has been left over (beyond the time appointed for its consumption) (Lev. 19:8)

507. Not to sanctify blemished cattle for sacrifice on the altar (Lev. 22:20) This text prohibits such beasts being set apart for sacrifice on the altar

508. That every animal offered up shall be without blemish (Lev. 22:21)

509. Not to inflict a blemish on cattle set apart for sacrifice (Lev. 22:21)

510. Not to slaughter blemished cattle as sacrifices (Lev. 22:22)

511. Not to burn the limbs of blemished cattle upon the altar (Lev. 22:22)

512. Not to sprinkle the blood of blemished cattle upon the altar (Lev. 22:24)

513. Not to offer up a blemished beast that comes from non-Israelites (Lev. 22:25)

514. That sacrifices of cattle can only take place when they are at least eight days old (Lev. 22:27)

515. Not to leave any flesh of the thanksgiving offering until the morning (Lev. 22:30)

516. To offer up the meal-offering of the Omer on the morrow after the first day of Passover, together with one lamb (Lev. 23:10).

517. Not to eat bread made of new grain before the Omer of barley has been offered up on the second day of Passover (Lev. 23:14).

518. Not to eat roasted grain of the new produce before that time (Lev. 23:14).

519. Not to eat fresh ears of the new grain before that time (Lev. 23:14).

520. To bring on Shavu'ot loaves of bread together with the sacrifices which are then offered up in connection with the loaves (Lev. 23:17-20)

521. To offer up an additional sacrifice on Passover (Lev. 23:36)

522. That one who vows to the L-rd the monetary value of a person shall pay the amount appointed in the Scriptural portion (Lev. 27:2-8)

523. If a beast is exchanged for one that had been set apart as an offering, both become sacred (Lev. 27:10)

524. Not to exchange a beast set aside for sacrifice (Lev. 27:10)

525. That one who vows to the L-rd the monetary value of an unclean beast shall pay its value (Lev. 27:11-13)

526. That one who vows the value of his house shall pay according to the appraisal of the kohein (Lev. 27:11-13).

527. That one who sanctifies to the L-rd a portion of his field shall pay according to the estimation appointed in the Scriptural portion (Lev. 27:16-24)

528. Not to transfer a beast set apart for sacrifice from one class of sacrifices to another (Lev. 27:26)

529. To decide in regard to dedicated property as to which is sacred to the Lord and which belongs to the kohein (Lev. 27:28).

530. Not to sell a field devoted to the Lord (Lev. 27:28)

531. Not to redeem a field devoted to the Lord (Lev. 27:28)

532. To make confession before the L-rd of any sin that one has committed, when bringing a sacrifice and at other times (Num. 5:6-7)

533. Not to put olive oil in the meal-offering of a woman suspected of adultery (Num. 5:15)

(continued)

APPENDIX (*continued*)

534. Not to put frankincense on it (Num. 5:15)
535. To offer up the regular sacrifices daily (two lambs as burnt offerings) (Num. 28:3)
536. To offer up an additional sacrifice every Shabbat (two lambs) (Num. 28:9)
537. To offer up an additional sacrifice every New Moon (Num. 28:11)
538. To bring an additional offering on Shavu'ot (Num. 28:26-27)
539. To offer up an additional sacrifice on Rosh Hashanah (Num. 29:1-6)
540. To offer up an additional sacrifice on Yom Kippur (Num. 29:7-8)
541. To offer up an additional sacrifice on Sukkot (Num. 29:12-34)
542. To offer up an additional offering on Shemini Atzeret, which is a festival by itself (Num. 29:35-38)
543. To bring all offerings, whether obligatory or freewill, on the first festival after these were incurred (Deut. 12:5-6)
544. Not to offer up sacrifices outside (the Sanctuary) (Deut. 12:13)
545. To offer all sacrifices in the Sanctuary (Deut. 12:14)
546. To redeem cattle set apart for sacrifices that contracted disqualifying blemishes, after which they may be eaten by anyone, (Deut. 12:15)
547. Not to eat of the unblemished firstling outside Jerusalem (Deut. 12:17)
548. Not to eat the flesh of the burnt-offering (Deut. 12:17). This is a Prohibition applying to every trespasser, not to enjoy any of the holy things. If he does so, he commits a trespass
549. That the kohanim shall not eat the flesh of the sin-offering or guilt-offering outside the Courtyard (of the Sanctuary) (Deut. 12:17)
550. Not to eat of the flesh of the sacrifices that are holy in a minor degree, before the blood has been sprinkled (on the altar), (Deut. 12:17)
551. That the kohein shall not eat the first-fruits before they are set down in the Courtyard (of the Sanctuary) (Deut. 12:17)
552. To take trouble to bring sacrifices to the Sanctuary from places outside the land of Israel (Deut. 12:26)

553. Not to eat the flesh of beasts set apart as sacrifices, that have been rendered unfit to be offered up by deliberately inflicted blemish (Deut. 14:3)
554. Not to do work with cattle set apart for sacrifice (Deut. 15:19)
555. Not to shear beasts set apart for sacrifice (Deut. 15:19)
556. Not to leave any portion of the festival offering brought on the fourteenth of Nissan unto the third day (Deut. 16:4)
557. Not to offer up a beast that has a temporary blemish (Deut. 17:1)
558. Not to bring sacrifices out of the hire of a harlot or price of a dog (apparently a euphemism for sodomy) (Deut. 23:19)
559. To read the portion prescribed on bringing the first fruits (Deut. 26:5-10)
561. That eight species of creeping things defile by contact (Lev. 11:29-30)
562. That foods become defiled by contact with unclean things (Lev. 11:34)
563. That anyone who touches the carcass of a beast that died of itself shall be unclean (Lev. 11:39)
564. That a lying-in woman is unclean like a menstruating woman (in terms of uncleanness) (Lev. 12:2-5)
565. That a leper is unclean and defiles (Lev. 13:2-46)
566. That the leper shall be universally recognized as such by the prescribed marks So too, all other unclean persons should declare themselves as such (Lev. 13:45)
567. That a leprous garment is unclean and defiles (Lev. 13:47-49)
568. That a leprous house defiles (Lev. 14:34-46)
569. That a man, having a running issue, defiles (Lev. 15:1-15)
570. That the seed of copulation defiles (Lev. 15:16)
571. That purification from all kinds of defilement shall be effected by immersion in the waters of a mikvah (Lev. 15:16)
572. That a menstruating woman is unclean and defiles others (Lev. 15:19-24)
573. That a woman, having a running issue, defiles (Lev. 15:25-27)

(continued)

APPENDIX (*continued*)

574. To carry out the ordinance of the Red Heifer so that its ashes will always be available (Num. 19:9).
575. That a corpse defiles (Num. 19:11-16).
576. That the waters of separation defile one who is clean, and cleanse the unclean from pollution by a dead body (Num. 19:19-22)
577. Not to drove off the hair of the scall (Lev. 13:33)
578. That the procedure of cleansing leprosy, whether of a man or of a house, takes place with cedar-wood, hyssop, scarlet thread, two birds, and running water (Lev. 14:1-7)
579. That the leper shall shave all his hair (Lev. 14:9)
580. Not to pluck out the marks of leprosy (Deut. 24:8)
581. Not to curse a ruler, that is, the King or the head of the College in the land of Israel (Ex. 22:27)
582. To appoint a king (Deut. 17:15)
583. Not to appoint as ruler over Israel, one who comes from non-Israelites (Deut. 17:15)
584. That the King shall not acquire an excessive number of horses (Deut. 17:16)
585. That the King shall not take an excessive number of wives (Deut. 17:17)
586. That he shall not accumulate an excessive quantity of gold and silver (Deut. 17:17)
587. That the King shall write a scroll of the Torah for himself, in addition to the one that every person should write, so that he writes two scrolls (Deut. 17:18).
588. That a Nazarite shall not drink wine, or anything mixed with wine which tastes like wine; and even if the wine or the mixture has turned sour, it is prohibited to him (Num. 6:3)
589. That he shall not eat fresh grapes (Num. 6:3)
590. That he shall not eat dried grapes (raisins) (Num. 6:3)
591. That he shall not eat the kernels of the grapes (Num. 6:4)
592. That he shall not eat of the skins of the grapes (Num. 6:4)
593. That the Nazarite shall permit his hair to grow (Num. 6:5)

594. That the Nazarite shall not cut his hair (Num. 6:5)
595. That he shall not enter any covered structure where there is a dead body (Num. 6:6)
596. That a Nazarite shall not defile himself for any dead person (by being in the presence of the corpse) (Num. 6:7)
597. That the Nazarite shall shave his hair when he brings his offerings at the completion of the period of his Naziriteship, or within that period if he has become defiled (Num. 6:9)
598. That those engaged in warfare shall not fear their enemies nor be panic-stricken by them during battle (Deut. 3:22, 7:21, 20:3)
599. To anoint a special kohein (to speak to the soldiers) in a war (Deut. 20:2).
600. In a permissive war (as distinguished from obligatory ones), to observe the procedure prescribed in the Torah (Deut. 20:10)
601. Not to keep alive any individual of the seven Canaanite nations (Deut. 20:16)
602. To exterminate the seven Canaanite nations from the land of Israel (Deut. 20:17)
603. Not to destroy fruit trees (wantonly or in warfare) (Deut. 20:19-20)
604. To deal with a beautiful woman taken captive in war in the manner prescribed in the Torah (Deut. 21:10-14)
605. Not to sell a beautiful woman, (taken captive in war) (Deut. 21:14)
606. Not to degrade a beautiful woman (taken captive in war) to the condition of a bond-woman (Deut. 21:14)
607. Not to offer peace to the Ammonites and the Moabites before waging war on them, as should be done to other nations (Deut. 23:7)
608. That anyone who is unclean shall not enter the Camp of the Levites (Deut. 23:11)
609. To have a place outside the camp for sanitary purposes (Deut. 23:13)
610. To keep that place sanitary (Deut. 23:14-15)
611. Always to remember what Amalek did (Deut. 25:17)
612. That the evil done to us by Amalek shall not be forgotten (Deut. 25:19)
613. To destroy the seed of Amalek (Deut. 25:19)

Index